Major Problems in the History
of American Workers

MAJOR PROBLEMS IN AMERICAN HISTORY SERIES

GENERAL EDITOR

THOMAS G. PATERSON

Major Problems
in the History
of American Workers

DOCUMENTS AND ESSAYS

EDITED BY
EILEEN BORIS
HOWARD UNIVERSITY

NELSON LICHTENSTEIN
UNIVERSITY OF VIRGINIA

D. C. HEATH AND COMPANY
Lexington, Massachusetts   Toronto

Address editorial correspondence to:

D. C. Heath
125 Spring Street
Lexington, MA 02173

Acquisitions Editor: James Miller
Developmental Editor: Sylvia Mallory
Production Editor: Tina V. Beazer
Designer: Sally Thompson Steele
Production Coordinator: Charles Dutton
Permissions Editor: Margaret Roll

Cover: *Street Scene, Twelfth Avenue,* 1928, by Reginald Marsh. Courtesy of Hirschl & Adler Galleries, Inc., New York.

International Standard Book Number: 0–669–19925–7

Library of Congress Catalog Card Number: 90–82495

10 9 8 7 6 5 4 3 2

12-12-96

To Daniel

Preface

A generation ago, only a handful of U.S. colleges and universities offered courses in labor history. Few scholars within the historical profession studied the subject. If a student had an interest in the history of work, trade unions, working-class living standards, or labor law, he or she most likely would find these topics taught in the departments of economics and sociology, or in schools of law and industrial relations.

Today, the history of labor—including the history of work in its broadest social context—stands far closer to what historians consider central problems in the American past. Of the several reasons for this transformation, three stand out. First, the history profession itself underwent a substantial democratization after World War II, with many newcomers entering the discipline from immigrant backgrounds or working-class families. Then came the 1960s, which filled graduate seminars with students eager to write a politically engaged "history from the bottom up" that might uncover the mass movements, social ideas, and historical circumstances that produced radical change in the American past. Finally, the globalization of economic life and the contemporary difficulties of U.S. capitalism have made the study of work enormously relevant, not only to historians but also to political economists, students of economic development, and business school professionals.

Labor history has flourished and grown; hundreds of courses are now taught throughout the country. Specialized journals devoted to the subject and numerous conferences and symposia engage scholars. Most important, what we usually consider the traditional subject matter of American history—politics, business expansion, and international diplomacy—can no longer be investigated without reference to the popular moods and shifting class relations of the workplace and civic community. Thus our understanding of the Civil War and World War II, of the rise of the railroads and the birth of the automobile industry, and of the changing fortunes of the political parties and their leading politicians have all been enriched, and in some cases transformed, by the last few decades of labor history scholarship.

This renaissance in the study of the history of American workers has been accompanied by a vast redefinition and elaboration of the subject. Today one cannot study the history of labor without exploring the changing structure of the family, the character of race relations, the history of American culture and social ideas, the technology of work, the organization of business enterprise, and the legal and political history of reform and reaction. In short, the lines dividing labor history from the general study of U.S. society and politics are fading.

In this book of readings, we have selected documents and essays exemplifying this expanded sense of what constitutes a history of the American working class. We include accounts of strikes, trade unions, and collective bargaining, but also studies of rural farm life, women's work culture, slavery, emancipation, management theory, and labor law. The chapters are arranged in a general chronological order, but we have tried to offer documents throughout the text that demonstrate the way in which particular themes flow from one generation to the next. Labor history is a contentious field, and the documents and readings in this anthology, like those that appear in other volumes in the Major Problems in American History Series, are intended to introduce students to a broad range of arguments and interpretations.

Each chapter in this book opens with a brief introduction to its topic, followed by a selection of relevant documents and essays by experts in the field. The documents offer authentic voices from each era, sometimes descriptive and sometimes engaged in passionate debate. As you will see for yourself, historical documents can yield different meanings, depending on the politics and interpretative framework of the historian who reads and evaluates them. The essays sometimes reveal a set of counterposed viewpoints; in other cases we have chosen selections to demonstrate how historians and other scholars complement each others' work to build a rounded sense of the past. Headnotes, setting the readings in historical and interpretive perspective, introduce each chapter's documents and essays. For those who wish to explore topics in more depth, a list of books and articles for further reading appears at the end of each chapter. A photographic essay portraying Americans at work, and an appendix of labor statistics are also featured.

Detailed and constructive written reviews were provided by Alan Dawley, Melvyn Dubofsky, Dana Frank, Joshua Freeman, J. Carroll Moody, Daniel Nelson, Mary Beth Norton, and Roy Rosenzweig. We would like to thank Mary Blewett, Heidi Hartmann, Barbara Melosh, Marcus Rediker, Leslie Rowland, and Laurel Thatcher Ulrich for their help in selecting the documents and essays. Steve Babson, Pete Daniels, Thomas Featherstone, Barbara Pepper, and Harry Rubinstein assisted us in preparing the photographic section. Finally, we are grateful to Thomas Paterson of the University of Connecticut, general editor of the Major Problems in American History Series, who got us started and helped us shape the volume; to Heath editors Sylvia Mallory and James Miller, who nurtured the work through to final manuscript; and to production editor Tina Beazer and permissions editor Margaret Roll.

E. B.

N. L.

Contents

CHAPTER 4
Slavery and the Transition to Free Labor
Page 124

CHAPTER 5
From Peasant to Proletarian
Page 171

C H A P T E R 6
The Organization of Labor
Page 229

C H A P T E R 7
Cultures of the Workplace
Page 275

PHOTOGRAPH ESSAY
Americans at Work in the Industrial Era
Page 309

CHAPTER 8
The Managerial Ethos
Page 318

CHAPTER 9
Industrial Unionism During the Great Depression
Page 361

CHAPTER 10
Labor and the State
Page 408

C H A P T E R 11
Race, Gender, and Industrial Unionism: World War II and Its Aftermath
Page 462

C H A P T E R 12
Trade Unions in the Postwar Order
Page 496

C H A P T E R 13
The Postwar Working Class
Page 540

C H A P T E R 14
Workers and Their Unions in Troubled Times
Page 579

C H A P T E R 15
The Future of Work
Page 634

A P P E N D I X
American Labor: A Statistical Portrait
Page 683

The Meaning of Work
and the History of Labor

⚜

What constitutes the history of American workers? To answer this question is to confront a series of intensely political choices about how a society works, who is powerful and powerless, and what are the hopes and aspirations of ordinary people. The very notion that we might gain insight from studying the history of labor implies that workers and their employers may not have identical interests and that classes do in fact exist in our society. These ideas seem to contradict much of the contemporary American ethos. Moreover, most labor historians believe that there is something unique and important about how people act in the workplace and what they think about their everyday work; that the hours spent at labor—whether in the home, the field, the office, the factory, or on the road—somehow shape people in a way uniquely different from, but not unrelated to, the ways in which their gender, region, religion, family status, and ethnic and racial background do. Obviously these are contentious propositions, far too important to be left to historians alone. Today the history of American workers is a subject to which sociologists, economists, political scientists, and historians turn their special talents and unique perspectives.

⚜ E S S A Y S

The following three essays demonstrate several different approaches to working-class history. In the first, David Brody of the University of California, Davis, a pioneer in the field, shows how a bitter nineteenth-century debate among economists opened the door to the study of working people and their nascent trade-union organizations. These early labor economists broke from the rigid anti-union stance of classical economics, only to create their own highly institutional brand of labor history, which was in turn assailed by a generation of cultural and social historians who came of age in more recent years. One of these new scholars, Elizabeth H. Pleck of the Wellesley College Center for Research on Women, incorporates in the second essay some important insights from feminist and sociological theory. She presents an illuminating discussion of the way long-

range changes in the family's structure and function contribute to our understanding of the history of production itself. Finally, Michael Reich, an economist
at the University of California, Berkeley, offers a far-reaching schema to explain
how the organization of work has changed over the past two centuries. A careful
student of economic history, Reich posits three stages in the evolution of American capitalism, each of which generated, often amidst much conflict, a new labor
system in harmony with the technological and economic requirements of its era.

The New Labor History

DAVID BRODY

. . . When one looks at urban history or at the history of the family or of
women, one is in fact also looking in large degree at the history of workers,
as well. . . . The study of labor history has a distinctive historiography,
however, that sets it somewhat apart from other aspects of American social
history. In this essay, I would like to start with some accounting of the
historical study of workers as it developed in America, and then proceed
to trace its recent evolution into a thriving part of the new social history.

The spirit of discovery is strongly felt by scholars seeking to reconstruct
the historical experience of ordinary people. They know they are breaking
into fresh ground and doing so by means of research methods unknown to
earlier generations of historians. That sense of discovery applies to modern
labor historians also, and for the same reasons. But labor history is not a
new field. It has a long and honorable tradition going back into the late
nineteenth century. The scope of that earlier history, however, was very
narrowly defined: only the institutions of labor—trade unions, collective
bargaining, politics, public policy—were proper subjects of study. . . . For
labor history, what is "new" is always quite clear. It is the determined
effort to move beyond the study of institutions to the study of workers
themselves. Other fields, such as urban and political history, have gone
through a similar struggle, but none has had to battle against so entrenched
an institutional perspective as that which dominated American labor history
for so many years.

The roots of the subject go back to a great struggle in the late nineteenth
century, between two schools of economics. The classical school, dominant
in the academies, was highly abstract and deductive. It drew on a set of
eternal principles and operated on the assumption of perfectly competitive
markets. From this elaborate theoretical framework came highly conservative conclusions. Classical economics argued against any intrusion on the
natural operation of the marketplace—against any regulation of business
activity, against legislative protection of workers and consumers, and,
above all, against trade unions and collective bargaining. In response, there
sprang up a rival school, whose intellectual origins derived from the German
universities that American graduate students began to attend in growing

David Brody, "Workers and Work in America: The New Labor History," in *Ordinary People
and Everyday Life* (Nashville: American Association for State and Local History, 1983) pp.
139–155. Reprinted with permission of AASLH Press.

numbers after the Civil War. The focus was on empirical research, on the study of the economy as it actually operated. From the 1870s onward, bureaus of labor statistics began to gather quantitative evidence, and economic institutions came under closer scrutiny. This "revolt against formalism," as the philosopher Morton G. White has termed it, was in part an intellectual struggle, an attempt to redefine the subject of economics, and in part it was political, an effort to legitimize trade unionism and encourage social and labor legislation. With the formation of the American Economic Association in 1886, this new institutional economics came of age.

Central to its empirical approach was historical study. That was especially stressed by the Germans, who indeed called themselves historical economists. History was one of the crucial ways of breaking out of the abstractions of the classical economics, of creating an empirical base for understanding the way economic systems operated and changed, over time. From the 1880s onward, the historical study of labor began, rooted not in the historical profession that was simultaneously emerging, but in institutional economics. The pioneering scholar was John R. Commons, who settled at the University of Wisconsin. Although Commons did a good deal of contemporary labor economics, his orientation was primarily historical. He began by gathering together the records of workers in America, a task wholly neglected until that time. This enormous undertaking resulted in the publication of the multivolume *A Documentary History of Industrial Society*. With that as a base, Commons and his students launched the first attempt to write a serious history of American workers. *A History of Labour in the United States*, published in four volumes from 1918 to 1935, remains today the fundamental account, the most comprehensive treatment of the American labor movement in its formative years. Although other centers of research sprang up, most notably at Johns Hopkins, Commons's preeminence never wavered, and his numerous students built up what became known as the Wisconsin school of labor history.

Its practitioners were labor economists, and the training they received defined the way they would approach history. They were interested almost exclusively in labor institutions. A huge monographic literature grew up dealing with the histories of individual unions or cataloguing particular structural features of internal union government and variations among collective-bargaining practices. The narrative histories, when they were undertaken, tended to be dismal recitations of events. In part, that was because the labor economists had no literary traditions on which to draw; but in part, too, it was a reflection of the way they defined their subject. Institutions, not people, concerned them, and neither the inherent drama nor the underlying social forces tended to find much place in their accounts. There was also a deep conservatism in the historical work of the labor economists. Their institutional approach had been devised to justify the trade-union movement, and, having accomplished that, they became its defenders. It is perhaps inherent in an institutional approach not to raise larger questions about what is being studied. Many of the economist-historians, too, were practitioners in the field, serving as arbitrators, labor-relations consultants, and government experts. The best of them, like Philip A. Taft, saw the subject very much from the inside. They knew well many labor leaders, and they understood in their bones the way trade unions operated. Such intimacy could produce deeply informed history; it did not lend itself to critical or detached assessment.

The Wisconsin school was singularly fortunate to have, in the person of Selig Perlman, a creative scholar capable of working out the theoretical underpinnings of the Commons approach. Perlman was an exceptional figure in the Commons circle. He had been a youthful Marxist in Europe; he was widely read in European history; he had a speculative cast of mind and, perhaps not incidentally, a quite elegant writing style. In *A Theory of the Labor Movement* (1928), Perlman argued that American workers were "job conscious," that is, that their collective activity sprang from a desire to protect interests on the job and, above all, to defend their job rights in what they saw as a world of restricted opportunity. Job consciousness was by no means unique to America; it was felt no less by European workers. What was exceptional about the American trade-union movement was that it genuinely expressed the job consciousness of its followers. The underlying point had already been addressed by V. I. Lenin, who had argued that, without the leadership of a vanguard of intellectuals, workers were incapable of rising above trade-union consciousness. The distinctive feature of American trade unionism, answered Perlman, was precisely that it was resistant to such penetration. It had not permitted outsiders—intellectuals, radicals, professors—to take over the movement and redirect it toward class struggle and Socialist politics. Although not entirely clear about the sources of this remarkable immunity, Perlman did know that it fostered an "organic" labor movement, one that arose from and truly expressed the will of the working class. Perlman's analysis obviously rested on assumptions about the character of American workers; but that had never been the focus of his research—he had merely reasoned back from his conception of job-conscious unionism and from a sensitive reading of the American conditions acting on labor. While acknowledging that flaw, Perlman's students never moved to correct it. *A Theory of the Labor Movement* was a powerful intellectual defense of the Wisconsin school, but not one calculated to lift its focus beyond the categories of labor institutionalism.

At the time that I was a history graduate student in the 1950s, the Commons tradition was still very much alive and flourishing. Virtually all the work in labor history was being done by labor economists. In 1955, Lloyd Ulman published his brilliant and encyclopedic *The Rise of the National Trade Union*; in 1957 and 1959, Philip Taft published his definitive two-volume history of the American Federation of Labor; and the next year, Walter Galenson brought out his detailed history of the launching of the industrial-union movement, *The CIO Challenge to the AFL*. The Harvard Labor-Management History Series, under the editorship of the eminent labor economist John T. Dunlop, was turning out a steady stream of books. After I finished my thesis in 1958, Dunlop asked me to write a book for the series. In a backhanded way, the invitation said a good deal about the labor history field. It was an experiment, Dunlop told me. He was curious to see what a *historian* might do with the subject he had in mind—a history of trade unionism in the meat industry. That the notion was novel was evident to me due to the trouble my revised thesis was having at the Harvard Press. The labor economists who read my study of steelworkers before the 1930s could not see what contribution I was making to their field. It was, in fact, because of stalemated reviews (I think my manuscript received a record number of readings) that Dunlop became familiar with my work. As a syndic of Harvard Press, he had been called on to decide the issue— which he did, in my favor.

These small events, besides what they revealed of John Dunlop's lively and generous mind, also reflected important changes going on in labor economics and in history. Among younger economists like Gary Becker, the institutional approach was giving way to more theoretical concerns. Human resources had a great vogue in the 1960s, and neoclassical market analysis dominates labor economics today. Although it left behind a rear guard of institutionalists—Taft was churning out books until his death in 1976—that shift opened up the field of labor history. At the same time, the historical profession was changing. History had traditionally been a genteel field, and it had not treated workers as a proper subject of study. When the profession opened up, it did so by recruiting from rural America. It is no accident that the frontier and section, not the city, dominated American historiography for the first third of the twentieth century. The civil rights struggle of the last twenty years has tended to obscure the extent to which American society had been broadly discriminatory in earlier years. Among other things, the elite white-collar occupations had been reserved for white Anglo-Saxon males: not only blacks and women but Catholics and Jews need not apply. A survey of the roster of the American Association of University Professors for that period reveals few women, but more women than people of recent immigrant extraction. As those barriers fell, after World War II, the sons of immigrants and working people entered the historical profession, and some of them began exploring questions related to their own backgrounds, including the history of workers.

No bell struck. The 1950s was an age of political quiescence, of consensus. Not much encouragement could be expected from senior scholars; nor was a labor history topic likely to open any doors in the lean job market of those years. I was perhaps more fortunate than others, in having as my mentor at Harvard Oscar Handlin, the pioneering scholar in immigration history. Even so, I was the only member of my seminar to work on a labor history dissertation, and only two or three of Handlin's long line of students ever did so. Here and there across the country, a scattering of other graduate students were moving in the same direction as well. The members of that first generation—Herbert Gutman, Melvyn Dubofsky, David Montgomery—each had his own intellectual odyssey. My own began with an interest in mass thinking, from a reading of Walter Lippmann, and in wartime repression, from a reading of Katherine Ann Porter's novella *Pale Horse,*

Pale Rider. What intrigued me most was the way these issues related to the experience of immigrant workers. Other neophyte labor historians almost certainly shared a similar identification with working-class life. And each one, as he launched his research, was also launching an assault on the institutionalism of the old labor history.

The 1950s constituted a golden age of American historiography. There came of age a remarkable generation of historians—Richard Hofstadter, David Potter, C. Vann Woodward, Oscar Handlin—who emphasized style, analysis that moved on multiple levels, the creative application of the social sciences to the past. All of this stood in shocking contrast to the mechanical research, the one-dimensional analysis, the wooden writing of the existing labor history literature. Young scholars like myself wanted to bring the subtlety and imagination that we saw in Hofstadter's *Age of Reform* or Handlin's *The Uprooted* to the writing of labor history. We wanted to raise the level of the craft. That, almost by definition, meant broadening the focus of labor history. There was a richer history to be explored and more complex questions to be answered than could be found in the story of trade unions. The latter would have to be studied, of course, but as part of the larger history of workers in America. And this conformed, ultimately, to the personal identification that had led us to labor history, in the first place. So, almost as soon as historians entered the field, it was given a thrust in the direction of social history.

Our initial success was, of course, limited. We had to grapple with basic problems of research and conceptualization. For his dissertation study of industrial conflict during the 1870s, Herbert Gutman discovered a rich record in local labor newspapers. David Montgomery uncovered similarly untapped sources for his thesis on labor reform and radical Republicanism, which appeared as his pioneering book *Beyond Equality* (1967). In my case, I originally intended to study the great strike wave of 1919 and its sources in the experience of immigrant workers in wartime America. When that proved too much to handle, I narrowed the topic down to the 1919 steel strike. The material was abundant, for the war period as well as afterward, and my working hypothesis seemed to make sense for the steelworkers. My thesis director, Oscar Handlin, on returning from a sabbatical year in the summer of 1955, approved of what I was doing and suggested that I include a background chapter on the industry and its workers. Handlin's suggestion—casually made, I think—set me off in a new direction. In the end, the "background chapter" turned into two-thirds of the study. What was crucial was the discovery of rich library materials—four volumes of a federal analysis of labor conditions in the steel industry, two statistical volumes on immigrants in the industry in the Dillingham Reports on Immigration, the Pittsburgh Survey, investigations of competition in the steel industry, including stenographic copies of testimony and exhibits in the antitrust suit against United States Steel, and much else from trade journals, company reports, and the labor press. Although I later did research at other libraries, the bulk of what I needed was sitting on the shelves of Widener Library, hitherto unknown to me, and, if known to others, never exploited by them. This material, the fruit of an intense public interest in the steel industry during the Progressive period, enabled me to reconstruct the history of American steelworkers as it had been shaped by technology, management policy, immigration, community, and trade unionism. Into this larger framework I fitted my original interest in the 1919 steel strike.

How large a part accident and discovery played in my writing of *Steelworkers in America: The Nonunion Era* should be all too apparent. But there was nothing accidental about the questions I was asking: *Why did workers come to America? What was their experience inside its mills and factories? How did they accommodate themselves to industrial life? What were the sources of their acquiescence and/or militancy?* These were the kinds of questions inevitably posed by the first generation of historians embarking on the study of labor history. It was in our ability to deal with these questions that we fell short. No one today—certainly no dissertation writer—would settle for my thesis research or cast the subject so broadly. The approved strategy in labor history, as in social history generally, is to cut out a small piece, a local study, and to treat it in depth. Several of Handlin's students, although not in labor history, were actually doing precisely that, just as I was finishing up. . . . For labor history, in any case, the first forays signified more a sense of promise than of actual achievement in writing the history of workers in America.

In the meantime, labor history was carving its place out within the historical profession. The scholarly superstructure developed swiftly—major archives in Detroit, in Atlanta, at Penn State, and elsewhere, a first-rate journal, and regional associations in many parts of the country. The volume of scholarship grew enormously: the annual bibliography in *Labor History* for 1973 listed sixteen pages of articles, as well as fifty-eight dissertations completed that year. The best books in the field attained a standard of craftsmanship the equal of anything to be found elsewhere in the profession. Sidney Fine's *Sit-Down: The General Motors Strike of 1936–1937* was a model of historical reconstruction based on exhaustive research. Irving Bernstein wrote superb narrative history of American labor during the 1920s and 1930s in his *The Lean Years* and *The Turbulent Years*, as did Melvyn Dubofsky for the Industrial Workers of the World in *We Shall Be All*. Most of the first generation of writing, and much even of the 1970s, dealt with the familiar subjects of labor history—leaders, strikes, organizations, politics. The groundwork was thereby also being laid for future work in the field, however. Far more than would have been the case in the 1950s, labor historians of the next decade were strongly positioned for exploiting fresh possibilities of writing the social history of American workers.

The most important influence came from England. Excepting Frederick Jackson Turner's "The Significance of the Frontier in American History" (1893), probably no single historical work has been so eagerly embraced or has set off so strong a surge of American scholarly activity as E. P. Thompson's *The Making of the English Working Class*. The leading figure in a brilliant constellation of English social historians that included Eric

Hobsbawm, George Rudé, and Brian Harrison, Thompson examined dimensions of working-class experience scarcely dreamed of by American
students. Class, Thompson argued, "is a *cultural* as much as an economic
formation." Following Marx, Thompson found "class experience . . .
largely determined by the productive relations into which men are born—
or enter voluntarily." But then: "Class-consciousness is the way these
experiences are handled in cultural terms: embodied in traditions, value
systems, ideas, and institutional forms." Although attentive to the economic
forces unleashed by the industrial revolution, Thompson's book was made
compelling by his brilliant evocation of an emergent working-class culture.
Among the themes that were most striking were Thompson's treatment of
the religious roots of industrial morality, the inner meaning of early labor
politics and reform, and, most important, the habits and customs of working
people as they moved from a preindustrial to an industrial world. Thompson
did more than map out a new terrain of working-class life for exploration.
By his own loving attention to the concrete and specific, he helped to
legitimize the close local study of workers that characterizes so much of
the recent research in American labor history. Most of all, the example of
his historical imagination—his fertile effort to re-create an earlier world of
working people—fired the ambitions of American scholars. They would
seek out and bring to life the hidden history of American working-class
culture.

The Thompsonian influence found its most comprehensive expression
in Herbert Gutman's pioneering essay, "Work, Culture, and Society in
Industrializing America." Gutman became the principal American exponent
of the Thompsonian approach. An inspiring teacher, Gutman set his many
graduate students at the University of Rochester to work on themes suggested by the English social historians. In increasing numbers, dissertations
and monographs began to appear—evangelical religion among Lynn shoemakers, the craft traditions of Danbury hatters, leisure in Fall River and
Lynn, the New England agrarianism of the Lowell textile girls, the cultural
life of Philadelphia workers before the Civil War. The most fully realized
of these early forays was Alan Dawley's *Class and Community: The Industrial Revolution in Lynn*. All of this work focused on the industrializing
phase of American working-class experience. All of it was local in orientation. All of it was inspired by English examples, and, almost always, the
influence was explicitly and gratefully acknowledged.

Very quickly, however, the English models were modified to accommodate to what was specific to the American experience. The ethnic factor,
especially, had to be taken into account, for, historically, immigrants had
made up the bulk of America's industrial labor force. To a large degree,
labor historians realized, the cultural dimensions of American working-class
experience took ethnic forms. In his study of iron molders of Troy, New
York, for example, Daniel Walkowitz treated them first as workers, then
considered their Irish associational activities, and finally revealed that the
web of ethnic relationships with police and politicians made the molders a
powerful presence in Troy in the years after the Civil War. Ethnic identity

was a shaping force for labor solidarity, evident in such various ways as the strike militancy of Slavic miners, the labor boycott as an Irish device in New York City, and the role of ethnic groups in the local labor politics of the Knights of Labor. Other studies stressed ethnocultural tensions as an obstacle to class developments, as, for example, in the Kensington riots of 1844 or in the conflicts between Irish and Cornish hard-rock miners and between French-Canadian and American textile workers. In *The Indispensable Enemy*, Alexander Saxton identified the hatred of the Chinese as a defining experience in California working-class life in the nineteenth century.

The ethnic approach, as it was pushed further, opened up new doors for understanding the work experience in America. In an illuminating study of the Amoskeag mills of Manchester, New Hampshire, for example, Tamara Hareven revealed how important the family system was in the recruitment and work patterns of the French Canadian cotton workers. The movement of immigrants into American industry, we now see, was not random, but—rather flowed through well-defined networks based on family and village ties. Deeper complexities emerge from a recent study of Italians, Poles, and blacks in Pittsburgh during the first third of the twentieth century. Although the three groups arrived with identically low skills, they experienced very different work careers in Pittsburgh. The Italians gravitated to casual and outdoor labor, avoided the factories, and moved up into entrepreneurial occupations. The Poles concentrated in the factories and remained there, with little upward mobility, for generation after generation. The blacks likewise did factory work, but never achieved the stable patterns of the Poles. These differences were attributable partly to ethnic preferences, especially the different preferences of the Italians and the Poles, but partly also to the relationship between family structures and job opportunities. Once inside an industrial plant, Polish workers secured substantial control over recruitment; almost invariably, sons entered the factories through family and personal connections. That, in turn, strengthened the tight family structures of the Polish working-class communities. Sons handed their pay over to their families, lived at home until they married, settled in the same neighborhoods afterward, and rarely moved far up the occupational ladder. The sons of black workers, on the other hand, could not rely on their fathers for jobs. The result was a quite different family pattern among working-class blacks: young people left at an early age, and the predominant unit was the isolated nuclear family of parents and children. The ethnic orientation has thus permitted the exploration of intricacies of working-class experience that would have been wholly inaccessible to earlier generations of labor historians.

The scholars studying ethnicity and work, unlike those interested in ethnicity and working-class culture, would probably not classify themselves as labor historians. This points to a second force, beyond that deriving from England, that has strongly advanced the historical study of workers in America, namely the growth of the new social history in all its guises. The hallmark throughout has been an unremitting focus on the "plain people"—to use Peter Knights' phrase—and these are in the main working people. The compartmentalizing of fields . . . necessarily are eroding, as historians press forward in their studies of the "plain people." The social historian may start out thinking he is studying city life, politics, or immigrants, and, depending on where his research carries him, may discover himself on the terrain of other disciplines. In the preceding paragraph on work and ethnicity, the attentive reader should have noticed that the key linkage occurs through family structure. . . . Questions of social mobility also figure strongly in the discussion. . . . Such fruitful intermingling of interests enlivens the new social history generally and enormously expands the pool of information available for any given field. As compared to twenty years ago, today's labor historian can draw on a vastly larger literature exploring the history of the American worker.

He is able also to borrow from what is innovative in the new social history. Quantitative methodology, never of much interest to the Commons school, has become an important tool in labor history. A number of old questions have thereby yielded fresh answers. By measuring the occupational composition of its membership, for example, Alan Dawley has shown that the organization of the Knights of St. Crispin was not an artisan revolt against the modernization of the shoe industry. The social origins and career lines of trade-union leaders have been traced in Warren Van Tine's *The Making of the Labor Bureaucrat, 1870–1920*. As more complex questions are tackled, more sophisticated use is sure to be made of computers and statistical analysis. This, in turn, depends on another kind of borrowing from the new social history, namely, from the innovative themes it is addressing. Labor historians now commonly deal with questions of social mobility, neighborhoods, family patterns, and living standards in their studies of working-class communities.

So far, we have treated the new labor history as essentially the beneficiary of influences coming from elsewhere; but there have been forces at work very specific to the study of labor history. One was ideological. Labor history, Eric Hobsbawm has remarked, "is by tradition a highly political subject." It had not been so in the United States, at least not in Hobsbawm's sense. Not Marxists, but the followers of Commons and Perlman dominated, and they wrote a labor history celebratory of pure-and-simple unionism. There was an American radical school, exemplified especially in the prolific writings of Philip Foner, but it was vastly less consequential than its European counterparts. Only in the 1960s did a strong radical wave sweep the American field; but, when it did so, it took forms very much encouraging of a social history orientation.

In part, that was the doing of E. P. Thompson and other English social historians, who wrote out of a Marxist tradition; American enthusiasts who seized on their brilliant findings tended to absorb their class framework, as well. More crucial, probably, were two developments indigenous to the American radical scene. One was the corporate-liberal interpretation advanced by James Weinstein in his *The Corporate Ideal in the Liberal State*. Far from challenging the power of American business, Weinstein argued, liberal reform was really a strategy by the corporate sector to shore up the status quo. Among Weinstein's key themes was the easy co-optation of the labor movement: unions were a ready partner of big business in the battle against socialism and the incipient radicalism of American workers. By so denigrating American trade unionism, the corporate-liberal argument weakened the legitimacy of traditional labor history and encouraged scholars to focus their attention more directly on the experience of the workers themselves. The positive impulse in that direction—and powerful it was— came from the New Left. From the late 1960s onward, partly as a result of the surge of labor militancy in the United States and in Europe, partly as a result of the waning energy of the student movement, the New Left shifted its ground and took up the cause of the worker. Rallying cries for "history from the bottom up" and for a "history of the inarticulate" were soon strongly felt within labor history. The initial tendency was to seek out the true history of American radicalism in the "self activity" of the workers. Much attention was given to mass militancy, as, for example, in Jeremy Brecher's *Strike!* The most influential of New Left labor historians, Staughton Lynd, extolled the insurgent movements of the 1930s and located their failure in the institutional rigidity of the Communist Party. The oral-history collection *Rank and File*, edited by Lynd and his wife, Alice, remains a powerful statement of the notion of the worker as indispensable actor of American labor history. The ideological sources of this writing, however, were quickly spent, and its balder formulations soon left behind; but the rank-and-file orientation survives. Among the younger generation of labor historians are many who passed through the radical movements of the 1960s; they retain from that experience a continuing determination not to be distracted from the hard task of writing labor history with workers at its center.

Nothing is more fascinating to the student of history than the way a new perception on the past opens up. In the early 1970s, such an event was happening in American labor history. Both social history and the English school had taught labor historians to see workers as members of communities, as bearers of religious beliefs, ethnic identities, political affiliations. Their specific identities as workers, especially as craft members, were likewise primarily related to their ways of life. Now a different focus emerged: what was the experience of workers on the job? While it is not altogether clear what prompted that question in the early 1970s, it certainly had roots in New Left traditions and in the rampant shop-floor unrest that was seen, for example, in the Lordstown strike of 1972. In the mysterious ways in which historical thinking moves, in any case, a number of writers at roughly the same moment began to study workers within the work place. They were, moreover, preoccupied with one theme—the ongoing struggle between workers and managers over control of the labor process.

Scholars have come to shop-floor history from two directions. One group, very much influenced by Harry Braverman's *Labor and Monopoly Capital: The Degradation of Work in the Twentieth Century*, has concerned itself with the managerial assault on the autonomy of workers. Taking as his text Frederick W. Taylor's *Principles of Scientific Management*, Braverman stressed above all the unceasing compulsion American management has felt to rationalize production. This imperative, Braverman argued, was inherent in the capitalist system, and the invariable consequence was the alienation of the worker from his work. Attracted by its implications for corporate capitalism, a group of radical economists have been drawn into the historical study of this problem. Their findings have been ably synthesized in Richard Edwards's *Contested Terrain: The Transformation of the Workplace in the Twentieth Century*. Labor-segmentation theory, a related argument developed by some of the same scholars, focuses on the way corporate employers secure the compliance of labor. Their workers become a permanent work force, fitted into a rationalized job structure and adequately rewarded, but also held in check by an ever-present reserve army of casual workers made up of women and minorities. Historians, while not on the cutting edge of this kind of analysis, have done important work in establishing the managerial context. Most notable on labor policy is Daniel Nelson's *Managers and Workers: Origins of the New Factory System*, and, on the larger managerial structure, Alfred D. Chandler's *Visible Hand: The Managerial Revolution in American Business*.

The other side of the story—the response of workers—has been very much the province of labor historians. They have been especially influenced by the work of David Montgomery. Montgomery has written provocatively on the autonomy of craft workers in the nineteenth-century factory and a workers' ethic of manliness underlying that independence, and on the evolution of the trade-union agreement as a device for formalizing and enforcing traditional work rules. He has identified the first two decades of the twentieth century as the critical period in the struggle over workers' control. The strike waves of those years constituted labor's response, largely futile, to management's aggressive deployment of machinery and managerial techniques in American factories. Like Gutman, Montgomery has been a prolific graduate teacher—the University of Pittsburgh became a major center in labor history during his tenure there—and his students have begun to explore on many fronts the themes of workers' control.

Another research strategy, rich in its potential, thus has opened up, pursuing the worker—not out into the community, but into the factory and at his workbench. What is especially important is the access that shop-floor history gives to the modern period of labor history. With a few notable exceptions, studies of working-class culture have been confined to the nineteenth century. The study of shop-floor activity will not be thus limited. The struggle of workers to retain control over the job and of managers to subordinate them to a rationalized system of production is a continuing story that does not end at any given stage of industrialization. Thus shop-floor history holds special significance for labor historians of the modern period, for it permits them to get at the experience of working people even in the age of mature collective bargaining. . . .

But what larger meaning will be invested in such a people's history? No clear synthesis has yet emerged. The new labor historian, for one, finds himself in a very different intellectual setting from the scholars of the Wisconsin school. By its nature, institutional history provided for its adherents a clear framework—none was clearer than the American trade union, with its well-defined structure and rules. On a larger scale, Selig Perlman's *Theory of the Labor Movement* performed the same function. As historians pushed out beyond trade union history, they necessarily left the safe haven of Perlman's explicit framework. The thrust of the current scholarship goes strongly against the construction of a new one. Research has focused itself on the intensive local study of workers. We have, moreover, developed an acute sense of the complexity and variety of American working-class experience, in which all lines of inquiry—family, ethnicity, mobility, technology, custom—converge to form an intricate network of connections. At its best, the new labor history has been highly imaginative at establishing linkages between various aspects of working-class experience and at conveying the totality of that experience at a given time and place; but such an approach, necessarily inward-looking, militates against systematic thinking about a new synthesis for American labor history.

For a while, *The Making of the English Working Class* seemed a sufficient guide. The enormous enthusiasm for Thompson's great book derived not only from our discovery of the richness of labor history, but equally from the expectation that, once we had acquired a comparable body of information, we would then go on to write our own *Making of the American Working Class.* Thompson's class formulation may serve admirably in the English setting. Thus, Gareth Stedman Jones, pushing his research into late nineteenth century, has written confidently of "the basic consistency of outlook reflected in the new working-class culture which spread over England after 1870." And further: "The distinctiveness of a working-class way of life was enormously accentuated. Its separateness and impermeability were now reflected in a dense and inward-looking culture." Like Gareth Stedman Jones, we have been busily gathering the evidence of American working-class culture; but labor historians cannot share Jones's confidence of discovering for American workers a "basic consistency of outlook" and a "distinctive . . . way of life."

Thompson's class analysis turned on the interaction between a settled population of English working people, especially cloth-making and metalworking artisans, and a new industrial order that was demonstrably antagonistic to working people's customs and values. Early America, advanced as England in most other ways, lacked such a pre-industrial laboring population. While colonial artisans have been intensively studied in recent years, such research has neither assumed nor discovered that the roots of an American working class are to be found in the laboring people of pre-industrial America. Unlike England, moreover, the recruits to American industrialism were sharply divided along ethnic, racial, and religious lines. And the defining issue—labor's struggle for political rights—was largely absent from the United States: the ballot came to American workers early and without much conflict. For all we have learned from Thompson and his English colleagues, American labor historians cannot expect to develop a new synthesis along the lines of *The Making of the English Working Class*. If not through the idea of a unified working-class culture, then where is the alternative approach for American labor history? No answer is yet at hand.

In this quandary, labor history is at one with the entire field of social history. The problem of synthesis served, indeed, as the theme of Bernard Bailyn's presidential address before the American Historical Association in 1981. The vitality of the new scholarship is evident at every hand—in the volume of research under way, in the accumulating monographic literature, in the prominence given social history within the historical profession. This momentum can be sustained, however, only if it leads to a synthesis that will provide guidance for future scholarship and, more important, help to reshape the existing perception of American social development. The truncated state of the field—rich in its findings, unclear as to larger meaning—places synthesis high on the agenda of American labor historians and of social historians generally.

Work and Family

ELIZABETH H. PLECK

. . . Efforts to mesh two important specialties, labor history and the history of the family, seem particularly worthwhile because in their concern for work and family these topics embrace two of the more fundamental areas of human activity and emotional investment. Some developments in labor and family history make it possible to examine the link between the two in some detail. Historians of labor, once concerned almost exclusively with the organization of labor unions, are now analyzing the significance of work itself. In the meantime, historians of the family, who initially focused on changes in household composition, have become increasingly interested in family norms, especially the changing emotional climate of the family. Ironically, these two rather similar trends (the shift in interest from organizational membership to changes in norms) have developed separately, as if families existed without workers and workers were devoid of families. One sociologist, in fact, has argued that modern industrial society and the corporation helped to propagate the "myth of separate worlds," the division between the spheres of work and of the family. Whatever the reasons for this inattention to the intersection of the two worlds, it seems obvious that the description of relationships between work and family makes for a richer and more complex social history.

A single sociological theory has informed most of the historical study of the relationship between work and family—this is that industrialization led to the separation of home and work. . . .

Functionalist theory assumes that industrialization fundamentally altered the balance between the family and other social institutions. Although

Elizabeth Pleck, "Two Worlds in One: Work and Family," in *Journal of Social History*, 10 (Winter 1976), pp. 178–189. Reprinted by permission of JSH.

the consequences arising from this separation of work and family were many, only one—the family's loss of its role in production—has been isolated as the crucial factor. A long list of other results has been attributed to the loss of the family's production function, including the decline of kinship as the basis of work organization, the loss of power for mothers and children, the revolt of youth against their parents, the emergence of adolescence as a separate life stage, and greater sexual freedom for young women. Some historians have minimized the extent of these social changes, or attributed them to causes other than the loss of the family's economic function. Not enough attention, however, has been paid to specifying the nature and scope of the family's loss of productive function—indeed, to whether such a loss of function occurred at all. . . .

Did industrialization cause the separation of home and work? Historians have modified or limited this interpretation without fundamentally challenging it. In this paper, I will first examine . . . historical work that partly refutes this interpretation, and then describe briefly two alternative emphases, also derived from contemporary work which present more promising lines of inquiry. Since issues in the history of work and family cross national boundaries, I have drawn on research in American and European social history. I have ordered the evidence from historical research, largely designed for purposes other than addressing this argument, into four different categories of arguments against the notion that industrialization created two distinct worlds for work and family.

1. Until recent times, separation of home and work characterized only the middle-class.

Historians of the Victorian family, as a case in point, have closely followed the functionalist emphasis on differentiation between family and work roles. Their descriptions of the Victorian middle-class family merely restates much of the sociological argument: the home was a place of repose where the breadwinner recuperated from the world of work. Only the husband earned an income and he alone moved between the two worlds. As family and work became increasingly separated, the Victorian home became more privatized, with separation of physical space for mothers and children and the division of the house between the more public and more private areas.

In this greater differentiation of function, a new role emerged for women: the glorification of motherhood. Mothers devoted increased hours of attention to their children. Removed from wage-earning, children became dependents in the family and took years preparing to enter the world of work. Husbands and wives increasingly inhabited two different emotional worlds—the task-preoccupied husband taking only a leisure time interest in the family, his expressive wife providing all the love and nurturance.

This argument points out the class dimension of a process—that work and family life first became separated among the middle classes where only one breadwinner was required to maintain the family. All the consequences of this new style of life—the glorification of motherhood, the new stages of childhood and adolescence, the segregation of fathers from their families—were attributed to the prosperity of these families and the loss of the productive role from the home. In this argument, the home, devoid of economic activity, served as a retreat from the world of work.

2. *Contrary to the functionalist assumption, production in the home declined gradually.*

Two systems of work, production on the farm or in the household and production in the factory coexisted for at least a century. The major form of home production was farming; as late as 1900, nearly two-thirds of all American families earned their living from the land. Nor did the development of industry simply end family enterprise. In the United States, France, England or Italy during the nineteenth century, daughters from farm families worked in the textile mills and returned home with wages and money for a dowry (or, at least in the United States, for their brother's education). Working sons and daughters often left the farm only to return with money which helped purchase capital improvements, thereby increasing the value of their inheritance.

Even with the organization of production in factories, many commodities were still produced at home. Everything from shoes, cigars and matchboxes to artificial flowers and buttons was made there. Even printing presses were located originally in shops next to the family living quarters. Some technological changes outside the home actually increased work within it. The sewing machine, located in a small corner of the family's apartment, made it possible to produce more garments at home, and as late as the 1880s, most apparel for American women, with the exception of cloaks, was made by families sewing in their apartments. With the introduction of new shears, for example, garments were cut at factories and parcelled out to sewing families. In fact, the lower wages of family workers at home led to a decline in craft shops and a rise in sweated labor.

Such commodity production, of course, gradually ended; however, the demise of the early handloom weavers in England has often been interpreted as the abrupt end of the family workshop. Actually, . . . home production declined much less rapidly in Western Europe than in England or the United States, and when handloom weaving finally disappeared in Europe, it was replaced by dressmaking in France, silk manufacturing in Italy and linen cloth making in Belgium. By the end of the nineteenth century the home economy still generated income and employment. In the cities, filled with migrants, taking boarders was a major wage-earning occupation of women, especially among childless married women with no outside employment. Around the turn of the century between 20% and 30% of American families accepted boarders. The persistence of all these forms of home production and services indicates considerable economic activity within the household.

Another development in the home economy was the rise of service industries. In some cases, wage-earners took work into their own homes (for example, laundresses), but such labor was performed mostly in the employer's home. While the most common category of female employment in the United States or in Western Europe around the turn of the century was domestic service, it was only one of a large list of home service occupations which included home repairs (plumbing, carpentry, repair and gardening) along with services outside the home (laundry and restaurants). Since homes purchased the services of workers, they continued to be centers of economic exchange, if not of commodity production.

The modifications of the functionalist interpretation accept the basic definitions of terms; they merely argue for a more precise dating of the decline in home production. The family workshop declined gradually—far more slowly in some European countries than in England or in America. Along with the organization of industry, home production grew and even prospered as it absorbed certain technological improvements. The two modes of work organization actually developed simultaneously for almost a century.

3. Market work moved outside the home but nonmarket work remained.

A new group of "home economists," that is, econometricians interested in the household as an economic unit, have challenged the old distinction between production and consumption. They point out that production and consumption are both merely allocations of time between monetized and nonmonetized activities. It takes time and purchased raw material to produce commodities—whether steel in a rolling mill or dinner at home. The steelworker receives wages for doing his labor while the housewife does not. The dinner is immediately "used" while the steel is exchanged for cash or credit. This perspective on work deemphasizes wage-earning, suggesting a much broader definition of "work" which includes nonmarket labor, most of which was (and is) performed by women.

Marxist historians also have emphasized the role of women in production; in maintaining and servicing the worker—the wife, according to Engels, "became the first domestic servant." For families only slightly above subsistence, these kinds of economic activities were the margin of survival. In Pittsburgh, for example, where around the turn of the century there were few municipal services in working-class districts, a steelworker who wanted clean clothes, water to bathe in or drink, or a cooked meal, required the services of a wife. Most unmarried male workers lived in boarding houses where there was at least one woman who performed this work. Beyond this direct form of maintenance, wives and children denied themselves food, garments, and heat in order to sustain and clothe the breadwinner. With increasing prosperity, wifely services were directed less toward family survival than toward maintaining high standards of cleanliness, child care, nutrition and leisure, all of which required greater time investments, and modern studies of housework (between 1920 and 1970) show no substantial change in the number of hours devoted to household tasks despite rising real wages and the introduction of more technology in the home. Even in the Victorian period, middle-class women—far from idle—

devoted a full week's work to housecare. The typical middle-class housewife hired a servant for the heavier tasks, but still performed most of her own cleaning. The one major change during this period was the increasing allocation of time to child care, an investment of the mother's hours occasioned as much by changing job requirements in middle-class work as by new sentiments towards children.

In connection with the pursuit of particular strategies of family fertility, it can be argued that reproduction was, in fact, a continuation of home production. In the view of some Marxists, children were commodities made in the home; that is, in a strictly economic sense, children were produced by time and labor and when mature, they repaid their parents' initial investment with either wages or free labor. Whether from farm or factory families they were needed as workers and as investments for their parents' old age. Parents purposely kept their daughters from marrying early in order to retain the extra wages. In so doing, they raised their daughters' marriage age, thereby lowering the number of future grandchildren. Thus these family strategies manipulated the production of labor power in the household.

Thus, to these two groups of economists, the family's functions at home and at work form part of the larger economic program; that is, productive activities within the home include the unpaid labor of a housewife along with her reproduction of children. By defining "work" in this manner, these groups of economists have revised the view of housework and also its relationship to paid employment. Still, these arguments only limit but do not contradict the functionalist interpretation. If one amended the argument to read, "industrialization caused a decline in the home production *of goods and services for exchange*," there would be no apparent objection from these theorists.

4. To a great extent, home and work were separated prior to industrialization.

Some historians are prone to argue that the separation of home and work occurred prior to factory production. Work in pre-industrial society was, of course, organized on a far smaller scale; it was often performed in households, on farms, or in craft shops. But if the question is one of whether families worked together in such settings, there is abundant evidence that they did not. To demonstrate that home and work were separated in pre-industrial society, one would begin by pointing out that the family in that period was *never integrated* as a work force. The level of population mobility was extremely high; between one- and two-thirds of the inhabitants in English and colonial American villages moved away in less than a decade. These migrants were adults, landless workers looking for jobs, or men impressed into the armies—or adolescents employed away from home as servants, apprentices, or live-in laborers. In colonial America the putting out of children with neighboring families was common. Even among children who lived at home, many worked as hired hands and servants for neighbors.

Sometimes these child laborers wanted to retain control over their own wages rather than contribute to the family economy. Where families worked the land together, death was so common that the family was often forced to employ outside workers. Such evidence contradicts the simplistic sociological notion that "in the earlier household economy, the members of the family daily worked together at home to produce their livelihood. . . ."

One might even argue that for a short interval economic and technological change created working families of this pure sociological model. Introduction of new machinery indeed led to the specialization of labor, thereby creating cottage industries where whole families produced commodities within the household. Family togetherness was even more usual among households in factory towns than in rural areas. However, the common residence of teenagers with the family was more frequent in industrial cities than in rural areas simply because adolescent children could find work in the mills. Thus, if the argument for the preindustrial integration of work and family is based solely on the fact of common residence in the family, then one cannot prove that work and family were integrated.

More substantially, one can argue that it was the subdivision of land rather than factory production that destroyed the functional unity of the family. Only because land was controlled by parents and economic opportunity was restricted was it possible for children to remain as family workers. Philip Greven's study of farmers in colonial Massachusetts traces the dissolution of the family work unit. In 17th century Andover adult children remained on these small farms, even postponing marriage, in return for their eventual inheritance of the property. As a result of the continued division of the land into smaller parcels, these Andover sons finally became less interested in inheriting the property and began to settle new farms far from their parents' residences.

As much or more unity of work and family was to be found in industrial settings as in farming areas. Some industries, like textile production in England, France, or the United States, employed the whole family. Sometimes English spinners hired their own sons as assistants. . . . In a similar American situation during the same period, Tamara Hareven reports that families recruited the laborers for the textile mills of Manchester, New Hampshire, and even controlled their placement within the factory's workrooms. Glassblowers, file makers and miners in France, England and the United States worked alongside their relatives. The extent of family control over conditions of work varied among industries; it is conceivable that families held greater sway in the textile industry, where women and children were often employed in the work force, than in heavy industries such as steel or machine production.

The argument concerning family cohesion in pre-industrial society proposes causes other than industrialization for the declining economic function of the family. Patterns of land inheritance largely determined the composition of the family work force. Landless wage laborers were as separated from their homes as modern proletarians. In fact, cottage industry and the employment of whole families in factories actually increased the unity of the family work force. The family's economic function was beginning to decline prior to industrialization, and in certain respects, it achieved a new unity as a result of industrial development.

In effect, the first three refutations amount only to slight modifications of functionalist theory; they try to show that the family lost its productive role only gradually, with rapid change occurring first for the bourgeoisie and subsequently for the working class, and with production for use continuing within the household. This fourth more drastic refutation of functionalist argument—that the family workplace was breaking down prior to industrialization—questions the cause of the decline but not the decline itself. Yet these backward or forward oscillations do little to advance the study of work and family. . . .

Beyond functionalist theory, two alternative perspectives apply to the study of the relationship between work and family. One, exchange theory, invokes a specific theoretical perspective to explain how changes in control over economic resources altered the family economy; a second emphasizes changes in the structures and norms in the workplace.

Exchange theory analyzes the relationship between work and family by examining the process of bargaining between family members. In this model, relatives with varying resources engage in any number of exchanges with each other. The outcomes—changes in family power, psychic rewards, or the psychological climate within the family—result from differential control of resources, that is, what holds the family (or any other social system) together is the norm of reciprocity, the assumption that one will receive payment in exchange for goods and/or services. According to this argument, one possible resource, although not the only one, is the income of family wage-earners. In studying the textile workers in Preston, England, Michael Anderson found a shift from normative kinship to calculative kinship, as the weight of community opinion, religion and tradition decreased, and the rational appraisal of mutual needs increased. Human needs—for housing, jobs, child care, nursing during sickness and assistance in old age—were met by family members, whose alternatives were largely determined by two factors: their relative possession of resources and the number of available partners. These structural conditions determined the whole content of kin relationships, even the pattern of household composition in Preston.

For all its analytic power in explaining the persistence of kinship in industrial society, certain objections may be made to exchange theory. Empirical studies in this perspective often define resources and rewards only in economic terms, forgetting that physical attractiveness, level of social skills, educational backgrounds and the potential for violence are resources as well. Exchange theory takes a highly instrumental view of interpersonal relations, assuming that "people engage in a kind of mental bookkeeping before they enter into relations and that they perform a periodic audit of the ones they have." Behavior is sometimes motivated by rational calculations but it is also influenced by personality needs, irrational factors, and the desire to emulate norms. Yet despite these weaknesses exchange theory has several advantages over functionalism. It shifts emphasis from the description of family functions to the interactive process (bargaining) between family members. And, it portrays the family as a potential arena of conflict rather than consensus between relatives with differing resources and needs.

From a second, less rigorously analytic perspective, one can examine how family norms determine one's position and perspective toward work. Specifically, this perspective describes the relationships between family life and changes in the salience, culture and scheduling of work. In their studies of women workers in nineteenth-century Europe, Joan Scott and Louise Tilly argue that despite new economic roles, women workers still defined themselves as members of the family enterprise. Even though changes in work and values eventually led to a decline in familialism, premodern values continued to persist in new environments and, in turn, determined behavior in these new locations. Under this analysis "behavior is less the product of new ideas than of the effects of old ideas operating in new or changing contexts." A diametrically opposite point of view is presented by Edward Shorter in *The Making of the Modern Family* where he argues that capitalism created rather immediate consequences, especially for young women working far from their familial homes. Removed from social controls and [economically] independent for the first time, these women sought and found sexual freedom, as reflected in the higher rate of legitimate and illegitimate births between 1750 and 1800. If women workers under capitalism achieved "economic independence" and thereby increased their sexual activity, one would have to show that 1) women's wages were high enough to insure independence, and 2) that women workers controlled their earnings. On both counts, the evidence goes against Shorter. Women's wages were less than men's (one-half of men's in the nineteenth century English garment industry, for example), too low to allow for residence separate from the family. The wages were often set lower, in fact, because employers assumed that women were living at home. A working woman was far less likely to control her own wages than her male counterpart; in 19th century France employers often gave the entire paycheck to the family of the working girl. As late as the 1920s most American working daughters living at home turned over their entire paycheck to their families and the ones living away from home donated at least half of their wages.

It is an odd commentary on the study of work and family that issues about changing commitment to work are posed only for women workers— who presumably experienced conflict between the two worlds, which male employees did not. The real issue is not whether capitalism altered or did not alter women's fundamental attitudes towards work and the family but that historians . . . have gone beyond functionalist theory to examine changing behavior in the workplace as well as in the family. The next stage, then, is to examine these changes within the context of *specific occupational cultures,* rather than to refer to the "capitalist marketplace" or to the general conditions of poverty.

How did the physical and emotional demands of work alter family life?

In many unskilled occupations, demands outside of working hours were minimal (thereby successfully dividing work and family into separate entities), but in as many others, time demands intruded on the worker's leisure and on the life of other family members. Most of the "absorptive" occupations were careers, whose characteristics sociologists have defined as a series of "age-graded," upwarded occupational changes. Some of these highly absorptive occupations were structured as "two-person" careers, involving the paid efforts of the husband and also the unpaid assistance of a wife (and sometimes of other family members). For some such careers, . . . work residence was combined with family living arrangements, such as the rectory, the embassy, the apartment above the family store or even the White House.

We know very little about the history of this category of occupations, which emerged in the 18th and 19th centuries, even though such careers reordered relationships in middle-class family life. What has been described as the "cult of domesticity" might be better understood as the family response to the emergence of the male career. For middle-class wives membership in charity organizations or social clubs or home entertaining was actually designed to advance a husband in his work. The emergence of the career may have had other consequences as well, perhaps delayed age at marriage or postponement of child-bearing. Possibly the fertility decline among the middle class in the 19th century was [as] much a response to the new male career as to changes in the level of prosperity, in middle-class values or in the wife's power.

Aside from the absorptiveness of any occupation, the additional characteristics of work—its structure, emotions, and norms—have transformed family life. Particular jobs reshaped the individual's personality by presenting a set of learning experiences that socialized his or her view of the world. Pessimism, insecurity, physical fatigue were often the consequences of menial work, just as self-esteem, control and autonomy were often psychological traits derived from bureaucratic tasks. New work experiences not only changed workers' perceptions but also introduced them to heretofore unavailable skills, such as when domestic servants in 19th-century France learned to read and write while at work. At the same time the experience in work coincided with altered levels of fertility. We know very little about this important connection, even though there is abundant information about the effects of occupational level on fertility. Yet it is clear that even within the same occupational stratum, only certain work was coincident with high fertility. Michael Haines has analyzed the reasons for high fertility among miners' families in England, Wales, Prussia and the United States around the turn of the century, arguing that in mining villages isolated from urban influences, premodern values towards the importance of children persisted. This, along with other factors—the absence of work opportunities for women, the men's relatively high wages and short period of peak earnings—contributed to high fertility.

Finally, the cultural milieu of work shaped leisure and family styles. Gareth Stedman Jones shows that by the end of the 19th century, the decline in the work day had increased the extent of working-class leisure for the whole family; he documents the rise of the new sex-segregated institutions among the working class—the pub, the men's clubs and sporting activities.

Changes in the scheduling of work also altered family life. Many labor historians have argued that despite the imposition of new scheduling, some workers continued to favor preindustrial habits of work, family, and leisure. As late as the middle- to late-19th century, industrial workers celebrated "St. Monday," a non-scheduled day of leisure from work. . . . Despite considerable scattered evidence about the effect of changes in scheduling on "family time," we need to know more about how the introduction of scheduled working hours and work days (or, for that matter night shifts), or the adoption of scheduled time in the schools changed family life. In addition to reducing the work hours during the day, the declining number of workdays and the sequencing of days or weeks away from work (that is, "holidays" or vacations), may have created more opportunities for family leisure. Any single change in the time or timing of school or work reverberated throughout the two worlds. Another aspect of scheduling change was the sequencing of the family life cycle with the world of work. The investigation of changes in these life cycle events (age at leaving home, marriage, birth of first and last child, widowhood) has occupied so much scholarly effort that little attention has been given to how the changing life cycle redounded on the world of work, although it is clear that an increase in family poverty—due to the absence of a mother's or child's labor—or more sexual freedom that often resulted from leaving the parental home can be understood as the changing intersection between the family's needs and the world of work.

To understand the history of work and family, historians must begin by rejecting theories based on "the myth of separate worlds," the separation of home and work under industrialization. They have raised objections and offered modifications of this argument without questioning its assumptions. One cannot study the relationship between work and family if it is assumed that the connections are only tangential. Functionalist analysis must be replaced by perspectives which examine how people reconciled the two worlds. I have suggested two possible approaches, although even in these alternative perspectives, there are difficulties and limitations. There is the danger for one thing of describing only one part of the process—how work affects family, or how family affects work. It will be necessary not only to follow the worker home from the job, but also to observe activity within the home and to study the influence of the family on the worker's partic-ipation in and involvement with work. If work and family form a larger whole, the social historian must specify how people move between the domains and demands of both worlds.

Capitalism, Class, and Labor History

MICHAEL REICH

Modes of Explanation in U.S. Labor History

The outpouring of scholarship in labor history and in social history in recent decades has literally turned two old fields upside down, in each case changing the focus of the subject matter and the principal explanatory orientation used to analyze it. . . . The old labor history focused primarily upon the evolution of U.S. labor unions and the experiences of organized workers in relation to their union leaders. Labor history was identified primarily with the history of official labor organizations.

By contrast, the subject matter of the new labor history has drawn attention to the diversity of U.S. workers' experiences, whether unionized or not, and the new social history has drawn attention to the everyday lives of all kinds of ordinary Americans, whether articulate or not. The new scholarship has provided a more rounded view of all Americans' historical experiences. It has given voice to hitherto neglected groups and shown how the working class and other groups have affected the historical process.

. . . [T]he principal explanatory orientation of the old labor history involved an articulated theoretical framework of industrial and labor development. Rapid and prosperous industrialization, together with the early achievement of liberal democratic political institutions, inevitably produced a working class, industrial relations system, and labor leadership with a specified functional character. Initial conditions in the United States differed from those in Europe and explain the differing characteristics of labor movements in each area.

In contrast, the new labor and the new social history utilize a theoretical framework that emphasizes historical contingency, with culture and consciousness rather than iron laws of macroeconomic or political development as the primary generating factors. Historical change is seen as contingent upon human action, which itself is informed by consciousness. Working-class culture, consciousness, and organization are seen as developing in a conflictual context, created by the unequal class relations and institutionalized power of industrializing capitalism. But the outcome of this process is not preordained, one way or another, and need not conform to any functional fit. . . .

The attention to contingency and culture certainly constitutes an important and welcome corrective to the theoretical approach of the old labor history. Yet, what has become of the economic forces and systematic determinants that loomed so large in the old scholarship? To some extent, they seem to be returning in the latest wave of the new labor history. . . .

One strand of this literature presents a new twist on an old labor history

Abridged from Michael Reich, "Capitalist Development, Class Relations, and Labor History," in J. Carroll Moody and Alice Kessler-Harris, eds., *Perspectives on American Labor History*. © 1989 by Northern Illinois University Press. Reprinted with permission of the publisher.

theme: changes in the organization of work during the process of industrialization displaced skilled artisans and small workshops and replaced them with less-skilled mass production workers employed in massive factories. But the changeover took much longer and was less linear in progression than was once thought, and skilled workers played a more active and class-conscious role than was previously thought. The historical diversity of the working class is thus now understood as partly rooted in the diversity of the labor process. Another strand reproduces some central themes of the new labor history: workers' culture at the workplace; the culture they bring to the workplace as well as the culture they create there, and not just economics and technology, play a constitutive role in the organization of work and the conflictual politics of industrial relations. . . .

Whereas the link to economic factors and the old labor history seems to be in the process of reconstruction, it does not yet seem to have been made in a systematic or synthesizing manner. . . . The new scholarship, goes the complaint, has been primarily addressed to microscopic case studies to the neglect of the recasting of grand and overarching themes. A new periodization and synthesis are needed.

The development of an integrative theoretical framework within which we could reinterpret the new scholarship certainly sounds desirable. But, how can it be constructed? . . .

This essay suggests that a new labor history synthesis must not only integrate culture and economics. It must also rest upon a more articulated overall conception of U.S. capitalist development than the new labor history has utilized thus far. To do so we need not return to the overly linear, deterministic, and functional theory of capitalist development of the old labor history. Proponents of a new radical political economics, including myself, have been working to improve and broaden our theories of capitalist development. Our approach emphasizes the constitutive importance of culture and politics in the evolution of economic structures. It is, I believe, complementary with the central contributions of the new labor history.

In a recent book, David M. Gordon, Richard Edwards, and I have tried to construct the outline of such an analysis. We developed a political-economic theory of macroeconomic development and drew from both the old and the new labor scholarship to offer an integrated interpretation of the history of the U.S. working class. Labor history, we proposed, should be embedded in a larger account of the dynamics of capitalist development and class conflict. The history of labor and labor struggles can be understood only if linked to macrodynamic developments, not just at the level of individual communities or workplaces but in the social and political order as a whole. . . .

A Stage Theory of Capitalist Development and Class Conflict

It is common to view capitalism as a distinct stage of human history. Yet, capitalism itself has undergone several decisive qualitative transformations, suggesting that capitalism has passed through successive stages of development. Since the 1820s, U.S. capitalism has undergone three major historical changes, each involving a new stage of development. The first stage, competitive capitalism, lasted until the 1890s. In this period slavery was abolished and the capitalist form of organizing production emerged dominant over production by independent artisans or family labor. This period was a stage of competitive capitalism because competition among capitalists became increasingly prevalent in most industries.

Competitive capitalism gave way to the second stage, monopoly capitalism, around the turn of the century, when immense concentrations of capital emerged. The large capitalists now became dominant not only over artisans and family labor but also over small capitalists and industrial workers. The Great Depression of the 1930s challenged this dominance, and a new stage of capitalism, contemporary capitalism, then followed.

In order to understand these decisive changes in U.S. capitalism, we need a theory of the stages of capitalist development that emphasizes the broader environment within which accumulation and change take place. The theory presented here begins with the observation that the institutions surrounding the process of capitalist accumulation must make a coherent structure, called the *social structure of accumulation,* or SSA, for successful capitalist accumulation to proceed.

The social structure of accumulation consists of the specific political, economic, social, and cultural environment within which the capitalist accumulation process is organized. These institutions include "economic" structures, such as the organization of producing firms and markets; the sources of raw materials, labor, and capital; the monetary and credit system; the pattern of state involvement in the economy; and the organization of work and the structure of labor markets. They encompass such international institutions as the organization of international trade, finance, and investment. Equally important, the institutions of the SSA crucially include "cultural" and "political" institutions such as the character of class consciousness, organization and conflict, and the nature of political coalitions and parties.

Once constructed, a social structure of accumulation passes through a life cycle that is connected to its ability to facilitate the capitalist accumulation process. A period of rapid economic growth depends upon the creation of a favorable SSA. But successful capital accumulation ultimately runs into its own limits, the limits imposed by the existing institutional structures or the limits created when it begins to destabilize those structures. With the onset of economic stagnation, the institutions of the structure of accumulation become further undermined. Class conflict is likely to intensify, as each group attempts to defend its existing position and offer and struggle for a vision of an alternative institutional arrangement.

A difficult and lengthy period of institutional reconstruction ensues, requiring experimentation with alternatives, collective action, and the forging of a new political consensus. This new consensus emerges when one class or coalition either overwhelms or reaches a compromise with competing classes or coalitions. Once put into place by the new consensus, the new institutions become consolidated and promote the next long boom. The key institutions continue to evolve during the boom, but in an already set framework.

The rise and decline of successive SSAs give rise to successive stages of capitalist development. Each SSA follows a life cycle characterized initially by exploration, next by consolidation, and finally by decay; the decay of one SSA overlaps with exploratory efforts to construct a new one. The new SSA is unlikely to resemble that of an earlier era because of changes in economic institutions, class structure, and political organization. Each period is likely to exhibit different structural dynamics.

The SSA approach, then, attempts to strike a balance between deterministic and contingent explanations. The boom comes to an end because of internal limits, specific to the period. But the resolution of the crisis, both the timing and terms on which it is resolved, are historically contingent. Consequently, the duration of both the boom and crisis periods are likely to be of uneven length.

The SSA approach offers several additional advantages. For economists, it raises historically contingent social and political factors to a greater level of importance than in conventional macroeconomic models. For historians, it allows us to examine what distinguishes different stages of capitalist development while also permitting variation across countries in the character of that development. The multidimensional approach contrasts with previous stage theories, which focused on technological spurts, movements in the relative prices of primary products, demographic shifts, or other single-factor explanations.

The life cycle of each distinct SSA produces, as a consequence, a specific long swing of the capitalist accumulation cycle. Long swings in capitalist development consist in alternating periods (of about twenty-five years each) of sustained relative prosperity and sustained relative stagnation. These have characterized the world capitalist economy since at least the early nineteenth century. I stress here relative prosperity and relative stagnation because the periods of stagnation that we identify exhibit relatively slow growth rather than no growth at all. Similarly, the periods of prosperity contain some years of recession and no growth, but these are not as frequent, severe, or sustained as in a period of relative stagnation. . . .

Three Stages in U.S. Labor History

Three qualitatively different social structures of accumulation have characterized the labor process and labor markets of the United States in the period from 1820 to the present. These three different (but overlapping) stages, in turn, have each proceeded through exploratory, consolidated, and decay phases. The interaction of macroeconomic dynamics and labor organization provide in each stage the mechanisms that lead to exploration, consolidation, and decay.

The first stage of the history of the U.S. working class consists of a period of initial proletarianization; its exploratory phase begins in about the 1820s, its consolidation in about the mid-1840s, and its decay phase lasts from the early 1870s to the mid-1890s. This process of initial proletarianization accompanied the development of competitive capitalism, the first stage of capitalist development in the United States.

In this period two great changes affected the development of the U.S. labor force: the abolition of slavery and its replacement by sharecropping in the cotton South, and the emergence of wage labor as the dominant form of employment in the rest of the nation. Our focus here is on the development of wage labor.

The initial scarcity of dependent wage labor forced employers to explore and ultimately rely upon diverse sources of labor supply: native white male farmers, young native women, children, immigrants, and artisans. These labor sources and the wage-labor market developed slowly and at uneven rates throughout the initial proletarianization period. The labor process in the capitalist factories remained equally diverse and in many instances untransformed from the precapitalist period; artisans in particular frequently retained considerable control over the organization of work.

In the period of relatively rapid growth, from the mid-1840s to the early 1870s, diverse internal systems of employer control over labor coexisted, corresponding largely to the respective characteristics of the labor supply. Small workshops typically were supervised by individual entrepreneur-owners, whereas larger factories often employed subcontracting schemes to organize the labor process. Labor markets also remained fragmented and highly imperfect in their competitive structure, divided into relatively distinct pockets. Competition among capitalists, however, began to grow over this period and became increasingly intense from the 1870s on.

The growth of intercapitalist competition, while providing an initial source of great dynamism, led first to increasing economic instability and then to stagnation. Especially after 1873, laissez-faire competition generated increasingly frequent and serious economic fluctuations. Since the national economy was becoming increasingly interdependent, farmers, workers, and businesses faced greater insecurities. Intense competition contributed to falling profit margins during the phase of relative stagnation, but widespread labor resistance, the growth of unionism, and traditional craft control over the labor process inhibited employer attempts to increase productivity or to cut real wages. The institutions of the competitive capitalist period did not permit employers to restore profit margins easily.

The social structure of the cotton South, it should be noted, also became less suited to facilitating national capitalist accumulation. The profits from slavery were both substantial and tended to mingle in a circulatory process with the profits from trade and wage labor. But the economic surplus generated in the postbellum era was scantier, reflecting both the growth of competition from foreign cotton suppliers and internal impediments inherent in the sharecropping system. Moreover, what little surplus was produced was less likely to enter the national banking system and become available for capitalist accumulation.

Seeking to construct a new SSA, employers began to search for means to restrain competition through mergers and tariff policy and to reduce the power of craft workers. Capital's search for a new social structure of accumulation was at first stimulated by declining profit rates and increased economic instability. It was given a further push by the spread of labor unrest from the 1870s on and by the rise of farmer movements in the 1880s and early 1890s.

But, in the crisis of the 1890s, the old institutions and coalitions broke up and new ones began to be formed, leading to a new SSA. Decisive labor defeats at Homestead and elsewhere in 1892, the electoral defeats of Populism and of an emergent farmer-worker coalition in 1896, the subsequent merger wave, and the drive for higher tariffs and overseas expansion each represent important events in the creation of this new social structure of accumulation, which we call the stage of monopoly capitalism.

Corresponding to this new stage of capitalist development, the second stage in the history of the U.S. working class consists in a period of homogenization. Its exploratory phase begins in the 1870s, a consolidation phase begins in the mid-1890s, and decay takes place in the period between the two world wars. Employers responded to their labor productivity problems in the late nineteenth century by reorganizing the workplace—mechanizing, increasing direct supervision of workers, and decreasing their reliance on skilled labor.

This reorganization, which later came to be called the *drive system*, increased capital-labor ratios, plant size, and the proportion of operatives in industry. Skill differentials fell slightly, a nationally competitive labor market was established, and employers now drew upon a vastly greater supply of labor. Although the ethnic and racial composition of the working class became much more diverse, the working conditions faced by the vast majority of workers became much more similar. For this reason, we describe the drive system as a homogenizing force.

The drive system alone did not constitute a sufficient innovation to usher in a new period of rapid capital accumulation. The new policies that consolidated the homogenization era centered on mechanisms to undercut worker opposition to the drive system: centralized personnel departments, cooperation with and cooptation of existing craft unions, and manipulation of ethnic and racial differences among workers. Such policies required enormous corporate size and were applied only after the great merger movement at the turn of the century. Once it was victorious over labor, big business still had to contend with opposition from other quarters: small business, middle-class Progressive reformers, and urban Socialists. These challenges were resolved during World War I.

The U.S. economic boom of the 1920s was largely made possible by the wartime consolidation of the victory of capital over labor. The boom nonetheless contained its own limits. Given the weak state of labor organization, the rapid growth of labor productivity generated by the drive system far outpaced the growth of wage rates. At the same time, the oligopolistic structure of industry prevented prices from falling; profits soared as a result, and income became distributed much more unequally. By the end of the decade, the consumer boom became based increasingly on debt and decreasingly on real consumer income. As a consequence, the level of economic activity became increasingly subject to the volatility of investment demand.

Economic contradictions, developing in the sociopolitical context of the second social structure of accumulation, made the economy vulnerable to a major crash. With the international economic rivalries of the period, the international institutions of the SSA were as seriously decayed as the domestic ones. The Great Depression then provided the context for the ensuing conflict over the content of the next social structure of accumulation.

In the 1930s class conflict intensified in both the industrial and political arenas. The primary industrial conflict involved, of course, the successful organization of unions among mass production industrial workers. The political conflict produced a realignment of political parties by 1936, analogous to but different in outcome from the realignment of 1896. Neither set of conflicts was resolved decisively until the war.

The third social structure of accumulation, which we call the stage of contemporary capitalism, was formed during and immediately after World War II. It was built upon three principal institutions that each differed substantially from their interwar counterparts. These consisted of a government commitment to avoid depressions and manage aggregate demand by active use of the tools of fiscal and monetary policy; U.S. military and economic leadership to stabilize and dominate the world market in a liberal world order; and the establishment of a limited capital-labor accord, a new system of labor relations that integrated the new industrial unions into a corporatist system of collective bargaining but excluded those groups that the industrial and craft unions had still failed to organize. The compromises inherent in the limited capital-labor accord meant that the postwar SSA was constructed on more favorable terms for a section of labor than was the prewar system.

Corresponding to this third stage of capitalism, the third stage in the history of the U.S. working class consists in a period of segmentation, with exploration beginning after World War I, consolidation beginning around World War II, and decay developing from the early 1970s to the present. The segmentation of labor both accompanied and helped facilitate the period of rapid growth in the United States after World War II. Large corporations had already explored segmentation mechanisms in the 1920s and early 1930s, but these were necessarily put aside for most of the Depression, as the conflict over the contours of industrial unionism became paramount. This conflict over the character of emergent industrial unionism gave way by the early 1950s to conflict within a contained and institutionalized system of collective bargaining that reflected major concessions to the unions.

In the postwar period of segmentation, greater distinctions emerged among unionized industrial workers, professional and technical workers, and workers in the secondary labor market. The expansion of the secondary labor market was facilitated by the break-up of sharecropping systems in the South, the extraordinary productivity growth of agriculture in all regions, and the rapid entry of women into wage labor. The development of divergent labor processes, pay rates, and skill levels and barriers among the three labor submarkets proceeded along both industrial and occupational lines.

By the early 1970s, this system of segmentation and the postwar institutional structure of accumulation more generally were showing signs of serious strain. The system of aggregate demand management, the structure of the international political economy, and the domestic limited capital-labor accord each were no longer functioning to promote prosperity, and a variety of alternative institutions were being explored.

In each period, then, the decline of a social structure of accumulation involved a shift from contained to disruptive class conflict. To be sure, the shift to a new social structure of accumulation did not occur as a mechanical process. Opposing groups presented and struggled for alternative visions of a new set of institutions that would resolve the current crisis. The institutions constructed ~ ~ not the only ones that would have worked; they were put into place because they did work and because they expressed the political power and success of a new governing coalition. In these ways, the changing character of labor-capital conflict was partly shaped by the macroeconomic context and partly helped to shape that context. . . .

✣ *F U R T H E R   R E A D I N G*

Robert Asher and Charles Stephenson, eds., *Labor Divided: Race and Ethnicity in United States Labor Struggles* (1990)

Rosalyn Baxandall, Linda Gordon, and Susan Reverby, eds., *America's Working Women: A Documentary History* (1976)

Harry Braverman, *Labor and Monopoly Capitalism* (1974)

Paul Buhle and Alan Dawley, eds., *Working for Democracy: American Workers from the Revolution to the Present* (1985)

Milton Cantor and Bruce Laurie, eds., *Class, Sex, and the Woman Worker* (1977)

John R. Commons et al., eds., *A History of Labor in the United States*, 4 vols. (1918–1935)

Mike Davis, *Prisoners of the American Dream* (1986)

Melvyn Dubofsky and Warren Van Tine, eds., *Labor Leaders in America* (1987)

Foster Rhea Dulles and Melvyn Dubofsky, *Labor in America* (1984)

Philip Foner, *History of the Labor Movement in the United States*, 5 vols. (1947–1983)

———, *Women and the American Labor Movement*, 2 vols. (1979–1980)

Michael Frisch and Daniel Walkowitz, eds., *Working-Class America* (1983)

Naomi Gerstel and Harriet Engel Gross, eds., *Families and Work* (1987)

Robert Gordon, Richard Edwards, and Michael Reich, *Segmented Work, Divided Workers* (1982)

James Green, ed., *Worker's Struggles, Past and Present* (1983)

———, *The World of the Worker: Labor in Twentieth Century America* (1978)

Carol Groneman and Mary Beth Norton, eds., *"To Toil the Livelong Day": America's Women at Work, 1780–1980* (1987)

William H. Harris, *The Harder We Run: Black Workers Since the Civil War* (1982)

Julius Jacobson, ed., *The Negro and the American Labor Movement* (1968)
Alice Kessler-Harris, *Out to Work* (1982)
Daniel J. Leab, ed., *The Labor History Reader* (1985)
Ruth Milkman, ed., *Women, Work, and Protest* (1985)
Marc S. Miller, ed., *Working Lives: The "Southern Exposure" History of Labor in the South* (1981)
Selig Perlman, *A Theory of the Labor Movement* (1928)
Karen Brodkin Sacks and Dorothy Remy, eds., *My Troubles Are Going to Have Trouble with Me: Everyday Trials and Triumphs of Women Workers* (1984)
Charles Stephenson and Robert Asher, eds., *Life and Labor* (1986)
Susan Strasser, *Never Done: A History of American Housework* (1982)
E. P. Thompson, *The Making of the English Working Class* (1963)
Robert H. Zieger, *American Workers, American Unions, 1920–1985* (1986)

CHAPTER 2

The Labor Systems
of Early America

⚕

When European settlers reached North American shores early in the seventeenth century, they brought along a whole set of values, customs, and laws that reflected an Old World poised halfway between its feudal past and bourgeois future. Feudalism no longer reigned in Western Europe, but almost all economic activity was heavily regulated so that it might conform to a world of hierarchy and deference. For example, the Tudor Industrial Code, enacted late in the sixteenth century, mandated compulsory labor for all able-bodied persons. Workers who refused to work at the rates set by local authorities were considered petty criminals and were subjected to whippings and forced labor in houses of correction.

Thus free labor in our modern sense was unknown when the English colonists of North America established their first farms, fisheries, and workshops in the seventeenth century. Workers were in short supply throughout the colonies, but instead of bidding wages higher, plantation owners, merchants, and sea captains sought to secure their laborers through various systems of coercion and servitude. In the Chesapeake region, a decreased supply of white servants and fear of rebellion among them led to the wholesale importation of African slaves. Farther north, indentured servants, who were bound to their masters for a set term of years, became an important source of colonial labor. In Pennsylvania, nearly two-thirds of all eighteenth-century immigrants had come as such servants.

In New England, the Pilgrim and Puritan settlements were more often based on subsistence farms and the artisan's workshop. Slavery and indentured servitude were less prevalent in New England than in regions of commercial agriculture, but even here production was bound up in a set of relationships that made the free exchange of goods and labor difficult.

Historians have become interested particularly in the nature of the household economy, both in New England and farther south. Were domestic-production units largely self-sufficient, or did the sale and purchase of crops and manufactured goods shape daily life even in these early years?

Historians have also probed the extent to which uniquely American condi-

*tions transformed the status of labor on this continent. Did the existence of a
large expanse of free land undermine traditional hierarchies? Did American
abundance advance, in equal proportion, the status of indentured servants, female members of the household, seafarers, and African slaves? And to what extent did the changing aspirations and beliefs of colonial workers mesh with the
larger movement for independence that became so powerful in the late eighteenth
century?*

✠ D O C U M E N T S

The first four documents reveal the conditions under which servants and slaves
labored in the New World. Writing to his parents in London, an indentured servant of the Virginia Company captures in the first document the unrewarded toil
of men struggling to survive in a land where freewheeling speculation became a
hallmark of the booming tobacco economy. The second document, lyrics sung to
a popular mid-seventeenth-century tune, chronicles the tasks of female servants
in Virginia. Not only were women from the British Isles responsible for the traditionally female work of cooking, sewing, and child rearing, but they were also
put to the "plow and cart" to such an extent that they sometimes saw their
lives little distinguished from those of African slaves. The third document compares different types of servitude, as observed by the Swedish botanist Peter
Kalm during his travels through the middle colonies between 1741 and 1751. Finally, the African experience of enslavement finds graphic expression in the
fourth document, an account of the middle passage that Olaudah Equiano wrote
in 1791, twenty-six years after his childhood capture. Given this wide range of
unfree labor in the American colonies, one might well ask, what conditions distinguish slavery from lesser forms of servitude?

The remaining documents suggest the diverse forms of free labor on northern farms and in northern seaports. From 1719 through 1755, Westborough, Massachusetts minister Ebenezer Parkman kept a diary, selections from which form
the fifth document. He recorded the farming responsibilities of a country pastor,
showing his reliance not only on servants and hired hands but also on the parishioners who labored in his fields in exchange for ministerial services. The
sixth selection humorously views such a world from the perspective of a country
parson's wife who lacked a maid for domestic chores. The final document, dated
1659, recounts the dangers that sailors faced on the high seas, as described by
first mate Edward Coxere.

An Indentured Servant's Letter Home, 1623

Loving and kind father and mother:

My most humble duty remembered to you, hoping in God of your good
health, as I myself am at the making hereof. This is to let you understand
that I your child am in a most heavy case by reason of the nature of the
country, [which] is such that it causeth much sickness, [such] as the scurvy
and the bloody flux and diverse other diseases, which maketh the body

very poor and weak. And when we are sick there is nothing to comfort us; for since I came out of the ship I never ate anything but peas, and loblollie (that is, water gruel). As for deer or venison I never saw any since I came into this land. There is indeed some fowl, but we are not allowed to go and get it, but must work hard both early and late for a mess of water gruel and a mouthful of bread and beef. A mouthful of bread for a penny loaf must serve for four men which is most pitiful. [You would be grieved] if you did know as much as I [do], when people cry out day and night—Oh! that they were in England without their limbs—and would not care to lose any limb to be in England again, yea, though they beg from door to door. For we live in fear of the enemy [Powhatan Indians] every hour, yet we have had a combat with them on the Sunday before Shrovetide [Monday before Ash Wednesday], and we took two alive and made slaves of them. But it was by policy, for we are in great danger; for our plantation is very weak by reason of the death and sickness of our company. For we came but twenty for the merchants, and they are half dead just; and we look every hour when two more should go. Yet there came some four other men yet to live with us, of which there is but one alive; and our Lieutenant is dead, and [also] his father and his brother. And there was some five or six of the last year's twenty, of which there is but three left, so that we are fain to get other men to plant with us; and yet we are but 32 to fight against 3000 if they should come. And the nighest help that we have is ten miles of us, and when the rogues overcame this place [the] last [time] they slew 80 persons. How then shall we do, for we lie even in their teeth? . . .

And I have nothing to comfort me, nor there is nothing to be gotten here but sickness and death, except [in the event] that one had money to lay out in some things for profit. But I have nothing at all—no, not a shirt to my back but two rags (2), nor no clothes but one poor suit, nor but one pair of shoes, but one pair of stockings, but one cap, [and] but two bands. My cloak is stolen by one of my own fellows, and to his dying hour [he] would not tell me what he did with it; but some of my fellows saw him have butter and beef out of a ship, which my cloak, I doubt [not], paid for. So that I have not a penny, nor a penny worth, to help me to either spice or sugar or strong waters, without the which one cannot live here. For as strong beer in England doth fatten and strengthen them, so water here doth wash and weaken these here [and] only keeps [their] life and soul together. But I am not half [of] a quarter so strong as I was in England, and all is for want of victuals; for I do protest unto you that I have eaten more in [one] day at home than I have allowed me here for a week. You have given more than my day's allowance to a beggar at the door; and if Mr. Jackson had not relieved me, I should be in a poor case. But he like a father and she like a loving mother doth still help me.

For when we go up to Jamestown (that is 10 miles of us) there lie all the ships that come to land, and there they must deliver their goods. And when we went up to town [we would go], as it may be, on Monday at noon, and come there by night, [and] then load the next day by noon, and go home in the afternoon, and unload, and then away again in the night, and [we would] be up about midnight. Then if it rained or blowed never so hard, we must lie in the boat on the water and have nothing but a little bread. For when we go into the boat we [would] have a loaf allowed to two men, and it is all [we would get] if we stayed there two days, which is hard; and [we] must lie all that while in the boat. But that Goodman Jackson pitied me and made me a cabin to lie in always when I [would] come up, and he would give me some poor jacks [to take] home with me, which comforted me more than peas or water gruel. Oh, they be very godly folks, and love me very well, and will do anything for me. And he much marvelled that you would send me a servant to the Company; he saith I had been better knocked on the head. And indeed so I find it now, to my great grief and misery; and [I] saith that if you love me you will redeem me suddenly, for which I do entreat and beg. And if you cannot get the merchants to redeem me for some little money, then for God's sake get a gathering or entreat some good folks to lay out some little sum of money in meal and cheese and butter and beef. Any eating meat will yield great profit. Oil and vinegar is very good; but, father, there is great loss in leaking. But for God's sake send beef and cheese and butter, or the more of one sort and none of another. But if you send cheese, it must be very old cheese; and at the cheesemonger's you may buy very good cheese for twopence farthing or halfpenny, that will be liked very well. But if you send cheese, you must have a care how you pack it in barrels; and you must put cooper's chips between every cheese, or else the heat of the hold will rot them. And look whatsoever you send me—be it never so much— look, what[ever] I make of it, I will deal truly with you. I will send it over and beg the profit to redeem me; and if I die before it come, I have entreated Goodman Jackson to send you the worth of it, who hath promised he will. If you send, you must direct your letters to Goodman Jackson, at James- town, a gunsmith. (You must set down his freight, because there be more of his name there.) Good father, do not forget me, but have mercy and pity my miserable case. I know if you did but see me, you would weep to see me; for I have but one suit. (But [though] it is a strange one, it is very well guarded.) Wherefore, for God's sake, pity me. I pray you to remember my love to all my friends and kindred. I hope all my brothers and sisters are in good health, and as for my part I have set down my resolution that certainly will be; that is, that the answer of this letter will be life or death to me. Therefore, good father, send as soon as you can; and if you send me any thing let this be the mark.

ROT

Richard Frethorne,
Martin's Hundred

"The Trappan'd Maiden:
Or, The Distressed Damsel,"
(A Popular Song, Mid-Seventeenth Century)

This Girl was cunningly Trappan'd, sent to Virginny from England,
Where she doth Hardship undergo, there is no Cure it must be so:
But if she lives to cross the Main, she vows she'll ne'r go there again.

Tune of Virginny, or, When that I was weary, weary, O.

Give ear unto a Maid, that lately was betray'd,
  And sent into Virginny, O:
In brief I shall declare, what I have suffer'd there,
  When that I was weary, weary, weary, weary, O.

[Since] that first I came to this Land of Fame,
  Which is called Virginny, O,
The Axe and the Hoe have wrought my overthrow,
  When that I was weary, weary, weary, weary O.

Five years served I, under Master Guy,
  In the land of Virginny, O,
Which made me for to know sorrow, grief and woe.
  When that I was weary, weary, weary, weary O.

When my Dame says 'Go' then I must do so.
  In the land of Virginny, O.
When she sits at Meat, then I have none to eat,
  When that I am weary, weary, weary, weary, O.

The Cloath[e]s that I brought in, they are worn very thin,
  In the land of Virginny, O,
Which makes me for to say, 'Alas, and Well-a-day!'
  When that I am weary, weary, weary, weary, O.

Instead of Beds of Ease, to lye down when I please,
  In the Land of Virginny, O;
Upon a bed of straw, I lye down full of woe,
  When that I am weary, weary, weary, weary, O. . . .

So soon as it is day, to work I must away,
  In the Land of Virginny, O;
Then my Dame she knocks, with her tinder-box,
  When that I am weary, weary, weary, weary, O. . . .

If my Dame says 'Go!' I dare not say no,
  In the Land of Virginny, O;
The Water from the Spring, upon my head I bring,
  When that I am weary, weary, weary, weary, O.

When the Mill doth stand, I'm ready at command,
  In the Land of Virginny, O;
The Morter for to make, which makes my heart to ake,
  When that I am weary, weary, weary, weary, O.

When the Child doth cry, I must sing 'By-a-by!'
  In the Land of Virginny, O;

No rest that I can have, whilst I am here a Slave,
  When that I am weary, weary, weary, weary, O. . . .

Then let Maids beware, all by my ill-fare,
  In the Land of Virginny, O;
Be sure to stay at home, for if you do here come,
  You all will be weary, weary, weary, weary, O.

But if it be my chance, Homewards to advance,
  From the Land of Virginny, O;
If that I, once more, land on English Shore,
  I'll no more be weary, weary, weary, weary, O.

Traveler Peter Kalm on Unfree Labor
in Pennsylvania, 1753

Servants. The servants which are employed in the English-American colonies are either free persons or slaves, and the former, again, are of two different classes.

1. Those who are entirely free serve by the year. They are not only allowed to leave their service at the expiration of their year, but may leave it at any time when they do not agree with their masters. However, in that case they are in danger of losing their wages, which are very considerable. A man servant who has some ability gets between sixteen and twenty pounds in Pennsylvania currency, but those in the country do not get so much. A maidservant gets eight or ten pounds a year. These servants have their food besides their wages, but they must buy their own clothes, and whatever they get of these as gifts they must thank their master's generosity for.

Indenture. 2. The second kind of free servants consists of such persons as annually come from Germany, England and other countries, in order to settle here. These newcomers are very numerous every year: there are old and young of both sexes. Some of them have fled from oppression, under which they have labored. Others have been driven from their country by religious persecution, but most of them are poor and have not money enough to pay their passage, which is between six and eight pounds sterling for each person. Therefore, they agree with the captain that they will suffer themselves to be sold for a few years on their arrival. In that case the person who buys them pays the freight for them; but frequently very old people come over who cannot pay their passage, they therefore sell their children for several years, so that they serve both for themselves and for their parents. There are likewise some who pay part of their passage, and they are sold only for a short time. From these circumstances it appears that the price on the poor foreigners who come over to North America varies considerably, and that some of them have to serve longer than others. When their time has expired, they get a new suit of clothes from their master and some other things. He is likewise obliged to feed and clothe them during the years of their servitude. Many of the Germans who come hither bring money enough with them to pay their passage, but prefer to be sold, hoping that during their servitude they may get a knowledge of the language and character of the country and the life, that they may the better be able to consider what they shall do when they have gotten their liberty. Such servants are preferable to all others, because they are not so expensive. To buy a negro or black slave requires too much money at one time; and men or maids who get yearly wages are likewise too costly. But this kind of servant may be gotten for half the money, and even for less; for they commonly pay fourteen pounds, Pennsylvania currency, for a person who is to serve four years, and so on in proportion. Their wages therefore are not above three pounds Pennsylvania currency per annum. . . . When a person has bought such a servant for a certain number of years, and has an intention to sell him again, he is at liberty to do so, but is obliged, at the expiration of the term of servitude, to provide the usual suit of clothes for the servant, unless he has made that part of the bargain with the purchaser. . . .

3. The *negroes* or blacks constitute the third kind. They are in a manner slaves; for when a negro is once bought, he is the purchaser's servant as long as he lives, unless he gives him to another, or sets him free. However, it is not in the power of the master to kill his negro for a fault, but he must leave it to the magistrates to proceed according to the laws. Formerly the negroes were brought over from Africa, and bought by almost everyone who could afford it, the Quakers alone being an exception. But these are no longer so particular and now they have as many negroes as other people. However, many people cannot conquer the idea of its being contrary to the laws of Christianity to keep slaves. There are likewise several free negroes in town, who have been lucky enough to get a very zealous Quaker for their master, and who gave them their liberty after they had faithfully served him for a time.

At present they seldom bring over any negroes to the English colonies, for those which were formerly brought thither have multiplied rapidly. In regard to their marriage they proceed as follows: in case you have not only male but likewise female negroes, they may intermarry, and then the children are all your slaves. But if you possess a male negro only and he has an inclination to marry a female belonging to a different master, you do not hinder your negro in so delicate a point, but it is of no advantage to you, for the children belong to the master of the female. It is therefore practically advantageous to have negro women. . . .

Olaudah Equiano Survives
the Middle Passage, 1791

. . . The first object which saluted my eyes when I arrived on the coast, was the sea, and a slave ship, which was then riding at anchor, and waiting for its cargo. These filled me with astonishment, which was soon converted into terror, when I was carried on board. I was immediately handled, and tossed up to see if I were sound, by some of the crew; and I was now persuaded that I had gotten into a world of bad spirits, and that they were going to kill me. Their complexions, too, differing so much from ours, their long hair, and the language they spoke, (which was very different from any I had ever heard) united to confirm me in this belief. Indeed, such were the horrors of my views and fears at the moment, that, if ten thousand worlds had been my own, I would have freely parted with them all to have exchanged my condition with that of the meanest slave in my own country. When I looked round the ship too, and saw a large furnace of copper boiling, and a multitude of black people of every description chained to-gether, every one of their countenances expressing dejection and sorrow, I no longer doubted of my fate; and, quite overpowered with horror and anguish, I fell motionless on the deck and fainted. . . .

I now saw myself deprived of all chance of returning to my native country, or even the least glimpse of hope of gaining the shore, which I now considered as friendly; and I even wished for my former slavery in preference to my present situation, which was filled with horrors of every kind, still heightened by my ignorance of what I was to undergo. I was not long suffered to indulge my grief; I was soon put down under the decks, and there I received such a salutation in my nostrils as I had never ex-perienced in my life: so that, with the loathsomeness of the stench, and crying together, I became so sick and low that I was not able to eat, nor had I the least desire to taste any thing. I now wished for the last friend, death, to relieve me; but soon, to my grief, two of the white men offered me eatables; and, on my refusing to eat, one of them held me fast by the hands, and laid me across, I think the windlass, and tied my feet, while the other flogged me severely. I had never experienced any thing of this kind before, and although not being used to the water, I naturally feared that element the first time I saw it, yet, nevertheless, could I have got over the nettings, I would have jumped over the side, but I could not; and besides, the crew used to watch us very closely who were not chained down to the decks, lest we should leap into the water; and I have seen some of these poor African prisoners most severely cut, for attempting to do so, and hourly whipped for not eating. This indeed was often the case with myself. In a little time after, amongst the poor chained men, I found some of my own nation, which in a small degree gave ease to my mind. I inquired of these what was to be done with us? [T]hey gave me to under-stand, we were to be carried to these white people's country to work for them. I then was a little revived, and thought, if it were no worse than working, my situation was not so desperate; but still I feared I should be put to death, the white people looked and acted, as I thought, in so savage a manner; for I had never seen among any people such instances of brutal cruelty; and this not only shown towards us blacks, but also to some of the whites themselves. One white man in particular I saw, when we were permitted to be on deck, flogged so unmercifully with a large rope near the foremast, that he died in consequence of it; and they tossed him over the side as they would have done a brute. This made me fear these people the more; and I expected nothing less than to be treated in the same manner. I could not help expressing my fears and apprehensions to some of my countrymen; I asked them if these people had no country, but lived in this hollow place? (the ship) they told me they did not, but came from a distant one. "Then," said I, "how comes it in all our country we never heard of them?" They told me because they lived so very far off. I then asked where were their women? had they any like themselves? I was told they had. "And why," said I, "do we not see them?" They answered, because they were left behind. I asked how the vessel could go? [T]hey told me they could not tell; but that there was cloth put upon the masts by the help of the ropes I saw, and then the vessel went on; and the white men had some spell or magic they put in the water when they liked, in order to stop the vessel. I was exceedingly amazed at this account, and really thought they were spirits. I therefore wished much to be from amongst them, for I expected they would sacrifice me; but my wishes were vain—for we were so quartered that it was impossible for any of us to make our escape. . . .

At last, when the ship we were in, had got in all her cargo, they made ready with many fearful noises, and we were all put under deck, so that we could not see how they managed the vessel. But this disappointment was the least of my sorrow. The stench of the hold while we were on the coast was so intolerably loathsome, that it was dangerous to remain there for any time, and some of us had been permitted to stay on the deck for the fresh air; but now that the whole ship's cargo were confined together, it became absolutely pestilential. . . . The shrieks of the women, and the groans of the dying, rendered the whole a scene of horror almost inconceivable. Happily perhaps, for myself, I was soon reduced so low here that it was thought necessary to keep me almost always on deck; and from my extreme youth I was not put in fetters. . . .

. . . One day, when we had a smooth sea and moderate wind, two of my wearied countrymen who were chained together, (I was near them at the time,) preferring death to such a life of misery, somehow made through the nettings and jumped into the sea: immediately, another quite dejected fellow, who, on account of his illness, was suffered to be out of irons, also followed their example; and I believe many more would very soon have done the same, if they had not been prevented by the ship's crew, who were instantly alarmed. Those of us that were the most active, were in a moment put down under the deck, and there was such a noise and confusion amongst the people of the ship as I never heard before, to stop her, and get the boat out to go after the slaves. However, two of the wretches were drowned, but they got the other, and afterwards flogged him unmercifully, for thus attempting to prefer death to slavery. . . .

Ebenezer Parkman's Record of a Rural Minister's Diverse Work, 1726, 1728, 1748

April 1726

. . . 3. I preach'd upon the Same Text as last Sabbath, Ps. 25, 11. John Whood of Hopkinton at Dinner with us. He rode home his Horse which I had had to keep.

4. One of Mr. Ward's Cows went home. What man would not think it worth Noting that [he] has Seen the mighty Contests and Brawlings that are often made about the most inconsiderable things of this kind, and the Reflections cast upon the honesty and uprightness of those of Sacred Character (because they ought to be Examples to observe), if there is not a peculiar preciseness and Exactness in making up the minutest part of an account.

5. Silence Bartlet came to Live with us. Two of Neighbor Clarks Cows went away. My Hay growing very short, or my Tenderness towards this man would not have suffer'd me to Send them away. . . .

7. Mr. Rice's Mare went away after Lecture. I preach'd this Day on 2 Cor. 1, 12. I very Eagerly expected Mr. Barrett, having sent to him in good Season, but (as it has happened these Three Times with him) I was disappointed.

8. Another of Mr. Wards Cows was Sent home.

9. This Day the Last of Mr. Wards Cows and his Horse went away. N.B. The 5th and 6th Neighbor Clark and his Son ploughed (with my Mare and Mr. Wards Horse) my Stubble, and the 8th and 9th Neighbor Clark with my Boy went on (as aforesaid) in ploughing and sowing of Wheat and Rye and Barley.

10. This Day was our sacrament. I preach'd upon Lamt. and 2 Cor. 1, 12. I have great Reason to express all gratitude to God for his presence with me, inasmuch as I trust I had much of the presence and spirit of God with me.

11. Robert Henry came to live with me. Neighbor Clark Sow'd My Oats, and Some Peas. William Clark Harrow'd till Eleven o'Clock and then Robert took the Work. . . .

July 1728

29. I assisted with my own hands in the Carting, etc.

30. Having got in my Hay, Rice, Barley, and Wheat, I dismiss'd Thomas Kendal for a while. Now we are intirely alone . . . having no Servant nor any one in the House. Our Loneliness gives Scope for Thought. God Sanctifie our solitude, and help us to improve in acquaintance with Himself. There was much Lighting in the North almost the whole Evening.

Reprinted from Francis G. Walett, ed. *The Diary of Ebenezer Parkman*, 1703–1782. First part, 1719–1755 (Worcester, Mass.: American Antiquarian Society, 1974). By permission of the Society.

June 1748

24. Exeeding Hott dry Season. Joseph and Ebenezer mowing and raking. P.M. came Mr. Stephen Fay with a Warrant from Captain Edward Baker Esquire with which he press'd Joseph Bowker, my Young Man, into the service! I went over to the Captain to see if nothing could be done to release him. The Captain said he would do his utmost: and accordinly Sent his son to try to hire Robert Cook, and he should offer him 50£. Nay not come without him if 60£ would procure him. I am afraid of the Temptation of too great Anxiety—but I beseech God to enable me to put my Trust in Him! and Committing all to Him, to be at Rest! Joseph went to Lieutenant Tainters who I am perswaded would do what in him lies. Two or Three Things made this impressing feel the worse. Its falling out at this Season, when I cannot get any Body in his stead; and it being on Friday when I was more disturb'd: (It was So exactly when Captain Baker press'd Thomas Winchester) And when they want but one Man out of the whole Town. My Dauter Mary not return'd from Marlborough till this p.m. Dr. Gotts young man, Breed, and Mrs. Sally Gott rode up with her in Mr. Lorings Chair, but Breed and Sally return'd. N.B. They inform me that Mrs. Smith was lately seiz'd with a Lethargy—and her Friends from Cape Ann are Sent for.

25. Still exceeding Hot, but was oblig'd to turn out and Pole Hay both Yesterday and to Day also. Joseph Bowker is oblig'd to go to the Frontiers and accordingly left us. May God be his Guardian and his Helper, and return him in Safety! The Interruptions I have had prevent my preparing more than part of an Exercise for tomorrow.

Ruth Belknap, a Country Parson's Wife, on "The Pleasures of a Country Life," c. 1782

> Up in the morning I must rise
> Before I've time to rub my eyes.
> With half-pin'd gown, unbuckled shoe,
> I haste to milk my lowing cow.
> But, Oh! it makes my heart to ake,
> I have no bread till I can bake,
> And then, alas! it makes me sputter,
> For I must churn or have no butter.
> The hogs with swill too I must serve;
> For hogs must eat or men will starve.
> Besides, my spouse can get no cloaths
> Unless I much offend my nose.
> For all that try it know it's true
> There is no smell like colouring blue.
> Then round the parish I must ride

Ruth Belknap, "The Pleasures of a Country Life," © 1782 in *Collections of the Massachusetts Historical Society* (Boston: Massachusetts Historical Society: MDCCCXCI), 6th series, Vol. 4, pp. 228–229.

And make enquiry far and wide
To find some girl that is a spinner,
Then hurry home to get my dinner.

If with romantic steps I stray
Around the fields and meadows gay,
The grass, besprinkled with the dews,
Will wet my feet and rot my shoes.

If on a mossy bank I sleep
Pismires and crickets o'er me creep,
Or near the purling rill am seen
There dire mosquitos peirce my skin.
Yet such delights I seldom see
Confined to house and family.

All summer long I toil & sweat,
Blister my hands, and scold & fret.
And when the summer's work is o'er,
New toils arise from Autumn's store.
Corn must be husk'd, and pork be kill'd,
The house with all confusion fill'd.
O could you see the grand display
Upon our annual butchering day,—
See me look like ten thousand sluts,
My kitchen spread with grease & guts,— . . .

Yet starch'd up folks that live in town,
That lounge upon your beds till noon,
That never tire yourselves with work,
Unless with handling knife & fork,
Come, see the sweets of country life,
Display'd in Parson B———'s wife.'

First Mate Edward Coxere Describes a Storm at Sea, 1659

The third day of the ninth month, 1662, we sailed for England, and had a fair wind. The 11th instant it proved a storm. It continued so violent that we lay without sail in the sea, driving. The 12th, about 4 in the morning, we having not seen no land from the time we came out of Portugal, being now, as we reckoned, in the Channel between England and France, still driving without sail, and the sea like mountains, I went to the master and told him I feared we might be near the coast of France, by Guernsey or Jersey, where near lay the Race of Alderney, a dangerous place, and that it would be convenient to get the ship about, and let her lay with her head towards the coast of England.

The master thought well so to do; upon which I with some of the seamen went forward by the foresail, the yard being lowered close down, and made fast one yard-arm of the sail well fast with ropes lest, whilst we

Reprinted from *Adventures by Sea of Edward Coxere*, edited by E. H. W. Meyerstein (1945) by permission of Oxford University Press.

loosed the other part of the sail to flat her about, the whole sail should through the violence of the wind blow away. We having loosed the lee sail, the yard a-portlands, put the helm a-weather, to bear up before the wind. The strength of the wind, with the seas like mountains, pressed the lee side of the ship under water, that through the weight of the water on the deck to leeward, and the wind and sea pressing her down that the ship lay on her side like a log in the sea, and could not bear up, but lay along as sinking, insomuch that the men did lament their conditions and for their poor wives and children, for we discerned nothing but death before our eyes. We loosed the spirit-sail, thinking thereby to make the ship bear up before the wind. The spirit-sail was no sooner loose but the wind blew the sail all to pieces, and [it] flew into the sea.

We being now in despair, looking on every sea to have its commission with it to swallow us up, we in this condition looked on [one] another with sorrowful hearts, holding fast lest we might be washed overboard. In this juncture of time the Lord put it into my heart, being on the forepart of the ship, to get aft to the master along the weather side of the ship. Being got to him, I told him we must not lay so if we could help it. He told me he knew not what to do. I told him of cutting our mainmast overaboard. With that one of the seamen standing by clasped me in his arms, as overjoyed, as to say "Is there hopes yet?" We forthwith went to work and cut away the mainmast, with sails, yards and all belonging to it; but before we could get it clear of the ship, the sea, heaving the ship with so much force against the mast and yards that we feared it would a run through the bottom of the ship; but Providence prevented it, so that we got quit of it. . . .

Then our ship bore up before the sea. One of our men then got down in the hold by the pumps, for the hold itself was full of goods, seeing the water was in [the] hold that he was up to the arm-pokes. This was heart-breaking news again, looking then for the ship to forsake us every moment and sink to the bottom. At this report the master got down in the hold in the well to see, and being so affrighted, as he told me afterward, that fearing the ship would sink before he got up again, that he could hardly find the scuttle where he went down. We kept pumping for our lives, also kept the ship right before the great sea with all the care we could, lest it should fall on our side and sink us quite. We had now little to do but to steer right before the sea and pump. At this time I took a piece of chalk in my hand and went down in the well, and by the edge of the water in the hold I made a score, and then came up again to the pumps, which were out of order very much. After some little time I went into the hold again to see whether the score of the chalk were above the water, so as that [if] we gained with pumping then life, if under then death; but I found the water to be below the water [waterline of the ocean] about an inch. So then I had hopes, if our pumps deceived us not. With this news I encouraged our men to pump.

This began at 4 in the morning, till noon before we got the ship clear at which time we saw the land, which was the island of Alderney on the coast of France, the place I feared: so that we were forced to clap the ship against the sea again, otherways we should be lost on the coast of France.

The storm through the Lord's mercy did a little abate, for we were forced to make some small sail to get over to the coast of England. The nights being long, it being in the ninth month, we got sight of the land before day, yet was not certain what land it was, being night. At this time it fell stark calm. Our master being wet and almost beaten out, they all lay down to sleep, only myself and two men to pump. When day appeared, we looked earnestly to know what land it was. I got up on the foreyard and saw Portland. . . .

✤ E S S A Y S

In the first essay, Richard S. Dunn, a professor of history at the University of Pennsylvania, divides colonial British America into three regional labor systems: the Caribbean and the southern mainland, with their various forms of slavery; the mid-Atlantic, with its mixture of wage labor and servitude; and New England, with its reliance on free labor. He contends that the sale and purchase of crops and goods in a market economy quickly supplanted self-sufficient agriculture, even in New England, where household production proved so versatile and valuable. University of New Hampshire historian Laurel Thatcher Ulrich concurs in the second essay, demonstrating that domestic manufacturing, the housewife's realm in eighteenth-century America, depended on an interdependence among many different households. In contrast to Dunn, however, Ulrich emphasizes the degree of nonmarket exchange that took place, often through the well-developed network of friends, neighbors, and kin relied upon by so many rural women. In the final essay, historian Marcus Rediker of Georgetown University argues that the seamen of the Atlantic world constituted a prototype of the sometimes militant wage laborers who would become more numerous and powerful as the commercial capitalism of the colonial era changed into the industrial society of the nineteenth century. Were there any similarities among these different systems of labor in colonial America? And did the workers themselves, whether on a southern plantation, a New England farm, or a transatlantic bark, share a common outlook on their lives and their work?

Servants and Slaves: Portraits in White and Black

RICHARD S. DUNN

The history of labor in colonial America is a large subject because it embraces more than half the colonial population during a 170-year span, as well as labor practices in seventeenth- and eighteenth-century England, West Africa, Ireland, Wales, Scotland, and Germany, the chief catchment areas for immigrant colonial laborers. It is a complex subject because each region of British America evolved a distinctive labor system: in the Caribbean sugar colonies, a quick dependence on African slave labor; in the southern mainland colonies, a slow conversion from white servants to black slaves, with heavy use also of white family labor; in the mid-Atlantic col-

Richard S. Dunn, "Servants and Slaves: The Recruitment and Employment of Labor" in *Colonial British America*, eds. Jack Greene and J. R. Pole, 1984, pp. 157–158, 172–188. Reprinted with permission of Johns Hopkins University Press.

onies, a mix of family and wage labor with immigrant servants and slaves; and in New England, a prime reliance upon native-born family and wage labor. Finally, it is a difficult subject because it treats the history of the inarticulate—laboring men and women who left few records or artifacts and who must be studied chiefly through the observations of their employers. It is much harder to reconstruct the bygone experiences and work habits of obscure servants and slaves than those of prominent planters and merchants, yet the effort must be made if we are to comprehend the labor systems of colonial America. . . .

I will define a colonial laborer as any person who performed manual labor, with or without wages, for a head of household: a slave, a servant, an apprentice, a wage laborer, or a dependent family worker. This definition *excludes* a great many colonial manual workers: self-employed small farmers and craftsmen, because they were independent producers; tenant farmers, because they were semi-independent producers; and members of the armed forces, because they were employed by the state rather than by individual entrepreneurs. . . .

By the mid-eighteenth century the American colonists had developed four strikingly different labor systems in the Caribbean, the southern mainland, the mid-Atlantic colonies, and New England. Let us briefly consider the functional aspects of each system and compare some of their social and economic characteristics.

In the Caribbean, ever since the days of Hawkins and Drake the English had pursued economic exploitation more than full-scale settlement. The sugar boom of the 1640s legitimated this tendency. Not only did the sugar planters convert from white to black workers but they became totally dependent upon massive slave imports. Between 1640 and 1780 the islanders bought about 1,225,000 Africans to stock their slave gangs, keeping just enough white overseers, doctors, and clerical workers on hand to maintain control. This social mode, a small cadre of white masters driving an army of black slaves, was totally without precedent in English experience. Already by 1680 in Barbados the gulf between the privileged gentry and the unprivileged laborers was much greater than at home. At this date the Barbados slaves outnumbered their masters by only two to one. By 1750 the Barbados ratio had climbed to four to one. In the Leeward Islands the ratio was seven to one: in the parish of St. Mary, in Antigua, as of 1767 only 65 whites paid taxes, and they held an average of 86 slaves apiece. Jamaica was the chief English sugar island by 1750, and it had a slave ratio of ten to one. A few hundred big entrepreneurs owned all of the best acreage and farmed on a very large scale. They raised cattle, cut timber, and cultivated indigo, cocoa, pimento, ginger, coffee, and cotton, but sugar was by far the most important crop. Surveys of the island taken in 1739, 1768, and 1832 disclose that half or more of the Jamaican slaves were attached to sugar estates, living and working in village-sized compounds. By 1814 in Westmoreland Parish, Jamaica, half of the slaves lived in gangs of 200 or more, and only 10 percent were placed in gangs of less than 30. While the black laborers were thus congregated into factorylike units, many of their employers had retired to England as absentees, leaving their estates in the hands of attorneys and overseers. . . .

To illustrate what can be learned by close study of Caribbean plantation records, let us consider the slave labor system in the Westmoreland sugar district of western Jamaica, as documented by the estate records of Mesopotamia plantation and by the diary of a Westmoreland estate manager, Thomas Thistlewood. The Mesopotamia records provide the fullest documentation yet found for any Caribbean slave community; they include eighty-five inventories of the slave force taken between 1736 and 1832. By correlating these inventories, we can reconstruct the careers of eleven hundred individual slaves, often from birth (or purchase) to death. Thistlewood's diary is the most minutely detailed day-by-day record yet discovered for the activities of any colonial planter. He kept this diary for thirty-six years, from his arrival in Jamaica in 1750 to his final illness in 1786, and he discloses almost more than the reader can bear about the underside of slave management.

Reading through Thistlewood's diary, one wonders how the slaves he dealt with could possibly endure such a regime and why they did not rebel far more frequently and violently. Thistlewood's first job in Jamaica was to manage a cattle pen in a remote mountain district. During the twelve months he held this job, in 1750–51, Thistlewood lived alone with forty-two slaves most of whom were African-born. In the first few days Thistlewood was there, the owner of the pen inspected the place and showed him how to manage the slaves: he ordered that the head slave, driver Mulatto Dick, be tied to an orange tree in the garden and given nearly three hundred lashes "for his many crimes and negligencies." It was nine days before Dick emerged from his cabin to go back to work. Thistlewood got the message: in the next twelve months he had 35 slaves whipped a total of 52 times. The punishment ranged from 50 to 150 lashes per whipping. In his diary Thistlewood recorded that he kept a slave mistress, with whom he had intercourse almost nightly. He also had sex with nine of the other fifteen females who lived at the pen. Thistlewood frequently reported that the slaves were shirking their work. Nine of them ran away at least once, and two of them disappeared repeatedly. All of them complained of hunger and kept stealing food. Several became violent: one man hacked a woman with a machete, and two men pulled knives when they were cornered. Yet Thistlewood was never personally threatened. He quit the job because he quarreled with the owner, not the slaves. Indeed, he went on lengthy hunting and fishing trips with some of the men whom he had flogged and whose wives he had raped, and he distributed rum, food, and other presents all round on leaving.

Turning to the Mesopotamia records, one begins to understand why these Jamaican slaves were not more rebellious: they were trapped into a labor routine that kept them exhausted, enervated, sickly, and dull. Mesopotamia was a fairly typical Jamaican sugar production unit, staffed by a labor gang that fluctuated in size between 250 and 350 during the last century of Jamaican slavery. Between 1762 and 1832, when the Mesopotamia records are most complete, nearly twice as many slaves died as were born on this estate, and the work force was sustained by introducing 147 new Africans—mostly male teenagers—and 278 "seasoned" slaves, bought from neighboring estates. During this seventy-year span only 4 slaves were sold, 12 were manumitted, and 9 escaped. Slaves born at Mesopotamia had a definite occupational advantage over slaves purchased from the slave ships or from other estates: they held the lion's share of the supervisory, craft, and domestic jobs. To some extent craftworkers and domestics secured preferential employment for their children, but the key factor was color. By 1832, 10 percent of the Mesopotamia slaves were mulattoes and quadroons, and these people were always assigned domestic or semiskilled jobs.

The majority of the Mesopotamia laborers were field workers, kept busy six days a week, year round, with twelve hours of monotonous drudge labor: digging cane trenches, weeding and dunging the young cane, tending the cattle, and harvesting the mature cane. The slaves were given simple hand tools and no labor-saving devices. Much of their work would have been performed by draft animals in English or North American agriculture. Sugar was then, as it is now, a seasonal crop, but the overseers stretched out the tasks to keep the slaves fully occupied at all times. The Mesopotamia records show a clear correlation between slave occupation and longevity: field workers broke down in health more quickly, and died younger, than craftworkers. Furthermore, females survived this labor routine better than males. During this seventy-year span 105 more males than females died at Mesopotamia, so that female workers considerably outnumbered male workers on this estate by 1832. A large majority of the field workers were women, even on the First Gang, which performed the heaviest field labor.

The Mesopotamia women who worked so hard produced few living children. Between 1762 and 1832 about half of the female slaves aged eighteen to forty-five were childless, and those who did raise children had small families. The disease environment, dietary deficiencies, and the debilitating labor regimen were probably the most important factors in explaining this infertility. It cannot be a pure coincidence that the Jamaican population began to increase naturally almost immediately after emancipation, when many women withdrew from field labor. According to the Mesopotamia records, about 20 percent of the slave deaths on this estate were attributable to diet and bad hygiene. The absentee owners of Mesopotamia were upset by the high mortality and the low fertility; they attempted to encourage motherhood by excusing from labor women with five or more children. The owners were bothered a good deal more, however, by the fact that so many of their slaves were elderly or invalids. A surprisingly large number of Mesopotamia slaves lived into their sixties and seventies. Although the owners kept adding young male workers, most of the labor was performed by women, and at any one time about 20 percent of the adult slaves were too sick or old for productive labor. Thus at Mesopotamia the Caribbean slave labor system proved to be inefficient as well as inhumane.

Turning to the southern mainland colonies, we find not one labor system but several. At one extreme, the South Carolina low-country rice planters employed slave labor practices reminiscent of those in the West Indies. In a parish like St. James Goose Creek, adjacent to Charleston, blacks outnumbered whites by four to one as early as the 1720s. The slaves were congregated into large work gangs, as in Jamaica, and compelled to plant, hoe, harvest, thresh, and husk the rice by hand. In the 1760s about half of the slaves in the low country were African-born; adult male slaves heavily outnumbered adult female slaves; and 40 percent of the blacks lived and worked in large gangs of at least fifty. At the opposite extreme, in the North Carolina piedmont, an entirely different labor system was in operation. Orange County, one of the few piedmont counties with surviving pre-revolutionary tax records, was a district of corn, wheat, and livestock agriculture. The taxpayers were small farmers of English, Scotch-Irish, or German stock who had migrated south from the Chesapeake or the mid-Atlantic colonies. In 1755 only 10 percent of the Orange County householders owned any slaves, and no planter in the county possessed as many as ten.

A third southern labor system, in many respects a median system combining features of the South Carolina low country and the North Carolina piedmont, was to be found in the Chesapeake, especially in the oldest settled tidewater counties of Virginia and Maryland. Here the tobacco planters, while just as interested as their South Carolina or Jamaica counterparts in making money through the exploitation of cheap labor, were also trying to shape a society in which both rich and poor whites had status and could feel comfortably at home. Between the 1680s and the 1750s they created an elaborately tiered social and economic hierarchy with slave laborers at the base, convict and indentured servants ranked next, then tenant farmers, then small landholders, then middling planters, and a handful of large planters—one to five [in] each county—at the top. By mid-century, slaveholding was very widely distributed throughout Virginia and Maryland. No Chesapeake county was so heavily tilted towards slave labor as the South Carolina rice parishes, but only the remote western frontier counties were without significant slave holdings. In 1755 the population in fourteen of the sixty-three Chesapeake counties was more than half black; all of these counties were in Virginia, served by the James, York, and Rappahannock rivers, where the African slave traders principally brought their cargoes. Maryland had noticeably fewer slaves at this date, which helps to explain why the planters from the upper Chesapeake were especially eager for convict servants. Even in the Virginia counties with the largest black populations slaveholding was far from universal. . . . [I]t appears that fewer than half of the small planters and tenant farmers in the Chesapeake were slaveholders in the 1760s and 1770s. . . .

While Chesapeake slavery was certainly not as brutal or repressive as in the Caribbean, the slaveholders seem to me to have stymied black resistance pretty effectively and to have thwarted most forms of black achievement.

In order to set up a meaningful comparison with Jamaican slavery as documented by the Mesopotamia estate records and Thomas Thistlewood's diary, let us consider parallel collections of evidence concerning the slave labor system in the northern neck of tidewater Virginia: the papers of the Tayloe family of Mount Airy, overlooking the Rappahannock, and the diary of Landon Carter, who lived next-door to the Tayloes at Sabine Hall. The Tayloes and the Carters were far from being representative Chesapeake slaveholders. They were among the largest entrepreneurs in the Chesapeake: the slave communities at Mount Airy and at Sabine Hall were equivalent in size to the slave community at Mesopotamia, Jamaica. John Tayloe I held 167 slaves at Mount Airy in 1747; his grandson held 383 slaves at Mount Airy in 1809, as well as hundreds of other slaves elsewhere in the Chesapeake. . . . How does Virginia slavery, as documented by the Tayloes and Landon Carter, chiefly differ from Jamaican slavery?

In the first place, the Tayloes and Carters saw themselves as patriarchs, in the fullest sense of the term, and this impelled them to manipulate their black workers' private lives and not simply to exploit their labor. In Jamaica, Thomas Thistlewood kept a diary in order to preserve his sanity, but in Virginia, Landon Carter kept a diary in order to nurture his self-image of father/ruler over his white family and black slaves. Through this diary the reader can follow Carter's efforts to supervise the work of his slaves, and manage their lives, for his own profit and their moral betterment. Carter moved constantly among the Sabine Hall field workers as well as the domestics, badgering them to work and doctoring them when sick. He would stay for hours in the threshing house in order to make the threshers work faster and more carefully. He knew his slaves as individuals, identifying some 150 blacks in his diary by name. His comments on slave behavior were almost invariably negative, for despite his wealth and status, Carter suffered acutely from paranoia. His diary in the 1760s and 1770s was a dumping ground, filled with diatribes against the people who betrayed him: his children and grandchildren and his slaves. In Carter's view, the Sabine Hall slaves, through "villanous lazyness," were constantly frustrating his best-laid plans. Thus carpenter Jimmy, who should have been building a corn house, was too lame to work, his legs swollen from wearing tight shoes. Far from feeling sorry for Jimmy, Carter punished this "splay footed rascal" by prohibiting him from going home at night to his wife, who lived on another quarter. Carpenter Tony, who should have been building Carter's garden fence, "goes on pretending with his scheme of old age creeping and whindling about often pretending to be sick." Plowman Manuel also had a scheme: to kill off Carter's oxen and horses by miring them in the mud. Body servant Nassau's strategy was to be constantly drunk.

. . . Carter played his role of patriarch ineptly, and his slaves knew how to outmaneuver and humiliate him. But they did so at great physical and psychic cost. Some of them escaped, at least briefly: Carter reports about forty runaways (mainly short-term) over a twenty-year span. Some of them were flogged: Carter reports twenty whippings in the year 1770 alone. Worse than the whippings must have been the endless intrusion, inspection, and harassment by this crabbed, obnoxious master. The slaves who knew Carter best, such as his body servant Nassau, were the ones most likely to run away. When Lord Dunmore called upon the Virginia slaves to revolt against their masters in 1775, fourteen of Carter's people fled to the British governor. This upset the proud old man very much. He dreamed one night that the runaways, looking "most wretchedly meager and wan," came back and begged for his help. But in truth, Carter's slaves had had quite enough of his help.

Landon Carter can be dismissed, and perhaps he should be, as an aberrant mental case. But the slaves who lived next-door at the Tayloes' Mount Airy plantation were also manipulated and intruded upon to a high degree. Admittedly, they worked less hard and lived much better than the slaves at Mesopotamia, Jamaica. Over a sixty-year span the Mount Airy records show that nearly twice as many slaves were born as died on this plantation. The labor pattern was designed to achieve total self-sufficiency: the field workers raised corn and pork in addition to tobacco, and they tended their gardens in off-hours; slave spinners and weavers made cloth from local cotton and wool; slave shoemakers tanned and dressed local leather; the smiths and joiners made wagons, ploughs, and hoes and shod horses; and the carpenters, masons, and jobbers erected and repaired buildings. Work logs kept by the overseers show a definite seasonal rhythm, with the harvest frenzy in midsummer and a long slack period in the winter. A third of the Mount Airy black workers were domestics or craftworkers, and women did much less of the heavy field labor than at Mesopotamia.

On the other hand, the lives of the Mount Airy slaves were continually disrupted by the Tayloes' practice of moving workers from one quarter to another or from one plantation to another and by their frequent sale of surplus slaves. . . . In 1792 John Tayloe III advertised: "For Sale 200 Virginia born, men, women and children, all ages and descriptions." At least 50 Mount Airy slaves were among those sold that year. Between 1809 and 1828 John Tayloe III sold 52 Mount Airy slaves, mainly teenage girls. Between 1828 and 1860 his sons moved 364 Mount Airy slaves to other Tayloe properties, about half of them to distant cotton plantations in Alabama. By this method the Tayloes kept the Mount Airy work force well organized for maximum productivity, with a high percentage of prime-aged male laborers. They clearly played favorites, keeping the domestics and craftworkers they liked best, together with their children, at Mount Airy. But among the field workers, husbands and wives generally lived at separate work quarters, and children were customarily taken from their parents at an early age. Thus the Tayloes' constant shuffling of the slave population, while sensible from a business viewpoint, was destructive of black family life.

To turn from the plantation slavery of tidewater Virginia to the farm, shop, and household environment of the mid-Atlantic colonies is to enter a different world. It was, to be sure, a variegated world, incorporating such laborers as the Yankee tenants, who staffed many of the baronial estates in the Hudson Valley; the Scottish tenants, who preserved their peculiar "farmtoun" style of husbandry in East Jersey; the African slaves, who labored on Quaker farms in West Jersey; the German redemptioners, who worked in rural Pennsylvania; and the Ulster servants, who bound themselves to masters in Philadelphia. But throughout this region the labor pattern differed in three important respects from the labor patterns of the Chesapeake and the Caribbean. First, the mid-Atlantic employers relied overwhelmingly on white labor, not black; and on apprentices, servants, and wage workers, not slaves. Second, they made heavy use of non-English imported white labor, especially Scotch-Irish and German immigrants. Third, the mid-Atlantic employment pattern more closely resembled the pattern in Britain or Europe than that in the plantation colonies. Agricultural laborers raised small grain crops and tended livestock, urban laborers were trained for crafts or tended shops, and female laborers were engaged for domestic service—all much as in the Old World.

Towns were more central work places in the mid-Atlantic economy than in the southern plantation economies; and since we will be focusing upon farm labor when discussing New England, it is appropriate to focus upon urban labor in the mid-Atlantic region. The premier town in this region during the eighteenth century was Philadelphia, which grew from around two thousand inhabitants in 1690 to nine thousand in 1740 and twenty-five thousand in 1776. By the Revolution, Philadelphia was the largest town and employment center in British America. Unhappily, many of the Philadelphia laborers—apprentices, servants, slaves, journeymen, and other wage workers (most particularly the female workers)—are impossible to find in the existing records. Some of them surface in the Philadelphia tax records for 1693, 1709, 1756, 1767, 1769, 1772, 1774, and 1775, in the twenty-four hundred inventories of estates filed between 1682 and 1780, in the newspapers, or in business records kept by merchants, shopkeepers, and artisans. But in many respects the Philadelphia servant or wage laborer remains a more shadowy figure than the Jamaica or Virginia slave.

Our understanding of labor practices in pre-revolutionary Philadelphia has been strongly colored by the example and the writings of Benjamin Franklin. He started out as a bound apprentice, became a wage-earning journeyman, and quickly rose through skill and hard work to be a self-employed printer, bookseller, and newspaper editor. And though he retired from the printing business at age forty-two, he was tremendously proud of his workingman's roots and of his craft as a printer, which enabled him to work with his hands and exercise his brain simultaneously. Franklin's *Autobiography* devotes considerable space to a description of the labor climate in Philadelphia from 1723, when he arrived as a runaway apprentice, to the 1730s, when he established himself as a successful printer. But the *Autobiography* was written for propaganda purposes; it is far more selective and less candid than the private diaries of Thomas Thistlewood and Landon Carter. Looking back as an old man upon his youth, Franklin was more concerned with character building than with the work practices in his printing shop. He encourages the reader to believe that any laborer, through industry, sobriety, and frugality, can rise up in the world. He introduces vignettes of lazy, drunken apprentices and journeymen as exemplars of behavior to avoid. He also contrasts the openness of the Philadelphia labor market with the proletarian restrictiveness of opportunity in London, where he also labored as a journeyman printer. Thanks to Franklin, we have tended to assume that Philadelphia provided an ideal environment for the struggling workingman and that most, if not all, of its inhabitants enjoyed expanding opportunities and a rising standard of living.

Recently this rosy picture has been challenged. A group of historians more influenced by E. P. Thompson's *The Making of the English Working Class* than by Franklin's *Autobiography* has been investigating servitude and slavery in Philadelphia, as well as job opportunities, wages, prices, and the distribution of wealth. Their findings suggest that while laborers in this town enjoyed generally favorable working and living conditions into the 1740s, their circumstances deteriorated badly in the next thirty years. Initially, as elsewhere in seventeenth-century America, the pioneers who founded Philadelphia relied heavily upon bound labor. The early inhabitants brought with them numerous indentured servants, and they purchased a shipload of 150 African slaves in 1684. . . . Philadelphians who died in the 1680s, during the first decade of settlement, held more slaves and servants per capita than at any later date. During the next forty years, from 1690 to 1730, servant imports were low, and slave imports were also fairly low. During this period Philadelphians did not abandon bound labor. Rather, they recruited apprentices and journeymen locally in the urban English fashion or hired migrant laborers from other colonies, such as seventeen-year-old Benjamin Franklin from Boston in 1723. And as the town grew rapidly and the local labor market expanded, Philadelphians bought many of the African slaves and the Irish and German servants who were shipped into the city between 1729 and 1775. These immigrant laborers came in overlapping waves: slave shipments in 1729–41, followed by shipments of German and Irish servants in 1732–56, then slave shipments in 1759–65 (at a time when it was impractical to import servants because the British enrolled large numbers of them into the army during the Seven Years' War), and Irish servants again from 1763 to 1775.

Despite this large-scale infusion of bound labor the proportion of slaves and immigrant servants in the total Philadelphia labor force was probably not rising during the years 1729–62, and it was certainly declining during the years 1763–75. Immigrant servants had to be constantly replaced, since they soon earned their freedom, and slaves had to be replaced also, since they had little chance to develop family life in Philadelphia and were not reproducing themselves. When offered a choice, Philadelphia employers preferred servants to slaves; they bought Africans mainly when immigrant whites were unavailable. And probably Philadelphia employers preferred native-born to immigrant workers. If African slaves and Irish servants had been especially sought-after, one would expect that the rich merchants and professionals, who could pay top prices, would have snapped up most of them. But instead we find that Philadelphia artisans of modest means bought much of the immigrant bound labor. In 1745, two-thirds of the 253 servants imported into the city were bound to artisans, and in 1767 about half of the 905 slaves in Philadelphia were held by artisans.

During and after the Seven Years' War there was a decisive shift away from bound to free wage labor. From 1754 onward the Philadelphia Quakers campaigned actively against slave ownership. Meanwhile, many free white laborers were drawn to the city because the wartime business boom of 1754–63 drove wages up in Philadelphia for mariners, shipwrights, and other semiskilled workers. In the peacetime depression that followed, there was a labor glut, wages fell, and Philadelphia employers discovered that wage labor was cheaper than bound labor. . . . [T]he 1760s and 1770s saw a great constriction in job opportunities for mariners and unskilled laborers and a great increase in the number of underemployed and unemployed workers. . . . [T]he wages of unskilled and semiskilled workers were now no longer adequate to cover the minimum cost of food, rent, fuel, and clothing. The wives and children of the laboring poor had to find marginal employment if families were to survive. The city fathers had to devise new measures of poor relief for the destitute.

Had young Benjamin Franklin wandered into Philadelphia in 1763 instead of 1723, according to this interpretation, he would have had much more difficulty in picking himself up from the bottom. The pre-revolutionary labor surplus in Philadelphia among unskilled and semiskilled workers was a new phenomenon in America, for labor had always been scarce in the colonies. We will encounter a parallel labor surplus—which might be better described as a population surplus—in the farm villages of eastern Massachusetts during the generation before the Revolution. There was also a population surplus in the Chesapeake, but it developed thirty or forty years later, after the Revolution, when tidewater planters sold their superfluous slaves or moved them to new work places in the piedmont or further west and south. But if all the oldest settled parts of America were becoming overstocked with laborers during the late eighteenth century, there was a marked difference between the southern and northern methods of coping with this situation. In Virginia the use of slave labor became more widespread among all white householders, rich and poor; consequently, the institution of slavery became more deeply entrenched in the years between 1750 and 1800. In Philadelphia the opposite occurred: slavery was abolished after the Revolution, indentured servitude sharply declined, and both immigrant and native-born unskilled and semiskilled workers were thrown onto the free wage market.

. . . The Virginia slaveholders may have been patriarchal and pre-capitalistic, but as we have seen, the masters of Mount Airy continually sold their slaves or transferred them to new job assignments not of their choice in order to maintain an effective labor force. The businessmen of Philadelphia likewise manipulated their proletarian employees, but the unskilled workers who flocked to this town came out of free choice, and if they were underpaid they had the further option (which many exercised) of moving on to other places in America where labor was still scarce. I do not wish to minimize the plight of Philadelphia's laboring poor, but they did have an ultimate freedom that was not available to their counterparts in England (where unskilled labor was in permanent surplus) nor to the Afro-American slaves in the Chesapeake and the Caribbean.

In New England, the chief singularity of the labor system was that during the eighteenth century nearly all work was performed by native-born whites. After the great Puritan migration of the 1630s had ended, the New England colonists imported few white servants or black slaves from abroad. . . . The few blacks were employed chiefly in the coastal towns, especially Newport and Boston. In addition to this slave labor, the New Englanders got the local Indians to do some of their dirty work. In 1774 a third of the Indians living in Rhode Island were boarding with white families, employed as servants. On the island of Nantucket the merchants who organized the whaling industry maneuvered the local Indians into manning the whaling boats. But Indians were no longer numerous in New England, having been nearly annihilated in the wars of the seventeenth century. Censuses of the four New England colonies taken during the 1760s and 1770s indicate that the Indians and Negroes together formed a tiny nonwhite minority—only a little over 3 percent of the regional population. The descendants of the Puritans, with their well-established reputation for clannish hostility to strangers and aliens, thus performed most of the labor assigned elsewhere in America to immigrant servants and slaves.

The New Englanders were the only American colonists to develop a homogeneous society, closely resembling in ethnic composition the society their ancestors had known in England. But the New Englanders did not perpetuate the mother country's sharp social division between the propertied, privileged upper and middling orders and the propertyless, unprivileged wage laborers. On the contrary, New England was the most egalitarian sector of colonial America, far less stratified than the Caribbean or Chesapeake colonies and somewhat less stratified than the mid-Atlantic colonies.

To be sure, New England had a growing poverty problem in the mid-eighteenth century. In Boston, more pronouncedly than in Philadelphia, unskilled wage workers began to resemble the permanently depressed laboring poor of England. A very large number of mariners were congregated in the coastal towns. In 1740 it was calculated that 74 percent of the fishing, coasting, and long-distance merchant ships in the American colonies sailed from New England ports. During the war years, wages on naval, privateering, and merchant ships were high; when shipping declined and wages plummeted during peacetime, some seamen quit, but many others became trapped into careers of unattractive, irregular, low-paying wage work. The wages of Boston seamen did not keep pace with commodity prices, and their probated estates declined significantly in value between 1685 and 1775. Sailors ranked below shoemakers and tailors as the most depressed occupational group in Boston. But the plight of the mariners was not indicative of the New England labor system as a whole. Most of the unskilled and semiskilled work in this region was performed on farms and not at sea. To get a sense of farming conditions, we must turn to the country villages, where the majority of New Englanders lived and worked.

Eighteenth-century New England farmers seem to have used formally bound labor—indentured servants or wage workers hired by the year—less than did Pennsylvania or Virginia farmers. For example, in Bristol, Rhode Island, two-thirds of the householders in 1689 had no live-in servants. Every one of these Bristol households included at least one adult woman—a wife, a grown daughter, or a female live-in servant—because men could not or would not do the cooking, needlework, cleaning, and processing of raw farm produce that every household required. Furthermore, nine out of ten Bristol households in 1689 included children, and overall there were 3.2 children per household. While this census does not tell which of these children were old enough to work, a later Bristol census, taken in 1774, divides the population between males and females over sixteen (hence old enough for full-scale work) and boys and girls up to sixteen (too young for work). On average there were three white workers per household. More than a third of these Bristol "adults" were listed as singles: . . . as unmarried sons and daughters. The same pattern reappears in a colonywide census of Massachusetts taken in 1764, which shows 3.4 nonworking children per household and 3.6 "adults." The mean Massachusetts household size of 7.0 white persons in 1764 is very much larger than the mean household size of 4.8 persons found in mid-eighteenth-century England and larger also than the white households of small planters in the Caribbean or the Chesapeake.

. . . [T]hese large Massachusetts households generated a great deal of family labor. . . .

Clearly the labor systems in the several regions of colonial America diverged remarkably from each other by 1775. And clearly these divergences held consequences for the future. The New England method, with its prime reliance upon family labor and supplementary help from hired hands and neighbors, was cumbersome and inefficient, but it was a functional method, and one that the New Englanders would carry westward with them after the Revolution as they set up new family farms in Ohio and beyond. The Philadelphia method, with its increasing reliance upon underpaid wage labor supplied by a pool of unskilled and semiskilled workers, was exploitive and inhumane, but it too was a functional method that capitalistic entrepreneurs would utilize as they built new western cities and recruited factory workers after the Revolution. The Chesapeake method, with its prime reliance upon unpaid labor by chattel slaves, appears to me to have been rather more exploitive and inhumane than labor practices further north, but here again was a functional method that cotton planters would carry westward after the Revolution as they set up new plantations in Alabama and elsewhere in the Deep South. But the Caribbean method of slave labor, in my view, was becoming truly dysfunctional by 1775. The sugar planters could sustain their work force only through continuous recourse to the

African slave trade, and their labor management was so patently inhumane that the abolitionists in England were able to mount an effective parliamentary attack upon them. When Parliament voted to close the slave trade in 1806, the Caribbean labor system was placed in jeopardy, pointing the way towards emancipation of the West Indian blacks and the near paralysis of the West Indian sugar industry. There are of course other reasons for the collapse of the sugar planters. But they were the only colonists in British America whose labor system went bankrupt, in both a moral and a business sense.

Housewives and Household Labor in Colonial America

LAUREL THATCHER ULRICH

By English tradition, a woman's environment was the family dwelling and the yard or yards surrounding it. Though the exact composition of her setting obviously depended upon the occupation and economic status of her husband, its general outlines were surprisingly similar regardless of where it was located. The difference between an urban "houselot" and a rural "homelot" was not as dramatic as one might suppose.

If we were to draw a line around the housewife's domain, it would extend from the kitchen and its appendages, the cellars, pantries, brewhouses, milkhouses, washhouses, and butteries which appear in various combinations in household inventories, to the exterior of the house, where, even in the city, a mélange of animal and vegetable life flourished among the straw, husks, clutter, and muck. Encircling the pigpen, such a line would surround the garden, the milkyard, the well, the henhouse, and perhaps the orchard itself—though husbands pruned and planted trees and eventually supervised the making of cider, good housewives strung their wash between the trees and in season harvested fruit for pies and conserves.

The line demarking the housewife's realm would not cross the fences which defined outlying fields of Indian corn or barley, nor would it stretch to fishing stages, mills, or wharves, but in berry or mushroom season it would extend into nearby woods or marsh and in spells of dearth or leisure reach to the shore. Of necessity, the boundaries of each woman's world would also extend into the houses of neighbors and into the cartways of a village or town. Housewives commanded a limited domain. But they were neither isolated nor self-sufficient. Even in farming settlements, families found it essential to bargain for needed goods and services. For prosperous and socially prominent women, interdependence took on another meaning as well. Prosperity meant charity, and in early New England charity meant personal responsibility for nearby neighbors.

None of this was unique to New England. In fact, each aspect of female life described here can be found in idealized form in the Bible in the description of the "virtuous woman" of Proverbs, chapter 31. The Puritans called this paragon "Bathsheba," assuming rather logically that Solomon could only have learned such an appreciation for huswifery from his mother. Forgotten in their encomia to female virtue was the rooftop bather whose beauty brought King David to grief. In English and American sermons Bathsheba was remembered as a virtuous housewife, a godly woman whose industrious labors gave mythical significance to the ordinary tasks assigned to her sex.

As described in Proverbs, Bathsheba is a willing servant to her family: "She riseth also while it is yet night, and giveth meat to her household."

She is a skilled manufacturer: "She seeketh wool, and flax, and worketh willingly with her hands."

She is a hard-working agriculturist: "With the fruit of her hands she planteth a vineyard."

She is a resourceful trader: "She is like the merchants' ships; she bringeth her food from afar."

Because her realm includes servants as well as young children, her ability to direct, to inspire, and to nurture others is as important to her success as hard work. "She openeth her mouth with wisdom; and in her tongue is the law of kindness." Her industry and her charity give legitimacy to her wealth. Though dressed in silk and purple, "strength and honour are her clothing" and "she stretcheth out her hand to the poor." Her goal is not public distinction but private competence. Although her husband is "known in the gates," her greatest reward is in looking well to "the ways of her household." In doing so, she earns the devotion of her children, the praise of her husband, and the commendation of God.

To describe this virtuous Bathsheba is to outline the major components of the housekeeping role in early America. . . . For most historians, as for almost all antiquarians, the quintessential early American woman has been a churner of cream and a spinner of wool. Because home manufacturing has all but disappeared from modern housekeeping, many scholars have assumed that the key change in female economic life has been a shift from "production" to "consumption," a shift precipitated by the industrial revolution. This is far too simple, obscuring the variety which existed even in the pre-industrial world. . . .

. . . A careful examination of the contents of their kitchens and chambers suggests the varied complexity as well as the underlying unity in the lives of early American women.

Let us begin with Beatrice Plummer of Newbury, Massachusetts. Forgetting that death brought her neighbors into the house on January 24, 1672, we can use the probate inventory which they prepared to reconstruct the normal pattern of her work.

With a clear estate of £343, Francis Plummer had belonged to the "middling sort" who were the church members and freeholders of the Puritan settlement of Newbury. As an immigrant of 1653, he had listed himself as a "linnen weaver," but he soon became a farmer as well. At his death, his loom and tackling stood in the "shop" with his pitchforks, his hoes, and his tools for smithing and carpentry. Plummer had integrated four smaller plots to form one continuous sixteen-acre farm. An additional twenty acres of salt marsh and meadow provided hay and forage for his small herd of cows and sheep. His farm provided a comfortable living for his family, which at this stage of his life included only his second wife, Beatrice, and her grandchild by a previous marriage. Had not death prevented him, he might have filled this January day in a number of productive ways, moving the loom into the sparsely furnished hall, for example, or taking his yoke of oxen to the wood lot "near the little river" to cut wood for the large fireplace that was the center of Beatrice's working world.

The house over which Beatrice presided must have looked much like surviving dwellings from seventeenth-century New England, with its "Hall" and "Parlor" on the ground floor and two "chambers" above. A space designated in the inventory only as "another Roome" held the family's collection of pots, kettles, dripping pans, trays, buckets, and earthenware. Perhaps this kitchen had been added to the original house as a lean-to, as was frequently the case in New England. The upstairs chambers were not bedrooms but storage rooms for foodstuffs and out-of-season equipment. The best bed with its bolster, pillows, blanket, and coverlet stood in the parlor; a second bed occupied one corner of the kitchen, while a cupboard, a "great chest," a table, and a backless bench called a "form" furnished the hall. More food was found in the "cellar" and in the "dairy house," a room which may have stood at the coolest end of the kitchen lean-to.

The Plummer house was devoid of ornament, but its contents bespeak such comforts as conscientious yeomanry and good huswifery afforded. On this winter morning the dairy house held four and a half "flitches" or sides of bacon, a quarter of a barrel of salt pork, twenty-eight pounds of cheese, and four pounds of butter. Upstairs in a chamber were more than twenty-five bushels of "English" grain—barley, oats, wheat, and rye. (The Plummers apparently reserved their Indian corn, stored in another location, for their animals.) When made into malt by a village specialist, barley would become the basis for beer. Two bushels of malt were already stored in the house. The oats might appear in a variety of dishes, from plain breakfast porridge to "flummery," a gelatinous dish flavored with spices and dried fruit. But the wheat and rye were almost certainly reserved for bread and pies. The fine hair sieves stored with the grain in the hall chamber suggest that Beatrice Plummer was particular about her baking, preferring a finer flour than came directly from the miller. A "bushell of pease & beans" found near the grain and a full barrel of cider in the cellar are the only vegetables and fruits listed in the inventory, though small quantities of pickles, preserves, or dried herbs might have escaped notice. Perhaps the Plummers added variety to their diet by trading some of their abundant supply of grain for cabbages, turnips, sugar, molasses, and spices.

Even without additions they had the basic components of the yeoman diet described in English agricultural literature of the seventeenth century. Although the eighteenth century would add a little chocolate or tea as well as increasing quantities of tiny "petators" to the New England farmer's diet, the bread, cider, and boiled meat which fed Francis and Beatrice Plummer also fed their counterparts a century later.

Since wives were involved with early-morning milking, breakfast of necessity featured prepared foods or leftovers—toasted bread, cheese, and perhaps meat and turnips kept from the day before, any of this washed down with cider or beer in winter, with milk in summer. Only on special occasions would there be pie or doughnuts. Dinner was the main meal of the day. Here a housewife with culinary aspirations and an ample larder could display her specialties. After harvest Beatrice Plummer might have served roast pork or goose with apples, in spring an eel pie flavored with parsley and winter savory, and in summer a leek soup or gooseberry cream; but for ordinary days the most common menu was boiled meat with whatever "sauce" the season provided—dried peas or beans, parsnips, turnips, onions, cabbage, or garden greens. A heavy pudding stuffed into a cloth bag could steam atop the vegetables and meat. The broth from this boiled dinner might reappear at supper as "pottage" with the addition of minced herbs and some oatmeal or barley for thickening. Supper, like breakfast, was a simple meal. Bread, cheese, and beer were as welcome at the end of a winter day as at the beginning. In summer, egg dishes and fruit tarts provided more varied nutrition.

Preparing the simplest of these meals required both judgment and skill. . . . The most basic of the housewife's skills was building and regulating fires—a task so fundamental that it must have appeared more as habit than craft. Summer and winter, day and night, she kept a few brands smoldering, ready to stir into flame as needed. The cavernous fireplaces of early New England were but a century removed from the open fires of medieval houses, and they retained some of the characteristics of the latter. Standing inside one of these huge openings today, a person can see the sky above. Seventeenth-century housewives *did* stand in their fireplaces, which were conceived less as enclosed spaces for a single blaze than as accessible working surfaces upon which a number of small fires might be built. Preparing several dishes simultaneously, a cook could move from one fire to another, turning a spit, checking the state of the embers under a skillet, adjusting the height of a pot hung from the lugpole by its adjustable trammel. The complexity of fire-tending, as much as anything else, encouraged the one-pot meal.

The contents of her inventory suggest that Beatrice Plummer was adept not only at roasting, frying, and boiling but also at baking, the most difficult branch of cookery. Judging from the grain in the upstairs chamber, the bread which she baked was "maslin," a common type made from a mixture of wheat and other grains, usually rye. She began with the sieves stored nearby, carefully sifting out the coarser pieces of grain and bran. Soon after supper she could have mixed the "sponge," a thin dough made from warm water, yeast, and flour. Her yeast might have come from the foamy "barm" found on top of fermenting ale or beer, from a piece of dough saved from an earlier baking, or even from the crevices in an unwashed kneading trough. Like fire-building, bread-making was based upon a self-perpetuating chain, an organic sequence which if once interrupted was difficult to begin again. Warmth from the banked fire would raise the sponge by morning, when Beatrice could work in more flour, kneading the finished dough, and shape the loaves, leaving them to rise again.

Even in twentieth-century kitchens with standardized yeast and thermostatically controlled temperatures, bread dough is subject to wide variations in consistency and behavior. In a drafty house with an uncertain supply of yeast, bread-making was indeed "an art, craft, and mystery." Not the least of the problem was regulating the fire so that the oven was ready at the same time as the risen loaves. Small cakes or biscuits could be baked in a skillet or directly on the hearth under an upside-down pot covered with coals. But to produce bread in any quantity required an oven. Before 1650 these were frequently constructed in dooryards, but in the last decades of the century they were built into the rear of the kitchen fireplace, as Beatrice Plummer's must have been. Since her oven would have had no flue, she would have left the door open once she kindled a fire inside, allowing the smoke to escape through the fireplace chimney. Moving about her kitchen, she would have kept an eye on this fire, occasionally raking the coals to distribute the heat evenly, testing periodically with her hand to see if the oven had reached the right temperature. When she determined that it had, she would have scraped out the coals and inserted the bread— assuming that it had risen enough by this time or had not risen too much and collapsed waiting for the oven to heat.

Cooking and baking were year-round tasks. Inserted into these day-by-day routines were seasonal specialties which allowed a housewife to bridge the dearth of one period with the bounty of another. In the preservation calendar, dairying came first, beginning with the first calves of early spring. In colonial New England cows were all-purpose creatures, raised for meat as well as for milk. Even in new settlements they could survive by browsing on rough land; their meat was a hedge against famine. But only in areas with abundant meadow (and even there only in certain months) would they produce milk with sufficient butterfat for serious dairying. Newbury was such a place.

We can imagine Beatrice Plummer some morning in early summer processing the milk which would appear as cheese in a January breakfast. Slowly she heated several gallons with rennet dried and saved from the autumn's slaughtering. Within an hour or two the curd had formed. She broke it, drained off the whey, then worked in a little of her own fresh butter. Packing this rich mixture into a mold, she turned it in her wooden press for an hour or more, changing and washing the cheesecloth frequently as the whey dripped out. Repacking it in dry cloth, she left it in the press for another thirty to forty hours before washing it once more with whey, drying it, and placing it in the cellar or dairy house to age. As a young girl she would have learned from her mother or a mistress the importance of thorough pressing and the virtues of cleanliness. She may also have acquired some of the many English proverbs associated with dairying. Taking her finished mound to the powdering tub for a light dusting, she perhaps recalled that "much saltness in white meat is ill for the stone."

The Plummer inventory gives little evidence of the second stage of preservation in the housewife's year, the season of gardening and gathering which followed quickly upon the dairy months. But there is ample evidence of the autumn slaughtering. Beatrice could well have killed the smaller pigs herself, holding their "hinder parts between her legs," as one observer described the process, "and taking the snout in her left hand" while she stuck the animal through the heart with a long knife. Once the bleeding stopped, she would have submerged the pig in boiling water for a few minutes, then rubbed it with rosin, stripped off the hair, and disemboweled it. Nothing was lost. She reserved the organ meats for immediate use, then cleaned the intestines for later service as sausage casings. Stuffed with meat scraps and herbs and smoked, these "links" were a treasured delicacy. The larger cuts could be roasted at once or preserved in several ways. With wine, ginger, mace, and nutmeg, pork could be rolled into a cloth and pickled as "souse." But this was an expensive—and risky—method. Beatrice relied on more common techniques. She submerged some of her pork in brine, trusting the high salt concentration and the low temperature in the dairy house to keep it untainted. She processed the rest as bacon. Each "flitch" stood in salt for two or three weeks before she hung it from the lugpole of her chimney for smoking. In the Plummer house "hanging bacon" must have been a recurring ritual of early winter.

Fall was also the season for cider-making. The mildly alcoholic beverage produced by natural fermentation of apple juice was a staple of the New England diet and was practically the only method of preserving the fruit harvest. With the addition of sugar, the alcoholic content could be raised from five to about seven percent, as it usually was in taverns and for export. The cider in the Plummer house was probably the common farm variety. In early winter the amber juice of autumn sat hissing and bubbling in the cellar in the most active stage of fermentation, a process which came to be described poetically as the "singing of the cider." . . .

All that we know of Beatrice Plummer of Newbury reveals her as a woman who took pride in huswifery. A wife who knew how to manage the ticklish chemical processes which changed milk into cheese, meal into bread, malt into beer, and flesh into bacon was a valuable asset to a man, as Francis Plummer knew. But not long after his death Beatrice married a man who did not appreciate her skills. To put it bluntly, he seems to have preferred her property. Like Francis Plummer before him, Edmund Berry had signed a prenuptial contract allowing Beatrice to retain ownership of the estate she had inherited from her previous husband. Subsequently, however, Edmund regretted his decision and began to hound Beatrice to tear up the paper. . . .

The tumult which thrust her into court gives life to the assemblage of objects found in her Newbury kitchen, and it helps to document the central position of huswifery in the self-definition of one northern New England woman.

Beatrice Plummer represents one type of early American housewife. Hannah Grafton represents another. Chronology, geography, and personal biography created differences between the household inventories of the two women, but there are obvious similarities as well. Like Beatrice Plummer, Hannah Grafton lived in a house with two major rooms on the ground floor and two chambers above. At various locations near the ground-floor rooms were service areas—a washhouse with its own loft or chamber, a shop, a lean-to, and two cellars. The central rooms in the Grafton house were the "parlour," with the expected featherbed, and the "kitchen," which included much the same collection of utensils and iron pots which appeared in the Plummer house. Standing in the corner of the kitchen were a spade and a hoe, two implements useful only for chipping away ice and snow on the December day on which the inventory was taken, though apparently destined for another purpose come spring. With a garden, a cow, and three pigs, Hannah Grafton clearly had agricultural responsibilities, but these were performed in a strikingly different context than on the Plummer farm. The Grafton homelot was a single acre of land standing just a few feet from shoreline in the urban center of Salem.

Joshua Grafton was a mariner like his father before him. His estate of £236 was modest, but he was still a young man and he had firm connections with the seafaring elite who were transforming the economy of Salem. When he died late in 1699, Hannah had three living children—Hannah, eight; Joshua, six; and Priscilla, who was just ten months. This young family used their space quite differently than had the Plummers. The upstairs chambers which served as storage areas in the Newbury farmhouse were sleeping quarters here. In addition to the bed in the parlor and the cradle in the kitchen, there were two beds in each of the upstairs rooms. One of these, designated as "smaller," may have been used by young Joshua. It would be interesting to know whether the mother carried the two chamber pots kept in the parlor upstairs to the bedrooms at night or whether the children found their way in the dark to their parents' sides as necessity demanded. But adults were probably never far away. Because there are more bedsteads in the Grafton house than members of the immediate family, they may have shared their living quarters with unmarried relatives or servants.

Ten chairs and two stools furnished the kitchen, while no fewer than fifteen chairs, in two separate sets, crowded the parlor with its curtained bed. The presence of a punch bowl on a square table in the parlor reinforces the notion that sociability was an important value in this Salem household. Thirteen ounces of plate, a pair of gold buttons, and a silver-headed cane suggest a measure of luxury as well—all of this in stark contrast to the Plummers, who had only two chairs and a backless bench and no discernible ornamentation at all. Yet the Grafton house was only slightly more specialized than the Newbury farmhouse. It had no servants' quarters, no sharp segregation of public and private spaces, no real separation of sleeping, eating, and work. A cradle in the kitchen and a go-cart kept with the spinning wheels in the upstairs chamber show that little Priscilla was very much a part of this workaday world.

How then might the pattern of Hannah Grafton's work have differed from that of Beatrice Plummer? Certainly cooking remained central. Hannah's menus probably varied only slightly from those prepared in the Plummer kitchen, and her cooking techniques must have been identical. But one dramatic difference is apparent in the two inventories. The Grafton house contained no provisions worth listing on that December day when Isaac Foot and Samuel Willard appeared to take inventory. Hannah had brewing vessels, but no malt; sieves and a meal trough, but no grain; and a cow, but no cheese. What little milk her cow gave in winter probably went directly into the children's mugs. Perhaps she would continue to breast-feed Priscilla until spring brought a more secure supply. In summer she might make a little cottage cheese or at harvest curdle some rich milk with wine or ale for a "posset," but she would have no surplus to process as butter or cheese. Her orchard would produce fresh apples for pie or puffs for autumn supper, but little extra for the cellar. Her three pigs might eventually appear, salted, in the empty barrels stored in the house, but as yet they represented only the hope of bacon. Trade, rather than manufacturing or agriculture, was the dominant motif in her meal preparations.

In colonial New England most food went directly from processor or producer to consumer. Joshua may have purchased grain or flour from the mill near the shipbuilding center called Knocker's Hole, about a mile away from their house. Or Hannah may have eschewed bread-making altogether, walking or sending a servant the half-mile to Elizabeth Haskett's bakery near the North River. Fresh meat for the spits in her washhouse may have come from John Cromwell's slaughterhouse on Main Street near the congregational meetinghouse, and soap for her washtubs from the soap-boiler farther up the street near the Quaker meetinghouse. Salem, like other colonial towns, was laid out helter-skelter, with the residences of the wealthy interspersed with the small houses of carpenters or fishermen. Because there was no center of retail trade, assembling the ingredients of a dinner involved many transactions. Sugar, wine, and spices came by sea; fresh lamb, veal, eggs, butter, gooseberries, and parsnips came by land. Merchants retailed their goods in shops or warehouses near their wharves and houses. Farmers or their wives often hawked their produce door to door. . . .

In such a setting, trading for food might require as much energy and skill as manufacturing or growing it. One key to success was simply knowing where to go. Keeping abreast of the arrival of ships in the harbor or establishing personal contact with just the right farmwife from nearby Salem village required time and attention. Equally important was the ability to evaluate the variety of unstandardized goods offered. An apparently sound cheese might teem with maggots when cut. Since cash was scarce, a third necessity was the establishment of credit, a problem which ultimately devolved upon husbands. But petty haggling over direct exchanges was also a feature of this barter economy.

Hannah Grafton was involved in trade on more than one level. The "shop" attached to her house was not the all-purpose storage shed and workroom it seems to have been for Francis Plummer. It was a retail store, offering door locks, nails, hammers, gimlets, and other hardware as well as English cloth, pins, needles, and thread. As a mariner, Joshua Grafton may well have sailed the ship which brought these goods to Salem. In his absence, Hannah was not only a mother and a housewife but, like many other Salem women, a shopkeeper as well.

There was another highly visible activity in the Grafton inventory which was not immediately apparent in the Plummers'—care of clothing. Presumably, Beatrice Plummer washed occasionally, but she did not have a "washhouse." Hannah did. The arrangement of this unusual room is far from clear. On December 2, 1699, it contained two spits, two "bouldishes," a gridiron, and "other things." Whether those other things included washtubs, soap, or a beating staff is impossible to determine. In a seaport town a building with a fire for heating rinse water, boiling laundry, and drying clothes could have been the base for a thriving home industry. But there is no evidence of this in the Grafton inventory. Like the "butteries" and "dairies" which appear in other New England houses, this room may have retained a specialized English name while actually functioning as a multipurpose storage and service room. With its spits and gridiron Hannah Grafton's "washhouse" may have served as an extra cooking space, perhaps on occasions when all fifteen chairs in the parlor were filled.

But on any morning in December it could also have been hung with the family wash. Dark woolen jackets and petticoats went from year to year without seeing a kettle of suds, but linen shifts, aprons, shirts, and handkerchiefs required washing. Laundering might not have been a weekly affair in most colonial households, but it was a well-defined if infrequent necessity even for transient seamen and laborers. One can only speculate on its frequency in a house with a child under a year. When her baby was only a few months old, Hannah may have learned to hold little Priscilla over the chamber pot at frequent intervals, but in early infancy, tightly wrapped in her cradle, the baby could easily have used five dozen "clouts" and almost as many "belly bands" from one washing to another. Even with the use of a "pilch," a thick square of flannel securely bound over the diaper, blankets and coverlets occasionally needed sudsing as well.

Joshua's shirts and Hannah's own aprons and shifts would require careful ironing. Hannah's "smoothing irons" fitted into their own heaters, which she filled with coals from the fire. As the embers waned and the irons cooled, she would have made frequent trips from her table to the hearth to the fire and back to the table again. At least two of these heavy instruments were essential. A dampened apron could dry and wrinkle while a single flat-iron replenished its heat.

As frequent a task as washing was sewing. Joshua's coats and breeches went to a tailor, but his shirts were probably made at home. Certainly Hannah stitched and unstitched the tucks which altered Priscilla's simple gowns and petticoats as she grew. The little dresses which the baby trailed in her go-cart had once clothed her brother. Gender identity in childhood was less important in this society than economy of effort. It was not that boys were seen as identical to girls, only that all-purpose garments could be handed from one child to another regardless of sex, and dresses were more easily altered than breeches and more adaptable to diapering and toileting. At eight years of age little Hannah had probably begun to imitate her mother's even stitches, helping with the continual mending, altering, and knitting which kept this growing family clothed.

In some ways the most interesting items in the Grafton inventory are the two spinning wheels kept in the upstairs chamber. Beatrice Plummer's wheel and reel had been key components in an intricate production chain. The Plummers had twenty-five sheep in the fold and a loom in the shed. The Graftons had neither. Children—not sheep—put wheels in Hannah's house. The mechanical nature of spinning made it a perfect occupation for women whose attention was engrossed by young children. This is one reason why the ownership of wheels . . . had a constancy over time unrelated to the ownership of sheep or looms. In the dozen inventories taken in urban Salem about the time of Joshua Grafton's death, the six non-spinners averaged one minor child each, the six spinners had almost four. Instruction at the wheel was part of the almost ritualistic preparation mothers offered their daughters. Spinning was a useful craft, easily picked up, easily put down, and even small quantities of yarn could be knitted into caps, stockings, dishcloths, and mittens.

Unfortunately, there is no documented event in Hannah Grafton's life corresponding to Beatrice Plummer's colorful appearance in court. But a cluster of objects in the chamber over her kitchen suggests a fanciful but by no means improbable vignette. Imagine her gathered with her two daughters in this upstairs room on a New England winter's day. Little Priscilla navigates around the end of the bedstead in her go-cart while her mother sits at one spinning wheel and her sister at the other. Young Hannah is spinning "oakum," the coarsest and least expensive part of the flax. As her mother leans over to help her wind the uneven thread on the bobbin, she catches a troublesome scent from downstairs. Have the turnips caught on the bottom of the pot? Has the maid scorched Joshua's best shirt? Or has a family servant returned from the wharf and spread his wet clothes by the fire? Hastening down the narrow stairs to the kitchen, Hannah hears the shop bell ring. Just then little Priscilla, left upstairs with her sister, begins to cry. In such pivotal but unrecorded moments much of the history of women lies hidden. . . .

. . . Hannah Grafton and Beatrice Plummer were . . . "typical" New England housewives of the period 1650–1750. . . . Hannah's punch bowl and her hardware shop exemplify both the commerce and the self-conscious civilization of coastal towns. Beatrice's brewing tubs and churn epitomize home manufacturing and agrarian self-sufficiency as they existed in established villages. Each type of housekeeping could be found somewhere in northern New England in any decade of the century. Yet these . . . women should not be placed in rigidly separate categories. Wealth, geography, occupation, and age determined that some women in any decade would be more heavily involved in one aspect of housekeeping than another, yet all

. . . women shared a common vocation. Each understood the rhythms of the seasons, the technology of fire-building, the persistence of the daily demands of cooking, the complexity of home production, and the dexterity demanded from the often conflicting roles of housekeeper, mother, and wife.

The thing which distinguished these women from their counterparts in modern America was not, as some historians have suggested, that their work was essential to survival. "Survival," after all, is a minimal concept. Individual men and women have never needed each other for mere survival but for far more complex reasons, and women were *essential* in the seventeenth century for the very same reasons they are essential today—for the perpetuation of the race. . . . English husbands could live without cheese and beer. Nor was it the monotony of these women's lives or the narrowness of their choices which really set them apart. Women in industrial cities have lived monotonous and confining lives, and they may have worked even harder than early American women. The really striking differences are social.

. . . [T]he lives of early American housewives were distinguished less by the tasks they performed than by forms of social organization which linked economic responsibilities to family responsibilities and which tied each woman's household to the larger world of her village or town.

For centuries the industrious Bathsheba has been pictured sitting at a spinning wheel—"She layeth her hands to the spindle, and her hands hold the distaff." Perhaps it is time to suggest a new icon for women's history. Certainly spinning was an important female craft in northern New England, linked not only to housework but to mothering, but it was one enterprise among many. Spinning wheels are such intriguing and picturesque objects, so resonant with antiquity, that they tend to obscure rather than clarify the nature of female economic life, making home production the essential element in early American huswifery and the era of industrialization the period of crucial change. Challenging the symbolism of the wheel not only undermines the popular stereotype, it questions a prevailing emphasis in women's history.

An alternate symbol might be the pocket. In early America a woman's pocket was not attached to her clothing, but tied around her waist with a string or tape. (When "Lucy Locket lost her pocket, Kitty Fisher found it.") Much better than a spinning wheel, this homely object symbolizes the obscurity, the versatility, and the personal nature of the housekeeping role. A woman sat at a wheel, but she carried her pocket with her from room to room, from house to yard, from yard to street. The items which it contained would shift from day to day and from year to year, but they would of necessity be small, easily lost, yet precious. A pocket could be a mended and patched pouch of plain homespun or a rich personal ornament boldly embroidered in crewel. It reflected the status as well as the skills of its owner. Whether it contained cellar keys or a paper of pins, a packet of seeds or a baby's bib, a hank of yarn or a Testament, it characterized the social complexity as well as the demanding diversity of women's work.

Workers on the High Seas: Shipboard Solidarity, 1700–1750

MARCUS REDIKER

God damn them that fails each other.
Seaman's Toast, 1721

Seamen were one of the most militant groups of workers in the eighteenth-century British empire. Their expressions of solidarity, whether uttered over a cool can of punch at sea or amid the hot commotion of a port-side riot against impressment, grew increasingly common through the course of the century. The material origins of such sentiments lay in the collective experience of work at sea. . . .

The seaman occupied a pivotal position in the creation of international markets and a waged working class as well as in the worldwide concentration and organization of capital and labor. During the early modern period, merchant capitalists organized themselves, markets, and a working class in increasingly transatlantic and international ways. As capital came to be concentrated in merchant shipping, masses of workers, numbering twenty-five thousand to forty thousand at any one time between 1700 and 1750, were, in turn, concentrated in this vibrant branch of industry. The huge numbers of workers mobilized for shipboard labor were placed in relatively new relationships to capital—as free and fully waged laborers and to each other. Seamen were, by their experiences in the maritime labor market and labor process, among the first collective laborers. In historical terms, this new collective worker did not possess traditional craft skills, did not own any means of production such as land or tools (and therefore depended completely upon a wage), and labored among a large number of like-situated people. The collective worker, exemplified by the seaman, was the proletarian of the period of "manufacture" and would, of course, become a dominant formal type of laborer with the advent of industrial capitalism.

Early modern maritime workers, by linking the producers and consumers of the world through their labors in international markets, were thus central to the accumulation of wealth on a scale previously unimagined. At the same time, they were crucial to the emergence of new relations between capital and labor. This essay focuses on the organization of maritime labor and some of the challenges to it. After some opening remarks on the maritime labor market, it investigates the labor process at sea between 1700 and 1750, examining the ship as a work environment with its own complex division and organization of labor and technology. Then it turns to the struggles over the labor process, working conditions, and the control of the workplace, emphasizing the ways in which seamen resisted

Marcus Rediker, "The Anglo-American Seaman as Collective Worker, 1700–1750," in Stephen Innes, ed., *Work and Labor in Early America* (Chapel Hill: University of North Carolina Press, 1988), pp. 252–286. Reprinted with permission of the author and Cambridge University Press.

the capitalist organization of production or deflected it toward other purposes of their own. The study concludes with observations on the relationships among the rise of North Atlantic capitalism, maritime work, and the sailors' efforts not to fail each other.

The maritime labor market took shape within the buzz and the hustle of the seaports that handled the commerce of the North Atlantic. Vessels of all varieties (ships, brigs, schooners, hoys, and many others involved in the coastal and deep-sea trades) clogged English, American, and West Indian harbors. Merchants bustled from ship to ship, pausing to watch with satisfaction as dockworkers and seamen lowered the last bale of cargo into a vessel's full belly or to argue furiously with shipbuilders over the cost of repairs. Captains and customs officials haggled, cursed, and winked at each other. Bloodied butchers and deft-dealing pursers stocked the merchant craft with salt beef and pork, and hawkers and peddlers tendered their wares along the stone-and-log wharves. Slaves, indentured servants, and day laborers toiled under the sharp gaze of overseers, lifting from ship's hold to shore's warehouse the commodities of the world. On the vessels, on the quays, or in the nearby alehouses, seamen in Monmouth caps and tarred breeches quizzed merchant captains about destinations and wages, just as they asked each other about the sturdiness of a particular ship or the character of her captain.

These seamen worked in a labor market that was international in character, a fact of first importance that is shown in the work lives of John Young and Edward Coxere. Young, apparently seized by British authorities from a French privateer during the War of Spanish Succession and quickly charged with treason, tried to explain to the High Court of Admiralty how the vicissitudes of an international work experience had got him into his present predicament. He proceeded to outline where his worldwide labors had taken him. Born in Spitalfields, he went to sea at "14 or 15 years of Age," apprenticed to a Captain John Hunter. During the next twelve years, he traveled from London to Barbados and Jamaica, sailed and fought aboard three West Indian privateers, went "sugar droghing" in the Caribbean coastal trade, found his way in a merchant ship back to London, and then, in various voyages, on to Bristol, the African coast, Virginia, Lisbon, Genoa, Leghorn, and Cartagena. Ned Coxere, a late-seventeenth-century merchant seaman and privateersman, summed up his maritime experience this way: "I served the Spaniards against the French, then the Hollanders against the English; then I was taken by the English out of a Dunkirker; and then I served the English against the Hollanders; and last I was taken by the Turks, where I was forced to serve then against English, French, Dutch, and Spaniards, and all Christendom." Not surprisingly, this able sailor spoke English, Spanish, French, Dutch, and the Mediterranean lingua franca. Coxere was truly an international workingman, finally refusing to participate in the nationalistic violence of the era of trade wars and becoming, instead, a pacifist and a Quaker.

Both Young and Coxere worked among men who, it must have seemed, came from almost everywhere: from every corner of England, America, and the Caribbean; from Holland, France, Spain, and all of Europe; from Africa and even parts of Asia. Regional, national, and ethnic identities abounded in the ships of the world, even though the Navigation Acts had required that three of four seamen on English ships be subjects of the crown. Such requirements were rarely enforced, especially in times of war and labor scarcity, when even the British state admitted that half or more of ships' crews might be foreign.

The global deployment of thousands of seamen in the early eighteenth century was predicated upon the broad and uneven process of proletarianization, through which these men or their forebears were torn from the land and made to sell their labor power on an open market to keep body and soul together. The major sources for stocking the labor market with "hands" were dispossession—the displacement or eviction of rural producers, most notably by the enclosure of arable farmland—and population growth, which forced the offspring of agrarian laborers or waged workers themselves to sell their mind and muscle for money. England, of course, was known for its teeming share of these "masterless men and women" in the early modern period. Population growth and dispossession, each with its own oscillating rhythm, combined to swell the number of those who in some way worked for a wage to some 60 percent of Britain's people by the beginning of the eighteenth century. Between 1700 and 1750, the process of proletarianization seems to have stabilized: population growth reached a certain plateau, showing perhaps a small upturn in the 1740s. The numbers of colonists in North America grew both naturally and by immigration throughout the period, and the population of the British West Indies increased only through the massive importation of Africans. There was, with a few exceptions, a general shortage of maritime labor in both areas between 1700 and 1750. But the dominant, overarching tendency, particularly in Britain and America, was toward ever greater employment of waged labor. Seamen were fitting symbols of the trend.

A labor market is defined as "those institutions which mediate, affect, or determine the purchase and sale of labor power." Here, our understanding of maritime labor is deficient, for the practices of labor market entrepreneurs have not been carefully studied. It is clear that crimps—"agents who traded in recruits when men were in great demand either for the armed forces or to man merchant vessels on the point of sailing"—were crucial to the maritime labor market, certainly in England if not in the New World until the late eighteenth century. An equally important if shadowy figure was the "spirit," described by Edward Barlow as "one of those who used to entice any who they think are country people or strangers and do not know their fashion or custom, or any who think they are out of place and cannot get work, and are walking idly about the streets." Spirits promised great wages and often gave advances in money. Those who accepted their offers often found themselves apprenticed as sailors or sold as indentured servants bound to America. Such recruiters operated from gin shops, alehouses, inns, and taverns, where they often seized indebted sailors and paid off their bills. In exchange, crimps and spirits gained the right to sell the seaman's services to outward-bound vessels, usually sailing to distant parts of the globe, and to receive the sailor's advance pay. Some crimps did not adhere even to these minimal standards of conduct, preferring instead to raid the pubs; handcuff, drag off, and incarcerate drunk sailors; and then sell them to merchant captains in search of labor. Probably most of the contracting of maritime labor was handled in less formal and exploitative ways, especially in the New World, where labor was scarce and wages were higher, through the pubs, inns, or taverns where merchants, ship captains, mates, and seamen gathered and through which information of shipping circulated. Seamen also peddled their own skills in the port cities by going from vessel to vessel, jumping aboard, asking the ship's route, pay, and fare. A man who did not possess adequate skills was hired by a master as a ship's boy or as an apprentice to some member of the crew.

Maritime labor in all English Atlantic ports was seasonal and often casual. The rhythms of climate dictated employment opportunities by icing harbors, by fixing the growing seasons of commodities such as sugar and tobacco, or by making parts of the world dangerous with disease or hurricane. Seafaring jobs were most easily found in late spring, summer, and fall, though the demand for labor in each port varied according to the commodities shipped, their destinations, and the length of the shipping season. Many mariners were unable to find year-round employment. Numerous landed occupations, however, were equally seasonal, and, for some, "sailoring was normally a casual employment, into and out of which they drifted as they found employment harder to come by on sea or on land." Such opportunities were always greater and more lucrative during war years. Employments connected to shipping "were notorious then, as later, as precarious occupations." Yet throughout the eighteenth century, it was increasingly the case for Jack Tar that, "once a sailor, the chances were that he would always be a sailor." By 1750, seafaring had become a lifelong occupation for increasing numbers of waged workers.

Seafaring labor consisted mainly of loading, sailing, and unloading the merchant vessel. The essence of the labor process was, quite simply, the movement of cargo. The ship, in many ways prefiguring the factory, demanded a cooperative labor process. Waged workers, the preponderant majority of whom did not own the instruments of their production, were confined within an enclosed setting to perform, with sophisticated machinery and under intense supervision, a unified and collective set of tasks. Large parts of this labor would be performed at sea in isolation from the rest of the population. The character of seafaring work and its lonely setting contributed to the formation of a strong laboring identity among seamen.

By 1700, seafaring labor had been fully standardized. Sailors circulated from ship to ship, even from merchant vessels to the Royal Navy, into privateering or piracy and back again, and found that the tasks performed and the skills required by each were essentially the same. They encountered a basic division of labor on each merchant ship, consisting of a master, a mate, a carpenter, a boatswain, a gunner, a quartermaster, perhaps a cook, and four or five able or ordinary seamen. A larger or more heavily manned ship included a second mate, a carpenter's mate, and four or five more common tars. This division of labor allocated responsibilities and structured working relations among the crew, forming a hierarchy of laboring roles and a corresponding scale of wages.

The organization of labor on each ship began with the master, the representative of merchant capital, who was hired "to manage the navigation and everything relating to [the ship's] cargo, voyage, sailors, etc." Frequently a small part owner himself, the master was the commanding officer. He possessed near-absolute authority. His ship was "virtually a kingdom on its own," his power "well nigh unlimited," and, all too frequently, to the muttering of his sailors, he ruled it like a despot. His primary tasks were navigation, tending the compasses, steering the vessel, and transacting the business throughout the voyage. He procured the ship's provisions and usually inflicted the punishments. Except on the largest of ships, he ran one of the two watches.

The mate, whose powers were vastly inferior to those of the master, was second in the chain of command. He commanded a watch and oversaw the daily functioning of the ship. He was charged with the internal management of the vessel, setting the men to work, governing the crew, securing the cargo, and directing the ship's course. The mate needed a sure knowledge of navigation, since he was to take charge of the vessel in the event of the master's death, a not uncommon occurrence at any time during the age of sail.

The carpenter, an important specialist in a wooden world, was responsible for the soundness of the ship. He repaired masts, yards, boats, and machinery; he checked the hull regularly, placing oakum between the seams of planks, and used wooden plugs on leaks to keep the vessel tight. His search for a leak often required that he wade through stagnant bilge water with vapors strong enough "to poison the Devil." His was highly skilled work which he had learned through apprenticeship. Often he had a mate whom he in turn trained.

The boatswain, like the mate, functioned as something of a foreman. He summoned the crew to duty, sometimes by piping the call to work that brought the inevitable groans and curses from the off-duty crew. His specific responsibilities centered on the upkeep of the rigging. He had to be sure that all lines and cables were sound and that sails and anchors were in good condition. . . .

The quartermaster did not require special training. Rather, he was an experienced, or "smart," seaman who was given an additional shilling or two per month to assist the mates. He provided an extra hand in storage, coiling cables, and steering the vessel. The cook, on the other hand, generally was truly "remarkable for his inability to cook." Often a wounded seaman no longer able to perform heavy labor, his status was rather low. According to the doleful and never-ending complaints of the ship's people, he brought no distinctive talents to his job.

The common seaman, Jack Tar himself, was a "person trained in the exercise of fixing the machinery of a ship, and applying it to the purposes of navigation." He needed to know the rigging and the sails as well as how to steer the ship, to knot and splice the lines, and to read the winds, weather, skies, and the mood of his commander. There were two categories of seamen: the able seaman, who fully knew his trade, and the ordinary seaman, usually a younger and less-experienced man. The latter was still learning the mysteries of tying a clove hitch or going aloft to reef in a sail in a blustery thunderstorm. In sum, a merchant ship, like a man-of-war, required a wide variety of skills; it was "too big and unmanageable a machine" to be run by novices. . . .

There were, of course, many variations of this standard division of labor, depending upon the related factors of trade route, cargo carried, and ship size. . . . Ships in the African trade were most heavily manned, for security against slave uprisings and as a safeguard against raging mortality, and often bore twenty to twenty-five men on a 200-ton vessel. Slaving voyages took ten to eleven months. Ships of the East India Company were, by eighteenth-century standards, mammoth, often as large as a man-of-war at 300–500 tons, and manned to survive a voyage enduring two years or more. Although ship size varied with the type of trade, the larger the ship's home port, the larger the ship and its crew were likely to be. . . .

The tendency of masters and mates to specialize in certain voyages indicates another crucial part of the maritime division of labor: the distribution of knowledge on board the ship. Masters and mates, as we have seen, needed to know how to use the principles of navigation, but the rest of the crew did not. Yet this separation of mental and manual labor was never complete—indeed, never could become as complete—as it would in later industrial production. The knowledge of seafaring was still contained largely within a broad system of apprenticeship, but one in which the perils of life at sea placed grave limits upon the advisability of keeping trade secrets. Only later, with the introduction of officers' schools and a growing social distance between the lower deck and the quarterdeck, would a consistent separation of conception from execution emerge. Much could be and was learned about navigation through observation of the daily work routine. Consequently, older and more experienced seamen, whatever their formal position, minimized the differential in knowledge that separated the top of the ship's labor hierarchy from its bottom.

The watch, another decisive element in the social arrangement of each ship, was perhaps the most basic unit for organizing the steady work of sailing the ship. . . . Each watch served four hours on duty, then four hours off, alternating in work shifts (also called watches) around the clock. The dogwatch, between 4:00 and 8:00 P.M., was subdivided into two-hour shifts. This produced a total of seven shifts, ensuring that a watch would not work the same hours each day. Each sailor alternately worked a ten- and a fourteen-hour workday. . . . Everyone made a roughly equivalent contribution by helping to keep the ship on course at the highest possible speed.

Even when off duty, one was never far from work. Anytime, anywhere, one might hear the mate's fearful cry: "Up every soul nimbly, for God's sake, or we all perish." . . . Situations of crisis mobilized both watches in urgent cooperation.

The ship's technical division of labor, while demanding cooperation and interdependence, was also highly graded and specialized relative to the total number of men employed. A crew of twelve usually was divided into five or six different ranks and an equal or greater number of pay stations. Rarely did more than four or five occupy equal positions in the laboring hierarchy. Rank, knowledge, watch, and pay were objective lines of demarcation and division within the ship's crew. The organization of work in the merchant service assembled a complex and collective unit of labor, only to separate that unit into shifting, overlapping, task-oriented components. . . .

The first stage of most voyages was loading the ship. Here, seamen, dockworkers, and other laborers collectively handled and hoisted the casks, bales, hogsheads, cases, ballast, provisions, and stores into the vessel's hold. In addition to the human strength involved in lifting, several mechanical devices were used to load the ship. Seamen used a wide array of tackle (an arrangement of ropes, pulleys, slings, and hooks) not only to lift and lower cargo into the ship but also to support the masts, extend the rigging, or expand the sails. . . . The heaviest tasks required the use of the capstan or its smaller and, in the merchant service, more popular counterpart, the windlass. These machines consisted of a "strong massy column of holes" into which seamen inserted bars or levers called handspikes. This machine worked on the same principle as a horse mill: seamen walked in a circle, and it required "some dexterity and address to manage the handspec to the greatest advantage; and to perform this the sailors must all rise at once upon the windlass, and, fixing their bars therein, give a sudden jerk at the same instant, in which movement they are regulated by a sort of song or howl pronounced by one of their number." . . . In heaving or hoisting, it was necessary that the men work to the chant of "Together!" acting "all in concert, or at the same instant." Seafaring labor, in its work chants and songs, revealed its profoundly collective nature. . . .

Once the cargo had been loaded and secured, work shifted from handling the goods to handling the ship. Three basic chores now confronted the crew: steering the ship, managing the rigging, and working the sails, the skillful performance of which determined the speed and sometimes the profitability of the voyage. Steering the ship, along with the associated duties of keeping lookout and sounding, was a central part of the work effort. The helmsman directed the ship's course with the use of the compass, the sun, the moon, and the stars, according to the officer of the watch. Each sailor took a turn at the helm. The lookout acted as an additional pair of eyes for the helmsman. In shallow water, soundings were taken to determine depth. These, with the aid of charts, helped to establish the vessel's location.

The rate of the ship's progress depended directly on the labors performed on the riggings and the sails. There were two kinds of rigging: the standing rigging (shrouds, stays, forestays, and backstays) was the collection of ropes that supported the masts, and the running rigging (braces, sheets, halyards, crew lines, and brails) was used "to extend and reduce the sails, or arrange them to the disposition of the wind." A series of lines running through blocks, or pulleys, were used to manage the sails, and, although much of this work was done from the deck, frequently a sailor had to climb aloft "hand-over-hand," carefully using the "horses" (rigging made expressly for sailors to stand upon or hold) to adjust a sail or a rope. Rigging work also demanded a superior knowledge of tying and connecting ropes, whether by hitches or knots, using lanyards or lashings, or splicing one piece of hemp to another. The strong but nimble fingers of the seaman deftly arranged a cat's-paw, a flemish eye, a sheepshank, a timber hitch, or a diamond knot.

Most deep-sea ships were either two- or three-masted vessels with a complex arrangement of sails, consisting of the course sails, topsails, and gallant sails as well as the smaller staysails, studding sails, and jibs, among many others. Sailors positioned the sails to accelerate or modify the ship's course by backing, balancing, reefing, shortening, furling, or loosing the enormous pieces of canvas. The tars scuttled from the deck to the tops, as high as sixty to seventy-five feet on most merchantmen, expanding this sail or reducing that one, according to the directions and strength of the winds. As in the loading of cargo, work on the helm, the rigging, and the sails required careful coordination. . . .

The maritime labor process was extraordinarily dangerous. Records do not exist that allow the computation of death rates for maritime industries and the comparison of these to rates for other occupations. . . . [A] crucial part of the seaman's socialization was to learn to endure physical trial and minimal provisions. As Edward Barlow explained in 1696, those men who "were not used to hardship and had not known the lack of drink" were the first to collapse and die in hard times. Quite apart from the dangers of scurvy, rheumatism, typhus, yellow fever, ulcers, and skin diseases, seamen had to contend with an extensive range of disabilities and afflictions that resulted from their work. Frequently lifting or pulling, seamen were peculiarly susceptible to hernia or the "bursted belly," as they preferred to call it. It was not unusual to lose a finger to a rolling cask, for an arm or leg to be broken by shifting cargo, or for a hand to be burned in tarring ropes. And of course numberless men drowned and "took their habitation among the haddocks."

One of the most hazardous aspects of the labor process was the dispensation of discipline, the necessary and bloody complement of the increasing productivity of seafaring labor in the eighteenth century. This "class discipline at its most personal and sadistic" . . . resulted in masters' and mates' inflicting many disabling injuries upon the common men of the deep. Having been beaten nearly senseless with a pitch mop, John Laws cried to George Burrell: "Captain, you have ruined me. I shall never be my own Man again." Such beating often produced what seamen called the "Falling Sickness." John Marchant, caned in 1735 by mate John Yates, was, as he told the High Court of Admiralty, "troubled with a diziness in his Head . . . in so much that he cannot go aloft without danger of falling down." Others considered themselves "incapable of going to sea," since they were, in their words, "damnify'd" like a piece of cargo. Seamen also suffered injury in battle against men-of-war, privateers, pirates, or coastal raiders. Upon discovering in 1713 that their captain had changed the voyage to a more dangerous destination, William Howell penned a protest for his shipmates, saying "that they did not hire themselves to fight" and properly wondering "In case they should lose a Legg or an Arme who would maintaine them and their Familys." It was a good question, for lucky was the seaman who, after fifteen years of service, could say, "I had my health and was able to seek for more employment."

The deep-sea sailor labored on a frail vessel surrounded by omnipotent forces of nature, and this situation imparted a special urgency to cooperative labor. Upon hitting a rock or being overtaken by a turbulent squall, many crews realized that they had to turn out, all hands high, to "work for our Lives." . . . Their life-and-death [experiences reveal] the massive confrontation between the seaman and his work. The labor was physical. It required extraordinary strength, stamina, dexterity, and agility. The labor was also dangerous. It required courage and a continual renewal of initiative and daring.

Many smaller but still crucial chores filled out the shipboard routine of labor. These included shadow work such as overhauling the rigging, coiling ropes, repairing and oiling gear, changing and mending sail canvas, tarring ropes, cleaning the guns, painting, swabbing and holystoning the deck, and checking the cargo. Such maintenance made it possible for seafaring work to be almost perpetual. Since the forces of nature dictated many of the tasks to be performed at sea, shadow work was used to fill the hours not directly devoted to sailing the ship. These chores made up one of the most contested domains of the labor process. How much and what kinds of work were seamen willing to give for their wages? This question had to be answered through a process of negotiation on every change of crew.

One of the central features of seafaring work was its social visibility. Work was a public activity, and crews were extremely sophisticated in judging the quality of each man's contribution. Everyone knew how to perform the basic tasks, and most men had been on other ships and had seen every chore, from the captain's duties downward, executed by others. Consequently, even the lowest ordinary seaman considered himself a judge of his officers. Further, work was closely scrutinized, since collective well-being depended on it. There was considerable pressure to demonstrate one's skills, and when a man could do a job better than his superior, it was rarely a secret. When a captain was unskillful in his station, a crew might follow his incorrect orders with precision just to expose his ignorance. A drunken captain shouting incoherent orders put the ship's company "in great fear and danger of their Lives." Fortunately, seamen were usually able to counteract such danger through their own knowledge of the labor process. . . .

This extensive knowledge of shipboard affairs frequently translated into severe problems for the captain. He found that some of his men were of an "unruly and Ungovernable Disposition" or a "grumbling unwilling mind." Captains endlessly groused about crew members they described as "self-willed" and "obstinate." Such intransigence usually came from one of two sources: either the seaman was new and unaccustomed to the nature of work and authority on board ship, or, knowing the ways of the merchant service, he objected to the manner in which the ship was being run. . . . Many such seamen had their own ideas about the social relations of work at sea. The organization, the pace, and the process of work became the focus of an often fierce struggle for control.

One way seamen attempted to expand their control over the labor process was by trying to enforce their own notions of what constituted a proper crew. In 1705 John Tunbridge deserted the *Neptune* because "the Ship had not hands enough on board to work her." Seamen commonly complained that their vessels were "too weakly man'd." In 1722 sailors refused to proceed in a voyage from London to northern Europe because the "Master had not eleven hands on board" as he had promised in his "first Agreement." In Charleston, South Carolina, in 1736, a crew of sea-men was brought on board the *Fenton* only to walk out en masse when they discovered how much pumping would be required to control a riverlike leak. . . . This form of protest, something of a preemptive strike, was, from the seaman's point of view, limited in its effectiveness. During times of peace, maritime workers were so abundant that they could not exert much pressure without fear of dismissal. Those who made up the reserve navy of the unemployed, those put out of work by the demobilization of the Royal Navy, waited anxiously for any vacant berth. During wartime, with the navy and privateers scouring the seas, labor was so scarce that ships often had no alternative but to sail with smaller crews. Seamen usually took their advantage in the form of higher wages.

Given the limits of this tactic, many mariners resorted to the work stoppage. Some stoppages were primarily defensive, used by seamen to preserve the privileges that previous generations of seafarers had won. They insisted, for example, that their work regimen was to be relaxed while they were in harbor. . . . A significant number of work stoppages resulted from individual acts of defiance. In 1735 Captain Joseph Barnes asked Henry Twine, his carpenter, "what he came to Sea for if he would not do his Business and Duty as Carpenter." Twine "replyed that he came to Sea for his Pleasure and would do what he pleased and nothing more." Actions of this sort in the workplace were highly visible and carried expansive social meanings, affording examples, even encouragement, to others. Oc-casionally, they precipitated collective actions. Everyone on board breathed (and worked) a bit more easily within the space created by the successful confrontation. . . .

Desertion was one of the most chronic and dangerous problems faced by the merchant capitalists of the shipping industry. Merchants bought the seaman's labor power in a contractual exchange. Monthly wages were paid for work on a specified voyage. Vast bodies of legislation and legal opinion were produced in an effort to guarantee that exchange. In signing a set of articles, the legal agreement between owner and captain and crew, seamen were usually required to affirm that they would not "go away from, Quit or leave the said Ship . . . in any port abroad, or go on board of any other Ship whatsoever," unless impressed or required to by force. But seamen always reserved to themselves the right to terminate that contract, to take their chances with the law, and to demonstrate that labor power was a commodity unlike any other. What merchant capitalists and their apologists saw as "the natural unsteddiness of seamen" was in fact the use of autonomous mobility to set the conditions of work.

The tactic of desertion was used in complex and sometimes ingenious ways. Seamen resorted to desertion to stay out of areas where they were likely to be pressed into the Royal Navy. . . .

Desertion was also used to avoid sailing into disease-ridden climates. . . .

Perhaps most crucially, desertion was used to escape the grasp of a brutal master or mate. In 1706, after one of their fellow tars had jumped overboard and eventually drowned in an attempt to escape the "severity" of their captain, William Bedford, John Lade, and John Tunbridge collectively deserted. They "being not able to suffer his Tirany any longer took the Boate and came on Shore." . . . Mariners endlessly alleged in court that a captain's cruelty was a primary reason for running from one ship to another.

On many occasions, the mere threat of desertion was enough to wrest an advantage from a captain. Some seamen threatened to desert during harsh weather, and others swore they would leave if a drunken and abusive mate were continued in service. One can imagine the fears of Captain Joseph Chapman in 1725, when two seamen "endeavoured to perswade all the Foremastmen on board to leave and desert the said Ships Service" while the ship was full of slaves. Four men deserted, and if the Africans "had revolted . . . there could not have been sufficient force to suppress them."

Desertion was encouraged by the extraordinary competition waged between the Royal Navy and the merchant service for the sailor's labor power. During war years, the bidding grew especially intense as privateers joined the rivalry, offering Jack Tar the prospects of greater riches for less work. Merchant captains were notorious for spiriting seamen away from the king's ships by offering high wages and generous allotments of rum. The sailor, even during peacetime, could shuttle back and forth between these two enterprises with great profit. . . .

The sprawling nature of the international labor market and the empire made desertion extremely attractive. Many seamen, like those who congregated in Massachusetts, migrated to the edges of the empire, where seafaring labor was scarce, taking advantage of high wages and better working conditions. Many a tar was willing "to leave the ship . . . if he could better himselfe," and such betterment was not hard to find in the West Indies.

By 1700, the plantation mode of production in the Caribbean had developed to the point that free wage labor there had become something of an anomaly. A crippling mortality affected practically every ship that sailed into West Indian ports, and this, combined with the scarcity of free labor, created a situation in which sailors quickly seized an advantage. Desertion served to destabilize the labor market and drive wages up. As one merchant captain explained in 1717, "It was and is usuall for Marriners of Ships who were and are hired at monthly wages to leave and desert their respective services at Jamaica and other parts in the west Indies and to ship and enter themselves into the Service of Ships att much greater wages by the Run." Once free of command, seamen were footloose in the port towns, "rambling to and fro about the Country," as one disapproving captain put it. They looked to sell their dear labor for "the run home" to London. "A Rambler in the West Indies," who made two pounds per month on the voyage to Jamaica, stood to make ten to twenty pounds and ten gallons of rum for the passage back to London. Such bargains drastically reduced the literal exploitation of maritime labor. . . .

Desertion also served as a firm demarcation of the captain's authority and as an affirmation of the sailor's own power. As Henry Fielding perceptively observed during his voyage to Portugal in 1754, the ship captain found that "it was easier to send his men on shore than to recall them. They acknowledged him to be their master while they remained on shipboard, but did not allow his power to extend to the shores, where they no sooner set their feet than every man became *sui juris,* and thought himself at full liberty to return when he pleased."

Desertion was, in all, an essential component of seafaring labor: . . . it affirmed the "free" in free wage labor. In so doing, it went far beyond and frequently contradicted the free wage labor imagined and endorsed by the merchant capitalist who paid for that labor and the merchant captain who supervised it. Merchants, masters, and governmental officials made resolute efforts to control the autonomous mobility of maritime workers. They issued acts and proclamations against straggling seamen in ports, they ran advertisements in newspapers for deserters, they sued incessantly in court, and they tried to implement a seaman's registry and a certificate system to identify sailors and make their labor readily available. The large measure of power held by these figures gave them some success in controlling Jack's mobility, for the seaman was not only free to find a job but also free to starve if he was unable to find one. Yet mobility was an essential component in the seaman's strategy for survival. The mariner had to maintain a continuity of income when often there was no continuity of available work. . . . [F]ree laborers in the colonial port cities were able to count on little more than 200–250 days of work per year. Jack Tar's rhythm of keeping body and soul together and the merchant's rhythm of capital accumulation did not move in the same motions. As a form of struggle and a means of survival, desertion had a pervasively wide circulation among maritime workers. The seafarer's mobility was a central part of his strategy to control the means of finding employment. It was a mobility made effective by the amorphous collective network through which rumor, reputation, and information circulated among sailors of the English Atlantic.

The tactic of work stoppage was a form of collective disobedience that often shaded into the more ominous crime of mutiny. Most mutinies between 1700 and 1750 were fleeting affairs, ranging from the downing of tools to the violent, almost always temporary seizure of ships. According to merchant captains, sailors formed "cabals" among themselves, and support usually coalesced around a particularly defiant member of the crew. For example, Captain Thomas King, in 1723, called Peter Lester a "mutineer," a man with whom "most part of the Sailors seemed to be in a cabal." King tried to maneuver Lester out of the ship but had "much difficulty . . . for noe Violence cou'd be us'd where the Major part of the Ships Company were inclin'd to favour him." Off the African coast in 1736, another crew attempted "to raise a mutiny" in response to the harsh punishments administered by their captain for work-related offenses. One of the sailors was placed in irons for his role in the rising. When asked by the captain of another merchant vessel why they were so angry, the seamen said, "By God, they would not be serv'd so, no Man shou'd confine any of them, for they were one and all resolved to stand by one another." . . .

In 1714 the crew of the *St. Joseph* "all as one" refused to go any further once their captain had changed the destination from that stipulated in their original agreement. In other disputes, seamen swore "they would stand by one another and stand Knock for Knock . . . meaning they would Resist" their master "by Force." To avert a captain's wrath over some anonymous misdeed, sailors often must have "turned freemasons and kept a secret." Not for nothing did seamen call each other "Brother Tar."

Mutiny sometimes took on a more permanent and material form; that is, it ceased to be a redressive and defensive posture and assumed the aggressive stance of piracy. Sailors then expropriated the workplace and arranged it anew. Since piracy represented a social world constructed apart from the ways of the merchant and the captain—and, hence, apart in significant ways from capital—robbery at sea can illuminate certain aspects of the labor process as seen by those whose lives were shaped by it.

Almost all early eighteenth-century pirates had worked in the merchant shipping industry, and piracy was deeply imbued with the collectivistic tendencies produced by life and labor at sea. Against the omnipotent authority of the merchant shipmaster, pirates elected their captain and other officers. Against the hierarchical pay system of the merchant service, pirates distributed their plunder in markedly egalitarian fashion. Pirates also exhibited a pervasive consciousness of kind.

The nature of the tasks performed by a seaman did not change for the bold tar who exchanged a life of legal trade for one of illegal plunder. In either employ, the same work had to be performed. Yet once among pirates, the intensity of labor decreased dramatically, because pirate ships were hugely overmanned. An average vessel of two hundred tons carried eighty or more men, but a merchant ship of equivalent size contained only thirteen to seventeen hands. These outlaws maintained the maritime division of labor but strictly limited its tendency to function as a hierarchy of status and privilege. They also altered its relation to income. There were, among pirates, only three pay stations for some eighty men, rather than five or six slots for fifteen sailors. Even more revealing, pirates abolished the wage.

They considered themselves risk-sharing partners rather than a collection of "hands" who sold their muscle on an open market.

Some mariners cast their lots with pirates in order to escape hard labor. As pirate Joseph Mansfield said in 1722, "the love of Drink and a Lazy Life" were "Stronger Motives with him than Gold." Admiral Edward Vernon, taking sixteen suspected pirates aboard his man-of-war, said that, since he needed "hands for the pump, it might be of service to carry them out of the way of falling into their old Courses, and that it might be a Means to learn them . . . working," which, Vernon noted, "They turned Rogues to avoid." . . . And as Woodes Rogers, the governor of the Bahama Islands, long-experienced in battles against sea robbers, said of pirates, "For work they mortally hate it." Samuel Buck, a long-time resident of the Bahamas, agreed: "Working does not agree with them."

The social contours of piracy, while fully congruent with the labor process at sea, were often formed in violent antipathy to that world of work from which many seamen gladly escaped. "Lower class utopias," writes Christopher Hill, for centuries aimed "to abolish wage-labour altogether, or drastically to reduce the working day." The social organization of piracy, even though based upon a relatively new form of collectivism, was part of that tenacious tradition that linked medieval peasants, seventeenth-century radicals such as the Diggers and Levellers, and the free wage laborers of the eighteenth century.

Perhaps the most telling evidence, much of it dating from the later eighteenth century, of the increasingly collective consciousness and activity among seamen lay in their resort to the strike. Given, in fact, the logic of collectivism that informed seafaring work, it comes as no surprise that the very term "strike" evolved from the decision of seamen, in 1768, to strike the sails of their vessels and, thereby, to cripple the commerce of the empire's capital city. The strike may have been born of shipboard cooperation, but, as a concept in language and in practical political and economic activity, it began to circulate with increasing velocity among all of those men and women involved in collective industrial labor.

These are some of the many ways in which the relationships initiated by the concentration of labor on the ship were soon transformed by seamen into a new basis for the organization of community. Sharing almost every aspect of life, separated from family and church, seafarers forged new social relations. Their new solidarity was often undercut by the diversity of the men who made their livings by the sea as well as by the mobility and dispersion that were essential features of their work. Yet for all of these men, self-protection—from harsh conditions, excessive work, and oppressive authority—was necessary to survival. Too often, claimed Edward Barlow, when under command "all the men in the ship except the master" were "little better than slaves." Social bonds among sailors arose from the very conditions and relations of their work. These men possessed a concrete and situational outlook forged within the power relations that guided their lives. Theirs was a collectivism of necessity. . . .

⚜ *FURTHER   READING*

Ira Berlin, "Time, Space, and the Evolution of Afro-American Society on British Mainland America," *American Historical Review*, 85 (1980), 44–78

T. H. Breen, "Back to Sweat and Toil: Suggestions for the Study of Agricultural Work in Early America," *Pennsylvania History* 49 (1982), 241–258

Lois Green Carr and Lorena S. Walsh, "The Planter's Wife: The Experience of White Women in Seventeenth-Century Maryland," *William and Mary Quarterly* 34 (1977), 542–571

Christopher Clark, "The Household Economy, Market Exchange and the Rise of Capitalism in the Connecticut Valley, 1800–1860," *Journal of Social History* 13 (1979), 169–189

Richard S. Dunn, *Sugar and Slaves: The Rise of the Planter Class in the English West Indies, 1624–1713* (1972)

James A. Henretta, "Families and Farms: Mentalite in Pre-Industrial America," *William and Mary Quarterly* 35 (1978), 3–32

Stephen Innes, ed., *Work and Labor in Early America* (1988)

Joan Jensen, *Loosening the Bonds: Mid-Atlantic Farm Women, 1750–1850* (1986)

Jesse Lemisch, "Jack Tar in the Streets: Merchant Seamen in the Politics of Revolutionary America," *William and Mary Quarterly* 25 (1968), 371–407

John L. McCuster and Russell R. Menard, *The Economy of British America, 1607–1789* (1985)

Michael Merrill, "Cash Is Good to Eat: Self-Sufficiency and Exchange in the Rural Economy of the United States," *Radical History Review* 4 (1977), 41–71

Edmund Morgan, *American Slavery, American Freedom: The Ordeal of Colonial Virginia* (1975)

Richard B. Morris, *Government and Labor in Early America* (1946)

Gary Nash, *Race, Class, and Politics: Essays on American Colonial and Revolutionary Society* (1986)

Marcus Rediker, *Between the Devil and the Deep Blue Sea: Merchant Seamen, Pirates, and the Anglo-American Maritime World, 1700–1750* (1987)

———, "Good Hands, Stout Heart, and Fast Feet: The History and Culture of Working People in Early America," in Geoff Eley and William Hunt, eds., *Reviving the English Revolution* (1988)

Sharon V. Salinger, *"To Serve Well and Faithfully": Labor and Indentured Servants in Pennsylvania, 1682–1800* (1987)

Carole Shammas, "Black Women's Work and the Evolution of Plantation Society in Virginia," *Labor History* 26 (1985), 5–28

Abbott Emerson Smith, *Colonists in Bondage: White Servitude and Convict Labor in America, 1607–1776* (1947)

Billy Smith, *The "Lower Sort": Philadelphia's Laboring People, 1750–1800* (1990)

Charles G. Steffen, *The Mechanics of Baltimore: Workers and Politics in the Age of Revolution, 1763–1812* (1984)

Rolla M. Tryon, *Household Manufactures in the U.S., 1640–1860* (1917)

Laurel Thatcher Ulrich, *Good Wives: Image and Reality in the Lives of Women in Northern New England, 1650–1750* (1980)

Alfred Young, *The Democratic Republicans of New York: The Origins, 1763–1797* (1967)

———, "George Robert Twelves Hewes [1742–1840]: A Boston Shoemaker and the Memory of the American Revolution," *William and Mary Quarterly* 38 (1981), 561–623

CHAPTER
3

From the Artisan's Republic
to the Factory System

⚜

When Philadelphians celebrated the newly ratified U.S. Constitution in 1791, masters, journeymen, and apprentices marched through the streets under banners that announced the unity reigning within each craft; only seventy years later, in the era when northern men rallied in support of the Union, urban workmen no longer felt it possible to march in the same ranks with merchants and manufacturers, who now employed them. In 1865 most Americans were farmers, and artisans working in traditional ways still produced most manufactured goods. But the egalitarianism of the early-nineteenth-century workshop had been replaced by a gaping social chasm that divided wage laborers in almost every trade from the factory owners and great merchants of the Civil War era.

The artisanal world had been characterized by small-scale production, local markets, skilled craftsmanship, and a self-reliant sense of community and citizenship. Early-nineteenth-century workmen thought of themselves as masters both in their household and in their trade, the upholders of an equal-rights tradition whose roots stretched back to the American Revolution. White women, blacks, and unskilled immigrants would obviously have an ambiguous relationship to this tradition. However, many historians have found in republicanism, the ideology that links civil virtue and personal independence to self-government, a powerful standard by which nineteenth-century workers judged and rejected the new men of wealth and power, who seemed to rise so quickly and to challenge so dramatically the values and livelihood of America's producing classes.

Factories, banks, railroads, and mines did not appear overnight. In nineteenth-century America, as in many underdeveloped nations today, large, mechanized enterprises existed alongside extensive systems of home production and the craft-based trades. In fact, the process of industrialization had a patchwork quality that deskilled and depressed some trades and skipped others entirely. In New York and Philadelphia, a process of ''metropolitan industrialization'' created a marvelously heterogeneous working class divided by skill, race, sex, and nationality. In contrast, the textile industry, which put its mills on isolated sites along the New England rivers, generated a more homogeneous class of workers.

At the famous Lowell, Massachusetts mills, Boston capitalists recruited thousands of young farm women and housed them in dormitory-like boarding houses. The textile factories of Rhode Island and Pennsylvania more typically employed whole families, relying heavily on a brutal system of child labor.

To what extent did these textile operatives share the same outlook as the more skilled artisans? Could women share with their menfolk the equal-rights ideology that sustained antebellum workingmen? Or was the republicanism of these artisans an obstacle to gender equality and class consciousness?

✣ D O C U M E N T S

The rise of the factory system revolutionized the shoemaking trade in the pre–Civil War era. The first four documents offer a glimpse of the work culture and protest traditions of Lynn, Massachusetts, workers in the shoe industry. In sketching apprenticeship life during the days of the old-time shoe workshop, David Johnson, a Lynn resident, re-creates in the first document the masculine work culture that members of the Mutual Benefit Society of Journeymen Cordwainers celebrated in the 1844 "Cordwainer's Song," reprinted here as the second document. Their proud republican world view had little meaning for female shoebinders like "Constance," who, in the third document, from the pages of the *Awl*, the newspaper of Lynn's artisan shoemakers, complains of her exclusion from the male fraternity. The fourth document, a reporter's account of a mass meeting of Lynn women during the Great Strike of 1860, demonstrates that both men and women drew upon the equal-rights tradition to attack wage slavery, but it also exposes persistent and deep gender divisions within the shoemaking work force.

The fifth document, testimony from the Pennsylvania State Senate, uncovers some of the horrors of the early textile mills and shows that their workers sought state regulation of excessive hours, child labor, and other exploitive conditions. Finally, in the sixth document, a voice from the Lowell Female Labor Reform Association demonstrates how women made their own ideologically charged attack upon wage slavery.

Why might workers have chosen to turn to the state rather than to their own organizations to fight the factory system? What roles did the increasing division of labor, and employer-hiring practices, play in the inability of so many workers to find common ground?

David Johnson Remembers Apprenticeship Life in the Artisan Shoe Shop, 1830

. . . A boy while learning his trade was called a "seamster"; that is, he sewed the shoes for his master, or employer, or to use one of the technicalities of the "craft," he "worked on the seam." Sometimes the genius of one of these boys would outrun all limits. One of this kind, who may be called Alphonzo, worked on the seam for a stipulated sum. He seemed

David N. Johnson, *Sketches of Lynn* (Lynn: Thomas P. Nichols, 1880), pp. 30, 32–35, 59–62.

to regard his work as an incidental circumstance. When he left the shop at night he might be expected back the next morning: but there were no special grounds for the expectation. He might drop in the next morning, or the next week. He left one Saturday night and did not make his appearance again until the following Thursday morning. On entering the shop he proceeded to take off his jacket as though there had been no hiatus in his labor. His master watched him with an amused countenance to see whether he would recognize the lapse of time. At length he said, "Where have you been, Alphonzo?" Alphonzo turned his head in an instant, as if struck with the preposterousness of the inquiry, and exclaimed, "Me? I? O, I've been down to Nahant." The case was closed. . . .

In almost every one of these shops there was one whose mechanical genius outran that of all the rest. He could "temper wax," "cut shoulders," sharpen scrapers and cut hair. The making of wax was an important circumstance in the olden time. To temper it just right so that it would not be too brittle and "fly" from the thread, or too soft and stick to the fingers, was an art within the reach of but few, or if within reach, was attained only by those who aspired to scale the heights of fame, and who, "while their companions slept, were toiling upward in the night." Such a one eyed his skillet of melted rosin as the alchemist of old viewed his crucible wherein he was to transmute the baser metals into gold. When the rosin was thoroughly melted, oil or grease was added until the right consistency was supposed to be nearly reached, the compound being thoroughly stirred in the meantime. Then the one having the matter in charge would first dip his finger in cold water and then into the melted mass, and taking the portion that adhered to his finger, would test its temper by pulling it, biting it, and rolling it in his hands. If found to be too hard, more oil or grease would be added, but very cautiously, as the critical moment was being reached. Then the test would be again applied. When the right result was supposed to be nearly gained, a piece of wax would be passed around among the crew for a confirmatory verdict. If the judgment of the master of ceremonies was indorsed, the experiment ended, and the mixture was poured into a vessel of cold water—usually the "shop-tub"—to cool sufficiently to be "worked." . . .

The shop-tub was an indispensable article in every shop. In early times, before the manufactures of wooden ware had become plenty and cheap, some rudely-constructed wooden vessel of home manufacture served the purpose. Afterwards a paint-keg or a firkin with the top sawed off, and still later a second-hand water-pail, was made to do service.

The theory was that the water of the shop-tub was to be changed every day. As this water was used for *wetting* the "stock"—which meant all the sole leather put into the shoe—and also often used for washing hands, it was somewhat necessary that it should be changed occasionally. The shifting of the "tub" often devolved upon the boy of the shop, except when he was too bright. In that case he "shirked" with the rest of the crew. This was the sort of boy that looked out of the attic window of the dormitory where he slept, to see if the smoke was gracefully curling from the shop's chimney, in the gray of the morning as he stretched himself for a supplementary snooze.

The man who had an "eye" for cutting "shoulders" occupied a niche of distinction among his fellow-craftsmen. If it was not necessary that he should have a "microscopic eye"—which Mr. Pope [the eighteenth-century English poet] tells us man does not need because he "is not a fly,"—it was needful that he should have a "geometric eye" when called upon to adjust the "shoulder" to "convex" and "concave" edges. To do this successfully required little less than a stroke of genius. Two cents was the usual price for cutting a "shoulder," and an experienced cutter would gather in each week quite a pile of the larger-size coppers of those days, whose purchasing power of many things was twice as great as at present. . . .

Perhaps one of the sorest experiences a boy had in old times in learning the "craft," was that which came from *breaking awls*. In order to fully appreciate the situation, the reader must take a survey of the whole field. It was a period of low wages. Awls were the most expensive "kit" used by the shoemaker. . . .

The awls were of two kinds, diamond and round, so called from the shape of their points. The diamond-shaped were usually preferred, as they were thought to be less liable to become dulled by use; but the so-called round awls—these were rather flatted at their points—were often used by "don" workmen, as they were less liable to "cut" the "upper." The awls first in use in this country were of English manufacture. The name of the manufacturer was stamped upon each awl, and there were three kinds, more or less in use, some fifty or more years ago when those of American make began to take their place. These were known as the Allerton, Wilson, and Titus awls, respectively. After the introduction of the American awl, the English article was not held in very high esteem by workmen employed upon ladies' shoes. They were badly shaped, and the points were left unfinished. The Allerton and Wilson had usually too long a crook, while the Titus was faulty in the opposite direction, being too straight, especially for certain kinds of work. They had, however, two important recommendations—they were better tempered, and therefore less liable to break, and their cost was only one-half, or less, that of the American awl.

Before the English awl was used, it was necessary to finish the points. This was sometimes done by grinding, sometimes by filing, and sometimes by sandpaper; and the points were smoothed off on a "whet-board," or by rubbing them on the pine floor. The man who could do this job skillfully was considered something of a genius. As already intimated, a boy could spoil a day's wages by breaking a few awls. If he was working on the seam on "long reds," and had a lot of extra hard soles on hand—some *hemlock tanned leather* for instance,—he had gloomy forebodings of the peril of the situation. If the master was a "hard" one, and the boy somewhat careless, there would most likely be an appeal to the "stirrup," whenever accidents of this kind rose above the average in frequency. . . .

"Cordwainers' Song," 1844

(Tune—"My Bible Leads to Glory")

The cause of labor's gaining,
The cause of labor's gaining,
The cause of labor's gaining,

    Throughout the town of Lynn.

Chorus
    Onward! onward! ye noble-hearted working men;
    Onward! onward! and victory is yours.

Arouse the working classes, &c.
Unite the free cordwainers, &c.
Let JUSTICE be our motto, &c.
Come, join us, all true hearted, &c.
Our prices are advancing, &c.
The WOMEN, too, are *rising,* &c.
New members daily join us, &c.
Our victory is certain, &c.
We'll *stitch* our SOLES still closer, &c.
Let all protect free labor, &c.
There'll soon be joy and gladness, &c.

Constance, "On the Art of Shoemaking," 1845

Great was his genius, and *inventive* thought!
Who first the curious *shoe* so nicely wrought,
Before this trade, others must soon retreat;
None will forego, this covering for their feet.

Without her shoe, what lady would be *seen*?
Take them away, what woman could be *Queen*?
Even the *Chinese* skill, in all the arts;
Will find this competition in these parts.

The town of Lynn in history is found:
Let all her sons be proud to have her named,
The very rocks with legions, rife are crowned;
And all the place with romance, still abound.

The lack of knowledge *see,* we cannot plead;
Our public schools give all the chance to *read,*
And learned men and great, with *faces* wise,
Will from the land of shoes, henceforth arise.

And now the Awl and Needle are combined,
Ladies your talent show, with intellect refined;
Though *men* still take the lead in politics and shoes,
Yet, when they ask our aid, oh! let us not refuse!

But help them in this work, with willing heart and hand,
And let not man be left alone, within this happy land;
Yet when we own this claim, (let not despotic sway,)
Arouse the woman's wrath, (and that *old* term, Obey.)

A Reporter's Account of Lynn Women's Mass Meeting During the Great Strike, 1860

. . . About noon, the procession from Lynn, consisting of about 3,500 men, preceded by a brass band, entered the village green, escorted by 500 Marbleheaders. The sight from the hotel steps was a very interesting one. Four thousand men, without work, poor, depending partially upon the charities of their neighbors and partially upon the generosity of the tradesmen of their town, giving up a certainty for an uncertainty, and involving in trouble with themselves many hundreds of women and children, while to a certain extent the wheels of trade are completely blocked, and no immediate prospect of relief appears. Their banners flaunted bravely. Their inscriptions of "Down with tyranny," "We are not slaves," "No sympathy with the rich," "Our bosses grind us," "We work and they ride," "No foreign police," and many others of like import, read very well and look very pretty, but they don't buy dinners or clothing, or keep the men at work or the women at home about their business. By this strike $25,000 *weekly is kept from circulation in Lynn alone,* and who can say what the effect will be on the storekeepers, dealers in articles of home consumption, if such a state of drainage is kept up for any great length of time? . . .

The most interesting part of the whole movement took place last evening, and will be continued tonight. I refer to the mass meeting of the binders and stitchers held by the female strikers at Liberty Hall. . . .

There are two classes of workers—those who work in the shops and those who work at home—the former use the machines and materials of the bosses, while the latter work on their own machines, or work by hand, furnishing their own materials. It is evident that the latter should receive higher pay than the former, and the report not having considered this fact, was subjected to severe handling. The discussion which followed was rich beyond description—the jealousies, piques and cliques of the various circles being apparent as it proceeded. One opposed the adoption of the report because, "the prices set were so high that the bosses wouldn't pay them." Cries of "Put her out," "Shut up," "Scabby," and "Shame" arose on all sides; but, while the reporters were alarmed, the lady took it all in good part, and made up faces at the crowd. The Chairman stated that, hereafter, Pickleeomoonia boots were to be made for three cents a pair less, which announcement was received with expressions of dismay, whereupon he corrected himself, and said they were to be three cents higher; and this announcement drew forth shouts and screams of applause. "There, didn't I *say* so?" said an old lady behind me. "You shut up," was the response of her neighbor; "you think because you've got a couple of machines you're some; but you ain't no more than anybody else." At this point some men peeped in at the window—"Scat, scat, and put 'em out," soon drove them away, and the meeting went into a Committee of the Whole, and had a grand chabbering for five minutes. Two ladies, one representing the machine

---

Howard, "The Bay State Strike," *New York Times,* Feb. 29, 1860, p. 3.

interest, and the other the shop girls, became very much excited, and were devoting themselves to an *exposé* of each other's habits, when the Chairman, with the perspiration starting from every pore, said in a loud and authoritative tone of voice: "Ladies! look at me; stop this wranglin'. Do you care for your noble cause? Are you descendants of old Molly Stark or not? Did you ever hear of the spirit of '76? [Yes, yes, we've got it.] Well, then, do behave yourselves. There ain't nobody nowhere who will aid you if you don't show 'em that you're regular built Moll Starks over agin." [Cheers, clappings, &c.] . . .

A proposition to march in the procession was the next topic which drew forth discussion. Some thought that proper minded women would better stay at home than be gadding about the streets following banners and music. To this there was some assent, but when a younger girl asked the last speaker what she meant by talking that way, when everybody in Lynn knew that she had been tagging around on the sidewalk after the men's processions the last week. . . .

Some of the statements were quite interesting. A Mrs. Miller said that she hired a machine on which she was able to make $6 per week—out of that she paid—for the machine, $1; for the materials, $1.50; for her board, $2; for bastings, $1;—making $5.50 in all, which left her a clear profit of only fifty cents a week. One of the bosses says, however, that if a woman is at all smart she can make $10 per week with her machine, which would be clear $3, sure. In fact, from remarks which were dropped around I judge that Mrs. Miller's estimate is rather low. The leading spirit of the meeting, Miss Clara Brown, a very bright, pretty girl, said that she called at a shop that day and found a friend of hers hard at work on a lot of linings. She asked what she was getting for them, and was told *eight cents for sixty.* "Girls of Lynn," said Clara, "*Girls* of Lynn, do you hear that and will you stand it? Never, Never, NEVER. Strike, then—strike at once; demand 8½ cents for your work when the binding isn't closed and you'll get it. Don't let them make niggers of you; [Shame, there are colored persons here.] I meant Southern niggers:—keep still; don't work your machines; let 'em lie still till we get all we ask, and then go at it, as did our Mothers in the Revolution."

This speech was a good one; it seemed to suit all parties, and they proposed to adjourn to Tuesday night, when they would have speeches and be more orderly. Canvassing Committees were appointed to look up female strikers and to report female "scabs." And with a vote of thanks to the Chairman, the meeting adjourned to meet in Lyceum Hall. . . .

Textile Operative William Shaw's Testimony on Child Labor in Pennsylvania's Textile Mills, 1838

. . . The greatest evils known are, first, the number of hours of labor, and the number of young children employed. Has worked in four different factories in nine years; in John P. Crozier's, nearly three years; Samuel

Riddle's, nearly two years; Joseph Dean, nearly two, and Jonathan Hatch, nearly one year, and now at Jos. Fleming's; is twenty-six years old. At Fleming's, about fifty persons employed; about eighteen females; about four children under twelve years old; about fifteen under eighteen years old. The proportion of children varies in different establishments; has known more than one-fourth to be children under twelve years of age; under twenty years, would include, in many cases, three-fourths; not many are apprenticed; they are usually hired to employers by parents and guardians. The hours vary in different establishments; in some I have worked fourteen and a-half hours. I have known work to commence as early as twenty minutes past four o'clock, in the summer season, and to work as late as half an hour before eight, P.M., an hour and a-half allowed for breakfast and dinner, when the hands all leave to go to dinner—children and all; the ringing of the bell was the notice to begin, and docking wages the penalty; the foreman rings the bell and stops the machinery. In the cities, the engineer rings the bell and stops the machinery.

The period of labor is not uniform; in some cases, from sun to sun. It is most common to work as long as they can see; in the winter they work until eight o'clock, receiving an hour and a-half for meals; an hour and a half is the entire time allowed for going, eating and returning; and that time is often shortened by the ringing of the bell too soon.

The labor of the children is, in some cases, excessive—in others it is not. The children are employed at spinning and carding. The question of excessive labor is more upon the kind of work; carding is the hardest work; their work is regulated by the operation of the machinery, at carding; and they must stand during the whole time; considers twelve or fourteen hours labor excessive at either branch for a child. I have known children of nine years of age to be employed at spinning—at carding, as young as ten years. Punishment by whipping, is frequent; they are sometimes sent home and docked for not attending punctually; never knew both punishments to be inflicted; generally the children are attentive, and punishments are not frequent. The carder, or person having charge of the children, inflicts the chastisement.

Boys and girls work together; no attention is paid by the manufacturer, or others in the factory, to the personal cleanliness of the children. Rules, sometimes printed, are posted in some of the factories, for the government.

The children are tired when they leave the factory; has known them to sleep in corners and other places, before leaving the factory, from fatigue. The younger children are generally very much fatigued particularly those under twelve years of age; has not heard frequent complaints of pain; more of being worried; has known the children to go to sleep on arriving at home, *before* taking supper; has known great difficulty in keeping children awake at their work; has known them to be struck, to keep them awake.

The children *are* more healthy when they first enter the factories, than afterwards; they lose colour, loss of appetite, and sometimes, not frequently, complain themselves; has known them to be compelled in some instances, to quit the factories, in consequence of ill health, particularly females. Boys quit frequently to go to trades; has known no deformity produced by the labor.

Parents are favorable to a reduction of hours; I think no attention is paid to education during the time they are employed in factories, except what they receive from Sabbath schools, and some few at night schools, when they are in an unfit condition to learn; the children attend Sabbath school with great reluctance; many will not attend in consequence of the confinement of the week.

No particular attention is paid to morals; the boys and girls are not kept separate in the factories; they have different water closets; generally separated only by a partition; obscene language is frequently used; not often by females; profane language is frequently used; care is seldom taken to prevent these things; if their work is done, it is all that is required; girls and boys work together and talk together; no pains are taken to ventilate factories; sometimes the windows are nailed down; sometimes fifty are employed in one room; in small factories, as few as ten; has never known a thermometer to be kept in the rooms; in the winter they are generally kept too cold. The machinery is propelled in the city by steam, in the country by water. In the carding room, the air is frequently filled with flyings. The only instance of a contageous disease being generated in a factory, was near Baltimore, some years ago, when the yellow fever broke out in the factory of the Messrs Buchanan's, when it was not in the city. The superintendents are generally careful in their language, not to set a bad example.

The wages of children are not regulated by the number of hours they labor; I have known some to get no more than fifty cents per week; I have known some to get as much as $1.25; the common rate is $1.00; oftener less than greater; most of the children are boys.

Amelia, a Woman Worker, Protests
Lowell Wage Slavery, 1845

. . . For the purpose of illustration, let us go with that light-hearted, joyous young girl who is about for the first time to leave the home of her childhood, that home around which clusters so many beautiful and holy associations, pleasant memories, and quiet joys; to leave, too, a mother's cheerful smile, a father's care and protection; and wend her way toward this far famed "city of spindles," this promised land of the imagination, in whose praise she has doubtless heard so much.

Let us trace her progress during her first year's residence, and see whether she indeed realizes those golden prospects which have been held out to her. Follow her now as she enters that large gloomy looking building—she is in search of employment, and has been told that she might

From "Voices from Lowell," 1845, in Philip Foner, ed., *The Factory Girls*, 1977, pp. 135–138, (Urbana: University of Illinois Press, 1977).

here obtain an eligible situation. She is sadly wearied with her journey, and withal somewhat annoyed by the noise, confusion, and strange faces all around her. So, after a brief conversation with the overseer, she concludes to accept the first situation which offers; and reserving to herself a sufficient portion of time in which to obtain the necessary rest after her unwonted exertions, and the gratification of a stranger's curiosity regarding the place in which she is now to make her future home, she retires to her boarding house, to arrange matters as much to her mind as may be.

The intervening time passes rapidly away, and she soon finds herself once more within the confines of that close noisy apartment, and is forthwith installed in her new situation—first, however, premising that she has been sent to the Counting-room, and receives therefrom a Regulation paper, containing the rules by which she must be governed while in their employ; and lo! here is the beginning of mischief; for in addition to the tyrannous and oppressive rules which meet her astonished eyes, she finds herself compelled to remain for the space of twelve months in the very place she then occupies, however reasonable and just cause of complaint might be hers, or however strong the wish for dismission; thus, in fact, constituting herself a slave, a very slave to the caprices of him for whom she labors. Several incidents coming to the knowledge of the writer, might be somewhat interesting in this connection, as tending to show the prejudicial influence exerted upon the interests of the operative by this unjust requisition. The first is of a lady who has been engaged as an operative for a number of years, and recently entered a weaving room on the Massachusetts Corporation: the overseers having assured her previous to her entrance, that she should realize the sum of $2.25 per week, exclusive of board; which she finding it impossible to do, appealed to the Counting-room for a line enabling her to engage elsewhere but it was peremptorily refused. . . .

But to return to our toiling Maiden,—the next beautiful feature which she discovers in this *glorious* system is, the long number of hours which she is obliged to spend in the above named close, unwholesome apartment. It is not enough, that like the poor peasant of Ireland, or the Russian serf who labors from sun to sun, but during one half of the year, she must still continue to toil on, long after Nature's lamp has ceased to lend its aid— nor will even this suffice to satisfy the grasping avarice of her employer; for she is also through the winter months required to rise, partake of her morning meal, and be at her station in the mill, while the sun is yet sleeping behind the eastern hills; thus working on an average, at least twelve hours and three fourths per day, exclusive of the time allotted for her hasty meals, which is in winter simply one half hour at noon,—in the spring is allowed the same at morn, and during the summer is added 15 minutes to the half hour at noon. Then too, when she is at last released from her wearisome day's toil, still may she not depart in peace. No! her footsteps must be dogged to see that they do not stray beyond the corporation limits, and she *must*, whether she will or no, be subjected to the manifold inconveniences of a large crowded boarding-house, where too, the price paid for her accommodation is so utterly insignificant, that it will not ensure to her the common comforts of life; she is obliged to sleep in a small comfortless, half ventilated apartment containing some half a dozen occupants each; but no matter, *she is an operative*—it is all well enough for her; there is no "abuse" about it; no, indeed; so think our employers,—but do we think so? time will show. . . .

Reader will you pronounce this a mere fancy sketch, written for the sake of effect? It is not so. It is a real picture of "Factory life"; nor is it one half so bad as might truthfully and justly have been drawn. But it has been asked, and doubtless will be again, why, if these evils are so aggravating, have they been so long and so peacefully borne? Ah! and why have they? It is a question well worthy of our consideration, and we would call upon every operative in *our* city, aye, throughout the length and breadth of the land, to awake from the lethargy which has fallen upon them, and assert and maintain their rights. We call upon you for action—*united and immediate action*. But, says one, let us wait till we are stronger. In the language of one of old, we ask, when shall we be stronger? Will it be the next week, or the next year? Will it be when we are reduced to the service conditions of the poor operatives of England? for verily we shall be and that right soon, if matters be suffered to remain as they are. Says another, how shall we act? we are but one amongst a thousand, what shall we do that our influence may be felt in this vast multitude? We answer there is in this city an Association called the Female Labor Reform Association, having for its professed object, the amelioration of the condition of the operative. Enrolled upon its records are the names of five hundred members—come then, and add thereto five hundred or rather five thousand more, and in the strength of our united influence we will soon show these *drivelling* cotton lords, this mushroom aristocracy of New England, who so arrogantly aspire to lord it over God's heritage, that our rights cannot be trampled upon with impunity; that we will no longer submit to that arbitrary power which has for the last ten years been so abundantly exercised over us.

One word ere we close, to the hardy independent yeomanry and mechanics, among the Granite Hills of New Hampshire, the woody forests of Maine, the cloud capped mountains of Vermont, and the busy, bustling towns of the old Bay State—ye! who have daughters and sisters toiling in these sickly prison-houses which are scattered far and wide over each of these States, we appeal to you for aid in this matter. Do you ask how that aid can be administered? We answer through the Ballot Box. Yes! if you have one spark of sympathy for our condition, carry it there, and see to it that you send to preside in the Councils of each Commonwealth, men who have hearts as well as heads, souls as well as bodies; men who will watch zealously over the interests of the laborer in every department; who will protect him by the strong arm of the law from the encroachments of arbitrary power; who will see that he is not deprived of those rights and privileges which God and Nature have bestowed upon him—yes,

From every rolling river,
From mountain, vale and plain.

We call on you to deliver
Us, from the tyrant's chain:

And shall we call in vain? We trust not. More anon.

⚓ *E S S A Y S*

Because it provides such a classic example of the replacement of artisan labor by the factory system, the evolution of the shoemaking industry in its American capital, Lynn, Massachusetts, has long captured historians' interest. Alan Dawley of Trenton State College finds that the mechanization of shoe manufacture enhanced the power of Lynn's entrepreneurial class, while it robbed artisan producers of their authority and independence. Dawley argues that women's presence in the Great Strike of 1860 offers a notable example of the inclusive character of the equal-rights doctrine. But Mary H. Blewett of the University of Lowell sees a less sanguine meaning in women's involvement. She finds that a female commitment to home and family could impede labor solidarity, and notes that Lynn's male artisans drew upon the moral authority of women to aid their own struggle, not to advance the factory girls' cause.

How did the rise of the factory system change the character of the shoemaking work force? What accounts for the different views of Dawley and Blewitt toward the 1860 strike? What other circumstances could have contributed to the strikers' defeat?

Lynn Shoemakers: Class Solidarity in the Great Strike

ALAN DAWLEY

For two centuries after the initial white settlement of New England, profit hungry investors and frustrated fortune hunters encountered powerful restraints on economic development. They were impeded by Puritan strictures against profiteering, by mercantilist regulations of the economy, and by environmental backwardness. But they persevered, and by the second quarter of the nineteenth century their boundless ambition for gain had achieved significant breakthroughs in extending the principles and practices of [the] marketplace directly into the sphere of production.

Leading the way were shoes and textiles, which stood first and second in the industrial statistics of New England from the first statistical surveys in the 1830s through the Civil War. Together these industries carved great basins of industrialization out of the hilly, rock-ribbed countryside that straddled the Merrimack and Connecticut River valleys and ran inland from the shores of Rhode Island and eastern Massachusetts. Lynn lay in one of these basins stretching from Boston to the White Mountains and including the major manufacturing cities of Lowell, Lawrence, Haverhill, Salem, Manchester, and Newburyport, plus several other smaller cities in Massachusetts, New Hampshire, and Maine. Furthermore, dozens of additional villages in the country imitated the enterprise of the more renowned urban centers, and in some of these hamlets outworkers for the shoe industry labored in the shadow of a local textile mill. Everywhere central shops, factories, and warehouses were shouldering their way in among the artisan shops, hay barns, livery stables, and grist mills that represented the vanishing era of economic restraint.

Lynn manufacturers joined the headlong rush toward unimpeded economic development. Between 1830 and 1836 they increased production by two-thirds, making this a time of "feverish excitement" when the character of the town changed "more rapidly and more essentially than at any previous period in her history." The number of streets and buildings nearly doubled in these years, and the physical strain on the community was compounded by social dislocation. The only thing that held back the rapacity of the entrepreneurs was the fearsome grip of panic, which took hold in 1837 and stopped them in their tracks. For the next seven years, they chafed at the restraints of the prolonged depression in the industry and organized through the Whig party to improve their prospects by increasing the tariff on imported shoes. But foreign competition was no longer a major factor in the industry, and when the domestic market finally responded to the proddings of the manufacturers in the mid-1840s, those who had survived congratulated themselves on being sounder and stronger than their fallen competitors and rushed ahead with renewed vigor. Another period of feverish expansion ensued between 1845 and 1850; boosted by the rapidly lengthening railroad network, shoe production came close to doubling. . . . Freed from the restraints of the past, the marketplace did not produce Adam Smith's version of stable, self-regulating progress, but manic cycles of expansion and contraction.

The main resource for expansion was labor. Increased output in the prefactory era was directly proportional to an increase in the number of shoemakers, and employers calculated profits in these terms: so many hands, so many dollars. During business upturns, they hired hand over fist; for every three employees of a Lynn firm in 1845, there were five in 1850. . . . Like the declining dominions of the Old South which were sending slave laborers to the more profitable cotton lands of the West, rural New England yielded up its laborers to employers who mined the area as if it were filled with gold. Making the transfer from farming to shoemaking was not difficult for the rural inhabitants, who had worked with their hands from childhood. What teenage girl did not know how to stitch and sew? What man who mended harnesses and repaired saddles could not learn the gentle craft of shoemaking, especially now that cutting was done by specialists? So for a quarter of a century the land readily gave up its people.

But no resource, however abundant, is inexhaustible. Employers quickly depleted the areas close to the cities, and they had to range ever further afield. Driven by gold fever, shoe manufacturers ventured into northern New Hampshire and Vermont, while textile employers prospected as far away as upstate New York and Canada in search of young female operatives. Competition among the employers was compounded by the migration of labor out of the region; enough Massachusetts natives moved to New York to make the number living there in 1850 almost equal to the total number of people employed by the entire Massachusetts boot and shoe industry. The shoe industry felt these pressures in the form of a diminishing marginal product in the branch where competition for labor was most keen—binding. In the 1830s each binder stitched an average of 934 pairs a year, but by 1850 the number had fallen below 700. . . .

Because textile recruiters sent most of the ready women without children to the factories, the boot and shoe firms had difficulty finding full-time binders and, instead, had to rely on new recruits who bound shoes intermittently between their other chores at home. "Women's nimble fingers," wrote one observer, "were found inadequate to the demand."

The geographical outreach of the outwork system heightened the manufacturers' dilemma by making production most sluggish at the frontiers of expansion. Transportation of raw materials to the fringes of the system 150 miles from Lynn consumed two or three weeks, and the return trip doubled the time lost in transit. When this delay was added to the easy going work pace logged by farmer shoemakers, the result was a waiting time that ranged as high as six to nine months before a pair of shoes was finished. The further the system expanded without changing its technological base the more difficulty it encountered reaching its objectives. As the distance and time between the various steps in the manufacturing process increased and as it became harder to get binding done quickly, the method of sending work out of town, originally designed as a means of raising peak seasonal output, was beginning to have just the opposite result. The gold rush was coming to a close.

Deus ex machina

The manufacturers' problem was resolved by a deus ex machina in the form of a sewing machine. Minor modifications of the original invention enabled an operator to bind the uppers in a fraction of the time it took by hand. Therefore the manufacturer no longer had to expand the geographical frontiers of his labor force and instead could cut back the total number of female employees and hire a greater proportion from among residents of Lynn. The importance of the machine was emphasized by a newspaper closely identified with the manufacturers: "The introduction of sewing machines for stitching and binding of shoes was the result of an absolute necessity."

Since the uppers were made of cloth or light leather, the same machine could be used for binding uppers and mending a dress. Initially, the cost of the machines restricted their use to people with substantial savings, but their price steadily declined from the $75 to 100 range of the early 1850s to a level around $20 in the early 1860s, before Civil War inflation drove the price up again. Newspaper ads were frequently addressed to "the lady operator and the shoe manufacturer" and strained to make the point that they were for family use, as well as for manufacturing. The ads were effective, and soon "almost every house" in Lynn sported a sewing machine; the number of sewing machines per capita was more than the number of hogs had ever been in preindustrial Lynn.

However, the trend in manufacturing was unmistakably away from the household and toward the factory. The first machines were tried out and proved in the shops of three of the larger manufacturers in 1852. Because they employed two to three times as many people as the average firm, these manufacturers were more deeply entangled in the contradictions of the outwork system than the smaller employers and were especially eager for a way out. Their initiative spread, and by 1855 most of the leading manufacturers had begun to use sewing machines. Sometimes smaller contractors set up independent stitching shops, but usually the manufacturers outfitted rooms of their own. From this point on through 1880 the trend in female employment was downward, even as total output rose: between 1850 and 1860 the number of women employed declined 40 percent, while their output doubled. Both speed and quality were enhanced by bringing operators and machines together under one roof, so that only one-fifth of the women employed in 1875 were left working at home.

From the outset, the stitching shops looked strikingly like factories. The gathering of as many as three or four dozen women in one room and the clatter of their machines were such a contrast to the picture of a woman quietly at work in her own kitchen that everyone agreed a fundamental change had taken place.

The invention of the sewing machine opened a new frontier, which "soon transformed the old fashioned 'shoe-binders' into a new and more expansive class of 'machine girls' whose capacity for labor was only limited by the capabilities of the machines over which they presided. Iron and steel came to the aid of wearied fingers and weakened eyes. This was the beginning of a new era, which is destined to produce results big with lasting benefit to our flourishing city."

Glowing enthusiasm for the factory system appeared in an 1860 federal census report on the boot and shoe industry. Describing the sewing machine as a "crowning invention," the article said that along with a sole-cutting machine it was bringing about "a silent revolution" in manufacturing. The report sensed the shoe industry was "assuming the characteristics of a factory system, being conducted in large establishments of several stories, each floor devoted to a separate part of the work, with the aid of steam-power, and all the labor-saving contrivances known to the trade. It is safe to predict that this change will go on until the little 'workshop' of the shoemaker, with its 'bench' and 'kit,' shall become a thing of the past, as the 'handcard' and the great and little 'spinning wheel' have disappeared from other branches of the clothing manufacture." This report jumped the gun by a few years, but because the major forms of factory organization were fully represented in machine stitching, and because the model of textile industry was so compelling, it is not surprising that the report assumed the inevitability of a full-scale factory system.

The Great Strike

The manufacturers' enthusiasm for machines and factories did not spread to the shoemakers. Binders and journeymen looked back over a quarter century of social dislocation, and now in the 1850s they feared that once again the manufacturers were up to no good. The first sewing machines introduced into the city "aroused the ire" of the binders, who saw them as another incursion on their household independence. A delegation of binders tried to block the spread of the new devices by visiting a central shop where one had been installed and requesting the operator to cease her work on the grounds that the machine "would ultimately be the ruin of the poor workingwomen." These early machines, which cost a third to a half of a binder's annual income, were clearly implements designed to benefit only capitalists; both the binders who went into the stitching shops and the shrinking group of those who worked at home continued to regard the new methods of production with extreme distrust. Each binder knew that the labor the new devices saved could well be her own, and what good, she wondered, could possibly come of something that eliminated hundreds of jobs each season.

The binders' ire was mollified for a time by the declining price of the sewing machine (making it more accessible for family use) and by the persistence of high levels of employment in the shoe industry. But when the Panic of 1857 brought the shoe business to a standstill, and workers all over the city were given the sack, the twin pressures of depression and displacement converged on shoemaker families to force discontent to the surface again, as in the 1830s and 1840s. The tensions between shoemakers and their bosses were apparent at two mass meetings held on the edge of winter in the depression's first year. As journeymen shoemakers and other laboring men of the community filed into Lynn's rustic Lyceum Hall, the chill November air reminded them of the blankets, overcoats, cordwood, and provisions they would need in the coming months, and of the long winter layover looming ahead when they would have little or no income. They listened with growing indignation while businessmen and politicians proposed emergency public relief, as if the honest workingmen of Lynn were nothing but paupers. Were they not able-bodied men willing to work?

At a second community meeting the following week, these sentiments buried the proposals for public relief. "Would it not be better," asked one opponent of charity, "for the show manufacturers to give full price—to say to the workman we will give you a little something to do until business is better?" And he added, "Let the rich come forward and say we will give you ten per cent of the profits we have made." The idea was radical enough to prompt a quick rejoinder from a shoe manufacturer and leather dealer named John B. Alley that the purpose of the meeting was not to degrade business for the benefit of labor. Alley was an up-and-coming politician on his way to the House of Representatives polishing the techniques of rhetorical compromise; he endorsed the work ethic but argued present circumstances made public relief a practical necessity.

Despite Alley's compromise, this debate set a tone of hostility for encounters between shoemakers and shoe manufacturers during the next three years. Eight months later several hundred journeymen sweltered through a July meeting in the Lyceum to consider a strike to raise wages. No action was taken immediately, but economic distress kept up a steady pressure, and by the spring of 1859 journeymen had established the Lynn Mechanics Association and had begun publishing the *New England Mechanic*. The Association and the *Mechanic* continued operation for the remainder of the year, becoming a solid core of organizational strength among the journeymen. Finally, in the winter of 1860 all the years of anxiety over the effects of machine stitching combined with the years of depression to produce a mounting frustration that burst forth in the Great Shoemakers Strike.

The biggest strike the United States had ever experienced hit the whole upper New England basin like a driving "Nor'easter." The shoe centers along the North Shore bore the full brunt of the storm, where a clear majority of shoemakers joined the strike, and it also swept inland to secondary towns and outwork villages. All in all, probably a minimum of 20,000 people quit work, somewhat more than half the employees living in this region and a third of the 60,000 employees of all Massachusetts firms. The progress of the strike was given large play in most of the region's major newspapers, and national journals sent illustrators and reporters to the scene. The experience left an indelible mark on folk memory, and for a generation it was recalled with the frequency and vividness people usually reserved for earthquakes or hurricanes. . . .

Lynn was at the center of the storm. The strike began on Washington's Birthday, a date the journeymen picked to demonstrate they were acting in the best traditions of the Republic. They believed the producers were the bone and sinew of society, and in a community of interdependent households the producers should be able to unite and carry everyone along with them. The dimensions of their success were revealed in the scope and style of demonstrations and parades held in support of the strike. In six weeks, five processions passed through the streets of Lynn, each with 1000 or more people in the line of march, plus hundreds of sympathizers in the sidelines. The largest demonstration occurred on March 16; besides strikers from Lynn marching in ward units, the 6000 people who crowded into the procession included companies of militia and firemen, brass bands, and several out-of-town strike delegations. . . .

The strikers immersed themselves in the pageantry of waving banners and brightly festooned uniforms to show that their strike had the support and expressed the will of the general community. The presence of the militia companies and firemen—themselves mostly laboring men in special uniforms—emphasized the interdependence among the householders of an artisan community. The organization of the strikers into ward units bespoke the ties of neighborhood fraternity and sorority. The joint participation of men and women expressed the solidarity of all who labored in the craft.

The strike processions, therefore, emrged from the customs and traditions of preindustrial society. They were festivals of the old artisan way of life presented in the context of the new system of industrial capitalism. Influences from the past and forces leading to the future simultaneously fashioned the present event.

The presence of women was a noteworthy feature of the processions. Without the action of women, it is questionable whether the strike would have occurred at all, and certainly without them it would have been far less massive in its impact. Women's grievances helped cause it; their demands shaped its objectives; their support ratified it as a community undertaking. Whether they worked at home or in the manufacturers' shops, all women employees earned piece wages, and both home and shop workers focused their demands on an increase in wages. They held their own strike meetings, did their own canvassing in Lynn and nearby towns to win support, and turned out in strength for the big street demonstrations. The laborer, they contended, was worthy of her hire.

The demonstration on March 7 was held in their honor. Escorted by a detachment of musket-bearing militia, 800 women strikers started at Lynn Common and marched in the falling snow for several hours past the central shops on Lynn's major thoroughfares. Their action was a bold violation of the cultural code that stipulated women should not venture beyond kitchen hearth and church pew. The keepers of this code of True Womanhood were middle-class families in retreat from the disorder of urban life into their parlors, sewing circles, and church clubs. But workingwomen were bound to no such cult of domesticity. For several generations their labor had mingled with that of other producers, just as their protests had blended with the journeymen, and they were not about to renounce their own heritage of Equal Rights.

At the head of their procession they carried a banner with an inscription taken from the Equal Rights philosophy: "AMERICAN LADIES WILL NOT BE SLAVES: GIVE US A FAIR COMPENSATION AND WE LABOUR CHEERFULLY." Slavery had long been the measure of the ultimate degradation of labor, the point to which the shoe bosses seemed to be driving their employees. With the execution of John Brown only three months before the strike, artisans felt the immediacy of the conflict between slavery and Free Soil, and analogies linking manufacturers to slavemasters flowed freely. One speaker at a mass meeting declared it was not necessary to go to "bleeding Kansas" to find oppressors of labor; there were plenty who had been "drawing the chains of slavery, and riveting them closer and closer around the limbs of free laboring men at home." . . . The Equal Rights tradition contenanced a limited version of feminism: women who worked should be accorded a place of honor among the ranks of toilers, should be paid a fair and equal compensation, and should take an active role in defending the rights of labor. But this was the extent of labor feminism: when it came to critical strike strategy, to political affairs, and to final arbitration in domestic matters, men ought to be in charge. Thus the cultural environment of the strike was filled with symbols of manhood which could hardly appeal to women strikers. The call to "stand for your rights like men!" must have left women seated in their chairs.

The "Cordwainers' Song" rallied shoemakers to the defense of the Tree of Liberty. Striking a classic Jeffersonian pose, the brave shoemakers prepared to shed their blood, should tyrants order their soldiers to fire. The tyrants of the song were the big shoe bosses of Lynn, especially those who practiced "dishonest competition" and affected an air of superiority in their dealings with the masses. But some of the manufacturers held the trust of the shoemaker, and four bosses received "Hurrahs!" when the Washington's Birthday marchers passed their central shops. One of the four reciprocated the holiday spirit by decorating his building with flags and bunting for the occasion. This was the kind of harmony between labor and capital many strike leaders hoped for. The week before Washington's Birthday, officers in the Mechanics Association had carried a bill of wages around to the manufacturers asking for voluntary agreement to pay the advanced rates. The committee even solicited contributions from the bosses to the strike fund! Shoemakers were not surprised when several manufacturers actually subscribed to pay; leading the list was a boss who "agreed to be taxed $300." Believing they represented the general will of their community, shoemakers found nothing strange in their plan to "tax" their neighbors.

Shoemakers prepared for the strike as members of the "producing classes." As producers they felt they were entitled to a fair reward for their toil, which they defined as an exchange of the goods they made for an equivalent value of food, clothing, shelter, and enjoyments. Anything less was cheating. Thus "monopolists" and "grinders" who cut their prices or cheapened their wares to increase their sales practiced "dishonest competition." In their train followed a host of unfortunate laborers forced to toil for a pittance on cheap goods until their existence approached the pauper labor of Europe. The dire result was the degradation of the earnings and reputations of "honest labor." When artisans divided their employers into "good bosses" and "bad bosses," they were not indulging in meaningless moralizing; they expressed a view of reality that conformed to the heritage of a community of householders.

Yet reality itself went well beyond this view. The central shop was no simple producer's household. The marketplace compelled manufacturers to adhere to the laws of competition, opposing the interest of those who bought labor to the interest of those who sold it. Moreover, shoemakers did not control the instruments of public authority. In the course of the strike, shoemakers were forced to face these disturbing facets of reality. The image of the artisan seemed to dissolve before their eyes, and in its place they saw an image of the industrial worker taking shape.

Shoemakers had to come to terms with the fact that manufacturers did not behave like fellow household producers. Only one came through on his pledge to the strike fund; the rest either reneged completely or paid only a trifling sum, such as a $20 contribution from the man who had agreed to be taxed $300. Worse than that, the manufacturers connived to break the back of the strike by hiring scab labor. They sent agents to ransack the surrounding states for workmen and hired "everything in the shape of a shoemaker." To the manufacturer, business was business, and the laws of the marketplace were more compelling than the will of the majority. With debts to pay, orders to fill, and customers to keep, manufacturers were not about to suspend the quest for profits just because the shoemakers desired it. But to the shoemakers, the manufacturers' effort to keep up production, after promising "to help us through, if we would strike and stick for a few weeks," was an outrageous betrayal. In a retrospective article fuming with indignation, two strike leaders snarled that the manufacturer, virtually without exception, tried to "defeat and disgrace us." One of the leaders told a group of binders in early April that the events of the past few weeks proved "the interest of capital is to get as much labor for as little money as possible."

Shoemakers had interests and compulsions of their own. Money wages were the staff of life; no one could survive any longer on home-grown pork and greens. Because shoemakers were wholly dependent on their industrial income, the wages of industrial unemployment were debt and destitution. Going into debt during the winter layover was a normal experience for shoemakers, but every year since the Panic of 1857 getting out of debt in the spring had been unusually difficult. The manufacturers were "grinding us down so low that men with large families could not live within their own means." Neither could young men with little experience (who were given low-paid tasks) nor women of any age and skill (whose wages were the lowest in the industry). Wage earners of all types concluded that the degradation of free labor was at hand.

In a mood of bitter determination shoemakers vowed that if the manufacturers would not willingly raise their wages, then they must be compelled to do so through a complete cessation of labor. This feeling motivated some strikers to use force to win their objectives, a marked contrast to the holiday atmosphere of the strike processions. On the morning of the day after Washington's Birthday a crowd of strikers gathered in front of the Central Square railroad depot. It was apparent that most manufacturers intended to maintain business as usual, because they continued to send cases of shoe stock to the depot for shipment to outworkers. A considerable portion of the crowd was in favor of preventing all such cases from leaving Lynn. Many who assembled that morning were piqued by a hoax played on them the previous afternoon, when they had carried what appeared to be a case of shoe stock back to its owner, only to discover it was filled with leather scraps and floor sweepings. This provocation was heightened by the local city marshal who addressed the crowd in insulting terms that "only served to increase irritation and excitement among the strikers who heard them."

The marshal got another crack at the shoemakers the same afternoon. With a few deputies in tow he fell upon a handful of men who were dumping cases destined for scab outworkers off an express wagon. The marshal's force succeeded in replacing the cases on the wagon, but in the eyes of the strikers, the marshal was now firmly identified with the shoe bosses, and his office lost whatever majesty it might have had. Pursuing their own justice, the strikers attempted to cast down the cases once again, and when the marshal stood in their way, they pummeled him and his men with their fists. It was reported that one of the strikers drew a knife. Overpowered in this fracas, the marshal refrained from further adventures that afternoon, and several more cases were taken from the train depot and returned to the central shops. In addition, the pugnacious expressman who tried to defend his cargo was "badly hurt," and strikers roughed up at least one journeyman on his way home with fresh materials.

In the eyes of the manufacturers the interference with the flow of trade and the attack on the city marshal constituted a vile threat to the social order bordering on insurrection. Through friends in city government, they prevailed upon the mayor to call out the militia. In his letter to the commander of the Lynn Light Infantry, Co. D, Eighth Regiment of the Massachusetts Volunteers, the mayor took note that "bodies of men have tumultuously assembled in [Lynn], and have offered violence to persons and property, and have, by force and violence resisted and broken the laws of the Commonwealth; and that military force is necessary to aid the civil authority in suppressing the same." The men were called to appear at their armory the next morning "armed, equipped with ammunition." Then while the mayor went off to counsel moderation before a mass meeting of shoemakers, other city officials got in touch with the state attorney general, the sheriff of Essex County, a major general in the state militia, and the city officials and police chiefs of Boston and South Danvers. The manufacturers were taking no chances with unruly employees.

The next day, February 24, shoemakers arose with dawning amazement to find their community occupied by outside police and armed militia. In the morning a detachment of deputies from South Danvers stood guard at the train station to see that there was no more interference with the shipment of shoe materials, and at 1:00 o'clock a posse of twenty uniformed Boston policemen arrived at the depot. These professional law officers joined the militia at an inn named the Sagamore House, which had been converted into command headquarters for the day. Decisions were in the hands of the attorney general, the major general, the city marshal, and several aldermen; conspicuously absent from the Sagamore were the mayor, who had fallen ill, and the city councilors. Apparently with the aim of arresting those who were disorderly the day before, the Boston regulars were sent back into the streets. Led by the hated city marshal, they roved through town for two hours, stimulating near riots where ever they went. Hounded by hoots and hisses, pelted by stones and brickbats, they ran the gauntlet of a hostile crowd, participated in a "general melee in which several of the crowd were knocked down," and finally ended their tumultuous trek through town at the railroad depot in Central Square where it had begun.

Most residents of the community were outraged at this incursion on their right of self-government. . . . Widespread indignation apparently blocked the prosecution of the five men arrested that day. Though they were spirited away to Salem for safekeeping and arraigned and bound over to the grand jury in Lynn a few days later, there is no record that the grand jury was ever convened or that any of the men were ever convicted of riotous conduct. The five benefited from community opposition to the odious actions of manufacturers and public officials, even though only one of the men arrested was a long-standing, propertied resident of Lynn. The others were newcomers, immigrants living in poverty, including the Irishman reported to have pulled a knife.

The turmoil of the first three days of the strike was the worst fury of the storm. On the evening of the third day the outside police and state officials left town, and the temporary soldiers dismantled their rifles and went home. That was the end of violence. But the passions stirred up in these days imparted a force and momentum to the strike that carried it through six weeks of mass organizing on a scale never before seen in American industry. While manufacturers hunted for scabs, teams of strike canvassers combed the neighborhoods of Lynn and visited a score of other shoe towns to mobilize support. Thousands of people were organized into strike processions, with thousands more watching. On the days of the processions, dozens of kitchens kept up a steady outpouring of food to provide refreshment to those who marched. In addition, there were rallies in Central Square, mass meetings in Lyceum Hall, and frequent meetings of the strike leadership in the Mechanics Association and the Ladies' Association of Binders and Stitchers.

Support of nonshoemakers was also mobilized. Besides other laboring men who marched in the fire and militia companies (with the conspicuous absence of the infamous Lynn Light Infantry), the city's retail businessmen were called upon to aid the strikers. Most grocers and provisions dealers were compelled to defer collection of shoemakers' bills, regardless of their opinion of the strike, but because of neighborhood ties and revulsion against the military invasion of their community, many retailers actively sympathized with the strikers. One lumber dealer, for example, gave shoemakers free access to a stand of trees he owned so they would not have to purchase cordwood. Several politicians also came forth, though their effort to curry favor with the voters led them into some strange political contortions. Congressman John B. Alley sent a donation of $100 to the strike fund, but after bending over backwards to be identified as a friend of labor he spun around and lectured the shoemakers on the foolishness and futility of their strike, intoning the perpetual murmur of the manufacturers, "the interests of the manufacturer and the journeymen are identical."

The strike was carried through March on high spirits, but by the beginning of April it was fast losing momentum, and within another two weeks it had subsided. Though a substantial number of manufacturers were paying higher wages by the end of the strike, the shoemakers were completely frustrated in their other goal of getting their employers to sign the bill of wages and thereby accede to the principle that shoemakers collectively had a voice in determining their wages. In this regard, the strikers were defeated partly by the decentralized character of bottoming (enabling manufacturers to get shoes bottomed by outworkers with less organization and militancy than Lynn artisans) and partly by the very economic factors that had caused the strike in the first place. To someone with no means of support except his labor, even low wages are better than no wages. Finally, the manufacturers' ability to lay their hands on the instruments of institutionalized violence (even though the effectiveness of the local police force on their behalf was nullified by the shoemakers) put the coercive power of the state on their side and tipped the balance of power their way. Coming after several decades of social dislocation caused by the growth of industrial capitalism, the Great Strike exposed the class fears and hatreds generated by the rising order. In the expanding marketplace, the manufacturer was both the hunter and the hunted, predator and prey. He sharpened his weapons, knowing that creditors and competitors did the same. Thus when a committee of his employees politely asked that he disarm, he politely refused, and when disorderly bands of employees broke his weapons in the street, he gave them a taste of martial law. For their part, the workers knew that the weapons of competition, though they be aimed at business competitors, struck them first. When it came to businessmen buying cheap and selling dear, employees' livelihoods could only suffer. And unless they could act collectively and affectively in their own cause, each would stand alone, the hunted and the prey. . . .

Conflict Among Lynn's Shoemakers

MARY BLEWETT

. . . This essay examines the relationship between gender and work in the shoe industry in Essex County, Massachusetts, before the Civil War. Large numbers of men and women were employed in the putting-out system of domestic production as the boot and shoe industry of New England expanded prior to 1860. Pre-industrial methods of shoemaking involved an initially close relationship between work and family, production and the home, in which the interrelationships of gender and work can be observed. Men and women shared the work and traditions of artisan life in the family, but each gender experienced work, culture and consciousness in different ways. What were the attitudes of male artisans toward women who worked in shoe production and how did these attitudes shape artisan ideology? Did the cultural traditions and ideology of artisan life reflect or serve the interests of pre-industrial women workers who were drawn into production in the early nineteenth century? How did the differences in gender and work affect the ability of artisans to protest the rise of industrialization?

The pre-industrial phase of New England shoe production was a golden age of artisan life, and shoemakers were central to the rise of worker protest

Mary Blewett, "Early Nineteenth-Century Divisions among Shoemakers: Factory Girls, Homeworkers, and Male Artisans" in *Journal of Social History,* 17 (Winter 1983–84), pp. 221–230, 233–239. Reprinted with permission.

against early industrial capitalism. The group experience of training and work in the apprentice system and its traditions of mutual obligation defined artisan culture. Its locus was the shoe shop where the craft was learned and practiced. Decentralized production allowed groups of male artisans significant control over the process of work and fostered a strong tradition of militant resistance to the reorganization of production by employers. Its mechanics' ideology . . . rested on the labor theory of value and republicanism as a political heritage from the American Revolution. . . . The ideology of artisan culture also included perceptions of gender relationships in the family and at work which defined and separated the roles of men and women and based collective action on the craftsman and householder.

For women workers, the pre-industrial period was a time of submersion in the family and in the family wage economy. The sexual division of labor placed them outside of the vitality of life, politics and work which centered in the artisan shop. While male artisans defended their craft and its traditions before 1860, women workers experienced the cutting edge of change in the reorganization of work after 1780: a sexual division of labor which denied them craft status, the disassociation of their work from the family labor system, the increasingly direct contact of the individual worker with the employer, the isolation and vulnerability of the outworker and the mechanization and centralization of work in the factory. These changes in women's work affected artisan shoemakers. They faced a loss of control over the coordination of production and a loss of wages for the family economy. In the 1850s mechanization and centralization of women's work altered the size and composition of the male work force, a factor which helped precipitate in 1860 the largest pre–Civil War demonstration of labor protest. However, for many women workers in factory production, the artisan tradition of collective resistance represented neither their work nor their cultural experience. This new generation of female factory workers came into conflict with the striking shoemakers of Lynn over the objectives and strategy of the regional strike in 1860. This division of interests weakened labor protest in 1860 and pointed to the conflict between ideology and reality in the gender perceptions of New England artisans. Women shared the work in shoe production with men, but after 1860 they would need to create an ideology to justify labor protest based on their distinct experience. To understand this experience before 1860 will enrich the meaning of worker culture in early industrialization. The submersion of women's work experience within artisan culture has obscured the penetration of home-life and the work process by early capitalism and has sustained the illusion of the early nineteenth-century family as a refuge from the market place. The failure of artisans to perceive and accommodate the interests of women as workers weakened their ability to challenge the reorganization of work by early industrial capitalism.

How did women come to share the work of artisans? . . . Before the expansion of the artisan system, shoemakers had worked alone in the kitchens of their houses (or other people's houses), in an el or an attached shed. This was a domestic setting for work where shared family labor might have evolved as in hosiery making or spinning and weaving in England. However, with the expansion of the artisan system and an increase in production, shoemaking required its own work space to accommodate several men and boys on various levels of the craft. A small out-building called a "ten footer" began to appear in Essex County by the 1780s as a self-contained work area for men. Many wives must have been pleased to rid their kitchens of the clutter, dirt and smell of the shoemaker's paraphenalia. . . .

The motive for the recruitment of women in shoemaking families to new work appears to have been made in the context of a shift in the control of profits as production expanded between 1780 and 1810. Production was expanded by merchant capitalists who bought leather and provided it to shoemakers. The merchant capitalist owned the shoes and marketed them. This control over raw materials meant control of profits as all cordwainers knew, and master shoemakers borrowed capital if they could to purchase leather. Those shoemakers who owned no leather and who accepted work from capitalists had only their labor from which to profit. They divided up the work among the men in their shops and augmented their wage income from labor by recruiting additional family members for work: their women. The male head of the shoemaking family disciplined and controlled women's work in the home. The merchant capitalist, who had no control over the assignment of work in the artisan shop or family, welcomed the new potential for production. As entrepreneurs, they paid no wages directly to women workers and did not need to supervise their work. By adapting to the new work, women added their traditional household labor to their family's income in ways which continued to permit them to combine family and work roles.

Why didn't the apprentices do the sewing of uppers to meet the needs of expanded production? They had learned the skill as part of their apprenticeship, and some did sew uppers whenever bottlenecks in production occurred. Specialization in sewing uppers, however, would have disrupted the apprenticeship system as an orientation to the male world of the artisan and to its work, rituals and hierarchy of subordination and dominance, as well as limiting the various services apprentices provided for the master and journeymen. To use apprentices would not have solved the labor shortage in an expanding market, for in a few years apprentices would become journeymen, no longer available to sew seams. Some more dependable source of new labor was needed, one which the capitalist would accept in the interests of expanded production, yet would not have to pay wages or supervise. The utilization of women in shoemaking families was a solution that would avoid changes in the apprentice system, meet the needs of both capitalist and artisan and threaten no alteration in the traditional patterns of gender formation. The origins of the sexual division of labor in the shoemaking craft was a conscious decision made by artisans and accepted by merchant capitalists to expand production.

Historians of the New England shoe industry have regarded the recruitment of female labor in the late eighteenth century as the natural evolution or inevitable outgrowth of women's involvement in household work or as the fitting of an excess female population in Essex County into a work process which drew on their abilities as needle workers. The recruitment of women in shoemaking families was instead a carefully controlled assignment of work designed to fit the role of women and to maintain gender relationships in the family, while preserving the artisan training system in its social as well as its craft aspect. Women were recruited to only a small part of the work, the sewing of the upper part of the shoe, and not to the craft itself. They were barred from apprenticeships and group work and isolated from the center of artisan life: the shoe shop. The artisan shop has come to be seen by historians as the center of pre-industrial political and cultural life for New England shoemakers and the source of the ideology and consciousness which many regard as representing the origins of the American working class. It was a world of men and boys.

The introduction of the sexual division of labor into an artisan craft represented a major change in the mode of production. Work was redefined and relocated, new words were coined and new procedures devised for supervision. The work assigned to women took on social meanings appropriate to their gender. Female family members adapted their traditional needle skills to hand sew the leather uppers of shoes in their kitchens without disrupting their domestic duties or their child care tasks. Needle work on leather uppers, a relatively clean part of the job, was accompanied by a new tool designed exclusively for women's work: the shoe clamp. The woman shoeworker would not have to straddle a shoemaker's bench, but would use a long, flexible wooden clamp which rested on the floor and which she held between her knees, holding the pieces of shoe upper together and freeing her hands to ply her needle. Her work was given a new name: shoebinding, which became a major category of women's work in the early nineteenth century.

Binders in shoemaking families earned no wages between the 1780s and the 1810s, but they did contribute their labor to family production and to the wage it commanded. The emergence of shoebinding testified to the adaptability and persistence of women's labor in household production. At this time, women in Essex County had few alternatives to hard, seasonal agricultural work or barter to add income to their families. The introduction of the sexual division of labor into an artisan craft was carefully controlled, guaranteeing the subordinate role of women by separating the work of shoebinding from any knowledge of the other various skills of the craft and by maintaining separate work places for men and women. These patterns survived the transformation of the industry into the factory system and, therefore, constituted a fundamental social dimension of work.

Although shoebinders worked in their kitchens where domestic tasks and child care continued, the artisan shop and its demands for work intruded. No work in the shop could proceed without a few pairs of sewn uppers. The binder's work in her kitchen was essential to the timing and pace of production in the shop, and she had to keep ahead of the requirements of the shop workers with a ready supply of sewn uppers. Her kitchen was transformed into a workplace where external demands from the ten footer shaped her time and tasks. The collective nature of men's work in the shoe shop, the locus of artisan culture, supported a militant tradition of resistance to the reorganization of production. This tradition did not mirror the experience of women workers who had no craft status and did not share in the political and religious discussions in the shop. The relationship of binders to this tradition was limited by their isolation from group production and mediated through their role in the family.

There were, however, limits to the capacity of female members of shoemaking families to fulfill the needs of the shoe shop for sewn uppers. Increasing numbers of shoes per lot strained the family labor system. Around 1800, ten to fourteen pairs of shoes made up a unit of production. By 1820 fifty, sixty and seventy pairs per lot were common, as most capitalists had organized cutting operations into central shops. Because shoebinding was typically combined with domestic work, the capacity of the binder who was both wife and mother to complete work on large lots had limits. In a pinch for more labor, shoemakers recruited the wives and daughters of neighbors, but this required some kind of a payment. Gradually after 1810, shoebinding, while still performed in the home, shifted to work paid first in goods (often factory-made textiles) and later in wages, provided to the worker by the shoe boss, and increasingly disassociated from the family labor system. . . .

By the 1830s shoe manufacturers had assumed much of the responsibility for hiring binders for wages and replaced husbands and fathers as employers. Even if her husband made shoes, a binder might work on uppers for ladies' boots while her spouse made coarse work shoes for Southern slaves. This disassociation of women's work from the family labor system affected the ability of the shoemaker to coordinate the work process. The shoe boss assumed responsibility not only for hiring female workers, often from non-shoemaking families, but also directed and coordinated the work process from his central shop. The shoemaker had to wait, sometimes for hours, for the shoe boss to provide him with bound uppers. The shift in the coordination of the work of binding and making to the central shop represented a decline in the power of artisans to exert control over the work process.

The disassociation of shoebinding and shoemaking, the direct payment of wages to the binder and the increasing control of women's work by the shoe boss made it essential for binders to organize themselves in order to protest against their employers. . . . Although these women sought and received the support of organized shoemakers especially in Lynn, the shoebinders created separate societies to represent their interests and acted independently. They did not challenge the sexual division of labor, but saw themselves as women workers unjustly treated by their employers and organized to demand a response to their grievances. They also attempted to utilize the mechanics' ideology in new ways to justify their protest and argue for new rights for women. . . .

By 1833 there were about 1,500 women in Lynn who earned wages as shoebinders. A wage cut prompted over half of them to organize the "Female Society of Lynn and vicinity for the protection and promotion of Female Industry." In their public statements, the shoebinders voiced the mechanics' ideology, blending it with expressions of their grievances as wage earners and using it as a defense of the worth of their labor as female members of artisan families. Most important, however, was their claim to new rights: the right to public action as women and the right to support themselves respectably and independently on their wages, independently in the sense of making a significant contribution to the family wage economy.

The Lynn binders who organized the Female Society met at the Friends' Meetinghouse on December 30, 1833 where, as the *Lynn Record* noted, women as well as men could speak freely in public. They were joined a few days later by 125 binders who met at the Methodist church in neighboring Saugus and adopted the same objectives, ideology and constitution. In the preamble to the society's constitution, the Lynn binders pointed to ". . . a manifest error, a want of justice, and reasonable compensation to the females; which calls imperiously for redress. While the prices of their labour have been reduced, the business of their *employers* has appeared to be improving, and prosperous, enabling them to increase their wealth. *These things ought not so to be!*" Their demand for higher wages was based on the labor theory of value. As workers, they believed they were not earning a just compensation; their independence and respectability was threatened. Furthermore, this economic injustice enriched the shoe boss. This was a violation of the dignity of their labor and a "moral outrage."

To redress their grievances, the shoebinders of Lynn demanded an extension of the equal rights doctrine of the artisan tradition to women. "Equal rights should be extended to all—to the weaker sex as well as the stronger." Many of the women who attended the society's first meeting on December 30, 1833, the preamble claimed, either supported themselves or their families on their earnings as binders and had become dependent on their wage labor. The disadvantages that women experienced "by nature and custom" should not be aggravated by "unnecessary and unjust" treatment as workers. The preamble expressed the belief that ". . . women as well as men, have certain inalienable rights, among which is the right at all times of 'peaceably assembling to consult upon the common good'." In this, the Lynn binders were responding to criticism that they were forming a combination against the manufacturers which endangered the town's prosperity. They replied that the shoe bosses combined together themselves to hold down wages and to pay the binders in store orders for goods. The women in the Lynn society equated their interests as workers with the interests of the community, regarding the welfare of the town as consisting, ". . . not in the aggrandizement of a few individuals, but in the general prosperity and welfare of the industrious and laboring classes."

The preamble went on to criticize the recent reduction in wages for shoebinding which prevented them from obtaining "a comfortable support." This concept represented the shoebinders' claim to a just wage, a feminine version of the "competency" sought by artisans, an income sufficient to support their families and permit a little savings for old age. However, in computing the wage which would earn them their comfortable support, the shoebinders used as a measure—not their work in production—but their duties and responsibilities as female members of artisan families. The shoebinders used their gender roles as the wives, daughters and widows of New England mechanics to insist upon a wage level that would confer dignity and independence on them. They calculated the price of the household services that a wife performed as a seamstress, washwoman, nurse and maid and demanded a wage high enough to cover these expenses. By extending the analogy of wage work into their domestic sphere, the wives of mechanics who bound shoes were bridging over the gap between work and domesticity. For a daughter, wages should be high enough to cover room, board and personal upkeep so as not to constitute a drain upon her father's income nor induce her to leave home for factory work. As for a mechanic's widow with dependents, her wage level should ensure a livelihood without the necessity of applying to the town for poor relief.

To be effective the Lynn shoebinders' society had to organize all working women in the local industry, whatever their attachment to the mechanic's family or dependence on their earnings. However, the ideology which the society's members borrowed from the artisan tradition and which they reshaped to their experiences of gender hierarchy within the family betrayed a contradiction between their demands for equal rights for men and women workers and the calculations of a just wage for women. Equal rights for women as workers suggested the primacy of work; wages computed on the expenses of household services indicated that, in family terms, domestic duties were primary for women. For the Lynn shoebinders, their gender role in the family and in artisan ideology transformed the labor theory of value into a measure of their domestic work.

The artisan shoemakers of Lynn promptly offered their support to the Female Society in early 1834, voting as a group to refuse to take work from any manufacturer not agreeing to the wages demanded by the binders. When the Lynn shoemakers had organized a Society of Journeymen Cordwainers in 1830 to defend the wages and privileges of the craft, they regarded the low wages paid to the shoebinders as an injury to themselves as male heads of families. "Look and see how they [the shoe bosses] have depressed the price of female labor, and reduced it down to almost nothing! This has an effect on us as husbands, as fathers, and as brothers." They perceived the grievances of the binders strictly in family terms. . . .

By the summer of 1834 the Lynn shoebinders' society was in trouble; three-fourths of its members were working for wages below the society's scale or had not paid their dues. One of the society's leaders, probably the President Mary A. Russell, used the *Lynn Record* of June 18 to urge the lagging membership to become "a band of sisters, each considering the welfare of the society as her own peculiar interest." She referred to the example of ". . . that liberty which other females have, that of setting their own prices upon their work." In what appeared to have been a reference to the March 1834 turnouts of the Lowell textile operatives, the writer urged a similar firmness and determination from the binders to become "equally free from oppression." Plans to divide work, share wages during dull times, start a manufacturing cooperative and exhortations to "think seriously, make exertions, be not discouraged" produced little response. . . .

Working women in New England shoe production . . . experienced a sense of consciousness as a gender, defined not only by domesticity but also by their work for wages. Shoebinders did not face a shift of production out of the home, but an assignment of new work for women in the home and its intensification in the outwork system. The sexual division of labor in shoe production reinforced the idea of a separate sphere for women and provided a class basis for the cult of domesticity among working women. By the 1830s, however, the family labor system had given way to the employment of women directly by the shoe boss in the outwork system. Sharing the bonds of womanhood both in work and in their domestic sphere, shoebinders in 1834 tried to organize themselves in terms of a female community of workers committed to self improvement and the improvement of society. Mary Russell actively sought to extend the idea of sisterhood as an organizing principle, but the shoebinders of Lynn could only respond hesitantly. The conditions under which many shoebinders labored—isolated from each other, employed by the shoe boss outside a group labor system and combining wage work with domestic responsibilities—discouraged collective activity. The tensions between their relationship to the artisan system and its equal rights ideology and their subordinate role as females in the family were exposed by their arguments for a just wage for women. Neither the social relations of the artisan family nor the realities of working as a woman for a shoe boss encouraged the shoebinder of Lynn to identify with her working sister in the Lowell mills or conceive of herself as a worker capable of supporting herself who could unite with her peers to protest mistreatment.

The efforts of the Lynn Female Society had limited success in 1834. Payments in store orders were temporarily suspended, but wages for binding shoes never even approached the wages offered to women workers in textile factories. Instead of raising wages to local shoebinders, shoe bosses in Eastern Massachusetts built networks of rural outworkers throughout the region extending into New Hampshire and Maine. By 1837, more women (15,366) were involved in shoe production in Massachusetts than female workers (14,759) in cotton textile factories. The decline in the importance of the shoemaking family as a work unit left wives increasingly dependent on their shoemaker husbands for economic support. As the shoe bosses became more important to the coordination of production and the recruitment of binders, the relationship between the shoemaker and his employer changed. The shoemaker was regarded less and less as a middle-man in the recruitment of outwork for the boss, who now ran the central shop and directed the work of both binder and maker. This change in the relationship between shoeworker and shoe boss plus the pressure on the family wage economy may be underlying reasons for the outbursts of collective activity among Essex County shoemakers in the 1840s.

The decade of the 1840s represented a high point of activism among shoemakers in Eastern Massachusetts, who organized on a regional basis and held conventions with other working men and women. The Cordwainers' Mutual Benefit Society of Lynn began to publish a labor paper, *The Awl*, in 1844 and tried to summon support for the society among women including shoebinders. In the first issue of the *Awl* on July 17, 1844, the editors developed a constituency and a set of objectives which limited and subordinated women's relationship to their organization. Oblivious to the implications for women of the disassociation of shoebinding from the family labor system and into a vulnerable isolation from group work and artisan ideology, the shoemakers' society in the 1840s perceived women as persons whose lives were defined primarily by family and morality. . . .

In the first issue, the clearest statement of the aims of the society was contained in a draft circular to "all brothers of the craft" throughout New England. The organization was seeking uniform wages for shoemaking in all New England shoe towns in order to restore the economic and social status of shoemakers in a society which they perceived as rapidly developing invidious class distinctions. The denial of a competency or reasonable income which would support an artisan's family comfortably and supply for old age threatened the equality and rights which freemen had won in the American Revolution. The society of cordwainers was especially sensitive to the declining status of those whose only wealth lay in the useful pursuit of a trade. The *Awl* championed the fundamental values of manly labor and linked its interests with all mechanics and artisans, as well as with the female operatives in the textile mills of New England, and with all working people, male or female, free or slave, who could not live decently and respectable in the economy of the 1840s.

At a meeting of the society on June 29, 1844, the members agreed to urge "the ladies" to lend their support and influence to the men's organization. Membership in the society was, however, defined by craft. The sexual division of labor prevented women from becoming members by learning the craft, although the society did accept as members three women trained as cordwainers: Mrs. Eliza Tuttle and two female apprentices. The appeal for the presence of the ladies at the society's meetings became a persistent theme in the *Awl* during its year and a half of publication. The presence of these ladies, like the membership of Mrs. Tuttle, was to be used for its exemplary and, more importantly, for its moral influence. These requests for women to attend the society's meetings every Saturday night at the Town Hall were predicated not on their status as wageearners or their work as shoebinders, but on their abilities as wives, mothers and sweethearts to persuade other shoemakers in Lynn to join. The economic interests of most women in the objectives of the society were assumed to be familial: by bettering the wages of men—be they husbands, fathers or sons—women's own interests would be served.

In the December 21 issue of the *Awl*, the editors published under the title, "Woman," a special appeal for female support which illustrated how they viewed the nature of women and the limits this view placed on women's involvement in the activities of the society. Women were perceived as moral beings and were called upon to "hallow and enoble" the objectives of the society. The appeal to them was based on their capacity for self-sacrifice. The editors sought to enlist their energies to serve the interests of others; "the poor and down-trodden" and "her lovely sisters toiling . . . to gain a scanty subsistance." . . . The *Awl* regarded women's power as moral, unselfish and spiritual, not as material, self-interested or political. These attitudes seemed to blind the cordwainers' society to the vulnerability and isolation of shoebinders.

The appeal of the *Awl* for female participation was deeply ambivalent. If women were seen as essentially moral and spiritual, characteristics that suggested gentility and the pious, private virtues that historians have identified as the cult of true womanhood, the ideology of the cordwainers' society pointedly rejected the values of the genteel, non-working classes who by their unearned wealth and leisured lives threatened the basic values of artisan culture. This side of their attitudes toward women revealed a fear of genteel or middle-class social behavior in females within their own families which would unfit them for the useful life of a mechanic's wife. . . .

The cordwainers' society claimed benefit to shoebinders who associated with the organizations, but the advice offered by the society suggests that the cordwainers refused to confront the implications of the isolated situation of most shoebinders in comparison with the collective nature of their own work. The folklore of artisan life in the 1840s and 1850s reflected the growing tensions between the shoemakers and the shoe boss over the quality of work turned into the central shop. Some shoe bosses treated their artisans with careful courtesy, while others did not. Shoemakers expressed resentment against hard bosses like Christopher Robinson of Lynn who tried in the late 1840s to alter the standards of work. Attempts to limit supplies or inspect work still in the shop were stoutly resisted. The cordwainers of Essex County were better able than the individual shoebinder to resist attempts by the shoe boss to control and discipline the work process.

In an early appeal for female participation in the September 11, 1844 issue, the shoebinders were exhorted by the editors of the *Awl* to come to the society's meetings and identify any shoe boss in Lynn who had cheated women by the order system. The order system was an arrangement by which wages were paid in goods rather than in cash, a profitable convenience for merchants and shoe bosses and, according to the *Awl*, one of the greatest evils of the system of production. Widows with dependents were urged to point out the manufacturers who discounted their wages by 10% if they insisted on cash. Name the boss, the appeal went on, so that the world will know him. The strategy of publicly humiliating shoe bosses by focusing the moral power of indignant women on their oppressors did not persuade any shoebinders to come forward. . . .

On the whole, the cordwainers' society of Lynn received little support from shoebinders. Its ideology implied a limited and subordinated role for most women. Its strategy to threaten the shoe bosses with public shame made the individual shoebinders even less likely to make an issue of mis-treatment, fearing a stratagem which would focus the combined anger of Lynn shoe manufacturers on her and deprive her of work.

In the 1840s and 1850s the number of women working as shoebinders in Massachusetts grew rapidly, and by 1855, 32,826 women were recorded as employed in the boot and shoe industry in comparison with 22,850 employed in cotton textiles. The number of women employed by Essex County shoe bosses grew from 7,027 in 1837 to 12,395 in 1855, an increase of 76%. By 1855 shoe manufacturing in Essex County had developed four major centers of outwork: Danvers and South Danvers, Haverhill (located near the New Hampshire border, Lynn and its neighbor Marblehead. These four centers of production accounted for 51% of all females in Massachu-setts who worked in shoe production, and Lynn manufacturers who listed 11,021 women workers in 1855 had developed an extensive outwork system which reached beyond Eastern Massachusetts into Southern New Hamp-shire and Maine.

Low wages, irregular employment and low productivity plagued both the shoebinder and the shoe boss in the outwork system. Binding shoes was often characterized by intensive periods of effort over several weeks' duration followed by long periods of no shoebinding at all. . . . [T]he shoe bosses came to rely on a relatively small group of steady binders for most production, while employing a widespread and numerous group of casual binders whose work was conducted at irregular intervals. Account books from the 1840s also illustrate a further division of labor within the tasks which the binders performed which limited their earnings. A woman might be assigned only part of the work on uppers, for example, only the most poorly paid work of "closing" or sewing up side seams rather than "fitting" or seaming cloth linings into the upper which earned better pay. The debit side of the account books revealed the continuation of the custom of "fur-nishing" by which the binder assumed the costs of thread, needles and lining material, thereby further reducing her wages. Much of women's work on shoes continued to be conducted separate from the family labor system by the wives and daughters of non-shoemaking families: farmers, other artisans, mariners and laborers. Work had not yet left the home, but the home setting of women's work was less and less likely to reverse the traditions and values of the shoemakers' craft.

With the invention of the sewing machine for leather in 1852 and the subsequent introduction of the factory system, the wages and the work available to shoebinders began to decline. But the adaptation of the sewing machine for cloth to stitch leather uppers did not immediately separate home and work for shoebinders. Neither did mechanization of women's work create a large scale factory system. Over the decade between 1855 and 1865, the process of shoe production slowly evolved toward the steam-powered factory, but the work process retained many features of pre-industrial production, including the sexual division of labor. John B. Nichols, who had succeeded in converting the I. M. Singer sewing machine to stitch light leather, went to Lynn in 1852 in the employ of Singer who had sold exclusive rights to lease his new machines in Essex County to three Lynn manufacturers. Nichols organized stitching rooms for them and instructed young women in the use of the leather sewing machine. By 1855 several other sewing machine companies: Grover & Baker, Wheeler & Wilson and Nichols & Bliss, were producing and selling machines for work on leather uppers. Shoebinding as women's needle work in the home seemed to face oblivion.

In the shoe centers of Lynn and Haverhill, the shoebinders organized to resist the introduction of the machines. A. S. Moore, one of Singer's agents in Essex County and the employer of machine operatives in Lynn, faced a committee of angry binders in 1852 who tried to pressure Moore and the women operatives to abandon the machines. In Haverhill shoebinders and shoemakers expressed bitterness at Isaac Harding who had brought the first stitching machines into town in 1853. Some of the women shook their fists in the face of Daniel Goodrich, Harding's partner. The binders were convinced that the machine would destroy their work. Many must have realized that centralized machine operations would force them to choose between their domestic duties and their ability to earn wages. Contributing to their distress was their unfamiliarity with the sewing machine for cloth. The marketing strategy of the early sewing machine companies concentrated on the use of the machines for the manufacture of clothing and shoes, ignoring the potential they would later realize in the domestic market for family sewing. Several experienced Haverhill binders who worked for the firm of Sawyer & Wheeler tried the new machines without success and gave up in despair.

Although the binders were correct to fear mechanization, the system of household production accommodated itself to the introduction of the leather stitching machine. Not all work on uppers was mechanized. Suspicions regarding customer acceptance of machine stitched shoes somewhat retarded mechanization. But if hand work was still available in the home, the wages for shoebinding fell rapidly as the productivity of machine work rose and labor costs declined. In 1860 the piece rate for machine sewing was estimated at one quarter the price of hand work, while the operative earned nearly three times as much as the binder. The shoebinder faced an uncertain future, working more intensively if she could obtain the work and at a severe wage reduction. Some binders rented or purchased leather stitching machines with hand cranks or foot treadles for use at home. Estimates differ on the extent of home use of stitching machines. They were expensive; in the mid-1850s the price ranged between $75 to $125. The most widespread use of home operated machines was apparently in Lynn, Salem and Marblehead where manufacturers rented machines to be used at home. Home use of a machine allowed women workers to continue to combine domestic duties with wage work and escape the discipline and long hours of centralized production. Until the introduction of steam power and the invention of a pegging machine to mechanize the work of shoe-makers, followed in 1862 by the McKay stitcher, home operations by foot power provided work for many women in their homes.

Some of the shoe manufacturers centralized stitching operations by adding a story to central shops where the leather was cut out or had two story buildings constructed to contain the activities of the central shop on the ground floor and the stitching room on the second floor. Stitching was also sub-contracted by the central shop owners to shops like that of John B. Nichols of Lynn which specialized in stitching uppers. The pre-industrial isolation of the female shoeworker from other operations in production was thereby maintained despite centralization. The work force in these little shops of thirty to fifty workers were "girls," that is, young unmarried women who left their homes to work all day at stitching machines. *The Lynn News* estimated in 1855 that there were 1,500 to 1,800 sewing machines in operation and that most of them were run in shops by young women who earned an average weekly wage of about $6.00. Many of these young women were members of local families, but by 1860 a sizeable portion of them had left their homes in the towns of Eastern Massachusetts, New Hampshire, Maine and the Maritime Provinces of Canada to board with families in Lynn and Haverhill and work for the attractive wages in the shoe shops. In the 1850s native-born, young New England women were abandoning work in the textile mills in the Merrimack Valley for employment in the shoe shops of Essex County.

The depression years of the late 1850s created a crisis in the rapidly changing New England shoe industry. The crisis involved a collapse in the pre-industrial wage patterns of the family economy as shoe manufacturing moved toward mechanization, centralization and the factory system. In the early 1850s an expanding market for boots and shoes in the developing West had drawn additional male workers into the process of bottoming: the attachment by hand of machine or hand-sewn uppers to soles. Heeling and finishing operations were reorganized and performed separately along with cutting operations in the central shops. Groups of workmen in the surrounding towns of Essex County served by a network of teamsters bottomed shoes for Lynn and Haverhill shoe bosses, but an even more extensive rural outwork system, reaching into Central New Hampshire and Southern Maine and served by railroad, supplied additional male workers for bottoming.

Machine productivity by female factory operatives increased the demand for bottomers, and Irish and German immigrants as well as migrants from New England came to the shoe towns of Massachusetts, crowding the local labor market. While the numbers of men who worked as bottomers increased, stimulated by machine productivity, the sex ratio of male to female shoeworker sharply reversed. The numbers of women employed in Massachusetts shoe production dropped off steadily in the 1850s. In Lynn the number of females employed on shoes shrank sharply by 41% between 1850 and 1860. The mechanization of women's work intensified the hard conditions of labor for both men and women involved in outwork in Essex

County. The productivity of the new machine stitchers had stimulated the demand for bottomers, while cutting the demand for shoebinders. By contemporary estimates, one factory girl at her stitching machine could supply enough work for twenty bottomers, while replacing eleven binders. The woman who operated a sewing machine at home still faced the custom of "furnishing," that is, providing thread, needles and lining materials. A considerable gap developed after 1855 between the wages of factory operatives and the wages of women working at home whether by hand or by machine.

Downward pressure on wages during the hard times after 1857 cut sharply into the shoemaker's family wage and helped precipitate the largest American demonstration of labor protest prior to the Civil War. A regional strike, beginning in February 1860 and spearheaded by activities in Natick and Lynn, disrupted production. The values and patterns of the pre-industrial family economy confronted the emerging factory system. This confrontation divided not only the workers and their employers, but also divided the strikers into groups promoting the family wage economy through the artisan tradition and groups of female factory operatives whose place in centralized production and whose status as temporary residents of the shoe city created a different set of interests in the 1860 strike.

The strikers in Lynn, led by the bottomers, hoped to organize the country shoemakers to refuse outwork, while they simultaneously halted production in the Lynn shops. Important to this strategy was the interruption of teamster activities which carried sewn uppers and cut soles to country workshops. Significantly, the first serious conflict in Lynn involved express teams which carried shoe uppers machine-sewn by female factory workers to Marblehead bottomers for the John Wooldredge Company. Wooldredge had pioneered both the adoption of the Singer sewing machine in 1852 and the introduction of steam power in 1858 for heeling and stitching operations. His firm symbolized the emerging factory system.

The strike leadership in Lynn had been considering the organization of the 3,000 shoebinders and stitchers as an auxiliary force to encourage community support and boycott uncooperative shoe bosses. Their decision to organize women workers was made after a violent incident on February 23 between strikers and expressmen which provoked widespread regional criticism in the press, precipitated the arrival of outside police forces and threatened to undermine the crucial support of shoemakers in the neighboring towns of Essex County for the strike. In 1860 the Lynn strike committee attempted to utilize the moral stature of women for the same family and community purposes as had the Lynn cordwainers' society in the 1840s. Women's participation would restore morality to the strike, help generate community support in Lynn and throughout Essex County and mitigate criticism. The involvement of local women would erase the images of violence and disorder and emphasize the nature of the strike as a defense of the New England family.

The strike committee in Lynn was not, however, prepared to acknowledge or represent the interests of the female factory operatives whose leaders quickly seized control of the women's meetings. The interests of these women workers, who were nearly 40% of the female work force in Lynn by 1860, conflicted with artisan conception of the family wage economy. The factory operatives disagreed with the advancement of the wages of male shoeworkers as the only objective in the strike and convinced the women workers of Lynn to strike for higher wages as binders and stitchers. They also began to organize women workers in the neighboring towns of Danvers, Newburyport and Marblehead. Realizing the importance of their strategic position to stop work in centralized production, the factory girls in Lynn proposed a coalition with female homeworkers to raise wages in both categories of work: homework for wives and mothers and factory work for single girls. This alliance of gender represented a bridge between the pre-industrial patterns of women's work and the developing factory system. Unity as a gender would protect the wages of the married and the unmarried, the homeworkers and the shop girls, by linking the cause of working women to the new sources of wages and power in factory work. Mechanization and centralization of women's work had meant higher wages for factory workers, but reduced the numbers of women employed, relegated wives and mothers to homework and depressed the wages of outworkers. For homeworkers, an alliance with the young factory girls represented a real chance in 1860 for women working at home to make a valuable connection with the new industrial workers. In return, factory girls could anticipate marriage and a chance to work at home for decent wages. The family wage economy would be protected by a coalition of women workers acting together on behalf of their own interests.

The factory girls, led by twenty-one year old Clara Brown, a native of Massachusetts, who boarded in Lynn with a shoemaker's family, won several crucial votes on raising women's wages in the strike meetings held by Lynn women. They challenged the male strike committee for leadership of the women workers and to articulation of their interests. The factory girls identified with other women in the industry as workers and as a gender, not unlike the brothers of the craft. The ideology of artisan life did not figure in their vision of an alliance of women workers at home and in the shops, nor did they identify with the bottomers on familial or on ideological grounds. Conscious of the power of factory stitchers in this alliance whose productivity could shut down production in the industry and halt outwork, Clara Brown declared: "Girls of Lynn, . . . strike at once . . . Don't work your machines; let them lie still until we get all we ask." At a later meeting she challenged: ". . . we've got the bosses where we can do as we please with 'em. If we don't take the work, what can the bosses do?"

The male strike committee quickly moved to oppose this unwelcome development. The committee members failed, however, to persuade the women at a meeting on February 28 to reconsider the list of wage demands which had been adopted the night before: a wage list which in the eyes of the striking shoemakers overvalued factory stitching and jeopardized homework. They feared that if the women's wages were raised, all stitching of uppers would be centralized in factories and homework eliminated. For the bottomers, the best protection for the family wage lay in obtaining higher wages for men's work and maintaining homework for women. In a bold move, the strike committee and its supporters among the women home-workers ignored the high wage list adopted by votes taken at several of the women's meetings and substituted a lower list of wages which they circulated as the official wage list for the women workers of Lynn to sign. On March 2 the supporters of the men's strike committee and the factory girls confronted each other at a tumultuous meeting. James Dillon, representing the bottomers, pleaded for the support of the women as wives and mothers of shoemakers and appealed to them not to alienate the bosses of the stitching shops by demanding an "unfair" increase in wages. Other speakers dismissed the shop girls as interested only in money and in "the right to switch a long-tailed skirt [extravagant dress]." Wage decisions, it was argued at the March 2 meeting, should be made by "sober, and discreet women" and not by "laughing" and "thoughtless girls." Clara Brown countered by insisting that the machine girls of Lynn had the power to protect homeworkers, but that the factory girls would only strike for "something worth having." She pointed out that the low wage list prepared by the homeworkers actually cut wages on factory work. Despite her warnings, representatives of the bottomers' committee persuaded the majority of the women at the meeting to reject the high wage list and the factory girls, accept their recommendations on behalf of the family and community in Lynn and join the striking men in great show of community support for the strike.

The legendary parade of striking women on a snowy March day through the streets of Lynn represented a great victory for the defenders of de-centralized production and for the artisan tradition in Lynn. The images of the women's procession printed in the pages of *Frank Leslie's Illustrated Newspaper* have come to epitomize the involvement of women in the 1860 strike, but these sketches obscured the battle which took place over the relationship of women workers to the strike. The political stance of the majority of the women workers who rejected the strategy of the factory girls and supported the bottomers was reflected in the familial values on one of their banners:

> Weak in physical strength but strong in moral courage, we dare to battle
> for the right, shoulder to shoulder with our fathers, husbands and brothers.

The decision of the homeworkers to support the men's strike committee was taken at the risk of ignoring the implications of mechanization, the factory system and the potential of the shop girls who, as workers in centralized production, represented the reorganization of industrial life in Lynn. Many Lynn women continued to support the bottomers until the strike slowly fell apart in late March, while the factory girls who boarded in Lynn returned to work or to their homes.

The bottomers of Lynn had fought in 1860 to maintain the traditions and ideology of decentralized production, including women's work in the home. The artisan ideology had operated successfully to unite the heterogeneous work force of male workers—rural migrants, Irish, Germans and shoemakers in country shops and shoe towns—in the 1850s, but cut off the new female factory workers from contributing to labor protest. The leaders of the Lynn strike failed to perceive or respond to the strategic potential of female machine operators in centralized production and had ignored and opposed their articulated interests. The perceptions which shoe-making artisans had developed of work and gender made it difficult for them to regard women as fellow-workers outside of family relationships, to include them in the ideology and politics built on artisan life or see in the experience of working women what awaited all workers as capitalism in the New England shoe industry moved toward the factory system. . . .

This overview of changes in women's work in New England shoe production and the relationship of women shoeworkers to the artisan tra-dition suggests that tension between women workers and the family values of artisan culture remained constant and unresolved as work reorganized during the shift toward industrialization from 1780 to 1860. Contradictions between perceptions of the proper gender role for women in the family and their consciousness as workers in production prolonged these tensions for women workers into the early factory system and the 1860 strike. This struggle, most visible during moments of labor protest, had been initiated by the recruitment of women into production in the artisan system and maintained by the differences in the location of work and the exposure of the individual worker to the increasing control of the work process by the employer. For the most part, women shoeworkers negotiated those tensions between family and work within the value system of artisan ideology, but in doing so they built limits into their consciousness as workers and into their ability to act together as women to defend their interests or claim new rights. The gender perceptions of artisan ideology as articulated by male shoeworkers in antebellum New England defined the role of women primarily as family members and as moral agents in society. Gender-based ideology and work experience cut women off from the most vital tradition of collective resistance in the early nineteenth century.

✦ F U R T H E R   R E A D I N G

Mary H. Blewett, *Men, Women, and Work: Class, Gender, and Protest in the New England Shoe Industry, 1780–1910* (1988)

Alan Dawley, *Class and Community: The Industrial Revolution in Lynn* (1976)

Thomas Dublin, *Women and Work: The Transformation of Work and Community in Lowell, Massachusetts, 1826–1860* (1979)

Paul G. Fahler, *Mechanics and Manufacturers in the Early Industrial Revolution: Lynn, Massachusetts, 1780–1860* (1981)

Philip S. Foner, ed., *The Factory Girls* (1977)

Brian Greenberg, *Worker and Community: Response to Industrialization in a Nine-teenth-Century American City, Albany, New York, 1850–1884* (1985)

Susan Hirsch, *Roots of the American Working Class: The Industrialization of Crafts in Newark, 1800–1860* (1978)

James L. Huston, "Facing an Angry Labor: The Americn Public Interprets the Shoemakers' Strike of 1860," *Civil War History* 28 (1982), 197–212

Gary Kulik, "Pawtucket Village and the Strike of 1824: The Origins of Class Conflict in Rhode Island," *Radical History Review* 17 (1978), 5–37

Bruce Laurie, *Artisans into Workers* (1989)

———, *Working People of Philadelphia, 1800–1850* (1980)

David Montgomery, *Beyond Equality: Labor and the Radical Republicans, 1862–1872* (1967)

———, "The Shuttle and the Cross: Weavers and Artisans in the Kensington Riots of 1844," *Journal of Social History* 5 (1972), 411–446

———, "The Working Classes of the Pre-Industrial City, 1780–1830," *Labor History* 9 (1968), 3–22

Jonathan Prude, *The Coming of the Industrial Order: Town and Factory Life in Rural Massachusetts, 1810–1860* (1983)

Howard Rock, *Artisans of the New Republic: The Tradesmen of New York City in the Age of Jefferson* (1979)

Stephen J. Ross, *Workers on the Edge: Work, Leisure, and Politics in Industrializing Cincinnati, 1878–1890* (1985)

Christine Stansell, *City of Women: Sex and Class in New York, 1789–1860* (1986)

William A. Sullivan, "The Industrial Revolution and the Factory Operative in Pennsylvania," *Pennsylvania Magazine of History and Biography* 78 (1954), 476–494

E. P. Thompson, "Time, Work-Discipline, and Industrial Capitalism," *Past and Present* 38 (1967), 56–97

Daniel J. Walkowitz, *Worker City, Company Town: Iron and Cotton-Worker Protest in Troy and Cohoes, New York, 1855–1884* (1978)

Anthony F. C. Wallace, *Rockdale: The Growth of an American Village in the Early Industrial Revolution* (1978)

Caroline Ware, *The Early New England Cotton Manufacture* (1931)

Norman Ware, *The Industrial Worker, 1840–1860* (1924)

Sean Wilentz, *Chants Democratic: New York City and the Rise of the American Working Class, 1788–1850* (1984)

CHAPTER
4

Slavery and the Transition
to Free Labor

᛭

*Artisans' struggle against the factory system proved to be a central theme in
northern industrial society, while slavery and emancipation defined southern economic and social life. Historians now recognize that cotton pickers, cane cutters,
household servants, and slave carpenters were also part of working-class America. So too were the tenant farmers, sharecroppers, and farm laborers who
emerged from the southern agricultural economy after the Civil War. Black labor
had built the antebellum southern economy, and its cotton exports generated the
single greatest source of capital that industrialized America.*

*But was the slave system of the American South merely a more exploitative
form of northern "wage slavery"? Were plantation owners simply agricultural
capitalists who availed themselves of a particularly low-cost class of laborers?
And what did the slaves think of their own servitude? How did they resist, and
how did they accommodate the will of their masters? Historians have debated
these issues for years. Many now think of the antebellum South as a society
quite different from that of the North, and one characterized by its own peculiar
set of social relations. Some masters did hire out their slaves by the month or
year to mines, docks, and workshops, but most considered plantation agriculture
the highest and best use of their human property because it insured their political and social dominance in a society fundamentally at odds with that of the
bourgeois, capitalist North.*

*The plantation ruling class could hardly be expected to relinquish its power
voluntarily, and it took a war of revolutionary proportions to abolish slavery in
the American South once and for all. Although the Union armies freed the
slaves, the labor question formed the heart of Reconstruction politics in the years
immediately after the war. A bitter conflict over the character and control of agricultural labor became central to the meaning of blacks' freedom and emancipation. Would the former slaves become peasant proprietors cultivating their own
land, or rural wage laborers supervised by old-regime slavemasters? Would
women be forced to work in the fields, as they had under slavery, or would
their labor be of a more domestic sort? And finally, would the former slaves*

*have access to education, the franchise, and political organizations that repre-
sented their own interests? The outcome of this intensely fought struggle, in
which northern capital and the federal government had a significant stake,
would prove decisive in shaping the class structure and the political life of the
southern states for generations afterward.*

✣ *D O C U M E N T S*

Plantation management was a complicated task, involving the coordination of
many types of labor. Planters often kept detailed operational records in diary
and account books. A page from such a log, listing slaves, animals, and other
tools of production, appears as the first document. In the second document, Solomon Northup, a free black kidnapped into slavery, describes cotton planting
and harvesting on the Bayou Boeuf in Avoyelles Parish, Louisiana. While both
sexes engaged in such field work, planters designated some jobs as "women's
work," as is seen in the third document, which comprises selections from the
oral histories that elderly ex-slaves offered federal historians in the 1930s. The
fourth document, a planter's advice on rearing slave children, sustains abolitionists' charges that masters bred slaves for the market in the Old South. But not
all slaves worked on plantations; the black abolitionist Frederick Douglass had
been hired out as a shipyard apprentice while still a slave. In the fifth document,
he shows how competition with slave laborers kindled a racist response among
those white workers whose wages they undercut.

The last three selections illustrate the difficulty of creating a class of free
wage laborers in the postwar South. The sixth document records one way in
which northern unionists sought to instill the virtues of "free labor" among the
former slaves. Here Captain Charles Soule addresses the recently freed population of Orangeburg District, South Carolina, on their responsibilities as wage laborers. But his advice on the rewards of hard work contrasts sharply with the
sentiments expressed in the seventh document, a petition to the president of the
United States from the freedmen of Edisto Island, South Carolina. The poverty
and inequality endemic to the sharecropping system are revealed in the final document, Ned Cobb's account of his life working on shares in the second decade
of the twentieth century.

A Record of Plantation Management, 1850

**Daily Records of Passing Events on *Pleasant Hill* Plantation During the Week
Commencing on *22* Day of *Sept.*, 185*0*, *Jones* Overseer***

Sunday

Monday   *A very dry time and verry warm. Waggon went to Clinton with 6
                Bales Cotton & 5 Mules & Back*

Tuesday   *A verry warm and dry day wanting rain verry much. Finished cutting
                Hay in Orchard to day verry healthy in Country*

Wednesday

Thursday   *A verry warm dry dusty day, Cotton wanting rain verry much, open-
                ing two fast, I had my Cogs put away in oat house, Put one Man to
                David Jacksons Jack I hear of but little Sickness*

Friday   *A shower of rain after noon with a good deal of Thunder. I went to
                saw Mill with one waggon after plank for fences, 3 Boys pressed 6
                Bales & broke the ferrale. The Cotton pickers lossed about two hours
                by the rain*

Saturday

---

* Handwritten entries appear in italics.

Daily Records of Cotton Picked on _Pleasant Hill_ Plantation During the Week Commencing on _21st_ Day of _Octr._, 1850, _Jones_ Overseer

NAME	NO.	MONDAY	TUESDAY	WEDNESDAY	THURSDAY	FRIDAY	SATURDAY	Week's Picking Brought Forward
Sandy	1	Ginning	Pressing	Ginning	Ginning	Ginning	Ginning	
Scott	2	Clearing	Pressing	Clearing	Clearing	Hauling corn		64
Solomon	3	Clearing	Hauling rails	Clearing	Gone to Clinton	Hauling		54
Bill	4	Clearing	Do	Clearing	Clearing	Hauling		30
Jerry	5	Clearing	Clearing	Clearing	Clearing	Do Do		90
Isaac	6	Clearing	Clearing	Clearing	Clearing	Do Do		70
Jim	7	Sick	Sick	Sick	Sick	Sick		Sick
Dotson	8	Gone after shoes	Clearing	Clearing	Clearing	Ho corn		60

The Planter's Annual Record of his Negroes upon *Pleasant Hill* Plantation, During the year 1850, *E. J. Capell* Overseer

MALES

NAME	AGE	VALUE AT COMMENCEMENT OF THE YEAR	VALUE AT END OF THE YEAR
John	70	$ 50.00	75.00
Tom	49	1000.00	1200.00
Sandy	38	600.00	800.00
Edmund	35	1000.00	1300.00
Jerry	40	700.00	950.00
Solomon	38	700.00	950.00
William	24	1000.000	1100.00
Charles	10	500.00	650.00
Tom	5	250.00	275.
Monroe	4	200.00	225.
Aaron	3	175.00	200
Jerry	1	75.00	100

FEMALES

NAME	AGE	VALUE AT COMMENCEMENT OF THE YEAR	VALUE AT END OF THE YEAR
Hannah	60	$100.00	125.00
Mary	34	800.00	900.00
Fanny	23	800.00	900.00
Rachel Sen.	32	675.00	750.00
Lucy	28	600.00	750.00
Azaline	13	600.00	700.00
Sarah	9	350.00	450.00
Harriet	8	300.00	400.00
Melissa	3	100.00	125.00
Carolina	3	150.00	150.00
Laura	1	100.00	125.00

The Planter's Statement of the Expenses of *Pleasant Hill* Plantation, During the Year 185_0_, ——— Overseer

	TO WHOM, HOW, WHEN AND WHERE PAID, &c.	SUM
Overseer's wages,	To Tom, Cash, Febry 1st Paid at home	10.00
	To R. M. Jenkins at Thickwood Precinct on	
Taxes,	27th of January 1851 for 1850	53.00
Pork, bacon, &c.,	None purchased	
	To 3 Barrels of Molasses @ 21¢ To Clauss	
Corn, flour, &c.,	& McCombs	25.20
	B Sara on the 7th Feby	
	To 10 New Plows part in Centi & part at	
Implements & tools,	home Jan 1st	51.00
	1 Two horse Waggon 1 Cart & Sundries	
	Septr 30th	140.00
	1 Sett Harness 1 Sett Cart Do	
	1 Bellows for Shop Oct. 30th	60.00
Bale rope & bagging,	To Cash paid for 477½ yds Rope	33.14
	" 　　　for 445 yds. Bagging	56.60
Blacksmith, carpenter		
&c.,	To Cash paid Carpenter	190.00
	Cash paid Blacksmith	7.25
Physician and		
apothecary,	To Cash paid J. R. Caulfield & Drug Store	21.00

The Slave Solomon Northup's View of Cotton Planting and Harvesting, 1854

. . . The ground is prepared by throwing up beds or ridges, with the plough—back-furrowing, it is called. Oxen and mules, the latter almost exclusively, are used in ploughing. The women as frequently as the men perform this labor, feeding, currying, and taking care of their teams, and in all respects doing the field and stable work, precisely as do the ploughboys of the North.

The beds, or ridges, are six feet wide, that is, from water furrow to water furrow. A plough drawn by one mule is then run along the top of the ridge or center of the bed, making the drill, into which a girl usually drops the seed, which she carries in a bag hung round her neck. Behind her comes a mule and harrow, covering up the seed, so that two mules, three slaves, a plough and harrow, are employed in planting a row of cotton. This is done in the months of March and April. Corn is planted in February. When there are no cold rains, the cotton usually makes its appearance in a week. In the course of eight or ten days afterwards the first hoeing is commenced. This is performed in part, also, by the aid of the plough and mule. The plough passes as near as possible to the cotton on both sides, throwing the furrow from it. Slaves follow with their hoes, cutting up the grass and cotton, leaving hills two feet and a half apart. This is called scraping cotton. In two weeks more commences the second hoeing. This time the furrow is thrown towards the cotton. Only one stalk, the largest, is now left standing in each hill. In another fortnight it is hoed the third time, throwing the furrow towards the cotton in the same manner as before, and killing all the grass between the rows. About the first of July, when it is a foot high or thereabouts, it is hoed the fourth and last time. Now the whole space between the rows is ploughed, leaving a deep water furrow in the center. During all these hoeings the overseer or driver follows the slaves on horseback with a whip. . . . The fastest hoer takes the lead row. He is usually about a rod in advance of his companions. If one of them passes him, he is whipped. If one falls behind or is a moment idle, he is whipped. In fact, the lash is flying from morning until night, the whole day long. The hoeing season thus continues from April until July, a field having no sooner been finished once, than it is commenced again.

In the latter part of August begins the cotton picking season. At this time each slave is presented with a sack. A strap is fastened to it, which goes over the neck, holding the mouth of the sack breast high, while the bottom reaches nearly to the ground. Each one is also presented with a large basket that will hold about two barrels. This is to put the cotton in when the sack is filled. The baskets are carried to the field and placed at the beginning of the rows.

When a new hand, one unaccustomed to the business, is sent for the first time into the field, he is whipped up smartly, and made for that day to pick as fast as he can possibly. At night it is weighed, so that his capability in cotton picking is known. He must bring in the same weight each night following. If it falls short, it is considered evidence that he has been laggard, and a greater or less number of lashes is the penalty.

An ordinary day's work is two hundred pounds. A slave who is accustomed to picking, is punished, if he or she brings in a less quantity than that. There is a great difference among them as regards this kind of labor. Some of them seem to have a natural knack, or quickness, which enables them to pick with great celerity, and with both hands, while others, with whatever practice or industry, are utterly unable to come up to the ordinary standard. Such hands are taken from the cotton field and employed in other business. Patsey, of whom I shall have more to say, was known as the most remarkable cotton picker on Bayou Bœuf. She picked with both hands and with such surprising rapidity, that five hundred pounds a day was not unusual for her.

Each one is tasked, therefore, according to his picking abilities, none, however, to come short of two hundred weight. I, being unskillful always in that business, would have satisfied my master by bringing in the latter quantity, while on the other hand, Patsey would surely have been beaten if she failed to produce twice as much. . . .

The hands are required to be in the cotton field as soon as it is light in the morning, and, with the exception of ten or fifteen minutes, which is given them at noon to swallow their allowance of cold bacon, they are not permitted to be a moment idle until it is too dark to see, and when the moon is full, they often times labor till the middle of the night. They do not dare to stop even at dinner time, nor return to the quarters, however late it be, until the order to halt is given by the driver.

The day's work over in the field, the baskets are "toted," or in other words, carried to the gin-house, where the cotton is weighed. No matter how fatigued and weary he may be—no matter how much he longs for sleep and rest—a slave never approaches the gin-house with his basket of cotton but with fear. If it falls short in weight—if he has not performed the full task appointed him, he knows that he must suffer. And if he has exceeded it by ten or twenty pounds, in all probability his master will measure the next day's task accordingly. So, whether he has too little or too much, his approach to the gin-house is always with fear and trembling. Most frequently they have too little, and therefore it is they are not anxious to leave the field. After weighing, follow the whippings; and then the baskets are carried to the cotton house, and their contents stored away like hay, all hands being sent in to tramp it down. If the cotton is not dry, instead of taking it to the gin-house at once, it is laid upon platforms, two feet high, and some three times as wide, covered with boards or plank, with narrow walks running between them.

This done, the labor of the day is not yet ended, by any means. Each one must then attend to his respective chores. One feeds the mules, another the swine—another cuts the wood, and so forth; besides, the packing is all done by candle light. Finally, at a late hour, they reach the quarters, sleepy and overcome with the long day's toil. Then a fire must be kindled in the cabin, the corn ground in the small hand-mill, and supper, and dinner for the next day in the field, prepared. All that is allowed them is corn and bacon, which is given out at the corncrib and smoke-house every Sunday morning. Each one receives, as his weekly allowance, three and a half pounds of bacon, and corn enough to make a peck of meal. That is all— no tea, coffee, sugar, and with the exception of a very scanty sprinkling now and then, no salt. . . .

Twentieth-Century Women Recall Their Work Lives in Slavery, 1930s

. . . I had to do everythin' dey was to do on de outside. Work in de field, chop wood, hoe corn, till sometime I feels like my back surely break. I done everythin' 'cept split rails. I never did split no rails.

This race coming up now don't know nothing 'bout hard work. Over there, see a road all turned up and you would see men and women both throwing up dirt and rocks; the men would haul it off and the women would take picks and things and get it up. You could, any day see a woman, a whole lot of 'em making on a road. Could look up and see ten women up over dar on the hill plowing and look over the other way and see ten more. I have done ever thing on a farm what a man done 'cept cut wheat.

I split rails like man. I used a iron wedge drove into the wood with a maul.

Marster Boles didn't have many slave on de farm, but lots in brickyard. I toted bricks and put 'em down where dey had to be. Six bricks each load all day. I fired de furnace for three years. Standin' front wid hot fire on my face. Hard work, but God was with me.

At night de men chops wood and hauls poles to build fences and de women folks has to spin four cuts of thread and make all de clothes. Some has to card cotton to make quilts and some weave and knits stockin's. Marse give each one a chore to do at night and iffen it warn't did when we went to bed, we's whipped. One time I fells plumb asleep befo' I finished shellin' some corn.

My young mistress name Catherine. When her marry, I was give to them for a housemaid, 'cause I was trim and light complected lak you see I is dis very day. Young missie say, "You come in my room Delia, I wants to see if I can put up wid you." I goes in dat room, winter time mind you, and Miss Charlotte sets down befo' de fire. Well, she allowed to me, "Delia, put kettle water on de fire." So I does in a jiffy. Her next command was: "Would you please be so kind as to sweep and tidy up de room?" I do all dat, then she say, "You is goin' to make maid, a good one!" She give a silvery giggle and says, "I just had you put on dat water for to see if you was goin' to make any slop. No, No! You didn't spill a drop, you ain't goin' to make no sloppy maid, you just fine." Then her call her mother in. "See how pretty Delia's made dis room, look at them curtains, draw back just right, observe de pitcher, and de towels on de rack of de washstand, my I'm proud of her!" She give old mistress a hug and a kiss and thank her for de present. Dat present was me. De happiness of dat minute is on me to dis day.

Dey was a big weavin' room where de blankets was wove, and cloth for de winter clothes. Linda Herndon and Milla Edwards was de head weavers; dey looked after de weavin' of de fancy blankets. De cardin' and spinnin' room was full of niggers. I can hear dem spinnin' wheels now turnin' round and saying hum-m-m-m, hum-m-m-m.

Mammy Rachel stayed in de dyein' room. She knew every kind of root, bark, leaf, and berry dat made red, blue, green, or whatever color she wanted. Dey had a big shelter where de dye pots set over de coals. Mammy Rachel would fill de pots with water, den she put in de roots, bark and stuff and boil de juice out. Den she strain it and put in de salt and vinegar to set de color. After de wool and cotton done been carded and spun to thread, Mammy take de hanks and drop dem in de pot of boilin' dye. She stir dem round and lift dem up an down with a stick, and when she hang dem up on de line in de sun, dey was every color of de rainbow. When dey dripped dry dey was sent to de weavin' room.

When I was 13 years old my ol' mistress put me wid a doctor who learned me how to be a midwife. Dat was 'cause so many women on de plantation was catchin' babies. I stayed wid dat doctor, Dr. McGill his name was, for 5 years. I got to be good. Got so he'd sit down an' I'd do all de work.

When I come home, I made a lot o' money for old miss. Lots of times, didn't sleep regular or git my meals on time for three–four days. Cause when dey call, I always went. Brought as many white as culled children. I's brought lots of 'em an' I ain't never lost a case. You know why. It's cause I used my haid. When I'd go in, I'd take a look at de women, an' if it was beyond me, I'd say, "Dis is a doctor case. Dis ain't no case for a midwife. You git a doctor." An' dey'd have to get one. I'd jes' stan' before de lookin' glass, an I wouldn't budge. Dey couldn't make me.

A Planter on Child Rearing, 1836

I have a nurse appointed to superintend all my little negroes, and a nursery built for them. If they are left to be protected by their parents, they will most assuredly be neglected. I have known parents take out an allowance for their children and actually steal it from them, to purchase articles at some shop. Besides, when they would be honest to their offspring, from their other occupations, they have not the time to attend to them properly. The children get their food irregularly, and when they do get it, it is only half done. They are suffered, by not having one to attend to them, to expose themselves; and hence many of the deaths which occur on our plantations.

I have just stated that I have a nursery for my little negroes, with an old woman or nurse to superintend and cook for them, and to see that their clothes and bedding are well attended to. She makes the little ones, generally speaking, both girls and boys, mend and wash their own clothes, and do many other little matters, such as collecting litter for manure, &c. In this they take great pleasure, and it has the tendency to bring them up to industrious habits. The nurse also cooks for them three times a day; and she always has some little meat to dress for them, or the clabber or sour milk from the dairy to mix their food. In *sickness* she sees that they are well attended to; and from having many of them together, one is taught to wait upon the other. My little negroes are consequently very healthy; and from pursuing the plan I have laid down, I am confident that I raise more of them, than where a different system is followed.

Frederick Douglass Confronts Working-Class Racism, 1836

. . . Very soon after I went to Baltimore to live, Master Hugh succeeded in getting me hired to Mr. William Gardiner, an extensive ship-builder on Fell's Point. I was placed there to learn to calk, a trade of which I already had some knowledge, gained while in Mr. Hugh Auld's ship-yard. Gardiner's, however, proved a very unfavorable place for the accomplishment of the desired object. Mr. Gardiner was that season engaged in building two large man-of-war vessels, professedly for the Mexican government. These vessels were to be launched in the month of July of that year, and in failure thereof Mr. Gardiner would forfeit a very considerable sum of money. So, when I entered the ship-yard, all was hurry and driving. There were in the yard about one hundred men; of these, seventy or eighty were regular carpenters—privileged men. There was no time for a raw hand to learn anything. Every man had to do that which he knew how to do, and in entering the yard Mr. Gardiner had directed me to do whatever the carpenters told me to do. This was placing me at the beck and call of about seventy-five men. I was to regard all these as my masters. Their word was to be my law. My situation was a trying one. I was called a dozen ways in the space of a single minute. I needed a dozen pairs of hands. Three or four voices would strike my ear at the same moment. It was "Fred, come help me to cant this timber here,"—"Fred, come carry this timber yonder,"—"Fred, bring that roller here,"—"Fred, go get a fresh can of water,"—"Fred, come help saw off the end of this timber,"—"Fred, go quick and get the crow-bar,"—"Fred, hold on the end of this fall,"— "Fred, go to the blacksmith's shop and get a new punch,"—"Halloo, Fred! run and bring me a cold-chisel,"—"I say, Fred, bear a hand, and get up a fire under the steam-box as quick as lightning,"—"Hullo, nigger! come turn this grindstone,"—"Come, come; move, move! and *bowse* this timber forward,"—"I say, darkey, blast your eyes! why don't you heat up some pitch?"—"Halloo! halloo! halloo! (three voices at the same time)"—"Come here; go there; hold on where you are. D—n you, if you move I'll knock your brains out!" Such, my dear reader, is a glance at the school which was mine during the first eight months of my stay at Gardiner's ship-yard. At the end of eight months Master Hugh refused longer to allow me to remain with Gardiner. The circumstance which led to this refusal was the committing of an outrage upon me, by the white apprentices of the ship-yard. The fight was a desperate one, and I came out of it shockingly mangled. I was cut and bruised in sundry places, and my left eye was nearly knocked out of its socket. The facts which led to this brutal outrage upon me illustrate a phase of slavery which was destined to become an important element in the overthrow of the slave system, and I may therefore state them with some minuteness. That phase was this—the conflict of slavery with the interests of white mechanics and laborers. In the country this conflict was not so apparent; but in cities, such as Baltimore, Richmond, New Orleans, Mobile, etc., it was seen pretty clearly. The slaveholders, with a craftiness peculiar to themselves, by encouraging the enmity of the poor laboring white man against the blacks, succeeded in making the said white man almost as much a slave as the black slave himself. . . .

Until a very little while before I went there, white and black carpenters worked side by side in the ship-yards of Mr. Gardiner, Mr. Duncan, Mr. Walter Price and Mr. Robb. Nobody seemed to see any impropriety in it. Some of the blacks were first-rate workmen and were given jobs requiring the highest skill. All at once, however, the white carpenters swore that they would no longer work on the same stage with negroes. Taking advantage of the heavy contract resting upon Mr. Gardiner to have the vessels for Mexico ready to launch in July, and of the difficulty of getting other hands at that season of the year, they swore that they would not strike another blow for him unless he would discharge his free colored workmen. Now, although this movement did not extend to me in *form,* it did reach me in *fact.* The spirit which it awakened was one of malice and bitterness toward colored people *generally,* and I suffered with the rest, and suffered severely. My fellow-apprentices very soon began to feel it to be degrading to work with me. They began to put on high looks and to talk contemptuously and maliciously of "the niggers," saying that they would take the "country," and that they "ought to be killed." Encouraged by workmen who, knowing me to be a slave, made no issue with Mr. Gardiner about my being there, these young men did their utmost to make it impossible for me to stay. They seldom called me to do anything without coupling the call with a curse, and Edward North, the biggest in everything, rascality included, ventured to strike me, whereupon I picked him up and threw him into the dock. Whenever any of them struck me I struck back again, regardless of consequences. I could manage any of them *singly,* and so long as I could keep them from combining I got on very well. In the conflict which ended my stay at Mr. Gardiner's I was beset by four of them at once—Ned North, Ned Hayes, Bill Stewart, and Tom Humphreys. Two of them were as large as myself, and they came near killing me, in broad daylight. One came in front, armed with a brick; there was one at each side and one behind, and they closed up all around me. I was struck on all sides; and while I was attending to those in front I received a blow on my head from behind, dealt with a heavy hand-spike. I was completely stunned by the blow, and fell heavily on the ground among the timbers. Taking advantage of my fall they rushed upon me and began to pound me with their fists. With a view of gaining strength, I let them lay on for awhile after I came to myself. They had done me little damage, so far; but finally getting tired of that sport I gave a sudden surge, and despite their weight I rose to my hands and knees. Just as I did this one of their number planted a blow with his boot in my left eye, which for a time seemed to have burst my eye-ball. When they saw my eye completely closed, my face covered with blood, and I staggering under the stunning blows they had given me, they left me. As soon as I gathered strength I picked up the hand-spike and madly enough attempted to pursue them; but here the carpenters interfered and compelled me to give up my pursuit. It was impossible to stand against so many.

Dear reader, you can hardly believe the statement, but it is true and therefore I write it down; that no fewer than fifty white men stood by and saw this brutal and shameful outrage committed, and not a man of them all interposed a single word of mercy. There were four against one, and that one's face was beaten and battered most horribly, and no one said, "that is enough"; but some cried out, "Kill him! kill him! kill the d—n nigger! knock his brains out! he struck a white person!" I mention this inhuman outcry to show the character of the men and the spirit of the times at Gardiner's ship-yard; and, indeed, in Baltimore generally, in 1836. As I look back to this period, I am almost amazed that I was not murdered outright, so murderous was the spirit which prevailed there. On two other occasions while there I came near losing my life. On one of these, I was driving bolts in the hold through the keelson, with Hayes. In its course the bolt bent. Hayes cursed me and said that it was my blow which bent the bolt. I denied this and charged it upon him. In a fit of rage he seized an adze and darted toward me. I met him with a maul and parried his blow, or I should have lost my life.

After the united attack of North, Stewart, Hayes, and Humphreys, finding that the carpenters were as bitter toward me as the apprentices, and that the latter were probably set on by the former, I found my only chance for life was in flight. I succeeded in getting away without an additional blow. To strike a white man was death by lynch law, in Gardiner's ship-yard; nor was there much of any other law toward the colored people at that time in any other part of Maryland. . . .

After learning to calk, I sought my own employment, made my own contracts, and collected my own earnings—giving Master Hugh no trouble in any part of the transactions to which I was a party. . . .

I was living among *freemen,* and was in all respects equal to them by nature and attainments. *Why should I be a slave?* There was *no* reason why I should be the thrall of any man. Besides, I was now getting . . . a dollar and fifty cents per day. I contracted for it, worked for it, collected it; it was paid to me, and it was *rightfully* my own; and yet upon every returning Saturday night, this money—my own hard earnings, every cent of it,—was demanded of me and taken from me by Master Hugh. He did not earn it; he had no hand in earning it; why, then should he have it? I owed him nothing. He had given me no schooling, and I had received from him only my food and raiment; and for these, my services were supposed to pay from the first. The right to take my earnings was the right of the robber. He had the power to compel me to give him the fruits of my labor, and this *power* was his only right in the case. . . .

A Northern Unionist Lectures Ex-Slaves on the Work Ethic, 1865

To the Freed People of Orangeburg District.

You have heard many stories about your condition as freemen. You do not know what to believe: you are talking too much; waiting too much; asking for too much. If you can find out the truth about this matter, you will settle down quietly to your work. Listen, then, and try to understand just how you are situated.

You are now free, but you must know that the only difference you can feel yet, between slavery and freedom, is that neither you nor your children can be bought or sold. You may have a harder time this year than you have ever had before; it will be the price you pay for your freedom. You will have to work hard, and get very little to eat, and very few clothes to wear. If you get through this year alive and well, you should be thankful.

Do not expect to save up anything, or to have much corn or provisions ahead at the end of the year. You must not ask for more pay than free people get at the North. There, a field hand is paid in money, but has to spend all his pay every week, in buying food and clothes for his family and in paying rent for his house. You cannot be paid in money,—for there is no good money in the District,—nothing but Confederate paper. Then, what can you be paid with? Why, with food, with clothes, with the free use of your little houses and lots. You do not own a cent's worth except yourselves. The plantation you live on is not yours, nor the houses, nor the cattle, mules and horses; the seed you planted with was not yours, and the ploughs and hoes do not belong to you. Now you must get something to eat and something to wear, and houses to live in. How can you get these things? By hard work—and nothing else, and it will be a good thing for you if you get them until next year, for yourselves and for your families. You must remember that your children, your old people, and the cripples, belong to you to support now, and all that is given to them is so much pay to you for your work. If you ask for anything more; it you ask for a half of the crop, or even a third, you ask too much; you wish to get more than you could get if you had been free all your lives. Do not ask for Saturday either: free people everywhere else work Saturday, and you have no more right to the day than they have. If your employer is willing to give you part of the day, or to set a task that you can finish early, be thankful for the kindness, but do not think it is something you must have. When you work, work hard. Begin early at sunrise, and do not take more than two hours at noon. Do not think, because you are free you can choose your own kind of work. Every man must work under orders. The soldiers, who are free, work under officers, the officers under the general, and the general under the president. There must be a head man everywhere, and on a plantation the head man, who gives all the orders, is the owner of the place. Whatever he tells you to do you must do at once, and cheerfully. Never give him a cross word or an impudent answer. If the work is hard, do not stop to talk about it, but do it first and rest afterwards. If you are told to go into the field and hoe, see who can go first and lead the row. If you are told to build a fence, build it better than any fence you know of. If you are told to drive the carriage Sunday, or to mind the cattle, do it, for necessary work must be done even on the Sabbath. Whatever the order is, try and obey it without a word. . . .

Captain Charles Soule

"We Demand Land": Petition by Southern Freedmen, 1865

Edisto Island S. C. Oct 28th, 1865.

To the President of these United States. We the freedmen Of Edisto Island South Carolina have learned From you through Major General O O Howard commissioner of the Freedman's Bureau. with deep sorrow and Painful hearts of the possibility of government restoring These lands to the former owners. We are well aware Of the many perplexing and trying questions that burden Your mind. and do therefore pray to god (the preserver of all. and who has through our Late and beloved President (Lincoln) proclamation and the war made Us A free people) that he may guide you in making Your decisions. and give you that wisdom that Cometh from above to settle these great and Important Questions for the best interests of the country and the Colored race: Here is where secession was born and Nurtured Here is were we have toiled nearly all Our lives as slaves and were treated like dumb Driven cattle. This is our home, we have made These lands what they are. we were the only true and Loyal people that were found in possession of these Lands. we have been always ready to strike for Liberty and humanity yea to fight if needs be To preserve this glorious union. Shall not we who Are freedman and have been always true to this Union have the same rights as are enjoyed by Others? Have we broken any Law of these United States? have we forfieted our rights of property In Land?— If not then! are not our rights as A free people and good citizens of these United States To be considered before the rights of those who were Found in rebellion against this good and just Government (and now being conquered) come (as they Seem) with penitent hearts and beg forgiveness For past offences and also ask if thier lands Cannot be restored to them are these rebellious Spirits to be reinstated in thier *possessions* And we who have been abused and oppressed For many long years not to be allowed the Privilige of purchasing land But be subject To the will of these large Land owners? God forbid. Land monopoly is injurious to the advancement of the course of freedom, and if Government Does not make some provision by which we as Freedmen can obtain A Homestead, we have Not bettered our condition.

We have been encouraged by Government to take Up these lands in small tracts, receiving Certificates of the same—we have thus far Taken Sixteen thousand (16000) acres of Land here on This Island. We are ready to pay for this land When Government calls for it. and now after What has been done will the good and just government take from us all this right and make us Subject to the will of those who have cheated and Oppressed us for many years God Forbid!

We the freedmen of this Island and of the State of South Carolina— Do therefore petition to you as the President of these United States, that some provisions be made by which Every colored man can purchase land. and Hold it as his own. We wish to have A home if It be but A few acres. without some provision is Made our future is sad to look upon. yess our Situation is dangerous. we therefore look to you In this trying hour as A true friend of the poor and Neglected race. for protection and Equal Rights. with the privilege of purchasing A Homestead—A Homestead right here in the Heart of South Carolina.

We pray that God will direct your heart in Making such provision for us as freedmen which Will tend to united these states together stronger

Than ever before—May God bless you in the Administration of your duties as the President Of these United States is the humble prayer Of us all.—

In behalf of the Freedmen
Henry Bram

Committee   Ishmael. Moultrie.
yates. Sampson

Ned Cobb on Sharecropping, 1913

. . . I've made a crop more or less every year, come too much rain or too much sun. I've had my cotton grow so fast as to grow to a weed. I've picked from many a stalk of cotton that growed so high until it was just a stalk, not many bolls I'd get for it. On the other hand, when the seasons just hit right, I've had stalks of cotton weren't no more than three foot high, just layin down with bolls. It don't take the tallest cotton to make a big crop.

In the year 1912, second crop I ever made on Miss Hattie Lu Reeve's place, good God it come a snap—and my cotton should have been thinned out, by right, but I weren't done choppin it out. And it come a cold day and and it sleeted on my crop. Done that again the next year, sleeted on that cotton in May, 1912, and 1913, too. And that cotton turned yellow as a fox and shedded off every leaf on it, but left the buds. I examined it and it looked terrible— in a day or two when the weather moderated, I examined my little old cotton and seed it was still alive, and them buds, after the sun hit em good, turnin hot after the snap of weather, little old cotton buds just kept livin and commenced a puttin out, flourishin. I just chopped it regular when I seed all that. And when I laid that cotton by, plowed it and put the dirt to it, it still looked weak and yellow. But it wouldn't die, it just kept a comin, kept a comin until it come out and made me that year eight good bales of cotton—1913. That was a high production for a one-horse farm. In them days people didn't make a bale to the acre. I had about eleven or twelve acres under cultivation and it weren't no first class land. But it was smooth land, easy to work. . . .

We hand-picked that cotton, all of it. Five years old, that's big enough to pick many a little handful, and my daddy had me out in the field pickin cotton before that. And I picked until I picked many a hundred pounds for my boy Vernon, for four years after I quit foolin with it myself. When I quit off pickin for Vernon I was able to pick as much as a hundred pounds a day—that was a little help to him. Pickin regular on my own farm, to pick up to three hundred pounds a day. The Bible says, once a man and twice a child—well, it's that way pickin cotton. I picked at the end of my cotton pickin days how much I picked at the start. . . .

Gathered that cotton from when it first opened up, around the latter part of August or the first week in September, and right through till it was all gathered. White man get out there and raise a big crop of cotton—when

I was a boy and after I was grown, every little Negro chap in the whole country around, as far as he had time to go get em, go get em and put em in his field pickin cotton. And his little crowd, maybe, if he had any chaps, they'd be pickin some on off-hours of school. Come home and go to pickin cotton. But mainly it was nigger children gathered the white man's crop when I come along. And if a chap had in mind that he didn't want to pick this man's cotton—chaps knowed whose cotton it was—mama and papa was sufficient to make him pick it. Carry that child out, some of em, in a white man's field, they'd work his little butt off with a switch if he didn't gather that cotton. You'd find some industrious white people that would work like colored; they was poor people, they'd get out there and pick. But ones that didn't care so much about stoopin down and pickin cotton, their cotton got ready—the little nigger chaps wasn't goin to school; scoop em up like flies and put em in the field.

Picked cotton in a sack—that's how we done it in this country, and other cotton countries I've heard spoke of. Put a sack on, long sack, sometimes the sack would be draggin behind you far enough that a little chap could walk up on the end of it. You'd have a strap to that sack, cross your chest and over your shoulder, resemblin to a harness, and the mouth of that sack right under your arm; you'd pick cotton and just drop it in there. That sack'd hold a full hundred pounds.

Take that sack and empty it in a big basket, cotton basket. White man would set it in his field, or a Negro, if it was his field and he had baskets. I used my own baskets, I made cotton baskets. Didn't pick my crops no other way but empty the cotton out of the sack and into the basket, and that relieved my sack, the weight of it on me, that would take it off, any amount of cotton I had picked in my sack.

I'd take my wagon to the field after me and my children done picked several baskets of cotton, stand it there and go to emptyin that cotton in the wagon. Set them baskets out there to keep a gatherin. I could nicely weigh my cotton in a basket then throw it on the wagon. Weighed my cotton right there, as I loaded it. My wife had good book learnin, she'd take the figures to the house—I could make figures but I didn't know enough to add em up: give her the book with the cotton figures on it, she'd add it up and tell me when I got a bale. That wagon had to move out of the field then. . . .

From my first startin off farmin after I married, even workin on halves, I had to carry my cotton to the gin. And when I got to where I rented, I'd gin at any gin I wanted to. I had mules able to do it; hitch them mules to my wagon, take em to the field; take em from the field to the barn; pull out from the barn to the gin. Drive up under a suction pipe; that suction would pull that lint cotton off the wagon and into them gins and the gins would gin it out—separate the lint from the seed and the seed would fall in a box. Another pipe carried the seed overhead from that box to a seed house out yonder. Didn't have nothin to do but go out there and open up that seed-house box and catch all my seed. Cotton went from the gin machines to a press—all them seeds and whatever trash was picked with that cotton done been ginned out. And a man at the press would work a lever and the press would press the cotton down into a box the shape of a bale so he could bale it off. He'd already have a underbaggin under it and he'd pull the top baggin down and wrap that cotton up, fasten them hooks, and bale it. . . .

Right there and then, and aint aimin to sell that cotton, you take that cotton back home and dump it off your wagon. It's used, startin at home— my mother, after the cotton come back from the gin, seed removed and leave the pure lint. I've seen her take a pair of cards, two cards each about as wide as my four fingers, and its made in the resemblance and in the manner and in the style of a mule brush. And she'd take one in one hand and lay a handful of that cotton on it, take the other card and comb it— that's called cardin batts—then change cards and comb it the other way until she got a nice clear batt of cotton in them brushes. And she'd have a quilt linin stretched out in the house and she'd take that batt of cotton, nice wad of cotton, and lay them batts all over that quilt; she could lay em as thick or thin as she wanted, then spread the next layer of cloth over it and sew the top layer and the bottom layer together around the edge— sewin that cotton in there and pullin it just tight enough to make it flat like she wanted a quilt. And when she sewed as far as she could reach, then she'd roll that quilt, take it loose from the corners of her frames, pull out them nails or small spikes and roll that quilt under, roll it under, just get it far enough, close enough, far as she could reach with her hand sewin. She'd do all around that quilt thataway, from one corner to the other. Had a bed quilt then, warm quilt, plied through with cotton. . . .

. . . If you want to sell your cotton at once, you take it to the market, carry it to the Apafalya cotton market and they'll sample it. Cotton buyin man cuts a slug in the side of your bale, reaches in there and pulls the first of it out the way and get him a handful, just clawin in there. He'll look over that sample, grade that cotton—that's his job. What kind of grade do it make? You don't know until he tells you. If it's short staple, the devil, your price is cut on that cotton. Color matters too, and the way it was ginned—some gins cuts up the cotton, ruins the staple. . . .

And so, I'd have my cotton weighed and I'd go up and down the street with my sample. Meet a white man, farmin man like myself, on the street; he'd see what I been offered for my sample—the buyer's marks would be on the wrapper—or I'd tell him. And he'd take that sample, unwrap it, look at it; he'd say, "Nate, I can beat you with your own cotton, I can get more for it than that."

Aint that enough to put your boots on! The same sample. He'd say, "Let me take your sample and go around in your place. I can beat what they offered you."

Take that cotton and go right to the man that had his bid on it and he'd raise it; right behind where I was, had been, and get a better bid on it. I've gived a white man my sample right there on the streets of Apafalya; he'd go off and come back. Sometime he'd say, "Well, Nate, I helped you a little on it but I couldn't help you much."

And sometime he'd get a good raise on it with another fellow out yonder. He'd bring my sample back to me with a bid on it. "Well, Nate, I knowed I could help you on that cotton."

That was happenin all through my farmin years: from the time I stayed on the Curtis place, and when I moved to the Ames place, and when I lived with Mr. Reeve, and when I moved down on Sitimachas Creek with Mr. Tucker, and when I lived up there at Two Forks on the Stark place, and when I moved down on the Pollard place and stayed there nine years. Colored man's cotton weren't worth as much as white man's cotton less'n it come to the buyer in the white man's hands. But the colored man's labor—that was worth more to the white man than the labor of his own color because it cost him less and he got just as much for his money.

✤ E S S A Y S

Comparing the work rhythms of plantation slaves to those of other preindustrial peoples, Eugene Genovese of Atlanta University explores the ways in which the slaves' African inheritance and plantation experience together forged a black work ethic that accommodated the otherwise harsh requirements of the slave system. Genovese contends that neither the planter class nor their slaves embraced bourgeois notions of time and work discipline. Most masters had to accommodate the slaves' preference for collective patterns of labor. After emancipation, blacks and whites, northerners and southerners waged a protracted struggle over the structure and content of the labor the former slaves would perform, as Columbia University historian Eric Foner shows in the second essay. While the freedmen and freedwomen sought their own homesteads, upon which only the adult males would be expected to labor regularly in the fields, northern officials wanted all the former slaves, men and women, to enter the labor market as wage workers. How fundamentally, therefore, did emancipation change the everyday work of black southerners? Does Foner find the same combination of collectivism and individualism among black laborers that Genovese claims to be a characteristic of slave culture itself?

The Plantation Work Ethic

EUGENE GENOVESE

. . . The slaveholders presided over a plantation system that constituted a halfway house between peasant and factory cultures. The tobacco and cotton plantations, which dominated the slave economy in the United States, ranged closer to the peasant than the factory model, in contradistinction to the great sugar plantations of the Caribbean, which in some respects resembled factories in the field; but even the small holders pushed their laborers toward modern work discipline. The planter's problem came to this: How could they themselves preserve as much as possible of that older way of life to which they aspired and yet convince their slaves to repudiate it? How could they instill factorylike discipline into a working population engaged in a rural system that, for all its tendencies toward modern discipline, remained bound to the rhythms of nature and to traditional ideas of work, time, and leisure?

They succeeded in overcoming this contradiction only to the extent that they got enough work out of their slaves to make the system pay at a level necessary to their survival as a slaveholding class in a capitalist world market. But they failed in deeper ways that cast a shadow over the long-range prospects for that very survival and over the future of both blacks and whites in American society. Too often they fell back on the whip and thereby taught and learned little. When they went to other incentives, as fortunately most tried to do, they did get satisfactory economic results, but at the same time they reinforced traditional attitudes and values instead of replacing them with more advanced ones.

The black work ethic grew up within a wider Protestant Euro-American community with a work ethic of its own. The black ethic represented at once a defense against an enforced system of economic exploitation and an autonomous assertion of values generally associated with preindustrial peoples. As such, it formed part of a more general southern work ethic, which developed in antagonism to that of the wider American society. A Euro-American, basically Anglo-Saxon work ethic helped shape that of southerners in general and slaves in particular and yet, simultaneously, generated a profound antithesis.

In the medieval Catholic formulation the necessity to work both derived from the Fall of Man and served as an expression of humility and submission. . . . To this stern doctrine of work as duty the slave opposed a religion of joy in life that echoed traditional Africa and, surprising as it may seem, even more firmly echoed the spirit of the plantation community itself. To speak of a "calling" or vocation for slaves would be absurd; but more to the point, worldly asceticism neither corresponded to the sensibilities shaped by the historical development from Africa to the New World nor could take root among a people who had no material stake in its flowering. . . .

The slaves' attitude toward time and work arose primarily from their own experience on the plantations of the South. Comparisons with Africa suggest some important cultural continuities. Traditional African time-reckoning focuses on present and past, not future. Time, being two-dimensional, moves, as it were, backward into a long past; the future, not having been experienced, appears senseless. This idea of time, which inhibited the appearance of an indigenous millennialism prior to Islamic and Christian penetrations, encouraged economic attitudes not readily assimilable to early bourgeois demands for saving, thrift, and accumulation. But, however strong the specifically African influence, even more important are those tendencies which characterize preindustrial agricultural peoples in general, for whom the Africans provided a variant or, rather, a series of variants. . . .

Traditional society measured its time by calendars based on agricultural and seasonal patterns, which themselves formed part of an integrated religious world-view. The year proceeded according to a certain rhythm, not according to equal units of time; appropriate festivals and rites broke its continuity and marked the points at which the human spirit celebrated the rhythm of the natural order. Not pure quantities of time obtained, but such flexible units as the beginning of planting and of the harvest. Time became subordinated to the natural order of work and leisure, as their servant rather than their master.

Whereas in peasant farming the work tasks and such natural conditions as the amount of daylight determine the length of the workday, the acceptable number and duration of breaks, and the amount and type of leisure, in factory work "the arbitrarily fixed time schedule determines the beginning and the end of work periods." In peasant societies work tasks such as planting and harvesting, which appear to conform to the demands of nature, have oriented the notation of time. E. P. Thompson argues convincingly that this "task orientation" has rendered work more humanly comprehensible: "The peasant or labourer appears to attend upon what is an observed necessity." For the preindustrial English community as a whole the distinction between "work" and "life" was much less clear than it was to become; the working day itself lengthened and contracted according to necessary tasks, and no great conflict appeared between the demands of work and those of leisure. One need not idealize the undoubtedly harsh physical conditions of preindustrial rural life to appreciate the force of Thompson's argument, especially since those who passed under industrial work discipline probably were themselves the ones who came most to idealize their previous existence and, thereby to heighten either their resistance or their despair. . . .

The advent of clock time represented more than a marking of regular work units—of minutes and hours—and of arbitrary schedules, for it supported the increasing division of labor and transformed that division of labor into a division of time itself. Capitalism production had to be measured in units of labor-time, and those units themselves took on the mysterious and apparently self-determining properties of commodities. When Benjamin Franklin said that time is money, he said much more than is generally understood. E. P. Thompson comments: "In a mature capitalist society all time must be consumed, marketed, put to *use;* it is offensive for the labour force merely to pass the time." Natural rhythms of work and leisure gave place to arbitrary schedules, which were, however, arbitrary only from the point of view of the laborers. The capitalists and those ideologues who were developing a new idea of rationality based on the demands of a rapidly developing economy saw the matter differently. The process of cultural transformation had to rest on economic and extra-economic compulsion and ultimately on violence. It served as the industrial equivalent of that which the West Indian slaveholders, with fewer inhibitions, called "seasoning." . . .

The slaves could not reckon time either according to preindustrial peasant models or according to industrial factory models. The plantations, especially the sugar plantations that dominated most of the slaveholding regions of the New World, although not of the United States, did resemble factories in the field, but even if we take them as our norm we cannot escape the implications of their preindustrial side. However much their economic organization required and tried to compel quasi-industrial discipline, they also threw up countervailing pressures and embodied inescapable internal contradictions.

The setting remained rural, and the rhythm of work followed seasonal fluctuations. Nature remained the temporal reference point for the slaves. However much the slaveholders might have wished to transform their slaves into clock-punchers, they could not, for in a variety of senses both literal and metaphoric, there were no clocks to punch. The planters, especially the resident planters of the United States and Brazil but even the typical West Indian agents of absentee owners, hardly lived in a factory world themselves and at best could only preach what the most docile or stupid slave knew very well they did not and could not practice. Since the plantation economy required extraordinary exertion at critical points of the year, notably the harvest, it required measures to capitalize on the slaves' willingness to work in spurts rather than steadily. The slaveholders turned the inclinations of the slaves to their own advantage, but simultaneously they made far greater concessions to the value system and collective sensibility of the quarters than they intended.

The slaveholders, as usual, had their way but paid a price. The slaves, as usual, fell victim to the demands of their exploiters but had some success in pressing their own advantage. Thus, the plantation system served as a halfway house for Africans between their agricultural past and their imposed industrial future. But, it froze them into a position that allowed for their exploitation on the margins of industrial society. The advantage of this compromise, from the black point of view, lay in the protection it provided for their rich community life and its cultural consolidation. The disadvantage lay in its encouragement of a way of life that, however admirable intrinsically, ill prepared black people to compete in the economic world into which they would be catapulted by emancipation. . . .

The black view of time, conditioned by the plantation slave experience, has provided a great source of strength for a people at bay, as one of Bishop A. G. Dunston's sermons makes clear:

> You know, that's the way God does it. Same as you can't hurry God—
> so why don't you wait, just wait. Everybody's ripping and racing and
> rushing. And God is taking his time. Because he knows that it isn't hurtin'
> nearly so bad as you and I think it's hurtin'—and that is the way he wants
> us to go. But by and by he brings relief. . . .

Black people, in short, learned to take the blow and to parry it as best they could. They found themselves shut out by white racism from part of the dominant culture's value system, and they simultaneously resisted that system both by historically developed sensibility and by necessity. Accordingly, they developed their own values as a force for community cohesion and survival, but in so doing they widened the cultural gap and exposed themselves to even harder blows from a white nation that could neither understand their behavior nor respect its moral foundations.

. . . The African tradition, like the European peasant tradition, stressed hard work and condemned and derided laziness in any form. Not hard work but steady, routinized work as moral duty was discounted. In this attitude African agriculturalists resembled preindustrial peoples in general, including urban peoples. The familiar assertion that certain people would work only long enough to earn the money they needed to live was leveled not only against day laborers but against the finest and most prestigious artisans in early modern Europe. . . .

The slaves' willingness to work extraordinarily hard and yet to resist the discipline of regularity accompanied certain desires and expectations. During Reconstruction the blacks sought their own land; worked it conscientiously when they could get it; resisted being forced back into anything resembling gang labor for the white man; and had to be terrorized, swindled, and murdered to prevent their working for themselves. This story was prefigured in antebellum times when slaves were often allowed garden plots for their families and willingly worked them late at night or on Sundays in order to provide extra food or clothing. The men did not generally let their families subsist on the usual allotments of pork and corn. In addition to working with their wives in the gardens, they fished and hunted and trapped animals. In these and other ways they demonstrated considerable concern for the welfare of their families and a strong desire to take care of them. But in such instances they were working for themselves and at their own pace. Less frequently, slaves received permission to hire out their own time after having completed the week's assigned tasks. They were lured, not by some internal pressure to work steadily, but by the opportunity to work for themselves and their families in their own way.

Many slaves voluntarily worked for their masters on Sundays or holidays in return for money or goods. This arrangement demonstrated how far the notion of the slaves' "right" to a certain amount of time had been accepted by the masters; how readily the slaves would work for themselves; and how far the notion of reciprocity had entered the thinking of both masters and slaves.

The slaves responded to moral as well as economic incentives. They often took pride in their work, but not necessarily in the ways most important to their masters. Solomon Northup designed a better way to transport lumber only to find himself ridiculed by the overseer. In this case it was in the master's interest to intervene, and he did. He praised Northup and adopted the plan. Northup comments: "I was not insensible to the praise bestowed upon me, and enjoyed especially, my triumph over Taydem [the overseer], whose half-malicious ridicule had stung my pride.''

From colonial days onward plantation slaves, as well as those in industry, mining, and town services, received payments in money and goods as part of a wider system of social control. These payments served either as incentive bonuses designated to stimulate productivity, or more frequently, as a return for work done during the time recognized as the slaves' own. Many planters, including those who most clearly got the best results, used such incentives. Bennet H. Barrow of Louisiana provides a noteworthy illustration, for he was not a man to spare the whip. Yet his system of rewards included frequent holidays and dinners, as well as cash bonuses and presents for outstanding work. In Hinds County, Mississippi, Thomas Dabney gave small cash prizes—a few cents, really—to his best pickers and then smaller prizes to others who worked diligently even if they could not match the output of the leaders. In Perry County, Alabama, Hugh Davis divided his workers into rival teams and had them compete for prizes. He supplemented this collective competition with individual contests. In North Carolina at the end of the eighteenth century Charles Pettigrew, like many others before and after him, paid slaves for superior or extra work.

The amounts sometimes reached substantial proportions. Captain Frederick Marryat complained that in Lexington, Kentucky, during the late 1830s a gentleman could not rent a carriage on Sundays because slaves with ready money invariably rented them first for their own pleasure. Occasionally, plantation records reported surprising figures. One slave in Georgia earned fifty to sixty dollars per year by attending to pine trees in his off hours. Others earned money by applying particular skills or by doing jobs that had to be done individually and carefully without supervision. Amounts in the tens and even hundreds of dollars, although not common, caused no astonishment.

The more significant feature of these practices, for the society as a whole if not for the economy in particular, was the regularity—almost the institutionalization—of payments for work on Sundays or holidays. Apart from occasional assignments of Sunday or holiday work as punishment and apart from self-defeating greed, not to say stupidity, which led a few masters to violate the social norm, Sunday was the slaves' day by custom as well as law. The collective agreement of the slaveholders on these measures had its origin in a concern for social peace and reflected a sensible attitude toward economic efficiency. But once the practice took root, with or without legal sanction, the slaves transformed it into a "right." So successfully did they do so that the Supreme Court of Louisiana ruled in 1836: "According to . . . law, slaves are entitled to the produce of their labor on Sunday; even the master is bound to remunerate them, if he employs them." Here again the slaves turned the paternalist doctrine of reciprocity to advantage while demonstrating the extent to which that doctrine dominated the lives of both masters and slaves. . . .

Underlying black resistance to prevailing white values, then, has been a set of particular ideas concerning individual and community responsibility.

It is often asserted that blacks spend rather than save as someone else thinks they should. But the considerable evidence for this assertion must be qualified by the no less considerable evidence of the heartbreaking scraping together of nickels and dimes to pay for such things as the education of the children, which will generally draw Anglo-Saxon applause, and the provision of elaborate funerals, which generally will not but which for many peoples besides blacks constitutes a necessary measure of respect for the living as well as the dead.

The slaves could, when they chose, astonish the whites by their work-time élan and expenditure of energy. The demands of corn shucking, hog killing, logrolling, cotton picking, and especially sugar grinding confronted the slaves with particularly heavy burdens and yet drew from them particularly positive responses.

With the exception of the Christmas holiday—and not always that—former slaves recalled having looked forward to corn shucking most of all. . . .

Certainly, the slaves had some material incentives. The best shuckers would get a dollar or a suit of clothes, as might those who found a red ear. But these incentives do not look impressive and do not loom large in the testimony. Those plantations on which the prize for finding a red ear consisted of a dollar do not seem to have done any better than those on which the prize consisted of an extra swig of whiskey or a chance to kiss the prettiest girl. The shucking was generally night work—overtime, as it were—and one might have expected the slaves to resent it and to consider the modest material incentives, which came to a special dinner and dance and a lot of whiskey, to be inadequate.

The most important feature of these occasions and the most important incentive to these long hours of work was the community life they called forth. They were gala affairs. The jug passed freely, although drunkenness was discouraged; the work went on amidst singing and dancing; friends and acquaintances congregated from several plantations and farms; the house slaves joined the field slaves in common labor; and the work was followed by an all-night dinner and ball at which inhibitions, especially those of class and race, were lowered as far as anyone dared.

Slavery, a particularly savage system of oppression and exploitation, made its slaves victims. But the human beings it made victims did not consent to be just that; they struggled to make life bearable and to find as much joy in it as they could. Up to a point even the harshest of masters had to help them do so. The logic of slavery pushed the masters to try to break their slaves' spirit and to reconstruct it as an unthinking and unfeeling extension of their own will, but the slaves' own resistance to dehumanization compelled the masters to compromise in order to get an adequate level of work out of them.

The combination of festive spirit and joint effort appears to have engaged the attention of the slaves more than anything else. Gus Brown, an ex-slave from Alabama, said simply, "On those occasions we all got together and had a regular good time." The heightened sense of fellowship

with their masters also drew much comment. Even big slaveholders would
join in the work, as well as in the festivities and the drinking, albeit not
without the customary patriarchal qualifications. They would demand that
the slaves sing, and the slaves would respond boisterously. Visitors expressed wonder at the spontaneity and improvisation the slaves displayed.
The songs, often made up on the spot, bristled with sharp wit, both ma-
licious and gentle. The slaves sang of their courtships and their lovers'
quarrels; sometimes the songs got bawdy, and the children had to be hustled
off to bed. . . .

But the songs also turned to satire. White participation in these festivals
was always condescending and self-serving, and the slaves' acceptance of
it displayed something other than childlike gratitude for small favors. They
turned their wit and incredible talent for improvisation into social criticism.
Occasionally they risked a direct, if muted, thrust in their "corn songs,"
as they came to be called.

> Massa in the great house, counting out his money,
> Massa in the great house, counting out his money,
> Oh, shuck that corn and throw it in the barn.
> Mistis in the parlor, eating bread and honey,
> Oh, shuck that corn and throw it in the barn.

More often, they used a simpler and safer technique. Ole Massa was always
God's gift to humanity, the salt of the earth, de bestest massa in de whole
wide worl'. But somehow, one or more of his neighbors was might bad
buckra. . . . Blacks—any blacks—were not supposed to sass whites—any
whites; slaves—any slaves—were not supposed to sit in judgment on masters—any masters. By the device of a little flattery and by taking advantage
of the looseness of the occasion, they asserted their personalities and made
their judgments.

A curious sexual division of labor marked the corn shuckings. Only
occasionally did women participate in the shucking. The reason for the
exclusion is by no means clear. Field women matched the men in hard
work, not only in picking cotton but in rolling logs, chopping wood, and
plowing. Yet at corn shuckings they divided their time between preparing
an elaborate spread for the dinner and taking part in quilting bees and the
like. As a result, the corn shuckings took on a peculiarly male tone, replete
with raucous songs and jokes not normally told in front of women, as well
as those manifestations of boyish prancing associated with what is called—
as if by some delightful Freudian slip—a "man's man."

The vigor with which the men worked and the insistence on a rigid
sexual separation raise the central question of the slaves' attitude toward
work in its relationship to their sense of family and community. The sense
of community established by bringing together house and field slaves and
especially slaves from several plantations undoubtedly underlay much of
the slaves' positive response, and recalled the festivities, ceremonials, and
rituals of traditional societies in a way no office Christmas party in an
industrial firm has ever done. And corn shucking, like hog killing, had a

special meaning, for at these times the slaves were literally working for themselves. The corn and pork fed them and their families; completion of these tasks carried a special satisfaction.

From this point of view the sexual division of labor, whatever its origin, takes on new meaning. In a limited way it strengthened that role of direct provider to which the men laid claim by hunting and fishing to supplement the family diet. Even the less attractive features of the evening in effect reinforced this male self-image. Nor did the women show signs of resentment. On the contrary, they seem to have grasped the opportunity to underscore a division of labor and authority in the family and to support the pretensions of their men. Slavery represented a terrible onslaught on the personalities and spirit of the slaves, and whatever unfairness manifested itself in this sexual bias, the efforts of male and female slaves to create and support their separate roles provided a weapon for joint resistance to dehumanization. . . .

The evidence from the sugar plantations is especially instructive. Louisiana's sugar planters reputedly drove their slaves harder than any others in the slave states. Such reputations are by no means to be accepted at face value, but they certainly drove them hard during the grinding season. Yet, slaves took to the woods as limited and local runaways more often during the spring and summer months than during the autumn grinding season, when the work reached a peak of intensity and when the time for rest and sleep contracted sharply. Once again, the small material incentives cannot account for the slaves' behavior.

The slaves brought to their labor a gaiety and élan that perplexed observers, who saw them work at night with hardly a moment to catch their breath. Many, perhaps most, found themselves with special tasks to perform and special demands upon them; by all accounts they strained to rise to the occasion. The planters, knowing that the season lasted too long to sustain a fever pitch of effort, tried to break it up with parties and barbecues and at the very least promised and delivered a gala dinner and ball at the end. Ellen Betts, an ex-slave from Texas, recalled: "Massa sho' good to dem gals and bucks what cuttin' de cane. When dey git done makin' sugar, he give a drink called 'Peach 'n' Honey' to de women folk and whiskey and brandy to de men." Another ex-slave, William Stone of Alabama, said that the slaves were "happy" to work during the sugar harvest " 'cause we knowed it mean us have plenty 'lasses in winter."

Still, the demands of the sugar crop meant the sacrifice of some Sundays and even the Christmas holiday. The slaves showed no resentment at the postponement of the holiday. It would come in due time, usually in mid-January, and the greater their sacrifices, the longer and fuller the holiday would likely be. For the slaves on the sugar plantations Christmas did not mean December 25; it meant the great holiday that honored the Lord's birth, brought joy to His children, and properly fell at the end of the productive seasons.

Cotton picking was another matter. One ex-slave recalled cotton-picking parties along with corn-shucking parties but added, "Dere wasn't so much foolishness at cotton pickin' time." The slaves missed, in particular, the fellowship of slaves from other plantations. An exchange of labor forces on a crash basis sometimes occurred, and ex-slaves remembered precisely those times warmly. The planters had to have their cotton picked at about the same time and could not easily exchange labor forces. But the neighborly tradition was too strong to be denied entirely, and when a planter fell dangerously behind, others would come to his aid. Unable to take time away from their own work unless well ahead of schedule, friendly planters had to send their slaves after hours to pick by moonlight. The slaves, instead of becoming indignant over the imposition, responded with enthusiasm and extra effort. Many of them later recalled this grueling all-night work as "big times," for they were helping their own friends and combining the work with festivity. Bonuses, parties, and relaxed discipline rewarded their cooperation. Scattered evidence suggests less whipping and harsh driving during the cotton-picking season on some plantations but the opposite on others.

Some planters congratulated themselves on their success in getting a good response during the critical cotton harvest. Virginia Clay visited Governor Hammond's noteworthy plantation in South Carolina and enthusiastically reported on the magnificent singing and general spirit of the slaves, and Kate Stone was sure that "the Negroes really seemed to like the cotton picking best of all." Henry William Ravenel, in his private journal, made an interesting observation that provides a better clue to the slaves' attitude. Writing in 1865, immediately after their emancipation, he declared that the slaves had always disliked planting and cultivating cotton and would now prefer almost any alternative labor. The picking season must have struck the slaves as a mixed affair. It meant hard and distasteful work and sometimes punishment for failure to meet quotas, but also the end of a tough season, prizes for good performances, and the prelude to relaxation and a big celebration. Yet, the special spirit of the season was not strong enough to carry the slaves through the rigors of labor; the whip remained the indispensable spur. . . .

Whatever the origins of the slaves' strong preference for collective work, it drew the attention of their masters, who knew that they would have to come to terms with it. Edmund Ruffin, the South's great soil chemist and authority on plantation agriculture, complained that the pinewoods of North Carolina were set afire every spring by inconsiderate poor whites who cared nothing for the damage they did in order to provide grazing land for their few cows. He added that the slaves also set many fires because they intensely disliked collecting turpentine from the trees. This work was light and easy in Ruffin's estimation, but the slaves resisted it anyway because it had to be performed in isolation. "A negro," Ruffin explained from long experience, "cannot abide being alone and will prefer work of much exposure and severe toil, in company, to any lighter work, without any company." . . .

The powerful community spirit and preference for collective patterns of working and living had their antithesis in an equally powerful individualism, manifested most attractively during and after Reconstruction in an attempt to transform themselves into peasant proprietors. This particular kind of individualism has also had less attractive manifestations, from the creation of the ghetto hustler and the devil-take-the-hindmost predator to the creation of a set of attitudes that many blacks hold responsible for a chronic lack of political unity. Certainly, the old collective spirit remains powerful, as the very notion of a black "brotherhood" demonstrates, but it does rest on a contradictory historical base. The work ethic of the slaves provided a firm defense against the excesses of an oppressive labor system, but like the religious tradition on which it rested, it did not easily lend itself to counterattack. Once the worst features of the old regime fell away, the ethic itself began to dissolve into its component parts. Even today we witness the depressing effects of this dissolution in a futile and pathetic caricature of bourgeois individualism, manifested both in the frustrated aspirations so angrily depicted in E. Franklin Frazier's *Black Bourgeoisie* and in violent, antisocial nihilism. But we also witness the continued power of a collective sensibility regarded by some as "race pride" and by others as a developing black national consciousness. . . .

Emancipation and the Reconstruction of Southern Labor

ERIC FONER

. . . Of the many questions raised by emancipation, none was more crucial for the future of both blacks and whites in Southern society than the organization of the region's economy. Slavery had been first and foremost a system of labor. And while all Republicans agreed that "free labor" must replace slavery, few were certain how the transition should be accomplished. "If the [Emancipation] Proclamation makes the slaves actually free," declared the *New York Times* in January 1863, "there will come the further duty of making them work. . . . All this opens a vast and most difficult subject." . . .

By 1865, hundreds of thousands of slaves scattered throughout the South had become, under federal auspices, free workers. The most famous of these "rehearsals for Reconstruction" occurred on the South Carolina Sea Islands. When the U.S. Navy occupied Port Royal in November 1861, virtually all the white inhabitants fled to the mainland, leaving behind some 10,000 slaves long accustomed to organizing their own labor. The system of labor employed on mainland rice and Sea Island cotton plantations, in which slaves were assigned daily tasks rather than working in closely supervised gangs, gave these blacks a unique control over the pace and length of the workday.

Excerpts from *A Short History of Reconstruction* by Eric Foner. Copyright © 1990 by Eric Foner. Reprinted by permission of Harper & Row, Publishers, Inc.

Sea Island blacks, it quickly became clear, possessed their own definition of the meaning of freedom. When the planters fled, the slaves sacked the big houses and destroyed cotton gins; they then commenced planting corn and potatoes for their own subsistence, but evinced considerable resistance to growing the "slave crop," cotton. But blacks were not to chart their own path to free labor, for in the navy's wake came Northern military officers, Treasury agents, investors, and a squad of young teachers and missionaries known collectively as Gideon's Band, the men fresh from Harvard, Yale, or divinity school, the women from careers as teachers and work in the abolitionist movement. Each group had its own ideas about how the transition to freedom should take place.

The most highly publicized Northerners on the islands, the Gideonites were also the least powerful. More influential were Treasury officials, army officers, and those, lured by the fabulously high price of cotton, who proposed to employ the ex-slaves as paid plantation laborers. In 1863 and 1864, Treasury agents auctioned Sea Island land seized for nonpayment of taxes. Despite efforts by the Gideonites to secure preferential treatment for blacks, only a small portion of the land went to groups of freedmen. Many plantations ended up in the hands of army officers, government officials, and Northern speculators and cotton companies. Eleven were purchased by a consortium of Boston investors that included Edward Atkinson, agent for six Massachusetts textile firms, and Edward S. Philbrick, assistant superintendent of the Boston & Worcester Railroad.

Motivating Atkinson and Philbrick was a typically American combination of reform spirit and desire for profit. In the eyes of these antislavery entrepreneurs, Port Royal offered the perfect opportunity to demonstrate that "the abandonment of slavery did not imply the abandonment of cotton" and that blacks would work more efficiently and profitably as free laborers than as slaves. Sent to the Sea Islands to oversee the experiment, Philbrick sought to create a model free labor environment, with blacks neither exploited by their employers nor lapsing into dependency upon the government. He opposed efforts to allow blacks access to land at below the market price, insisting, "no man . . . appreciates property who does not work for it." He failed to consider the possibility that the former slaves had worked for the land during their 250 years of bondage.

Was the free labor experiment a success? One Gideonite, William C. Gannett, believed so, pointing to an improvement in black living conditions—wooden chimneys replaced by brick, better clothing, a more varied diet. Philbrick himself remained uncertain. Personally, it was lucrative enough, earning him $20,000 in 1863 alone. But the freedmen continued to prefer growing provision crops to cotton. By 1865, concluding that blacks "will not produce as much cotton in this generation as they did five years ago," he divided his plantations into small parcels, sold them to the laborers, and returned to Massachusetts. In the end, the experiment underscored both the ambiguities within the concept of free labor itself and the conflicting interests lurking beneath the effort to reconstruct the Southern society.

Northern investors understood free labor to mean working for wages on plantations; to blacks it meant farming their own land and living largely independent of the marketplace. . . .

[Behind this dispute] was a broader question suggested by the end of slavery: Should the freedmen be viewed as ready to take their place as citizens and participants in the competitive marketplace, or did their unique historical experience oblige the federal government to take special action on their behalf? Although they had generally accepted the expansion of national authority during the war, many reformers still espoused laissez-faire ideas. Assistance begets dependence, insisted Sea Island teacher William C. Gannett; the sooner blacks were "thrown upon themselves, the speedier will be their salvation."

At the other end of this ideological spectrum stood Radicals advocating an act of federal intervention comparable in scope to emancipation—the division of planter lands among the freedmen. The most persistent Congressional supporter of such a measure was George W. Julian, chairman of the House Committee on Public Lands, who insisted that without land reform, the freedmen would find themselves reduced to "a system of wages slavery . . . more galling than slavery itself." The creation of the Freedmen's Bureau in March 1865 symbolized the widespread belief among Republicans that the federal government must shoulder broad responsibility for the emancipated slaves, including offering them some kind of access to land.

The Bureau was empowered to distribute clothing, food, and fuel to destitute freedmen and oversee "all subjects" relating to their condition in the South. Despite its unprecedented responsibilities, it was clearly seen as a temporary expedient, for its life-span was initially limited to one year. Massachusetts Sen. Charles Sumner had proposed establishing the Bureau as a permanent agency with a secretary of Cabinet rank, but such an idea ran counter to strong inhibitions against long-term guardianship. In one respect, however, the Freedmen's Bureau appeared to promise a permanent transformation of the condition of the emancipated slaves. For Congress authorized it to divide abandoned land and confiscated land into forty-acre plots for rental to freedmen and loyal refugees and eventual sale. While hardly a definitive commitment to land distribution, the law establishing the Bureau clearly anticipated that the government would aid some blacks to become independent farmers in a "free labor" South.

While Congress deliberated, a victorious Gen. William T. Sherman added a new dimension to the already perplexing land question. On January 12, 1865, at the urging of Secretary of War Edwin M. Stanton, who had joined him in Savannah, Sherman gathered twenty leaders of the city's black community, mostly Baptist and Methodist ministers. The conversation revealed that these black leaders possessed a clear conception of the meaning of freedom. Garrison Frazier, a Baptist minister who had known bondage for sixty years before purchasing his liberty in 1857, defined freedom as "placing us where we could reap the fruit of our own labor." The best way to accomplish this, he added, was "to have land, and . . . till it by our own labor." Four days later, Sherman issued Special Field Order

No. 15, setting aside the Sea Islands and a portion of the lowcountry rice coast south of Charleston, extending thirty miles inland, for the exclusive settlement of blacks. Each family would receive forty acres of land, and Sherman later authorized the army to loan them mules. (Here, perhaps, lies the origin of the phrase "forty acres and a mule" that would soon echo throughout the South.) By June, some 40,000 freedmen had been settled on 400,000 acres of "Sherman land." Here in coastal South Carolina and Georgia, the prospect beckoned of a transformation of Southern society more radical even than the end of slavery. . . .

. . . Beginning in 1865, and for years thereafter, Southern whites throughout the South complained of the difficulty of obtaining female field laborers. Planters, Freedmen's Bureau officials, and Northern visitors all ridiculed the black "female aristocracy" for "acting the *lady*" or mimicking the family patterns of middle-class whites. White employers also resented their inability to force black children to labor in the fields, especially after the spread of schools in rural areas. Contemporaries appeared uncertain whether black women, black men, or both were responsible for the withdrawal of females from agricultural labor. There is no question that many black men considered it manly to have their wives work at home and believed that, as head of the family, the male should decide how its labor was organized. But many black women desired to devote more time than under slavery to caring for their children and to domestic responsibilities like cooking, sewing, and laundering.

The shift of black female labor from the fields to the home proved a temporary phenomenon. The rise of renting and sharecropping, which made each family responsible for its own plot of land, placed a premium on the labor of all family members. The dire poverty of many black families, deepened by the depression of the 1870s, made it essential for both women and men to contribute to the family's income. Throughout this period, a far higher percentage of black than white women and children worked for wages outside their homes. Where women continued to concentrate on domestic tasks, and children attended school, they frequently engaged in seasonal field labor. Thus, emancipation did not eliminate labor outside the home by black women and children, but it fundamentally altered control over their labor. Now blacks themselves, rather than a white owner or overseer, decided where and when black women and children worked. . . .

Nowhere were blacks' efforts to define their freedom more explosive for the entire society than in the economy. Freedmen brought out of slavery a conception of themselves as a "Working Class of People" who had been unjustly deprived of the fruits of their labor. To white predictions that they would not work, blacks responded that if any class could be characterized as lazy, it was the planters, who had "lived in idleness all their lives on stolen labor." It is certainly true that many blacks expected to labor less as free men and women than they had as slaves, an understandable aim considering the conditions they had previously known. "Whence comes the assertion that the 'nigger won't work'?" asked an Alabama freedman. "It comes from this fact: . . . the freedman refuses to be driven out into the field two hours before day, and work until 9 or 10 o'clock in the night, as was the case in the days of slavery."

Yet freedom meant more than shorter hours and payment of wages. Freedmen sought to control the conditions under which they labored, end their subordination to white authority, and carve out the greatest measure of economic autonomy. These aims led them to prefer tenancy to wage labor, and leasing land for a fixed rent to sharecropping. Above all, they inspired the quest for land. Owning land, the freedmen believed, would "complete their independence."

To those familiar with the experience of other postemancipation societies, blacks' "mania for owning a small piece of land" did not appear surprising. Freedmen in Haiti, the British and Spanish Caribbean, and Brazil all saw ownership of land as crucial to economic independence, and everywhere former slaves sought to avoid returning to plantation labor. Unlike freedmen in other countries, however, American blacks emerged from slavery convinced that the federal government had committed itself to land distribution. Belief in an imminent division of land was most pervasive in the South Carolina and Georgia lowcountry, but the idea was shared in other parts of the South as well, including counties that had never been occupied by federal troops. Blacks insisted that their past labor entitled them to at least a portion of their owners' estates. As an Alabama black convention put it: "The property which they hold was nearly all earned by the sweat of *our* brows."

In some parts of the South, blacks in 1865 did more than argue the merits of their case. Hundreds of freedmen refused either to sign labor contracts or to leave the plantations, insisting that the land belonged to them. On the property of a Tennessee planter, former slaves not only claimed to be "joint heirs" to the estate but, the owner complained, abandoned the slave quarters and took up residence "in the rooms of my house." Few freedmen were able to maintain control of land seized in this manner. A small number did, however, obtain property through other means, squatting on unoccupied land in sparsely populated states like Florida and Texas, buying tiny city plots, or cooperatively purchasing farms and plantations. Most blacks, however, emerged from slavery unable to purchase land even at the depressed prices of early Reconstruction and confronted by a white community unwilling to advance credit to sell them property. Thus, they entered the world of free labor as wage or share workers on land owned by whites. The adjustment to a new social order in which their persons were removed from the market but their labor was bought and sold like any other commodity proved in many respects difficult. For it required them to adapt to the logic of the economic market, where the impersonal laws of supply and demand and the balance of power between employer and employee determine a laborer's material circumstances.

Most freedmen welcomed the demise of the paternalism and mutual obligations of slavery and embraced many aspects of the free market. They patronized the stores that sprang up throughout the rural South, purchasing "luxuries" ranging from sardines, cheese, and sugar to new clothing. They saved money to build and support churches and educate their children. And they quickly learned to use and influence the market for their own ends. The early years of Reconstruction witnessed strikes or petitions for higher wages by black urban laborers including Richmond factory workers, Jackson washerwomen, New Orleans and Savannah stevedores, and mechanics in Columbus, Georgia. In rural areas, too, plantation freedmen sometimes bargained collectively over contract terms, organized strikes, and occasionally even attempted to establish wage schedules for an entire area. Blacks exploited competition between planters and nonagricultural employers, seeking work on railroad construction crews and at turpentine mills and other enterprises offering pay far higher than on the plantations.

Slavery, however, did not produce workers fully socialized to the virtues of economic accumulation. Despite the profits possible in early postwar cotton farming, many freedmen strongly resisted growing the "slave crop." "If ole massa want to grow cotton," said one Georgia freedman, "let him plant it himself." Many freedmen preferred to concentrate on food crops and only secondarily on cotton or other staples to obtain ready cash. Rather than choose irrevocably between self-sufficiency and market farming, they hoped to avoid a complete dependence on either while taking advantage of the opportunities each could offer. As A. Warren Kelsey, a representative of Northern cotton manufacturers, shrewdly observed:

> The sole ambition of the freedman at the present time appears to be to become the owner of a little piece of land, there to erect a humble home, and to dwell in peace and security at his own free will and pleasure. If he wishes, to cultivate the ground in cotton on his own account, to be able to do so without anyone to dictate to him hours or system of labor, if he wishes instead to plant corn or sweet potatoes—to be able to do *that* free from any outside control. . . . That is their idea, their desire and their hope.

Historical experience and modern scholarship suggest that acquiring small plots of land would hardly, by itself, have solved the economic plight of black families. Without control of credit and access to markets, land reform can often be a hollow victory. And where political power rests in hostile hands, small landowners often find themselves subjected to oppressive taxation and other state policies that severely limit their economic prospects. In such circumstances, the autonomy offered by land ownership tends to be defensive, rather than the springboard for sustained economic advancement. Yet while hardly an economic panacea, land redistribution would have had profound consequences for Southern society, weakening the land-based economic and political power of the old ruling class, offering blacks a measure of choice as to whether, when, and under what circumstances to enter the labor market, and affecting the former slaves' conception of themselves.

Blacks' quest for economic independence not only threatened the foundations of the Southern political economy, it put the freedmen at odds with both former owners seeking to restore plantation labor discipline and Northerners committed to reinvigorating staple crop production. But as part of the broad quest for individual and collective autonomy, it remained central to the black community's effort to define the meaning of freedom. Indeed, the fulfillment of other aspirations, from family autonomy to the creation of schools and churches, all greatly depended on success in winning control of their working lives and gaining access to the economic resources of the South.

Northern journalists who hurried south at the end of the Civil War telegraphed back reports of a devastated society. Where the great armies had fought and marched, vast scenes of desolation greeted the observer. The Shenandoah Valley, Virginia's antebellum breadbasket, appeared "almost a desert," its barns and dwellings burned; bridges demolished, fences, tools, and livestock destroyed. Northern Alabama, having endured three years of fighting, and the state's central counties, which felt the wrath of the Union cavalry early in 1865, offered vistas of "absolute destitution." Along Sherman's track in Georgia and South Carolina, the scars of battle were everywhere. A white Georgian in August described in his diary a railroad journey through "a desolated land. Every village and station we stopped at presented an array of ruined walls and chimneys standing useless and solitary . . . thanks to that destroying vandal."

Even apart from physical devastation, the widespread destruction of work animals, farm buildings, and machinery, and the deterioration of levees and canals, ensured that the revival of agriculture would be slow and painful. So too did the appalling loss of life, a disaster without parallel in the American experience. Thirty-seven thousand blacks, the great majority from the South, perished in the Union Army, as did tens of thousands more in contraband camps, on Confederate Army labor gangs, and in disease-ridden urban shanty-towns. Nearly 260,000 men died for the Confederacy—over one-fifth of the South's adult white male population. The region, moreover, was all but bankrupt, for the collapse of Confederate bonds and currency wiped out the savings of countless individuals and the resources and endowments of colleges, churches, and other institutions.

Agricultural statistics reveal the full extent of the economic disaster the South had suffered. Between 1860 and 1870, while farm output expanded in the rest of the nation, the South experienced precipitous declines in the value of farm land and the amount of acreage under cultivation. The number of horses fell by twenty-nine percent, swine by thirty-five percent, and farm values by half. The real value of all property, even discounting that represented by slaves, stood thirty percent lower in 1870 than its prewar figure, and the output of the staple crops cotton, rice, sugar, and tobacco, and food crops like corn and potatoes, remained far below their antebellum levels. Confederate Gen. Braxton Bragg returned from the war to his "once prosperous" Alabama home to find "*all, all* was lost, except my debts."

Despite the grim reality of desolation and poverty, the South's economic recovery involved more than rebuilding shattered farms and repairing broken bridges. An entire social order had been swept away, and on its ruins a new one had to be constructed. The process by which a new social and economic order replaced the old followed different paths in different parts of the South. But for black and white alike, the war's end ushered in what South Carolina planter William H. Trescot called "the perpetual trouble that belongs to a time of social change."

For the majority of planters, as for their former slaves, the Confederacy's defeat and the end of slavery ushered in a difficult adjustment to new race and class relations and new ways of organizing labor. The first casualty of this transformation was the paternalist ethos of prewar planters. A sense of obligation based on mastership over an inferior, paternalism had no place in a social order in which labor relations were mediated by the impersonal market and blacks aggressively pressed claims to autonomy and equality. "The Law which freed the negro," a Southern editor wrote in 1865, "at the same time freed the master, all obligations springing out of the relations of master and slave, except those of kindness, cease mutually to exist." And kindness proved all too rare in the aftermath of war and emancipation. Numerous planters evicted from their plantations those blacks too old or infirm to labor, and transformed "rights" enjoyed by slaves—clothing, housing, access to garden plots—into commodities for which payment was due.

"The former relation has to be unlearnt by both parties," wrote one planter, but except for the obligations of paternalism, ideas inherited from slavery displayed remarkable resiliency. For those accustomed to the power of command, the normal give-and-take of employer and employee was difficult to accept. The employer, many planters believed, should be the sole judge of the value of his laborers' services. One white North Carolinian hired a freedman in the spring of 1865, promising to give him "whatever was right" after the crop had been gathered. Behavior entirely normal in the North, such as a freedman leaving the employ of a Georgia farmer because "he thought he could do better," provoked cries of outrage and charges of ingratitude.

Carl Schurz and other Northerners who toured the South in 1865 concluded that white Southerners "do not know what free labor is." To which many planters replied that Northerners "do not understand the character of the negro." Free labor assumptions—economic rationality, internal self-discipline, responsiveness to the incentives of the market—could never, planters insisted, be applied to blacks. "They are improvident and reckless of the future," complained a Georgia newspaper. Nor was another free labor axiom, opportunity for social mobility, applicable in the South. A Natchez newspaper informed its readers: "The true station of the negro is that of a servant. The wants and state of our country demand that he should remain a servant."

The conviction that preindustrial lower classes share an aversion to regular, disciplined toil had a long history in both Europe and America. In the Reconstruction South, this ideology took a racial form, and although

racism was endemic throughout nineteenth-century America, the requirements of the plantation economy shaped its specific content in the aftermath
of emancipation. Charges of "indolence" were often directed not against
blacks unwilling to work, but at those who preferred to labor for themselves.
"Want of ambition will be the devil of the race, I think," wrote Kemp P.
Battle, a North Carolina planter and political leader, in 1866. "Some of my
most sensible men say they have no other desire than to cultivate their
own land in grain and raise bacon." On the face of it, such an aspiration
appears ambitious enough, and hardly unusual in the nineteenth-century
South. But in a plantation society, a black man seeking to work his way
up the agricultural ladder to the status of self-sufficient farmer seemed not
an admirable example of industriousness, but a demoralized freedman unwilling to work—work, that is, under white supervision on a plantation.

The questions of land and labor were intimately related. Planters quickly
concluded that their control of black labor rested upon maintaining their
own privileged access to the productive land of the plantation belt. Even
if relatively few freedmen established themselves as independent farmers,
plantation discipline would dissolve since, as William H. Trescot explained,
"it will be utterly impossible for the owner to find laborers that will work
contentedly for wages alongside of these free colonies." At public meetings
in 1865, and in their private correspondence, planters resolved never to
rent or sell land to freedmen. In effect, they sought to impose upon blacks
their own definition of freedom, one that repudiated the former slaves'
equation of liberty and autonomy. "They have an idea that a hireling is
not a freedman," Mississippi planter Samuel Agnew noted in his diary. . . .

Between the planters' need for a disciplined labor force and the freedmen's quest for autonomy, conflict was inevitable. Planters attempted
through written contracts to reestablish their authority over every aspect
of their laborers' lives. "Let everything proceed as formerly," one advised,
"the contractual relation being substituted for that of master and slave."
These early contracts prescribed not only labor in gangs from sunup to
sundown as in antebellum days, but complete subservience to the planter's
will. One South Carolina planter required freedmen to obey the employer
"and go by his direction the same as in slavery time." Many contracts not
only specified modes of work and payment, but prohibited blacks from
leaving plantations, entertaining visitors, or holding meetings without permission of the employer.

Such provisions proved easier to compose than to enforce. Planters
quickly learned that labor contracts could not by themselves create a submissive labor force. On the aptly named Vexation plantation in Texas,
blacks in September 1865 were said to be "insolent and refusing to work."
The employees of Louisiana's former Confederate governor, Thomas O.
Moore, set their own pace of work, refused to plow when the ground was
hard, and answered his complaints in a "disrespectful and annoying" manner. Conflict was endemic on plantations throughout the South. Some blacks
refused to weed cotton fields in the rain. Others would not perform the
essential but hated "mud work" of a rice plantation—dredging canals and

repairing dikes—forcing some rice planters "to hire Irishmen to do the ditching." House servants, too, had their own ideas of where their obligations began and ended. Butlers refused to cook or polish brass, domestics would not black the boots of plantation guests, chambermaids declared that it was not their duty to answer the front door, serving girls insisted on the right to entertain male visitors in their rooms.

Southern whites were not the only ones to encounter difficulty disciplining former slaves. During and immediately after the war, a new element joined the South's planter class: Northerners who purchased land, leased plantations, or formed partnerships with Southern planters. These newcomers were a varied, ambitious group, mostly former soldiers anxious to invest their savings in this promising new frontier and civilians lured South by press reports of "the fabulous sums of money to be made in the South in raising cotton." Joined with the quest for profit, however, was a reforming spirit, a vision of themselves as agents of sectional reconciliation and the South's "economic regeneration." As an Illinois man farming in Texas wrote: "I am going to introduce new ideas here in the farming line and show the beauties of free over slave labor."

Southern planters predicted that the newcomers would soon complain about the character of black labor, and they were not far wrong. The very "scientific" methods Northerners hoped to introduce, involving closely supervised work and changes in customary plantation routines, challenged the more irregular pace of work preferred by blacks and their desire to direct their own labor. As time passed, the Northern planters sounded and acted more and more like Southern. Some sought to restore corporal punishment, only to find that the freedmen would not stand for it. Perhaps the problem arose from the fact that, like Southern whites, most of the newcomers did not believe recently emancipated blacks capable of "self-directed labor." If the freedmen were to become productive free laborers, said the *New York Times* with unintended irony, "it must be done by giving them new masters." Blacks, however, wanted to be their own masters. And, against employers both Southern and Northern, they used whatever weapons they could find in the chaotic economic conditions of the postwar South to influence the conditions of their labor.

Blacks did, indeed, enjoy considerable bargaining power because of the "labor shortage" that followed the end of slavery. Particularly acute in sparsely populated Florida and the expanding cotton empire of the Southwest, competition for labor affected planters throughout the South. "The struggle seems to be who will get the negro at any price," lamented Texas planter Frank B. Conner. Planters, he concluded, must band together to "establish some maximum figure," stop "enticing" one another's workers, and agree that anyone "breaking the established custom should be driven from the community."

The scarcity of labor was no mirage. Measured in hours worked per capita, the supply of black labor dropped by about one-third after the Civil War, largely because all former slaves were determined to work fewer hours than under slavery, and many women and children withdrew altogether from the fields. But the "labor shortage" was a question not only of numbers, but of power. It arose from black families' determination to use the rights resulting from emancipation to establish the conditions, rhythms, and compensation of their work. . . .

Despite the intensity of their conflict, neither former master nor former slave possessed the power to define the South's new system of labor. A third protagonist, the victorious North, also attempted to shape the transition from slavery to freedom. To the Freedmen's Bureau, more than any other institution, fell the task of assisting at the birth of a free labor society. The Bureau's commissioner was Gen. Oliver Otis Howard, whose close ties to the freedmen's aid societies had earned him the sobriquet "Christian General." Although temporary, Howard's agency was an experiment in social policy that, a modern scholar writes, "did not belong to the America of its day." Its responsibilities can only be described as daunting; they included introducing a workable system of free labor in the South, establishing schools for freedmen, providing aid to the destitute, aged, ill, and insane, adjudicating disputes among blacks and between the races, and attempting to secure for blacks and white Unionists equal justice from the state and local governments established during Presidential Reconstruction. The local Bureau agent was expected to win the confidence of blacks and whites alike in a situation where race and labor relations had been poisoned by mutual distrust and conflicting interests. Moreover, the Bureau employed, at its peak, not more than 900 agents in the entire South. Only a dozen served in Mississippi in 1866, and the largest contingent in Alabama at any time comprised twenty. "It is not . . . in your power to fulfill one tenth of the expectations of those who framed the Bureau," Gen. William T. Sherman advised Howard. "I fear you have Hercules' task."

At first glance, the Bureau's activities appear as a welter of contradictions, reflecting differences among individual agents in interpreting general policies laid down in Washington. But unifying the Bureau's activities was the endeavor to lay the foundation for a free labor society. To the extent that this meant putting freedmen back to work on plantations, the Bureau's policies coincided with the interests of the planters. To the extent that it prohibited coercive labor discipline, took up the burden of black education, sought to protect blacks against violence, and promoted the removal of legal barriers to blacks' advancement, the Bureau reinforced the freedmen's aspirations. In the end, the Bureau's career exposed the ambiguities and inadequacies of the free labor ideology itself. But simultaneously, the former slaves seized the opportunity offered by the Bureau's imperfect efforts on their behalf to bolster their own quest for self-improvement and autonomy. . . .

In the war's immediate aftermath, federal policy regarding black labor was established by the army. And the army seemed to many freedmen to have only one object in view—to compel them to return to work on the plantations. In the spring and early summer of 1865, military commanders issued stringent orders to stem the influx of freedmen into Southern cities. Military regulations forbade blacks to travel without passes from their employers or be on the streets at night and prohibited "insubordination" on their part. In several cities, postwar black political organization began with protests against army policies. A group of Memphis free blacks condemned the rounding up of "vagrants" for plantation labor: "It seems the great slave trade is revived again in our city." In July, Secretary of War Stanton instructed Southern commanders to discontinue pass requirements and cease interfering with blacks' freedom of movement. But the assumption underpinning military policy, that the interests of all Americans would be best served by blacks' return to plantation labor, remained intact as the Freedmen's Bureau assumed command of the transition to free labor.

The idea of free labor, wrote a Tennessee agent, was "the noblest principle on earth." Like Northern Republicans generally, Bureau officers held what in retrospect appear as amazingly utopian assumptions about the ease with which Southern labor relations could be recast in the free labor mold. Blacks and whites merely had to abandon attitudes toward labor, and toward each other, inherited from slavery, and the market would do the rest. "Let it be understood that a fair day's wages will be paid for a fair day's work," Gen. Robert K. Scott, the Bureau's chief officer in South Carolina, announced, "and the planter will not want for reliable and faithful laborers." With the Bureau acting as midwife at its birth, the free market would quickly assume its role as arbiter of the South's economic destinies, honing those qualities that distinguished free labor from slave—efficiency, productivity, and economic rationality—and ensuring equitable wages and working conditions.

In fact, this social vision was to a large extent irrelevant to the social realities the Bureau confronted. The free labor ideology rested on a theory of universal economic rationality and the conviction that all classes in a free labor society shared the same interests. In reality, former masters and former slaves inherited from slavery work habits and attitudes at odds with free labor assumptions, and both recognized, more clearly than the Bureau, the irreconcilability of their respective interests and aspirations. The free labor social order, moreover, ostensibly guaranteed the ambitious worker the opportunity for economic mobility, the ability to move from wage labor to independence through the acquisition of productive property. Yet what became of this axiom in an impoverished society where even the highest agricultural wages remained pitiably low, and whose white population was determined to employ every means at its disposal to prevent blacks from acquiring land or any other means of economic independence?

Establishing themselves in the South in the summer and fall of 1865, Bureau agents hoped to induce Southerners to "give the system a fair and honest trial." To planters' desire for a disciplined labor force governed by the lash, agents responded that "*bodily coercion* fell as an incident of slavery." To the contention that blacks would never work voluntarily or respond to market incentives, they replied that the problem of economic readjustment should be viewed through the prism of labor, rather than race. . . .

The "two evils" against which the Bureau had to contend, an army officer observed in July 1865, were "cruelty on the part of the employer and shirking on the part of the negroes." Yet the Bureau, like the army, seemed to consider black reluctance to labor the greater threat to its economic mission. In some areas agents continued the military's urban pass systems and vagrancy patrols, as well as the practice of rounding up unemployed laborers for shipment to plantations. Bureau courts in Memphis dispatched impoverished blacks convicted of crimes to labor for whites who would pay their fines. "What a mockery to call those 'Freedmen' who are still subjected to such things," commented a local minister.

United as to the glories of free labor, Bureau officials, like Northerners generally, differed among themselves about the ultimate social implications of the free labor ideology. Some believed the freedmen would remain a permanent plantation labor force; others insisted they should enjoy the same opportunity to make their way up the social ladder to independent proprietorship as Northern workers; still others hoped the federal government would assist at least some blacks in acquiring their own farms. Howard believed most freedmen must return to plantation labor, but under conditions that allowed them the opportunity to work their way out of the wage-earning class. At the same time, he took seriously the provision in the act establishing his agency that authorized it to settle freedmen on confiscated and abandoned lands. In 1865, Howard and a group of sympathetic Bureau officials attempted to breathe life into this alternative vision of a free-labor South.

. . . [T]he Bureau controlled over 850,000 acres of abandoned land in 1865, hardly enough to accommodate all the former slaves but sufficient to make a start toward creating a black yeomanry. Howard's subordinates included men sincerely committed to settling freedmen on farms of their own and protecting the rights of those who already occupied land. In Louisiana, Thomas Conway, the Bureau's assistant commissioner, leased over 60,000 acres to blacks. . . . Most dedicated of all to the idea of black landownership was Gen. Rufus Saxton, a prewar abolitionist who directed the Bureau in South Carolina, Georgia, and Florida during the summer of 1865. Saxton had already overseen the settlement of thousands of blacks on lands reserved for them under Gen. Sherman's Field Order 15. In June 1865 he announced his intention to use the property under Bureau control to provide freedmen with forty-acre homesteads "where by faithful industry they can readily achieve an independence."

Initially, Howard himself shared the radical aims of Conway and Saxton. At the end of July 1865 he issued Circular 13, which instructed Bureau agents to "set aside" forty-acre tracts for the freedmen as rapidly as possible. But [President] Andrew Johnson, who had been pardoning former Confederates, soon directed Howard to rescind his order. A new policy, drafted in the White House and issued in September as Howard's Circular 15, ordered the restoration to pardoned owners of all land except the small amount that had already been sold under a court decree. Once growing crops had been harvested, virtually all the land in Bureau hands would revert to its former owners. . . .

The restoration of land required the displacement of tens of thousands of freedmen throughout the South. The army evicted most of the 20,000 blacks settled on confiscated and abandoned property in southeastern Virginia. The 62,000 acres farmed by Louisiana blacks were restored to their former owners; as the wife of a New Orleans editor observed, Gen. Joseph S. Fullerton, who succeeded Conway, "can't seem to hustle out fast enough the occupants of confiscated property." . . .

Nowhere, however, was the restoration process so disruptive as in the Georgia and South Carolina lowcountry. On more than one occasion freedmen armed themselves, barricaded plantations, and drove off owners attempting to dispossess them. Black squatters told one party of Edisto Island landlords in February 1866, "you have better go back to Charleston, and go to work there, and if you can do nothing else, you can pick oysters and earn your living as the loyal people have done—by the sweat of their brows." Bureau agents, black and white, made every effort to induce lowcountry freedmen to sign contracts with their former owners, while federal troops forcibly evicted those who refused. In the end, only about 2,000 South Carolina and Georgia freedmen actually received the land they had been promised in 1865.

The events of 1865 and 1866 kindled a deep sense of betrayal among freedmen throughout the South. Land enough existed, wrote former Mississippi slave Merrimon Howard, for every "man and woman to have as much as they could work." Yet blacks had been left with

> no *land,* no *house,* not so much as [a] place to lay our head. . . . Despised by the world, hated by the country that gives us birth, denied of all our writs as a people, we were friends on the march, . . . brothers on the battlefield, but in the peaceful pursuits of life it seems that we are strangers.

Thus, by 1866 the Bureau found itself with no alternative but to encourage virtually all freedmen to sign annual contracts to work on the plantations. Its hopes for long-term black advancement and Southern economic prosperity now came to focus exclusively on the labor contract itself. By voluntarily signing and adhering to contracts, both planters and freedmen would develop the habits of a free labor economy and come to understand their fundamental harmony of interests. Agents found themselves required to perform a nearly impossible balancing act. Disabusing blacks of the idea that they would soon obtain land from the government, and threatening to arrest those who refused to sign a contract or leave the plantations, agents simultaneously insisted on blacks' right to bargain freely for employment and attempted to secure more advantageous contracts than had prevailed in 1865. Some Bureau officers approved agreements in which the laborer would receive nothing at all if the crop failed and could incur fines for such vaguely defined offenses as failure to do satisfactory work or "impudent, profane or indecent language." More conscientious agents revoked contract provisions regulating blacks' day-to-day lives and insisted that laborers who left plantations before the harvest must be paid for their work up to the date of departure. And virtually all agents insisted that planters acknowledge that their power to employ physical coercion had come to an end.

The Bureau's role in supervising labor relations reached its peak in 1866 and 1867; thereafter, federal authorities intervened less and less frequently to oversee contracts or settle plantation disputes. To the extent that the contract system had been intended to promote stability in labor relations in the chaotic aftermath of war and allow commercial agriculture to resume, it could be deemed a success. But in other ways, the system failed. For the entire contract system in some ways violated the principles of free labor. Agreements, Howard announced soon after assuming office, "should be free, *bona fide* acts." Yet how voluntary were labor contracts signed by blacks when they were denied access to land, coerced by troops and Bureau agents if they refused to sign, and fined or imprisoned if they struck for higher wages? Propertyless individuals in the North, to be sure, were compelled to labor for wages, but the compulsion was supplied by necessity, not by public officials, and contracts did not prevent them from leaving work whenever they chose. Why, asked the New Orleans *Tribune* again and again, did the Bureau require blacks to sign year-long labor contracts when "laborers throughout the civilized world"—including agricultural laborers in the North—could leave their employment at any time? To which one may add that even the most sympathetic Bureau officials assumed that blacks would constitute the rural labor force, at least until the natural working of the market divided the great plantations into small farms. "Idle white men" were never required to sign labor contracts or ordered to leave Southern cities for the countryside, a fact that made a mockery of the Bureau's professed goal of equal treatment for the freedmen.

Howard always believed that the Bureau's policies, viewed as a whole, benefited the freedmen more than their employers, especially since civil authorities offered blacks no protection against violence or fraud and the courts provided no justice to those seeking legal redress. He viewed the system of annual labor contracts as a temporary expedient, which would disappear once free labor obtained a "permanent foothold" in the South "under its necessary protection of equal and just laws properly executed." Eventually, as in the North, the market would regulate employment. Yet in the early years of Reconstruction, operating within the constraints of the free labor ideology, adverse crop and market conditions, the desire to restore production of the South's staple crops, and presidential policy, Bureau decisions conceived as temporary exerted a powerful influence on the emergence of new economic and social relations, closing off some options for blacks, shifting the balance of power in favor of employers, and helping to stabilize the beleaguered planter class. . . .

So began the forging of a new class structure to replace the shattered world of slavery. It was an economic transformation that would culminate, long after the end of Reconstruction, in the consolidation of a rural proletariat composed of the descendants of former slaves and white yeomen, and of a new owning class of planters and merchants, itself subordinate to Northern financiers and industrialists. The historian, however, must avoid telescoping the actual course of events into a predetermined, linear progression. A new set of labor arrangements did not spring up overnight, and there was no preordained outcome to the workings of what one federal official described as "the new *system* of labor if system it may be called, when there is endless confusion, and absurd contradiction."

In some parts of the South, planters in the early postwar years found it almost impossible to resume production, notably in the sugar and rice kingdoms, where the estates of exceptionally wealthy aristocracies lay in ruins. The war had devastated the expensive grinding and threshing mills and the elaborate systems of dikes, irrigation canals, and levees and thoroughly disrupted the labor system. Only a handful of Louisiana's sugar plantations operated at all in 1865; the rest stood idle, overgrown with weeds, and the crop amounted to only one-tenth of that raised in 1861. In the rice region, "labor was in a disorganized and chaotic state, production had ceased, and . . . the power to compel laborers to go into the rice swamp utterly broken." . . .

Where agricultural production did resume, a variety of arrangements often coexisted in the same area, sometimes on the same plantation. In the early years of Reconstruction, payments included cash wages, paid monthly or at year's end, a share of the crop, divided collectively among the entire labor force or among smaller groups of workers; various combinations of wage and share payments; time-sharing plans in which freedmen worked part of the week for the planter and part on their own land; wages in kind; and cash wages for specific tasks.

Beneath the welter of arrangements, however, certain broad patterns may be discerned. In 1865 and 1866, a majority of labor contracts involved agreements between planters and large groups of freedmen. Payment was generally either in "standing wages" withheld until year's end, or, more frequently, "share wages"—a share of the crop sometimes paid collectively to the workers and divided among themselves and sometimes allocated according to their working capacity. In the contracts of 1865, the shares paid to the freedmen were usually extremely low, sometimes as little as one-tenth of the crop. In effect, moreover, the postponement of payment to the end of the year represented an interest-free extension of credit from employee to employer, as well as a shifting of part of the risk of farming to the freedmen. The practice not only left share workers penniless in the event of a poor crop, but offered numerous opportunities for fraud on the part of planters, some of whom deducted excessive fines for poor work or other infractions, or presented freedmen with bills for rations that exceeded the wages due them.

In 1866 and 1867, the freedmen's demand for an improvement in their economic condition and greater independence in their working lives set in motion a train of events that fundamentally transformed the plantation labor system. Blacks' desire for greater autonomy in the day-to-day organization of work produced a trend toward the subdivision of the labor force. Gang labor for wages persisted where planters had access to outside capital and could offer high monthly wages, promptly paid. Thanks to an influx of Northern investment, this was the case on sugar plantations that managed to resume production. On many sugar plantations in 1866 and 1867, however, squads of a dozen or fewer freedmen replaced the gangs so reminiscent of slavery. Generally organized by the blacks themselves, these squads sometimes consisted entirely of members of a single family, but more often included unrelated men. By 1867 the gang system was disappearing from the cotton fields.

The final stage in the decentralization of plantation agriculture was the emergence of sharecropping. Unlike the earlier share-wage system, with which it is often confused, in sharecropping individual families (instead of large groups of freedmen) signed contracts with the landowner and became responsible for a specified piece of land (rather than working in gangs). Generally, sharecroppers retained one-third of the year's crop if the planter provided implements, fertilizer, work animals, and seed, and half if they supplied their own. The transition to sharecropping occurred at different rates on different plantations and continued well into the 1870s, but the arrangement appeared in some areas soon after the Civil War.

To blacks, sharecropping offered an escape from gang labor and day-to-day white supervision. For planters, the system provided a way to reduce the cost and difficulty of labor supervision, share risk with tenants, and circumvent the chronic shortage of cash and credit. Most important of all, it stabilized the work force, for sharecroppers utilized the labor of all members of the family and had a vested interest in remaining until the crop had been gathered. Yet whatever its economic rationale, many planters resisted sharecropping as a threat to their overall authority and inefficient besides (since they believed blacks would not work without direct white supervision). A compromise not fully satisfactory to either party, the system's precise outlines remained a point of conflict. Planters insisted sharecroppers were wage laborers who must obey the orders of their employer and who possessed no property right in the crop until they received their share at the end of the year. But sharecroppers, a planter complained in 1866, considered themselves "partners in the crop," who insisted on farming according to their own dictates and would not brook white supervision. Only a system of wages, payable at the end of the year, he concluded, would allow whites to "work in accordance with our former management." But precisely because it seemed so far removed from "our former management," blacks came to prefer the sharecropping system.

If freedmen in the cotton fields rejected the gang labor associated with bondage, those in the rice swamps insisted on strengthening the familiar task system, the foundation of the partial autonomy they had enjoyed as slaves. "We want to work just as we have always worked," declared a group of freedmen in South Carolina's rice region, and to attract labor, rice planters found themselves obliged to let the blacks "work . . . as they choose without any overseer." Out of the wreck of the rice economy and blacks' insistence on autonomy emerged an unusual set of labor relations. Some planters simply rented their plantations to blacks for a share of the crop or divided the land among groups of freedmen to cultivate as they saw fit. Others agreed to a system of labor sharing in which freedmen worked for two days on the plantation in exchange for an allotment of land on which to grow their own crops.

Thus, the struggles of early Reconstruction planted the seeds of new labor systems in the rural South. The precise manner in which these seeds matured would be worked out not only on Southern farms and plantations, but also on the Reconstruction battlefields of local, state, and national politics.

✢ *F U R T H E R   R E A D I N G*

Ira Berlin, *Slaves Without Masters: The Free Negro in the Antebellum South* (1974)
—— and Herbert Gutman, "Natives and Immigrants, Free Men and Slaves: Urban Workingmen in the Antebellum American South," *American Historical Review* 88 (1983), 1175–1200
—— et al., eds., *Freedom: A Documentary History of Emancipation, 1861–1867*, Series I, Volumne I: *The Destruction of Slavery* (1985); Series I, Volumne II: *The War Time Genesis of Free Labor: The Upper South* (1990); Series I, Volumne III: *The War Time Genesis of Free Labor: The Lower South* (1990)
Pete Daniel, *Breaking the Land: The Transformation of Cotton, Tobacco, and Rice Cultures since 1880* (1985)
W. E. B. Du Bois, *Black Reconstruction in America, 1860–1880* (1935)
Barbara Jeanne Fields, *Slavery and Freedom on the Middle Ground: Maryland During the Nineteenth Century* (1985)
Robert W. Fogel and Stanley L. Engerman, *Time on the Cross: The Economics of American Negro Slavery* (1974)
Eric Foner, *Politics and Ideology in the Age of the Civil War* (1980)
——, *Nothing but Freedom: Emancipation and Its Legacy* (1983)
——, *Reconstruction: America's Unfinished Revolution* (1988)
Eugene Genovese, *The Political Economy of Slavery* (1965)
——, *Roll, Jordon, Roll: The World the Slaves Made* (1974)
Herbert Gutman, *Slavery and the Numbers Game: A Critique of "Time on the Cross"* (1975)
Jacqueline Jones, " 'My Mother Was Much of a Woman': Black Women, Work, and the Family Under Slavery," *Feminist Studies* 8 (1982), 235–269
Peter Kolchin, *Unfree Labor: American Slavery and Russian Serfdom* (1987)
Phillip D. Morgan, "Work and Culture: The Task System and the World of Low-country Blacks, 1700–1880," *William and Mary Quarterly* 39 (1982), 564–599
Roger L. Ransom and Richard Sutch, *One Kind of Freedom: The Economic Consequences of Emancipation* (1977)
Willie Lee Rose, *Rehearsal for Reconstruction: The Port Royal Experiment* (1964)
Robert S. Starobin, *Industrial Slavery in the Old South* (1970)
Deborah Gray White, *Ar'n't I a Woman?: Black Women in the Plantation South* (1986)

Jonathan M. Wiener, *Social Origins of the New South: Alabama, 1860–1885* (1978)
Harold Woodman, "Sequel to Slavery," *Journal of Southern History* 43 (1977), 523–554
———, "Post–Civil War Southern Agriculture and the Law," *Agricultural History* 53 (1979), 319–337
Gavin Wright, *The Political Economy of the Cotton South* (1978)

CHAPTER 5

From Peasant to Proletarian

✣

*During the forty years before the end of World War I, millions of peasants, ru-
ral laborers, and village tradesmen emigrated from Europe, the Mexican border-
lands, French Canada, and the southern states. Most settled in the centers of
industry and commercial agriculture that spread in a giant arc from New England through the Midwest and on to the great farms and mines of California.
This transformation of rural people into a wage-earning proletariat was a
worldwide phenomenon that swelled the populations of Shanghai, Buenos Aires,
and Berlin as well as those of Chicago, Detroit, and Buffalo. By 1920 one out
of eight U.S. residents had been born abroad; in many cities and regions, a
large majority of the working class were either immigrants or the sons and
daughters of immigrants.*

*Historians once conceived of America as a ''melting pot'' in which a process
of cultural assimilation and upward mobility rapidly homogenized these newcomers. But today, scholars are more impressed with the vitality and integrity of
these rural cultures, and with the remarkable struggle immigrant communities
waged to nurture traditional values of work and family even in the midst of an
urban, industrial environment over which they seemed to have so little control.
A process of ''chain migration'' ensured that individual neighborhoods would
long retain a particular ethnic flavor: in some instances, an entire block might
be populated by the former residents of a single Sicilian village or North Caro
lina county. Likewise, choice and circumstance often linked particular immigrant
groups to the job opportunities that opened up in specific regional industries: for
example, French-Canadians in the textile mills of Woonsocket, Rhode Island;
Finns along the Seattle waterfront; and Lithuanian Jews in the clothing factories of Baltimore. Black migrants from the U.S. South could find little work
other than employment in personal service, although the labor shortages of
World War I opened up thousands of jobs in meatpacking, steel, and other
heavy industries to African-American males.*

*What impact did these ethnic, racial, and gender divisions have on work-
ing-class America? Certainly some employers took advantage of this heterogeneity
to structure their work forces along ethnically hierarchical lines that would enable them to suppress unions and more easily control those who toiled in their
factories and mills. Protestant males of northern European extraction usually
held the supervisory positions; unemployed blacks were sometimes recruited as
strikebreakers. Racial prejudice, gender discrimination, and ethnic rivalry within*

the working class also made organization and resistance difficult. But could the ethnic solidarity of these same workers enhance their capacity for militancy and self-organization? Did they find in their peasant heritage social values that they could use to question the legitimacy of industrial capitalism itself?

✢ D O C U M E N T S

Much of what we know about the work life of immigrant labor was first recorded by Progressive Era reformers eager to ameliorate deplorable workplace conditions. In the first document, industrial-relations investigator John Fitch describes the eighteen- to twenty-four-hour "long turn" worked by pre–World War I immigrant steelworkers, and notes its devastating impact on their family and community life. In the second document, labor economist John R. Commons, a pioneering historian of American labor, offers a congressional investigating committee a structural analysis of the sweatshop system in the Jewish garment trades. Lewis Hine's famous photographs captured the evils of child labor and of unsanitary sweatshops for the National Child Labor Committee; the third selection comprises examples of Hine's tenement-life scenes.

The next two documents provide an insight into the African-American migration experience. We get a sense of why blacks moved North in the fourth document, consisting of letters published during 1917 in *The Chicago Defender*, a major black newspaper. The fifth document records the argument made by some black leaders for opening up factory jobs to black women, who were thought to adjust well to the pace of machine-driven work. The final set of documents suggests a comparison between industrial and agricultural labor and the role played by ethnicity in the deployment of the work force. In the sixth document, California beet growers exemplify the racist attitudes of the dominant culture in their 1911 evaluation of their Mexican and Japanese workers. Migrant laborers testify before a Truman-era investigating committee, in which they describe a labor-contract system not much different from that of the beet-field workers a half-century before, while unionized agricultural workers complain of competition from undocumented immigrants before a 1952 session of Congress in the seventh document. The last document shows the response of the Congress of Industrial Organizations (CIO) to migrant labor in the early post–World War II years.

Investigator John Fitch Describes
Steel's Long Shift, 1912

There is a very large class of workmen in the steel industry, many thousands of them throughout the country, who work consecutively either eighteen hours or twenty-four hours regularly every two weeks. This is so because the two shifts alternate working nights, the day shift of one week becoming the night shift of the next and so on. When the plant works only six days, this can be accomplished without difficulty, but in a seven-day plant it is made possible only through the institution known as the "long turn." The night crew can change to the day shift by working through Saturday night until Sunday noon, an eighteen-hour period. The former day crew then relieves them and works until Monday morning, thus putting in another eighteen-hour period and getting itself on to the night shift for the week. The more general custom, however, is for the day shift to get in line for night work by working a full twenty-four-hour period, Sunday and Sunday night, finishing Monday morning. That puts the night crew on to Monday's day shift and allows them twenty-four hours off duty. Where the change is made every week, each crew works six days in one week and eight in the next.* In some plants the change is made only each two weeks. In that case, each man works the long turn once a month.

It is in the blast furnaces that the long turn comes with regularity. Federal census figures in 1910 show that there were 28,429 wage-earners employed in blast furnaces in the United States in 1909. The Federal Bureau of Labor investigators found that in a blast furnace plant nine-tenths of the employes [sic] work seven days a week. Nine-tenths of 38,429 is 34,586, which is the number of men in the blast furnaces who work either eighteen or twenty-four hours once or twice each month in 1909. But that isn't all. There were 647 open-hearth furnaces in 1909 with over 15,000 men tending them. Many of them work a part of every Sunday, and a considerable proportion are regular twelve-hour, seven-day workmen. And that isn't all. The number of mill wrights, engineers, yard laborers, furnace tenders, and guards in steel mills throughout the United States who have been regularly working twelve hours a day and seven days a week cannot be conjectured from data in my possession. It is a positive fact, however, that there is an enormous number of them. If we could ascertain the total number of seven-day workmen in 1910, we should find it to have been, I think, well over 50,000. A great majority of these worked twenty-four hours twice each month. . . .

Social Effects of a 12-Hour Day

But all these things are more or less beside the point. Supposing it were true that the twelve-hour work is easy and that there were no physical indications of overstrain. The big fact, the only really vital and significant fact, remains that a twelve-hour schedule denies a man all true leisure. It isn't leisure for a man to sit on a bench in a steel mill waiting for his turn any more than it is for [a] motorman at a street crossing, waiting for the signal to proceed, or a machinist at his lathe, between times of increasing the tension. I have yet to hear of a steel company official choosing to spend his rest periods sitting on a bench beside a blooming mill, or picking out a blast furnace yard as a place to sleep. On the other hand, I am not recommending automobiles or golf as the necessary forms of recreation for the steel workers, but I do insist that it is the workman's right to spend his leisure hours outside the mill yard, and that is something that the twelve-hour day denies him.

---

* There are fourteen working days in one week—unless you think that a man who works twelve hours each twenty-four is doing only a half day's work at a time.

In October, 1910, I talked with an employe of the Cambria Steel Company, an independent concern, who had one week a ten-hour day and next week a fourteen-hour night, and who every other Saturday night went out and worked through until Sunday night, a twenty-four-hour shift. It took him an hour to get from his home to the mill and another hour to go back. So his actual time away from home was twelve hours on day shift and sixteen hours at night.

"It's pretty hard to get rested in summer when you're on the night turn," he told me, "It's too hot to sleep well daytimes. But in the winter you can drop down and go to sleep anywheres, you're so tired. The day shift isn't so bad—ten hours long—but after you've worked the Sunday long turn, you're used up pretty bad. It takes several days to get over it." . . .

In November, 1910, I was in Lackawanna, N.Y., the home of the Lackawanna Steel Company, which is also an independent concern. It was there that I met the man . . . who worked fifty-six hours out of a possible seventy-two, at one time last fall. I called upon him in his home.

"Of course," he told me, "such a schedule is pretty hard on a man; I'm dead for a week after working the long shift. And then, you know, if you're a church man, it makes it pretty hard to attend services; I can't ever go Sunday morning. And Sunday night it's hard to go because I go to work extra early Monday morning. I get out to prayer-meeting only every other week, when I am on the day shift, and it's absolutely impossible to have a full meeting of the church at any time because the men work on different shifts." . . .

It was this man's wife who gave me a little insight into the burden of the long shift upon the housekeeper. "It's just about as hard for me as it is for him," she said. "He has to be at work at seven o'clock in the morning, so I have to get up at half past five to get his breakfast; and then he doesn't get home until after six and so it's pretty late before I get the work done. And on Monday mornings, when he goes to work earlier, I get up at half past four. But the worst thing about it all is that it's terribly uncertain. Sometimes he works a long turn when I don't expect it and sometimes he doesn't when I thought he was going to. If we plan for an evening out together, like as not he will come home early for supper and tell me that he has got to go back to the mill and work all night. We don't ever plan things any more; we just take an evening's pleasure together whenever we happen to have it."

"It's a great strain on a man," another at Lackawanna told me. "I could stand eight hours all right, but the twelve-hour schedule is a terribly nerve racking thing. I am only twenty-seven years old and my nerves are getting pretty bad. It's simply a killing pace in the steel works, and no pleasure in it. Most of the skilled men that I know are just trying to save their money until they get a stake and go out into something else before the industry kills them." . . .

Economist John R. Commons Denounces the "Sweating System," 1901

The term "sweating," or "sweating system," originally denoted a system of subcontract, wherein the work is let out to contractors to be done in small shops or homes. "In practice," says the report of the Illinois Bureau of Labor Statistics, "sweating consists of the farming out by competing manufacturers to competing contractors of the material for garments, which in turn is distributed among competing men and women to be made up." . . . In the sweating system the foreman becomes a contractor, with his own small shop and foot-power machine. In the factory system the workmen are congregated where they can be seen by the factory inspectors and where they can organize or develop a common understanding. In the sweating system they are isolated and unknown.

The position of the contractor or sweater now in the business in American cities is peculiarly that of an organizer and employer of immigrants. The man best fitted to be a contractor is the man who is well acquainted with his neighbors, who is able to speak the languages of several classes of immigrants, who can easily persuade his neighbors or their wives and children to work for him, and who in this way can obtain the cheapest help. During the busy season, when the work doubles, the number of people employed increases in the same proportion. All the contractors are agents and go around among the people. Housewives, who formerly worked at the trade and abandoned it after marriage, are called into service for an increased price of a dollar or two a week. Men who have engaged in other occupations, such as small business and peddling, but who are out of business most of the year, are marshaled into service by the contractor, who knows all of them and can easily look them up and put them in as competitors by offering them a dollar or two a week more than they are getting elsewhere. Usually when work comes to the contractor from the manufacturer and is offered to his employees for a smaller price than has previously been paid, the help will remonstrate and ask to be paid the full price. Then the contractor tells them, "I have nothing to do with the price. The price is made for me by the manufacturer. I have very little to say about the price." That is, he cuts himself completely loose from any responsibility to his employees as to how much they are to get for their labor. The help do not know the manufacturer. They cannot register their complaint with the man who made the price for their labor. The contractor, who did not make the price for their labor, claims that it is of no use to complain to him. So that however much the price for labor goes down, there is no one responsible for it.

There is always cutthroat competition among contractors. A contractor feels more dependent than any of his employees. He is always speculating on the idea of making a fortune by getting more work from the manufacturer than his neighbor and by having it made cheaper. Usually when he applies for work in the inside shop he comes in, hat in hand, very much like a beggar. He seems to feel the utter uselessness of his calling. Oftentimes the contractor is forced to send work back because he cannot make it under the conditions on which he took it; yet he does not dare to refuse an offer for fear the manufacturer will not give him more of his work. So he tries to figure it down by every device, and yet, perhaps, in the end is forced to send it back. . . .

Tenement-Life Scenes of Lewis Hine, 1911

Children carried garments from the factory to be sewn at home. In fieldnotes accompanying this photograph, Lewis Hine wrote, "A load of kimonos just finished. Girl very reticent. Thompson St., N.Y." (National Archives)

Reflecting on this New York City scene, Hine noted, "Mrs. Lucy Libertine and family: Johnnie, 4 years old, Mary 6 years, Millie 9 years, picking nuts in their basement tenement, 143 Hudson St. Mary was standing on the open mouth of the bag holding the cracked nuts [to be picked], with her dirty shoes on, and using a huge, dirty jacknife." (National Archives)

African-American Letters on Migrating North, 1917

Memphis, Tenn., May 5, 1917.

Dear Sir: I saw your add in the Chicago Defender papa and me being a firman and a all around man I thought I would write you. prehaps You might could do me lots of good. and if you can use me any way write me and let me No. in my trade or in foundry work. all so I got a boy 19 years old he is pretty apt in Learning I would Like to get him up there and Learn him a trade and I have several others would come previding if there be an opening for them. So this is all ans. soon

Algiers, La., May 16–17.

Sir: I saw sometime ago in the Chicago Defender, that you needed me for different work, would like to state that I can bring you all the men that

From "Letters Home from Black Migrants to the North," 1916–1918, Emitt Scott, ed., in *Journal of Negro History*, 4 (July 1919), pp. 305–306. Reprinted by permission of the Association for Study of Afro-American Life and History, Inc.

you need, to do anything of work. or send them, would like to Come my self Con recomend all the men I bring to do any kind of work, and will give satisfaction; I have bin foreman for 20 yrs over some of these men in different work from R. R. work to Boiler Shop machine shop Blacksmith shop Concreet finishing or putting down pipe or any work to be did. they are all hard working men and will work at any kind of work also plastering anything in the labor line, from Clerical work down, I will not bring a man that is looking for a easy time only hard working men, that want good wages for there work, let me here from you at once.

Ellisville, Miss., 5/1/17.

Kind Sir: I have been takeing the Defender 4 months I injoy reading it very much I dont think that there could be a grander paper printed for the race, then the defender. Dear Editor I am thinking of leaving for Some good place in the North or West one I dont Know just which I learn that Nebraska was a very good climate for the people of the South. I wont you to give me some ideas on it, Or Some good farming country. I have been public working for 10 year. I am tired of that, And want to get out on a good farm. I have a wife and 5 children and we all wont to get our from town a place an try to buy a good home near good Schools good Churchs. I am going to leave here as soon as I get able to work. Some are talking of a free train May 15 But I dont no anything of that. So I will go to work an then I will be sure, of my leaving Of course if it run I will go but I am not depending on it Wages here are so low can scarcely live We can buy enough to eat we only buy enough to Keep up alive I mean the greater part of the Race. Women wages are from $1.25 Some time as high as $2.50. just some time for a whole week.

Hoping Dear Editor that I will get a hearing from you through return mail, giving me Some ideas and Some Sketches on the different Climate suitable for our health.

P. S. You can place my letter in Some of the Defender Columns but done use my name in print, for it might get back down here.

African-American Leaders Laud Black Women's Progress in Industry, 1924

The Negro woman's sudden entrance into industry is a new adventure and a dramatic innovation. In the urgent quest for workers to "carry on" during the World War, she saw her longed-for opportunity, saw—as she visioned it—the end of the rainbow, and she came seeking it by thousands from her sunny, quiet southern home and plantation and placid housework and was at once swallowed up in the industrial centers in northern cities. Plucked so abruptly from the narrow spheres of such service as field hands, domestics and children's nurses, it is amazing to observe the transition and transformation of this same gentle, leisurely southern woman into the high-tension industrial worker in a large factory. Labor turnover, time clocks, piece work, output, maximum and minimum production, these words were unknown in her vocabulary a few years back. But today there are thousands of these girls and women, working tirelessly and patiently and steadily in our large industrial plants,—and *making good*.

At the close of the War and during the general depression in business which followed, many Negro girls were released and replaced with white help. It was a tragedy to the Negro girl, as she had not had time to lay aside anything for the rainy day, to gain needed experience and skill, and to overcome the impatience of the average employer and an antagonistic foreman. She was hired in a period of crisis, to fill the gap at the bottom of the scale,—the most undesirable and unskilled jobs in the factory were assigned to her. The idea seemed very general that she could not be trusted to do the skilled work in any event—usually she was not given an opportunity if white help could be secured. Wet and sloppy work, heavy and tedious, with little chance for advancement, and if she did succeed, it was by sheer grit and determination, as many have told me. She had to be able to outdo her white competitor; sometimes she failed through lack of experience, and this would cause employers to say she was not capable, when in most cases it was simply due to poor selective instinct on his part or lack of intelligence or adaptability in her particular case.

Left to the mercy of ignorant, prejudiced, intolerant foremen, what could be expected? However, the whole story is not so dark. Though her progress was retarded by the turn in events, still we know that she did retain some very worthwhile places and she has progressed in them wherever possible to semi-skilled and skilled jobs. It is worthy of note, that wherever an employer was humane and appreciative and gave his Negro help a chance to advance and a square deal in wages and working conditions, he had steady, cheerful workers—which refutes a charge so prone to be made about their being undependable. Employers have found her amiable in disposition, intelligent and more adaptable than the unskilled foreign worker for whom white social agencies are engaged in season and out to aid them to adjust themselves, develop technique and become capable, highly skilled workers. For the Negro girl there are no such agencies outside of a small work being done by the Y.W.C.A. in the City of Chicago. In my experience with both white and Negro girls, I have found no difference between them in capacity for work. . . .

The story of the Negro women employed at the Nachman Springfilled Cushion Company of Chicago, Illinois, may be of some value in understanding the whole situation. It will also show the splendid growth of a business whose enviable record for superior quality and excellence in manufactured products is the output of these same women power machine operators, who make the durable covers for the softly resilient springs.

In the beginning this company employed less than fifty persons. It was a simple matter for the heads of the firm to know each individual worker. Today there are between six and seven hundred on the pay-roll. The employment of such large numbers has tended to destroy any personal relation between employer and employees, and there is practically no contact with the workers. The making of these cushion covers was also a simple process in the beginning; they were used mostly for chair seats and a perfectly "green" girl who had never seen a power machine before could learn in a very few days to sew them. Today this firm manufactures cushions for all kinds of upholstered furniture, day-beds, mattresses, and automobile seats. Each unit-spring is enclosed in a separate pocket and these covers are made in two operations.

When I tell you we have girls who can sew from five to seven thousand pockets in a day, you will realize that they have become "peppy" and mastered the speeding-up in industry. They are put on piece work in about three weeks and we have many girls making from twenty to thirty dollars per week. An average girl can make eighteen dollars per week. This is good pay for a year round job.

There came a time when this large group of girls, with no previous factory experience and no one to encourage and reprove them or give them any personal attention whatever, were doing about as they pleased. They were very irregular in attendance,—a very serious matter to the firm, in trying to give prompt service and keep up production.

The cushion is an unfinished product and is delivered in large quantities to factories to be upholstered. The girls would say, "If we stay out we are the only losers, being on piece work." So the week would go something like this: Monday—bad; Tuesday—a little better; Wednesday—very good, being pay day; Thursday—very poor; Friday—somewhat better; Saturday—a half-day and the worst day of the week. The company was about three months behind in delivery of orders due to the fact that girls were given a chance to learn to operate the machines with pay, and many stayed just long enough to learn. Continually employing new help, of course, was responsible for poor quality of work as well as a large labor turnover and financial loss. The girls were disposed to be late for work and quit anywhere from a half-hour to fifteen minutes before closing time. There was considerable lack of respect for authority when it came to the forelady and inspector, as there was more or less a division of authority; so the firm had almost decided to release all the colored help, which meant a terrible blow to future opportunities. It was at this juncture that the Chicago Urban League was appealed to and they advised putting a Negro woman as Personnel Director in charge to save the situation if possible for these hundreds of girls. The work of this Director has been very interesting and to some considerable degree satisfactory to the firm. It must be acknowledged to the credit of the firm that they have done everything possible for the Director to carry out her plans.

Her first task was to establish confidence and good-will in the hearts of the workers for herself. This was done by bringing about some very needed improvements for the physical welfare of the workers, such as individual towels, rest-room, installing a wholesome lunch service, ice-water coolers on each floor during the summer months, having the space between the rows of machines widened seventeen inches so that the girls could swing the large work more easily in sewing, installation of ventilators. There was a need to develop a spirit of respect for those in authority and this has been brought about gradually by the careful handling of individual cases needing adjustment. It was necessary to educate those in authority as to their duty and responsibility as well as to require respect from the girls toward them.

The girls soon realized that if they had just cause for complaint, they were upheld; if they were in the wrong, their Director gave them a warning the first time that a second offense would mean dismissal, and it did mean just that. Misfits were gradually released; careless and poor operators were discharged; certain factory rules were established, such as for punctuality, attendance, general conduct. This was done after heart to heart talks with the girls and they were made to realize the necessity for these adjustments.

We have without doubt today, we believe, the best disciplined group of factory employees to be found. We have an average of 97% on time; 95%–98% on the job! Our production has increased steadily from about 250,000 pockets to an average of 400,000 per day and on special occasions when we have needed an increased production they have easily speeded up to 500,000. This is the output of about 170 operators. . .   Eighteen months ago we were three months behind in filling orders; today we guarantee a twenty-four hour delivery. Posting an hourly production scale on the bulletin board stimulates interest and it is great sport to watch the figures mount. We issue from time to time a printed bulletin or news sheet containing instructions and matters of general interest and information for the workers. We encourage the girls to larger earning effort by giving each girl a new dollar bill for every five dollars increase in her pay check; we also issue stars to the girls to wear on their caps, showing their rating,— one star for fifteen dollars; two stars for twenty dollars. . . .

Until the Negro woman in industry has had a longer factory experience, until she has acquired the modern industry complex, where they are employed in large numbers, they must be guided. In a few years they will have established themselves without question as to their ability and capacity for routine factory work. Then they may be counted upon to make their contribution and become an integral part of the great industrial systems of America. Give her time, give her guidance—most of all, give her opportunity.

Employer Views of Foreign Beet Workers, 1911

The opinions of growers as to the general desirability as laborers of the different races employed vary, of course, according to individual prejudices and local race feeling, but they have certain striking features in common.

The consensus of opinion as to the Chinese is decidedly favorable, particularly when they are contrasted in certain respects with other races at present employed. The Chinese are regarded as thoroughly honest, faithful, conscientious, and efficient, though slow workers. They require no watching, and are said always to keep their contracts, regardless of losses to themselves. Furthermore, they take an interest in the outcome of the crop that often approaches servility toward their employers. For instance, it is said in one district that after they had finished the thinning they would often leave several of the old men at the camp to cut out weeds as fast as they grew. In this case the contract for each operation—thinning, hoeing, or harvesting—was apparently a separate one.

The chief criticism of the Chinese is based on their slowness and their reluctance to adopt new methods. In one district where they were employed for ten years they are said to have worked without tools for several seasons. They did not understand the kind of work desired, and consequently did all the thinning with their fingers. Later they consented to use hoes, and gradually became proficient workmen.

In weighing growers' opinions of the Chinese it must be remembered, however, that these opinions are expressed nearly a decade after the race had largely disappeared from the industry, and furthermore, that they refer to selected members of the race with years of experience in American methods of work and contractual relations. There is at least a question whether the Chinese have not risen in the appreciation of growers with their scarcity and at the expense of the reputations of the races at present employed.

The Japanese are commonly praised for their industry, quickness, steadiness, sobriety, cleanliness, adaptability, and eagerness to learn American ways and customs. They are condemned for lack of commercial honesty and for the pursuit of their own interests regardless of the cost to their employers. Many instances are reported of their disregard of contract obligations. The question as to whether a contract shall be kept or broken is apparently, in these cases, a commercial one, the answer depending upon the amount of money involved. If the contract price, less advances already made by the grower, is greater than the expense of completing the work the contract will be fulfilled; if it is less, the contract will be broken. One instance is reported where a bond was required from the contractor for the faithful performance of his agreement. This was in the case of a sugar company which employs nearly 300 Japanese for the hand work of its own fields. These men are all hired through a single contractor, a Japanese, who has been employed by the company for several years.

The company in its contract with this man requires from him a bond, to cover penalties provided for in the agreement in the following cases: (1) If at any time both the contractor and his foreman should be found absent from the fields by officials of the company during working hours; (2) if at any time the work should be stopped by disagreements between the contractor and his men. In the latter case the penalty is $100 for each day work is so interrupted. The company regards this contractor as a very reliable man and worthy of their entire confidence.

The average Japanese contractor is said to be very shrewd in choosing opportune moments for increasing his demands. It is said that one device used in the harvesting season is to postpone the work as long as possible on the pretext of a scarcity of laborers and then to demand increased prices because the beets have increased in size during the delay. The grower in such cases must usually accede to the demands made or see his beets suffer from neglect in the fields. The bond in his contract (if the contract is so guaranteed) with the Japanese is rarely sufficient to recover the loss of his crop.

Sometimes when the contractor, contrary to the usual custom, hires his men by the day he is forced to demand an increase in the contract price because of the demands of his men for higher wages. Sometimes the contract price in such cases is contingent upon his ability to secure men at a certain rate. If the men succeed in securing a raise in wages the additional amount in either case is an expense, not to the contractor, but to the grower. The latter must harvest his crop or bear the large losses risked in an intensive culture like that of the sugar beet.

The extent to which the Japanese have forced prices up in the past ten years is illustrated by the history of prices paid for thinning in a certain district. For this work the men are paid by the hour for an eleven-hour day. When the Japanese first entered the district in large numbers in 1899, they worked at thinning for about $1 per day. Shortly after that they demanded and obtained 10 cents more per day. Since then their wages have gradually risen until in 1908 they were $1.65. During the thinning season of 1909 the men demanded 17 cents an hour, or $1.87 [sic] per day, but the "bosses" met and formally agreed to pay no more than $1.75 for eleven hours' work. The purpose of this agreement was to prevent overbidding for field workers. The men were forced to accept this rate of pay, but soon renewed their demands for the greater increase. At the time the special agent of the Commission visited this locality, no agreement had been reached.

In short, the Japanese are accused of the tactics pursued by other monopolists; that is, of local price cutting to repress competition, and of exorbitant increases in prices when, for the time being, competition is impossible.

In addition to lack of respect for contract obligations the Japanese are further accused of doing dishonest work. Often, when a flat rate has been made to cover the hand work of the entire season, it has been found that the Japanese would hoc out as many beets as possible in the thinning in order to make easier work of that operation and leave less work for the harvesting season. Sometimes, it is said, they would simply chop off the part of the beet showing above ground. Partly to remedy this evil the sliding scale of prices for topping and loading has been generally introduced. In justice to the Japanese, it should be said that they are not the only race accused of overthinning. The sliding scale is used in contracts with Mexicans in districts where only Mexicans are employed; and at present an attempt is being made to introduce this method of payment among the German-Russians in northern Colorado, for the same reason that led to its adoption among the Japanese in California.

As to Mexicans, conflicting opinions are expressed. Some employers complain that they are "hard to handle"; others say that they are much more tractable than the Japanese, who, they assert, are inclined to become conceited. All employers agree that the Mexicans lack ambition, and that they are addicted to the vices of drunkenness and gambling to an unusual degree. Consequently there is much complaint of their irregularity at work. In the face of this fact, however, some employers insist that the Mexican always keeps his contract. The reference here is doubtless to a practice of refraining from attempts to alter the terms of contracts rather than to the regularity with which the work called for is done.

In the two southern California districts where the force of field workers is predominantly Mexican, the Mexican is preferred to the Japanese. He is alleged to be more tractable and to be a better workman in one case. In the other he is said to be a quicker and better workman than the Japanese, but complaint is made that he is unreasonable. This is perhaps occasioned by a strike among the Mexicans for higher wages in the year 1908. This strike was broken by the temporary employment of German-Russians.

As previously stated, the Mexicans have been employed in several northern districts to provide competition against the Japanese. In at least one instance, already reported, it is said the Mexicans were soon "spoiled" by the Japanese, who persuaded them to be less careful in their work in order not to discredit Japanese standards.

To sum up, the Mexican is a fairly honest, efficient worker, whose usefulness is, however, much impaired by his lack of ambition and his proneness to the constant use of intoxicating liquor.

The East Indian has not yet had a fair trial in the industry. He is, of course, generally complained of on account of his uncleanliness, but this complaint is irrelevant in a consideration of his efficiency as a beet worker. So far as present experience goes, the East Indian is a slow but honest, steady, and exceedingly tractable workman. He is averse to entering into contracts, because he does not understand the contract system, but it is said that this aversion can be overcome after his confidence has been gained by his employers.

In the amount of work done in a day by individuals of different races the Japanese are far in the lead. The average Japanese can be counted upon to care for at least 12 acres during the season. The Mexicans and East Indians never average more than 7 or 8 acres. The explanation is that the Japanese not only works more rapidly—and less thoroughly—but that he also works longer hours.

Migrant Agricultural Labor Speaks Out, 1951–1952

Crew Leader "A" from Florida—Workers in Crew—70

Q. What time of the year did you go north up to Hendersonville [North Carolina]?

A. It was the 3d of June. . . . I stayed there the whole summer. . . . I was on the beans.

Q. When did you leave Hendersonville?

A. Around, it was the 9th of October.

Q. Did you get pretty steady work for your whole crew on that?

A. Reasonable. For 6 weeks we had pretty steady work and we had, you might say, nothing since then.

Q. What were you doing in August and September?

A. You might say nothing. Just scarcely getting along, just getting by.

Q. How did your gang make out?

A. They did better than I did, I didn't make enough to make expenses.

Q. Before, have you gone farther north or to some other place than Hendersonville?

A. No, sir.

Q. This is your regular deal, then?

A. Yes; that is right.

Q. Before this year did you do pretty good on this deal?

A. We haven't did any good in 3 years. In 3 years we didn't do much good either year.

Q. Did you try to get the North Carolina Employment Service to help you find some other place to go in August and September when you didn't have much to do?

A. I checked with them. As long as there is little work to do there, they are not going to turn you loose, more especially if you have a crew.

Q. Where you were, there was almost no work in August and September?

A. Practically no work; the rain fell so heavy it pretty near drowned the crop out. . . . It hasn't been so hot for 3 years.

Q. Do you figure on going up there again next year?

A. Well, I am not definite because I tried it three times and I don't know whether I am going to take that chance again.

Q. Have you had the same people (crew) the last 3 years?

A. Just the same number, not the same people . . . pretty near a new crew every year.

Let the testimony of a Texas-Mexican worker who came to our hearing at Phoenix, Ariz., speak for itself:

Q. Where is your home in Texas?

A. Weslaco, Tex. (Lower Rio Grande Valley).

Q. Why don't you stay down around Weslaco and work down there?

A. Well, I don't stay there because I can't make any money over there in that town.

Q. What is the reason you can't make any money there?

A. Well, because there is a lot of laborers in that town and they can't get any work. This year they promised us to pay 75 cents an hour. You can go anywhere to look for a job and you can't find any job. . . .

Q. Who promised you 75 cents?

A. Well, on the radio, I listen to the radio, and they took all the Nationals back to Mexico and so want to raise the price for us, but I and my brothers, my two brothers, was looking for a job all the way around the town and they couldn't find any, and myself started to work about 20 days after I got there, and I got started to get some people to get ready to come to Montana with me.

Q. I wanted to ask Mr. F—— about these Mexican Nationals in Texas. You say that you couldn't make any money there and wages were too low, there weren't any jobs because there was an abundance of other workers?

A. Yes.

Q. Were those other workers Mexican Nationals that came across the river?

A. Yes, sir; they crossed the river, and they worked for 3 or 4 days, dollar a day, two dollars and a half, and that is the reason we can't get jobs.

Q. You mean they paid them two dollars or two and a half?

A. Two and a half or three dollars.

Q. For how many hours?

A. Ten hours.

Q. They are getting about 25 cents an hour?

A. Yes.

Q. You spoke about the Mexican Nationals. Do you happen to know whether those are wetback Mexicans, or were those contract Mexicans that were brought in under the Government program? Which of those two was it that took most of the work around Weslaco?

A. Well, it is Mexicans that is from Mexico. They just crossed the river, and that is the reason they got a lot of laborers there in that town, and they don't get any jobs for us on farm labor.

U.S. Farm Workers Attack Competition from Illegal Migrants, 1952

Statement of George Stith, Gould, Ark., Agricultural Worker, Cotton Plantation

Mr. Chairman and members of the committee, my name is George Stith. My address is Star Route Box 5, Gould, Ark. All my life I have worked on cotton plantations. When I was 4 years old my family moved to southern Illinois, near Cairo. We picked cotton in southeast Missouri, and west Tennessee nearly every year. We later moved across the river into Missouri and share-cropped. In 1930 we moved back to Arkansas. I don't know whether I am a migratory worker or not, but we certainly did a lot of migrating.

In 1936 when I was share cropping in Woodruff County, Ark., I joined the union which was then called the Southern Tenant Farmers Union. It is now the National Farm Labor Union, A. F. of L. I have been a member of the union ever since. My wife and I farmed on shares, half to the landlord and half to us. In 1943 after the cotton was picked I went to Salem, N.J., to work in a canning plant. The job was arranged by our union and another A. F. of L. union that had contracts in the plants and some of the big farms of that State. For several years I went to work in New Jersey as soon as crops were laid by in the summer, and sometimes in the winter if there was a job open. My landlord didn't like for me to leave the plantation, but my wife stayed at home and took care of things. I saved all the money I made and intended to buy a farm of my own but I just couldn't make it. After the war the cotton planters in Arkansas started changing the old share-crop system. They bought more tractors and started doing part of the work the share cropper did, and instead of allowing a man half the proceeds of the crop, they changed to 60 percent to the landlord and 40 percent to the cropper. We saw that no matter how hard we worked and saved we could never buy a farm of our own. I started in to help build the National Farm Labor Union to better the wages and conditions of people like me. My wife and I work each year. We chop cotton in the spring and pick some cotton in the fall.

For a long time I had heard about labor shortages in the West and how Mexican workers were being imported. I was sure that no people would be imported from Mexico to work on farms in Arkansas. There were too many people living in the little towns and cities who go out to chop and pick cotton. There were others from the hill sections of Arkansas, Tennessee, and other nearby States who came in each fall to help pick the cotton.

The importation of Mexican nationals into Arkansas did not begin until the fall of 1949. Cotton-picking wages in my section were good. We were getting $4 per 100 pounds for picking. As soon as the Mexicans were brought in the wages started falling. Wages were cut to $3.25 and $3 per 100 pounds. In many cases local farm workers could not get jobs at all. The cotton-picking season which usually starts about the middle of September and ends the last of December, was cut short. By November 15 nearly all the cotton was out of the fields that year. I think there were about 25,000 Mexican nationals hired in 1949. In 1950 there was a small crop of cotton but more Mexicans were brought in to pick cotton and it was all picked out before the end of October. The cotton plantation owners kept the Mexicans at work and would not employ Negro and white pickers. As soon as a plantation owner finished picking his crop the Mexicans would be sent to another plantation. If there were some local workers picking cotton on the plantation they would be fired so the Mexicans could be employed. I think that was because they had to guarantee the Mexicans at least 4 days work a week. The Arkansas cotton picker wasn't guaranteed anything so he lost the job.

I would like to add to that statement that the farm worker in the State of Arkansas has been hit hard by the importation of foreign labor simply because the season of his work has been cut very short. He further sometimes finds himself, as I stated, without a job, because there seems to be some agreement between the plantation owners that they would employ Mexicans all the time, because in several cases we went to fields or had been picking cotton in fields and we would find a group of Mexican workers there and they would say, "I am sorry, I would like to use you, but we have these Mexicans here and we have got to see that they have work."

The American farm worker had no guaranty of a job, he had no social security, no unemployment compensation to live on during the winter. . . .

Statement of Juanita Garcia, Brawley, Imperial Valley, Calif., Migratory Farm Worker

Mr. Chairman and the committee, my name is Juanita Garcia. I live in Brawley, Calif. I work in the field and in the packing sheds. I lost my job in a packing shed about 2 weeks ago. I was fired because I belonged to the National Farm Labor Union. Every summer our family goes north to work. We pick figs and cotton. My father, my brothers, and sisters also work on the farms. For poor people like us who are field laborers, making a living has always been hard. Why? Because the ranchers and companies have always taken over.

When I was a small kid my dad had a small farm but he lost it. All of us used to help him. But [my] dad got older and worn out with worries every day. Lots of us kids could not go to school much. Our parents could not afford the expenses. This happened to all kids like us. Difficulties appear here and there every day. Taxes, food, clothing, and everything go up. We all have to eat. Sometimes we sleep under a leaky roof. We have to cover up and keep warm the best way we can in the cold weather.

In the Imperial Valley we have a hard time. It so happens that the local people who are American citizens cannot get work. Many days we don't work. Some days we work 1 hour. The wetbacks and nationals from Mexico have the whole Imperial Valley. They have invaded not only the Imperial Valley but all the United States. The nationals and wetbacks take any wages the ranchers offer to pay them. The wages get worse every year. Last year most local people got little work. Sometimes they make only $5 a week. That is not enough to live on, so many people cannot send their children to school.

Many people have lost their homes since 1942 when the nationals and wetbacks started coming. Local people work better but wetbacks and nationals are hired anyway.

Last year they fired some people from the shed because they had nationals to take their jobs. There was a strike. We got all the strikers out at 4:30 in the morning. The cops were on the streets escorting the nationals and wetbacks to the fields. The cops had guns. The ranchers had guns, too. They took the wetbacks in their brand-new cars through our picket line. They took the nationals from the camps to break our strike. They had 5,000 scabs that were nationals. We told the Mexican consul about this. We told the Labor Department. They were supposed to take the nationals out of the strike. They never did take them away.

It looks like the big companies in agriculture are running the United States. All of us local people went on strike. The whole valley was hungry because nobody worked at all. The melons rotted in the fields. We went out and arrested the wetbacks who were living in caves and on the ditches and we took them to the border patrol. But the national scabs kept working. Isn't the Government supposed to help us poor people? Can't it act fast in cases like this? We local farm workers are not giving up. The Government helped the ranchers last year. We are going to keep fighting against these terrible conditions. We ask your committee to help us and to tell President Truman the truth. . . .

CIO Resolution on Foreign Migrant Workers, 1951

The Congress of Industrial Organizations is deeply concerned with the working and living conditions of migrant workers. Workers from Puerto Rico, Mexico, and Caribbean nations working in the United States are particularly subject to exploitation and discrimination in ways destructive to our program of international friendship.

Hundreds of thousands of Mexicans have been encouraged to steal across the border and have found employment in industry as well as agriculture. Such illegal entrants are easy victims of exploitation, and their presence has dragged down wage scales throughout the Southwest.

The farm-labor bill passed by Congress this year ignored the recommendations of the President's Commission on Migrant Labor, took no steps to improve the recruitment of domestic workers, and authorized the importation of Mexicans under contract without steps to outlaw illegal entry or adequate safeguards.

The new Mexican agreement for bringing in contract workers extends for 6 months only, and authorizing legislation should be revised before it is renewed.

The Farm Placement Service of the United States Department of Labor was severely criticized by the President's Commission on Migratory Labor for not consulting with labor, as it does with the growers, and for permitting American standards to be adversely affected. Mexicans are still being brought in without proper procedures for proving that domestic workers cannot be found if proper conditions are offered. Methods for determining appropriate wages are inadequate, and rates as low as 50 cents an hour have been authorized.

More blame attaches to Congress than to the Department of Labor, its Bureau of Employment Security, and the Farm Placement Service. Although these agencies should be less subservient to the large growers and to farm bloc Senators and Representatives, Congress itself betrayed the American farm workers in the execution of the 1951 United States–Mexican farm-labor agreement without enabling legislation for an adequate program for full utilization of United States farm workers. The House and Senate Labor Committees were frozen out by the efforts of powerful Senators and Congressmen and jurisdiction given to the Agricultural Committees. We call upon Congress to start obeying its own laws for the conduct of its business in the field of migrant labor by assigning bills affecting farm workers to the Labor Committees clothed by law with exclusive jurisdiction over such legislation.

The CIO urges President Truman and Congress to put into effect the major recommendations of the President's Commission on Migratory Labor, including a minimum wage for agriculture and a constructive program for recruiting domestic workers, including Puerto Ricans, under decent conditions of employment and living. As an interim step, we urge Congress without further delay to take the measures for controlling illegal entrants recommended by President Truman, with adequate appropriations for the Farm Placement Service and the Immigration and Naturalization Service.

We urge the United States Department of Labor, in administering the Farm Placement Service and the Mexican contract-labor agreement, to carry out more effectively its solemn responsibility to protect American standards of living and to prevent exploitation of citizens of friendly nations. Where Mexicans or other foreign workers are admitted, they should have decent conditions, the right to join United States unions, and the full protection of our social legislation. We oppose the importation of foreign workers for any type of processing operation.

As part of the development of a constructive program for supplying agricultural labor, the United States Department of Labor should cease to permit the Farm Placement Service to give growers overwhelming consideration in its operations. The representatives of organized labor should be given a voice on general advisory committees and on all bodies dealing with the need for bringing in foreign workers and the conditions under which they are admitted.

This convention calls to the attention of our affiliates the importance of renewing their efforts to organize workers engaged in the processing or the growing of farm products. We favor continued close contact between the CIO and the free labor movements of Mexico and other nations of the Western Hemisphere for mutual consultation on the problem of migrant labor from those countries. . . .

⚵ *E S S A Y S*

The first essay is a pathbreaking study by the late historian Herbert Gutman. He argues that American working-class history has been characterized by a clash between generation after generation of rural immigrants, who imported their traditional "customs, rituals, and beliefs" into the United States, and an industrial system that emphasized the rigid time and work discipline believed to be essential to factory production. In the second essay, Wellesley College historian Jacqueline Jones considers the migration experience of a specific rural people, the African-Americans. Jones focuses on black women, who had to confront a new world of work in a virulently racist society. In the final essay, Ronald Takaki, who teaches ethnic studies at the University of California, Berkeley, explores the work lives of Hawaii's multicultural proletariat in that territory's sugar cane fields in the late nineteenth and early twentieth centuries. Compare the functioning of the contract system in large-scale agriculture to its deployment in the garment trades, as described in the documentary section of this chapter. To what extent was the experience of these Hawaiian laborers similar to that of the Eastern European immigrants and black migrants in the East?

The Cultures of First-Generation
Industrial Workers

HERBERT GUTMAN

Common work habits rooted in diverse premodern cultures (different in many ways but nevertheless all ill fitted to the regular routines demanded by machine-centered factory processes) existed among distinctive first-generation factory workers all through American history. We focus on two quite different time periods: the years before 1843 when the factory and machine were still new to America and the years between 1893 and 1917 when the country had become the world's industrial colossus. In both periods workers new to factory production brought strange and seemingly useless work habits to the factory gate. The irregular and undisciplined work patterns of factory hands before 1843 frustrated cost-conscious manufacturers and caused frequent complaint among them. Textile factory work rules often were designed to tame such rude customs. A New Hampshire cotton factory that hired mostly women and children forbade "spirituous liquor, smoking, nor any kind of amusement . . . in the workshops, yards, or factories" and promised the "immediate and disgraceful dismissal" of employees found gambling, drinking, or committing "any other debaucheries." . . . Manufacturers elsewhere worried about the example "idle" men set for women and children. Massachusetts family heads who rented "a piece of land on shares" to grow corn and potatoes while their wives and children labored in factories worried one manufacturer. "I would prefer giving constant employment at some sacrifice," he said, "to having a man of the village seen in the streets on a rainy day at leisure." Men who worked in Massachusetts woolen mills upset expected work routines in other ways. "The wool business requires more man labour," said a manufacturer, "and this we study to avoid. Women are much more ready to follow good regulations, are not captious, and do not clan as the men do against the overseers." Male factory workers posed other difficulties, too. In 1817 a shipbuilder in Medford, Massachusetts, refused his men grog privileges. They quit work, but he managed to finish a ship without using further spirits, "a remarkable achievement." . . .

Employers responded differently to such behavior by first-generation factory hands. "Moral reform" as well as . . . carrot-and-stick policies meant to tame or to transform such work habits. Fining was common. . . . Special material rewards encouraged steady work. A Hopewell Village blacksmith contracted for nineteen dollars a month, and "if he does his work well we are to give him a pair of coarse boots." In these and later years manufacturers in Fall River and Paterson institutionalized traditional customs and arranged for festivals and parades to celebrate with their workers a new mill, a retiring superintendent, or a finished locomotive. . . . Where factory work could be learned easily, new hands replaced irregular ones. A factory worker in New England remembered that years before the Civil War her employer had hired "all American girls" but later shifted to immigrant laborers because "not coming from country homes, but living as the Irish do, in the town, they take no vacations, and can be relied on at the mill all year round." Not all such devices worked to the satisfaction of workers or their employers. Sometime in the late 1830s merchant capitalists sent a skilled British silk weaver to manage a new mill in Nantucket that would employ the wives and children of local whalers and fishermen. Machinery was installed, and in the first days women and children besieged the mill for work. After a month had passed, they started dropping off in small groups. Soon nearly all had returned "to their shore gazing and to their seats by the sea." The Nantucket mill shut down, its hollow frame an empty monument to the unwillingness of resident women and children to conform to the regularities demanded by rising manufacturers.

First-generation factory workers were not unique to premodern America. And the work habits common to such workers plagued American manufacturers in later generations when manufacturers and most native urban whites scarcely remembered that native Americans had once been hesitant first-generation factory workers. To shift forward in time to East and South European immigrants new to steam, machinery, and electricity and new to the United States itself is to find much that seems the same. American society, of course, had changed greatly, but in some ways it is as if a film— run at a much faster speed—is being viewed for the second time: primitive work rules for unskilled labor, fines, gang labor, and subcontracting were commonplace. In 1910 two-thirds of the workers in twenty-one major manufacturing and mining industries came from Eastern and Southern Europe or were native American blacks, and studies of these "new immigrants" record much evidence of preindustrial work habits among the men and women new to American industry. . . . [S]killed immigrant Jews carried to New York City town and village employment patterns, such as the *landsmannschaft* economy and a preference for small shops as opposed to larger factories, that sparked frequent disorders but hindered stable trade unions until 1910. Specialization spurred anxiety: in Chicago Jewish glovemakers resisted the subdivision of labor even though it promised better wages. . . . American work rules also conflicted with religious imperatives. On the eighth day after the birth of a son, Orthodox Jews in Eastern Europe held a festival, "an occasion of much rejoicing." But the American work week had a different logic, and if the day fell during the week the celebration occurred the following Sunday. "The host . . . and his guests," David Blaustein remarked, "know it is not the right day," and "they fall to mourning over the conditions that will not permit them to observe the old custom." The occasion became "one for secret sadness rather than rejoicing." Radical Yiddish poets, like Morris Rosenfeld, the presser of men's clothing, measured in verse the psychic and social costs exacted by American industrial work rules:

purchase farmland. Their private letters to European relatives indicated a realistic awareness of their working life that paralleled some of the Lowell fiction: "if I don't earn $1.50 a day, it would not be worth thinking about America"; "a golden land so long as there is work"; "here in America one must work for three horses"; "let him not risk coming, for he is too young"; "too weak for America." Men who wrote such letters and avoided injury often saved small amounts of money, and a significant number fulfilled their expectations and quit the factory and even the country. Forty-four South and East Europeans left the United States for every one hundred that arrived between 1908 and 1910. . . . Immigrant expectations coincided for a time with the fiscal needs of industrial manufacturers. The Pittsburgh steel magnates had as much good fortune as the Boston Associates. But the stability and passivity they counted on among their unskilled workers depended upon steady work and the opportunity to escape the mills. When frequent recessions caused recurrent unemployment, immigrant expectations and behavior changed. . . . [P]easant "group consciousness" and "communal loyalty" sustained bitter wildcat strikes after employment picked up. The tenacity of these immigrant strikers for higher wages amazed contemporaries, and brutal suppression often accompanied them (Cleveland, 1899; East Chicago, 1905; McKees Rock, 1909; Bethlehem, 1910; and Youngstown in 1915 where, after a policeman shot into a peaceful parade, a riot caused an estimated one million dollars in damages). The First World War and its aftermath blocked the traditional route of overseas outward mobility, and the consciousness of immigrant steelworkers changed. They sparked the 1919 steel strike. The steel mill had become a way of life for them and was no longer the means by which to reaffirm and even strengthen older peasant and village life-styles. . . .

Even though American society itself underwent radical structural changes between 1815 and the First World War, the shifting composition of its wage-earning population meant that traditional customs, rituals, and beliefs repeatedly helped shape the behavior of its diverse working-class groups. The street battle in 1843 that followed Irish efforts to prevent New York City authorities from stopping pigs from running loose in the streets is but one example of the force of old styles of behavior. Both the form and the content of much expressive working-class behavior, including labor disputes, often revealed the powerful role of secular and religious rituals. In 1857 the New York City unemployed kidnapped a musical band to give legitimacy to its parade for public works. After the Civil War, a Fall River cotton manufacturer boasted that the arrival of fresh Lancashire operatives meant the coming of "a lot of greenhorns here," but an overseer advised him, "Yes, but you'll find they have brought their horns with them." A few years later, the Pittsburgh courts prevented three women married to coal miners from "tin-horning" nonstrikers. The women, however, purchased mouth organs. ("Tinhorning," of course, was not merely an imported institution. In Franklin, Virginia, in 1867, for example, a Northern white clergyman who started a school for former slave children had two nighttime "tin horn serenade[s]" from hostile whites.) Recurrent street demonstrations in Paterson accompanying frequent strikes and lockouts nearly always involved horns, whistles, and even Irish "banshee" calls. These had a deep symbolic meaning, and, rooted in a shared culture, they sustained disputes. A Paterson manufacturer said of nonstrikers: "They cannot go anywhere without being molested or insulted, and no matter what they do they are met and blackguarded and taunted in a way that no one can stand . . . which is a great deal worse than actual assaults." . . .

But the manufacturers could not convince the town's mayor (himself a British immigrant and an artisan who had become a small manufacturer) to ban street demonstrations. The manufacturers even financed their own private militia to manage further disorders, but the street demonstrations continued with varying effectiveness until 1901 when a court injunction essentially defined the streets as private space by banning talking and singing banshee (or death) wails in them during industrial disputes. In part, the frequent recourse to the courts and to the state militia after the Civil War during industrial disputes was the consequence of working-class rituals that helped sustain long and protracted conflicts.

Symbolic secular and, especially, religious rituals and beliefs differed among Catholic and Jewish workers fresh to industrial America between 1894 and the First World War, but their function remained the same. Striking Jewish vestmakers finished a formal complaint by quoting the Law of Moses to prove that "our bosses who rob us and don't pay us regularly commit a sin and that the cause of our union is a just one." ("What do we come to America for?" these same men asked. "To bathe in tears and to see our wives and children rot in poverty?") An old Jewish ritual oath helped spark the shirtwaist strike of women workers in 1909 that laid the basis for the International Ladies Garment Workers Union. A strike vote resulted in the plea, "Do you mean faith? Will you take the old Jewish oath?" The audience responded in Yiddish: "If I turn traitor to the cause, I now pledge, may this hand wither and drop off at the wrist from the arm I now raise." . . . Immigrant Catholic workers shared similar experiences with these immigrant Jews. A reporter noticed in 1910 at a meeting of striking Slavic steelworkers in Hammond, Indiana: "The lights of the hall were extinguished. A candle stuck into a bottle was placed on a platform. One by one the men came and kissed the ivory image on the cross, kneeling before it. They swore not to scab." Not all rituals were that pacific. That same year, Slavic miners in Avelia, Pennsylvania, a tiny patch on the West Virginia border, crucified George Rabish, a mine boss and an alleged labor spy. . . . That event was certainly unusual, but it was commonplace for time-honored religious symbols as well as American flags to be carried in the frequent parades of American workers. Western Pennsylvania Slavic and Italian coal miners in a bitter strike just east of Pittsburgh (eighteen of twenty thousand miners quit work for seventeen months when denied the right to join the United Mine Workers of America) in 1910 and 1911 carried such symbols. "These rural marches," said Paul Kellogg [*Survey* editor], "were in a way reminiscent of the old time agrarian uprisings which have marked English history." But theirs was the behavior of peasant and village Slavs and Italians fresh to modern industrial America, and it was just such tenacious peasant-worker protests that caused the head of the Pennsylvania State Police to say that he modeled his force on the Royal Irish Constabulary, not, he insisted, "as an anti-labor measure" but because "conditions in Pennsylvania resembled those in strife-torn Ireland." Peasant parades and rituals, religious oaths and food riots, and much else in the culture and behavior of early twentieth-century immigrant American factory workers were cultural anachronisms to this man and to others, including Theodore Roosevelt, William Jennings Bryan, Elbert Gary, and even Samuel Gompers, but participants found them natural and effective forms of self-assertion and self-protection.

The perspective emphasized in these pages tells about more than the behavior of diverse groups of American working men and women. It also suggests how larger, well-studied aspects of American society have been affected by a historical process that has "industrialized" different peoples over protracted periods of time. . . . Contact and conflict between diverse preindustrial cultures and a changing and increasingly bureaucratized industrial society also affected the larger society in ways that await systematic examination. Contemporaries realized this fact. Concerned in 1886 about the South's "dead"—that is, unproductive—population, the Richmond *Whig* felt the "true remedy" to be "educating the industrial morale of the people." The *Whig* emphasized socializing institutions primarily outside of the working class itself. "In the work of inculcating industrial ideas and impulses," said the *Whig*, "all proper agencies should be enlisted—family discipline, public school education, pulpit instruction, business standards and requirements, and the power and influence of the workingmen's associations." What the *Whig* worried over in 1886 concerned other Americans before and after that time. And the resultant tension shaped society in important ways. . . .

The same process also affected the shaping and reshaping of American police and domestic military institutions. We need only realize that the burning of a Boston convent in 1834 by a crowd of Charlestown truckmen and New Hampshire Scotch-Irish brickmakers caused the first revision of the Massachusetts Riot Act since Shays' Rebellion, and that three years later interference by native firemen in a Sunday Irish funeral procession led to a two-hour riot involving upward of fifteen thousand persons (more than a sixth of Boston's population), brought militia to that city for the first time, and caused the first of many reorganizations of the Boston police force. The regular contact between alien work cultures and a larger industrializing or industrial society had other consequences. It often worried industrialists, causing C. E. Perkins, the president of the Chicago, Burlington, and Quincy Railroad to confide in a friend in the late nineteenth century, "If I were able, I would found a school for the study of political economy in order to harden men's hearts." It affected the popular culture. A guidebook for immigrant Jews in the 1890s advised how to make it in the New World: "Hold fast, this is most necessary in America. Forget your past, your customs, and your ideals. . . . A bit of advice to you: do not take a moment's rest. Run, do, work, and keep your own good in mind." Cultures and customs, however, are not that easily discarded. So it may be that America's extraordinary technological supremacy—its talent before the Second World War for developing labor-saving machinery and simplifying complex mechanical processes—depended less on "Yankee know-how" than on the continued infusion of prefactory peoples into an increasingly industrialized society. The same process, moreover, may also explain why movements to legislate morality and to alter habits have lasted much longer in the United States than in most other industrial countries, extending from the temperance crusades of the 1820s and the 1830s to the violent opposition among Germans to such rules in the 1850s and the 1860s and finally to formal prohibition earlier in this century. Important relationships also exist between this process and the elite and popular nativist and racist social movements that have ebbed and flowed regularly from the 1840s until our own time, as well as between this process and elite political "reform" movements between 1850 and the First World War.

The sweeping social process had yet another important consequence: it reinforced the biases that otherwise distort the ways in which elite observers perceive the world below them. When in 1902 *The New York Times* cast scorn upon and urged that force be used against the Jewish women food rioters, it conformed to a fairly settled elite tradition. Immigrant groups and the working population had changed in composition over time, but the rhetoric of influential nineteenth- and early twentieth-century elite observers remained constant. Disorders among the Jersey City Irish seeking wages due them from the Erie Railroad in 1859 led the Jersey City *American Standard* to call them "imported *beggars*" and "*animals*," "a mongrel mass of ignorance and crime and superstition, as utterly unfit for its duties, as they are for the common courtesies and decencies of civilized life." . . .

Although the Civil War ended slavery, it did not abolish these distorted perceptions and fears of new American workers. In 1869 *Scientific American* welcomed the "ruder" laborers of Europe but urged them to "assimilate" quickly or face "a quiet but sure extermination." Those who retained their alien ways, it insisted, "will share the fate of the native Indian." Elite nativism neither died out during the Civil War nor awaited a rebirth under the auspices of the American Protective Association and the Immigration Restriction League. In the mid-1870s, for example, the Chicago *Tribune* called striking immigrant brickmakers men but "not reasoning creatures," and the Chicago *Post-Mail* described that city's Bohemian residents as "depraved beasts, harpies, decayed physically and spiritually, mentally and morally, thievish and licentious." The Democratic Chicago *Times* cast an even wider net in complaining that the country had become "the cess-pool of Europe under the pretense that it is the asylum of the poor." Most

Chicago inhabitants in the Gilded Age were foreign-born or the children of the foreign-born, and most English-language Chicago newspapers scorned them. . . . Here, as in the Jersey City *American Standard* (1859) and *The New York Times* (1902), much more was involved than mere ethnic distaste or "nativism." In quite a different connection and in a relatively homogeneous country, the Italian Antonio Gramsci concluded of such evidence that "for a social elite the features of subordinate groups always display something barbaric and pathological." The changing composition of the American working class may make so severe a dictum more pertinent to the United States than to Italy. Class and ethnic fears and biases combined together to worry elite observers about the diverse worlds below them and to distort gravely their perceptions of these worlds. . . .

These pages have fractured historical time, ranging forward and backward, to make comparisons for several reasons. One has been to suggest how much remains to be learned about the transition of native and foreign-born American men and women to industrial society, and how that transition affected such persons and the society into which they entered. "Much of what gets into American literature," Ralph Ellison has shrewdly observed, "gets there because so much is left out." That has also been the case in the writing of American working-class history, and the framework and methods suggested here merely hint at what will be known about American workers and American society when the many transitions are studied in detail. Such studies, however, need to focus on the particularities of both the groups involved and the society into which they enter. Transitions differ and depend upon the interaction between the two at specific historical moments. But at all times there is a resultant tension. [E. P.] Thompson writes:

> There has never been any single type of "the transition." The stress of the transition falls upon the whole culture: resistance to change and assent to change arise from the whole culture. And this culture includes the systems of power, property-relations, religious institutions, etc., inattention to which merely flattens phenomena and trivializes analysis.

Enough has been savored in these pages to suggest the particular importance of these transitions in American social history. And their recurrence in different periods of time indicates why there has been so much discontinuity in American labor and social history. The changing composition of the working population, the continued entry into the United States of nonindustrial people with distinctive cultures, and the changing structure of American society have combined together to produce common modes of thought and patterns of behavior. But these have been experiences disconnected in time and shared by quite distinctive first-generation native and immigrant industrial Americans. It was not possible for the grandchildren of the Lowell mill girls to understand that their Massachusetts literary ancestors shared a great deal with their contemporaries, the peasant Slavs in the Pennsylvania steel mills and coal fields. And the grandchildren of New York City Jewish garment workers see little connection between black ghetto unrest in the 1960s and the kosher meat riots seventy years ago. A half-century has passed since Robert Park and Herbert Miller published W. I. Thomas's *Old World Traits Transplanted*, a study which worried that the function of Americanization was the "destruction of memories." . . .

From Farm to City: Southern Black Women Move North, 1900–1930

JACQUELINE JONES

. . . The Great Migration of the World War I era represented a dramatic break with the past in several crucial respects. First, the sheer magnitude of the movement was striking. Between 1916 and 1921 an estimated half million blacks, or about 5 percent of the total southern black population, headed north (this number was larger than the aggregate figure for the preceding forty years). Compared with their predecessors, the new migrants more often came from the Deep South; they traveled longer distances to their final destination and relied on overland (rail) transportation rather than water transportation, and a greater proportion than previously chose to go to midwestern cities. In 1920 more than a fourth of the North's black population was concentrated in New York, Chicago, and Philadelphia, and their black communities were larger than any in the South. Still, blacks numbered no more than 9 percent of the total population of any urban area in the North, and only 2 percent of all northerners were black.

Contemporary observers, particularly nervous white southerners convinced that their entire supply of black labor was about to disappear overnight, provided melodramatic accounts of the initial population movement in the spring of 1916. Many assumed that the arrival of a train sponsored by a northern railroad company was enough to create havoc at a moment's notice and that black men, promised free transportation and outrageously high wages in return for their labor, would scramble aboard with only the shirts on their backs, without bothering to say good-bye to friends or family. In fact, the decision to leave was just as often a calculated one made by husbands and fathers as it was an impulsive act on the part of single men. In his survey of 506 male migrants to Pittsburgh in 1918, Abraham Epstein found that 300 were married (though single people predominated in the eighteen- to thirty-year age group). Thirty percent already had their families with them, and an almost equal number planned to have their wives and children join them as soon as possible.

The Great Migration, then, was frequently a family affair. Significantly, black men mentioned the degraded status of their womenfolk as one of the prime incentives to migrate, along with low wages and poor educational opportunities for their children. Husbands told of sexual harassment of wives and daughters by white men and of other forms of indignities woven into the fabric of southern society. One migrant to Chicago expressed satisfaction that his wife could now go into a shop and "try on a hat and if she don't want it she don't have to buy it." Another man in the same city, a stockyard worker, told an interviewer for the Commission on Race Relations that in Mississippi

> Men and women had to work in the fields. A woman was not permitted to remain at home if she felt like it. If she was found at home some of the white people would come to ask why she was not in the field and tell her she had better get to the field or else abide by the consequences. After the summer crops were all in, any of the white people could send for any Negro woman to come and do the family washing at 75 cents to $1.00 a day. If she sent word she could not come she had to send an excuse why she could not come. They were never allowed to stay at home as long as they were able to go. Had to take whatever they paid you for your work.

However, letters from potential migrants to the Chicago *Defender* (the largest black newspaper and an enthusiastic proponent of migration), indicate that most men expected their wives to continue to contribute to the family income, at least temporarily, in their new northern home. . . .

Some women during this period did have to make the decision to leave, find their way north, and locate housing without the aid of a trailblazing spouse. Single mothers from rural areas searched for a way north, because, as one South Carolina widow put it, "When you live on the farm, the man is the strength." Domestic servants in southern cities decided to find out for themselves the truth of reports that northern wages might be three or four times more than they were used to making. Strains on the household budget prompted daughters to strike out at an early age. A fifteen-year-old in New Orleans realized that her mother had "such a hard time" trying to make ends meet for a family of five and as the oldest child, she could lessen expenses at home and at the same time contribute extra cash to the family income by finding a job in Chicago. The plight of a Sea Island girl about the same age was less critical but no less compelling. In 1919 she left for New York City, hoping to escape from the loneliness of St. Helena's Island, where you "go to bed at six o'clock. Everything dead. No dances, no moving picture show, nothing to go to. . . ."

In general, demographic patterns of migration to different cities were determined by the nature of employment opportunities. Men almost invariably led the way north to cities like Pittsburgh and Detroit that offered industrial jobs for them but few positions outside domestic service for women. Chicago, with its more diversified female occupational structure, attracted single women and wives like Mrs. T of St. Louis, who preceded her husband to the city in order to investigate job conditions because, according to a Race Commission interviewer in 1920, she "doesn't always wait for him to bring something to her, but goes out herself and helps to get it."

Few migrants, male or female, abandoned the South totally or irrevocably. Some went back home frequently to join in community celebrations, to help with planting and harvesting on the family farm, or to coax friends north with their beautiful clothes and stories of good pay. A constant flow of letters containing cash and advice between North and South facilitated the gradual migration of whole clans and even villages. For example, the records of a Detroit social-welfare agency include the case of a young Georgia widow who moved to the city in 1922 to care for her ill niece. The woman returned south the following year and then went back to Detroit with one of her children, leaving the other three in the care of her mother-in-law. In 1925 she managed to convince the older woman (aged seventy) and her sister-in-law (aged fifty-nine) to join her in the North. There the three women pieced together a living for themselves and the four children by doing "day work" (domestic service on a daily basis). Thus the continuous renewal of personal ties through visits south and moves north meant that, at least for the first few years, the migrants maintained contact with their southern homes in both a physical and a cultural sense.

Paid Labor

The radical economic inequality of black working women in the urban North did not become apparent until the early twentieth century. Before that time, disproportionately large numbers of single and married black women worked for wages, but they and black men and white women were concentrated in essentially the same job category—domestic service. In a rough sense, all three groups were subjected to the same kinds of degrading working conditions characteristic of this form of employment. But as household conveniences and electricity lessened the need for elbow grease, new forms of business enterprise opened clerical and sales positions for white women. Commercial laundries gradually replaced laundresses, and personal service became increasingly associated with black women exclusively. For the most part, black female wage earners remained outside the expanding industrial economy, and the few who gained a foothold in factory work remained in the lowest-paying jobs. Despite the significant shift in white working women's options, the paid labor of black women exhibited striking continuity across space—urban areas in the North and South—and time—from the nineteenth to the early twentieth century. . . .

Although the war provided black men with their first opportunities in northern industrial employment, regardless of their personal talents or ambitions they rarely advanced beyond those jobs "reserved for the rawest recruits to industry." These were menial positions, subject to regular layoffs. Demobilization resulted in mass firings of black laborers in many plants, though some men retained their low-level jobs in the metalworking, automobile, and food processing industries. For example, in the Chicago meat-packing and slaughterhouses where they composed up to 70 to 80 percent of all workers in the 1920s, they were concentrated in jobs traditionally held by men with "no alternative," so difficult and disagreeable were the assigned tasks. Black men still constituted a labor force of last resort, and they could not look forward to gradual advancement for themselves or even for their sons. Moreover, black men's work patterns continued to diverge from those of white men, who moved into white-collar, managerial, and advanced technology jobs in increasing numbers. By 1930 two types of workers symbolized the status of all black male wage earners in the urban North—the New York City apartment house janitor and the Pittsburgh steelworker who manned a blast furnace during the hottest months of the year.

It is clear, then, that most male breadwinners suffered from chronic underemployment and sporadic unemployment, and that other household members had to supplement their irregular earnings. In 1930 from 34 to 44 percent of black households in the largest northern cities had two or more gainfully employed workers. Most apparent among black families was the high percentage of wives who worked outside the home—in 1920, five times more than the women in any other racial or ethnic group. The different cities showed some variation in this regard: In 1920, for example, 25.5 percent of black married women in Detroit, but 46.4 percent in New York, worked for wages (rates for all cities remained stable over the next decade). Variations between cities can be explained by reference to the local job situation for black men. In general, where men had access to industrial employment—in Pittsburgh and Detroit, for example—fewer wives worked than those in cities where large numbers of men could find little work outside domestic service. Jobs in the latter category were just as insecure as those in the industrial sector, but with the added disadvantage that they paid much less.

Black wives worked in greater proportion compared to white wives, but more significantly, they served as wage earners more often than immigrant wives of the same socioeconomic class. Not only did black husbands earn less than foreign-born men, their wives bore fewer children compared to immigrant women. The few children blacks had tended to establish independent households, or at least retain their wages for their own use, in greater proportion than the offspring of immigrant families. For example, based on her observations of black and immigrant neighborhoods in Manhattan in 1911, New York social worker Mary White Ovington suggested that the "marked contrasts" in the lives of women of the two races derived primarily from their respective households' "different occupational opportunities." The young white wife, she wrote in *Half a Man: The Status of the Negro in New York*, rarely "journeys far from her own home"; she departs from "her narrow round of domestic duties" to seek day or laundry work only if "unemployment visits the family wage earner." As the household grows in size over the years, its income is augmented by the wages of older sons and daughters who, "having entered factory or store, bring home their pay envelopes unbroken on Saturday nights" and turn them over to their mother. Gradually the family's standard of living improves, and the number and quality of its material possessions increases. As children depart from the household to marry, and the father's wage-earning capacity dwindles in proportion to his physical strength, the family falls on difficult times and "the end of the woman's married life is likely to be hard and comfortless."

The black woman, on the other hand, has a quite different family history. Ovington noted that she often begins "self-sustaining work" at the age of fifteen and remains in the labor force after marriage because of her husband's inability to support his family ("save in extreme penury") on his wages alone. The working black wife's day is more diverse and varied than that of the white homemaker, but she must sacrifice time with her children in return. Wrote Ovington, "An industrious, competent woman, [the black mother] works and spends, and in her scant hours of leisure takes pride in keeping her children well-dressed and clean."

A black woman must continue to work throughout her middle years because her wage-earning children tend to hand over to her "only such part [of their paychecks] as they choose to spare." Ovington disapprovingly noted that these young people were self-indulgent in their spending habits and often neglected the needs of their parents and siblings. The types of jobs available to sons and daughters served to lessen parental control; many "go out to service, accept long and irregular hours in hotel or apartment, travel for days on boat or train." Moreover, "factory and store are closed" to young women. Consequently the mother "must continue her round of washing and scrubbing." Yet old age did not necessarily bring with it unremitting drudgery and sorrow. According to Ovington, an elderly black woman often spent her last years engaged in productive labor at home, "treated with respect and consideration" in the household of her children. . . .

In general, black women's work in the North was synonymous with domestic service; although the racial caste system was more overtly brutal in the South, white Americans regardless of regional affiliation relegated black women to this lowliest occupational status. The exploitation of black domestics was thus a national, rather than a southern, phenomenon. In the three largest northern cities—New York, Chicago, and Philadelphia—the total number of servants declined by about 25 percent (from 181,000 to 138,000) between 1910 and 1920, but the proportion of black women in that occupational category increased by 10 to 15 percent. After World War I, black women constituted more than a fifth of all domestics in New York and Chicago, and over one-half in Philadelphia. Pittsburgh, with its heavy-industry jobs for black men, offered few alternatives for their wives and daughters; in 1920 fully 90 percent of black women in that city made their living as day workers, washerwomen, or live-in servants. The 108,342 servants and 46,914 laundresses not in commercial laundries totaled almost two-thirds of all gainfully employed black women in the North.

In their efforts to secure cheap domestic labor from the South, middle-class families at times engaged in deceitful practices. In the early 1920s, for example, a young Florida native was reduced to a state of involuntary servitude by a white family in a Chicago suburb. She eventually managed to escape but not before her employer "had kicked, beaten, and threatened her with a revolver if she attempted to leave." Yet such cases of violence and overt intimidation were relatively rare. Like southern mistresses, northern white women tyrannized their servants in more subtle ways. Indeed, though a migrant might endure a scolding delivered in a Brooklyn accent, or even broken English, instead of a southern drawl, she was likely to discover that the personal dynamics of the employer-employee relationship differed little between North and South.

Still, in the urban North the occupation of domestic service was shaped by the region's peculiar social structure and spatial arrangement and so diverged in certain ways from the southern case. For instance, in their new homes, migrant women encountered competition from white women for service jobs for the first time. After World War I, when white female factory workers lost their positions to returning soldiers, they displaced black domestics, at least temporarily, until they could find something better. Moreover, developments in household technology affected the number and kinds of jobs available. As the work associated with cleaning, heating, and lighting homes became more efficient and less messy, and as the latest laborsaving devices were installed in modern, expensive apartment units, the demand for servants declined. And finally, the traditional social hierarchy characteristic of service collapsed into two or three categories of work, leaving little room for upward mobility within households.

A profusion of new gadgets and technology, combined with domestic reformers' attempts to "professionalize" and "systematize" household management during this period, more often than not complicated the daily routine for servants and housewives alike. Illiterate cooks had no use for recipes, grocery lists, or filing systems. Gas and electric appliances could work miracles if used properly, but offered the resentful domestic an opportunity to wreak havoc on her employer's pocketbook and nerves. In 1922 a government researcher reported cases of laundresses who had either ruined clothes or broken equipment while using electric machines. Whirling washtubs and powerful clothes wringers endangered the arms and fingers of women accustomed to boiling clothes over an open fire or beating them on river rocks. Mistresses expressed their frustration toward employees who did not know "how to fold the clothes just so after they were ironed as well as wash them out according to rule." In sum, few white women were inclined to oversee the transformation of field hands into practitioners of the new "scientific" principles of domestic labor.

Like their southern sisters, black domestics in the North had their own strategies for coping with jobs they despised as much as needed. First and foremost, as a group they refused, whenever possible, to submit to the desire of white employers for live-in servants. Noted a study made by the Chicago School of Civics and Philanthropy in 1911, "[Married black women] are accused of having no family feeling, yet the fact remains that they will accept a lower wage and live under far less advantageous conditions for the sake of being free at night. That is why the 'day work' is so popular." Day work had distinct advantages; it conformed to the long-term checkered work schedule of most working mothers, and it allowed employees a certain amount of flexibility in choosing their mistresses and assignments. White women, who preferred a sustained commitment from "general houseworkers," retaliated against day workers with a variety of ruses to wring more labor from them at a cheap price. Mistresses advertised for a laundress to do a week's worth of washing, but then presented her with three times that amount—apparently freshly soiled—to launder for the agreed-upon wages. Some women promised but never delivered pay raises, while others insisted that the servant perform additional work for the white woman's neighbors for one day's pay.

When other kinds of jobs did become available, black women rarely hesitated to pursue them, though this fact is hardly reflected in occupational statistics for the first three decades of the twentieth century. For example, less than 3 percent of all black working women were engaged in manufacturing in 1900 compared with 21 percent of foreign-born and 38 percent of native-born white working women. By 1930 the comparable figures were 5.5 percent of gainfully employed black women (100,500 out of 1,776,922), 27.1 percent of foreign-born, and 19 percent of native-born white women. (These figures reveal the impact of the last group's opportunities in sales and clerical work.) Black women, about 10 percent of the total American female population, constituted only 5.4 percent of the country's female manufacturing workers and only 0.5 percent of all female employees in clerical occupations, though they were gainfully employed in disproportionately large numbers overall. Dressmakers who worked at home accounted for about one-fifth of all black women described under the heading "Manufacturing and Mechanical Pursuits" in the United States Census for 1930. The largest group of black female factory workers in the North included those in the clothing industry (16 percent of all black women factory workers). An equal number labored in cigar and tobacco factories in the South. Food processing workers (11 percent) constituted the next largest group.

Like their menfolk, black women entered the northern industrial labor force for the first time during World War I. A Women's Bureau survey of 11,812 black female employees in 150 plants in nine states found that most of the women were young (sixteen to thirty years old), and they worked at a variety of jobs. In war industry plants, they assembled munitions and manufactured gas masks, airplane wings, nuts, bolts, rivets, screws, rubber tires, tubes, and shoes. As railroad employees they cleaned cars, repaired ʼacks, sorted salvage, flagged trains, and worked in the yards. The needs ʼocal industries shaped black women's employment patterns in different ʼ. Over 3,000 black women in Chicago found jobs in meat-packing pì   In the Philadelphia area they worked in twenty-eight different indu   ʼncluding glass, garment, and candy factories.

ʼhs paid higher wages and offered more in the way of personal freedoˌ   ʼ to domestic service. In 1918 one black woman explained the decisˌ   ʼrself and her friends to take jobs in a railroad yard that paid $3 a   the colored women like this work and want to keep it. We are makinˌ   ʼre money at this than any work we can get, and we do not have to work as hard as at housework which requires us to be on duty from six o'clock in the morning until nine or ten at night, with might [sic] little time off and at very poor wages. . . ." The garment and railroad industries, in addition to government munitions factories, offered the highest wages to black women in industry—up to $15 to $20 per week. The prospect of hundreds of thousands of black women escaping the drudgery of service and entering the new technological age inspired the title of one extensive study conducted in 1919, "A New Day for the Colored Woman Worker."

Three aspects of black women's industrial employment during World War I indicated that their "progress" in this area was destined to be temporary if not altogether illusory. First, only a small number of black domestics and laundresses found alternate employment in manufacturing. The percentage of semiskilled operatives increased threefold from 1910 to 1920, but that gain represented only a small proportion (4.3 percent) of all black female workers engaged in nonagricultural pursuits immediately after the war. (A similar trend was evident among factory laborers.) Of the black women who did not till the soil in 1920, fully 80 percent were still maids, cooks, or washerwomen. Second, black women employed as industrial workers remained at the lowest rungs of the ladder in terms of wages and working conditions; for the most part they replaced white women who had advanced, also temporarily, to better positions. Finally, demobilization eroded even these modest gains. In October 1919 a writer for *World Outlook* acknowledged that "war expediency opened the door of industry" for black women, but that "in most cases, the colored woman is the 'marginal worker.' She is the last to be hired, the first to go." Those who managed to hold on to industrial jobs faced a constant struggle. As a New York woman remarked, "Over where I work in the dye factory, they expect more from a colored girl if she is to keep her job. They won't give a colored girl a break." . . .

Larger factories segregated black women in separate shops with inferior working, eating, and sanitary facilities. Smaller plants often refused to hire any black women at all, if the provision of separate areas would have been inefficient or too expensive. In other cases, the extent of white women's labor militancy and racial prejudice dictated hiring practices. During the 1920s, for example, white women factory workers in Philadelphia and machinery manufacturing operatives in Chicago went out on strike to protest the employment of black women in their plants. (The Chicago garment workers union was exceptional in that it successfully organized black women after they had been used as strikebreakers during the labor dispute of 1917.) Other companies integrated their nonunion female personnel with small numbers of strategically assigned black women to put their white employees on notice that cheap labor was readily available in the event of a protest or job action.

Because of the racially segregated female workplace, individual black and white women did not usually vie directly for the same jobs at the same time. However, the role of black women as a reserve labor force served to intensify interracial animosity and fear; the fluctuating economy caused many white women to worry constantly about their ability to hold on to a nonservice job. Employers readily took advantage of this situation. For these reasons, few white women embraced their black sisters (especially those who readily took better jobs—if only temporarily—as strikebreakers) in the struggle against industrial capitalism. Moreover, organized labor helped to perpetuate the lowly position of black women workers. As a trade union, the American Federation of Labor had no interest in the fate of unskilled wage earners. But even local chapters of internationals that had a potential black constituency (like the Amalgamated Meat Cutters and Butcher Workmen and the International Ladies Garment Workers Union [ILGWU] for the most part perceived the elimination of black women from the labor force to be in their own best interest. Unlike the Chicago ILGWU, these locals made little effort to organize black women. They unashamedly boasted "integrated" organizations, when in fact they might have no more than one or two black members. Separate groups of black female laborers lacked an advocate equivalent to their menfolks' Brotherhood of Sleeping Car Porters and thus had to engage in informal methods of protest—absenteeism, high turnover rates, careless work habits—or spontaneous job actions like walkouts in order to resist exploitation in the form of low wages and poor working conditions. . . .

If the history of black women in factory jobs is one of discrimination even more profound than that faced by immigrant women, the history of black women in clerical and sales work is one of complete exclusion. Ultimately, the reasons why black women as a group continued to make beds and wash dishes while white women were being hired as switchboard operators, stenographers, and sales clerks illustrate the complicated ways in which racial prejudice could shape the hiring policies of industrial and commercial capitalists. Employers did not necessarily forfeit their economic interests to their own racist impulses (though it is true that prejudice against women and blacks precluded an ideal, efficient work force in which tasks were assigned on the basis of ability, rather than on physical or cultural characteristics). Rather, for many establishments, discrimination proved to be good business in terms of employee and customer relations.

Like industrialists, employers of clerical, telephone, and sales personnel had to balance the cheapness of black female labor with the high costs of physical segregation. But to these employers, the "sexy saleslady" factor served as the primary reason for limiting low-paying but relatively high-status positions to white women, usually those of native parentage. As the Victorian era drew to a close, companies that sold consumer goods and services became increasingly self-conscious about their public image. . . . the most effective medium between public and product, according to advertising experts, was an attractive, well-spoken, and pliant young woman who invested whatever she was selling with her own charms. Tact and politeness were key ingredients in any successful public-relations position, but a pleasing physical appearance (or voice)—one that conformed to a native-born white American standard of female beauty—was an equally important consideration in hiring office receptionists, secretaries, department store clerks, and telephone operators.

For these reasons even black female high-school graduates could find few positions commensurate with their formal education. Stories of highly educated black women condemned to a lifetime of menial labor were legion. For example, a young graduate of the Cambridge Latin and High School, Addie W. Hunter, fulfilled certification requirements for civil service and clerical positions in Boston, but she had to work in a factory while she chased "the will-o-the-wisp of the possible job." She invested all of her meager savings in an unsuccessful lawsuit to gain a position for which she was qualified. In 1916, "out of pocket, out of courage, without at present, any defense in the law," she stated the obvious reason why other young women like herself would inevitably find their formal training wasted: "For the way things stand at present, it is useless to have the requirements. Color—the reason nobody will give, the reason nobody is required to give, will always be in the way."

The sexual and racial division of labor in Chicago stores and offices during the 1920s provides additional confirmation of these points. A clothing store in the city hired both black and white women, but the latter served as salesclerks and ate in a lunchroom on the first floor, while black women worked as maids and ate in the basement. Significantly, the country's largest employer of black clerical workers (1,050 in 1920) was Montgomery Ward, a mail-order establishment whose personnel had no direct contact with the customers they served. Even this company ran into public-relations problems. When black women were first hired during World War I, they had to eat their meals in local Loop restaurants, prompting complaints from the owners of these establishments "fearing the loss of old patrons in handling this new business." The company eventually built its own cafeteria in order to shore up its image and remove its black employees from public view. . . .

In most large cities during this period, commercial entertainment and vice districts were located in or near black residential areas. White law-enforcement officials sought to locate this type of activity, with its attendant drug and alcohol use, prostitution, gambling, and petty and organized crime, away from "respectable" (that is, white) neighborhoods. Many of the black people with jobs in the fields of legal or illegal entertainment were either employees of whites or consumers of services and goods marketed by whites. Young, attractive black women worked as dancers or waitresses in cabarets that catered to middle-class "slummers." This type of work provided little long-term financial security, but for some women it offered a glamorous alternative to assembly lines and kitchens.

Predictably, the physical concentration of urban vice gradually created disproportionate numbers of black prostitutes. The "incentives" for young women to make their living this way were largely negative ones—inability to support oneself by other means and force exerted by a pimp. Most of the domestic servants in brothels were young black women, at least some of whom were vulnerable to the importations of madames and patrons. A study of prostitution in New York City from 1900 to 1931 conducted by a Brooklyn College sociologist highlighted a number of themes characteristic of the profession in other northern cities as well. During the first three decades of the century, the "social evil" had gradually become concentrated in Harlem, a "civic twilight zone" that whites found to be "a convenient place in which to go on a moral vacation." Poor and without "influential friends," black women were arrested and convicted more often and received stiffer jail sentences than their white counterparts. No doubt many individual women struggled to preserve their self-respect under the most degrading of circumstances. Yet as a group, black prostitutes represented an extreme form of the victimization endured by all black women workers in terms of their health, safety, and financial compensation.

In conclusion, paid employment carried with it a "social message" for women in industrial America. To be sure, black and white female factory workers together heard a similar message about gender (specifically female–white male) relationships. Both groups labored under the watchful eye of foremen and they remained segregated from male workers. But black women's work experiences delivered an additional, more strident message about the social and economic consequences of racial discrimination. In factories, black women labored apart from even those who were already making less than men; they received task assignments more unpleasant and hazardous than those who already toiled under the worst of conditions.

Marriage intensified the differences between black and white working-class women. Although young working girls of both races might have indulged in romantic fantasies about marriage, few black women could count on a wedding to end their days of sustained wage earning. The "social message" of domestic service for black wives was especially clear. The white mistress–black maid relationship preserved the inequities of the slave system (at least some domestics made the analogy), and thus a unique historical legacy compounded the humiliations inherent in the servant's job. In the end, a black female wage earner encountered a depth and form of discrimination never experienced by a Polish woman, no matter how poor, illiterate, or lacking in a "factory sense" she was.

Household Responsibilities

As a form of productive labor, housework was not intrinsically demeaning. Black women of course performed the same services for their own families as they did for whites, though the two workplaces had radically different social consequences. This was true in the South as well as in the North, but life in northern cities made new kinds of household demands on black women even as it opened up new possibilities for them and their children. Any discussion of women's work in the home must begin with a description of the material dimensions of household and community life, for these, together with a culturally determined sexual division of labor, shaped domestic responsibilities.

Although the specific process of ghettoization varied from city to city, the Great Migration in general intensified patterns of racial segregation throughout the urban North. . . .

Small, congested, poorly equipped rooms, together with inclement winter weather and unfamiliar forms of household technology, changed the nature of housework for many migrant women. During his visits to the homes of Pittsburgh newcomers, Abraham Epstein noted that, though an apartment might be equipped with gas, many women persisted in using coal and wood to fuel their fires for cooking and laundry purposes, even in July; "being unaccustomed to the use of gas, and fearful of it, [they] preferred the more accustomed method of cooking." A similar situation existed in Philadelphia, where migrants continued to use familiar cooking equipment rather than feed coins into a kitchen meter for gas. Grease and soot from old kerosene or coal stoves smudged the few windows of tenement apartments and, by blocking out all light, necessitated the use of oil lamps day and night. The women who contributed to the family income by washing clothes worked under the most trying circumstances. Mrs. E. H. of Pittsburgh had to lug water from an outside pump by the stairs to her one-room apartment; it always seemed to be hot and damp and filled with ill children. On warm, sunny days, clothes might be hung outside in a back courtyard, but in cold or rainy weather, the laundry had to dry inside. Although not all migrants lived in large, multiple-unit dwellings (which were most characteristic of New York), few had the front porches that even washerwomen in the urban South depended upon.

Women who worked for money within their own homes faced a trade-off of sorts between taking care of their own children on the one hand and adding to the confusion in already overcrowded rooms on the other. At home, laundresses, seamstresses, and hairdressers had relative flexibility in terms of hours of work and childcare provisions. Yet, at the same time, their tiny apartments became "hotter, more cluttered, and more unhealthful." Moreover, this type of work was often unreliable and failed to provide adequate support for a family with children.

Despite their efforts to care for their own offspring and earn a living wage at the same time, black working mothers were held responsible for a variety of social ills related to family life, from the extraordinarily high black infant mortality rates characteristic of all northern cities to educational "retardation" and juvenile delinquency. Certainly, the gainful employment of mothers could at times adversely affect children, though through no fault of their own. Women with infants could not breastfeed regularly during the day; they had to substitute cow's milk or some other food (routinely prepared under less than ideal conditions) for this natural, nutritionally superior form of nourishment. Neighbors and relatives had their own domestic and financial responsibilities, and many could care for other children only sporadically. Some unattended children were locked in the home all day, while others took to the streets, "with keys tied around their necks on a ribbon" to seek out fun and mischief until their mothers returned from work. . . .

Social workers lamented the fate of children like Pittsburgh's Harry, age eleven, a thief, left to his own devices by a mother earning $3 a week in a service job that consumed all her time but a few hours each morning. . . .

Like mothers, fathers feared for their children. In 1917 one man, recently arrived in Cleveland, complained about ghetto "loffers, gamblers [and] pockit pickers"; "I can not raise my children here like they should be," he declared, "this is one of the worst places in principle you ever look on in your life." Yet few men could exercise any regular, systematic control over their children's whereabouts. Servants and factory laborers worked long hours outside their own neighborhoods. Those who were laid off or otherwise unemployed often gathered in places familiar to white employers looking for workers—a certain street corner, vacant lot, lunch room, or barbershop, for example. In other cases, Pullman porters, live-in domestics, and men who could find work only in a distant city were absent from home for extended periods. At times a husband had to stay in a boardinghouse near his job while his family lived elsewhere. . . .

Fathers were not the only wage earners to make an untimely departure from the black household and thus create extra work for wives and mothers. In the northern city, eldest daughters still helped their mother with the housework and childcare, but they lacked the subservience characteristic of the rural *paterfamilias* tradition. . . . Mothers considered clothes washing "as the proper share of housework" for adolescent girls; in some cases that meant that a ten- or twelve-year-old was responsible for doing the laundry for families with as many as ten members. Perhaps it was no wonder, then, that as more married women had to engage in day work during the recession of 1921–22, rates of "juvenile delinquency" (usually defined as truancy, vagrancy, or sexual activity) among black girls aged ten to eighteen noticeably increased; without rigorous parental oversight at least some girls chose the excitement of street life over scrubbing clothes. . . .

In supplying the household's necessities, migrant wives and mothers had to adjust to the North's cash economy. . . . Southern sharecroppers lived on the landlord's credit, and in some cases grew their own vegetables and raised hogs, cows, and chickens; they rarely saw more than a few dollars each month. Even in southern towns and cities, blacks often kept a few chickens and tended a small garden. But in the North these hedges against hard times were no longer available, and furthermore, a whole host of new, expensive necessities had appeared—warm clothing, shoes (for "all feet at least ten months in the year"), and large quantities of coal, gas, or kerosene. The migrant woman found that she had moved from semi-self-sufficiency to a consumer society. As her "stores of 'hog and hominy,' corn meal, syrup, and sweet potatoes" brought from Alabama dwindled, "the corner grocery, with its bewildering bright-colored canned goods, and other dazzling shops offer[ed] unusual opportunities for getting rid of money. . . .

In the North, the amount of work associated with household maintenance increased dramatically as wives sought to meet the daily needs of

lodgers, as well as those of their immediate families. Extended and augmented households served both economic and social functions. Because of
the youthfulness of the migrant population and the imbalanced sex ratio
among blacks in most northern cities (in favor of women in the East, men
in the Midwest), ghettos contained an unusually large number of single
persons, childless married couples, and parents with very few children.
(Fertility rates of northern urban black women were lower than those of
southern women, black or white, in cities or rural areas.) In seeking shelter
for themselves, then, blacks as a group faced problems shaped by both
demographic and economic considerations that made the enlarged household a compelling arrangement, if not an absolute necessity in many cases.

At least one-third of ghetto households between 1915 and 1930 contained
lodgers at any one time. . . . According to a recent study of urban adjustment among blacks and Poles in Pittsburgh from 1900 to 1930, maturing
black families relied increasingly on income from lodgers because they could
not count on their own sons and daughters for financial support. Polish
households, on the other hand, became more nuclear over the years; gradually children started to work and turn over their wages to their parents,
thereby lessening the need for boarders. Finally, black heads of household
were less able than their Polish counterparts to provide "meaningful economic contacts" for either their offspring or friends, fostering a greater
sense of individualism (with regard to finding and keeping jobs) among
black wage earners who lived together.

Female lodgers at times helped the mother of the household with ba-
bysitting, cleaning, and cooking. Indeed, case histories of extended and
augmented families suggest that at a certain point at least one woman
boarder became necessary to share the tremendous increase in housework.
Large households simply added to the domestic obligations of wives who
had little in the way of time, cash, and conveniences. Black women supported the lodging system by dint of muscle power and organizational
ability, and in the process they demonstrated how their homemaking skills
could help to supplement household income while benefiting the migrant
community. In the urban North, as in the rural and urban South, the
boundaries between family and kin, household and neighborhood remained
flexible and ever shifting.

Conclusion

Black migrants brought with them a way of looking at the world that
originated in the rural South and set them apart from equally poor white
country folk, as well as from city dwellers. Like other newcomers to the
city, they had to make basic adjustments related to finding a job, sustaining
kin relationships, and spending money and free time. But the process of
adjustment among blacks was shaped by long-standing Afro-American traditions and customs, and thus contrasted with that of various Eastern
European immigrant groups on the other hand and native-born white urban
in-migrants on the other. . . .

The expanded realm of political and educational activities in northern cities represented a tangible form of upward social mobility for black women migrants from the South. Few of these women could afford to define self-betterment (or even intergenerational advancement) according to the standards established by Eastern European immigrants and native-born whites—a move out of the congested city into the spacious suburbs, a move up out of unskilled work into a semiskilled or white-collar position. But if black wives and mothers had to continue to toil for wages outside their own homes, doing traditional "black women's work," they reaffirmed cultural priorities that had significant social, if not material, consequences for black people as a group. Like their emancipated grandmothers, they worked for the educational improvement of their children, and like their emancipated grandfathers, they cast votes on behalf of the political integrity of their own communities. This is not to suggest that black women lacked an interest in striving for improved housing or jobs; to the contrary, their stubborn eagerness to seek out better living quarters, to leave domestic service for factory work, and to drop out of the work force altogether whenever household finances permitted showed that they adhered to the family values shared by working-class women regardless of race. Nevertheless, the peculiar dynamics of racial prejudice in the North precluded a definition of mobility expressed in purely economic terms.

Gradually, a national perspective began to break down the insularity of ghetto life, and a former rural peasantry directly confronted modern industrial society. Likewise, white northerners came to understand that racial issues were no longer a distant regional or historical anachronism, as they had once believed. Noted the white journalist Ray Stannard Baker of the Great Migration: "On wide Southern farms [blacks] can live to themselves; in Northern cities they become part of ourselves." His observation pertained primarily to growing black political influence, for in a cultural and economic sense, ghetto residents remained apart from the larger white society. When the depression of the 1930s threw white folks out of work too, considerations of political expediency, not racial justice, influenced the responses of most elected officials to the plight of black people. These responses affected black women both as wage earners and as family members; for the first time since Reconstruction the work of wives and mothers entered the purview of national policymakers. . . .

Asian Immigrants Raising Cane: The World of Plantation Hawaii

RONALD TAKAKI

Paralleling the migration of Chinese to California was the movement of Chinese, Japanese, Korean, and Filipino laborers to Hawaii, an American economic colony that became a territory of the United States in 1900. Over

Ronald Takaki, *Strangers from A Different Shore: A History of Asian Americans* (Boston: Little, Brown, 1989), pp. 132–155. Copyright © 1989 by Ronald Takaki.

300,000 Asians entered the islands between 1850 and 1920. Brought here as "cheap labor," they filled the requisitions itemizing the needs of the plantations. Their labor enabled the planters to transform sugar production into Hawaii's leading industry. "It is apparent," declared the *Hawaiian Gazette* excitedly in 1877, "that Sugar is destined most emphatically to be 'King.'" But to be "King" the sugar industry required the constant importation of workers whose increasing numbers led to the ethnic diversification of society in the islands. For example, in 1853, Hawaiians and part-Hawaiians represented 97 percent of the population of 73,137 inhabitants, while Caucasians constituted only 2 percent and Chinese only half a percent. Seventy years later, Hawaiians and part-Hawaiians made up only 16.3 percent of the population, while Caucasians represented 7.7 percent, Chinese 9.2 percent, Japanese 42.7 percent, Portuguese 10.6 percent, Puerto Ricans 2.2 percent, Koreans 1.9 percent, and Filipinos 8.2 percent.

Hawaii was ethnically very different from the mainland. In 1920, Asians totaled 62 percent of the island population, compared to only 3.5 percent of the California population and only 0.17 percent of the continental population. Constituting a majority of the population in Hawaii, Asians were able to choose a different course than their mainland brethren. Powered by "necessity" yet buoyed by "extravagance," they responded in their own unique ways to the world of plantation Hawaii. . . .

Asian immigrants were not prepared for their experiences as plantation workers in Hawaii. They had come from societies where they labored to provide for their families within a context of traditions and established rules and obligations. They had greater control over their time and activities, working with family members and people they knew. "In Japan," a plantation laborer said, "we could say, 'It's okay to take the day off today,' since it was our own work. We were free to do what we wanted. We didn't have that freedom on the plantation. We had to work ten hours every day." The Filipino *tao*, or peasant farmer, followed the rhythm of the day, the weather, and the seasons in the Philippines. He worked in the fields with his wife and children, driving the carabao before him and urging his family workers to keep pace with him. *Hana-hana*—working on the plantation in Hawaii—was profoundly different.

Though laborers still awoke early as they did in the old country, they were now aroused by the loud screams of a plantation siren at five in the morning. . . .

After the 5:00 A.M. plantation whistle had blown, the *lunas* (foremen) and company policemen strode through the camps. "Get up, get up," they shouted as they knocked on the doors of the cottages and the barracks. "Hana-hana, hana-hana, work, work." A Korean remembered the morning her mother failed to hear the work whistle and overslept: "We were all asleep—my brother and his wife, my older sister, and myself. Suddenly the door swung open, and a big burly luna burst in, screaming and cursing, "Get up, get to work." The luna ran around the room, ripping off the covers, not caring whether my family was dressed or not." . . .

"All the workers on a plantation in all their tongues and kindreds, 'rolled out' sometime in the early morn, before the break of day,'' reported a visitor. One by one and two by two, laborers appeared from "the shadows, like a brigade of ghosts.'' From an outlying camp, they came on a train, "car after car of silent figures,'' their cigarettes glowing in the darkness. In front of the mill they lined up, shouldering their hoes. As the sun rose, its rays striking the tall mill stack, "quietly the word was passed from somewhere in the dimness. Suddenly and silently the gang started for its work, dividing themselves with one accord to the four quarters of the compass, each heading toward his daily task.'' The workers were grouped by the foremen into gangs of twenty to thirty workers and were marched or transported by wagons and trains to the fields. Each gang was watched by a luna, who was "almost always a white man.'' The ethnicity of the gangs varied. Some of them were composed of one nationality, while others were mixed. One luna said he had workers of all races in his gang, including Hawaiians, Filipinos, Puerto Ricans, Chinese, Japanese, Portuguese, and Koreans.

There were gangs of women workers, too, for women were part of the plantation work force—about 7 percent of all workers in 1894 and 14 percent in 1920. Most of the women workers—over 80 percent of them—were Japanese. Women were concentrated in field operations, such as hoeing, stripping leaves, and harvesting. My grandmother Katsu Okawa was a cane cutter on the Hana Plantation, and my aunt Yukino Takaki was an *hapaiko* worker, or cane loader, on the Puunene Plantation. Though women were given many of the same work assignments as men, they were paid less than their male counterparts. Japanese-female field hands, for example, received an average wage of only fifty-five cents per day in 1915, compared to the seventy-eight cents Japanese-male field hands received.

Women also worked in the camps: they washed laundry, cooked, and sewed clothes. "I made custom shirts with hand-bound button holes for 25 cents,'' recalled a Korean woman. "My mother and sister-in-law took in laundry. They scrubbed, ironed and mended shirts for a nickel a piece. It was pitiful! Their knuckles became swollen and raw from using the harsh yellow soap.'' On the Hawi Plantation, my grandmother Katsu Okawa operated a boarding house where she fed her husband and eight children as well as fifteen men every day. . . .

The most regimented work was in the fields. "We worked like machines,'' a laborer complained. "For 200 of us workers, there were seven or eight lunas and above them was a field boss on a horse. We were watched constantly.'' A Japanese woman, interviewed years later at the age of ninety-one, said: "We had to work in the canefields, cutting cane, being afraid, not knowing the language. When any *haole* [white] or Portuguese luna came, we got frightened and thought we had to work harder or get fired.'' . . .

One of the most tedious and backbreaking tasks was hoeing weeds. Laborers had to "hoe hoe hoe . . . for four hours in a straight line and no talking,'' said a worker. "Hoe every weed along the way to your three rows. Hoe—chop chop chop, one chop for one small weed, two for all big ones." They had to keep their bodies bent over. They wanted to stand up and stretch, unknotting twisted bodies and feeling the freedom of arched backs. The laborers cursed the lunas, "talking stink" about the driving pace of the work: "It burns us up to have an ignorant *luna* stand around and holler and swear at us all the time for not working fast enough. Every so often, just to show how good he is, he'll come up and grab a hoe and work like hell for about two minutes and then say sarcastically, 'Why you no work like that?' He knows and we know he couldn't work for ten minutes at that pace." The lunas were just plain mean "buggas." Laborers also did "hole hole" work, the stripping of the dead leaves from the cane stalks. To protect themselves against the needles of the cane leaves, they wore heavy clothing. Still, as they left the fields each day, they found their hands badly cut by the cane leaves. . . .

As they worked, laborers wore *bangos* hanging on chains around their necks—small brass disks with their identification numbers stamped on them In the old country, they had names, and their names told them who they were, connecting them to family and community; in Hawaii, they were given numbers. The workers resented this new impersonal identity. Laborers were "treated no better than cows or horses," one of them recalled. "Every worker was called by number, never by name." . . .

When the cane was ripe, lunas on horseback led the workers out into the fields to harvest the crop. . . .

Cutting the ripe cane was dirty and exhausting work. As the workers mechanically swung their machetes, they felt the pain of the blisters on their hands and the scratches on their arms. "When you cutting the cane and you pulling the cane back," a worker said, "sometimes you get scratched with the leaves from the cane because they have a little edge just like a saw blade." Their heavy arms, their bent backs begged for a break, a moment of rest. . . .

Twelve feet in height, the cane enclosed and dwarfed the Asian workers. As they cleared the cane "forests," cutting the stalks close to the ground, they felt the heat of the sun, the humidity of the air, and found themselves surrounded by iron red clouds of dust. They covered their faces with handkerchiefs; still they breathed the dust and the mucus they cleared from their noses appeared blood red. "The sugar cane fields were endless and the stalks were twice the height of myself," a Korean woman sighed. "Now that I look back, I thank goodness for the height, for if I had seen how far the fields stretched, I probably would have fainted from knowing how much work was ahead. My waistline got slimmer and my back ached from bending over all the time to cut the sugar cane." . . .

Collecting the cane stalks, the workers tied them into bundles and loaded them onto railway cars. A train then pulled the cane to the mill where engines, presses, furnaces, boilers, vacuum pans, centrifugal drums, and other machines crushed the cane and boiled its juices into molasses and sugar. Inside the mill, laborers like my uncle Nobuyoshi Takaki felt like they were in the "hold of a steamer." The constant loud clanking and whirring of the machinery were deafening. . . .

At four-thirty in the afternoon, the workers again heard the blast of the plantation whistle, the signal to stop working. "Pau hana," they sighed, "finished working." Though they were exhausted and though they thought they were too tired to hoe another row of cane or carry another bundle of stalks, they suddenly felt a final burst of energy and eagerly scrambled to the camps. . . .

Planters claimed they treated their workers with "consideration and humanity," seeking "in every possible way to advance their comfort and make them contented and happy." But their purpose was not entirely humanitarian. Planters understood clearly that it was "good business" to have their laborers "properly fed": it "paid" to have a "contented lot of laborers," for they would then be able to extract a "good day's work" from them.

The paternalism of the planters was also intended to defuse the organizing efforts of the workers. A plantation manager explained how laborers were "capable of comprehending the difference between kind words, kind acts, kind wages generally and ruffian roughness and abuse." Paternalism was designed to pacify labor unrest. "We should avail to get our house in order before a storm breaks," planters told themselves. "Once the great majority of the laboring classes are busy under conditions which breed contentment . . . we can expect a gradual and effectual diminution of the power of the agitating [labor] element." Planters agreed that "humanity in industry pays."

Plantation paternalism also served to maintain a racial and class hierarchy. White plantation managers and foremen supervised Asians, constituting 70 to 85 percent of the work force. They saw their role as "parental" and described Koreans as "childlike" and Filipinos as "more or less like children" "by nature." The vice president of H. Hackfield and Company sent managers a circular informing them that the Filipino was "very incapable of caring for himself." Left entirely to his own resources, the Filipino was likely to spend his money on "fancy groceries" and consequently to be insufficiently nourished. Managers should "look after" Filipino laborers. Planters explained their paternalism in terms of white racial superiority. They had spread "Caucasian civilization" to Hawaii, where they as members of "a stronger race" had to supervise and care for Asian and Hawaiian laborers. "Where there is a drop of the Anglo-Saxon blood, it is sure to rule."

Behind paternalism was the "necessity" of coercion. Planters believed that they should control their workers with "the strong hand." "There is one word which holds the lower classes . . . in check," they declared, "and that is Authority." The plantation organization resembled a system of military discipline. . . .

As "generals," plantation managers devised an intricate system of rules and regulations for their "troops." They required their workers to be "industrious and docile and obedient," "regular and cleanly in their personal habits," punctual for work and rest, and present on the plantation at all times. To punish workers for violating the rules, planters developed an elaborate system of fines, which specified a charge for virtually every kind of misconduct. . . .

Where fines did not work, harsher penalties were employed. Asked how he would punish a contract laborer for idleness, a planter replied: "We dock him; we give him one one-half or three-quarters of a day of wages; and if he keeps it up we resort to the law and have him arrested for refusing to work." Sometimes planters used physical punishment to intimidate the workers. Chinese workers on the Olowalu Plantation were allowed five to fifteen minutes for lunch and were "kicked" if they did not return promptly to work. . . . The Hawaiian government had outlawed whipping, but the law did not always reflect reality. . . . A worker graphically described the tiered structure of strict supervision: "Really, life on the plantation is one of restrictions, unwritten rules and regulations imposed upon the inhabitants by the manager who is assisted by his various ranks of overseers and lunas to see to it that the people obey these regulations and do the amount and nature of the work that is expected of them. . . . In conclusion I say that life on a plantation is much like life in a prison."

To strengthen their authority over their ethnically diverse work force, planters developed an occupational structure stratifying employment according to race. Skilled and supervisory positions were predominantly occupied by whites. In 1882, for example, 88 percent of all lunas and clerks were white, while 28.5 percent of the laborers were Hawaiian and 48.3 percent were Chinese. None of the lunas were Chinese. In 1904, the Hawaiian Sugar Planters' Association passed a resolution that restricted skilled positions to "American citizens, or those eligible for citizenship." This restriction had a racial function: it excluded Asians from skilled occupations. They were not "white" according to federal law and hence ineligible to become naturalized citizens. In 1915, Japanese laborers were mostly field hands and mill laborers. There were only one Japanese, one Hawaiian, and two part-Hawaiian mill engineers; the remaining forty-one mill engineers (89 percent) were of European ancestry. A racial division was particularly evident in supervisory positions: of the 377 overseers, only two were Chinese and seventeen Japanese; 313 of all overseers (83 percent) were white. . . .

After federal law terminated the contract-labor system in 1900, planters used their centralized organization, the Hawaiian Sugar Planters' Association, to institute mechanisms to keep wages low. In a "Confidential Letter" to plantation managers on July 24, 1901, the association called for island conventions of managers to form wage-fixing agreements: "The deliberations of Island conventions at which managers would meet should be behind closed doors as it would be embarrassing to have such proceedings published." To carry out this plan, the association established a central labor bureau to coordinate all employment of Asian laborers and to set wage rates. Laborers were warned they should not try to leave their assigned plantations to bargain for higher wages, for they would not be hired by another plantation unless they could show a certificate of discharge. To provide incentives for their workers to increase their productivity, the association introduced a "bonus system" in 1910. . . . But the bonus also kept the workers from leaving the plantation. The bonus was paid only once a year, and workers forfeited it if they left the plantation before bonus time. . . .

To control their workers, planters tied other "strings." They utilized a multitiered wage system, paying different wage rates to different nationalities for the same work. Japanese cane cutters, for example, were paid ninety-nine cents a day, while Filipino cane cutters received only sixtynine cents. Planters also cultivated nationalistic consciousness among the laborers in order to divide them. They appealed to the "race pride" of the Filipino laborers to urge them to work as hard as the Japanese laborers. One Filipino work-gang leader, giving instructions in Ilocano, declared to his men: "We are all Filipinos, brothers. We all know how to hoe. So, let's do a good job and show the people of other nations what we can do. Let us not shame our skin!" The planters' divide-and-control strategy promoted interethnic tensions that sometimes erupted into fistfights in the fields and riots in the camps. On the Spreckelsville Plantation on Maui in 1898, for example, three hundred Japanese, wielding sticks and clubs, drove a hundred Chinese laborers from the camps. A year later, during a riot involving Chinese and Japanese workers on the Kahuku Plantation on Oahu, sixty Chinese were wounded and four killed.

But plantation workers did not concentrate their discontent against each other; rather, they usually directed their rage outward against their bosses and the system, seeking to gain greater control over the conditions of their labor and a greater share of the profits they had produced. Not passive and docile as the managers wanted them to be, they actively struggled to improve the quality of their lives on the plantation in many different ways.

Occasionally workers fought back violently. They retaliated against mean overseers for physical abuse and mistreatment. Numerous instances of workers assaulting and beating up cruel and unfair lunas can be found in the records. On a Maui plantation in 1903, for example, after an Irish luna had hit a laborer, he was attacked by a gang of Chinese workers and buried under a ten-foot pile of cane stalks. In 1904, on the Waipahu Plantation, two hundred Korean laborers mobbed the plantation physician, claiming he had killed a Korean patient with a kick to the abdomen. Sometimes workers aimed their anger at property, especially the dry cane fields that were easy targets for arson. After the police had broken up a demonstration of protesting Chinese laborers on the Waianae Plantation in 1899, a fire swept through its cane fields.

But while planters worried about direct labor resistance, they also had to watch for subtle and ingenious actions. . . .

. . . Everywhere workers engaged in day-to-day resistance, trying to minimize the amount of labor their bosses extracted from them. Many workers feigned illness in order to be released from work. . . . Laborers became skilled practitioners in the art of pretending to be working. On the Kohala Plantation on the island of Hawaii, a luna discovered that supervising Japanese women in the fields could be frustrating. In his diary, supervisor Jack Hall complained: "It always seemed impossible to keep them together, especially if the fields were not level. The consequence was that these damsels were usually scattered all over the place and as many as possible were out of sight in the gulches or dips in the field where they could not be seen, where they would calmly sit and smoke their little metal pipes until the luna appeared on the skyline, when they would be busy as bees."

To escape from work and daily drudgery, sliding numbly into recalcitrance, many plantation laborers resorted to drugs—opium and alcohol. . . . A Filipino worker remembered how "drinks were readily available because just about everyone knew how to make 'swipe wine.' You just ferment molasses with water and yeast and in a week it's ready. And if you distilled that, you got clear liquor ten times stronger than any gin you could buy from the store."

Planters complained that the use of drugs made it "impossible" to get from their laborers "anything like a fair day's work." "No employees can drink booze and do six honest days' work in a week," managers grumbled. . . . After saturating themselves with opium or alcohol on the weekends, laborers were "unfit for work" on Monday. Inspecting the camps on Mondays, plantation managers sometimes found a third of their men "dead drunk."

Drugs eased, perhaps made more bearable, the emptiness plantation laborers felt on the weekends as well as the boredom of their meaningless and routine work during the week. "There was very little to do when work was over," recalled a Chinese laborer, "and the other fellows who were having a good time smoking asked me to join them, so then in order to be a good sport I took up opium smoking, not realizing that I would probably have to die with it." "If we don't smoke," another Chinese worker said, "we feel as if something were gnawing at our insides. The opium fumes will drive away that feeling and lift us out of our misery into a heaven of blissful rest and peace." Momentarily at least, drugs enabled workers to escape the reality of the plantation and to enter a dream world where they could hear again the voices of fathers, mothers, and other loved ones. . . .

But drugs were self-destructive and offered only temporary euphoria, and plantation workers often sought a more permanent form of escape— *ha'alele hana,* desertion from service. Until Hawaii became a U.S. territory in 1900, the contract-labor system was legal in the islands and plantation laborers under contract were bound by law to serve three-to-five-year terms. . . . Thousands of contract laborers fled from their assigned plantations before the completion of their contracts. In 1892, Marshal Charles B. Wilson calculated that 5,706 arrests, or one third of the total arrests made between 1890 and 1892, were for desertion.

Planters constantly worried about their contract laborers running away. "On the island of Maui," the *Pacific Commercial Advertiser* observed in 1880, "scarcely a day passes which does not bring along some member of the police force in search of absconding Chinese plantation laborers, who are making quite a business of shipping [signing a labor contract], drawing large advances, and then 'clearing out' causing their employers much inconvenience and expense." . . .

. . . Generally staying on the plantations only as long as they were required by their contracts, Chinese workers moved in search of better employment opportunities. Many became rice farmers, making the swamplands yield rich harvests, and others settled in nearby villages and opened small stores. "My grandfather Len Wai worked on a plantation and operated a store during after-work hours," stated Raymond Len. "The store did well and he went full time into it after his contract was up." Most Chinese ex-plantation laborers went to Honolulu, where they lived in a bustling Chinatown.

Thousands of Japanese workers also left the plantations after their contracts had been fulfilled. . . . After annexation and the prohibition of contract labor in the Territory of Hawaii, laborers were no longer bound to the plantations, and planters anxiously witnessed an exodus of Japanese laborers to the mainland. In their camps, Japanese workers read circulars and advertisements about higher wages in California. In 1906 the *Hawaiian Star* reported: "The 'American fever,' as it is called among the Japs, appears to be causing a lot of agitation among them. Local Japanese papers contain the advertisement of Hasagawa, who recently got a license to solicit laborers, calling for 2,000 Japanese to go to the coast at once. The advertisement offers wages of from $1.35 per day up, stating that men who are good can make from $2 to $4 per day." In their efforts to stem the Japanese movement to the mainland, planters asked the Japanese Consul in Hawaii to issue circulars in Japanese instructing Japanese laborers to remain on the plantation. In 1903 the consul urged his countrymen to "stay at work steadily on the plantations and not go to an uncertainty on the mainland." Ignoring the consul's advice, Japanese laborers continued to migrate to the mainland in search of the highest bidder for their labor. By early 1907, 40,000 Japanese had left Hawaii for the West Coast.

But in March President Theodore Roosevelt suddenly issued an executive order prohibiting the passage of Japanese from Hawaii to the mainland. . . . At a mass meeting in Honolulu, Japanese laborers angrily denounced Roosevelt's restriction: "It enslaves us permanently to Hawaii's capitalists!" Trapped by law in Hawaii, Japanese workers saw they had no choice but to struggle for a better life in the islands.

Most of them saw that the struggle would have to be a collective one, and that their most powerful weapon was the strike. But they also realized the planters had the power to retaliate brutally. Past experiences had taught them some harsh lessons. In 1891, for example, two hundred striking Chinese laborers had protested unfair deductions from their wages and marched to the courthouse in Kapaau on the island of Hawaii. The plantation managers ordered them to return to their camps; late in the afternoon, the strikers left the courthouse. But as they were walking back to the camps, they were confronted by policemen armed with bullock whips. In fear, one or two of the strikers stooped to pick up stones. Suddenly, according to a newspaper report, the Chinese strikers found themselves "in the midst of a general onslaught," and were "ruthlessly overridden and welted with the bullock whips." Pursuing the fleeing Chinese strikers, the policemen attacked the Chinese camp. They "demolished every window, strewed the premises inside and out with stones, seized every Chinaman they came across, and yanked forty or more by their queues. . . . Chinamen were seen with their tails twisted about the pommel of a saddle, dragged at a gallop."

Planters believed their repression of strikes had been justifiable because contract laborers could not legally strike: they were bound by contract to work for a specified term of years and could be arrested and punished in the courts for violating the agreement. But the Organic Act of 1900, which established Hawaii as a territory of the United States on June 14, abolished the contract-labor system.

Months before the Organic Act took effect, plantation workers anticipated their freedom. On April 4, Japanese workers in Lahaina struck. Upset over the deaths of three mill hands who had been crushed under a collapsed sugar pan, the laborers blamed management carelessness for the accident and refused to work. The strikers seized the mill and the town. For ten days, they defiantly "continued to meet, to parade in the town under Japanese flags, to drill, and even, unhindered by anyone, demolished the house and property of a store clerk who would not give them credit." . . .

In 1900, over twenty strikes swept through the plantations as 8,000 workers withheld their labor from the bosses. While the strikes were led and supported mainly by Japanese workers, two of them involved inter-ethnic cooperation. On June 22, Chinese and Japanese laborers on the Puehuchu Plantation struck to protest the retention of part of their wages, a provision contained in their original labor contracts. Five months later, forty-three Japanese and Portuguese women field hands on the Kilauea Plantation demanded that wages be raised from eight dollars to ten dollars a month. Though the striking women were locked out by the management, they stood together and won their wage increases.

After 1900, management-labor conflict became even more intense. As they organized themselves and initiated strike actions, workers found themselves facing the power of the state. This occurred during the 1906 Waipahu Plantation strike. Demanding higher wages, Japanese laborers struck, and plantation manager E. K. Bull immediately requested police assistance. Forty-seven policemen armed with rifles were assigned to the plantation. They functioned as Bull's private army. The policemen marched in review on the plantation grounds to intimidate the strikers with a show of force; patrolling the camps, they stopped and questioned all stragglers. During a tense moment of the negotiations, Bull threatened to use the police to evict the strikers from their homes in the camps. Unintimidated, the seventeen hundred Japanese strikers forced Bull to grant concessions in order to end the strike.

The Waipahu Plantation strike of 1906 underscored the importance of collective labor action. Labor violence and arson were individualistic as well as sporadic actions; they did not seriously undermine planter control. Recalcitrance and drunkenness represented resistance but did not change conditions in the workplace. Desertion enabled dissatisfied workers to escape, leaving intact the mechanisms of planter discipline and regimentation. But striking constituted a particularly effective expression of labor resistance, for it could lead to a positive transformation of the plantation structure. Moreover, striking could enable men and women of various nationalities to gain a deeper understanding of themselves as laborers, to develop a working-class identity and consciousness.

Divided by the political strategy of the planters and by their diverse national identities, workers initially tended to define their class interests in terms of their ethnicity. Thus, at first they organized themselves into "blood unions"—labor organizations based on ethnic membership: the Japanese belonged to the Japanese union and the Filipinos to the Filipino union.

The most important manifestation of "blood unionism" was the Japanese strike of 1909. Protesting against the differential-wage system based on ethnicity, the strikers demanded higher wages and equal pay for equal work. They noted angrily how Portuguese laborers were paid $22.50 per month while Japanese laborers earned only eighteen dollars a month for the same kind of work. "The wage is a reward for services done," they argued, "and a just wage is that which compensates the laborer to the full value of the service rendered by him. . . . If a laborer comes from Japan and he performs the same quantity of work of the same quality within the same period of time as those who hail from the opposite side of the world, what good reason is there to discriminate one as against the other? It is not the color of the skin that grows cane in the field. It is labor that grows cane."

The Japanese strikers struggled for four long months. The strike involved 7,000 Japanese plantation laborers on Oahu, and thousands of Japanese workers on the other islands supported their striking compatriots, sending them money and food. Japanese business organizations such as the Honolulu Retail Merchants' Association contributed financially to the strike fund, and the Japanese Physicians' Association gave free medical service to the strikers and their families. A strong sense of Japanese ethnic solidarity inspired the strikers. Stridently shouting banzai at rallies, they affirmed their commitment to the spirit of Japan—*yamato damashii*. They told themselves they must "stick together" as Japanese to win the strike.

The strike reflected a new consciousness among Japanese workers, a transformation from sojourners to settlers, from Japanese to Japanese Americans. In their demand for a higher wage, the strikers explained: "We have decided to permanently settle here, to incorporate ourselves with the body politique [sic] of Hawaii—to unite our destiny with that of Hawaii, sharing the prosperity and adversity of Hawaii with other citizens of Hawaii." Gradually becoming settled laborers, they now had families to support, children to educate, and religious institutions to maintain. Hawaii was becoming home for the Japanese laborers, and they asked what kind of home Hawaii would be for them. The strikers argued that the unsatisfactory and deplorable conditions on the plantations perpetuated an "undemocratic and un-American," class-divided society of "plutocrats and coolies." Such a pattern of social inequality was injurious to Hawaii in general. Fair wages would encourage laborers to work more industriously and productively, and Hawaii would enjoy "perpetual peace and prosperity." The goal of the strike was to make possible the formation of "a thriving and contented middle class—the realization of the high ideal of Americanism."

But the planters pressured the government to arrest the Japanese strike leaders for "conspiracy." Then they broke the strike by hiring Koreans, Hawaiians, Chinese, and Portuguese as scabs and began importing massive numbers of Filipinos to counterbalance the Japanese laborers. Three months after the strike, however, the planters eliminated the differential-wage system and raised the wages of the Japanese workers.

An ethnically based strike seemed to make good political sense to Japanese plantation laborers in 1909, for they constituted about 70 percent of the entire work force. Filipinos represented less than one percent. But the very ethnic solidarity of the Japanese made it possible for planters to use laborers of other nationalities to break the "Japanese" strike. Eleven years later, Japanese workers found that they had been reduced proportionately to only 44 percent of the labor force, while Filipino workers had been increased to 30 percent. Organized into separate unions, workers of both nationalities came to realize that the labor movement in Hawaii and their strike actions would have to be based on interethnic working-class unity.

In December of 1919, the Japanese Federation of Labor and the Filipino Federation of Labor submitted separate demands to the Hawaiian Sugar Planters' Association. The workers wanted higher wages, an eight-hour-day, an insurance fund for old retired employees, and paid maternity leaves. Their demands were promptly rejected by the planters. The Japanese Federation of Labor immediately asked the managers to reconsider their decision and agreed to declare a strike after all peaceful methods had been tried. The Japanese leaders knew there was "no other way but to strike." "Let's rise and open the eyes of the capitalists," they declared. "Let's cooperate with the Filipinos"—"back them up with our fund" and "our whole force." The Japanese leaders thought both labor federations should not act precipitously, however. Rather, both unions should prepare for a long strike and plan a successful strategy.

But the Filipino Federation of Labor felt the time for action had arrived. Consequently, on January 19, 1920, Pablo Manlapit, head of the Filipino union, unilaterally issued an order for the Filipinos to strike and urged the Japanese to join them. In his appeal to the Japanese Federation of Labor, Manlapit eloquently called for inter-ethnic working-class solidarity: "This is the opportunity that the Japanese should grasp, to show that they are in harmony with and willing to cooperate with other nationalities in this territory, concerning the principles of organized labor. . . . We should work on this strike shoulder to shoulder."

Meanwhile, 3,000 Filipino workers on the plantations of Oahu went out on strike. They set up picket lines and urged Japanese laborers to join them. "What's the matter? Why you hanahana [work]?" the Filipino strikers asked their Japanese co-workers. Several Japanese newspapers issued clarion calls for Japanese cooperation with the striking Filipinos. The *Hawaii Shimpo* scolded Japanese workers for their hesitation: "Our sincere and desperate voices are also their voices. Their righteous indignation is our righteous indignation. . . . Fellow Japanese laborers! Don't be a race of unreliable dishonest people! Their problem is your problem!" . . . On January 26, the Japanese Federation of Labor ordered the strike to begin on February 1. United in struggle, 8,300 Filipino and Japanese strikers— 77 percent of the entire plantation work force on Oahu—brought plantation operations to a sudden stop. . . .

Aware of the seriousness of the challenge they faced and determined to break the strike, planters quickly turned to their time-tested strategy of divide and control. The president of C. Brewer and Company, one of the corporate owners of the sugar plantations, informed a plantation manager: "We are inclined to think that the best prospect, in connection with this strike, is the fact that two organizations, not entirely in harmony with each other, are connected with it, and if either of them falls out of line, the end will be in sight." The planters isolated the Filipino leadership from the Japanese Federation of Labor and created distrust between the two unions. They offered Manlapit a bribe, and suddenly, to the surprise of both the Filipino and Japanese strikers, Manlapit called off the strike, condemning it as a Japanese action to cripple the industries of Hawaii. But, on the rank-and-file level, many Filipinos continued to remain on strike with the Japanese. Escalating their attack on the Japanese, the planters slandered the Japanese strikers as puppets of Japan and claimed they were seeking to "Japanise" the islands. . . .

To break the strike directly, planters enlisted Hawaiians, Portuguese, and Koreans as strikebreakers. They knew that Koreans had a particular enmity for the Japanese, and the planters had consistently used Koreans to help break Japanese strikes. During the 1920 strike, Korean laborers under the leadership of the Korean National Association announced: "We place ourselves irrevocably against the Japanese and the present strike. We don't wish to be looked upon as strikebreakers, but we shall continue to work . . . and we are opposed to the Japanese in everything." More than one hundred Korean men and women organized themselves into a Strikebreakers' Association and offered their services to the Hawaiian Sugar Planters' Association.

Planters served forty-eight-hour eviction notices to the strikers, forcing them to leave their homes and find shelters in empty lots in Honolulu. Crowded into encampments during the height of the influenza epidemic, thousands of workers and their family members fell ill and 150 died. . . . Under such punishing and chaotic conditions, the strikers could not hold out indefinitely and were compelled to call off the strike in July.

Though they had been soundly beaten, the workers had learned a valuable lesson from the 1920 strike. Filipinos and Japanese, joined by Spanish,

Portuguese, and Chinese laborers, had participated in the first major interethnic working-class struggle in Hawaii. Men and women of different ethnicities, realizing how the 5:00 A.M. whistle had awakened all of them and how they had labored together in the fields and mills, had fought together for a common goal. And as they walked the picket lines and protested at mass rallies together, they understood more deeply the contribution they had made as workers to the transformation of Hawaii into a wealthy and profitable place.

During the strike, as the workers reached for a new unity transcending ethnic boundaries, leaders of the Japanese Federation of Labor questioned the existence of two separate unions—one for the Japanese and one for the Filipinos—and suggested the consolidation of the two federations into one union. They insisted that Japanese workers must affiliate with Filipino, "American," and Hawaiian workers, for as long as all of them were laborers they should mutually cooperate in safeguarding their standard of living. On April 23, the Japanese Federation of Labor decided to become an interracial union and to call the organization the Hawaii Laborers' Association—a new name trumpeting a feeling of multiethnic class camaraderie.

One of the leaders of the Hawaii Laborers' Association articulated this new and developing class perspective. The fact that the "capitalists" were "haoles" and the laborers Japanese and Filipinos was a "mere coincidence," explained Takashi Tsutsumi. Japanese and Filipinos had acted as "laborers" in "a solid body" during the 1920 strike. What the workers had learned from their struggle, Tsutsumi continued, was the need to build "a big, powerful and non-racial labor organization" that could "effectively cope with the capitalists." Such a union would bring together "laborers of all nationalities." The 1920 strike had provided the vision—the basis for a new union: in this struggle, Japanese and Filipino workers had cooperated against the planter class. "This is the feature that distinguishes the recent movement from all others." Tsutsumi observed. "There is no labor movement that surpasses the recent movement of Japanese and Filipinos." Tsutsumi predicted that a "big" interracial union would emerge within ten years, springing from a "Hawaiian-born" leadership. "When that day comes," he concluded, "the strike of 1920 would surely be looked upon as most significant." . . .

⚓ *F U R T H E R   R E A D I N G*

James Barnett, *Work and Community in the Jungle: Chicago's Packinghouse Workers, 1894–1922* (1987)

John Bodnar, *Workers' World: Kinship, Community and Protest in an Industrial Society* (1982)

————, Roger Simon, and Michael P. Weber, *Lives of Their Own: Blacks, Italians, and Poles in Pittsburgh, 1900–1960* (1982)

Albert Camarillo, *Chicanos in a Changing Society: From Mexican Pueblos to American Barrios in Santa Barbara and Southern California, 1848–1930* (1979)

Lawrence Cardosa, *Mexican Emigration to the United States, 1897–1931* (1980)

John Cumbler, *Working-Class Community in Industrial America: Work, Leisure and Struggle in Two Industrial Cities* (1979)

Sarah Deutsch, *No Separate Refuge: Culture, Class, and Gender on an Anglo-Hispanic Frontier in the American Southwest, 1880–1940* (1987)

Hasia Diner, *Erin's Daughters in America* (1983)

Donna R. Gabaccia, *From Italy to Elizabeth Street* (1983)

Mario Garcia, *Desert Immigrants: The Mexicans of El Paso, 1880–1920* (1981)

Evelyn Nakano Glenn, *Issei, Nisei, War Bride: Three Generations of Japanese American Women in Domestic Service* (1986)

James Grossman, *Land of Hope: Chicago, Black Southerners, and the Great Migration* (1989)

Herbert Gutman, *Power and Culture: Essays on the American Working Class* (1987)

———, *Work Culture, and Society in Industrializing America* (1976)

Tamara K. Hareven, *Family Time and Industrial Time: The Relationship Between Family and Work in a New England Industrial Community* (1982)

Jacqueline Jones, *Labor of Love, Labor of Sorrow: Black Women, Work, and the Family from Slavery to the Present* (1985)

David M. Katzman, *Seven Days a Week: Women and Domestic Service in Industrializing America* (1978)

Gerd Korman, *Industrialization, Immigrants, and Americanizers: The View from Milwaukee* (1967)

Barrington Moore, *Social Origins of Dictatorship and Democracy: Lord and Peasant in the Making of the Modern World* (1966)

Michael J. Piore, *Birds of Passage: Migrant Labor and Industrial Societies* (1979)

Daniel T. Rodgers, "Tradition, Modernity, and the American Industrial Worker," *Journal of Interdisciplinary History* 7 (1977), 655–681

Judith K. Smith, *Family Connections: A History of Italian and Jewish Immigrant Lives in Providence, Rhode Island* (1985)

Joe William Trotter, Jr., *Black Milwaukee: The Making of an Industrial Proletariat, 1915–45* (1985)

Virginia Yans-McLaughlin, *Family and Community: Italian Immigrants in Buffalo, 1880–1930* (1977)

Olivier Zunz, *The Changing Face of Inequality: Urbanization, Industrial Development, and Immigrants in Detroit* (1982)

C H A P T E R
6

The Organization of Labor

⚕

Between the 1880s and the First World War, American workers organized themselves into a series of trade unions and political groups designed to sustain their livelihoods and project a vision of the society they hoped to construct. This was an era of enormous social ferment and economic change during which urbanization took a leap forward, women entered the work force in large numbers, mills and factories reached enormous scale, and a substantial segment of American business became national in scope. American businesspeople—especially those at the helm of new industries like steelmaking, electrical manufacturing, and automobile production—bitterly resisted the rise of labor organizations, but trade unionism nevertheless grew steadily in this era, especially in construction, clothing, and mining. By the peak of the World War I employment boom, unions enrolled almost 20 percent of the working class.

In this new world, American unionists experimented with a variety of organizational structures and ideological perspectives. Craft unionism, along the lines pioneered by Samuel Gompers and Adolph Strasser of the Cigar Makers Union, established itself quite firmly in trades like carpentry, printing, and plumbing and among railroad engineers and conductors. The new unions often sustained their power by restricting entry to their trade, frequently at the expense of women, blacks, and Asians. But others struggled to build unions of a far more inclusive sort, from the Knights of Labor in the 1880s, industrywide unions like the United Mine Workers and the short-lived American Railway Union in the 1890s, to the pre–World War I Industrial Workers of the World, which sought nothing less than the organization of the entire working class into ''One Big Union.'' In general, socialists and radicals tended to have more influence in trade unions organized along industrial rather than craft lines, although Eugene V. Debs, the great socialist leader of these years, did have many enthusiastic followers among skilled craft workers, especially in the garment trades and metal-cutting industries.

One way to explain the divergent character of American union organizations is to look more closely at the industries that these unions sought to organize. American unions have usually reflected, in both their organizational structure and ideological outlook, the character of the industry in which they have sought to function. Thus the craft unions of the American Federation of Labor flourished in trades where the individual worker's skill was still paramount and where competitive conditions in the industry kept management divided. In con-

*trast, unionists have often sought to build labor organizations enrolling workers
in all job categories—industrial unionism—in those economic sectors where
businesses have grown large or where industry instability has been so great, as
in coal mining and the needle trades, that a strong union can limit wage and
price competition and impose a certain level of industrial stability.*

*What role then does ideology play in maintaining the organizational struc-
ture and economic practices of American unions in the years before World War
I? To what extent were John Commons and Selig Perlman right about the "job
consciousness" of American workers? What kinds of unions have espoused the
more visionary aspirations of socialists such as Eugene V. Debs?*

✣ D O C U M E N T S

The first document, a description of a Labor Day parade in 1889 by the *Boston
Herald*, reflects the degree to which unionists took pride in their movement and
saw it as a cornerstone of all society. Samuel Gompers, president of the American Federation of Labor, defends the right to strike in the second document,
which compares the use of this weapon in labor's arsenal to the struggle waged
by the House of Commons to make the British crown accountable to the people.
In the third document, Edward O'Donnell, a prominent Boston unionist, makes
it clear that labor organizations should be for men only. A sizable group of
women, however, did find their way into the union movement, which prompted
Alice Henry of the Women's Trade Union League to discuss the merits of local
unions composed of women alone, as the fourth document shows. The last two
documents present, respectively, the 1905 preamble of the Industrial Workers of
the World and an attack on craft-union autonomy written in 1911 by William
Trautmann, an IWW founder.

"Labor's Great Army," 1889

An army, with banners flying and music sounding, on its march to the
battlefield, is a grand and inspiring spectacle. . . . An army in days of peace,
with its pomp of ordered motion and its glowing colors and glitter of weapons, is always an attractive sight, charming the gazers, young and old, for
a little while, away from the commonplaces of the everyday struggle for
bread and wealth. . . . But an industrial army, such as Boston witnessed
yesterday parading its historic streets, with a record of invincible patience,
an ever widening purpose of righteous achievement, is a sight more attractive, a spectacle more impressive. It means more for the future than
all the battlefields that have been drenched with human blood. It is a
celebration of the partial reign of the common people.

So excellent were the exhibitions of all the different crafts that it would
be almost invidious to particularize any as the chief ornaments. Yet, perhaps
to most people, the "floats" of the carpenters, by their striking contrast
of the old log cabin of the fathers with a modern building caused the greatest
impression and suggested, in addition, the immense strides in quality of
work made by the workers in the last few years, just as the procession
suggests in a larger way the immense strides made by the workers them-

selves in securing the recognition of their important position in the body politic. The industrial army of yesterday seemed to feel that the workers are the base of the heaven-seeking pyramid of civilization, and that, if that is not well founded and secure, the top must topple. . . .

Union 33 of Boston was most profuse in its exhibition of mottoes. . . . One was a huge saw made of wood and painted quite realistically. On one side was the inscription, "We are organized to elevate," and on the reverse, "Set on eight hours." Another device was a carpenter's square enlarged to a fairly heroic size. The inscription was: "We are all square union men; non-union men are not square."

Other mottoes which attracted especial attention were these: "Honest labor never rusts: up with wages, down with trusts." "Nine hours a day has paved the way: eight hours a day has come to stay." "Less work, more recreation." "We build the cities." "Those who build palaces should not dwell in hovels."

The Operative Tailors' Union gave some very sharp raps. They were accompanied by two large open wagons, trimmed and decorated, one drawn by four horses, and bearing a representation of a tailor shop in active operation with men engaged in cutting, sewing and pressing. The other wagon was fitted to resemble the interior of a room in a tenement house, with all its squalor and misery. The first wagon bore a large sign inscribed: "Away with the filthy scab tenement house labor. We will investigate a few tenement houses for $20." The second bore simply the pregnant remark: "Twenty coats a day's work."

Samuel Gompers Defends the Strike, 1899

The working people find that improvements in the methods of production and distribution are constantly being made, and unless they occasionally strike, or have the power to enter upon a strike, the improvements will all go to the employer and all the injuries to the employees. A strike is an effort on the part of the workers to obtain some of the improvements that have occurred resultant from bygone and present genius of our intelligence, of our mental progress. We are producing wealth today at a greater ratio than ever in the history of mankind, and a strike on the part of workers is, first, against deterioration in their condition, and, second, to be participants in some of the improvements. Strikes are caused from various reasons. The employer desires to reduce wages and lengthen hours of labor, while the desire on the part of employees is to obtain shorter hours of labor and better wages, and better surroundings. Strikes establish or maintain the rights of unionism; that is, to establish and maintain the organization by which the rights of the workers can be the better protected and advanced against the little forms of oppression, sometimes economical, sometimes political—the effort on the part of employers to influence and intimidate workmen's political preferences; strikes against victimization; activity in the cause of the workers against the blacklist. . . .

It required 40,000 people in the city of New York in my own trade in

1877 to demonstrate to the employers that we had a right to be heard in our own defense of our trade, and an opportunity to be heard in our own interests. It cost the miners of the country, in 1897, sixteen weeks of suffering to secure a national conference and a national agreement. It cost the railroad brotherhoods long months of suffering, many of them sacrificing their positions, in the railroad strike of 1877, and in the Chicago, Burlington, and Quincy strike, of the same year, to secure from the employers the right to be heard through committees, their representatives . . . Workmen have had to stand the brunt of the suffering. The American Republic was not established without some suffering, without some sacrifice, and no tangible right has yet been achieved in the interest of the people unless it has been secured by sacrifices and persistency. After a while we become a little more tolerant to each other and recognize all have rights; get around the table and chaff each other; all recognize that they were not so reasonable in the beginning. Now we propose to meet and discuss our interests, and if we can not agree we propose in a more reasonable way to conduct our contests, each to decide how to hold out and bring the other one to terms. A strike, too, is to industry as the right that the British people contended for in placing in the House of Commons the power to close the purse strings to the Government. The rights of the British people were secured in two centuries—between 1500 and 1700—more than ever before, by the securing of that power to withhold the supplies; tied up the purse strings and compelled the Crown to yield. A strike on the part of workmen is to close production and compel better terms and more rights to be acceded to the producers. The economic results of strikes to workers have been advantageous. Without strikes their rights would not have been considered. It is not that workmen or organized labor desires the strike, but it will tenaciously hold to the right to strike. We recognize that peaceful industry is necessary to successful civilized life, but the right to strike and the preparation to strike is the greatest preventive to strikes. If the workmen were to make up their minds tomorrow that they would under no circumstances strike, the employers would do all the striking for them in the way of lesser wages and longer hours of labor.

An A.F.L. View of Women Workers, 1897

The invasion of the crafts by women has been developing for years amid irritation and injury to the workman. The right of the woman to win honest bread is accorded on all sides, but with craftsmen it is an open question whether this manifestation is of a healthy social growth or not.

The rapid displacement of men by women in the factory and workshop has to be met sooner or later, and the question is forcing itself upon the leaders and thinkers among the labor organizations of the land.

Edward O'Donnell, "Women as Bread Winners—the Error of the Age." *American Federationist* 4, No. 8 (October 1897).

Is it a pleasing indication of progress to see the father, the brother and the son displaced as the bread winner by the mother, sister and daughter?

Is not this evolutionary backslide, which certainly modernizes the present wage system in vogue, a menace to prosperity—a foe to our civilized pretensions? . . .

The growing demand for female labor is not founded upon philanthropy, as those who encourage it would have sentimentalists believe; it does not spring from the milk of human kindness. It is an insidious assault upon the home; it is the knife of the assassin, aimed at the family circle—the divine injunction. It debars the man through financial embarrassment from family responsibility, and physically, mentally and socially excludes the woman equally from nature's dearest impulse. Is this the demand of civilized progress; is it the desire of Christian dogma? . . .

Capital thrives not upon the peaceful, united, contented family circle; rather are its palaces, pleasures and vices fostered and increased upon the disruption, ruin or abolition of the home, because with its decay and ever glaring privation, manhood loses its dignity, its backbone, its aspirations. . . .

To combat these impertinent inclinations, dangerous to the few, the old and well-tried policy of divide and conquer is invoked, and to our own shame, it must be said, one too often renders blind aid to capital in its warfare upon us. The employer in the magnanimity of his generosity will give employment to the daughter, while her two brothers are weary because of their daily tramp in quest of work. The father, who has a fair, steady job, sees not the infamous policy back of the flattering propositions. Somebody else's daughter is called in in the same manner, by and by, and very soon the shop or factory are full of women, while their fathers have the option of working for the same wages or a few cents more, or take their places in the large army of unemployed. . . .

College professors and graduates tell us that this is the natural sequence of industrial development, an integral part of economic claim.

Never was a greater fallacy uttered of more poisonous import. It is false and wholly illogical. The great demand for women and their preference over men does not spring from a desire to elevate humanity; at any rate that is not its trend.

The wholesale employment of women in the various handicrafts must gradually unsex them, as it most assuredly is demoralizing them, or stripping them of that modest demeanor that lends a charm to their kind, while it numerically strengthens the multitudinous army of loafers, paupers, tramps and policemen, for no man who desires honest employment, and can secure it, cares to throw his life away upon such a wretched occupation as the latter.

The employment of women in the mechanical departments is encouraged because of its cheapness and easy manipulation, regardless of the consequent perils; and for no other reason. The generous sentiment enveloping this inducement is of criminal design, since it comes from a thirst to build riches upon the dismemberment of the family or the hearthstone cruelly dishonored. . . .

But somebody will say, would you have women pursue lives of shame rather than work? Certainly not; it is to the alarming introduction of women into the mechanical industries, hitherto enjoyed by the sterner sex, at a wage uncommandable by them, that leads so many into that deplorable pursuit. . . .

Unionist Alice Henry on Why Women Need Their Own Local Unions, 1915

The commonest complaint of all is that women members of a trade union do not attend their meetings. It is indeed a very serious difficulty to cope with, and the reasons for this poor attendance and want of interest in union affairs have to be fairly faced.

At first glance it seems curious that the meetings of a mixed local composed of both men and girls, should have for the girls even less attraction than meetings of their own sex only. But so it is. A business meeting of a local affords none of the lively social intercourse of a gathering for pleasure or even of a class for instruction. The men, mostly the older men, run the meeting and often are the meeting. Their influence may be out of all proportion to their numbers. It is they who decide the place where the local shall meet and the hour at which members shall assemble. The place is therefore often over a saloon, to which many girls naturally and rightly object. Sometimes it is even in a disreputable district. The girls may prefer that the meeting should begin shortly after closing time so that they do not need to go home and return, or have to loiter about for two or three hours. They like meetings to be over early. The men mostly name eight o'clock as the time of beginning, but business very often will not start much before nine. . . .

Where the conditions of the trade permit it by far the best plan is to have the women organized in separate locals. The meetings of women and girls only draw better attendances, give far more opportunity for all the members to take part in the business, and beyond all question form the finest training ground for the women leaders who in considerable numbers are needed so badly in the woman's side of the trade-union movement today.

Those trade-union women who advocate mixed locals for every trade which embraces both men and women are of two types. Some are mature, perhaps elderly women, who have been trade unionists all their lives, who have grown up in the same locals with men, who have in the long years passed through and left behind their period of probation and training, and to whose presence and active coöperation the men have become accustomed. These women are able to express their views in public, can put or

Alice Henry. "The Woman Organizer." *The Trade Union Woman.* New York: D. Appleton and Co., 1915.

discuss a motion or take the chair as readily as their brothers. The other type is represented by those individual women or girls in whom exceptional ability takes the place of experience, and who appreciate the educational advantages of working along with experienced trade-union leaders. I have in my mind at this moment one girl over whose face comes all the rapture of the keen student as she explains how much she has learnt from working with men in their meetings. . . . Always she is quick enough to profit by the men's experience, by their ways of managing conferences and balancing advantages and losses. . . .

But with the average girl today the plan does not work. The mixed local does not, as a general rule, offer the best training-class for new girl recruits, in which they may obtain their training in collective bargaining or cooperative effort. . . . Many of the discussions that go on are quite above the girls' heads. And even when a young girl has something to say and wishes to say it, want of practice and timidity often keep her silent. . . .

The girls, as a rule, are not only happier in their own women's local, but they have the interest of running the meetings themselves. They choose their own hall and fix their own time of meeting. Their officers are of their own selecting and taken from among themselves. The rank and file, too, get the splendid training that is conferred when persons actually and not merely nominally work together for a common end. Their introduction to the great problems of labor is through their practical understanding and handling of those problems as they encounter them in the everyday difficulties of the shop and the factory and as dealt with when they come up before the union meeting or have to be settled in bargaining with an employer.

Preamble of the Industrial Workers of the World, 1908

The working class and the employing class have nothing in common. There can be no peace so long as hunger and want are found among millions of working people and the few, who make up the employing class, have all the good things of life.

Between these two classes a struggle must go on until the workers of the world organize as a class, take possession of the earth and the machinery of production, and abolish the wage system.

We find that the centering of management of the industries into fewer and fewer hands makes the trade unions unable to cope with the ever growing power of the employing class. The trade unions foster a state of affairs which allows one set of workers to be pitted against another set of workers in the same industry, thereby helping defeat one another in wage wars. Moreover, the trade unions aid the employing class to mislead the

Reprinted with permission from ed., Joyce L. Kornbluh, *Rebel Voices: An IWW Anthology* (Ann Arbor: University of Michigan, 1964), p. 8.

workers into the belief that the working class have interests in common with their employers.

These conditions can be changed and the interest of the working class upheld only by an organization formed in such a way that all its members in any one industry, or in all industries if necessary, cease work whenever a strike or lockout is on in any department thereof, thus making an injury to one an injury to all.

Instead of the conservative motto, "A fair day's wage for a fair day's work," we must inscribe on our banner the revolutionary watchword, "Abolition of the wage system."

It is the historic mission of the working class to do away with capitalism. The army of production must be organized, not only for the every day struggle with capitalists, but also to carry on production when capitalism shall have been overthrown. By organizing industrially we are forming the structure of the new society within the shell of the old.

IWW Founder William Trautmann Explains Why Strikes Are Lost, 1911

After a tremendous epidemic of strikes a few years ago, . . . there seems to be at present a relapse all around. "The workers have gone to sleep" thinks the superficial observer and the uninformed outside world.

This seems, indeed, to be the truth. However, a relapse in numerical strength would amount to little: economic depression could be attributed as the cause.

But deplorable would it be if there were in reality a relapse in the aggressive attitude, in the revolutionary feelings of the workers.

This spirit of revolt manifesting itself a few years ago in somewhat rough actions and expressions seemed to mark the beginning of a general awakening of large masses of workers, and yet there seems to be nothing left of the spontaneous, widespread tendency of revolt.

For this there must be reasons. Such powerfully exploding forces cannot be destroyed altogether, or be dammed in by repressive measures. . . .

If occasionally larger bodies of workers become involved in these demonstrations of revolt, politicians and labor (mis)leaders are quickly on hand to suggest termination of the conflict, with the promise of speedy arbitration. These leaders of labor often even threaten to engage union strikebreakers if the workers refuse to obey their mandates. In some cases the places of striking workers have been filled by other members of these so-called unions so as to suppress any rebellion against the leaders and the capitalist class whom they serve. But seldom is anything more heard of the results of such conciliatory tactics, or of any determined stand on the part of the workers to enforce the terms of such settlements. Their power once crushed after having been exercised with the most effective precision, also destroys their

Reprinted with permission from ed., Joyce L. Kornbluh, *Rebel Voices: An IWW Anthology* (Ann Arbor: University of Michigan, 1964), pp. 18–24.

confidence; and the organization through which they were able to rally the forces of their fellow workers for concerted action disappears. . . .

What Is Craft Autonomy?

It is a term used to lay down restrictive rules for each organization which adheres to the policy of allowing only a certain portion of workers in a given industry to become members of a given trade union. Formerly, as a rule, a craft was determined by the tool which a group of workers used in the manufacturing process. But as the simple tool of yore gave way to the large machine, the distinction was changed to designate the part of a manufacturing process on a given article by a part of the workers engaged in the making of the same.

For instance, in the building of a machine the following crafts are designated as performing certain functions, namely:

The workers preparing the pattern are pattern-makers.

The workers making cores are core makers.

The workers making molds and castings are molders. . . .

The workers preparing and finishing the parts of machines are machinists.

The workers polishing up the parts of machines are metal polishers. . . .

The workers putting on copper parts are coppersmiths.

The workers putting on the insulation parts are steamfitters.

This line of demarkation [sic] could thus be drawn in almost every industry.

Now these various crafts, each contributing its share in the production of an article, are not linked together in one body, although members of these crafts work in one plant or industry.

They are separated in craft groups. Each craft union zealously guards its own craft interests. The rule is strictly adhered to that even if the protection of the interests of a craft organization is detrimental to the general interests of all others no interference is permitted. This doctrine of non-interference in the affairs of a craft union is what is called "craft or trade autonomy." . . .

Take, for example, the first street car workers' strike in San Francisco . . . Not only were all motormen, conductors and ticket agents organized in one union, but the barnmen, the linemen and repairers, and many of the repair shop workers enlisted in the union, also the engineers, the firemen, the electricians, the ashwheelers, oilers, etc., in the power stations. They all fought together. The strike ended with a signal victory for the workers; this was accomplished because the workers had quit their work spontaneously. But hardly had they settled down to arrange matters for the future, and to make the organization still stronger, when they found themselves confronted with the clamor of "craft autonomy rules."

They were told that the electricians in the power houses, linemen and line repairers had to be members of the International Brotherhood of Electrical Workers. The workers heard to their amazement that the engineers had to be members of the International Union of Steam Engineers.

The firemen, ashwheelers and oilers were commanded to withdraw at once from the Street Car Employees' Union, and join the union of their craft. The workers in the repair shops were not permitted under trade autonomy rules to form a union embracing all engaged therein. They had to join the union of their craft, either as machinists, molders, polishers or woodworkers, and would not be permitted to be members of any other organization. . . .

In the second strike of street car workers in 1907 the absolute failure, the complete disaster, was solely due to the fact that the workers, separated in several craft groups, could not strike together and win together. Similar cases, by the hundreds, could be enumerated to show what grave injuries craft autonomy inflicts upon the workers. And if the investigator will follow the investigation of facts and underlying causes, he will be surprised to see how the employers take advantage of this dividing-up policy. He will see how the capitalist gleefully helped to pit one portion of the workers against others in the same or other industries, so that the latter, while kept busy fighting among themselves, had no time nor strength to direct their fights against the employers and exploiters. . . .

What more is needed to convince the workers of the reason: "Why Strikes Are Lost"?

The Sacredness of Contracts

[W]ith the separation from other groups of workers a craft or sectarian spirit was developed among members of each of the trade organizations. . . ."Gains at any price" even at the expense of others, has become the governing rule. The rule of "non-interference" made sacred by the decrees of those who blatantly pose as leaders of labor, permitted one craft union to ride roughshod over the others. . . .

A great victory is proclaimed in print and public when one or the other of such craft organizations succeeds in getting a contract signed with an individual employer, or, what is considered still better, if it is comsummated with an association of employers in a given industry. But actuated by that sectarian spirit these contracts are considered to be inviolable. Not so much by the employers, who will break them any time when it will be to their advantage; but by the workers who are organized in craft unions. Imbued with their sectarian ideas, by the terms of such a contract they are in duty bound to protect the interests of the employers if the latter should have controversies with other craft unions. Thus the workers consent to being made traitors to their class.

Small wonder, therefore, that in that period between 1901 and 1905, the time that these lessons and conclusions are drawn from, the employers were able to check first, then to retard, and finally to paralyze the workers in any efforts to secure by their organized efforts permanently improved conditions in their places of employment. . . .

No wage worker, if he has any manhood in him, likes to be a strike-breaker of his own free will. That there are thousands of strikebreakers in America is due to the discriminative rules of the American Federation of Labor unions. . . . But the history of strikes proves that where no restrictive measures are enforced, the workers in one plant instinctively make common cause; they stand together in every conflict with their employers.

No so when the lash of a sacred contract is held over their head. The breaking of a contract, in most of the cases, means suspension from the union. It means that the union agrees to fill the places of men or women who suspend work in violation of contracts. This is so stipulated in most of the agreements with the employers. . . .

Now in that strike of butcher workmen in the stock yards they look to the engineers, the firemen and others to quit their jobs. They expected the teamsters to walk out in their support as the latter themselves had gained their demands only by the support of all. And really all the members of these craft unions were prepared and ready to lay down their tools. The strike would have been won within 24 hours if all had stood together. The employers realized that. They sent for their labor lieutenants. Over 25 labor leaders conjointly helped to force the workers back to their stations. Drivers already walking out were told to return or their places would be filled by other union men. The engineers were commanded to abide by their contract with the companies. Union printers, members of the Typographical Union, employed in the printing plants of the stock yards, were escorted every day through the picket lines of the poor strikers with permit badges pinned to their coats, issued by their union, so that the strikers' pickets would not molest these "licensed" strikebreakers. . . . All appeals to the manhood of these union strikebreakers were in vain. Stronger than their sense of duty and of solidarity in the struggle of members of their own class, was the "iron gag and chain of craft union non-interference" *The contracts were the weapons in the hands of the capitalists, by which the craft unionists were forced to wear the stigma of strikebreakers.* . . .

The craft unionists, forced by the lieutenants of the employing class—because most of the craft union leaders are indirectly their servants—defeated themselves. They shattered not only their own hopes, but the hopes, the confidence, the aspirations of thousands and tens of thousands, who had thought, after all, that unionism meant: "Solidarity, Unity, Brotherly Support in Hours of Strike and Struggle." . . .

✥ E S S A Y S

In the first essay, historian Jama Lazerow of the University of Puget Sound portrays the Knights of Labor at their zenith in 1886. Although they opposed strikes, Lazerow explains that the Knights were often effective trade unionists and proponents of a popular labor ideology that was deeply rooted in evangelical Protestantism and political values long associated with patriotism and American democracy.

The most successful of these trade unions, which organized the skilled workers of the municipal building trades, are carefully dissected in American University historian Michael Kazin's portrait of the San Francisco Building Trades Council, which appears here as the second essay. The council's powerful leaders, sometimes dubbed the barons of labor, controlled much of their trade, but only by narrowing labor's vision. In the final selection, Alice Kessler-Harris of Rutgers University explores one dimension of that conservative outlook, the AFL's sexual ideology. Male craft unionists of the Gompers era often excluded women from their organizations, both because they endorsed the home-and-motherhood vision of women's place and because they feared, sometimes rightly, that employers would use cheap female labor to depress the wage level and working conditions of male workers. What forms of unionism were most successful in the Gompers era? What kinds of unions most threatened employers?

Power and Respectability: The Knights of Labor

JAMA LAZEROW

On a bright autumn morning in 1886, some ten to fifteen thousand working people gathered in Boston's South End for the first Labor Day parade in the city's history. Thousands lined the sidewalks of the parade route, while hundreds more stood on balconies and rooftops to catch a glimpse of this army of organized workers. At the head of the three mile procession were leaders of the Knights of Labor and the trade unions. Behind them, disciplined ranks of tailors, printers, iron moulders, shoemakers, and building tradesmen led workers from every stratum of the labor force through the city's busiest downtown streets. . . . Although day laborers and factory operatives participated in the demonstration, the skilled trades comprised the main body of the marchers. "Honest labor was to the front," the editor of a Knights paper wrote, "there paraded there the foundation of our very social being—the creator of all the wealth, the bone and sinew of all our industries. . . ."

This workers' movement had . . . arisen overnight. In 1885, the Knights of Labor comprised barely a handful of local assemblies in the city. The Central Labor Union (CLU), an umbrella organization for the skilled trades, contained only three strong unions: the carpenters, the plasterers, and the printers. Between the fall of 1885 and the following summer, however, working people everywhere began to organize and to act. . . . By Labor Day 1886, organized labor claimed at least 25,000 Boston workers, probably five times its strength a year before.

The Knights of Labor was the most powerful workers' organization to emerge from this movement. Indeed, John Swinton, the era's foremost labor editor, named Boston "the banner city of the KL." By July 1886, the Order had swelled to seventy-nine locals with a membership of nearly 16,000. Moreover, its influence was remarkably widespread. When a Mas-

Jama Lazerow, "The Workingman's Hour: The Knights of Labor in 1886," *Labor History*, 21 (Spring 1980): pp. 200–215, 217–220.

sachusetts militia company was ordered to ride a boycotted railroad, half of the men refused to board, claiming to be Knights members. . . .

The rise of the Knights of Labor . . . was part of a dramatic upsurge of labor activity, whose focus was the national movement for the eight hour day. In 1884, the Federation of Organized Trades and Labor Unions, precursor to the American Federation of Labor, had resolved that "eight hours shall constitute a legal day's work from and after May 1, 1886." By late 1885, local trade unions across the country had begun raising the demand in meetings and rallies. In Boston, the CLU began organizing in early November. While the Knights did not endorse the strike itself, they supported shorter hours as an ideal and often participated in the CLU's agitational meetings. Knights leaders, many of whom had fought for the eight hour day in the 1860s, regularly addressed the gatherings.

The building trades, the most experienced and politically advanced sector of Boston's working class, took the lead in organizing for the strike. In mid-April, the carpenters, painters, plumbers and bricklayers presented the employers of their respective trades with various demands. Several unions called for a new wage standard, in addition to the eight hour day. The Master Builders Association (MBA), an employers' organization comprising most of the large building contractors in the city, refused to negotiate on the grounds that the workers had ignored the fundamental law of supply and demand and the necessity for profit-making. The issue thus joined, the men prepared to strike. As the hour of the walkout approached, the Carpenters' Union called for a demonstration of all trades at Fanueil Hall. The massed workers resolved:

> That this is the workingman's hour, and afrighted capital begins to understand that labor has rights which it is bound to respect—giving promise that the hour is at hand when the producer of wealth shall claim his own, and freely share in the gains and honors of advanced civilization.

On May 3, 1886, six months of labor agitation for the eight hour day climaxed in a massive strike of nearly 7,000 carpenters, painters, and plumbers. With building in the city at a standstill, many small contractors acceded to the demands shortly after the walkout began. The MBA, however, moved swiftly to assure the public and the men that it would stand firm. Their leader, William Sayward, revealed the gravity with which he and his organization viewed this movement. "The principle for which we are standing," he insisted, "is something altogether beyond the superficial question of eight hours, or nine hours, or any number of hours as being the proper limit for a day's labor—it is the principle of resisting any intrusion or dictation by any organization or society in the details of our private business."

Despite this resistance, the initial phase of the strike was a resounding success, revealing a vibrant and growing labor movement. Picketing strikers, who turned out by the hundreds every morning, were effective in blocking the importation of scab labor. Many went to the railroad stations and persuaded incoming workmen, usually in a peaceful manner, to return home. At night, the individual trades met and spirits ran unusually high. New members, sometimes as many as sixty or seventy in a night, were initiated into the various unions. Plumbers in the surrounding towns of Cambridge, Somerville, Chelsea, Dorchester, and Quincy walked out in solidarity with the strikers. In Boston itself, the movement provided the opportunity for wage strikes by clothing workers, tailors, and cigar makers.

On May 15, the strike reached its high point [when] 2,500 workers met at the carpenters' strike headquarters for a mass celebration. But on the 17th, Norcross Brothers, a member of the Master Builders, offered a nine hour day as a compromise proposal. Believing that this move was intended as an MBA "feeler," the carpenter leadership advocated compromise on the grounds that "half a loaf is better than none at all." But the next day, the employers' association repudiated the concession. On the 20th, the president of one of the carpenters' unions shocked an assemblage of 2,000 men by announcing the end of the strike. It is likely that he had reached a private agreement with the MBA, which subsequently offered an experimental nine hour system based on an hourly wage with provisions for overtime pay.

Though many of the striking carpenters at first expressed disapproval of the settlement by vigorously chanting, "No! No!," they ratified their leadership's decision and returned to work the following day. The painters now moved quickly to end their strike. Here, too, there was opposition from the rank-and-file, who barely voted the necessary two-thirds majority. The plumbers held out until mid-June when they too capitulated. By this time, the employers who had acceded to the eight hour demand during the strike had reinstated the ten hour system.

Though the eight-hour-strike ended in defeat, its very occurrence, coupled with the meteoric rise of the Knights of Labor, marked a crucial episode in the history of Boston labor. The depression of the 1870s had nearly wiped out the viable movement trade unionists had built in the 1850s and 1860s. When the labor movement re-emerged in the 1880s, the factory system and industrial concentration had given rise to a more visible and distinct working class. This "division of society into classes" had an ambiguous influence upon both labor and the society at large. For many in the business and professional classes, class division was a source of both hope and fear: they hoped that progress, government, and order would flow from labor organization, yet they feared that if the "wrong elements" emerged victorious, the result would be chaos, disorder, and class strife. For workers, while the return of prosperity in the 1880s offered possibilities for organization and material advancement, the fact that these new opportunities emerged in a society with an increasingly distinct working class may be a key to certain tensions within the labor movement. On the one hand, the agitation and strikes of 1886 represented the culmination of a struggle for autonomy and independence through the shorter workday and, thus, escape from wage-earning status. On the other hand, increasingly visible class distinctions encouraged the bread-and-butter orientation which would dominate a later era, as many came to accept the permanence of their position as workers.

Boston workers were part of a national upsurge of strike and union activity in 1886. Some labor historians have described this movement as a battle between an atavistic and rather muddle-headed Knights of Labor and a forward-looking, pragmatic trade unionism. Others have portrayed the Knights as an organization with a vision, with principles which were "democratic" and even "radical." The terms in which these arguments are cast are misleading. In the Boston case, categories such as radical/conservative or forward-looking/backward-looking are simply not useful in understanding the period. Further, nearly all historians have characterized society's response to the movement as one of repression and condemnation. This, too, seems to be mistaken. A detailed look at Boston labor activity in 1886 reveals a picture quite different from standard treatments of the subject.

Historians have not properly understood the interdependence of the labor movement in the 1880s. In Boston, the Knights and the CLU arose together, finding in each other mutual support and commonality of doctrine and interest. They both appealed primarily to the skilled trades, both adhered to a deeply-felt reform tradition, and both recognized the importance of social reconstruction. . . .

The founding of the CLU in April 1878 marked the revival of the Boston labor movement after the grim years of the 1873 depression. Organized by unions of printers, tailors, hatters, and cigar makers, the group found support among leaders of the Knights, such as George McNeill and Albert Carlton. During the first part of the 1880s, in fact, when internal differences threatened to destroy the CLU, its survival had much to do with the aid and encouragement received from the Knights.

While the Knights have traditionally been cast as "reformers" in contrast to a more "practical" trade union movement, the Boston CLU was ideologically similar to the Order. These trade unionists advocated the shorter workday, industrial safety, cooperative enterprise, and the abolition of child and prison labor. In its charter, the CLU affiliate unions declared their intention

> . . . to form an organization capable by the weight of its numbers of speaking with authority on all matters of mutual interest to the various trades . . . to unite the various trades for all purposes affecting the interests of the working class in general; to begin not in the interests of any particular trade or union, but equally for the welfare of all.

Many Boston Knights, moreover, were leading trade unionists and members of the CLU. This was particularly true of local organizers in the city. These men shed doubt upon the contention of some historians that the Knights were muddle-headed, old-fashioned reformers. Francis Pickett, who organized sixteen Knights locals during the spring of 1886 alone, was both a member of the executive board of District Assembly 30 and a leading trade unionist. During the 1870s, as a young man, he learned brick and

stone masonry in Brockton and became involved with the Knights there.
An effective speaker, he was appointed chief of the educational corps for
the District and often spoke at eight hour meetings organized by the CLU.
He joined the Boston Anarchist Club in 1887 and later became labor editor
at the *Herald.* In the 1890s he was a union leader in the building trades
and served one term as president of the CLU. Pickett was thirty-two in
1886. . . .

Frank Foster was another young Knights leader. A native of Palmer,
Massachusetts, he came to Boston in 1880 and was elected president of
the Cambridge Typographical Union two years later. In 1883, as a member
of the Knights of Labor and the Central Labor Union, he was a delegate
to the national convention of the Federation of Organized Trades and Labor
Unions. Between 1883 and 1886, Foster edited the Knights paper, the
Haverhill *Laborer,* in which he advocated the eight hour day, cooperation,
and labor legislation. In 1887, he became a leading officer of the state AFL,
playing a key role in its formation. . . .

The Knights, then, were not out-of-date reformers but practical men
with a vision who were inextricably intertwined with the trade union movement of their day. More important to understanding the Order's role in the
labor movement, however, is the specific nature and roots of its ideology,
an often ambiguous concoction. Static categories such as radical/
conservative and forward-looking/backward-looking ignore the Knights'
complexity. Rather, a new set of concepts are necessary to capture the
dynamic aspects of the organization and its historical role.

A product of the late nineteenth century, the Knights imbibed the
powerful currents of their time—republicanism, nationalism, and evangelical Protestantism. As numerous historians of American political and social
thought have pointed out, these traditions often came together, particularly
in rhetoric, in the notion of America as an "experiment." Frequently,
groups premised their beliefs and actions on the exigencies of maintaining
that "sacred trust," usually a millennial blend of freedom, equality, and
individualism. The Knights laid claim to this tradition, arguing that they
were purifiers in a corrupt world. Perceiving the emergence of a new aristocracy (Capital), a perennial American fear, they saw themselves as the
"new hope."

George McNeill, the most prominent of the Boston Knights leaders,
revealed all of the essential elements of this tradition in a speech at a
meeting of District Assembly 30 in April 1886. McNeill told of a vision he
had had, standing on the steps of the Capitol building in Washington.
Looking westward, he said, he had seen on the horizon "what appeared
to be a terrible conflagration as a flame, as tongues and fangs of flame,
shot upward and outward." Then, "the scene changed," he said, "and
there in the calm blue canopy of the heavens I saw the full rounded glory
of the setting sun." The promise of the latter rested with the labor movement. McNeill posed the choice facing Americans: "whether this grand
republic, born and baptized in blood, should go down at last in red and
fiery flame, or whether, when it had served its purpose to humanity, it

should simply go down like the golden glory of the setting sun, full of hope and promise of a brighter and grander day." For McNeill "the success or failure of the republican experiment rests with us."

McNeill revealed still more about the Knights' perception of themselves and of their historic role by linking . . . their struggle against tyranny to the Revolutionary War, still vivid in the American memory. Like the rest of his speech, his remarks were cast in religious language and imagery. "I am glad to welcome you here tonight," he said, "on this 19th day of April, a day ever dear to the heart of every American . . . and as this is the anniversary of the day when the Christian soil of virgin villages were stained in the blood of our fathers, and as they died to put down that chattel system of slavery, so we stand here remembering that blood shed and that sacrifice. . . ."

This speech reveals the main traditions comprising Knights of Labor ideology. The Knights saw the equal rights tradition of republicanism as their own and believed it was threatened by consolidated capital. This notion was prevalent in the trade union movement as well. During the eight hour strike, the carpenters accused the Master Builders Association of betraying American principles by the "unrepublican" character of their name. The term "master," they declared, was "foreign and offensive to our sense of citizenship, as well as offensive to the fundamental principles on which the republic is based." . . .

The Knights, then, pictured themselves as a counterweight to rising greed, corruption, monopoly, and intemperance. It is within this ideological framework that their often contradictory role must be understood. For as inheritors of the republican tradition, they were both vigilant guardians of freedom and democracy and proponents of law, order, and nation. Their insistence of defending the "nation" could involve stopping violence in a labor demonstration as well as striking against greedy capitalists.

This tension between activism and conservatism, militance and moderation, may best be seen in the image the Knights projected of themselves. The "true Knight," the order's leaders insisted, was "sober, respectable, conservative, modest, nonopportunistic, lawful, respectful, educated." This last virtue was especially important. The more you think, they told workingmen, "the better you can express your ideas. . . . Learn to think, and you will learn to write, and by thinking, writing and talking, you can work out your own salvation." The Knights, then, perceived themselves as educated, respectable, and honest American workingmen fighting for their rightful share of advanced civilization as well as the restoration of right and justice. This self-image led to concerted action for better wages, shorter hours, and a full range of labor legislation, but also to moderation and prudence in the face of an agitated laboring population.

Generally, the Knights opposed the use of walkouts as a regular weapon against employers. Instead, they favored arbitration as the best tool for settling labor disputes. This tendency may be a clue to their precipitant decline after 1886. With an executive board and centrally coordinated local leadership, the Knights were in an ideal position to argue on behalf of an agitated working class. Consistently, however, they failed to provide militant leadership. Though Knights leaders spoke at eight hour meetings, the Order did not participate in the strike itself. In a four month strike by tailors which began in March 1886, the Knights executive board repeatedly aggravated relations with the men by negotiating wages without consultation and without putting their decisions to a vote. Some of the workers accused their negotiators of acting in the employers' interest by settling quickly because a Knights convention was pending. At one point the basters openly defied orders from the executive board to return to work.

Typical of the Knights' handling of labor disputes was the abortive strike at a South Boston factory in early 1886. Here a picture emerges of militant and aroused workers and a moderate, even restraining Knights of Labor leadership. On March 19, 600 employees at the Norway Iron Works demanded a wage increase of 15% to cover the reduction instituted two years earlier. They met with local Knights in South Boston, voicing a general consensus for immediate action against the plant. They were persuaded, however, to return to work until the executive board decided on a course of action. Before leaving the meeting with the Knights the workmen vowed to strike if they were denied their demands. A member of the executive board and five representatives of the men, all of whom had worked at the factory for over ten years, then negotiated with the shop's superintendent. The agreement they reached called for the employees to return to work for the same wages and hours, with the company's promise that "as soon as the price of the manufacturing item had advanced and as soon as the income of the company would warrant," a raise would be granted.

In contrast to the Knights' aversion to strikes, the trade unions endorsed the weapon, their major focus in 1886 being the movement for a shorter workday. Given the Knights' public support for the CLU's eight hour meetings, it may be that the two organizations served different functions for a single movement with common goals. Moreover, the arguments for shorter hours during this period reveal the limited and often conservative nature of the CLU's ideological leadership. While some unionists argued that less work would allow workers more time to cultivate their minds, other leaders stressed more immediate problems. They pointed to the physical damage inflicted by long hours, and more importantly to the fact that a shorter workday would "spread the work." The advent of widespread unemployment, they argued, had given rise to competition for jobs, allowing owners to pay low wages. With shorter hours, more men would be employed, thus reducing competition and raising wages.

In the 1860s, the most significant aspect of the eight hour demand had been its class nature. By establishing a specific part of the day which could not be purchased by an employer, working people challenged the prevalent concept of private property and struck a blow for freedom from wage slavery. In the 1880s, the demand for the eight hour day still carried these radical implications for many workers, particularly in the building trades. These men drew upon a sixty year history of shorter hour struggles and an even older tradition of trade union organization. They comprised the most advanced and experienced element of Boston labor. For them, the eight hour day was a long-cherished goal. Workers without this long tradition, however, might have been attracted by shorter hour agitation because the meetings provided an opportunity to come together, not because they had a strong ideological commitment to the demand itself. And, in fact, only the building trades actually struck for the eight hours when the appointed day arrived.

A CLU eight hour circular released in early January 1886 illustrates the attitude of many trade union organizers and their understanding of the workers' general consciousness. Its message stressed the material aspects of the shorter hours question. "Overwork and machinery," it read, "combine to increase the army of the unemployed. Every unemployed man is an obstacle to our common advancement. An army of unemployed men is an army of obstacles. To remove them, they must be employed by reducing the hours of labor. Let us act!"

The trend in eight hour agitation becomes clearer when we compare the 1886 movement with a similar one in 1890. Again, there were references to the rights of "free born American citizens," the threat of slavery, and the linking of the eight hour day with the emancipation of slaves. As AFL leader Frank Foster put it, "the man whose hours of toil are fixed for him by another is not free." Other trade union leaders spoke of the laborer's right to control his working time. But here the similarities with 1886 end. First, the 1890 strike, called by the AFL, was far more orderly, organized, and well-planned. The Federation decided that only the carpenters would walk out on May 1, with the rest of the union movement supplying financial and moral support. In essence, one sector of the working class struck on behalf of labor as a whole. More importantly, there was a new tone to the arguments for the eight hour day. While the carpenters spoke of labor's "free-born rights," they gave an indication of their orientation in claiming "the right to name both the price and the length of our day's labor, the same as any other merchant selling his commodity."

The tensions and ambiguities within the labor movement in the 1880s were exploited by the more sophisticated elements of Boston's business and professional classes. The newspaper press and many politicians, particularly a new breed in the Democratic Party, perceptively recognized that unions could be used to great advantage if handled properly. As the Democratic *Globe* pointed out, it was not organized labor but unorganized and disorderly labor that the nation had to fear. While many in the middle and upper classes still refused to recognize the existence of class distinctions, they did acknowledge the emergence of a large wage-earning population. They argued that America could avert the class conflict so prevalent in Europe by channeling labor in a moderate and orderly direction.

Herein lay a new posture toward labor organization. Frank Foster recognized the general mood in Boston when he noted in January 1886 that the "great dailies" had recently evinced a change in attitude. While the

Globe was the most receptive, all of the major newspapers in the city were generally friendly to the growing union movement. This tolerant atmosphere legitimated organizational activities, but it also encouraged moderation and conciliation.

Publishers encouraged cooperation, arbitration, and peaceful settlement as a way of avoiding any possibility of militant or violent action. The main strategy was to present labor as a conservative force and, in particular, to use the Knights as an example worthy of emulation. In March 1886, when the Knights of Labor successfully negotiated a wage increase for the employees of the Boston Metropolitan Horsecar Company, the *Globe* devoted the entire front page of its Sunday edition to the honesty, orderliness, and peaceful approach of the Order. The *Post*, another Democratic paper, also encouraged labor to support arbitration and follow the conservatism of the Knights. Reviewing a recent strike, the editor condemned the "ugly temper" evinced by some workers who had "forgotten the Order's principles." He was certain, however, that the organization would support "such force as may be necessary to control the more ill-disposed of their number."

The Democratic party was particularly concerned with the labor issue, often working closely with the Knights to secure passage of labor measures in the state legislature. In this way, Democrats believed, social harmony would be assured. As the *Globe* put it, while the European social order will surely be torn asunder from within, "our working people are partners in political and social concern, shareholders in government, and hence have the power as well as the right to secure what justly belongs to them." The importance of the labor vote, of course, was a key consideration in Democratic thinking. "The plain people of Massachusetts," the *Globe* editorialized, "will best serve their own interests by standing by the party that always stands by them."

Indeed, many Boston politicians had awakened to labor's potential at the polls. Their response to Boston's first Labor Day parade illustrates their concern. The 15,000 demonstrators filed past the State House, hoping to be reviewed by the governor. While he did not attend, many city politicians were on hand, including Boston's first Irish Catholic mayor, Hugh O'Brien. "It was frequently remarked," the Democratic *Post* reported, "that there were a good many voters in line.". . .

While the *Globe* joined the other papers in the city in opposing the eight hour strike, it continued to present the workmen in a favorable light. "Who are these strikers?" the editor asked. "Are they not the very flower of Massachusetts manhood? Those who whisper that this portends revolution have missed the mark. There is no portion of the community more ready to defend law and order. . . ." William Shields, head of the Boston Carpenters' Union and later a national officer of the Brotherhood of Carpenters' and Joiners, verified this conservative image of the strikers. "If there were a disturbance in the street at this very moment," he declared, "the laboring men would assist in quelling it." At the outset of the strike, in fact, Shields warned his men to stop scab labor by peaceful persuasion only. If violence should erupt in the streets, he told his audience, you must stop it. . . .

The problem of the labor movement's conservatism and its relationship to middle class support is highlighted by the passage of state labor legislation during this period. In 1886, with heavy Knights and CLU promotion, Democratic elements in the Massachusetts legislature secured several measures, most importantly the State Arbitration Bill. Arbitration, as the *Post* put it, was the "savior from violence." The *Globe*, throughout 1886, consistently backed the legislation and the concept which lay behind it. The editor never tired of pointing out that the "labor problem" could only be solved if both classes were fair, rational, cooperative and met on terms of mutual interest. Arbitration was the antidote to labor's potential disruptive threat.

What was the immediate effect of the State Board of Arbitration? The board's first task was to bring striking workers back to work. Once business was in operation again, negotiations could begin. The first annual report of the commission pointed to an "increasing aversion to strikes" on the part of working people. Since they had to air their grievances before a panel, both sides chose their positions more carefully, the board reported. This made both sides more reasonable in their demands and more receptive to compromise. However, while workers showed good faith in coming to terms, employers often used the proceedings as a pretext to get their employees back on the job and then refused to participate further in the discussions. This tactic, quite naturally, often took the wind out of the aggrieved workers' sails. Moreover, in its first year of operation, the board was generally impotent in dealing with recalcitrant employers.

This close-up look at the events of 1886 in one community suggests that historians have been insensitive to the complexities of the labor movement in the 1880s. The imposition of false dichotomies has obscured the ambiguities within both organizations and ideologies. The movement was Janus-faced. It sought power and respectability. Although militant, it was also committed to conciliation. It crusaded for change but within time-honored American traditions. It was these tensions that certain elements of Boston's middle class exploited by encouraging the formation of conservative labor organizations and aiding in their integration into the polity and economic structure.

The events of 1886 marked the emergence of a viable and growing workers' movement in Boston. While the May strike had been defeated, the upsurge in labor activity revealed a movement undreamed of a year before. The thousands of working people at Boston's first Labor Day parade gave notice of a new spirit and, to many, of a new order. The march demonstrated, as the editor of the *Transcript* remarked, "their own existence—the strength and spread of the idea of the union of wage-earners for an aggressive self-protection." The kind of "self-protection" the movement would ultimately promote, however, was not at all clear in 1886. That would depend upon the resolution of tensions and ambiguities within the labor movement in the future.

Union Power in the Building Trades

MICHAEL KAZIN

Each evening, journeyman carpenter George Farris returned to his San Francisco hotel room and faithfully jotted down one or two impressions of the day in a leather-bound diary. "Like the job first rate, all the men are nice fellows, though all of them don't belong to Union 22, and I am liable to get in trouble for working with them," he wrote in May, 1902. San Francisco was then in the midst of a building boom, and business agents for the [Building Trades Council] BTC and its largest union were trying to catch interlopers on their closed-shop turf.

Like most carpenters at the time, Farris was, by necessity, a temporary worker in a variety of settings. One week, he would lay thick joists in a downtown structure with a crew of twelve; a month later, he worked alone, sawing and nailing exposed girders called "rustic" on a new Victorian-style residence. Although a loyal unionist, Farris was then in his fifties and had to take what jobs he could find, even if nonunion craftsmen would be toiling alongside him. His terse accounts of the life of a working mechanic in the Progressive era provide a rare personal glimpse into both the business of construction and the struggle between employers and the BTC for control of the labor process and the allegiance of the individual worker. . . .

In 1906, a retired San Francisco carpenter named James Brannock wrote that building tradesmen were no longer the highly skilled lords of yesteryear. They needed few tools, worked faster with mill-made parts, and were "under the eyes of a foreman or boss constantly," . . . Historians of carpentry have affirmed this view. At the turn of the century, according to Robert A. Christie, the introduction of machine-made wooden parts allowed contractors to hire "the 'green hand'—a woman, an immigrant, or child—who displaced a score of carpenters at half the wages of one." Division of the trade into such "degraded" specialties as door-hanging and floor-laying began to occur at the same time.

George Farris only partly fits this gloomy portrait of skill dilution and a loss of control. On the one hand, he was at the mercy of foremen and contractors who harried him for working too slowly and sometimes did not pay him until he had agreed to start a new job for them. On the other hand, Farris traveled around San Francisco (and Oakland, after the earthquake and fire of 1906), plying his trade at a remarkably diverse range of tasks and demonstrating a flexibility not accounted for by modern critics of "de-skilling." He was, in turns, a floor layer, constructor of everything from stairs to coalbins to bulkheads . . . , a foundation foreman, a finisher, and

Michael Kazin, "The Closed Shop Empire: From Job Site to Labor Temple," in *Barons of Labor: The San Francisco Building Trades and Union Power in the Progressive Era*, 1986, pp. 82–85, 94–100, 102–106. Reprinted by permission of University of Illinois Press.

a carver of hardwood fixtures for a luxurious dining room. Farris also sought to embellish his skills: he studied mechanical and architectural drawing and owned a small library of technical books. While performing a variety of tasks could be tiresome the aging carpenter never wrote that he had lost or declined a job because it required knowledge he did not possess. . . .

A stalwart unionist who kept up his dues even when out of work for a stretch, Farris nevertheless bent organizational rules whenever necessary. He once worked on a Sunday and feared his weekday co-workers "would find it out and report to the Union." Farris usually viewed the visit of a business agent with alarm. "The Trades Council delegate was around this forenoon," he wrote in 1909. "The plumber thought I did not have a Card but I have.". . .

George Farris ended his diary in 1910, a dejected and lonely man. The fifty-seven-year-old bachelor could then find work only at nonunion sites in the East Bay at more than a dollar below scale and was constantly afraid of a visit from the "walking delegate" (business agent) or the BTC. However, on Labor Day, Farris donned his best clothes and, as he had done each year since 1890, joined Local 22's contingent in a big parade down Market Street. "Our flag and banner shows the ravage of time," he reflected with uncharacteristic sentiment in his room that night, "but we would not change them for new ones."

Why did Farris maintain his loyalty to a union whose representatives were a constant threat to his livelihood whenever he practiced his trade on an open-shop job or with craftsmen who did not possess a paid-up working card from the BTC? The answer is partly cultural and psychological. Belonging to a respected union with several thousand members allowed a man a certain pride in his associations and an identity which could make an anonymous life seem a bit less insignificant. However, George Farris's willingness to transcend his gripes about nosy business agents also stemmed from a recognition that building trades unionism in San Francisco decisively mediated the relationship between employer and craftsman. The maintenance of a wage scale above that of other workers, the scrutiny of any practices that would increase hours or speed up the pace of labor, and the blanket enforcement of closed-shop regulations were elements of a mutual ethic which softened the hard edges of the market economy. Even a disgruntled carpenter with little interest in union affairs was glad to have the big stick of organization on his side. . . .

Craftsmen in the nineteenth century had routinely set their own wage rates and work rules, but the growth of large manufacturing corporations and industrywide employer associations in the 1890s forced international unions to retreat to an emphasis on collective bargaining. However, in well-organized cities like San Francisco, the old way could still function. The BTC represented not only every building craft but also teamsters who transported materials to job sites and factory workers who made wooden and metal fixtures. Within this closed-shop empire, sympathetic strikes seldom had to be called; the *threat* of united action was sufficient.

However, labor's power was vigorously exercised against individual

contractors who disobeyed a BTC dictum. The employer would be summoned to appear before the BTC Executive Board. Any firm which failed
to respond to the "subpoena" of [BTC President P. H.] McCarthy's
"court" could be placed on probation or labeled "unfair," thus depriving
it of skilled workers. Not surprisingly, most of the accused presented themselves and pled their cases. All but a few apologized or swore ignorance
of the transgression, usually hiring a nonunion worker. Sometimes, the
inquiry took on a humiliating tone, as in this report from 1913: "Young
Mr. Sheridan appeared in response to citation [and] was questioned at some
length as to his intentions and attitude toward union labor. He promised
to abide by the laws and rules of the Council; and the Board recommends
that Sheridan & Son be placed on probation until such time as the Council
is satisfied that the firm will live up to the laws of this Council." The BTC
routinely fined the guilty party a minimum of fifty dollars and donated the
money to a hospital or home for the aged.

    With such tactics, the BTC effectively dominated the bulk of small
contractors, especially those who hired journeymen in only one or two
trades, but large employers were not so easily intimidated. McCarthy and
his men had to exert pressure in a measured fashion to avoid either tearing
the fabric of industrial harmony or backing down significantly in their
resolve.

    A revealing example of this process occurred in the fall of 1908 during
the construction of the First National Bank building in downtown San
Francisco. Willis Polk, the skyscraper's architect, wanted to save $2,300
for his clients, the general contracting firm of Smith and Watson, by casting
in a workshop the ornate ceiling of the bank directors' conference room
rather than hiring plasterers to do the entire job on site. One Sunday,
McCarthy discovered that nonunion casters were building the ceiling. He
ordered all plasterers not to report for work and demanded a meeting with
Polk. The next morning, Smith and Watson threatened to import enough
plasterers from the East to flood the market. But that day, when the noon
whistle sounded, the employers watched unhappily as every one of their
hundreds of workers, from a variety of trades, packed up his tools and
walked off the job. On Tuesday evening, after talking with McCarthy, Willis
Polk "admitted" that plasterers were superior to casters for the task in
question. On Wednesday morning, all trades returned to work, and affiliated
members of the BTC began erecting the expensive ceiling. Labor's muscle,
tactfully applied, had won the day.

    The most tangible fruits of union power were high wages and the eight-
hour day. Fluctuations in the construction industry retarded pay increases
but never forced union craftsmen to lower their scales. Moreover, most
building workers received wages at least a dollar a day higher than those
paid to the skilled metal and printing trades. Hod carriers even earned more
than machinists . . . ! By 1900, with few exceptions, construction tradesmen
enjoyed a work schedule of eight hours a day and forty-four hours a week
(pay envelopes were distributed after a half-day on Saturday). Although
national standards for the industry were also quite high, the San Francisco

building trades led their counterparts in all other large cities. McCarthy boasted that superior wages insured greater productivity: "We can in this city do one and a quarter as much as the men in Chicago can and feel better, leaving the establishment in the evening."

BTC leaders passed judgment on all demands for more pay and shorter hours, but local unions made and usually enforced their own trade rules. These regulations, some of which originated in the eighteenth century, wove self-respect into the fabric of each working life. Employers attacked them as archaic, arbitrary, and inefficient. But trade rules guaranteed workers a measure of autonomy and humane treatment, and unionists always defended them, even if they adopted a "get along, go along" philosophy while performing the work itself. A decentralized industry left ample room for flexibility in this regard.

San Francisco building unions stressed rules of four types. These limited the power of supervisors, regulated members becoming contractors, restricted output to a human pace, and controlled the number and use of apprentices. On a given job, contractors, by offering bonuses, could entice workers to evade the rules, but the fact that they existed in meticulous detail probably deterred most violations.

Practically every local required foremen to be union members and severely curtailed their authority. The Bay Area District Council of Carpenters stated that any foreman "using abusive language or in any way domineering over the members employed under him, with a view of rushing them at their work, thus preventing good workmanship" would be fined up to fifty dollars for each offense. The Painters obligated foremen to report "delinquent members" to business agents. Contractors could not join a union and were thus, by definition, barred from working alongside their employees.

However, many mechanics did look forward to becoming contractors, and locals had to spell out whether or not members could use their union status as a stepping stone to self-employment. The Steam and Operating Engineers took a firm stand against subcontracting: "Any member owning, leasing, hiring, supplying, procuring or causing to be furnished any hoisting or portable engine or boiler on building of construction work" immediately forfeited his membership and had to wait an unspecified period before he could gain readmittance. The Painters, more typically, were lenient, stating only that a member could not hold union office while he was employing others. The object of these regulations was to warn prospective contractors that they could not straddle indefinitely the divide between boss and mechanic.

In 1931, an anti-union publicist charged that restriction of output had almost ruined the building industry. The anonymous writer cited a variety of rules from the heyday of union control: bricklayers who limited themselves to 850 bricks a day, electricians who would not install more than eleven outlets in eight hours, and painters who refused to use a brush more than four inches wide. Employers considered the routine withholding of labor the most outrageous of all union rules, a direct affront to their ideal of profitable, efficient production. A few contractors who had once been journeymen realized that specific "stints" actually insured quality work and were not only devices to stretch out the job, but the institution still distressed them. It was a daily reminder that craftsmen wielded a critical degree of control over production.

In fact, San Francisco union rules never specifically limited output. The District Council of Carpenters did penalize "any member found guilty of pace setting, or rushing members," but the infraction was only vaguely defined. Carpenters interviewed in the late 1920s claimed that the rule was never really used to restrict production. As a student of the Buffalo building trades discovered in the 1950s, "Flexibility, informality, and exchange of favors characterize relations. Each one is adjusted . . . on the basis of the relative strength and interests of the parties."

However, all union members were prohibited from supplying any but the smallest, most inexpensive tools. "I took my iron mitre box [to work] this morning," George Farris wrote of a simple device which guides the cut of a saw, "but I may bring it home as the Union don't allow carpenters to use them." Painters could take only putty knives and dust cloths to the job; while plumbers were forbidden to furnish a long list of implements including, "hack saw blades, force pump . . . stocks, dies, cutters, taps, risers, augers, forges . . . pipe wrenches or tongs over 18 inches long."

One motivation for these rules was egalitarian: if employers required men to bring an array of tools to the job, only established journeymen with reliable transportation would find work. But the limits on tools were also a method of preserving the craftsman's sphere. It was the contractor's responsibility to submit a bid, buy materials, and schedule the different phases of construction. Asking workers to provide expensive tools, which, after all, were a form of capital, was illegitimate unless they were also invited to share equally in management prerogatives and in the profits themselves.

These restrictions did not mean that building unionists opposed mechanization itself. Construction lagged far behind other American industries in adopting power-driven tools and other labor-saving devices. BTC locals, while their members may have benefited from technological backwardness, almost never tried to stop the introduction of machinery. *Organized Labor* even suggested that journeymen take classes in the use of power tools and counseled that workers who continued to educate themselves would "always command the maximum wage." McCarthy looked forward to a six-hour workday once mechanization had been applied to every craft. This philosophical acceptance of new technology cost BTC unions little either in the numbers or working conditions of their members. . . .

One tradition that unionists defended adamantly was the regulation of apprenticeship programs. In other industries, mass immigration and the increasing subdivision of crafts had made formal apprenticeship systems largely obsolete. However, each of the skilled building trades clung to the institution, despite the rise of private training schools in some parts of the country. Unionists believed that a worker who had passed through an apprenticeship was more versatile and thus could command higher wages and respect from employers. Moreover, sons of journeymen could more easily secure a place in the trade as long as unions decided who could become an apprentice. . . .

The government of the BTC can be compared to that of an aggressive and often tyrannical city-state. Organized for expansionist purposes, it was ultimately stymied by its own isolation. But internally, the Sparta of California labor was an almost impregnable fortress. For over two decades, its leaders managed to defeat all opponents within an apparatus that was, in striking ways, a forerunner of the CIO unions of the 1930s.

The BTC combined features of both an industrial federation and a coordinating body in which about fifty formally autonomous crafts participated . . . Delegates to the BTC were elected by a proportional system: three delegates for a union with one hundred members or less and one delegate for each additional one hundred dues-payers. The Executive Board followed the model of the U.S. Senate: each local, regardless of its size, had one representative. Locals were free to choose their own delegates, but the BTC Constitution clearly stated where supreme power resided: a majority of the BTC could reject delegates "who, in its judgment, are considered undesirable or detrimental to the best interests" of the organization. The BTC also had the right to expel an entire local for "disobedience, rebellion, or treason," accusations frequently hurled at those who opposed McCarthy. BTC leaders sometimes interfered with a local's election if they felt the outcome was crucial to their own political interests. Usually, however, the benefits of siding with the "court faction" made sanctions against opponents unnecessary.

Local councils wielding such influence were not unique to San Francisco in the Progressive era. The first American "city central," the Mechanics' Union of Trade Associations, was founded in Philadelphia in 1827, and its successors careened through the nineteenth century, gaining during hard-fought strikes or political campaigns and then floundering at the first defeat or economic slump. In the aftermath of World War I, local federations in Seattle and Chicago organized new sectors of the work force and led them in massive strikes that shut down steel mills, shipyards, and meatpacking plants.

Building tradesmen eagerly joined their own separate citywide federations. The interrelated nature of the crafts and the local nature of the industry convinced them that coordination was both possible and desirable. As in San Francisco, carpenters, whose brotherhood already operated as a quasi-industrial union of woodworking crafts, initiated and dominated most building trades councils. Once organized, these councils quickly relegated international unions (so called because they operated both in Canada and the United States) to a minor role in local affairs. From their headquarters in Indianapolis or Washington, D.C., international officials had neither the money nor the legal right to enforce their will on members in

San Francisco or other cities. During strikes, they had to acquiesce to the better-informed judgment of local leaders. Prior consent from national head-quarters for a walkout was a rarity in the building trades.

In San Francisco, the BTC almost entirely superseded the power of the internationals. McCarthy and his men created several new locals—laborers, hodcarriers, housemovers, and glaziers—and balked at affiliating them with the international organizations in their respective crafts. More established locals like the Painters and Plumbers had roots in local asso-ciations dating back to the 1850s and 1860s which predated their "parent" bodies. Given this history, BTC leaders understandably refused to relin-quish control to officials sitting thousands of miles away who would not have to pay the costs or bear the brunt of potential battles.

McCarthy and his allies did have to allow locals a measure of autonomy. District councils existed in certain key trades—carpenters, painters, cement workers, and electricians. These represented unions from the entire Bay Area, providing suburban members with an alternative to the weaker BTCs in outlying counties. District officers sometimes appealed to their inter-national union when they felt abused by the McCarthy juggernaut. But international bureaucrats respected the might of the San Francisco barony and usually sided with its leaders in their squabbles with pesky affiliates.

. . . Business agents employed by the BTC were the human glue connecting individual workers and their locals with the hierarchy . . . Instead of the petty grafters and despots who plagued construction in eastern metropo-lises, "walking delegates" in San Francisco acted more like labor police-men. They enforced union rules, collected information from shop stewards at job sites, and reported directly to the BTC Executive Board which was their only legitimate source of funds.

Many locals hired their own business agents, but only the BTC's men could "pull a job" when more than one trade was involved. Thus, agents for locals became distinctly subordinate officials with a mélange of small, short-lived projects to oversee; they were barred from enjoying the inde-pendence and wealth of their counterparts in other well-organized cities like Chicago and New York. Beginning in 1904, BTC delegates voted to give themselves veto power over whom locals chose as their agents. . . .

The BTC treated its prized employees well. Wages for the three regular business agents . . . kept pace with the scale of the highest paid crafts. When Charles Nelson served concurrently as a San Francisco supervisor and BTC agent, he received $168 monthly for his union work but only $100 from the city. The BTC also purchased automobiles for Nelson and his colleagues—no small prerequisite at a time when ownership of the machines was still mostly limited to professionals and businessmen. Compared by their superiors to the "general in the field," business agents were the mobile linchpins of an organization whose members were scattered throughout the Bay Area.

Many locals were not willing vassals, but all had to bow to the gravita-tional pull of BTC officials in routine matters. Jurisdictional disputes, which had historically set craft against craft in a fratricidal struggle for jobs, were kept to a minimum. Locals quarreling over jurisdiction had to bring their cases to a special BTC committee and abide by its decision or face harsh punishment: a short strike by other trades against the offender, expulsion from the BTC, or, at the extreme, the organization of a dual union. Once the rebel local capitulated, however, it was usually readmitted to full membership.

Building unionists who tried to restrain or topple McCarthy's rule faced tremendous difficulties. Locals that differed greatly in size, leadership, and the nature of the work performed were easily controlled by a centralized administration which held the tacit allegiance of all non-protestors . . . Local 22 of the United Brotherhood of Carpenters and Joiners stayed unflinchingly loyal to its best-known member throughout the Progressive era. Chartered in 1882 by nine ex-Knights of Labor, "Big 22" became, under McCarthy, the largest building trades union in the West. By 1905, it had 2,000 members and retained this number until World War I. Local 22, however, did not have the town to itself. The subdivision of carpentry into separate crafts and the bond of ethnicity spawned eight different locals, each affiliated with the United Brotherhood. The Amalgamated Carpenters, a separate group imported from England which stressed mutual insurance, also had six San Francisco branches. In a boom town for unionism, many concerns catered to the avid clientele.

Elections for Local 22 officers were occasions for a purging of the BTC's enemies, either real or imagined. Wrapping themselves in the mantle of a glorious past when McCarthy and his predecessors had won the eight-hour day and the closed shop, loyalists branded their opponents "would-be destroyers of the labor movement" and promised to uphold the *status quo*. . . . In 1917, after the annual election of officers, *Organized Labor* crowed, "One lone aspirant made a bid for financial secretary against the incumbent . . . but it did not take 'opponent' long to realize that he was 'not running'.". . .

Unskilled laborers, in stark contrast to San Francisco's closed-shop pattern, were the forlorn stepchildren of the building trades. Organized as a purely local operation in 1901, the United Laborers Union quickly signed up 4,000 members but lost all but 1,000 of these when unemployed workingmen swarmed into the city after the 1906 earthquake and fire. Thereafter, most of the city's approximately 25,000 day laborers (overwhelmingly Irish and Italian immigrants) were at the mercy of employers under little pressure to hire unionists. Contractors for large, well-publicized projects, like the Municipal Railroad and Civic Center, had to operate a closed shop or face a storm of criticism. But transients and occasionally even prisoners did the heavy, menial work on streets, sewers, and private buildings. San Francisco was a "union town" for only those day laborers who had luck or a friend in city hall.

To exacerbate the problem, the BTC treated the United Laborers with benign contempt. Members repeatedly asked McCarthy to declare an eight-hour workday on private construction, already the statutory limit on municipal contracts, but BTC leaders always counseled patience, perhaps fearing that skilled unionists would never support a struggle for their less privileged brethren. Meanwhile, William Dwyer, who commanded the United Laborers for many years, often signed up casual laborers on the few closed-shop jobs in the city for a reduced initiation fee of $2.50 and then denied them membership after the project ended. When three delegates from the union cursed McCarthy for refusing to approve a raise in their scale, they tasted the president's wrath in the form of a unique resolution: "Any delegate taking the name of any executive officer . . . in vain or speaking deprecatingly of him" was barred from holding a post or even *speaking* in both the BTC and his own local for a year after committing the offense.

Periodically, building unionists outraged by such methods would announce a drive to reform the BTC, but, during McCarthy's reign, their efforts never progressed past that initial stage. They put forth no ideological themes other than an abstract belief in democracy, and, indeed, the very impermanence of the coalitions made agreement on any but *ad hoc* grievances unthinkable. Because they had no sustained, coherent opposition, BTC leaders could caricature dissidents as jealous men who clamored to smash a worthy structure they could not control. Internal rivals shared neither their experience nor their access to power and thus had to endure what most building workers probably considered to be a benevolent dictatorship.

The Labor Movement's Failure to Organize
Women Workers

ALICE KESSLER-HARRIS

"The organization of women," wrote Fannia Cohn, an officer of the International Ladies Garment Workers Union to William Green, newly elected president of the American Federation of Labor, "is not merely a moral question, but also an economic one. Men will never be certain with their conditions unless the conditions of the millions of women are improved." Her letter touched a home truth and yet in 1925, the year in which Cohn's letter was written, the A. F. of L., after nearly forty years of organizing, remained profoundly ambivalent about the fate of more than eight million wage-earning women.

During those four decades of industrial growth, the women who worked in the industrial labor force had not passively waited to be organized. Yet their best efforts had been tinged with failure. Figures for union members are notoriously unreliable, and estimates fluctuate widely. But something like 3.3 percent of the women who were engaged in industrial occupations in 1900 were organized into trade unions. As low as that figure was, it was

Alice Kessler-Harris, "Where are The Organized Women Workers." Reprinted from *Feminist Studies*, volume 3, number 1/2 (Fall, 1975), pp. 92–105 by permission of the publisher, Feminist Studies, Inc.

to decline even further. Around 1902 and 1903 trade union membership among women began to decrease, reaching a low of 1.5 percent in 1910. Then, a surge of organization among garment workers lifted it upwards. A reasonable estimate might put 6.6 percent of wage-earning women into trade unions by 1920. In a decade that saw little change in the relative proportion of female and male workers, the proportion of women who were trade union members quadrupled, increasing at more than twice the rate for trade union members in general. Even so, the relative numbers of wage-earning women who were trade union members remained tiny. One in every five men in the industrial workforce belonged to a union, compared to one in every fifteen women. Although more than 20 percent of the labor force was female, less than 8 percent of organized workers were women. And five years later, when Fannia Cohn was urging William Green to pay attention to female workers, these startling gains had already been eroded.

Figures like these have led historians of the working class to join turn-of-the-century labor organizers in lamenting the difficulty of unionizing female workers. Typically, historians argue that the traditional place of women in families, as well as their position in the workforce, inhibited trade unionism. Statistical overviews suggest that these arguments have much to be said for them. At the turn of the century, most wage-earning women were young, temporary workers who looked to marriage as a way to escape the shop or factory. Eighty-five percent of these women were unmarried and nearly half were under twenty-five years old. Most women worked at traditionally hard-to-organize unskilled jobs: a third were domestic servants and almost one quarter worked in the garment and textile industries. The remainder were scattered in a variety of industrial and service jobs, including the tobacco and boot and shoe industries, department stores, and laundries. Wage-earning women often came from groups without a union tradition: about one half of all working women were immigrants or their daughters who shared rural backgrounds. In the cities, that figure sometimes climbed to 90 percent.

For all these reasons, women in the labor force unionized with difficulty. Yet the dramatic fluctuations in the proportions of organized working women testify to their potential for organization. And the large numbers of unions in which the proportion of women enrolled exceeded their numbers in the industry urge us to seek further explanations for the small proportions of women who actually became union members.

No apparent change either in the type of women who worked or in the structure of jobs explains the post-1902 decline in the proportion of unionized women. On the contrary, several trends would suggest the potential for a rise in their numbers. The decline began just at the point when union membership was increasing dramatically after the devastating depression of 1893–1897. The proportion of first-generation immigrant women who were working dropped after the turn of the century only to be matched by an increase in the proportion of their Americanized daughters who worked. Married women entered the labor force in larger numbers suggesting at once a more permanent commitment to jobs and greater need for the se-

curity unions could provide. Large declines in the proportion of domestic
workers reduced the numbers of women in these isolated, low-paying, and
traditionally hard-to-organize jobs. At the same time, increases in office
and clerical workers, department store clerks, and factory operatives, offered fertile areas from promoting unionization among women. Strenuous
organizing campaigns by and among women in all these areas achieved few
results.

Although cultural background, traditional roles, and social expectations
hindered some unionizing efforts, they were clearly not insurmountable
barriers. Given a chance, women were devoted and successful union members, convinced that unionism would serve them as it seemed to be serving
their brothers. In the words of a seventeen-year-old textile worker, "We
all work hard for a mean living. Our boys belong to the miners' union so
their wages are better than ours. So I figured that girls must have a union.
Women must act like men, ain't?" In the garment workers union where
women were the majority of members, they often served as shop "chair-
ladies" and reached positions of minor importance in the union structure. . . . In these unions, women arrested on picket lines thought highly
enough of the union to try to save it bail money by offering to spend the
night in jail before they returned to the line in the morning.

In mixed unions, women often led men in militant actions. Iowa cigar
makers reported in 1899 that some striking men had resumed work, while
the women were standing pat. Boot and shoe workers in Massachusetts
were reported in 1905 to be tough bargainers. "It is harder to induce women
to compromise," said their president, "they are more likely to hold out to
the bitter end . . . to obtain exactly what they want." The great uprising
of 1909 in which 20,000 women walked out of New York's garment shops
occurred over the objections of the male leadership, striking terror into the
hearts of Jewish men afraid "of the security of their jobs." Polish "spool
girls" protesting a rate cut in the textile mills of Chicopee, Massachusetts,
refused their union's suggestion that they arbitrate and won a resounding
victory. Swedish women enrolled in a Chicago Custom Clothing Makers
local, lost a battle against their bosses' attempt to subdivide and speed up
the sewing process when the United Garment Workers union, largely male,
agreed to the bosses' conditions. The bosses promptly locked out the
women forcing many to come to terms and others to seek new jobs. At
the turn of the century, female garment workers in San Francisco and
tobacco strippers, overall and sheepskin workers, and telephone operators
in Boston ran highly successful sex-segregated unions.

If traditional explanations for women's failure to organize extensively
in this period are not satisfying, they nevertheless offer clues to understanding the unionization process among women. They reveal the super-
ficiality of the question frequently asked by male organizers and historians
alike: "Why don't women organize?" And they encourage us to adopt
economist Theresa Wolfson's more sensitive formulation: "Where are the
organized women workers?" For when we stop asking why women have

not organized themselves, we are led to ask how women were, and are, kept out of unions.

The key to this question lies, I think, in looking at the function that wage-earning women have historically played in the capitalist mode of production. Most women entered the labor force out of economic necessity. They were encouraged by expanding technology and the continuing division of labor which in the last half of the nineteenth century reduced the need for skilled workers and increased the demand for cheap labor. Like immigrant men, and blacks today, women formed a large reservoir of unskilled workers. But they offered employers additional advantages. They were often at the mercy of whatever jobs happened to be available in the towns where their husbands or fathers worked, and they willingly took jobs that offered no access to upward mobility. Their extraordinarily low pay and exploitative working conditions enabled employers to speed up the process of capital accumulation. Their labor was critical to industrial expansion, yet they were expected to have few job-related aspirations and to look forward instead to eventual marriage. Under these circumstances, employers had a special incentive to resist unionization among women. As John Andrews, writing in the 1911 Report on the Condition of Women and Child wage earners, put it: ". . . the moment she organizes a union and seeks by organization to secure better wages she diminishes or destroys what is to the employer her chief value."

If the rising numbers of working women are any gauge, women for the most part nicely filled the expectations of employers. Traditional social roles and the submissive behavior expected of women with primary attachments to home and family precisely complemented the needs of their bosses. To those women whose old world or American family norms encouraged more aggressive and worldly behavior—Russian Jews, for example—unionization came easier. Yet, for the most part, women fought on two fronts: against the weight of tradition and expectation, and against employers. If that were not enough, there was yet a third battlefront.

Unionists, if they thought about it at all, were well aware of women's special economic role. Samuel Gompers, head of the American Federation of Labor, editorialized in 1911 that some companies had "taken on women not so much to give them work as to make dividends fatter." In a competitive labor market unionists tended to be suspicious of women who worked for wages and to regard them as potentially threatening to men's jobs. "Every woman employed," wrote an editor in the A. F. of L. journal, *American Federationist*, "displaces a man and adds one more to the idle contingent that are fixing wages at the lowest limit."

Since employers clearly had important economic incentives for hiring women, male trade unionists felt they had either to eliminate that incentive, or to offer noneconomic reasons for restricting women's labor-force participation. In the early 1900s they tried to do both. In order to reduce the economic threat, organized labor repeatedly affirmed a commitment to unionize women wage earners and to extract equal pay for them. Yet trade unionists simultaneously argued that women's contributions to the home and their duties as mothers were so valuable that women ought not to be in the labor force at all. Their use of the home-and-motherhood argument had two negative effects: it sustained the self-image on which the particular exploitation of women rested, and it provided employers with a weapon to turn against the working class as a whole.

Buttressed by the grim realities of exploitative working conditions and the difficulties of caring for children while working ten or more hours a day, and supported by well-intentioned social reformers, the argument to eliminate women from the work force, in the end, held sway. It was, of course, impossible to achieve, so the A. F. of L. continued to organize women and to demand equal pay for equal work. But genuine ambivalence tempered its efforts. The end result was to divide the working class firmly along gender lines and to confirm women's position as a permanently threatening underclass of workers who finally resorted to the protection of middle-class reformers and legislators to ameliorate intolerable working conditions. The pattern offers us some lessons about what happens to the work force when one part of it attacks another.

The published sources of the A. F. of L. reveal some of the attitudes underlying A. F. of L. actions, and I have focused attention on these because I want to illustrate not only how open and prevalent the argument was, but because the A. F. of L.'s affiliated unions together constituted the largest body of collective working-class opinion. We have amassed enough evidence by now to know that the A. F. of L. was a conservative force whose relatively privileged members sacrificed the larger issues of working-class solidarity for a piece of the capitalist pie. In the creation of what labor economist Selig Perlman called "a joint partnership of organized labor and organized capital," the Federation cooperated extensively with corporation-dominated government agencies, sought to exclude immigrants, and supported an imperialist foreign policy. Its mechanisms for dealing with the huge numbers of women entering the labor force are still unclear. Yet they are an integral part of the puzzle surrounding the interaction of ideological and economic forces in regulating labor market participation.

In the period from 1897 to 1920, the A. F. of L. underwent dramatic expansion. It consolidated and confirmed its leadership over a number of independent unions, including the dying Knights of Labor. Membership increased from about 265,000 members in 1897 to more than four million by 1920, and included four-fifths of all organized workers. In the same period, the proportion of women working in the industrial labor force climbed rapidly. Rapid and heady expansion offered a golden opportunity for organizers. That they didn't take advantage of it is one of the most important facts in the history of labor organizing in America.

Union leaders were sure that women did not belong in the work force. Anxious about losing jobs to these low-paid workers, they tried instead to drive women out of the labor force. "It is the so-called competition of the unorganized defenseless woman worker, the girl and the wife, that often tends to reduce the wages of the father and husband," proclaimed Samuel Gompers. And the *American Federationist* was filled with tales of men displaced by women and children. "One house in St. Louis now pays $4 per week to women where men got $16," snapped the journal in 1896. "A local typewriter company has placed 200 women to take the place of unorganized men," announced an organizer in 1903.

The Federation's fears had some basis. In the late nineteenth and early twentieth century, new technology and techniques of efficiency pioneered by Frederick Taylor eroded the control and the jobs of skilled workmen, replacing them with managerial experts and the unskilled and semiskilled. Skilled members of the A. F. of L. who might appropriately have directed their anger at the way technology was being manipulated, lashed out instead at women who dared to work. Gompers offers a good example. In an article published in 1904, he declared, "The ingenuity of man to produce the world's wealth easier than ever before, is utilized as a means to pauperize the worker, to supplant the man by the woman and the woman by the child. . . ." Some of the least appropriate bitterness was expressed by Thomas O'Donnell, secretary of the National Spinners Union whose constituency, once largely female, had been replaced by men after the Civil War. The advent of simple electric-powered machinery caused him to complain that "the manufacturers have been trying for years to discourage us by dispensing with the spinning mule and substituting female and child labor for that of the old time skilled spinners. . . ."

Real anxieties about competition from women stimulated and supported rationalizations about woman's role as wife and mother. Working men had argued even before the Civil War that women belonged at home, and both the harsh conditions of labor and the demands of rearing a family supported their contention. But the women who worked for wages in the early 1900s were overwhelmingly single, and often supported widowed mothers and younger siblings with their meager pay. An argument that could have been used to improve conditions for all workers was directed at eliminating women from the work force entirely. By the early 1900s it had become an irrepressible chorus. "The great principle for which we fight," said the A. F. of L.'s treasurer in 1905, "is opposed to taking . . . the women from their homes to put them in the factory and the sweatshop." "We stand for the principle," said another A. F. of L. member, that it is wrong to permit any of the female sex of our country to be forced to work, as we believe that the man should be provided with a fair wage in order to keep his female relatives from going to work. The man is the provider and should receive enough for his labor to give his family a respectable living." . . . No language was too forceful or too dramatic. "The demand for female labor," wrote an official of the Boston Central Labor Union in 1897, is "an insidious assault upon the home . . . it is the knife of the assassin, aimed at the family circle." The *American Federationist* romanticized the role of women's jobs at home, extolling the virtues of refined and moral mothers, of good cooking and even of beautiful needlework and embroidery.

These sentiments did not entirely prevent the A. F. of L. from attempting to unionize women. Gompers editorialized on the subject in 1904: "We . . . shall bend every energy for our fellow workmen to organize and unite in trade unions; to federate their effort without regard to . . . sex." Yet the limited commitment implied by the wish that women would get out of the work force altogether was tinged with the conviction and perhaps the hope that women would in the end, fail. The Federation's first female organizer, Mary Kenny, had been appointed as early as 1892. But the Federation had supported her only half-heartedly and allowed her position to expire when she gave up the job to marry. It was 1908 before the organization appointed another woman, Annie Fitzgerald, as full-time organizer. While Gompers and others conceded the "full and free opportunity for women to work whenever and wherever necessity requires," Gompers did not address himself to the problem of how to determine which women were admissible by these standards, and his actions revealed that he thought their numbers relatively few. The A. F. of L. repeatedly called for an end to discriminatory pay for women and men: "Equal compensation for equal service performed." The demand was a double-edged sword. While it presumably protected all workers from cheap labor, in the context of the early 1900s labor market it often functioned to deprive women of jobs. The Boston Typographical Union, noted one observer, saw "its only safety in maintaining the principle of equal pay for men and women. . . ." Officials must have been aware that equal compensation for women often meant that employers would as soon replace them with men. It was no anomaly, then, to find an A. F. of L. organizer say of his daughters in 1919 that though he had "two girls at work [he] . . . wouldn't think of having them belong to a labor organization."

When the A. F. of L. did organize women, its major incentive was often the need to protect the earning power of men. Women were admitted to unions after men recognized them as competitors better controlled from within than allowed to compete from without. "It has been the policy of my associates and myself," wrote Gompers in 1906, "to throw open wide the doors of our organization and invite the working girls and working women to membership for their and our common protection." *American Federationist* articles that began with pleas that women stay out of the work force concluded with equally impassioned pleas to organize those who were already in it. Alice Woodbridge, writing in 1894, concluded an argument that women who worked for wages were neglecting their duties to their "fellow creatures" with the following statement: "It is to the interest of both sexes that women should organize . . . until we are well organized there is little hope of success among organizations of men." The A. F. of L. officially acknowledged competition as a primary motivation for organizing women in 1923. "Unorganized they constitute a menace to standards established through collective action. Not only for their protection, but for the protection of men . . . there should be organization of all women. . . ."

These were not of course the only circumstances of which men suspended their hostility toward women's unions. Occasionally in small towns female and male unions in different industries supported each other against the hostile attacks of employers. Minersville, Pennsylvania miners, for example, physically ousted railroad detectives who tried to break up a meeting of female textile workers. The women in this case were the daughters, sisters and sweethearts of miners. Far from competing with men for jobs, women were helping to support the same families as the miners. Similarly, women and men in newly established industries could cooperate more effectively in unionizing together. The garment industry saw parallel but equally effective organization among its various branches. Though female organizers complained bitterly of the way they were treated, male leadership depended on the numerical majority of female workers to bargain successfully with employers and did not deny women admission. Yet, even here, union leadership successfully eliminated "home work" without offering to the grossly underpaid and often needy female workers who did it a way of recouping their financial losses.

Occasional exceptions notwithstanding, the general consequence of union attitudes toward women was to isolate them from the male work force. Repeatedly women who organized themselves into unions applied for entry to the appropriate parent body only to be turned down or simply ignored. Pauline Newman, who had organized and collected dues from a group of candy makers in Philadelphia, in 1910 offered to continue to work with them if the International Bakery and Confectionery Workers union would issue a charter. The International stalled and put them off until the employers began to discharge the leaders and the group disintegrated. Waitresses in Norfolk, Virginia suffered a similar fate. Mildred Rankin, who requested a charter for a group of fifteen was assured by the local A. F. of L. organizer that she was wasting her time. "The girls were all getting too much money to be interested," was his comment on denying the request. New York's International Typographical Union refused to issue female copyholders a charter on the grounds that they were insufficiently skilled. When the group applied to the parent A. F. of L. for recognition, they were refused on the grounds that they were within the ITU's jurisdiction. The Women's Trade Union League got little satisfaction when it raised this issue with the A. F. of L.'s executive council the following year. Though the Federation had agreed to issue charters to black workers excluded from all-white unions, it refused to accord the same privilege to women. The parent body agreed only to "take up the subject with the trade unions and to endeavor to reach an understanding" as far as women were concerned.

A strong union could simply cut women out of the kinds of jobs held by unionized men. This form of segmenting the labor market ran parallel to, and sometimes contradicted the interests of employers who would have preferred cheap labor. A Binghamton, New York, printing establishment, for example, could not hire women linotype operators because "the men's union would not allow it." The technique was as useful for excluding racial minorities as it was for restricting women. Like appeals to racist beliefs, arguments based on the natural weakness of women worked well as a rationale, as the following examples will indicate. Mary Dreier, then President of the New York Chapter of the Women's Trade Union League, recalled a union of tobacco workers whose leaders refused to admit women because "they could only do poor sort of work. . . . because women had no colour discrimination." A Boston metal polishers union refused to admit women. "We don't want them," an official told a Women's Bureau interviewer. "Women can only do one kind of work while men can polish anything from iron to gold and frame the smallest part to the largest," and besides, he added, "metal polishing is bad for the health."

Women were often excluded from unions in less direct but equally effective ways. The International Retail Clerks Union charged an initiation fee of $3, and dues of 50¢ a month. Hilda Svenson, a local organizer in 1914, complained that she had been unable to negotiate a compromise with the International. "We want to be affiliated with them," she commented, "but on account of the dues and initiation fee we feel it is too high at the present time for the salaries that the girls in New York are getting." Sometimes union pay scales were set so high that the employer would not pay the appropriate wage to women. Joining the union could mean that a female printer would lose her job, so women simply refused to join.

Though the A. F. of L. supported its few female organizers only halfheartedly, male organizers complained of the difficulty of organizing women. Social propriety hindered them from talking to women in private or about moral or sanitary issues. Women felt keenly the absence of aid. When the Pennsylvania State Federation of Labor offered to finance the Philadelphia Women's Trade Union League's program for organizing women, its secretary pleaded with Rose Schneiderman to take the job. "We have never had a wise head to advise, or an experienced worker," she wrote.

But even membership in a union led by men guaranteed little to women. Such well known tactics as locating meetings in saloons, scheduling them at late hours, and ridiculing women who dared to speak deprived women of full participation. And unions often deliberately sabotaged their female members. Fifteen hundred female street railway conductors and ticket agents, dues-paying members of New York City's Amalgamated Street Workers Union, complained in 1919 that their brother union members had supported a reformers' bill to deprive them of their jobs. When the women discovered they had been betrayed they resigned from the union and formed their own organization sending women throughout the state to Albany "to show them that they . . . were able to take care of their own health and morals." To no avail. Eight hundred of the 1500 women lost their jobs and the remaining 700 continued to work only at reduced hours. Supporting union men was not likely to benefit women either. Mary Anderson, newly appointed head of the Women's Bureau, got a frantic telegram from a WTUL organizer in Joliet, Illinois, early in 1919. The women in a Joliet steel plant who, in return for the promise of protection, had supported unionized men in a recent strike, were fighting desperately for jobs that the union now insisted they give up. The company wanted to retain the women, but union men argued the work was too heavy for them.

As the idea of home-and-motherhood was used to exclude women from unions, so it enabled unionized workers to join legislatures and middle-class reformers in restricting women's hours and regulating their working condition through protective labor legislation. The issue for the Federation's skilled and elite corps of male workers was clearly competition. Their wives did not work for wages, and most could afford to keep their daughters outside the marketplace. In an effort to preserve limited opportunity, they attacked fellow workers who were women, attempting to deny them access to certain kinds of jobs. Abused by employers who valued women primarily for their "cheap labor," women were isolated by male workers who were afraid their wages and their jobs would fall victim to the competition. Arguments used by male workers may have undercut their own positions, confirming the existence of a permanent underclass of workers and locking men psychologically and economically into positions of sole economic responsibility for their families. Appeals to morality and to the duties of motherhood obscured the economic issues involved, encouraging women and men alike to see women as impermanent workers whose major commitment would be to families and not to wage earning. Women would, therefore, require the special protection of the state for their presumably limited wage-earning lives.

The argument reached back at least as far as the 1880s and it was firmly rooted in the idea that the well-being of the state depended on the health of future mothers. But the line between the interests of the state and those of working men was finely drawn, and occasionally a protagonist demonstrated confusion about the issue. A few examples will illustrate the point. The cigar maker, Adolph Strasser, testifying before a Congressional Committee in 1882, concluded a diatribe against the number of women entering the trade with a plea to restrict them. "Why?" asked his questioner. "Because," replied Strasser, "I claim that it is the duty of the government to protect the weak and the females are considered among the weak in society." Nearly forty years later, a Women's Bureau investigator reported that the Secretary of the Amalgamated Clothing Workers Union, fearful that women were taking jobs from men, had argued that women were "going into industry so fast that home life is very much in danger, not to mention the propagation of the race. As the idea spread, it took on new forms, leading a Boston streetcar union secretary to acknowledge that "he would not care to see [women] employed as conductors. . . . It coarsened [them] to handle rough crowds on cars. But in more sophisticated form, the argument for protective legislation appeared as a patriotic appeal to enlightened national self-interest. "Women may be adults," argued one A. F. of L. columnist in 1900, "and why should we class them as children? Because it is to the interest of all of us that female labor should be limited so as not to injure the motherhood and family life of a nation." Sometimes pleas were more dramatic. . . .

Gompers, as well as other Federation officials, at first opposed the idea of legislation. But in the period following World War I, their attitudes changed, perhaps as a result of what seemed like an enormous increase in the number of women in the industrial labor force. The A. F. of L. encouraged the Department of Labor to set up a Women's Bureau to defend the interests of wage-earning women. The Bureau, on investigation, found that many union officials viewed unionization and protective legislation as alternate means to the same goal: better working conditions. Sara Conboy, United Textile Workers' official and a WTUL activist, told a Women's Bureau interviewer that she believed in "legislation to limit long hours of work for women where and when the union [was] not strong enough to limit hours." Some unionized workers thought legislation surer and faster or remarked that it was more dependable than possibly untrustworthy union leaders. A. J. Muste, then secretary of the Amalgamated Textile Workers Union of America preferred unionization, but was said to have believed that legislation did not hinder organization and might be essential in industries with many women and minors. But some women union leaders were not so sanguine. Fannia Cohn of the International Garment Workers Union only reluctantly acquiesced to the need for protective legislation. "I did not think the problem of working women could be solved in any other way than the problem of working men and that is through trade union organization," she wrote in 1927, "but considering that very few women are as yet organized into trade unions, it would be folly to agitate against protective legislation." Cohn laid the problems of female workers on the absence of organization.

In any event, exclusion from unions merely confirmed the discomfort many women felt about participating in meetings. Italian and Southern families disliked their daughters going out in the evenings. Married and self-supporting women and widows had household duties at which they spent after-work hours. Women who attended meetings often participated reluctantly. They found the long discussions dull and were often intimidated by the preponderance of men. Men, for their part, resented the indifference of the women and further excluded them from leadership roles, thereby discouraging more women from attending. Even fines failed to spark attendance. Some women preferred to pay them rather than to go to the meetings.

Self-images that derived from a paternalistic society joined ethnic ties in hindering unionization. Wage-earning women, anxious to marry, were sometimes reluctant to join unions for what they felt would be a temporary period. Occasionally, another role conflict was expressed: "No nice girl would belong to one," said one young woman. An ILG organizer commented that most women who did not want to join a union claimed that "the boss is good to us and we have nothing to complain about and we don't want to join the union." A woman who resisted unionization told an organizer that she knew "that $6 a week is not enough pay but the Lord helps me out. He always provides . . . I won't ever join a union. The Lord doesn't want me to." A recent convert to unionism apologized for her former reticence. She had always scabbed because church people disapproved of unions. Moreover she and her sister had only with difficulty, she told an organizer, overcome their fear of the Italian men who were organizing their factory.

Exceptions to this pattern occurred most often among women whose ethnic backgrounds encouraged both wage labor and a high level of social consciousness, as in the American Jewish community, for example. Young Jewish women constituted the bulk of the membership of the International Ladies Garment Workers Union in the period from 1910 to 1920. Their rapid organization and faithful tenure is responsible for at least one quarter of the increased number of unionized women in the second decade of the twentieth century. And yet, they were unskilled and semi-skilled workers, employed in small, scattered shops, and theoretically among the least organizable workers. These women, unionized at their own initiative, formed the backbone of the ILGWU, which had originally been directed toward organizing the skilled, male cutters in the trade.

As it became clear to many laboring women that unionists would offer them little help, many women turned to such middle-class allies as the Women's Trade Union League. Established in 1905, the WTUL, an organization founded by female unionists and upper-middle class reformers, offered needed financial and moral support for militant activity. Its paternalistic and benevolent style was not unfamiliar to women and those who came from immigrant families seemed particularly impressed with its Americanizing aspects. Young immigrant girls spoke with awe of the "fine ladies" of the WTUL and did not object to the folk-dancing classes that were part of the Chicago League's program. But help from these nonwage-earning women came at a price. Working women who became involved in the WTUL moved quickly from working class militance to the search for individual social mobility through vocational training, legislation, and the social refinements that provided access to better paying and rapidly increasing clerical and secretarial jobs. Rose Schneiderman illustrates this syndrome well. Beginning as a fiery organizer of the hat-and-cap makers, she moved through the WTUL to become Secretary of the New York State Department of Labor. Like the WTUL, which had begun by organizing women into trade unions, she began in the 1920s to devote herself to attaining protective legislation, even borrowing some of the arguments used by men who did not wish women to compete with them.

By this time many working women were themselves moving in the direction of legislative solutions to exploitative working conditions. It seemed to be the most accessible solution to the problems of exploitation. Female workers interviewed by the Women's Bureau at first felt that both women and men should be included in any legislation. Later, they asked that office workers were exempted. Other women acquiesced reluctantly. "I have always been afraid," wrote a supervisor in a Virginia silk mill, "that if laws were made discriminating for women, it would work a hardship upon them.'' By 1923 she had changed her mind: ''. . . it would in time raise the entire standard rather than make it hard for women.'' As women came to accept the necessity for legislation, they, like men, saw it as an alternative to unionization and rationalized its function in terms of their female ''roles.'' A Women's Bureau agent noted of the reactions to a 48-hour law passed in Massachusetts that ''the girls felt that legislation establishing a 48-hour week was more 'dignified' and permanent than one obtained through the union as it was not so likely to be taken away.'' By the mid-1920s only business and professional women remained staunchly opposed to protective legislation.

Within this framework of trade-union ambivalence and the real need of wage-earning women for some form of protection employers who were particularly anxious that women not unionize pressed their advantage. Using crude techniques, rationalized by the home-and-motherhood argument, they contributed more than their share toward keeping women out of unions. In the small businesses in which women most often worked, employers used a variety of techniques to discourage organization, some of them familiar to men. Department store employees whose union membership became known were commonly fired. Many stores had spy systems so that employees could not trust their coworkers. Blacklists were common. A representative of the year-old retail clerks union testifying before a Congressional Committee in 1914 was afraid even to reveal the number of members in her union. Owners of New York's garment shops, fighting a losing battle by 1910, nevertheless frequently discharged employees who were thought to be active organizers or union members.

Other tactics were no more subtle. Employers often played on ethnic and racial tensions in order to prevent women from unionizing. Rose Schneiderman, who formed the Hat and Cap Makers Union in 1903, fought against bosses who urged immigrant workers to stick to the ''American shop''— a euphemism for an antiunion shop. Jewish owners sometimes hired only Italian workers who were thought to be less prone to unionization than Jews. Others hired ''landsmen'' from the same old country community, hoping that fraternal instincts might keep them from striking. Blacks were played off against whites. Waitresses picketing Knab's restaurant in Chicago were met with counterpickets paid by the employers. A representative of the waitresses union reported indignantly that the employer ''placed colored pickets on the street, colored women who wore signs like this, 'Gee, I ain't mad at nobody and nobody ain't mad at Knab.' '' When the nonunion pickets attracted a crowd, police moved in and arrested the union members. The women were further discouraged by trials engineered by employers who had previously given ''every policeman a turkey free.''

Police routinely broke up picket lines and outdoor union meetings. Women who were accused of obstructing traffic or were incited into slapping provocateurs were arrested. More importantly, women who might have been interested in unionization were intimidated by police who surrounded open air meetings or by department store detectives who mingled obtrusively with potential recruits. Department store owners diverted workers from street meetings by locking all but one set of doors or sending trucks, horns honking full blast, to parade up and down the street in which a meeting was scheduled.

Small employers formed mutual assistance associations to help them resist their employees' attempts to unionize. The Chicago Restaurant Keepers Association, for example, denied membership to any "person, firm or corporation . . . having signed agreements with any labor organization." Garment manufacturers in both New York and Chicago created protective associations to combat what they called "the spreading evil of unionism." In small towns, the power of town officials was called into play. Ann Washington Craton, organizing textile workers in Minersville, Pennsylvania, was warned by the town burgess: "You are to let our girls alone . . . Mr. Demsky will shut the factory down rather than have a union. . . . The town council brought this factory here to provide work for worthy widows and poor girls. We don't intend to have any trouble about it."

Employers justified continued refusal to promote women or to offer them access to good jobs on the grounds that women's major contribution was to home and family. When they were challenged with the argument that bad working conditions were detrimental to that end, they responded slowly with paternalistic amelioration of the worst conditions and finally by acquiescing to protective labor legislation. Often concessions to workers were an effort to undercut mounting union strength, as for example when department store owners voluntarily closed their shops one evening a week. Some employers introduced welfare work in their factories, providing social workers, or other women, to help smooth relationships between them and their female employees. Mutual benefit associations, sometimes resembling company unions, were a more familiar tactic. Though they were presumably cooperative and designed to incorporate input from workers, membership in them was compulsory and dues of ten to twenty-five cents per month were deducted from wages. In return employees got sickness and health benefits of varying amounts but only after several months of continuous employment. A 1925 investigation of one widely publicized cooperative association operated by Filene's department store in Boston revealed that in all its twelve years, only store executives had ever served on its board of directors.

Manufacturers seemed to prefer legislation regulating the hours and conditions of women's work to seeing their workers join unions. One, for example, told the Women's Bureau of the Department of Labor that a uniform 48-hour week for women would equalize competition and would, in any event only confirm existing conditions in some shops. Some went even further hoping for federal legislation that would provide uniform standards nationwide.

When occasionally employers found it in their interests to encourage unionism they did so in return for certain very specific advantages. One of these was the union label. In the garment industry the label on overalls in certain parts of the country assured higher sales. To acquire the right to use it, some employers rushed into contracts with the United Garment Workers and quite deliberately urged their workers into the union. New York garment manufacturers negotiated a preferential union shop, higher wages, and shorter hours with the ILGWU in return for which the union agreed to discipline its members and to protect employers against strikes. The garment manufacturers' protective association urged employers to "make every effort to increase the membership in the union so that its officers may have complete control of the workers and be enabled to discipline them when necessary." Southern textile mill owners, otherwise violently opposed to unions, were similarly interested in the disciplinary functions of unionism. They would, an observer reported, modify their opposition "if the purposes of the union were to improve the educational, moral, and social conditions of the workers."

In general, however, employers made valiant attempts to keep women out of unions. The paternalism, benevolence, and welfare they offered in compensation were supported by other sectors of their society, including the trade unions. Middle-class reformers and government investigators had long viewed the harsh conditions under which women worked as detrimental to the preservation of home and family, and government regulation or voluntary employer programs seemed to many an adequate alternative. Unions played into this competitive structure adopting the home-and-motherhood argument to restrict women's labor-force participation. In the process they encouraged women to see their interests apart from those of male workers.

Limited labor-force opportunities, protective labor legislation and virtual exclusion from labor unions institutionalized women's isolation from the mainstream of labor. Not accidentally, these tendencies confirmed traditional women's roles, already nurtured by many ethnic groups and sustained by prevailing American norms. Together they translated into special behavior on the part of female workers that isolated them still further from male workers and added up to special treatment as members of the labor force.

In acquiescing, women perhaps bowed to the inevitable, seeking for themselves the goals of employers who preferred not to see them in unions, of male workers who hoped thereby both to limit competition and to share in the advantages gained, and of middle-class reformers who felt they were helping to preserve home and motherhood. Echoing labor union arguments of twenty years earlier, Women's Bureau head Mary Anderson defended protective legislation in 1925 on the grounds that such laws were necessary to conserve the health of the nation's women.

A final consequence for women was to lead them to search for jobs in non-sex-stereotyped sectors of the labor market. Employers' needs in the rapidly expanding white-collar sector led women increasingly toward secretarial and clerical work. Vocational education to train women for office jobs, teaching, and social work expanded rapidly in the early twentieth century. Working women rationalized these jobs as steps up the occupational ladder; state and local governments and employers provided financial aid; and middle-class women launched a campaign to encourage women to accept vocational training. It took an astute union woman like Fannia Cohn to see what was happening. She drew a sharp line between her own function as educational director of the International Ladies Garment Workers Union and the functions of the new schools. Her hope was to train women to be better union members, not to get them out of the working class.

The parallel development of protective legislation and vocational education confirmed for many working women their marginal positions in the labor force, positions they continued to rationalize with obeisance to marriage and the family. As Alice Henry said of an earlier group of female wage-earners, "they did not realize that women were within the scope of the labor movement." Fannia Cohn understood what that meant. That hard-headed and clear-sighted official of the ILGWU prefaced a call for a revolution in society's view of women with a plea for an end to competition between working women and men. Because it was destructive for all workers, she argued, "this competition must be abolished once and for all, not because it is immoral, yes inhuman, but because it is impractical, it does not pay." But in the first two decades of the twentieth century, the moral arguments prevailed—releasing some women from some of the misery of toil, but simultaneously confirming their place in those jobs most conducive to exploitation.

✣ *F U R T H E R   R E A D I N G*

Robert Christie, *Empire in Wood* (1965)

Melvyn Dubofsky, *We Shall Be All: A History of the Industrial Workers of the World* (1969)

Melvyn Dubofsky and Warren Van Tine, eds., *Labor Leaders in America* (1987)

Nancy Schrom Dye, *As Equals and as Sisters: Feminism, the Labor Movement, and the Women's Trade Union League of New York* (1981)

Leon Fink, *Workingmen's Democracy: The Knights of Labor and American Politics* (1982)

Joan Jensen and Sue Davidson, eds., *A Needle, a Bobbin, a Strike* (1984)

Stuart Kaufman, *Samuel Gompers and the Origins of the American Federation of Labor, 1848–1896* (1973)

Michael Kazin, *The Barons of Labor: The San Francisco Building Trades and Union Power in the Progressive Era* (1987)

Alice Kessler-Harris, *Out to Work: A History of Wage-Earning Women in the United States* (1982)

John Laslett, *Labor and the Left: A Study of Socialist and Radical Influences in the American Labor Movement, 1881–1924* (1970)

Bernard Mandel, *Samuel Gompers: A Biography* (1963)

Robin Miller Jacoby, "The Women's Trade Union League and American Feminism," *Feminist Studies* 3 (Fall 1975), 126–140

Richard Oestreicher, *Solidarity and Fragmentation: Working People and Class Consciousness in Detroit, 1875–1900* (1986)

Michael Rogin, "Voluntarism: The Political Functions of an Anti-Political Doctrine," *Industrial and Labor Relations Review* 15 (July 1962), 521–535

Nick Salvatore, *Eugene V. Debs, Citizen and Socialist* (1982)

Shelton Stromquist, *A Generation of Boomers: The Pattern of Railroad Labor Conflict in Nineteenth-Century America* (1987)

Warren Van Tine, *The Making of the Labor Bureaucrat* (1973)

C H A P T E R
7

Cultures of the Workplace

✢

In recent years historians have come to realize that the daily routine maintained by almost all workers is a product not just of the formal hierarchies established by management nor of the institutional apparatus of the trade union. Instead, everyday life in the workplace is shaped by a particular work culture, consisting of the ideology and practices with which workers stake out a relatively autonomous sphere of action on the job, a realm of informal, customary values and rules that are changed only slowly as one generation of workers merges into the next.

Of course, the range of such work cultures is enormously varied, and some are far more pleasant and communal than others. The single greatest factor determining the character of a work culture may well be the predominant gender in the work force. Men and women often bring their own culture-bound expectations to the job and socialize in different ways. Meanwhile, the organization of the work and the technology of production structure the kinds of informal associations that one worker can make with another. Thus the friendship pattern of a department-store clerk might be quite different from that of a hospital nurse. The vital cooperation of a longshore gang might evoke a sense of solidarity far greater than the more individualized work practices of a long-haul truck driver.

A focus on work culture prompts us to ask several questions. What kinds of informal rules and behavioral norms guide the interaction among workers and between employees and their supervisors, customers, and the general public? Under what circumstances have informal mechanisms restricted the pace and output of labor and socialized newcomers to the job? How have worker efforts to resist or accommodate managerial demands become institutionalized through trade unions, company-employment policies, and off-the-job voluntary associations? How do conceptions of manhood and womanhood define the world of work? In what ways do responsibilities toward home and children, which women carry with them to the workplace, shape the culture of sex-segmented occupations? And to what extent have work cultures based on skill and a common working environment transcended the antagonisms of gender, race, and ethnicity?

275

✤ D O C U M E N T S

In the first selection, United Mine Workers of America leader John Brophy recalls the work traditions and code of ethics that enabled him and his workmates
to face the dangers inherent in early-twentieth-century coal mining. The waitress's world differed dramatically from that of the miner's, but, as the second
document reveals, women who waited tables evolved a complex set of social
techniques useful for increasing their tips and easing their work. Nurses also
drew on a set of gender-based cultural norms to forge a work culture that affirmed their value as women but rejected unfavorable female stereotypes. In the
third document, a personal memoir of a hospital nursing apprentice, Ann Forrest
captures the acculturated experience of this craft as it existed in the late 1930s.
Here "soldiering," or a deliberate slowdown of work, was antithetical to the
work rules and culture of nursing. But as Antioch student Stanley Mathewson
found in 1931, and as the fourth document reveals, miners, machinists, errand
boys, and department-store clerks were among the wide range of laborers who
successfully resisted managerial efforts to increase the pace of work, thereby establishing an easier work routine and higher rate of pay.

In these examples, what characteristics most shaped the work culture: the
level of technology in the workplace, the characteristics of the workers, or management decisions about the work process and rate of pay? To what extent do
these diverse work settings evoke a sense of collective cooperation or a sense of
individual accomplishment?

Miner John Brophy Learns His Trade, 1907

. . . I got a thrill at the thought of having an opportunity to go and work
in the mine, to go and work alongside of my father. After . . . I got experience and some strength, and the ability to work with a little skill, I
was conscious of the fact that my father was a good workman; that he had
a pride in his calling. At that time all pit mining was hand work, as it were.
But he not only was concerned with seeing that his rib—the left side of
his workplace, which was known as the rib—was trimmed clean and clear
so that he kept a straight line, as it were, cut just like a brick wall. Alongside
the rib, paralleling it, would be the roadway on which the cars came to be
loaded.

It was a great satisfaction to me that my father was a skilled, clean
workman with everything kept in shape, and the timbering done well—all
of these things: the rib side, the roadway, the timbering, the fact that you
kept the loose coal clean rather than cluttered all over the workplace, the
skill with which you undercut the vein, the judgment in drilling the coal
after it had been undercut and placing the exact amount of explosive so
that it would do an effective job of breaking the coal from the solid—
indicated the quality of his work—it was all these things. . . .

[I]t was skill in handling the pick and the shovel, the placing of timbers,
and understanding the vagaries of the workplace—which is subject to certain pressures from the overhanging strata as you advance into the seam.

From John Brophy, *Memoir*, Columbia Oral History Collection (1955), pp. 95–104.

It's an awareness of roof conditions. And it's something else too. Under the older conditions of mining under which I went to work with my father, the miner exercised considerable freedom in his working place in determining his work pace and the selection of the order of time in the different work operations. Judgment was everywhere along the line, and there was also necessary skill. It was the feel of all this. You know that another workman in another place was a good miner, a passable miner, or an indifferent one. . . .

While he had all that independence and exercise of individual judgment in his work, it's not to say that that was the total situation for the miner, because there are over-all control situations in the total mine system. There was the flow and distribution of mine cars, which constitute a turn of cars — that is, a share of work opportunity by which the miner earns his day's wages, because he was paid by the ton. That has an over-all controlling influence on him. He must meet this turn of the cars or his earnings declined. Also, unless there are very good reasons, such as adverse conditions developing in the workplace, he is inclined to lose face with his fellow workers if he misses his turn because of poor workmanship.

It's true too that many of the dangers in the mine are local and individual to the miner. That is, they occur in his working place. No one can safeguard him but himself using his own judgment in securing proper safeguards.

There are other conditions, like the matter of ventilation. If ventilation is poor, then all the miners are affected. If ventilation is bad, then of course, the distress becomes evident and there is considerable disturbance among the men and an attempt to do something about it. In the case of gas explosions, in mines where there are explosive gases, a small pocket of gas is ignited by a naked light or by the black powder explosive used to shatter the coal. It may be that they light just a small pocket of gas and create no danger, so that it just burns out the gas. But quite often the area of gas is so extensive that when ignited it has a widespread effect — that is, the violence of the explosion may kill not only the people in the workplace but others in the entire mine area. Such an explosion, if extensive, shatters the ventilating system, then after-damp follows, the poisonous residue left from the igniting of the gas, with all the oxygen burned out — suffocates the people that are left alive. . . .

The miner is always aware of danger, that he lived under dangerous conditions in the workplace, because he's constantly uncovering new conditions as he advances in the workingplace, exposing new areas of roof; discovering some weakened condition or break which may bring some special danger. There is also the danger that comes from a piece of coal slipping off the fast and falling on the worker as he lays prone on the bottom doing his cutting. The worker has got to be aware of all these conditions that may be in coal, that may be in the roof.

Then there is this over-all condition which controls his life. . . . It's an awareness of danger in all its various aspects and the recognition that in some of the larger areas of operation in the mine proper he must cooperate with his fellows at the price of life or to ward off or guard against danger.

These are the peculiar complexes of the miner: he's a highly individualized worker—I'm speaking of the miner of my day and previous generations—who exercises a great deal of individual initiative in doing his work, in safeguarding himself in his individual workplace. He also must be concerned with his fellows in the larger aspect—the total mine—and he must be prepared to aid his fellows in time of danger. Everything else stops where there's danger. You react to the call for assistance at the moment when assistance may be required because while it may be somebody else today, it may be you tomorrow.

Then there is the further fact that the miner by and large lived in purely mining communities which were often isolated. They developed a group loyalty under all these circumstances. They were both individualists and they were group conscious. They had individual concerns and loyalties but they also had group concerns and group loyalties. It made them an extraordinary body of workers, these miners, because of these very special conditions, because involved in it was not only earning a livelihood, but a matter of health and safety, life and death were involved in every way. You find time and again miners, in an effort to rescue their fellow workers, taking chances which quite often meant death for themselves in an effort to rescue somebody else. . . .

Along with that is a sense of justice. There was the very fact that the miner was a tonnage worker and that he could be short weighed and cheated in various ways, and the only safeguard against it was organization. In that case it was important to have a representative of the miners to see that the weight was properly done and properly credited to the individual miner. There was the whole complex of circumstances that had been in the mining industry for generations which had been their experience. The miner in my day in the United States was aware that all knowledge didn't start with his generation, and that back of it were generations of other miners in other parts of the world, who had similar experiences, who had had their struggles, who had met situations in various ways and who had passed their knowledge on to their children and their children had passed it on.

Take my case. I think I have mentioned before that at least on one side of my family there are at least four generations of miners, and I say this with a sense of pride; very much so. I'm very proud of the fact that there is this long tradition of miners who have struggled with the elements. The nearest thing that I can compare it to—this miner's pride that grows out of his individual skill and his individual need and his cooperative relations with his fellows and his dependency upon the total operation to aid him in his daily output for his earnings—is the sailor. After all, the total operation for the seaman is the ship. He must maintain a certain standard, he must safeguard the ship because that's the element in which he operates, a changeable one. He has individual duties and he achieves individual skill as a sailor. But he must cooperate. There is a difference between a miner and a sailor. One is out on the surface; the other is underneath. The other thing is this, too. The difference is that every day a part of the miner's day is spent in his own small community with his family. It has certain elements of comparison, but there is that fundamental difference—that the miners live on the land in fixed communities and are there every day of the year, whereas the sailor does not. But both are equally dependent upon the good conduct on the operation, on the ship, in the mine. The miner depends upon good mine operation not only for a living but for life itself.

A Waitress And Her Customers, 1917

I received my first tip on the first day that I was a waitress. A shabby, dissipated wreck of a man came in and sat down on one of the stools at my counter. To my surprise, he ordered a forty-five cent meal. I became very busy and I did not at once remove his dirty dishes. A boy sat down on the stool vacated by this man and I took his order. When I was attempting to clear a place for it, I saw a greasy, dirty nickel on the counter. The boy gave it a little push towards me and said, "I guess this is yours."

"I thought it was yours," I said, and then I realized that I had been given a tip. I knew that it was customary to tip a waitress in more fashionable eating places but that it was done here, was a great surprise to me. Presently two mail carriers came in, one white and one colored, and each, when he left, gave me a dime. I had tipped colored boys many times but it was indeed a new experience to have one tip me.

The second place that I worked was Foyle's Tea Shop. One day when the waitresses were eating their lunch in the rear of the room, a plainly dressed woman entered and sat down at a table near the front.

"There's a lady at your table, Florence," said a waitress to a pretty girl who sat next to her.

"I don't care if there is," said Florence, "I'm tired and I'm going to eat my lunch. Somebody else can wait on her."

In a few minutes she returned to the waitresses' table and showed, lying on the palm of her hand, a bright new dime.

"Now aren't you sorry, Florence?" she asked, and then added, "All she asked for was a bowl of soup."

"Just my luck!" said Florence with a little grimace as she went on eating.

"That's a movie ticket," said the other girl as she slid the dime into her apron pocket.

But it was not until I reached the Café des Reflections that I began to realize the enormous importance of the tip in the life of the waitress. It was nothing unusual there, for a two meal girl to make $18.00 or $20.00 per week in tips, and the steady girl made still more. I myself, as a two meal girl, made $8.15 in tips in five days, and I was inexperienced and had the poorest station in the house.

"Did you make good today, girlie?" someone would always ask.

I would tell them how much I made.

Frances Donovan, *The Woman Who Waits* (Boston: Richard G. Badger, The Gorham Press, 1920), pp. 194–197.

"Well, you are new. You will do better after a while. The new girl always gets the front station and it's no good."

A station is a group of tables that is assigned to you. A back station is always better than a front station and "deuces" (tables for two) are better than larger tables. "I've got them three deuces at the back of the room," a girl will say, "and every time I have a couple sittin' at them three deuces, that means three quarters for me. You'd probably only get ten cents, where I'd get a quarter, because you ain't on to the game."

"I can even get a tip out of a woman," another will say. "I just stick around and act so darn nice that she can't resist. But whether it's a man or a woman, you got to stick around and act like you expected it, or you won't get no tip."

I was never very successful at working people for tips and never made over half what the other girls made. One night at Laconia Park I had an order from a man for a pitcher of Apollinaris water and grape juice. Owing to the wretched service at the soda fountain, I was a long time getting it. Later the same man ordered a round of sandwiches for his party, five in number.

"That was a nice party you had, kid," said the girl next to me, "how much did you get out of them?"

"Twenty cents," I answered.

"You didn't know how to handle him, then. I've had him several times and he's good for a half or a dollar always."

And one morning at breakfast in the servants' dining room, at the Meadow Lark Golf Club, the Cockney who had charge of the men's lockers said to me, "Well, Fannie, how much did Mr. L. come through with last night in the dining room?"

"Not a cent," I said cheerfully.

"Well then," he said, "you didn't give him service."

I protested mildly here.

"Well then, you didn't talk to him. That's where you lost out. You should have talked to him about his game. (The Cockney said "gyme.") No matter whether you know anything about golf or not you must say, 'And how many did you make it in today?' and if he says '87', you say, 'well, now that's not bad, you'll do better next time, no doubt, Mr. L., and anyway you've got a magnificent swing. I was looking out just as you drove off the ninth tee and I must say, Mr. L., you've surely got a swing.' Now that's the talk that brings them. After that he'd be good for a half or maybe a dollar. He expects a waitress to entertain him at dinner."

Letters from an Apprentice Nurse, 1939

January 12

I'm a nurse now. Been one a whole week. Don't ask me why I was accepted when there's a stack of applications that high in the office from

Ann Forrest, *Yes, Doctor!* (Siloam Springs, Arkansas: Bar D Press, 1939), pp. 9, 22–23, 28–29, 66–67.

real nurses asking for employment, "salary no object." Evidently eating and somewhere to sleep are the objects, for nurses do get maintenance and pay.

But I am a nurse. I'm not enthusiastic; I'm having to learn too much that I'd rather not know. I don't like seeing "life in the raw," and a lot of this is just glorified, uniformed drudgery.

And parts of the personal side make me sick. I mean SICK; it's nauseating to see the way nurses practically worship doctors. And I'm not wild about the manners of the profession. For the first time in my life I'm stepping back from a door to let a man pass through first: Doctors first, always. . . .

February 16

I'm having Experiences. Today a patient offered me a handful of silver for a quarter-grain or two of morphine. I was sorely tempted. With a few customers like that, I could soon reopen my hose shop—for somebody else to run. Oh, I could get away with it. I could always say I had lost my supply—dropped it in the bathroom, where it melted before I could pick it up. But no.

Besides, I don't know that I could be interested now in anything so different from hospital life as a business of my own would be. I think I'm being inoculated with the hospitalis virus, and now I know what is meant by the "insidious onset" of a disease. It certainly slipped up on me.

Ann, darling, I hope I never have need of something to help me hold to my religion. But I may. This P.M. we operated on an old man whose stomach had been inactive for five days, and found his intestines in such condition that he couldn't have lived another forty-eight hours, but, Ann, he died on the table. Dr. P. sewed him up quickly, and we got him back to his room. The circle nurse had given him a stimulant on the table, and Dr. Wood gave him another directly into the heart. The man is breathing now, although his pulse isn't yet perceptible, and the doctors have told the family that he can't live through the night. But he will react from his anaesthetic, and be able to tell his family goodbye.

The operation was his only chance, and it turned that he didn't have that, (tuberculous intestines, looked like pink freckles) but it's my first death, and it has upset me. I don't believe I'll ever be the ideal nurse, coolly efficient, but I will not become embittered. . . .

February 26

This is the darndest place. Everybody calls the cook, "Cook," and the orderly "Porter," but it's a big insult to call one of us "Nurse." If you were my patient, you'd be supposed to call me, "Miss Williams."

We are operating right and left this week. The OR is supposed to be the most glamorous department of the hospital, but I don't quite see why; everything except surgery is talked about in there. So far, I've heard more dirt dished there than anything else. If I could laugh at dirty jokes, I'd be one of the crowd; maybe I'll learn that, too.

. . . I'm not yet reconciled to the subordination of nurses. The infernal, eternal "Yes, Doctor" irritates me still. Somehow, it seems less servile to call their names. I can't explain that, but I always say, "Yes, Doctor Wood," etc. Nobody understands that but Drake; she said she felt that way, too, for the first hundred years. . . .

May 23

Tonight, or last night, rather, one of the patients was dead as she'll ever be. I gave her a stimulant which should have picked her up in fifteen minutes, but didn't; but in a few minutes she did start breathing—a sort of lifeless gasp. It was forty-five minutes before the pulse was perceptible.

Of course, what I did was my duty, and besides, I had to do it. But since the hypo took so long to take effect, think what would have happened if I had hesitated a few minutes in indecision, or had been careless in any way.

But sometimes I feel that I'd like a little crop rotation or something. What I really mean is that I'd like to plow under every third patient, or so. I must be getting to be an impersonal nurse, after all.

Popular patients are the hardest to take care of, because of their visitors. If I had a hospital, I'd bar visitors and flowers—and go broke in a week, I know, but it would be a peaceful week. . . .

A Student's View of "Soldiering," 1931

The worker upon entering industry is, of course, first aware of the direct pressure exerted by his fellow-workmen. In fact, a new worker will often practice restriction for a long time for no other reason than that the working group insists upon it. Later, he usually becomes familiar with the underlying causes, the indirect factors which make "regulation," in the eyes of his fellows, necessary.

The cases which follow indicate how potent a factor for restriction the pressure of the group may be. . . .

"Red," a beginner in industry, was working on an assembly line in a phonograph factory, producing small motors, on hourly rate. The line was turning out an average of only 30 motors a day. "Red" found it so easy to keep up his part of the work that he would pile up parts ahead of the next worker in the line. He would then move over and help perform the next operation until the other worker caught up. This went on until "Red" was shifted by the foreman to the final operation in the assembly line. Here he was in a position to work as fast as he liked so far as passing on his completed work was concerned, but he was constantly waiting for the man behind. In order not to appear slow this man had to put through a few more parts, which had its effect all along the assembly line. The process of speeding up developed slowly until the gang, which formerly put through about 30 motors a day, was turning out an average of 120 a day. To "Red's" surprise, the men objected strenuously to this increase, argued with him and even threatened to "meet him in the alley" unless he slowed down

---

Stanley Mathewson, *Restriction of Output Among Unorganized Workers* (New York: Viking, 1931), pp. 15–20.

his production. "Red" said that when production got up above 100 motors a day the threats became so insistent he began to fear "they might really mean something." However, "Red's" problem was "solved" by his transfer to another department. . . .

Tex, a southern boy, started to work for a mining company. He wanted to go into the mines, but he was too young to be put underground; so he was given a job in the electrical department running a coil-winding machine. He had never run such a machine, but found it quite easy to operate after he had been "shown how." The average output of the coils he was running had been 72 a day. When he began working, Tex knew no better than to make all the coils he could. The first day everything was new, but at the end of the second day he found that he had turned out 90 coils, 18 over the previous average output. If a new boy could produce as many as that on his second day, a much larger number might have been possible as he became better acquainted with his machine. Tex never found out what he might have done, however. He was frightened out of such an effort by two of the older workmen who approached him at the end of that second day and demanded, in a threatening manner, that he cut down his production.

On other jobs with this company, where Tex worked for several years, he encountered similar pressure. When he was given employment underground he was put to work with Tom, an experienced mine-electrician. One of their tasks was to get the material ready, haul it into the mine and put up about 600 feet of mine trolley-wire. The preparations for such a job usually took about a half day. Tex suggested a way in which this time could be cut in half. He was delighted when Tom fell in readily with his suggestion. The material was prepared, hauled into the mine and under the new plan they were ready to put it in place before the morning was half gone. Then Tex got a shock! Tom, instead of going right ahead and putting up the wire, quit work and ordered Tex to do the same. They spent the time "just fooling around" until the hours which had been saved were used up unproductively. . . .

A messenger boy received a lesson in the principle of "cooperation" on his first job. The duties of the messengers took them to offices and shops where interesting people were at work and where interesting things went on. When he joined the group, the other messengers had a habit of stopping here and there on their rounds. This custom had established a sort of standard time for each round. The new boy found that he could make his rounds a lot faster than was usual if he did not stop to chat with the stenographers and watch the mechanics. The other boys soon explained to him that if he hurried from place to place they would have to do the same. This would necessitate giving up the interesting visits to which they were accustomed.

During the first six weeks of Ellen's employment in a large department store, she was at the bargain tables. Sometimes the merchandise sold itself so fast she could hardly handle the customers; at other times, her table would contain such unattractive goods that, try as she would, she could not interest any one. To keep either the extremely slow or the extremely fast pace was very hard for Ellen, and at times her tallies showed alarmingly small totals. She would probably have been dropped if her fellow-workers had not helped her out by sharing their sales with her.

Some time later Ellen was transferred to another department. Here, freed from the excessive peaks and lags, she made a sales record for the department. As a result, the other girls were censured by the buyer for not being able to keep up with her. She was later put at the head of a section and needed the coöperation of the girls. Accordingly, she split her sales with them so that they would not be criticized when their tallies were compared with hers. This plan worked all right until Ellen decided that she was foolish to work on that basis. She began to restrict her efforts, rather than give away the result of her extra work.

✵ E S S A Y S

In the first selection, historian David Montgomery of Yale University describes a late-nineteenth-century world where their unique knowledge of the labor process offered male craftsmen substantial control of the workplace. Setting work rules, first informally and then through their unions, these machinists, iron molders, coal miners, and other skilled and semiskilled men developed an ethos of mutuality grounded in their masculine identity. Strikes, especially those undertaken to support other crafts, marked a willingness to defend their institutions and values against employer encroachments.

In the second essay, Barbara Melosh of George Mason University stresses the significance of gender identity in shaping work culture. Drawing on manuals, memoirs, and fiction, she re-creates the time when nursing was a craft taught through hospital apprenticeship, and not a profession learned in college. She analyzes the culture of the hospital-trained nurse: her commitment to work and sense of craft pride even in a society that generally denied women opportunities for both.

Are all work cultures as oppositional as those of the nineteenth-century craftsman? Could teaching positive self-esteem to nurses undermine the structure of authority in hospital workplaces?

Work Rules and Manliness in the World of the Nineteenth-Century Craftsman

DAVID MONTGOMERY

"In an industrial establishment which employs say from 500 to 1000 workmen, there will be found in many cases at least twenty to thirty different trades," wrote Frederick Winslow Taylor in his famous critique of the practices of industrial management which were then in vogue.

David Montgomery, "Workers' Control of Machine Production in the Nineteenth Century," *Labor History*, 17 (Fall 1976): pp. 485–509. Reprinted by permission of *Labor History*.

The workmen in each of these trades have had their knowledge handed down to them by word of mouth. . . . This mass of rule-of-thumb or traditional knowledge may be said to be the principle asset or possession of every tradesman. . . . [The] foremen and superintendents . . . recognize the task before them as that of inducing each workman to use his best endeavors, his hardest work, all his traditional knowledge, his skill, his ingenuity, and his good-will—in a word, his "initiative," so as to yield the largest possible return to his employer."

Big Bill Haywood put the same point somewhat more pungently, when he declared: "The manager's brains are under the workman's cap."

Both Taylor and Haywood were describing the power which certain groups of workers exercised over the direction of production processes at the end of the nineteenth century, a power which the scientific management movement strove to abolish, and which the Industrial Workers of the World wished to enlarge and extend to all workers. It is important to note that both men found the basis of workers' power in the superiority of their knowledge over that of the factory owners. It is even more important to note that they were referring not to "pre-industrial" work practices, but to the factory itself. . . .

My concern here [is] with the patterns of behavior which took shape in the second and third generations of industrial experience, largely among workers whose world had been fashioned from their youngest days by smoky mills, congested streets, recreation as a week-end affair and toil at the times and the pace dictated by the clock (except when a more or less lengthy layoff meant no work at all). It was such workers, the veterans, if you will, of industrial life, with whom Taylor was preoccupied. They had internalized the industrial sense of time, they were highly disciplined in both individual and collective behavior, and they regarded both an extensive division of labor and machine production as their natural environments. But they had often fashioned from these attributes neither the docile obedience of automatons, nor the individualism of the "upwardly mobile," but a form of control of productive processes which became increasingly collective, deliberate and aggressive, until American employers launched a partially successful counterattack under the banners of scientific management and the open shop drive.

Workers' control of production, however, was not a condition or state of affairs which existed at any point in time, but a struggle, a chronic battle in industrial life which assumed a variety of forms. Those forms may be treated as successive stages in a pattern of historical evolution, though one must always remember that the stages overlapped each other chronologically in different industries, or even at different localities within the same industry, and that each successive stage incorporated the previous one, rather than replacing it. The three levels of development which appeared in the second half of the nineteenth century were those characterized by 1) the functional autonomy of the craftsman, 2) the union work rule, and 3) mutual support of diverse trades in rule enforcement and sympathetic strikes. Each of these levels will be examined here in turn, then in con-

clusion some observations will be made on the impact of scientific management and the open shop drive on the patterns of behavior which they
represented.

The functional autonomy of craftsmen rested on both their superior
knowledge, which made them self-directing at their tasks, and the supervision which they gave to one or more helpers. Iron molders, glass blowers,
coopers, paper machine tenders, locomotive engineers, mule spinners,
boiler makers, pipe fitters, typographers, jiggermen in potteries, coal miners, iron rollers, puddlers and heaters, the operators of McKay or Goodyear
stitching machines in shoe factories, and, in many instances, journeymen
machinists and fitters in metal works exercised broad discretion in the
direction of their own work and that of their helpers. They often hired and
fired their own helpers and paid the latter some fixed portion of their own
earnings.

James J. Davis, who was to end up as Warren Harding's Secretary of
Labor, learned the trade of puddling iron by working as his father's helper
in Sharon, Pennsylvania. "None of us ever went to school and learned the
chemistry of it from books," he recalled. "We learned the trick by doing
it, standing with our faces in the scorching heat while our hands puddled
the metal in its glaring bath." His first job, in fact, had come at the age
of twelve, when an aged puddler devised a scheme to enable him to continue
the physically arduous exertion of the trade by taking on a boy (twelve-
year old Davis) to relieve the helper of mundane tasks like stoking the
furnace, so that the helper in turn could assume a larger share of the taxing
work of stirring the iron as it "came to nature." By the time Davis felt he
had learned enough to master his own furnace, he had to leave Sharon,
because furnaces passed from father to son, and Davis' father was not yet
ready to step down. As late as 1900, when Davis was living at home while
attending business college after having been elected to public office, he
took over his father's furnace every afternoon, through an arrangement the
two had worked out between themselves.

The iron rollers of the Columbus Iron Works, in Ohio, have left us a
clear record of how they managed their trade in the minute books of their
local union from 1873 to 1876. The three twelve-man rolling teams, which
constituted the union, negotiated a single tonnage rate with the company
for each specific rolling job the company undertook. The workers then
decided collectively, among themselves, what portion of that rate should
go to each of them (and the shares were far from equal, ranging from $19\frac{1}{4}$
cents, out of the negotiated $1.13 a ton, for the roller, to 5 cents for the
runout hooker), how work should be allocated among them, how many
rounds on the rolls should be undertaken per day, what special arrangements
should be made for the fiercely hot labors of the hookers during the summer,
and how members should be hired and progress through the various ranks
of the gang. To put it another way, all the boss did was to buy the equipment
and raw materials and sell the finished product. . . .

Three aspects of the moral code, in which the craftsmen's autonomy
was protectively enmeshed, deserve close attention. First, on most jobs

there was a stint, an output quota fixed by the workers themselves. As the laments of scientific management's apostles about workers "soldiering" and the remarkable 1904 survey by the Commissioner of Labor, *Regulation and Restriction of Output*, made clear, stints flourished as widely without unions as with them. Abram Hewitt testified in 1867 that his puddlers in New Jersey, who were not unionized, worked 11 turns per week (5½ days), made three heats per turn, and put 450 pounds of iron in each charge, all by arrangement among themselves. Thirty-five years later a stint still governed the trade, though a dramatic improvement in puddling furnaces was reflected in union rules which specified 11 turns with five heats per turn and 550 pounds per charge (a 104% improvement in productivity), while some nonunion mill workers followed the same routine but boiled bigger charges.

Stints were always under pressure from the employers, and were often stretched over the course of time by the combined force of competition among employers and improving technology. In this instance, productivity under union rules expanded more than three per cent annually over three and half decades. But workers clung doggedly to the practice, and used their superior knowledge both to determine how much they should do and to outwit employers' efforts to wring more production out of them. In a farm equipment factory studied in 1902, for example, the machine shop, polishing department, fitting department and blacksmith shop all had fixed stints, which made each group of workers average very similar earnings despite the fact that all departments were on piecework. . . . Similarly, Taylor's colleague Carl Barth discovered a planer operator who avoided exceeding the stint while always looking busy, by simply removing the cutting tool from his machine from time to time, while letting it run merrily on.

"There is in every workroom a fashion, a habit of work," wrote efficiency consultant Henry Gantt, "and the new worker follows that fashion, for it isn't respectable not to." A quiver full of epithets awaited the deviant: 'hog,' 'hogger-in,' 'leader,' 'rooter,' 'chaser,' 'rusher,' 'runner,' 'swift,' 'boss's pet,' to mention some politer versions. And when a whole factory gained a reputation for feverish work, disdainful craftsmen would describe its occupants, as one did of the Gisholt turret lathe works, as comprised half "of farmers, and the other half, with few exceptions, of horse thieves." On the other hand, those who held fast to the carefully measured stint, despite the curses of their employers and the lure of higher earnings, depicted themselves as sober and trustworthy masters of their trades. Unlimited output led to slashed piece rates, irregular employment, drink and debauchery, they argued. Rationally restricted output, however, reflected "unselfish brotherhood," personal dignity, and "cultivation of the mind."

Second, as this language vividly suggests, the craftsmen's ethical code demanded a "manly" bearing toward the boss. Few words enjoyed more popularity in the nineteenth century than this honorific, with all its connotations of dignity, respectability, defiant egalitarianism, and patriarchal male supremacy. The worker who merited it refused to cower before the foreman's glares—in fact, often would not work at all when a boss was watching. . . .

Finally, "manliness" toward one's fellow workers was as important as it was toward the owners. "Undermining or conniving" at a brother's job was a form of hoggish behavior as objectional as running more than one machine, or otherwise doing the work that belonged to two men. Union rules commanded the expulsion of members who performed such "dirty work," in order to secure employment or advancement for themselves. When the members of the Iron Heaters and Rollers Union at a Philadelphia mill learned in 1875 that one of their brothers had been fired "for dissatisfaction in regard to his management of the mill," and that another member had "undermined" the first with the superintendent and been promised his rolls, the delinquent was expelled from the lodge, along with a lodge member who defended him, and everyone went on strike to demand the immediate discharge of both excommunicates by the firm.

In short, a simple technological explanation for the control exercised by nineteenth-century craftsmen will not suffice. Technical knowledge acquired on the job was embedded in a mutualistic ethical code, also acquired on the job, and together these attributes provided skilled workers with considerable autonomy at their work and powers of resistance to the wishes of their employers. On the other hand, it was technologically possible for the worker's autonomy to be used in individualistic ways, which might promote his own mobility and identify his interests with those of the owner. The ubiquitous practice of subcontracting encouraged this tendency. In the needle trades, the long established custom of a tailor's taking work home to his family was transformed by his employment of other piece workers into the iniquitous "sweat shop" system. Among iron molders, the "berkshire" system expanded rapidly after 1850, as individual molders hired whole teams of helpers to assist them in producing a multitude of castings. Carpenters and bricklayers were lured into piece work systems of petty exploitation, and other forms of subcontracting flourished in stone quarrying, iron mining, anthracite mining, and even in railroad locomotive works, where entire units of an engine's construction were let out to the machinist who filed the lowest bid, and who then hired a crew to assist him in making and fitting the parts.

Subcontracting practices readily undermined both stints and the mutualistic ethic (though contractors were known to fix stints for their own protection in both garment and locomotive works), and they tended to flood many trades with trained, or semi-trained, workers who undercut wages and work standards. Their spread encouraged many craftsmen to move beyond reliance on their functional autonomy to the next higher level of craft control, the enactment and enforcement of union work rules. In one respect, union rules simply codified the autonomy I have already described. In fact, because they were often written down and enforced by joint action, union rules have a visibility to historians, which has made me resort to them already for evidence in the discussion of autonomy per se. But this intimate historical relationship between customary workers' autonomy and the union rule should not blind us to the fact that the latter represents a significant new stage of development.

The work rules of unions were referred to by their members as "legislation." The phrase denotes a shift from spontaneous to deliberate collective action, from a group ethical code to formal rules and sanctions, and from resistance to employers' pretentions to control over them. In some unions the rules were rather simple. The International Association of Machinists, for example, like its predecessors the Machinists and Blacksmiths' International Union and the many machinists' local assemblies of the Knights of Labor, simply specified a fixed term of apprenticeship for any prospective journeyman, established a standard wage for the trade, prohibited helpers or handymen from performing journeymen's work, and forbade any member from running more than one machine at a time or accepting any form of piece work payment.

Other unions had much more detailed and complex rules. There were, for example, sixty-six "Rules for Working" in the by-laws of the window-glass workers' Local Assembly 300 of the Knights of Labor. They specified that full crews had to be present "at each pot setting," that skimming could be done only at the beginning of blowing and at meal time, that blowers and gatherers should not "work faster than at the rate of nine rollers per hour," and that the "standard size of single strength rollers" should "be 40 × 58 to cut 38 × 56." No work was to be performed on Thanksgiving Day, Christmas, Decoration Day or Washington's Birthday, and no blower, gatherer or cutter could work between June 15 and September 15. In other words, during the summer months the union ruled that the fires were to be out. In 1884 the local assembly waged a long and successful strike to preserve its limit of 48 boxes of glass a week, a rule which its members considered the key to the dignity and welfare of the trade.

Nineteenth-century work rules were not ordinarily negotiated with employers or embodied in a contract. From the 1860s onward it became increasingly common for standard *wages* to be negotiated with employers or their associations, rather than fixed unilaterally as unions had tried earlier, but working rules changed more slowly. They were usually adopted unilaterally by local unions, or by the delegates to a national convention, and enforced by the refusal of the individual member to obey any command from an employer which violated them. Hopefully, the worker's refusal would be supported by the joint action of his shop mates, but if it was not, he was honor bound to pack his tool box and walk out alone, rather than break the union's laws. . . .

On the other hand, the autonomy of craftsmen which was codified in union rules was clearly not individualistic. Craftsmen were unmistakably and consciously group-made men, who sought to pull themselves upward by their collective boot straps. As unions waxed stronger after 1886, the number of strikes to enforce union rules grew steadily. It was, however, in union legislation against subcontracting that both the practical and ideological aspects of the conflict between group solidarity and upwardly mobile individualism became most evident, for these rules sought to regulate in the first instance not the employers' behavior, but that of the workers themselves. Thus the Iron Molders Union attacked the "berkshire" system by rules forbidding any of its members to employ a helper for any other purpose than "to skim, shake out and to cut sand," or to pay a helper out of his own earnings. In 1867, when 8,615 out of some 10,400 known molders in the country were union members, the national union legislated further that no member was allowed to go to work earlier than seven o'clock in the morning. During the 1880s the Brick Layers' Union checked subcontracting by banning its members from working for any contractor who could not raise enough capital to buy his own bricks. All building trades unions instructed their members not to permit contractors to work with tools along side with them. . . . All such regulations secured the group welfare of the workers involved by sharply rejecting society's enticements to become petty entrepreneurs, clarifying and intensifying the division of labor at the work place, and sharpening the line between employer and employee.

Where a trade was well unionized, a committee in each shop supervised the enforcement in that plant of the rules and standard wage which the union had adopted for the trade as a whole. The craft union and the craft local assembly of the Knights of Labor were forms of organization well adapted to such regulatory activities. The members were legislating, on matters on which they were unchallenged experts, rules which only their courage and solidarity could enforce. On one hand, the craft form of organization linked their personal interests to those of the trade, rather than those of the company in which they worked, while, on the other hand, their efforts to enforce the same rules on all of their employers, where they were successful, created at least a few islands of order in the nineteenth-century's economic ocean of anarchic competition.

Labor organizations of the late nineteenth century struggled persistently to transform workers' struggles to manage their own work from spontaneous to deliberate actions, just as they tried to subject wage strikes and efforts to shorten the working day to their conscious regulation. "The trade union movement is one of reason, one of deliberation, depending entirely upon the voluntary and sovereign actions of its members," declared the executive Council of the AFL. Only through "thorough organization," to use a favorite phrase of the day, was it possible to enforce a trade's work rules throughout a factory, mine, or construction site. Despite the growing number of strikes over union rules and union recognition in the late 1880s, the enforcement of workers' standards of control spread more often through the daily self-assertion of craftsmen on the job than through large and dramatic strikes.

Conversely, strikes over wage reductions at times involved thinly disguised attacks by employers on craftsmen's job controls. Fall River's textile manufacturers in 1870 and the Hocking Valley coal operators in 1884, to cite only two examples, deliberately foisted severe wage reductions on their highly unionized workers in order to provoke strikes. The owners' hope was that in time hunger would force their employees to abandon union membership, and thus free the companies' hands to change production methods. As the treasurer of one Fall River mill testified in 1870: "I think the question with the spinners was not wages, but whether they or the manufacturers should rule. For the last six or eight years they have ruled Fall River." Defeat in a strike temporarily broke the union's control, which had grown through steady recruiting and rule enforcement during years which were largely free of work stoppages.

The third level of control struggles emerged when different trades lent each other support in their battles to enforce union rules and recognition. An examination of the strike statistics gathered by the U.S. Commissioner of Labor for the period 1881–1905 reveals the basic patterns of this development. Although there had been a steady increase in both the number and size of strikes between 1881 and 1886, the following 12 years saw a reversal of that growth, as stoppages became both smaller and increasingly confined to skilled crafts (except in 1894). With that change came three important and interrelated trends. First, the proportion of strikes called by unions rose sharply in comparison to spontaneous strikes. Nearly half of all strikes between 1881 and 1886 had occurred without union sanction or aid. In the seven years beginning with 1887 more than two-thirds of each year's strikes were deliberately called by a union, and in 1891 almost 75 per cent of the strikes were official.

Secondly, as strikes became more deliberate and unionized, the proportion of strikes which dealt mainly with wages fell abruptly. Strikes to enforce union rules, enforce recognition of the union, and protect its members grew from 10 per cent of the total or less before 1885 to the level of 19–20 per cent between 1891 and 1893. Spontaneous strikes and strikes of laborers and factory operatives had almost invariably been aimed at increasing wages or preventing wage reductions, with the partial exception of 1886 when 20 per cent of all strikes had been over hours. The more highly craftsmen became organized, however, the more often they struck and were locked out over work rules.

Third, unionization of workers grew on the whole faster than strike participation. The ratio of strike participants to membership in labor organizations fell almost smoothly from 109 in 1881 to 24 in 1888, rose abruptly in 1890 and 1891 (to 71 and 86, respectively), then resumed its downward trend to 36 in 1898, interrupted, of course, by a leap to 182 in 1894. In a word, calculation and organization were the dominant tendencies in strike activity, just as they were in the evolution of work rules during the nineteenth century. But the assertion of deliberate control through formal organization was sustained not only by high levels of militancy (a persistently high propensity to strike), but also by remarkably aggressive mutual support, which sometimes took the form of the unionization of all grades of workers within a single industry, but more often appeared in the form of sympathetic strikes involving members of different trade unions.

Joint organization of all grades of workers seemed most likely to flourish where no single craft clearly dominated the life of the workplace, in the way iron molders, brick layers, or iron puddlers did where they worked. It was also most likely to appear at the crest of the waves of strike activity among unskilled workers and operatives, as is hardly surprising, and to offer evidence of the organizational impulse in their ranks. In Philadelphia's shoe industry between 1884 and 1887, for example, the Knights of Labor successfully organized eleven local assemblies, ranging in size from 55 to 1000 members, each of which represented a different craft or cluster of related occupations, and formulated wage demands and work rules for its own members. Each assembly sent three delegates to District Assembly 70, the highest governing body of the Knights for the industry, which in turn selected seven representatives to meet in a city-wide arbitration committee with an equal number of employers' representatives. Within each factory a "shop union" elected by the workers in that plant handled grievances and enforced the rules of the local assemblies, aided by one male and one female "statistician," who kept track of the complex piece rates.

There is no evidence that local assemblies of unskilled workers or of semi-skilled operatives ever attempted to regulate production processes themselves in the way assemblies of glass blowers and other craftsmen did. They did try to restrict hiring to members of the Knights and sometimes regulated layoffs by seniority clauses. For the most part, however, assemblies of operatives and laborers confined their attention to wages and to protection of their members against arbitrary treatment by supervisors. On the other hand, the mere fact that such workers had been organized made it difficult for employees to grant concessions to their craftsmen at the expense of helpers and laborers. Consequently, the owners were faced simultaneously with higher wage bills and a reduction of their control in a domain where they had been accustomed to exercise unlimited authority.

Moreover, workers who directed important production processes were themselves at times reluctant to see their own underlings organized, and frequently sought to dominate the larger organization to which their helpers belonged. A case in point was offered by the experience of the Knights of Labor in the garment industry, where contractors were organized into local assemblies of their own, supposedly to cooperate with those of cutters, pressers, tailors, and sewing machine operators. Contractors were often charged with disrupting the unionization of their own employees, in order to promote their personal competitive advantages. Above all, they tried to discourage women from joining the operators' assemblies. As the secretary of a St. Louis tailors' local assembly revealed, contractors who were his fellow Knights were telling the parents of operators that "no dissent [sic] girl belong to an assembly."

On the other hand, the experience of the Knights in both the shoe and garment industries suggests that effective unionization of women operatives was likely to have a remarkably radicalizing impact on the organization. It closed the door decisively both on employers who wished to compensate for higher wages paid to craftsmen by exacting more from the unskilled, and on craftsmen who were tempted to advance themselves by sweating others. In Philadelphia, Toronto, Cincinnati, Beverly, and Lynn both the resistance of the manufacturers to unionism and the level of mutuality exhibited by the workers leapt upward noticeably when the women shoe workers organized along with the men. Furthermore, the sense of total organization made all shoe workers more exacting in their demands and less patient with the protracted arbitration procedures employed by the Knights. Quickie strikes became increasingly frequent as more and more shoe workers enrolled in the Order. Conversely, the shoe manufacturers banded tightly together to destroy the Knights of Labor.

In short, the organization of all grades of workers in any industry propelled craftsmen's collective rule making into a more aggressive relationship with the employers, even where it left existing styles of work substantially unchanged. The other form of joint action, sympathetic strikes, most often involved the unionized skilled crafts themselves, and consequently was more directly related to questions of control of production processes. When Fred S. Hall wrote in 1898 that sympathetic strikes had "come so much in vogue during the last few years," he was looking back on a period during which organized workers had shown a greater tendency to walk out in support of the struggles of other groups of workers than was the case in any other period in the history of recorded strike data. Only the years between 1901 and 1904 and those between 1917 and 1921 were to see the absolute number of sympathetic strikes approach even *one-half* the levels of 1890 and 1891.

There were, in fact, two distinct crests in the groundswell of sympathetic strikes. The first came between 1886 and 1888, when a relatively small number of disputes, which spread by sympathetic action to include vast numbers of workers, caught public attention in a dramatic way. The Southwest railways strike of 1886, the New York freight handlers dispute of 1887, and the Lehigh coal and railroad stoppages of 1888 exemplified this trend. None of them, however, primarily involved control questions, in the sense they have been described here.

The second crest, that of 1890–92, was quite different. It was dominated by relatively small stoppages of organized craftsmen. In New York state, where the Bureau of Labor Statistics collected detailed information on such stoppages until 1892 (and included in its count strikes which were omitted from the U.S. Commissioner of Labor's data because they lasted less than a single day or included fewer than six workers), the number of establishments shut by sympathetic strikes rose from an average of 166 yearly between 1886 and 1889 to 732 in 1890, 639 in 1891, and 738 in 1892. Most of them involved the employees of a single company, like the 15 machinists who struck in support of the claims of molders in their factory or the four marble cutters who walked out to assist paper hangers on the same site. A few were very large. When New York's cabinet makers struck to preserve their union in 1892, for example, 107 carpenters, 14 gilders, 75 marble cutters and helpers, 17 painters, 23 plasterers, 28 porters, 12 blue stone cutters, 14 tile layers and helpers, 32 upholsterers, 14 varnishers, 149 wood carvers, and others walked out of more than 100 firms to lend their support.

Eugene V. Debs was to extol this extreme manifestation of mutuality as the "Christ-like virtue of sympathy," and to depict his own Pullman boycott, the epoch's most massive sympathetic action, as an open confrontation between that working-class virtue and a social order which sanctified selfishness. It is true that the mutualistic ethic which supported craftsmen's control was displayed in its highest form by sympathetic strikes. It is equally true, however, that the element of calculation, which was increasingly dominating all strike activity, was particularly evident here. As Fred S. Hall pointed out, sympathetic strikes of this epoch differed sharply from "contagious" strikes, which spread spontaneously like those of 1877, in two respects. First, the sympathetic strikes were called by the workers involved, through formal union procedures. Although figures comparing official with unofficial strikes are not available, two contrasting statistics illustrate Hall's point. The construction industry was always the leading center of sympathetic strikes. In New York more than 70 per cent of the establishments shut by sympathetic action between 1890 and 1892 were involved in building construction. On the other hand, over the entire period of federal data (1881–1905) no less than 98.03 per cent of the strikes in that industry were called by unions.

Second, as Hall observed, the tendency toward sympathetic strikes was "least in those cases where the dispute concerns conditions of employment such as wages and hours, and [was] greatest in regard to disputes which involve questions of unionism—the employment of only union men, the recognition of the union, etc." The rise of sympathetic strikes, like the rise of strikes over rules and recognition, was part of the struggle for craftsmen's control—its most aggressive and far-reaching manifestation.

It is for this reason that the practice of sympathetic strikes was ardently defended by the AFL in the 1890s. Building trades contracts explicitly provided for sympathetic stoppages. Furthermore, at the Federation's 1895 convention a resolution carried, directing the Executive Council to "convey to the unions, in such way as it thinks proper, not to tie themselves up with contracts so that they cannot help each other when able." The Council itself denied in a report to the same convention that it opposed sympathetic strikes. "On the contrary," it declared, "we were banded together to help one another. The words union, federation, implied it. An organization which held aloof when assistance could be given to a sister organization, was deserving of censure," even though each union had the right to decide its own course of action.

On the other hand, not all unions supported this policy by any means. Under the right conditions it was just as possible for work processes to be regulated by the rules of a craft union which stood aloof from all appeals to class solidarity, as it was for an individual craftsman to identify his functional autonomy to his employer's interests through subcontracting. Precisely such a solitary course was proudly pursued by the locomotive engineers and firemen. In general, where a union was strong enough to defy its employers alone and where no major technological innovations threatened its members' work practices, it tended to reach an accommodation with the employers on the basis of the latter's more or less willing recognition of the union's work rules. . . .

[E]mployers in many industries banded together in the early 1890s to resist sympathetic strikes, union rules and union recognition with increasing vigor and effectiveness. Sympathetic lockouts were mounted by employers' organizations to deny striking workers alternative sources of employment or financial support. Legal prosecutions for conspiracy in restraint of trade, including use of the Sherman Anti-Trust Act against the Workingmen's Amalgamated Council of New Orleans for the city-wide sympathetic strike of 1892, and court-ordered injunctions provided supplementary weapons. In this setting, unionized craftsmen suffered a growing number of defeats. Whereas less than 40 per cent of the strikes of 1889 and 1890 had been lost by the workers, 54.5 per cent of the strikes of 1891 and 53.9 per cent of those of 1892 were unsuccessful. This level of defeats was by far the highest for the late nineteenth century, and would not be approached again until 1904. The losses are all the more remarkable when one recalls that these were record years for union-called strikes (as opposed to spontaneous strikes), and that throughout the 1881 to 1905 period strikes called by unions tended to succeed in better than 70 per cent of the cases, while spontaneous strikes were lost in almost the same proportion. The explanation for the high level of defeats in calculated strikes of 1891 and 1892 lies in the audacity of the workers' demands. Official strikes over wages remained eminently successful. The fiercest battles and the bitterest losses pivoted around union rules and recognition and around sympathetic action itself.

Consequently trade unionists began to shy away from sympathetic strikes in practice, despite their verbal defenses, even before 1894. The statistical appearance of a crescendo of sympathetic strikes in 1894 followed by an abrupt collapse is misleading. Hall suggests that crafts other than the building trades were becoming hesitant to come out in sympathy with other groups, especially with workers from other plants, from 1892 onward. Although the New York data ends that year, it seems to bear him out in an interesting way. The total number of sympathetic strikes in New York was as great in 1892 as it had been in 1890. On the other hand, 67 per cent of those strikes had been in the building trades in 1890, as compared to 69 per cent in 1891 and 84 per cent in 1892. One wishes the figures had continued, so as to reveal whether the small numbers of such strikes after 1895 were confined to construction. In any event, even in 1892 more than 100 of the 120 establishments outside of the building trades which were hit by sympathetic strikes were involved in a single conflict, that of the cabinet makers. And the workers ultimately abandoned that battle in total defeat. In this context the resurgence of such strikes in 1894 appears as an aberration. Indeed, the Pullman boycott and the bituminous coal strike together accounted for 94 per cent of the establishments shut by sympathy actions in the first six months of that year.

. . . As craftsmen unionized, they not only made their struggles for control increasingly collective and deliberate, but also manifested a *growing* consciousness of the dependence of their efforts on those of workers in other crafts. They drew strength in this struggle from their functional autonomy, which was derived from their superior knowledge, exercised through self-direction and their direction of others at work, and both nurtured and in turn was nurtured by a mutualistic ethic, which repudiated important elements of acquisitive individualism. As time passed this autonomy was increasingly often codified in union rules, which were collectively "legislated" and upheld through the commitment of the individual craftsmen and through a swelling number of strikes to enforce them. Organized efforts reached the most aggressive and inclusive level of all in joint action among the various crafts for mutual support. When such actions enlisted all workers in an industry (as happened when women unionized in shoe manufacturing), and when they produced a strong propensity of unionized craftsmen to strike in support of each other's claims, they sharply separated the aggressive from the conservative consequences of craftsmen's autonomy and simultaneously provoked an intense, concerted response from the business community.

In an important sense, the last years of the depression represented only a lull in the battle. With the return of prosperity in 1898, both strikes and union organizing quickly resumed their upward spiral, work rules again seized the center of the stage, and sympathetic strikes became increasingly numerous and bitterly fought. Manufacturers' organizations leapt into the fray with the open shop drive, while their spokesmen cited new government surveys to support their denunciations of workers "restriction of output."

On the other hand, important new developments distinguished the first decade of the twentieth century from what had gone before. Trade union officials, who increasingly served long terms in full-time salaried positions, sought to negotiate the terms of work with employers, rather than letting their members "legislate" them. The anxiety of AFL leaders to secure trade agreements and to ally with "friendly employers," like those affiliated with the National Civic Federation, against the open shop drive, prompted them to repudiate the use of sympathetic strikes. The many such strikes which took place were increasingly lacking in union sanction and in any event never reached the level of the early 1890s.

Most important of all, new methods of industrial management undermined the very foundation of craftsmen's functional autonomy. Job analysis through time and motion study allowed management to learn, then to systematize the way the work itself was done. Coupled with systematic supervision and new forms of incentive payment it permitted what Frederick Winslow Taylor called "*enforced* standardization of methods, *enforced* adoption of the best implements and working conditions, and *enforced* cooperation of all the employees under management's detailed direction." Scientific management, in fact, fundamentally disrupted the craftsmen's styles of work, their union rules and standard rates, and their mutualistic ethic, as it transformed American industrial practice between 1900 and 1930. Its basic effect, as Roethlisberger and Dickson discovered in their experiments at Western Electric's Hawthorne Works, was to place the worker "at the bottom level of a highly stratified organization," leaving his "established routines of work, his cultural traditions of craftsmanship, [and] his personal interrelations" all "at the mercy of technical specialists."

Two important attributes of the scientific management movement become evident only against the background of the struggles of nineteenth-century craftsmen to direct their own work in their own collective way. First, the appeal of the new managerial techniques to manufacturers involved more than simply a response to new technology and a new scale of business organization. It also implied a conscious endeavor to uproot those work practices which had been the taproot of whatever strength organized labor enjoyed in the late nineteenth century. A purely technological explanation of the spread of Taylorism is every bit as inadequate as a purely technological explanation of craftsmen's autonomy.

Second, the apostles of scientific management needed not only to abolish older industrial work practices, but also to discredit them in the public eye. Thus Taylor roundly denied that even "the high class mechanic" could "ever thoroughly understand the science of doing his work," and pasted the contemptuous label of "soldiering" over all craft rules, formal and informal alike. Progressive intellectuals seconded his arguments. Louis Brandeis hailed scientific management for "reliev[ing] labor of responsibilities not its own." And John R. Commons considered it "immoral to hold up to this miscellaneous labor, as a class, the hope that it can ever manage industry." If some workers do "shoulder responsibility," he explained, "it is because certain *individuals* succeed, and then those individuals immediately close the doors, and labor, as a class, remains where it was."

It was in this setting that the phrase "workers' control" first entered the vocabulary of the American labor movement. It appeared to express a radical, if often amorphous, set of demands which welled up around the end of World War I among workers in the metal trades, railroading, coal mining, and garment industries. Although those demands represented very new styles of struggle in a unique industrial and political environment, many of the workers who expressed them could remember the recent day when in fact, the manager's brains had been under the workman's cap.

The Work Culture of Nurses

BARBARA MELOSH

. . . Hospital schools trained the overwhelming majority of nurses, and most of them inculcated their charges with a view of nursing that diverged rather sharply from leaders' visions. Apprenticeship stood at the center of the hospital school's method and mission. Although in part a managerial strategy, it was also an ideology of what nursing should be and a carefully articulated method for making young women into competent and committed nurses.

An early ethics manual advised that "to become a good trained nurse, development must come from three sides—the hands, the heart, and the head." Defenders of the hospital schools heartily endorsed that sentiment and would have approved the order as well. They valued the craft skills of nursing—gentle hands, a deft injection, careful handling of the patient in pain. The cold objectivity of an academic degree was no fit measure of "the nursing heart," and classroom work could do little to nurture the qualities of an ideal nurse: "a sense of honor, a sense of humor, a sense of order, a humane heart, patience and self-control." Superintendents of hospital schools confidently set out to mold their human material to these exacting requirements. For these women, nursing education was more than the mastery of a body of knowledge, it was a moral initiation: "The drilling and disciplining of the woman inside the nurse, the development of a right attitude of mind and right habits of life, are the most difficult as well as the most important part in the making of a nurse."

These sweeping objectives were both the weakness and the strength of the hospital schools. Setting out "to shape the young nurse's total personality," superintendents could claim broad authority over students' lives, and very broad prerogatives for themselves. The paternalistic discipline of the hospital could be petty and arbitrary, alienating independent young women. At times, the defense of craft skills and empathy verged on anti-intellectualism: some nurses resisted the very notion of liberal education with unreasoning vehemence. Yet the same ideology provided nurses with strong preparation and motivation to work. Rooted deeply in the realities of the ward, hospital programs gave nurses a direct socialization into the work they would do as graduates. Moreover, the insularity of the schools and the intensity of hospital life comprised a powerful rite of passage. Separated from the claims of the larger culture, a bit distant from its prescriptions for women, nursing students might find new and compelling models for female commitment to work.

Manuals, oral and written memoirs, and fiction reveal the emotional impact of the student nurse's apprenticeship. Graduates from the 1920s and the 1950s retell their experiences of training in strikingly similar ways: common perceptions and values blur the actual historical differences in their educations. These are narratives of initiation, of a journey from innocence to knowledge. As they begin, the narrator is an outsider describing the initial strangeness and threat of the hospital world. The trials and rituals of ward duty challenge her, and gradually she learns the skills and discipline of a nurse. Once inept at ward duties, frightened or repelled by hospital life, the young nurse comes to master her responsibilities and take pride in her abilities. Advancing through the training course, she gains the perspective and privileges of the insider. . . .

Hospital superintendents maintained strict control over students' work and social lives, exercising an authority that extended well past the normal limits of school or workplace discipline. Student nurses had to live in the hospital nursing residence, cut off from familiar surroundings, family, and friends. Long working hours, early curfews, and prohibitions against socializing with male co-workers further constrained their social lives. The demands of ward duty, as interpreted by the superintendent, reigned over all other considerations. A student nurse had little time that she could call her own. Superiors arranged her ward hours and classroom schedules, determined her meal times and study hours, and governed her hours of sleep. On or off duty, her appearance and demeanor had to conform to rigid standards of propriety. At one training school in 1918, for example, students were not permitted to cut their hair; in the 1930s, another superintendent forbad bleached hair. Supervisors inspected students' rooms and mustered their nurses before ward duty for inspection. One nurse remembered ruefully that everyone in the school was required to wear her uniform sixteen inches from the floor, regardless of her own height; the superintendent, a stickler for symmetry, wanted her students' hems to form an unbroken line when the group assembled. Even the most intimate bodily functions might come under the superintendent's relentless scrutiny. In an extreme example, one article urged superintendents to record each student's menstrual periods, to provide "anti-constipation" diets, and to segregate "fat and lean" groups in the dining room, with appropriate foods for each. Discipline, efficiency, and regularity could go no farther.

From her first days at school, the student nurse learned the elaborate rituals of hospital hierarchy. Advice manuals presented "hospital etiquette" as a symbol of respect for superiors and a sign of the nurse's own seriousness and responsibility. One description conveys the ceremonial quality of professional deference. "The head-nurse and her staff should stand to receive the visiting physician, and from the moment of his entrance until his departure, the attending nurses should show themselves alert, attentive, and courteous, like soldiers on duty." In the same way, entering students deferred to their nursing superiors, including superintendents, directors, head nurses, instructors, and students in the upper classes. In the 1920s, seniority systems applied even within the first-year class: students were arbitrarily ranked in the order that they arrived at the training school. . . .

In accepting the rigid codes of hospital hierarchy, the young woman left behind her old social life and adopted the new order of the hospital. One nurse novel dramatized this moment. Walking down the hall with her class, a probationer catches sight of an old friend, an intern who had convinced her to enroll in the training school. When she greets him warmly, he rebuffs her, enforcing the hospital code of formality and distance. As another new nurse discovers indignantly, the hospital's military respect for rank reversed the usual etiquette between men and women. "For the first time in my life, I'm stepping back from a door to let a man pass through first: Doctors first, always."

The probationary period, usually about three to six months, tested the young woman's commitment to nursing and her fitness for the work. The transition from laywoman to nurse began in earnest when the neophyte first entered the ward. In the teens and early 1920s, student nurses often took on ward duties within their first week at the hospital, and some probationers were assigned to full twelve-hour shifts. Through the 1920s and 1930s, such long hours became less common, but students still spent at least two to four hours a day on the ward during their first months. Set to work on menial tasks, the probationer underwent another form of ritual mortification and began to observe and adjust to hospital life.

One nurse, trained in the teens, humorously described her dawning awareness of a nurse's duties. "Who, I began to wonder, was to serve the lowly bedpans, hold the vomitus basins, change the smelly dressings, administer the blood transfusions and enemas?" . . . Another remembered her first day at school: she was sent to the operating room, where someone handed her an amputated foot to carry off. Under such duress, young women quickly revised their romantic visions of holding patients' hands and soothing fevered brows.

The structure and content of probationers' work clearly indicated the schools' emphasis on practical over academic credentials. Before 1920, theoretical education was often provided by different physicians who lectured on their specialties in a loosely organized curriculum. Exhausted students could give only perfunctory attention to the lectures, which were held at night or during breaks in a twelve-hour shift. Students often seized the opportunity for some much-needed sleep. Most schools began to organize more systematic classroom work and to hire full-time nursing faculty in the 1920s and 1930s, but student nurses continued to provide most of the hospital nursing service through 1950. Nursing arts—techniques of handling patients, giving routine care, and administering treatments—were taught in the classrooms, where students first practiced on "Mrs. Chase," the ubiquitous life-sized model, and then on each other. Later, on duty, students tested their skills under the supervision of an instructor or an advanced student, and gradually perfected their techniques in the constant repetition of the ward routine. Students had to perform credibly in their academic work, but the real test lay elsewhere.

Student nurses were evaluated after the first few months of probation, and the successful ones were honored in the ritual of capping. They still wore the stripes and pinafores of students, but they had attained the white caps that distinguished graduate nurses. They began to work full days on the ward, rotating through the hospital's different services. Soon after capping, the nurse took her first tour of night duty. Alone on the floor, she watched patients through the long hours of darkness. As a junior, or second-year, nurse, she might take charge of a busy ward during the day. Senior, or third-year, nurses, resplendent in their newly acquired whites, routinely ran the floors and helped to instruct less experienced students. At commencement, proud new nurses accepted their diplomas and the black bands that circle the white caps of graduate nurses.

To survive these rites of passage, the student had to acquire the stern discipline of the nurse. Strict rules of conduct offered young women a model of the controlled life. Her personal demeanor had to be schooled to the same standards. The impulsiveness of youth, the undisciplined license of lay life, had no place in the hospital. As the fictional Sue Barton begins her nursing career, a supervisor lectures the new students, "She has a grave responsibility and her manner should be in keeping with it. Personal adornment and personal pleasures must be put aside." . . . Tempered by experience, this control would make the nurse equal to the challenges of hospital life.

Professional demeanor helped nurses to defend their emotions against the shocks of hospital life, and discipline guided their adjustment to unfamiliar and threatening situations. Both the physical intimacy of nursing and its psychological associations with sex and death made the work "dirty." Nurses' access to patients' bodies violated the boundaries of normal social relationships. They touched strangers and matter-of-factly dealt with their mucus, blood, urine, feces, vomitus, and bile. Nursing brought women into sustained contact with sickness and death, experiences that evoked fear and disgust in laypersons. Through overt instruction and by example, student nurses learned inner discipline and shared rituals that helped to ward off their own uneasiness.

Memoirs and manuals contained anecdotes and special instructions on the hazards of male patients, acknowledging the cultural sensitivity of that relationship. As a long tradition of jokes, popular fiction, and pornography also shows, the nurse's physical contact with patients is charged with sexual associations. . . . [A] nurse revealed the presence and threat of these sexual associations when asked if she had gotten any specific instructions about caring for male patients. A 1953 graduate, she laughed nervously and said, "Now how do you mean that? No, no, no, no, never, never, never—we were not *female*—we were *nurses*."

Nurses were taught to use professional demeanor to dissociate themselves from the sexual intimations of physical contact. The nurse's professional poise and self-control framed the situation, marking it off from ordinary social encounters between men and women. Approaching her task impersonally, the young woman silently instructed her patient that their contact was strictly business. "No nurse can too soon learn the importance that tone and manner assume in such relations," one manual emphasized. Others advised nurses to maintain their professional distance by avoiding "familiarity." One admonished nurses never to tell patients their first names, and warned students that some patients might even "contrive to remove concealing drapes." Such advice defended the nurse's identity as a young woman from the contamination that patients might associate with her duties; as one discussion concluded, "Being a nurse in no way makes you less a lady."

If male patients could fluster an inexperienced nurse, her exposure to sick and dying patients posed an even more severe trial to her self-control. In oral and written memoirs, nurses portray their early experiences with death in sharp detail. Often intense and deeply moving, sometimes grotesque or comical, these stories show how nurses learned to accept their responsibility for patients and to manage the emotional strain of death.

For many, hard work helped to control emotions that might otherwise have become overwhelming. Over and over, nurses explained that they overcame their fear of the responsibility of night duty by throwing themselves into their tasks. Confronted with emergencies, nurses discovered their resources for coping. One nurse who entered training in 1918 almost immediately faced overflowing wards and morgues as influenza struck her city. An inexperienced probationer, she learned quickly to lay out corpses. "It had to be done, so you did it." Even under more ordinary circumstances, the busy routine of classes, ward duty, and study left little time for introspection.

More experienced nurses helped their charges to accept death as an inevitable part of their work. One nurse recalled the support of her supervising nurse during a difficult experience. As the hours crawled by on her first night duty, the student heard her patient lapse into Cheyne-Stokes respiration, the labored and erratic breathing of the dying. She called for the night supervisor, who questioned her about the patient's condition and then quietly confirmed the young woman's assessment. She asked the student about the nursing care she had given, and then concluded, "We have done everything we can to make this patient comfortable, but she is dying. There is nothing more you can do." In this understated way, the supervisor marked out the limits of nursing involvement. She commended the student for her careful observation and responsibility, and at the same time taught her to face a patient's impending death without guilt or panic.

Supervisors tacitly acknowledged students' emotions in the face of death, but they insisted on self-control. One nurse's memoir described her lonely watch with a young dying patient and her overwhelming emotion as the end approached. She resolved, "I must steady myself. It will never do to go to pieces like this at the last moment." The child died soon after, and she carried his body to the morgue. Reporting the death to her night supervisor, she rebelled inwardly against the older woman's calmness, yet drew strength from her example. Later in the night, the supervisor stopped by to comfort the student, but gently told her that she must develop a nurse's self-command. Another supervisor skillfully used the seniority system to bolster a quavering student. The young nurse controlled herself until her patient died, but then "became totally unstrung." She begged the head nurse not to leave her alone with the corpse, traditionally attended by a nurse until the undertaker arrived. The supervisor left the room but sent in "a little probationer. . . . Of course I tried to act brave then, for the sake of the other girl who had been there only a few days." Gradually she learned the nurse's stoic creed: "A nurse must take things as they come."

Such counsel was not easy to live by. Nurses' narratives indicate the emotional strain of their work. Intriguingly, their memories of patients' deaths usually include physical descriptions that are vividly realistic, even naturalistic. Nurses frequently recalled the trauma of the nurse's last service to her patient, the physical care of the corpse. No doubt they remembered this experience because it was especially unfamiliar and shocking to them as students, and their frank accounts were a way for them to come to terms with death. By naming feared realities, nurses claimed control over them. Yet the content and tone of these narratives reveal a lingering uneasiness. . . .

Manuals, novels, and prescriptive literature indicate the tension between prescriptions for work and for gender; to a striking degree, they dwell on the troublesome issue of professional demeanor. The ideology of discipline countered and challenged the dominant culture by inculcating young women with an image of female strength. Narratives of initiation during hospital apprenticeship show students overcoming the conflict between work and gender in resolutions that affirm women's control and competence on the job.

The literature struggled with the problem of maintaining professional demeanor and warned of the pitfalls of callousness and sentimentality, two words that constantly recur. Manuals tacitly acknowledged cultural claims on women in advising young nurses to guard against becoming hardened and cynical. Similarly, the authors of nursing novels addressed the cultural anomaly of female detachment through characters who were novices. In the novel *Into the Wind*, for example, a new student observes her more seasoned roommates with mixed feelings. "They're as human as your own family when they're grousing about having to get out of bed, and they're as—as impersonal as lamp-posts when they're ready to go *on,* as they call it." In the same fashion, the spirited probationer of a fictionalized memoir reflects doubtfully on the advice to remain objective: "I was deeply moved as I looked into her patient little face, wondering how a nurse could reconcile her two separate selves, one the indifferent, cold, calculating creature who took things impersonally, held fast to rules, crowded out all impulses of kindness: and the other gentle, tolerant, patient, and understanding." . . .

In place of religious faith was a pragmatic ideology that directed nurses to earthly goals, motivating them to learn emotional control for the sake of success in work. Prescriptive literature resisted the negative connotations of professional demeanor for women, rejecting the layperson's association of self-control with callousness. Didactic stories and advice left no room for doubt: the nurse had to achieve emotional discipline to do her work. This message appeared so predictably in manuals, memoirs, and novels that it sometimes took on a rehearsed quality, as one nurse's recollections illustrate: "We soon learned that we could not be nurses of calm judgment and steady nerves unless we detached ourselves entirely from the personal element in every case," she explained. "This does not mean that we were callous to human suffering but rather that we sought to relieve our feelings by skillful help rather than through emotion." Such control carried personal costs, as these sources conceded implicitly, but the rewards and satisfactions of successful nursing would outweigh the losses.

Initiation narratives powerfully reinforced this ideology. They portrayed students who resolve their doubt and ambivalence about professional distance in the certainty of a full commitment to nursing. . . .

I Was a Probationer traces a student's exposure to professional demeanor and her gradual acceptance of its underlying ideology. An intern observes the young nurse's dismay at a child's death and tells her, "You'll be able to take it as part of your work in time. . . . Time makes all of us callous. . . . If we let our emotions carry us away, we might not be able to do for the patient what must be done." As she learns to care for a badly burned patient, her senior nurse warns her about the excruciating pain she will inflict when she changes the dressings, and advises, "Now don't go under. Just remember it's another case. Say to yourself that you are trying to relieve suffering, that everything is being done that is humanly possible. I know how you'll feel."

As her training progresses, the student acquires the discipline of hospital life, and affirms the value of control. Nursing a patient with advanced gangrene, she reflects, "Two months before, I would have been revolted at the sight of her rotting foot, but now I accepted it without letting it touch me emotionally. That was the way nurses became callous to suffering, and I was beginning to see that it was a fortunate adjustment. Otherwise they could not endure the demands made upon them." This initiation is complete when she and her classmate begin to pass on the lesson to the new entering class. When a naive probationer gives an emotionally colored account of her patient's plight, the seasoned students admonish her sharply. "It's all right to have a certain amount of pity for suffering, but there's nothing about a pan of saffron vomit that makes me feel sentimental. Forget your feelings. You've got to face the repulsive side as well as the sentimental."

Didactic fiction often dramatized the culmination of apprenticeship, the moment when a student comes to identify herself as a nurse. Confronted with the test of a sudden emergency, Sue Barton thinks quickly and saves the day. She takes pride in this evidence of her developing skill and competence, and stops to reflect on her gradual transformation from laywoman to nurse when she returns briefly to her old world. On a short visit home, she feels distant from her once-familiar circle of family and friends. "Her real life was in the hospital now. . . . Invisible cords bound her to it, for she was a born nurse. She knew it, now." Some accounts explicitly pose the conflict between work and private life, especially romance. In one fictional example, Cherry Ames, the heroine of a series of nursing adventures, is called from the Christmas dance to cover a short-staffed floor. Changing from her black lace dress to hospital whites, she feels inspired by a new sense of duty. "The hospital uniform came first." . . . Such stories ran against cultural prescriptions for women, and indeed against a broader cultural emphasis on private life and leisure, to affirm the value of satisfying work.

One common feature of student culture suggests another level at which young women sought to resolve the conflicts between gender and work. Leaving their old identities behind, students frequently coined new names for one another. Memoirs and novels provide many examples. An especially rich source is the column "Calling All Nurses," a regular feature in *RN* that printed letters from nurses trying to locate former classmates or coworkers. In virtually every example, these names were neuter or masculine, perhaps symbolizing students' recognition of the "masculine" character of their work. Nurses often addressed their peers by their last names. Very likely this usage developed as an irreverent abbreviation of the hospital etiquette, which mandated formality. Common among men, the familiar use of last names was more unusual for women. Nurses also dubbed each other with inventive nicknames. Female or feminine tags were very rare;

one "Mother" Mount stood out from dozens of others. Sometimes pet names came from the medical language nurses shared; one pair of students named themselves "Morphine" and "Atropine." Many others were masculine diminutives, usually invented from students' surnames: Gertrude Peterson answered to "Pete," Iona McCoy was called "Mac," Helen L. Donoghue was "Donnie," and "Althea" was quickly shortened to "Al." Others resolutely defied gender classification, like "Smoky" Phillips, "Wicky" (Olive Wagner), and "Mergie" (Elsie M. Bernhoft). In renaming one another, student nurses selected names that pushed feminine associations into the background.

This distinctive culture did not go unchallenged as the enclosed female world of the hospital school became increasingly anachronistic. More colleges and universities began admitting "co-eds," the developing field of psychology celebrated romantic heterosexuality, and popular culture and social life focused more and more on the heterosexual couple. Responding uneasily to the mounting pressure on same-sex institutions, manuals advised students to moderate their relationships with other women. Overt references to homosexuality appear even in early prescriptive literature—even though nursing courses did not include basic material on sex and birth control until the 1950s and 1960s.

A 1900 manual cautioned, "Towards fellow probationers and the other nurses in the ward it is best not to be too familiar or too friendly; sudden, violent friendships are undesirable and unnecessary. . . . Sentimental, intense personal friendships between nurses are a mistake. . . . In some instances they must be regarded as forms of perverted affection; they are always unhealthy, since they make too great demands upon the emotions and nerve force, and are likely to assume undue proportions." . . . Such warnings were the most extreme expressions of the conflict between gender and work: the commitment to work was so anomalous for women that it might threaten heterosexuality itself.

Nonetheless, in a culture that defined love and marriage as the center of women's lives, the hospital schools, prescriptive literature, and nurses all affirmed the choice of work over marriage. One nurse remembered her decision to enter training school thus: "I was feeling serious—like a nun about to take the veil." Ethics manuals extolled the solid satisfactions of professional life, and urged students to approach their work "as singlemindedly as if there were no question that their lives were to be given to professional activities. The possibility of matrimony has wrecked many a career by hovering about the young woman, distracting her interest and proving in the end to be an illusion." . . .

The ideology and experience of training school reverberated in women's lives and work. Many nurses apparently shared the strong identification with their work that fiction and memoirs describe. As one nurse wrote in 1941, "There's something about nursing that gets into the blood." A married nurse who decided to return to work corroborated, "Giving up nursing is much harder than it might seem . . . this profession gets a 'hold' on you." For these nurses, apprenticeship culture nurtured the intense commitment to work that is more commonly associated with professional training and practice. In oral memoirs, even women who had not been employed for many years continued to identify themselves and to be identified by others as nurses. Frequently, neighbors and family drew on their skills and experiences, asking nurses about child raising problems or illness in the family and summoning them in emergencies. Some nurses used their skills in community agencies. One woman worked as a volunteer for the local visiting nurses' association, and a day care center solicited her for its board because she was a nurse. And most talked wistfully of going back to work someday. Nursing remained a part of them in a way that other women's work simply does not: waitresses, secretaries, teachers, or social workers seldom have such strong and enduring personal and social connections to their work. Memoirs and letters often corroborate the messages of prescriptive literature and fiction; as one editorial put it, "No true nurse ever really stops nursing though she may be far afield in her daily work. In her heart she is always a nurse."

Implicitly and overtly, the literature and culture of apprenticeship subverted the dominant ideology of woman's place. First, narratives of initiation undercut cultural ideals by testing prescribed characteristics of "femininity" against the demands of hospital life. As young women converted to the nursing creed, they came to see delicacy and refinement as mere squeamishness, and to view emotional expressiveness as suspect, often a sign of weak and facile sentimentality. Hospital discipline replaced these superficial responses with the mature realism of the nurse. Second, in a culture that valued women primarily in domestic roles, the schools presented the attractions of work outside the home. In their positive portrayals of women's competence, seriousness, and emotional control, the narratives promoted female commitment to work.

In the self-contained world of the hospital schools, such values could flourish. Set apart from the social life of their contemporaries, young women participated in a communal life arranged around work. Theirs was a woman's world: they enjoyed the support and camaraderie of other women as peers, and looked up to female models as they worked with more experienced students and supervisors. Few other institutions in the twentieth century could provide young women with a comparable experience of female autonomy. Seldom explicitly feminist in their ideology, the schools nonetheless empowered young nurses as women by expecting much of them, and by denying the cultural contradiction between femininity and commitment to work. . . .

✤ *F U R T H E R   R E A D I N G*

Cynthia Sondik Aron, *Ladies and Gentlemen of the Civil Service: Middle-Class Workers in Victorian America* (1987)

Susan Porter Benson, *Counter Cultures: Saleswomen, Managers, and Customers in American Department Stores, 1890–1940* (1986)

Patricia Ann Cooper, *Once a Cigarmaker: Men, Women, and Work Culture in American Cigar Factories, 1900–1919* (1987)

Margery Davies, *Woman's Place Is at the Typewriter, 1870–1930* (1982)

Sarah Eisenstein, *Give Us Bread but Give Us Roses* (1983)

Rick Fantasia, *Cultures of Solidarity: Consciousness, Action, and Contemporary American Workers* (1988)

Dee Garrison, *Apostles of Culture: The Public Librarian and American Society, 1876–1920* (1979)

Jacqueline Dowd Hall et al., *Like a Family: The Making of a Southern Cotton Mill World* (1987)

David Halle, *America's Working Man: Work, Home, and Politics Among Blue-Collar Property Owners* (1984)

Ken Kuster, *Know-How on the Job: The Important Working Knowledge of "Unskilled" Workers* (1978)

Micaela di Leonardo, et al., "Women's Work, Work Culture, and Consciousness," *Feminist Studies* 11 (Fall 1985), 491–557

Walter Licht, *Working for the Railroad: The Organization of Work in the Nineteenth Century* (1983)

Barbara Melosh, *"The Physician's Hand": Work Culture and Conflict in American Nursing* (1982)

David Montgomery, *The Fall of the House of Labor* (1987)

———, *Workers' Control in America* (1979)

Kathy Peiss, *Cheap Amusements* (1986)

Susan Reverby, *Ordered to Care: The Dilemma of American Nursing, 1850–1945* (1987)

Vicki L. Ruiz, *Cannery Women, Cannery Lives: Mexican Women, Unionization, and the California Food Processing Industry, 1930–1950* (1987)

Karen Brodkin Sacks, *Caring by the Hour: Women, Work and Organizing at Duke Medical Center* (1988)

Studs Terkel, *Working* (1972)

Patricia Zavella, *Women's Work and Chicano Families: Cannery Workers of the Santa Clara Valley* (1988)

Americans at Work in the Industrial Era

In this antebellum painting by Stanhope A. Forbes, *Forging the Anchor*, nineteenth-century work values and techniques are positively depicted. The work is cooperative and intrinsically important and engages both muscle and mind. On the right an apprentice stokes the fire while the tools of the blacksmith trade rest nearby. (Hagley Museum and Library)

In 1868 artist Stanley Fox offered *Harper's Bazaar* readers a sketch entitled *Women and Their Work in the Metropolis*. Note the homeworking mother who occupies the enlarged central panel. (Museum of American History)

In 1903 skilled workers in this Lynn, Massachusetts, shoe factory still cut and sorted leather with few tools and little direct supervision. (Hagley Museum and Library)

In a cotton field near Memphis, an early-twentieth-century plantation owner weighs the cotton picked by his hired hands after they have filled their hampers. (National Archives)

Black workers gather crude turpentine in a North Carolina pine forest in 1903. (Hagley Museum and Library)

During most of the twentieth century, office work has been organized according to Taylorite principles and segregated by gender, as in this office scene from the 1920s. (Culver Pictures)

Machinist Herman Backhoffer stands proudly beside his giant lathe at the Westinghouse turbine shop in Liston, Pennsylvania, just outside Philadelphia, in 1919. Such skilled northern European workers were among the most militant trade unionists in the World War I era and were often exceedingly hostile to the unskilled immigrants recently arrived from eastern and southern Europe. (Hagley Museum and Library)

By the early twentieth century, bread baking had moved from home to factory and had shifted from women's work to men's work, as this 1930 photograph of a commercial bakery near Philadelphia shows. (Hagley Museum and Library)

Anthracite miners in eastern Pennsylvania still used the pick, shovel, and hammer when this photograph was taken in 1930. Although the United Mine Workers of America would soon reorganize these coal fields and challenge the power of the Philadelphia-based railroads that owned these mines, the union could not forestall the postwar decline of anthracite as a heating fuel and the subsequent impoverishment of the region. (Hagley Museum and Library)

Wilmington, Delaware, leaders of the International Union of Marine and Shipbuilding Workers of America, CIO, sign their first contract with the Pusey and Jones Company in March 1941. Midcentury labor leaders often dressed as middle-class professionals, but in this bargaining ceremony the class divide is obvious. (Hagley Museum and Library)

During the Second World War, military aircraft were built by a work force of more than 2 million men and women. Here B-24s are being assembled at Ford's giant Willow Run factory outside Detroit. Contrary to popular impressions, this was not assembly-line work but resembled building construction instead. (Library of Congress)

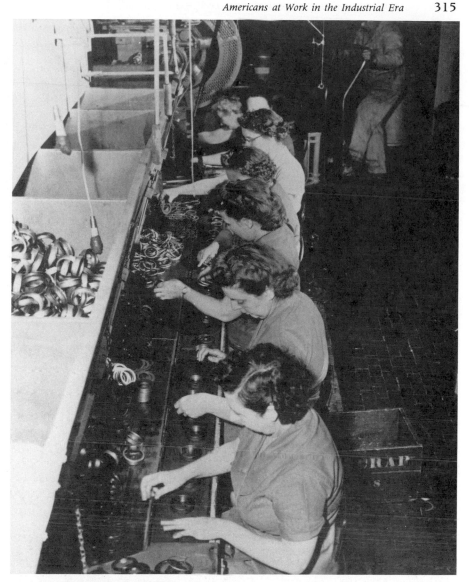

Women steadily increased their proportion of the paid-labor force during the twentieth century, but light assembly and inspection remained a job "ghetto" where women factory workers were usually concentrated, as in this auto-parts assembly line of the late 1940s. (The Archives of Labor and Urban Affairs, Wayne State University)

Led by local president Paul Silver, center, these postwar shop stewards at Detroit Steel Products (UAW Local 351) made the union's democratic influence felt at the point of production. Silver is wearing a UAW bowling sweater, indicating his support of the union campaign to build an integrated bowling league at a time when the sport was otherwise racially segregated. (AFL-CIO Metro Detroit)

Although the Taft-Hartley Act was not the "slave labor" law denounced by most contemporary trade-union leaders, its passage in 1947 did help bring the growth of the labor movement to a halt. Here a Detroit Labor Day float dramatizes union opposition to the new law. (Archives of Labor and Urban Affairs, Wayne State University)

The time clock, here being punched by employees of the Lukens Steel Company about 1950, was one of the most common technical innovations devised by the scientific-management movement. In the years before the First World War, the time clock had replaced the factory whistle as a device for regulating the blue-collar workday. (Hagley Museum and Library)

In 1989 thousands of union miners and their supporters were arrested by Virginia state police during the Pittston strike in the southwest corner of the state. The United Mine Workers union struck to defend the health and pension benefits of its members, but the conflict proved most notable for the strikers' mass civil disobedience and their spirited solidarity, here signified by the fatigue-style hunting clothes that many strikers adopted as a uniform. (William E. Lester, United Mine Workers of America)

The Managerial Ethos

✣

The manipulation of the production process and the active management of labor were not high priorities for the owners of most nineteenth-century enterprises. Until the turn of the century, skilled workers, foremen, and inside contractors did most of a firm's hiring, determined the pace of the work, and structured the production routine. Unskilled men and women workers were often subjected to a brutal "drive" system of hard and continuous labor, but their daily fate was almost entirely in the hands of their immediate supervisor, not the company's top executives, whose talents were instead directed toward finance and sales.

All this began to change around 1900. As industrial and commercial enterprises grew larger and the "labor problem" more acute, the owners of capital began to turn their attention inward toward the more efficient and predictable management of that most unpredictable factor in production: human labor. Frederick W. Taylor, the offspring of a wealthy Philadelphia family, is most closely associated with this new movement toward scientific management. Taylor thought that trained managers could increase the productivity of their enterprises many times over by systematically reorganizing machinery, payment schemes, and employee supervision—by intervening directly at the point of production where they had hardly ventured before. Many of Taylor's particular ideas, such as the progressive piece-rate pay plan, would prove unworkable, but his general outlook helped lay the basis for the twentieth century's infatuation with the idea of skilled managerial technique as the solution to almost all problems of the material world.

What did the unions think of Taylor's ideas? In what ways did the application of these ideas differ between skilled and unskilled labor; between men and women; and among workers in offices, factories, and transport? To what extent can the management of labor be a science?

✣ D O C U M E N T S

Just before his death in 1915, Frederick Taylor distilled some of his most important ideas in a final talk, reprinted here as the first document. By this time Taylor had become something of a cult figure among industrial managers and certain Progressive Era reformers, both of whom thought that a socially informed scientific management was the key to resolving contemporary problems of class antagonism. Taylorist ideas spread far beyond the factory, as the second document demonstrates. Here the planning director of Macy's department store explains her managerial role in this large bureaucracy. In the third document, Robert Schrank, a former unionist, offers a critical inside look at the managerial strata during the 1950s, when these executives enjoyed an era of great self-confidence. In the final selection, management expert Douglas McGregor uses the latest ideas in mid-twentieth-century social psychology to critique authoritarian-style Taylorism. McGregor's work was part of a larger trend toward personnel management, human relations, and various programs of participatory management that have flourished in the last quarter-century.

Frederick Winslow Taylor on the Principles of Scientific Management, 1916

By far the most important fact which faces the industries of our country, the industries, in fact, of the civilized world, is that not only the average worker, but nineteen out of twenty workmen throughout the civilized world firmly believe that it is for their best interests to go slow instead of to go fast. They firmly believe that it is for their interest to give as little work in return for the money that they get as is practical. The reasons for this belief are two-fold, and I do not believe that the workingmen are to blame for holding these fallacious views.

If you will take any set of workmen in your own town and suggest to those men that it would be a good thing for them in their trade if they were to double their output in the coming year, each man turn out twice as much work and become twice as efficient, they would say, "I do not know anything about other people's trades; what you are saying about increasing efficiency being a good thing may be good for other trades, but I know that the only result if you come to our trade would be that half of us would be out of a job before the year was out." That to the average workingman is an axiom; it is not a matter subject to debate at all. And even among the average business men of this country that opinion is almost universal. They firmly believe that that would be the result of a great increase in efficiency, and yet directly the opposite is true. . . .

The . . . reason why the workmen of this country and of Europe deliberately restrict output is a very simple one. . . . If, for example, you are manufacturing a pen, let us assume for simplicity that a pen can be made by a single man. Let us say that the workman is turning out ten pens per day, and that he is receiving $2.50 a day for his wages. He has a progressive foreman who is up to date, and that foreman goes to the workman and suggests, "Here, John, you are getting $2.50 a day, and you are turning out ten pens. I would suggest that I pay you 25 cents for making that pen." The man takes the job, and through the help of his foreman, through his own ingenuity, through his increased work, through his interest in his business, through the help of his friends, at the end of the year he finds himself turning out twenty pens instead of ten. He is happy, he is making

$5, instead of $2.50 a day. His foreman is happy because, with the same room, with the same men he had before, he has doubled the output of his department, and the manufacturer himself is sometimes happy, but not often. Then someone on the board of directors asks to see the payroll, and he finds that we are paying $5 a day where other similar mechanics are only getting $2.50, and in no uncertain terms he announces that we must stop ruining the labor market. We cannot pay $5 a day when the standard rate of wages is $2.50; how can we hope to compete with surrounding towns? What is the result? Mr. Foreman is sent for, and he is told that he has got to stop ruining the labor market of Cleveland. And the foreman goes back to his workman in sadness, in depression, and tells his workman, "I am sorry, John, but I have got to cut the price down for that pen; I cannot let you earn $5 a day; the board of directors has got on to it, and it is ruining the labor market; you ought to be willing to have the price reduced. You cannot earn more than $3 or $2.75 a day, and I will have to cut your wages so that you will only get $3 a day." John, of necessity accepts the cut, but he sees to it that he never makes enough pens to get another cut. . . .

The Development of Scientific Management

There has been, until comparatively recently, no scheme promulgated by which the evils of rate cutting could be properly avoided, so soldiering has been the rule.

Now the first step that was taken toward the development of those methods, of those principles, which rightly or wrongly have come to be known under the name of scientific management—the first step that was taken in an earnest endeavor to remedy the evils of soldiering; an earnest endeavor to make it unnecessary for workmen to be hypocritical in this way, to deceive themselves, to deceive their employers, to live day in and day out a life of deceit, forced upon them by conditions—the very first step that was taken toward the development was to overcome that evil. . . .

What is scientific management? It is no efficiency device, nor is it any group or collection of efficiency devices. Scientific management is no new scheme for paying men, it is no bonus system, no piece-work system, no premium system of payment; it is no new method of figuring costs. It is no one of the various elements by which it is commonly known, by which people refer to it. It is not time study nor man study. It is not the printing of a ton or two of blanks and unloading them on a company and saying, "There is your system, go ahead and use it." Scientific management does not exist and cannot exist until there has been a complete mental revolution on the part of the workmen working under it, as to their duties toward themselves and toward their employers, and a complete mental revolution in the outlook of the employers, toward their duties, toward themselves, and toward their workmen. And until this great mental change takes place, scientific management does not exist. Do you think you can make a great mental revolution in a large group of workmen in a year, or do you think you can make it in a large group of foremen and superintendents in a year? If you do, you are very much mistaken. All of us hold mighty close to our ideas and principles in life, and we change very slowly toward the new, and very properly too.

Let me give you an idea of what I mean by this change in mental outlook. If you are manufacturing a hammer or a mallet, into the cost of that mallet goes a certain amount of raw materials, a certain amount of wood and metal. If you will take the cost of the raw materials and then add to it that cost which is frequently called by various names—overhead expenses, general expense, indirect expense; that is, the proper share of taxes, insurance, light, heat, salaries of officers and advertising—and you have a sum of money. Subtract that sum from the selling price, and what is left over is called the surplus. It is over this surplus that all of the labor disputes in the past have occurred. The workman naturally wants all he can get. His wages come out of that surplus. The manufacturer wants all he can get in the shape of profits, and it is from the division of this surplus that all the labor disputes have come in the past—the equitable division.

The new outlook that comes under scientific management is this: The workmen, after many object lessons, come to see and the management come to see that this surplus can be made so great, providing both sides will stop their pulling apart, will stop their fighting and will push as hard as they can to get as cheap an output as possible, that there is no occasion to quarrel. Each side can get more than ever before. The acknowledgment of this fact represents a complete mental revolution.

What Scientific Management Will Do

I am going to try to prove to you that the old style of management has not a ghost of a chance in competition with the principles of scientific management. Why? In the first place, under scientific management, the initiative of the workmen, their hard work, their good-will, their best endeavors are obtained with absolute regularity. . . . That is the least of the two sources of gain. The greatest source of gain under scientific management comes from the new and almost unheard-of duties and burdens which are voluntarily assumed, not by the workmen, but by the men on the management side. . . . These new duties, these new burdens undertaken by the management have rightly or wrongly been divided into four groups, and have been called the principles of scientific management.

The . . . first of the new burdens which are voluntarily undertaken by those on the management side is the deliberate gathering together of the great mass of traditional knowledge which, in the past, has been in the heads of the workmen, recording it, tabulating it, reducing it in most cases to rules, laws, and in many cases to mathematical formulae, which, with these new laws, are applied to the co-operation of the management to the work of the workmen. This results in an immense increase in the output, we may say, of the two. The gathering in of this great mass of traditional knowledge, which is done by the means of motion study, time study, can be truly called the science. . . .

The next of the four principles of scientific management is the scientific selection of the workman, and then his progressive development. It becomes the duty under scientific management of not one, but of a group of men on the management side, to deliberately study the workmen who are under them; study them in the most careful, thorough and painstaking way; and not just leave it to the poor, overworked foreman to go out and say, "Come on, what do you want? If you are cheap enough I will give you a trial."

That is the old way. The new way is to take a great deal of trouble in selecting the workmen. The selection proceeds year after year. And it becomes the duty of those engaged in scientific management to know something about the workmen under them. It becomes their duty to set out deliberately to train the workmen in their employ to be able to do a better and still better class of work than ever before, and to then pay them higher wages than ever before. This deliberate selection of the workmen is the second of the great duties that devolve on the management under scientific management.

The third principle is the bringing together of this science of which I have spoken and the trained workmen. I say bringing because they don't come together unless some one brings them. Select and train your workmen all you may, but unless there is some one who will make the men and the science come together, they will stay apart. The "make" involves a great many elements. They are not all disagreeable elements. The most important and largest way of "making" is to do something nice for the man whom you wish to make come together with the science. Offer him a plum, something that is worthwhile. There are many plums offered to those who come under scientific management—better treatment, more kindly treatment, more consideration for their wishes, and an opportunity for them to express their wants freely. That is one side of the "make." An equally important side is, whenever a man will not do what he ought, to either make him do it or stop it. If he will not do it, let him get out. I am not talking of any mollycoddle. Let me disabuse your minds of any opinion that scientific management is a mollycoddle scheme.

I have a great many union friends. I find they look with especial bitterness on this word "make." They have been used to doing the "making" in the past. That is the attitude of the trade unions, and it softens matters greatly when you can tell them the facts, namely, that in our making the science and the men come together, nine-tenths of our trouble comes with the men on the management side in making them do their new duties. I am speaking of those who have been trying to change from the old system to the new. . . .

The fourth principle is the plainest of all. It involves a complete redivision of the work of the establishment. Under the old scheme of management, almost all of the work was done by the workmen. Under the new, the work of the establishment is divided into two large parts. All of that work which formerly was done by the workmen alone is divided into two large sections, and one of those sections is handed over to the management. They do a whole division of the work formerly done by the workmen. It is this real cooperation, this genuine division of the work between the two sides, more than any other element which accounts for the fact that there never will be strikes under scientific management. When the workman realizes that there is hardly a thing he does that does not have to be preceded by some act of preparation on the part of management, and when that workman realizes when the management falls down and does not do its part, that he is not only entitled to a kick, but that he can register that kick in the most forcible possible way, he cannot quarrel with the men over him. It is team work. There are more complaints made every day on the part of the workmen that the men on the management side fail to do their duties than are made by the management that the men fail. Every one of the complaints of the men have to be heeded, just as much as the complaints from the management that the workmen do not do their share. That is characteristic of scientific management. It represents a democracy, co-operation, a genuine division of work which never existed before in this world. . . .

A Macy's Manager on Department-Store Bureaucracy, 1925

It would not be possible to cover adequately in one paper such a subject as scientific management applied to department store practice. I have, therefore, chosen to limit my subject to what a planning department can do to help to introduce scientific management into department store practice. I should like to emphasize "*help* to introduce" because I feel that a planning department is not the only agency through which the principles of scientific management have become known or are finding expression. Such a department is merely a tool of management to assist management to do its job better.

Before pointing out the need for a planning department in a department store it may be well to review the conception of a planning department in a factory, the place where it originated. The department which Frederick W. Taylor originated is an agency primarily for the centralized control of production; that is, it not only devises and establishes better methods of operation, but it also provides for the proper scheduling and routing of work through the plant. . . .

Let us consider some of the major problems which a department store faces in trying to introduce better methods and in trying to increase individual efficiency. One of the greatest problems encountered is variety of work. Few persons realize that there are about twice as many employees behind the scenes in a store as there are in public view. These employees are engaged in occupations which are quite as important to the life of the

Eugenia Lies, "Improving Department Store Techniques," *Bulletin of the Taylor Society* 10 (August 1925): pp. 185–188.

store as selling. Varied as are the kinds of merchandise sold, and the appeals which must be made to sell it, still more varied are the jobs which are performed before and after the merchandise is offered for sale. First, it is handled by the Receiving Department, where a record is made of its receipt from the manufacturer or vendor and where it is marked and sent either to be kept in reserve stock or immediately to the selling floor. Before its sale is complete, the salesclerk's record of sale—the salescheck—must pass through the hands of a cashier and a wrapper or packer. The wrapped merchandise is then sent to the Delivery Department, where it is sorted and assigned to a delivery route. The driver then conducts it to the customer's door, and that is the end of a cycle as far as the merchandise is concerned—unless there is a complaint! If this happens—and cases are known to have occurred—the merchandise may make a trip back to the store, or at any rate will be the subject of investigation by the Adjustment Bureau, and will also occasion some correspondence carried on by the Correspondence Department. At all events, while the merchandise is being delivered, the Auditing Department will be using the record of its sale in computing the daily totals of transactions. These activities are inevitably a part of the routine of conducting a large distributing business. Other departments have been established to supplement various selling departments, such as the following manufacturing departments: Millinery Workroom, Mattress Factory, Carpet Workroom, Printing Shop, Photo Laboratory, and Picture Framing Department. Still others are needed for the work of building maintenance such as the Carpenter Shop, the Paint Shop, and the Engineer's Office. The coordination of the jobs performed in such a variety of departments to the end that the whole store operate as a unit is a task of gigantic proportions.

Not only does work vary in different departments; very often a great variety of operations of comparatively short duration must be performed on a single job. This is true even after the principle of division of labor has been utilized. Take as an example the work of a marker who attaches price tickets to articles of merchandise before they are sent to the selling departments. At one time, and even today in many stores, a salesclerk not only sold merchandise but marked it also. We, however, have taken the function of marking away from the salesclerk. Furthermore, we attempt to assign markers to certain departments. If we stop to consider the thousands of articles sold in one department, such as the Drug Department, we have some conception of the variety of operations and therefore the difficulties encountered in trying to standardize the job of marking.

A third factor which must be reckoned with in developing standards of performance is the tremendous fluctuation in business. To be sure there are certain periodical fluctuations which can be prognosticated. These would include a daily peak between the hours of 11 and 4, a weekly peak on Saturdays, and seasonal peaks at Easter and Christmas. By a careful analysis of past performance one can note with increasing accuracy where these peaks occur and can study their behavior. But in a merchandising business there will always be many valleys and peaks of which we can have no warning until they are upon us. These are caused by such uncontrollable factors as weather and style of merchandise.

The fact that many of the employees are in direct contact with our customers increases the difficulty of the problem and makes it imperative that we instruct our salesforce not merely in the mechanics of their job but also in the psychology of salesmanship.

All these factors make the work of determining standards of production for so many jobs more difficult. We have not found a solution for all cases, but we have gone far enough in our studies to recognize certain principles. In order to measure performance when so many operations are involved that it is impossible to set a separate standard of production for each, we attempt to find a common denominator of work. Where the fluctuations in the amount of work received or other conditions of work cannot be controlled, we measure average performance over a period of time against the standard set.

The function of our Planning Department is that which may be attributed to any agency of scientific management— . . . "to standardize policies, methods, equipment and tools." Our method of attack is to standardize procedure, supervise its installation and finally to follow up after the installation has been completed. We maintain these three well defined divisions of any piece of work, as they insure a comprehensive grasp of the problems and a check-up on progress made. For illustration, we make job analyses, to furnish the employment and training departments with job specifications, and to develop with these departments promotional plans and a standardized wage scale after the operations of the job have been standardized. In addition to the study of the individual jobs, an analysis of the relationship of one job to another is made in order to determine the most direct routing of work and the best layout of the department as a whole. The equipment—chairs, desks, tables, files, etc.—and the condition of work, lighting and ventilation are studied also. . . .

In discussing one or two specific problems which have been assigned to the Planning Department I shall not attempt to describe our methods of attacking each one individually. I shall rather limit myself to a statement of the problem and its solution.

One of our earliest assignments arose from the desire on the part of our executives to compensate our non-selling employees, in addition to their weekly salary, by some means which would be comparable to our commission payments to selling employees. At this time we were thinking of a non-selling bonus in terms only of attendance, punctuality, personal ratings and other factors not directly pertaining to production. After much thought and discussion it was decided that any kind of a bonus payment should be limited to a payment on production measured against standards of work set for each job. This was a new principle in the payment of such employees, and its acceptance made it necessary for us to discard the general attendance and punctuality bonus then in use. But in order to avoid the feeling in the organization that we were even indirectly reducing wages, we introduced a compensating more liberal vacation plan, which in dollars and cents would cost the organization just about as much as the bonus had cost. . . .

Another problem on which we have worked is the centralization and improvement of our personnel control record cards. We have no Personnel Manager in our store; we have, however, an Employment Manager and a Superintendent of Training, both of whom are responsible to the General Manager. For this reason we have always had an individual personnel record card in the Manager's office. This card was in a vertical file, and furthermore was not designed in such a way as to furnish a quick and all-inclusive understanding of the employee's record in the organization. For instance, it was not possible to obtain up-to-date information on the employee's error record without wading through a number of error slips which were enclosed in the folder. There was also a duplication of records in the Employment and Training Departments. We found that it was possible not only to design a card which would include all the information desired, arranged in such a way that almost at a glance the executive using it could know all the facts, but also to use a visible index file in which daily postings of records could be made with much greater ease. Furthermore, by using a special type of visible index equipment, we were able to file our references and application blanks in the same file with the active card. Thus we avoided a double file often felt necessary with a visible active card. . . .

A Unionist Explores Management Life in the 1950s, 1978

I went to a fancy Madison Avenue employment agency, and within a few days I was on a new job as a foreman in the machine-building and maintenance division of a small retail data-processing company. After spending so many years fighting the bosses and their managers, becoming part of management proved to be more traumatic than I had expected. . . .

I began to remember the things workers beefed about when I was a union officer. Now I was determined to pay attention to the conditions of work. After all, I rationalized, even the socialist brotherhood in any form had to have some kind of supervision. I kept asking myself: Could I supervise others without myself becoming a mechanical robot?

There were about forty-five men, almost all skilled workers, in the department. There was no union. My first efforts were to become familiar with the work as well as to straighten out job order systems and establish cost centers and parts inventory. The plant manager was pleased with what I was doing. "You're doing a great job, Bob, keep it up." Now, I thought, I can start paying attention to working conditions.

I started by improving the ventilation, cleaning up the toilets, building an eating area, getting the windows washed; generally making the physical surroundings more pleasant. The employees loved it; and with no urging

Robert Schrank, *Ten Thousand Working Days* (Cambridge: MIT Press, 1978), pp. 133–143.

on my part, production began to increase. I had become an instant success, yet I did not have to do anything as a foreman that I considered antithetical to the interests of the workers, whom I now called employees. . . .

My relations with the men in the department were easy-going. I would walk around checking on the work, doing quality control and at the same time kidding about the difficult jobs, sports, politics, and sex in about that order. Thinking back, second only to being competent as a toolmaker machinist, the most important management quality I would say I had was a good sense of humor. The work itself I sort of knew by rote, and I could get answers, too, by consulting others. That was never of any earth-shaking importance to me, so I would joke about what had to be done. The men would sort of laugh, yet they rushed to meet schedules. That turned out to make me look good. . . .

My efforts on behalf of the company were rewarded by promotions, first to chief plant engineer and then to division engineer responsible for three plants. As the demands of the job increased, I found myself increasingly committing more of my life to the company. To the envy of other managing engineers, I began to be consulted by the vice president in charge of production at the head office of the corporation. I was now mixing with the corporate executives, traveling first class, eating at 21 Club with three corporate vice presidents . . . Good food, fine wine, the best cigars. . . . I was moving up, and, by God, I liked it. . . .

I was now working for corporate headquarters. I found myself becoming more involved, absorbed, single-minded, with an excitement for equipment deadlines and new ideas that created in me a general sense of euphoria. Yet there was a difference between this kind of work and the labor movement. What was it? Slowly I was missing the old companionship, the wonderful conversation of all my friends in screw machines, turret lathes, and the machine shops. The management world was a circumspect one full of innuendo, nuance, correct dress, and carefully choreographed behavior. The result was little or no spontaneity, no feelings, no physical contact. All this meant zero sensuality. I was beginning to miss walking with my arm on another guy's shoulder at a union meeting. Doubts began to take root about whether I could make it as a corporate executive. . . .

Some doubts have grown in me about engineers and managers. The first has to do with management's ability to manage, and the second has to do with behavioral science notions about work, motivation, and job satisfaction. In my days as a union official, there was a fantasy that corporations were homogeneous, single-headed, efficient monsters systematically exploiting workers. Talk about being convinced by one's own propaganda! Institutions and professions now appear to me as tribal groups defending their turf—territoriality: their secrets, sacred bundles, and their leaders and tribal councils. When I moved from the union tribe to the corporate tribe, I learned some of their secrets. They were fumbling around pretty much like the rest of us, yet they were better able to conceal it through public relations, with its handouts, image building, color slide and sound shows. Then there is always the secrecy that is called up to "protect us from our competition" or from other tribes, but this is usually baloney since it is more often used to hide mistakes from the world at large. . . .

I think that engineers and managers would rate considerably higher on the alienation scale than most unionized workers. The competition of managers vying for recognition and position creates little trust, and that means little human contact or concern. The corporation I worked for was liberal and easy-going, but even there the higher up the totem pole you climbed, the faster they went for your jugular. . . .

Managers and engineers tend to lose their concern about people because of their total preoccupation with "the product." In my case, feed mechanisms, the product, took over most of my psychic energy. Such narrow frames of reference have an impact on how managers and engineers view other people. Preoccupied and obsessed with the product line, they can begin to view people, or the workers, as obstacles to reaching their objectives.

In the whole production matrix, people are probably the most frustrating for managers since they constitute the most difficult variable to control and predict. No matter how predictable society tries to make its members through its various socializing mechanisms, people continue to give managers the most trouble. Managers are always complaining about "those workers." "If only they would do what we tell them or learn to follow instructions, we would surpass all our quotas." It is this obsession with the product and the consequent neglect of human needs that could fill case-history books with stories of management's insensitivity to workers. This insensitivity is often turned around and explained as a "lack of worker motivation." Workers become strangers to many managers and are seen only as an extension of a piece of machinery in which a capital investment has been made. This leads to the engineering dream of eliminating the "human element" in production.

A good illustration of this phenomenon came up in a union negotiation. Sitting around the huge conference table in the mahogany paneled conference room during an intensive collective bargaining session with the Republic Steel Corporation, the company was reciting a litany of how much production time is lost as a result of lateness, extended coffee breaks, lunch time beyond the bell, and early quitting. The whole discussion seemed kind of absurd, so I kept encouraging the industrial engineers to give us the data on what the lost-time factor added up to. Out came the slide rules as the figures multiplied upward. "The company has 5,000 employees in this division. Estimated loss on starting time, seven minutes; on two coffee breaks, twelve minutes; and quitting ten minutes early. That makes a total of 2,400 hours a day." The company was very impressed with these figures. After all, they were clear evidence of the cost of malingering.

I said, "I would like to have a recess." It was agreed. The company representatives left the room, and the union committee remained. I asked the committee members how many times the average worker went to the toilet during the workday to pee or shit, and how long did each function take. . . . We calculated an average of twenty-eight or thirty minutes per employee lost a day in the toilet. I asked the committee if they would permit me to bargain away at least some of that time, or in other words, if we could reduce the toilet time in exchange, let's say, for a couple more holidays. Everyone appreciated the absurdity of this, but they were happy to join the dramatic fantasy that would reveal the production engineers' thought processes.

When the company representatives returned to the bargaining table, I put forth our propositions, in the course of which the absurdity of it all seemed to carry me away. "We are not only willing to reduce defecation time, but we have recently become aware of a pill that, taken each morning, would assure the employer of no defecation on company time." Noticing on the other side of the table the industrial engineers all playing with their slide rules, the committee members almost blew it with their giggling.

Charles Hunsteter, chief of production engineering, a pudgy fellow with thin strands of hair plastered to his sweaty forehead announced, "You think it's funny. Well 1,666 hours a day at $5.00 per hour labor and overhead cost, $5830 a day times 250 workdays a year: $1,500 million a year." The figures so excited him that he said, "Schrank, I don't know if you're kidding or serious, or what. But the fact is this could change our entire competitive position, and I would hope you would give our company first crack at it." Well, the poor committee members thought they would bust. The company attorney, a little more reality-oriented, was embarrassed by the joke and changed the subject. On the way out the door at the end of the session, Charlie said, "Schrank, you may be kidding, but this could be an extremely useful tool in production scheduling."

That incident epitomizes a particular kind of industrial engineering management viewpoint that I am amazed to find still prevails in some manufacturing companies. How to perfect a completely programmed person in order to eliminate the human element from technology continues to influence the thinking of at least some behavioral scientists and industrial engineers concerned with productivity and worker motivation. . . .

Social Science at the Service of Management, 1957

It has become trite to say that industry has the fundamental know-how to utilize physical science and technology for the material benefit of mankind, and that we must now learn how to utilize the social sciences to make our human organizations truly effective.

To a degree, the social sciences today are in a position like that of the physical sciences with respect to atomic energy in the thirties. We know that past conceptions of the nature of man are inadequate and, in many ways, incorrect. We are becoming quite certain that, under proper con-

Reprinted by permission of the publisher from *Management Review*, November 1957, © 1957. American Management Association, New York. All rights reserved.

ditions, unimagined resources of creative human energy could become available within the organizational setting.

We cannot tell industrial management how to apply this new knowledge in simple, economic ways. We know it will require years of exploration, much costly development research, and a substantial amount of creative imagination on the part of management to discover how to apply this growing knowledge to the organization of human effort in industry. . . .

The conventional conception of management's task in harnessing human energy to organizational requirements can be stated broadly in terms of three propositions. In order to avoid the complications introduced by a label, let us call this set of propositions "Theory X":

1. Management is responsible for organizing the elements of productive enterprise—money, materials, equipment, people—in the interest of economic ends.

2. With respect to people, this is a process of directing their efforts, motivating them, controlling their actions, modifying their behavior to fit the needs of the organization.

3. Without this active intervention by management, people would be passive—even resistant—to organizational needs. They must therefore be persuaded, rewarded, punished, controlled—their activities must be directed. This is management's task. We often sum it up by saying that management consists of getting things done through other people. . . .

Currently, the popular theme is "firm but fair." . . . It is reminiscent of Teddy Roosevelt's "speak softly and carry a big stick."

Is the Conventional View Correct?

The findings which are beginning to emerge from the social sciences challenge this whole set of beliefs about man and human nature and about the task of management. The evidence is far from conclusive, certainly, but it is suggestive. It comes from the laboratory, the clinic, the schoolroom, the home, and even to a limited extent from industry itself.

The social scientist does not deny that human behavior in industrial organization today is approximately what management perceives it to be. He has, in fact, observed it and studied it fairly extensively. But he is pretty sure that this behavior is *not* a consequence of man's inherent nature. It is a consequence rather of the nature of industrial organizations, of management philosophy, policy, and practice. The conventional approach of Theory X is based on mistaken notions of what is cause and what is effect.

Perhaps the best way to indicate why the conventional approach of management is inadequate is to consider the subject of motivation. . . .

Man is a wanting animal—as soon as one of his needs is satisfied, another appears in its place. This process is unending. It continues from birth to death. . . .

Management knows today of the existence of these needs, but it often assumes quite wrongly that they represent a threat to the organization. Many studies have demonstrated that the tightly knit, cohesive work group may, under proper conditions, be far more effective than an equal number of separate individuals in achieving organizational goals.

Yet management, fearing group hostility to its own objectives, often goes to considerable lengths to control and direct human efforts in ways that are inimical to the natural "groupiness" of human beings. When man's social needs—and perhaps his safety needs, too—are thus thwarted, he behaves in ways which tend to defeat organizational objectives. He becomes resistant, antagonistic, uncooperative. But this behavior is a consequence, not a cause. . . .

Above the social needs—in the sense that they do not become motivators until lower needs are reasonably satisfied—are the needs of greatest significance to management and to man himself. They are the *egoistic needs*, and they are of two kinds:

1. Those needs that relate to one's self-esteem—needs for self-confidence, for independence, for achievement, for competence, for knowledge.

2. Those needs that relate to one's reputation—needs for status, for recognition, for appreciation, for the deserved respect of one's fellows. . . .

The typical industrial organization offers few opportunities for the satisfaction of these egoistic needs to people at lower levels in the hierarchy. The conventional methods of organizing work, particularly in mass production industries, give little heed to these aspects of human motivation. If the practices of scientific management were deliberately calculated to thwart these needs, they could hardly accomplish this purpose better than they do. . . .

Finally—a capstone, as it were, on the hierarchy of man's needs—there are what we may call the *needs for self-fulfillment*. These are the needs for realizing one's own potentialities, for continued self-development, for being creative in the broadest sense of that term.

It is clear that the conditions of modern life give only limited opportunity for these relatively weak needs to obtain expression. The deprivation most people experience with respect to other lower-level needs diverts their energies into the struggle to satisfy *those* needs, and the needs for self-fulfillment remain dormant. . . .

We recognize readily enough that a man suffering from a severe dietary deficiency is sick. The deprivation of physiological needs has behavioral consequences. The same is true—although less well recognized—of deprivation of higher-level needs. The man whose needs for safety, association, independence, or status are thwarted is sick just as surely as the man who has rickets. And his sickness will have behavioral consequences. We will be mistaken if we attribute his resultant passivity, his hostility, his refusal to accept responsibility to his inherent "human nature." These forms of behavior are *symptoms* of illness—of deprivation of his social and egoistic needs.

The man whose lower-level needs are satisfied is not motivated to satisfy those needs any longer. For practical purposes they exist no longer. Management often asks, "Why aren't people more productive? We pay good wages, provide good working conditions, have excellent fringe benefits and steady employment. Yet people do not seem to be willing to put forth more than minimum effort."

The fact that management has provided for these physiological and safety needs has shifted the motivational emphasis to the social and perhaps to the egoistic needs. Unless there are opportunities *at work* to satisfy these higher-level needs, people will be deprived; and their behavior will reflect this deprivation. Under such conditions, if management continues to focus its attention on physiological needs, its efforts are bound to be ineffective.

People *will* make insistent demands for more money under these conditions. It becomes more important than ever to buy the material goods and services which can provide limited satisfaction of the thwarted needs. Although money has only limited value in satisfying many higher-level needs, it can become the focus of interest if it is the *only* means available. . . .

People, deprived of opportunities to satisfy at work the needs which are now important to them, behave exactly as we might predict—with indolence, passivity, resistance to change, lack of responsibility, willingness to follow the demagogue, unreasonable demands for economic benefits. It would seem that we are caught in a web of our own weaving. . . .

For these and many other reasons, we require a different theory of the task of managing people based on more adequate assumptions about human nature and human motivation. I am going to be so bold as to suggest the broad dimensions of such a theory. Call it "Theory Y," if you will.

1. Management is responsible for organizing the elements of productive enterprise—money, materials, equipment, people—in the interest of economic ends.

2. People are *not* by nature passive or resistant to organizational needs. They have become so as a result of experience in organizations.

3. The motivation, the potential for development, the capacity for assuming responsibility, the readiness to direct behavior toward organizational goals are all present in people. Management does not put them there. It is a responsibility of management to make it possible for people to recognize and develop these human characteristics for themselves.

4. The essential task of management is to arrange organizational conditions and methods of operation so that people can achieve their own goals *best* by directing *their own* efforts toward organizational objectives.

This is a process primarily of creating opportunities, releasing potential, removing obstacles, encouraging growth, providing guidance. It is what Peter Drucker has called "management by objectives" in contrast to "management by control." It does *not* involve the abdication of management, the absence of leadership, the lowering of standards, or the other characteristics usually associated with the "soft" approach under Theory X. . . .

Another way of saying this is that Theory X places exclusive reliance upon external control of human behavior, while Theory Y relies heavily on self-control and self-direction. It is worth noting that this difference is the difference between treating people as children and treating them as mature adults. After generations of the former, we cannot expect to shift to the latter over night. . . .

The ingenuity and the perseverance of industrial management in the pursuit of economic ends have changed many scientific and technological dreams into commonplace realities. It is now becoming clear that the application of these same talents to the human side of enterprise will not only enhance substantially these materialistic achievements, but will bring us one step closer to "the good society."

✦ E S S A Y S

In the first essay, Stephen Meyer of the University of Wisconsin, Parkside, explains how the deployment of the moving assembly line in 1914 emerged out of more than a decade of effort by the Ford Motor Company to speed up production, build new machines, standardize its products, and cope with a shortage of skilled workers. Mass production of the sort that Ford pioneered demanded an extreme division of labor, thousands of unskilled workers, and rigid factory discipline. Because of the assembly line's revolutionary implications, many early twentieth century managers thought that Ford's methods could be transferred from the factory to offices, restaurants, and stores. But in her essay on department-store saleswomanship, Susan Porter Benson of the University of Missouri, Columbia, shows that this was an impossible task. Department-store managers wanted as much control over their saleswomen as Henry Ford held over his workers, but the very nature of the department-store environment—the saleswoman/customer interchange—could not be so easily standardized or supervised.

What workers benefited from Taylorism? Where did it prove most successful? What internal contradictions characterized the new managerialism?

The Making of Ford's Assembly Line

STEPHEN MEYER

I have heard it said, in fact I believe that it's quite a current thought, that we have taken skill out of work. We have not. We have put a higher skill into planning, management, and tool building, and the results of that skill are enjoyed by the man who is not skilled.—Henry Ford, 1922

The dominant American attitude toward technology has been contained in the metaphor of "Prometheus unbound." Until recently, technology has been viewed generally as a powerful, positive, and autonomous force which,

Stephen Meyer, *The Five Dollar Day: Labor Management and Social Control in the Ford Motor Company, 1908–1921*, 1981, pp. 9–26, 29–36. Reprinted by permission of State University of New York Press.

once unleashed, has provided greater and greater levels of material comfort for the Western world. To be sure, Marxists and humanists have criticized the prevailing mood, but they generally have been unheeded. Historians of technology have tended to emphasize the lives of great inventors, their creations, and their entrepreneurial development. Usually, the social context of innovation and change has concerned the social environment of the inventor or its industrial and commercial exploitation. Frequently, when historians have addressed the subject of industrial technology, they have stressed the achievements of the captains of industry, the innovations in factory methods and techniques, and the satisfaction of consumer desires. Too often, they have isolated industrial technology from the objects of technical change and have neglected its impact on workers. To date, historians have not integrated fully the fields of social history and the history of technology.

Within this context, the experience of the Ford Motor Company represents an important case study for the integration of the history of technology and social history. . . . Undoubtedly, automotive production technology established the pattern for technical change in the modern mass production industries through the twentieth century. In the matter of a few years, a single industrial establishment demonstrated the transition from traditional craft forms of work to modern industrial ones. Additionally, in the popular mind, Henry Ford and the Ford Motor Company gave the world mass production with its modern dilemma of work and its discontents. While this popular view was only a partial truth, technical and organizational innovation in the Highland Park factory did represent, as [historian] Alfred Chandler noted, "the culmination of earlier developments in the metal working industries." Here, "the new technology was most fully applied" and "brought an enormously swift expansion in the output and productivity of a single factory." . . .

Generally, American advances in industrial technology have been attributed to a shortage of skilled labor. Most certainly, such was the case for the Ford factory. Technical change was the result of a phenomenal growth in the volume of Model T production and the concomitant expansion of [the] Ford labor force. In 1908, the Ford Motor Company employed an estimated 450 persons. By 1913, it grew to more than 14,000 workers. This growth created a monumental labor problem—a severe shortage of skilled mechanics who could machine and assemble parts for the popular Model T Ford. Consequently, the company hired large numbers of less-skilled and non-skilled American and immigrant workers. Prior to the rapid expansion in the workforce, Ford production workers were predominantly skilled American and German craftsmen. By 1914, three-quarters of the workforce was foreign-born and slightly more than half of the workforce came from southern and eastern Europe. Indeed, the workforce lacked traditional industrial skills. So, in the design of machines, the rationalization of work tasks and routines, and the rearrangement and integration of work processes, Ford managers and engineers found their technical solution to a social and economic problem. With advanced machine-tool technology, the division and subdivision of labor, and the novel techniques of line production and assembly, they relied on the traditional American solution to labor shortages. Technical and organizational innovation displaced skill. It permitted unskilled labor to perform work of high quality and in large quantities.

Specifically, Ford managers and engineers redesigned what they labelled the "mechanical element" of production. The "human element" had to conform to its new work tasks and routines. The result was the destruction of traditional patterns of work and discipline and the overall deterioration of conditions of work in the newly mechanized factory. In order to produce their incredibly popular automobile and to overcome their shortage of skilled labor, Ford managers and engineers brought together and implemented a number of interconnected technical and managerial innovations. In the end, they revolutionized automobile production and factory production in the modern world.

The specific components for the new Ford industrial system were not entirely new. Yet, taken together and systematically applied, they completely transformed factory production. First, Ford managers and engineers standardized the design of their product. This enabled them to specialize and routinize machine and work processes throughout the Ford plant. Second, they used the most recent advances in machine-tool technology. The new machines "transferred" skill into the design of sophisticated and complicated machines. Third, they analyzed, rationalized, and reorganized work tasks and routines. In effect, they "Taylorized" work processes and eliminated wasteful moments and motions in the performance of work. In other words, they followed the proposals of Frederick W. Taylor, the originator of scientific management Finally, they developed and extended the unique concepts of progressive production and progressive assembly. And, ultimately, they created an integrated industrial system. The result was a complete change in tasks and routines, a new occupational structure, and new forms of control in the various shops and departments of the Ford factory.

Founded in 1903, the Ford Motor Company followed the pattern of development of other early automobile manufacturers. . . . Automobile manufacture was a complicated process—first, the foundry production of castings and their machine production into individual parts; second, the assembly of these individual parts into components, such as a magneto or an engine; and, finally, the assembly of thousands of parts and components into the motor vehicle. The manufacture of parts and components often involved a substantial capital expenditure. At the same time, the infant automobile industry suffered from a volatile and fluctuating demand for its luxury product. Consequently, the Ford enterprise, like other early automobile manufacturers, reduced its financial risk through its concentration on the final assembly of automobiles. The company subcontracted the manufacture of various parts and components to outside machine shops and foundries. Gradually, as the company grew, it began to produce more and more of its own parts and components, such as engines, axles, transmis-

sions, chassis, bodies, and so forth. By the 1920s, most automobile manufacturers produced all of their major parts and components and left the
minor small ones to outside shops and factories. In the Ford Motor Company, the subsumption of part and component manufacture began in 1906
and rapidly accelerated with the manufacture of the popular Model T in
1908 and with the construction of the Highland Park plant in 1910.

Against this background, from the early years until the arrival of assembly lines in 1914, the Ford shops relied on customary craft methods
for the organization of production. To be sure, a long tradition of innovation
and change existed in American workshops and factories. But, at the same
time, a strong craft tradition delineated the boundaries for change in machines, work routines, and shop organization. . . .

For the craftsman, the skilled worker, or the contractor, their skill and
knowledge translated into power. Craft skills and knowledge meant status,
authority, and control over the performance of tasks within work groups.
Indeed, from the 1890s to the 1920s, the development of systematic and
scientific forms of management and control represented an effort to break
the hold of the autonomous craftsman on the work force and on work
procedures.

These customs and traditions formed the backdrop for the work patterns
in the early automobile shops and factories. And, most certainly, they
contained and restrained technical innovation in the Ford shops. For example, as late as 1912, Ford assembly procedures seemed rather routine.
A photograph of the Ford engine assembly room showed a large room with
row upon row of assembly benches. At the center of each bench was an
engine block, on the side a vise, and behind the block bins of parts. H. L.
Arnold, an industrial journalist, described traditional assembly operations
in the Ford plant:

> Ordinary shop practice stations the principal component in a convenient
> place on the shop floor . . . and proceeds with the assembly by bringing
> other components to the principal component and applying or fixing them
> to the principal component which remains in place until the assembly is
> completed.

. . . At the assembly bench, the skilled worker occupied a central place.
He began with a bare motor block, utilized a wide range of mental and
manual skills, and attached part after part. Not only did he assemble parts,
but he also "fitted" them. If two parts did not go together, he placed them
in his vise and filed them to fit. The work routines contained variations in
tasks and required considerable amounts of skill and judgment. Additionally, unskilled truckers served the skilled assemblers. When an assembler
completed his engine, a trucker carried it away and provided a new motor
block. The laborer also kept the assembler supplied with an adequate number of parts and components. Here, the division of labor was relatively
primitive—essentially, the skilled and the unskilled. Under normal conditions, a Ford motor assembler needed almost a full day of work to complete a single engine. . . .

In the Ford machine shops, the social relationships were much more dynamic and much less certain. From the 1880s on, factory managers and engineers devoted considerable attention to the productive efficiency of the machine shop. Yet, despite the efforts of Taylor and other systematic and scientific managers, craft customs and traditions, technological limitations, and market considerations hindered the efforts to manage and control independent machinists. For in spite of an increasing division of labor and an increasing technical sophistication, machinists still retained sufficient skill and knowledge to maintain some degree of functional autonomy.

By the turn of the century, technical and organizational innovation narrowed the range of the traditional machinist's skill. Both work tasks and basic machine tools became more specialized. But, the machinist still needed practical knowledge and manual ability. By this time, the division of labor progressed along the line of specialized work within the craft or the operation of specialized machine tools. For example, general workman, vise hand, die sinker, and tool maker represented specialties of the trade; lathe, planer, and milling machine operator represented specialized machine occupations. Nevertheless, even the specialized machinist exercised considerable intellectual and manual skills within a narrower range. . . .

Until the full mechanization of the Ford factory, which began around 1910, assemblers, molders, machinists, and many other production workers were skilled craftsmen. Additionally, large numbers of less-skilled and unskilled workers—helpers, assistants, laborers, truckers, and so forth—complemented and assisted this highly skilled workforce. Indeed, until its technological and organizational transformation, the early Ford factory was "a congeries of craftsmen's shops rather than an integrated plant."

The popular and practical design of the Model T Ford facilitated the technological and administrative transformation of the Ford factory. Gradually, as Model T sales increased and as production schedules stabilized, Ford and his engineers and managers began to realize the profound impact of product design on their factory operations. The standard design of the Model T influenced machine selection, work and task organization, and the integration of the entire plant. It facilitated the division of labor through the simplification of work routines. This, in turn, meant that some operations could be designed into machines. Finally, the systematic analysis of work and machines logically resulted in an equally systematic examination of the interconnected operations of the entire plant. To this end, the standard design proved a catalyst for innovation and for the integration of the entire Ford industrial system.

Henry Ford's personal contribution to this process was his dogged determination to realize his imaginative concept for the Model T Ford. . . . [H]e suggested a relationship between design and production methods:

> The way to make automobiles is to make one automobile just like another automobile, to make them all alike, to make them come through the factory alike—just like one pin is like another pin when it comes from the pin factory, or one match is like another match when it comes from the match factory.

Indeed, Ford had a deceptively simple idea—"a motor car for the great multitude," a complicated product for a mass market, with "the simplest designs." He wanted to produce a standardized automobile that could be manufactured like a pin or a match. . . .

Once initiated, the process of standardization had its own inexorable inner logic. It influenced each routine and operation throughout the entire plant. In 1916, John R. Lee, a Ford factory manager described this process:

> For the past eight years, the plan of the company has been steadfastly toward standardization. A single model chassis with a very limited number of bodies have been built in large quantities with the exercise of exacting thought and care in the development of mechanism and material which are especially adapted to the product.

Consequently, the factory became an integrated industrial system. As [industrial engineer] H. F. Porter observed, the flow of materials to and through the plant had to be balanced perfectly. "Lapses," he related:

> . . . would, if given any leeway here, cause untold havoc. Thorough standardization in one department, therefore, entails equally thorough standardization in all other interdependent departments.

As in the eighteenth-century textile mills, innovation in one area of production necessitated innovation in others. Technical advance in one shop created bottlenecks in other shops. And, these bottlenecks spurred innovation in technologically backward departments. . . .

Within this context, Ford had a sound economic logic in his oft-repeated statement that the customer could choose any color so long as it was black. Another color meant a deviation from a standard design and from standardized production procedures.

In the development of their novel methods and techniques of production, Ford managers and engineers worked within a rapidly evolving tradition of American technological innovation. In 1912, a special subcommittee of the American Society of Mechanical Engineers (ASME) detailed this tradition in its survey of "the present state of the art of industrial management." In this study, American mechanical engineers attempted to synthesize the new industrial ideas and practices which bore the general label, "scientific management." The subcommittee wanted to amalgamate the ideas of Taylor and his followers and successors. In the process, it developed the notion of "labor-saving management." And, it concluded that the new art of management emphasized two older principles, the division of labor and the transference of skill, and a more recent one, the new "mental attitude" on the part of industrial engineers and managers. . . .

This new mental attitude brought the method of science to industry. The result was "to extend the principle of the transference of skill to production, so that it completely embraces every activity in manufacture." Ultimately, each principle related to the skill of workers: the division of labor simplified skills, the transfer of skill shifted it to the machine, and the new mental attitude uncovered its fundamental elements, and relocated skills in the design of work tasks and routines, of machines, and of the entire integrated industrial system.

The new "scientific" division of labor was an important element in the evolution of mass production in the Ford factory. While Ford denied that "scientific management" or "Taylorism" formed the basis of his new industrial methods, most surely some elements of the new managerial tradition influenced the reorganization of work tasks and routines in the Highland Park plant. . . .

In fact, Taylor himself visited Detroit several times. In 1914, he addressed an assemblage of Detroit factory managers, superintendents, and foremen. Here, he commented favorably on the application and, in some instances, the autonomous development of his principles in the automobile industry. This industry, he said, was "the first instance in which a group of manufacturers had undertaken to install the principles of scientific management without the aid of experts." In Detroit, the practical men in automobile shops and factories independently developed and expanded on Taylor's general principles. And, Ford and his managers and skilled workers were at the forefront of technical innovation and change. . .

In 1914, H. L. Arnold commented on the Ford plant's "highly original and wonderfully effective cost-reducing methods." He then listed the basic principles for the Ford reorganization of work tasks and routines:

1. A broad survey of the field of effort with a wholly free and unfettered mind.
2. The careful examination of existing conditions.
3. The elimination of every needless muscular movement and expenditure of energy.

In effect, Ford managers and engineers Taylorized work tasks and routines in their modern automobile factory. They followed Taylor's idea that intellectual activity should be separated from manual work and should be located in a planning department. As Taylor noted: "the cost of production is lowered by separating the work of planning and the brain work as much as possible from the manual labor." Through their accurate and methodical studies of work tasks and routines, Ford managers and engineers—the brain workers—eliminated nonproductive moments and motions from the work routines.

Henry Ford detailed how the division of labor through time study changed the assembly procedures for pistons and rods. The "old plan" of assembly, he related, was:

> . . . a very simple operation. The workman pushed the pin out of the piston, oiled the pin, slipped the rod in place, put the pin through the rod and piston, tightened on screw, and opened another screw. That was the whole operation. The foreman, examining the operation, could not discover why it should take as much as three minutes. He analyzed the motions with a stop-watch. He found that four hours of a nine-hour day were spent walking. The assembler did not go off anywhere, but he did shift his feet to gather in his materials and to push away his finished piece. In the whole

task, each man performed six operations. The foreman devised a new plan: he split the operation into three divisions, put a slide on the bench and three men on each side of it, and an inspector at the end. Instead of one man performing the whole operation, one man then performed only one-third of the operation—he performed only as much as he could do without shifting his feet.

The reorganization of work resulted in a phenomenal increase in worker productivity. Under the old method, twenty-eight men assembled 175 pistons and rods in a nine-hour day; under the new one, seven men assembled 2,600 in an eight-hour day.

Arnold reported on the division of labor for hand and automatic machine work throughout the entire Ford plant. Managers and engineers possessed "actual stop-watch time" for thousands of operations. "Minute division of labor," he concluded:

> is effective in labor-cost reducing in two ways: first by making the workman extremely skilled, so that he does his part with no needless motions, and secondly by training him to perform his operation with the least expenditure of will-power, and hence with the least brain fatigue.

In this instance, Arnold revealed an important aspect of the managerial attitude about technical and organizational achievements. Needless to say, his concept of skill differed considerably from that of the craftsman. Moreover, his ideal worker was the mindless automaton who applied himself constantly and consistently with little thought. . . .

Next, improvements in machine-tool technology constituted a powerful force for the transformation of work routines and factory procedures. In fact, Ford industrial expansion occurred at the same time that machine tools underwent notable improvements in their design and construction. Until the early twentieth century, the general-purpose machine tool, which relied on the varied and complex skills of the machinist, prevailed in American workshops and factories. To be sure, some nineteenth-century industries developed their specialized machines for the volume production of nearly identical parts. Indeed, the automatic screw machine was a classic nineteenth-century example of the automatic and special-purpose machine. Additionally, the small arms, sewing machine, agricultural implement, and bicycle industries all made important contributions in the design of specialized machines for the manufacture of nearly identical parts. Nonetheless, due to technical limitations of the machines, these parts were not truly interchangeable, because they often required skilled mechanics to file and to "fit" the parts together. Undoubtedly, the new automobile industry sparked a most intense phase in the design and specialization of machine tools in the first decades of the twentieth century. As the new machine-tool technology acquired technical sophistication, the volume production of duplicate parts required little, if any skill. Furthermore, assembly operations no longer needed skilled machinists. And, Ford engineers and tool makers were in the forefront of technical innovation in machine shop practices. . . .

From 1910 to 1914, Ford engineers and tool makers fully utilized and further developed this new machine-tool technology. Ford plant superintendent Charles Sorensen reported that the move to Highland Park in 1910 "was followed by a tremendous expansion in equipment." . . . Indeed, the company invested staggering amounts of capital for the purchase and construction of specialized machines for the manufacture of the Model T Ford. By 1914, it spent $3.6 million for "plant, buildings, tanks and fixtures" and $2.8 million for "machine-tool equipment." For the manufacture of a single part, Ford engineers purchased the very best machines available. If a required machine did not exist on the market, they designed and built their own in the factory tool room. The company relied so thoroughly on the new productive technology that in 1914 the Highland Park plant had more than 15,000 machines and fewer than 13,000 workers. . . .

In addition to the purchase and construction of the most modern machine tools, Ford engineers designed and constructed special attachments, such as jigs, fixtures, and other mechanical devices, which transformed multipurpose machines into single-purpose ones. Not only engineers, but also skilled tool makers, experimental room hands, draftsmen, and metal pattern makers, developed and manufactured the novel machines and devices. In an era where craft skills and traditions still survived, little delineated the tasks of the college-educated engineer and the shop-bred mechanic. Both proved invaluable and essential for technical innovation in the Ford plant. The practical skilled workers, Arnold observed, "constitute the aristocracy of every shop." Moreover, they had to be good, experienced, and highly paid. "Nothing," he concluded, "is scamped or hurried in Ford's tool-making . . . , because economy in tool-making is rank extravagance." In the tool-making department, engineers and mechanics transferred skill from human to mechanical form in the design of machines and their attachments. . . .

Jigs and fixtures were work-holding devices which adapted multi- and special-purpose machines for the high volume production of identical parts. Technically, a jig held work but was not fastened to the machine. A fixture also held work but was fastened to the table or the bed of the machine. In 1912, the ASME Machine Shop Committee reported: "The development of jigs and fixtures for interchangeable manufacturing has been remarkable." These new mechanical devices, it added, insured "interchangeability, low production costs, and systematic production." Generally, engineers and machinists referred to fixtures as "furniture" or "appliances" since they were additions to the table or the base of the machine. Ford managers, engineers, and skilled workers called these devices "farmers' tools" because they allowed green farm hands to produce large amounts of high-quality work. . . .

Finally, progressive production and progressive assembly involved the arrangement of men and machines and the coordination and synchronization of productive operations. They were the next logical step from the division of labor and the advanced and specialized machine tools. Assembly lines and conveyors were central images of Ford mass production. But, they represented only one aspect of the new innovation in the industrial process. As Ford engineers labeled it, the fundamental notion was "progressive" or "continuous" production. Following this idea, Ford managers and engineers arranged sequentially all industrial operations to manufacture and to assemble automobile parts, components, and the final product. . . . Progressive production originated in the machine shops which produced finished metal parts around 1912 to 1913 and then gradually moved to assembly operations from 1913 to 1914. . . .

The basis of factory departments shifted from class of machine operation performed to type of product produced. Porter added that "the plan of manufacture carries the parts along from machine to machine, with comparatively little labor; far less labor than would be necessary if the departments were arranged by operations instead of work." Within a single year, true progressive or continuous production, not simply the orderly flow of material from machine to machine or department to department, became a reality. . . .

As a consequence of this innovation, materials handling became a central concern of Ford managers and engineers. Progressive production meant the constant and continuous movement of raw materials, parts, and components to and through the Highland Park factory. To facilitate this movement, Ford engineers developed a number of new devices, such as gravity work-slides and rollways to move work by hand, and endless chains and endless conveyor belts to transport parts and materials from location to location. Overhead craneways carried the heavier and bulkier items or batches of parts to and from storage. . . . [T]he mechanical movement of materials further eliminated the need for costly truckers and increased the amount of floor space for productive men and machines. . . .

E. A. Rumley [a journalist] observed that "the men stand elbow to elbow, like a line of soldiers." Moreover, as it moved from hand to hand, each part of the Model T had "its predetermined path through the machine shop."

From 1913 to 1914, Ford managers and engineers further refined their notion of progressive or continuous production with the creation of moving lines for the assembly of parts into automobile components and for the final assembly of parts and components into the Model T Ford. . . . To be sure, some experimentation was under way. For automobile assembly, the work-process was divided and subdivided and workers performed specialized operations. At first, teams of workmen moved from car to car and attached their part or component. However, materials did not move in the same manner as in the machine shops. Two examples illustrated the evolution and the advantages of the Ford assembly lines. One was the magneto assembly line, the first to develop; and the other was the chassis assembly line, the most difficult to implement, into which all other parts and components flowed.

The flywheel magneto provided the electrical charge to ignite the fuel of the Ford automobile. It was the first component to be assembled on a moving assembly line. Prior to May 1913, one Ford worker put together approximately 35 to 40 magnetos in a nine-hour day. A skilled assembler constructed the entire component. "The work was done by experienced men," H. L. Arnold noted, "but was not so uniformly satisfactory as was desired, and was costly . . . as all one-man assembly must of necessity be forever." In May 1913, Ford managers and engineers analyzed the work and subdivided it into twenty-nine separate operations. As in existing progressive machining operations, the assemblers passed the component from worker to worker by hand. The managers and engineers continued to redesign and to restructure the work and the assembly processes. They added a chain-driven conveyor to move the component from one worker to another. And, after March 1914, productivity dramatically increased—fourteen workers assembled 1,335 magnetos in an eight-hour day. Even though the working day was reduced by one hour, the assemblers more than doubled their average productivity and produced an average of 95 magnetos per person each day.

Ford engineers duplicated this procedure with varying degrees of difficulty in other assembly departments throughout the Highland Park factory from the late summer of 1913 through 1914. They created a coordinated and synchronized industrial system as a result of their efforts to provide for the progressive machine production of parts and the progressive assembly of these parts into components and finally the Model T Ford. As [Ford production chief] Sorensen recalled:

> What was worked at Ford was the practice of moving work from one quarter to another until it became a complete unit, then arranging the flow of these units at the right time and the right place to a moving assembly line from which came a finished product.

Hands, rollways, gravity slides, chain and belt conveyors, and overhead cranes moved materials from location to location. Men, machines and materials became an intricately interconnected mechanical organism.

Eventually, everything flowed to the chassis assembly line, where "from 1,000 to 4,000 separate pieces of each chassis component" streamed "daily, infallibly, and constantly." Begun in the late summer of 1913 and completed in the late spring of 1914, chassis assembly lines presented the greatest difficulty to Ford engineers. Until August 1913, Ford workers assembled the Model T chassis at a single location. . . . At the time, 250 skilled assemblers with the assistance of 80 "component carriers" assembled 6,182 chassis in the course of one month. [Journalist Fred H.] Colvin reported that the assemblers moved from chassis to chassis to attach their pieces or component. It required an average of $12\frac{1}{2}$ hours of one workman's time to put together a single chassis.

In August 1913, Ford managers and engineers began to analyze, experiment with, and systematize their procedures for chassis assembly. In September 1913, they connected the Model T chassis to a "rope and windlass" device and pulled it along a row of parts and components. Six assemblers and their helpers walked along with the chassis and attached the necessary parts and components as they went down the line. This resulted in a dramatic reduction of the assembly time for each chassis. It fell to an average of five hours and fifty minutes of a workman's time—a reduction of 50 percent. Next, in October, the mechanical device pulled the chassis along a line of 140 stationary assemblers. They stood at stations near supplies of parts and components and attached them as the chassis passed. The assembly time now averaged slightly less than three hours per worker. Additional changes in the length of the line and the number of stations further reduced the chassis assembly time. In January 1914, the engineers developed an "endless chain-driven" conveyor to pull the chassis along the line. In April 1914, they created a "man high" line to eliminate unnecessary and unproductive movements on the part of the workers. In the end, these experiments reduced chassis assembly time from $12\frac{1}{2}$ hours to one hour and thirty-three minutes.

By June 1914, Ford managers and engineers perfected the new chassis assembly line to their satisfaction and introduced it as a part of the normal industrial operations of the new mechanized Highland Park plant. Eighteen workmen performed the first two operations which set the chassis frames on two assembly lines. On these lines, unskilled assemblers performed the remaining forty-three operations to put together the Model T chassis. Mechanical conveyors delivered the parts and components to their stations. One hundred and forty-two workers assembled an average of 600 chassis in an eight-hour day. The average assembly time for each chassis under normal, as opposed to experimental, conditions was slightly under two hours of a worker's time. This was approximately one-sixth of the time that traditional methods and techniques of assembly required. . . .

In a few brief years, modern mass production became a reality in the Ford Highland factory. Within an extremely short period of time, Ford engineers and skilled workers transformed [the] traditional industrial process and broke ground for modern forms of integrated and synchronized production. Although difficult, the technical and organizational problems were not insurmountable. Nevertheless, the new industrial technology was a mixed social blessing, perhaps even a curse. It promised a material cornucopia for all. Yet, at the same time, it contained incredible social costs. The world of work would never be the same again. The new industrial technology made the worker's daily routine more monotonous and more repetitive. It dramatically altered the social structure of the shop, the factory, and, in fact, modern industrial society. And, it possessed or required new patterns of authority and control over the workforce. Indeed, the new industrial technology had a profound impact on modern social existence.

Taylorizing the Shopgirl

SUSAN PORTER BENSON

The control of selling and of the people who did it was by far the most persistent and troubling problem of department-store managers. . . . The

---

Susan Porter Benson, *Saleswomen, Managers, and Customers in American Department Stores, 1890–1940*, 1986. Reprinted with abridgements by permission of University of Illinois Press.

people behind the counters could enhance or doom management efforts to make the store efficient, profitable, and an effective agent of the culture of consumption. Managers could devise policies to improve their profit positions or their standing with the public, but the salespeople determined the success of such policies by the way in which they implemented them and through their own interactions with the store's clientele. Managers might advertise lavishly, but their expenditures were for naught if salespeople failed to follow up the interest they awakened in customers. Managers might frame stern policies to cut the costs of customer service, but if salespeople informed customers of these rules in a tactless way, they might turn out to be false economies. Managers might streamline their stock and choose assortments cannily, but merchandise would sell only if salespeople presented it convincingly to customers.

The task of devising a labor-management policy that would consistently and dependably turn the balance in their favor was an enduring preoccupation of department-store managers. They were, of course, not alone in feeling anxious and dissatisfied about their relations with their employees; labor militancy and changes in the organization of production had made labor management a nationwide preoccupation of businessmen, workers, and interested citizens by the 1890s. Department-store executives' tactics were in some ways similar to those of their factory counterparts, with whom they shared a desire for an efficient and tractable labor force. Both experimented with more humane and respectful treatment of workers, the paternalistic benefits known as welfare work, and money incentives, although department stores adapted each of these to the special conditions of large-scale retailing. In one respect, however, department-store and factory practice diverged dramatically. The unique element in department-store labor policy was the encouragement of skilled selling: the use of trained salesclerks to increase the size and number of sales transactions through merchandise information and sales psychology. It contrasted with self-service schemes, which department stores shunned before World War II, in that salespeople controlled the customer's access to the merchandise and actively influenced the course of a sales transaction. Department-store managers placed great faith in this hybrid strategy, asserting that it would enhance their public image and increase productivity while creating a contented, loyal, and respectful sales force.

In fact, the problems associated with selling were far less tractable, grounded in an emerging world of service work. . . . Department-store selling was not only one of the first of these new occupations—distinguished by their remove from production—to emerge but it also displayed the characteristics of service work in uncommonly high relief: the addition of the client to the usual worker-employer dyad was always implicit in service work, but the client was directly and emphatically present on the selling floor as he or she was not, for example, in a steam laundry. . . . Department-store managers were in the vanguard of the still-continuing effort to forge labor-management policies appropriate to the new situation. . . .

Department-store managers were going against the grain of prevailing labor-management trends in the twentieth century. They hoped to foster skill when the central tendency was to undermine it. They undertook to monitor that skill with the supervisory and accounting methods developed elsewhere to deskill and regiment workers. Even more, they attempted to harness skill in social interaction, a most unmanageable quality and one even harder to control than manual skill. In the factory, manual skill could ultimately if not easily be taken into the hands of management, mental and manual work divorced, and skill separated from the social relations of the workplace. In the store, however, the skill of selling was intimately and organically bound up with the social relations of the selling floor and the work group; only in the hands of the workers could it have the desired effect on sales. Ultimately, store managers had an apples-and-oranges problem: they were trying to combine elements that grew out of fundamentally different systems.

Equally troublesome were the problems of assessing and measuring the productivity of selling personnel. Those features of retailing which had limited department-store managers' efforts to systematize the store's organization had an even more dramatic effect on their attempts to mold the sales force. The central problem, wrote an industry observer in 1913, was that "[t]he best salesperson . . . is *not necessarily* the one that *has the largest book*"—book being selling-floor slang for the day's sales totals. High productivity, measured by sales alone, was not a reliable indicator of a salesperson's effectiveness. If an item was not sold properly, with due consideration for the customer's sensibilities, the store stood to suffer in the short run through the return of the merchandise and in the long run through the loss of the customer's goodwill. High production in a factory was, by contrast, a virtually unmixed blessing. On the selling floor, manner was at least as important as cumulative result: it mattered little if a worker stamped out a widget while in a high temper, but it made a great difference if a saleswoman sold a pair of stockings while in a grouchy mood. Moreover, a department could not function smoothly unless salespeople gave due attention to such non-selling tasks as stock work and display. Department-store managers never successfully integrated these intangibles into a clear measure of productivity.

Monitoring performance was as difficult as monitoring output. The complex social dynamics of selling were not easily reduced to clear directives; even had they been so, the close supervision necessary to enforce them would have jeopardized sales by annoying customer and salesperson alike. The core of scientific management in the factory—dividing and regularizing the work process—simply was not applicable to selling as it was defined in the palace of consumption. Non-selling workers often made change and wrapped packages, but the interaction between customer and salesperson could be neither subdivided nor standardized. Store executives had little choice but to allow salespeople broad latitude in dealing with the public.

The flow of work in retailing remained intractably irregular. Daily, weekly, and seasonal fluctuations were compounded by departmental variations, changes in fashion, the weather, and the moods of countless customers. Planning and staffing became monumentally difficult in the face of this endemic variability. Unlike factory managers, department-store managers could not regulate the flow of work, shift it from one department to another, or simply require overtime work to cope with a rush. Customers demanded to be served when and where they presented themselves; assuring service without astronomical personnel expenses was an enduring problem of the department-store executive. Unable to smooth out work load fluctuations, managers shifted the onus to their salespeople and demanded more intensive sales efforts to compensate for slow periods.

A fourth stumbling block on the road to tighter control of the work force was the public nature of the store. Labor policies were open for all to see, and concerned observers could easily question workers about the terms of their employment. The conditions under which goods were manufactured were not normally visible to the public, while the conditions under which they were sold were a public spectacle. Both organized and unorganized women shoppers were outraged at seeing overworked, underpaid women toil long hours in unhealthy surroundings; almost invariably, the same middle- and upper-class women who made up the backbone of the store's clientele spearheaded the campaigns for better conditions for working women. . . .

The Shopgirl: Class, Gender, and Selling

The selling staff of the typical department store by the 1890s was overwhelmingly working-class and overwhelmingly female, and these facts powerfully shaped labor policy. Class and gender in selling interacted in extremely complex ways, sometimes complementary and sometimes contradictory. Executives set out to change the class-based characteristics of their salespeople and to co-opt their gender-based characteristics, unwittingly entering a maze of difficulties from which they never extricated themselves.

Mid-nineteenth-century policies had built into department stores a class tension which bedeviled managers well into the middle of the twentieth century. Their methods of attracting customers and their policies toward the sales force conflicted sharply and sometimes explosively. The cultural demands of the growing urban middle and upper classes set the tone for the store, but department-store selling did not attract those of the same backgrounds. The comparatively low pay, long hours, and difficult working conditions as well as the popular image of the blowzy shopgirl usually drove middle-class working women into other employment such as clerical work. Working-class saleswomen behaved in ways that were grounded in their own cultural background but grated on their employers and their customers. Contemporary accounts of saleswomen frequently recall *Pygmalion*: some raved at the ingratitude of those who dared to be different from themselves; others winced at saleswomen's demeanor, language, and dress. Ungrammatical colloquialisms and familiar forms of address appalled employers;

one observer noted censoriously, "[T]he salespeople have become so forward as to call customers 'Dearie.' The use of such terms is a liberty which
the woman of finer sensibilities quickly resents." Dress also conveyed a
powerful class-laden message: customers were displeased when "approached by an employee who is overdressed and who bears on her person
marks of opulence which apparently do not accord with her position." The
social conflict that electrified relations between saleswomen and customers
was fundamentally of the store manager's own making: eager for the cheap
labor of uneducated women, viewing selling as semi-automatic, setting his
sights on an affluent clientele, he had created the problem of lackluster
selling for which he blamed his saleswomen.

While managers condemned clerks' class attributes out of hand, they
found much to recommend in their gender characteristics. Certain aspects
of women's culture dovetailed with managers' developing conceptions of
skilled selling. If class was a divisive factor in the clerk-customer relationship, gender was a unifying one. Qualities which had for a century been
encouraged in women—adeptness at manipulating people, sympathetic
ways of responding to the needs of others, and familiarity with things
domestic—fit nicely into a new view of selling. Managers urged saleswomen
to transfer skills from their domestic to their work lives; during the early
1920s, Filene's tested aspiring coat, suit, and dress saleswomen on their
knowledge of style and fabrics and their ability to choose "the correct
style" for different types of customer. Making the store more and more
like a home, executives encouraged saleswomen to act more and more like
hostesses, to treat their customers as guests. Empathy and responsiveness
constituted the irreducible core of selling skill. A writer in 1911 urged,
"Shop *with* the customer, not *at* her"; Macy's training director affirmed
in 1940 that "interest in the customer's problems" was the key to selling
success. Twentieth-century selling centered on the salesperson as a lay
psychoanalyst of the counter, the evangelist of the therapeutic ethic of the
culture of consumption. . . .

In department stores' formative years women's cheapness and cultural
characteristics dovetailed nicely. But as executives pursued their goal of
skilled selling more energetically, a contradiction between women's position
in the labor market and their role as skilled saleswomen emerged. Saleswomen constantly heard their supervisors emphasize the critical importance
of skilled selling, and understood from their daily experience their ability
to make or break a sale, but as women workers they remained low-paid
and low-valued in the labor-market hierarchy.

Defining the Problem: Pressures from Within and Without

While building, organizing, decorating, and systematizing the store, executives had slighted the critical area of selling—the interaction across the
counter. Convinced on the one hand that selling as men had practiced it
was an inborn talent, and on the other that attractive goods presented in
a luxurious environment would practically sell themselves, managers be-

tween 1850 and 1890 had believed that the ideal sales force was composed of neatly dressed, polite women who would sell mechanically and inoffensively. Certain that they needed only cogs on their wheels, department-store managers had wasted little time and energy on the development of their sales forces. They encouraged a passive style of selling in their employees, as described by a turn-of-the-century writer: " . . . His salespersons do not urge the customer to buy, and dilate upon the beauties of his wares. They simply hand the customer what he or she wants, and make a record of the sale. It is not his desire, the merchant says, to sell the customer what he does not want." Another observer noted that clerks' behavior varied in different grades of store: at the cheaper end of the spectrum, managers tolerated "rudeness, stupidity, and indifference," while in carriage-trade firms they demanded "intelligence, cheerfulness, and courtesy." . . .

In small ways in the 1890s and more intensely during subsequent decades, a disturbing conjunction of forces impelled managers to revise their views of their clerks. They began to realize that their irresistible ads, dazzling merchandise, and sumptuous stores had solved one set of problems—the attraction of crowds to the store—only by creating another—that of high overhead. The public spectacle of the department store was commercially viable only if customers spent more than they would from simple need or random impulse. Managers convinced themselves that only skilled selling could accomplish this . . . Cost-cutting in the non-selling departments made only a fractional difference in overhead costs, but the sale of a tie with a shirt or of three pairs of stockings instead of one dramatically decreased the proportion of fixed costs to selling price. . . . Managers concluded that selling was the bellwether that would lead the way to more profitable and efficient operations . . .

The combination of financial pressures within the store and external pressures from customers and social reformers pushed the department-store executive to frame a new role for his employees and new policies to deal with them. His balance sheets suggested that only skilled selling could reduce the impact of high fixed costs and maximize the effect of expensive advertising and service schemes. Aware of his image as an exploiter of women workers, he undertook to upgrade both the image and the actual experience of his saleswomen. On the one hand, he wanted to reap the goodwill benefits of broad-minded policies . . . On the other, he hoped that a fully trained, decently treated, and more refined type of clerk would be a more loyal and effective saleswoman. Whatever methods he used—simple kindness, welfare work, training, or financial incentives—the goal was the same: the development of skilled selling. The idea that the salesperson was the merchant's emissary to the public was the foundation of the emerging retail personnel wisdom, although it was a difficult lesson for many managers to learn. Even in the late 1920s, industry writers still felt it necessary to remind department-store executives of the pivotal place of salespeople in their store: "A manager has only one pair of eyes and only one pair of ears, but he needs more. So he must train his salespeople to keep their eyes and ears open for customers' sympathetic reactions. . . . To the public, our corporation is the girl behind the counter." There was respect for the salesperson in the new view, but there was also fear—and both were aspects of the retailer's uneasy recognition of the alarming power of a group which he had once considered no more than a passive adjunct to his elaborate store systems. . . .

Too often, discipline on the selling floor was all stick and no carrot, with harsh words underlined by elaborate systems of fines and penalties. Many stores appeared to assume their employees had criminal tendencies. Store detectives, spying floor managers, undercover agents, and cumbersome procedures for employees' purchases and for the removal of their personal property from the store kept them under constant and intrusive surveillance. Tardiness, small errors in filling out sales checks, and faults in procedure led to fines or some form of infantilizing public exposure and confession. Some stores required employees to sign a slip acknowledging the error; others demanded confessional interviews with supervisors; still others posted the names of the most frequent offenders. . . . The clerk who had to repay her employer the five dollars extra change she gave to a customer lost not just a few cents, but most of her week's salary. Such penalties alienated customers as well as workers. One customer, enraged when a clerk was fined for some accidental breakage, paid the saleswoman's fine and vowed never to return to the offending store. . . .

Still, the need to cultivate a cheerful, satisfied, and cooperative sales force led many retailers to moderate the harsher aspects of store discipline and to favor the carrot over the stick. As early as the mid-1890s, retail writers urged managers to "enforce justice and fairness." The hallmarks of the new approach were an appeal to the good nature of the clerk, "rewards for accuracy" rather than "fines for mistakes," and showing "the employee how he will *gain* if he endeavors to advance himself, rather than how he will *lose* if he does not." The enlightened approach curiously combined repentance for past injustices, a concern for public image, a consciousness of the importance of the salesperson, and a conviction that arbitrary treatment backfired. One observer smugly noted that an abusive employer might as well save his breath: "In rough tones, not unaccompanied by opprobrious language, he scolded the help, while they listened to him with sullen glances or cynical smiles. It was also noticeable that on his departure one or two employees began at once to do the very thing for which he had just blamed them, and which he had just forbidden." Warning that authoritarian pressure frequently sparked rebellion, another grimly noted that "if this is true of men, it must be even more true of the twentieth-century woman." . . .

Perhaps the most common method of avoiding capricious management practices was the rule book. Around the turn of the century, many retailers had begun to spell out both expected conduct and the penalty for violations. Rule books were a response to the growing size of department stores, a recognition of the need to end arbitrary practices, and a means of exacting genteel behavior from the sales force. One of the most pervasive and enduring of the new rules was that regarding dress; appearing first during the late 1890s, dress regulations were accepted practice by the 1920s. In 1929, for example, a survey of twenty-two stores in the New York metropolitan area showed that every store but one specified the color of saleswomen's clothing. Some managers required dark, inconspicuous clothing because they liked the uniformity it gave to the store's appearance. Others hoped that drab colors would minimize the "danger of display of poor taste and lack of background on the part of the employees," a hope they underlined by displaying clothing acceptable in style and color near employees' lunch rooms. But they also saw semi-uniform clothing as a subtle way of controlling employees' behavior. They worried that an overdressed saleswoman would behave in a high-handed way: "because she 'sports' good clothes and an exaggerated coiffure, [she] thinks she can lord it over all with whom she comes into contact, be it customer or fellow-employee." Conversely, dress codes enforced "a defined and appropriate 'class distinction' between the customer and the assistant, which is . . . very pleasant to the lady shopper."

Managers' kinder and less arbitrary treatment might improve the morale of the salespeople and brighten the atmosphere of the store, but it could also produce lackluster employees. In 1903, a buyer pointed out the perils of the rule-bound store: "It is responsibility that brings out character, that gives force and initiative, that puts man (or woman) 'on his mettle.' Good help is impossible where employees are treated like slaves or children." . . . Moreover, managerial whim continued to weigh heavily on the saleswoman. The move toward more humane and evenhanded treatment was spotty and inconsistent, as managers' attitudes toward seats for saleswomen show.

Early-twentieth-century reformers secured the passage of many state laws requiring the provision of seats for saleswomen, but it was another question entirely whether saleswomen would actually be permitted to use the seats. Managers early realized the wisdom of allowing idle saleswomen to sit down: it was "absurd to expect continual interest and civility" from someone who was on her feet nine hours or more and "the sight of unoccupied saleswomen seated, instead of standing, at their counters redounds to the reputation as well as to the pecuniary benefit of the store proprietor." Women's Bureau investigators during the 1920s, however, found widely varying management policies on this issue. In Oklahoma, for example, one saleswoman reported that she was treated as if she "were committing a crime" when she sat down; in a second store, managers instructed saleswomen "not to tire themselves by constant standing"; and in a third firm women were forbidden to sit by the first-floor manager but permitted to do so by the second-floor manager. . . .

Department-store managers rejected both the older ideal of the naturally gifted salesman and the late-nineteenth-century model of the passive, unskilled, order-taking saleswoman. They undertook to shape a whole new breed of clerks, no longer taking salespeople as they found them. Selling skill, twentieth-century style, could be codified and taught . . .

Convinced that the customary agents of early socialization—the home and the school—had failed, managers began to transform department stores into educational institutions. They blamed "unpropitious home surroundings and . . . defects in our educational system" for the fact that so many salespeople "frequently [spoke] and act[ed] in ways which [did] not commend them to people of refinement." Working-class and immigrant children were simply not being assimilated into the respectable middle-class mainstream fast enough to fill the places behind the counters of department stores. The schools, moreover, were falling short in their methods as well as in the ideology they taught: they did not encourage thinking, provided only "*admonition*" and not "EXPLANATION," failed to teach students to "ANALYZE, rather than *memorize*." These complaints are a measure of the distance between department stores' and manufacturers' labor requirements. Most of the latter would have been content had the schools inculcated the traditional virtues of hard work and obedience through admonition and memorization, while department-store managers wanted initiative and independent judgment grafted on as well. . . .

Managers were confident that the benevolent guidance of the store would transform the dismal product of an unfortunate home and a misguided school. Samuel Reyburn, president of Lord & Taylor and a key figure in department-store management circles in the 1920s and 1930s, spoke glowingly of the impact of the store environment on such a girl: "Constant contact with the woman who is in charge of her department will have an influence on her. Daily contact with other girls who have been subjected to influences in business will have an influence on her. Daily observations of customers in the building will influence her, and slowly she will change because of these influences. She will lower the tone of her voice, grow quiet in her manner, exhibit better taste in the selection of her clothes, become more considerate of others." But, Reyburn continued, this "natural" process was too slow and haphazard; the enlightened store would hurry it along in an organized, deliberate socialization campaign. . . .

Welfare Work

There were two major strands in this effort. The first, commonly known as welfare work, flourished during the first two decades of the twentieth century and merged into the personnel management movement of the 1920s. Training, the second, began in the early 1900s, was firmly established in the 1910s, and became widespread after 1920. Welfare work included store facilities and social service programs for workers, activities that were implicitly rather than directly didactic, while training taught everything from arithmetic to modern art to sales psychology to the proper way to fill in a sales check. Welfare work and training shared the goal of inculcating salespeople with a new outlook that would make them more effective at skilled selling. They frequently overlapped in execution, particularly in trying to modify the class and cultural perspective of the salesperson. Both offered certain benefits to workers at the same time as they demanded in return more compliant and efficient behavior. Finally, class and gender were central issues in both efforts. . . .

Welfare work combined workers' services and facilities—rest rooms, lounges, dining rooms, gymnasiums, infirmaries, libraries, vacation retreats, and savings banks—with some rudimentary education along the lines of personal hygiene, etiquette, and grammar classes. Some of the new facilities were spartan—a lunchroom might amount to some rickety benches and a table in a basement room—but others rivaled those provided for customers. Lord & Taylor's Fifth Avenue store, opened in 1914, had luxurious rest and recreation facilities for the store's employees, while in 1916 San Francisco's Emporium bought a thirty-two-acre resort and opened the lavish facilities to its workers for a nominal fee. Following the lead of Providence's Shepard's Company, a number of department stores during the 1900s and 1910s employed welfare secretaries to oversee these programs and to dispense advice and counseling to troubled employees. Some stores, notably Filene's, encouraged the formation of store organizations which functioned as company unions.

Welfare work in the store as in the factory had many meanings: it provided a much-improved work environment; it secured more efficient performance either directly or indirectly; and it enhanced the firm's public image. A store lunchroom, for example, served healthful, cheap lunches, gave workers quick service so that they could return punctually to the selling floor, and looked good in store publicity. Outings similarly provided good advertising and pleasant diversion along with an opportunity to build the store spirit which produced eager and efficient workers. . . .

Welfare work in department stores assumed the added burden of dampening the class conflict across the counter. One enthusiastic writer likened Jordan Marsh's employee facilities to a "high-class hotel," asking rhetorically: "If a girl, say, reared in humble surroundings, spends some part of her day amid pictures and cheerful furniture and tasteful rugs and books and sunlight, will she not insensibly acquire a clearer insight into the ideas and needs of the majority of the store's customers? Will she not, then, be better able to wait upon her trade deftly, sympathetically, and understandingly?" Some aspects of welfare programs served all four ends. Clinics, for example, increased efficiency, in one store reducing absenteeism so much that the work force could be cut by fifty-four people. Free or low-cost medical care was no small boon to the clerk who earned barely enough for the day-to-day necessities; suitably publicized, it created goodwill for the store. Finally, medical care could eradicate health problems related to class status and thus eliminate a jarring note in the palace of consumption: in the words of a journalist, "A customer is attracted to a person of wholesome appearance who will promptly and quite excusably shrink from a clerk whose hair shows the presence of vermin, or who is careless in controlling a cough." In the end, welfare work promised not only to mollify the customer and transform the working-class saleswoman—it held the hope of attracting the elusive "better class" of salesperson to an increasingly attractive and respectable workplace. . . .

Welfare work helped to change the popular image of the shopgirl by improving her working conditions and beginning to attack her class-based characteristics. Still, it provided no clear vision of what the new skilled salesperson would be like; clean towels, hot meals, and edifying literature could set the stage for skilled selling, but they could not write the script. This task fell to training programs. Tremendously varied in their specifics, these programs attempted to build upon the educational aspects of welfare work but focused more directly on the demands of department-store selling. Training sought both to increase immediate, quantifiable efficiency—for example, to teach saleswomen punctilious accuracy in filling out sales checks—and to develop the ability to cope creatively with situations requiring discretion instead of cut-and-dried compliance with rules. The second aim is most important because it defined and, insofar as possible, transmitted selling skill. Advocates of training assumed that their programs would have broad institutional benefits as well as positive effects on individuals; one writer argued, for example, that training programs would break down institutional barriers by bringing together people from different departments.

Training consisted of general education, merchandise training, and salesmanship training; all three were recognized by the mid-1900s. General education, building on welfare work's foundation, sought to fill the gaps left by inadequate family and school training. Courses ranged from grammar-school work for younger employees to university-level offerings for adults. Although this aspect of training did not speak explicitly to better selling performance, it grew out of the conviction that a better education would give an air of polish and efficient competence to the sales force. Attempting to convey middle-class values and behavior, arithmetic classes included Franklinesque exercises in personal budgeting, and English instruction prescribed a drawing-room version of standard English.

Merchandise training surveyed the historical development of a product, its manufacturing process, its properties, and its uses. It was a curious amalgam of high culture (in, for example, visits to museums), traditional womanly wisdom about homemaking and dress, new "scientific" information about the care of various fabrics and articles, and the dictates of fashion. The combination conveyed to the saleswoman a uniform notion of respectable "good taste." In the words of Helen Rich Norton, an important figure in retail training circles, "the broadest and most important of the aims" of retail training was to impress upon the students "[i]mproved standards of living, better habits of thought, higher interpretations, and ideals." Some attempts to reach this goal verged on the absurd: both the NRDGA and the *Dry Goods Economist* circulated films showing life in Palm Beach and Miami so that salespeople could develop the "mental 'atmosphere' " to advise resort-bound customers properly. Norton's textbook, *Retail Selling*, included five pages of essential French terms, suggesting that stores retain a French teacher to teach proper pronunciation to the sales force. Whether programs tried to apply a veneer of middle-class trappings or to remake the saleswoman's "inner consciousness," the target was the same: the saleswoman's class identity.

By contrast, salesmanship training built on the saleswoman's gender identity. Women had been trained to be consumers even before they were trained to be saleswomen; for example, their socialization encouraged them to pay attention to the style and construction of clothing. Such a consciousness became selling skill when saleswomen could guess a customer's size at a glance or estimate her budget by assessing the clothes she wore. Similarly, saleswomen had as women learned to deal with affect, to sense and meet people's needs. Once behind the counter, they had only to apply their interpersonal talents to dealing with their customers.

Training programs encouraged saleswomen to develop their social skills as well, so that they could create sales where there would have been none. Trainers counseled saleswomen to expand the individual sales transaction through suggestion selling and to set the stage for future sales by building up a clientele of customers. Suggestion selling was by far the most popular tactic urged upon salespeople; the literature is filled with inspirational pieces touting, quite correctly, its powers to expand profits and cut costs. Bosses exhorted saleswomen to size up each customer's budget and preferences in order to maximize her purchases each time she visited the store, suggesting a tie to go with a shirt—a second pair of hose—a handbag to match shoes—a good buy on dish towels. Suggestion selling could also serve as a form of speedup. Sanger Brothers of Dallas, for example, launched a major campaign for suggested sales in September 1921. The firm promised to maintain salaries despite the sharp postwar deflation if salespeople kept sales up to the old dollar levels, a task requiring them to increase the number of sales by from one-third to one-half. . . .

The Contradictions in Training

Despite managers' high hopes, training programs in fact ran into many obstacles which offset or negated their benefits. The great paradox in training saleswomen was that it succeeded best on the selling floor where store managers had the least reliable control. General education and store system could easily be taught in a traditional classroom setting, but the most critical part of training—that involving merchandise and interaction with customers—was more effectively learned through experience and participation. One writer maintained that fully 85 percent of training time should be spent in the selling department. . . . Yet training on the sales floor was usually conducted by the buyer and the sponsor, both of whom had a primary loyalty to their department and different ideas about selling skill than did upper management. Buyers were frequently and necessarily absent from the departments and, even when they were present, tended to emphasize the speedy sale of current stock more than the development of a sound selling staff for the future. Finally, they often imposed their idiosyncracies on their training efforts, conveying their own idea of selling skill rather than a uniform, storewide version.

The sponsor, a saleswoman assigned the duty of greeting, indoctrinating, and training newcomers to her department, appeared on the scene at the turn of the century. Her position was anomalous: her role as sponsor gave her authority over those who were technically her equals. Financial incentive reinforced the contradiction; if the sponsor spent too much time in training, her own sales totals and thus her reputation with her superiors would suffer. A sponsor was rarely well trained for her role, and her immediate supervisors begrudged any time she spent away from selling. But most disquieting of all was sponsors' great latitude in training: managers rarely knew precisely what they told new employees. Sponsors were dangerous because [they were] potentially subversive, but approximately half of the nation's department stores continued to use them between 1910 and 1940 because they provided a convenient and economical means of training.

Just as selling skill was best transmitted on the selling floor, so there it was forged. Management wisdom competed with on-the-job wisdom developed by saleswomen. Sometimes the two versions clashed, . . . but even when they coincided managers were eager to gain control of the transmission of knowledge. One of the signs of managers' new fearful respect for their salespeople was their desperate eagerness to solicit advice and suggestions, not just because it earned employees' goodwill but also because it was an important source of good ideas. Salespeople developed resourceful tactics for dealing with customers and had the best up-to-the-minute reading of demand, and managers were eager to appropriate that knowledge so that they could recycle it in training programs. . . . The use of sponsors was a similar attempt to harness shop-floor wisdom. Managers encouraged salespeople to turn in suggestions for better selling service and required them to fill out "call slips" whenever a customer requested an item that was out of stock and sometimes whenever they lost a sale. Such campaigns were potentially useful ways for upper management to learn what was happening on the sales floor; they served as a check on the performance of buyers and salespeople alike and spotlighted areas for special training efforts. . . .

A second built-in contradiction in sales training was that between managers' lofty goals for training programs and their practical scorn for selling as a function and for those who did the work. Managers hoped to induce their saleswomen to forget the mixed reputation of department-store selling and to think of it as a profession, a vocation conferring dignity on those who practiced it. . . .

Countering this rhetoric were the actual position of selling in the stores and the reality of training programs. The retail literature constantly urged executives to spend more time on the selling floor, teaching by example and proving management's respect for selling, yet department-store executives from buyers to general managers were notorious for fleeing to their offices at the first opportunity. Most retail executives in fact concentrated on merchandising, disdaining selling and assuming it would somehow be fostered by others. Scorn for selling went hand in hand with a low opinion of those who sold. . . .

The major method of assessing sales performance also belied managers' rhetoric about the professional nature of skilled selling. Sales force performance was evaluated by sales totals, through direct ratings by superiors, and through the reports of service shoppers. The first, as noted earlier, dangerously emphasized quantity at the expense of quality and the second was as subjective and arbitrary in the store as in other settings. Service shopping was the peculiar department-store form of evaluation, providing a comprehensive shop-floor view of selling through the use of undercover employees who posed as customers and reported on the service they received from salespeople. The shoppers were recruited by individual stores, supplied by schools of retailing, or hired from commercial shopping services such as the Willmark Service System. The women chosen as shoppers came from the same general social and economic strata as the department-store clientele as a whole; service shopping was thus doubly useful since it revealed the typical customer's standards for store service along with her assessment of the degree to which the sales force met those standards. Managers asked shoppers to rate salespeople on everything from "[e]vidence of taste and judgment" to honesty to whether they had a salesbook and pencil handy. Shoppings ranged from the completely secret, with no warning whatever to employees, to the relatively open, in which case employees were told what the shoppers were looking for as well as the week or month in which the shopping would take place; in all cases, of course, the individual shoppers remained unknown to the sales force. Managers almost always told the salespeople the results of the shopping reports and targeted low-rated areas for special training efforts, usually followed by repeated shoppings. A form of industrial espionage, service shopping impressed workers with their subordinate status and their bosses' distrust of them. . . .

The relationship between salespeople and their customers produced a final contradiction in skilled selling. Customers and managers wanted salespeople to be both deferential and authoritative, but the two characteristics clashed rather than complemented each other. The more managers urged their saleswomen to become experts on their merchandise and fashion, the more likely clerks were to resist the demand for deference. At the same time, managers zealously tried to prevent their salespeople from assuming terms of familiarity or equality with their customers, and retail periodicals were filled with outraged accounts of saleswomen who presumed that customers would share their tastes. Typical of the genre was a tale about a saleswoman who offered a collar to a "smart-looking business woman with an air of authority":

> "Here's one that we are selling lots of to stenographers and typewriters, and lots of us girls have bought 'em, too," the girl explained.
>
> Harriet saw a shade of resentment pass over the woman's face, as she set her lips firmly, dropped the collar and started to turn away.

Incentives for Skilled Selling

Department-store managers bolstered their rhetoric about the joys of professional selling with financial incentives. The notion of incentive was integral to welfare work: while medical care supplied by the store might well lead to greater loyalty and efficiency, it was also a reward in itself. Not so with training, which—especially in its more simplistic forms—offered no inherent benefit to the salesperson. Department-store managers therefore introduced a variety of incentives for skilled selling, borrowing schemes from their brothers in manufacturing. . . .

Store managers endlessly tinkered with salary systems because they worried that incentive payments overemphasized sales totals. Factory managers could simply pay incentives for each item that passed quality control, while retailers had no way of knowing if a sale was satisfactorily conducted. Managers feared that incentives would lead salespeople to slight those who were "just looking," indecisive, or small spenders. In their eagerness to boost their book, salespeople might oversell merchandise, thus increasing the store's proportion of costly returned goods. Moreover, incentive plans rewarded neither the intangibles involved in a sale (such as attitude, demeanor, and helpfulness) nor the performance of other sales floor duties (such as stock work, merchandise display, and cooperation with fellow workers). A writer in the *Dry Goods Economist* spoke for many of his colleagues when he stressed the connection between incentive payments and training: "it is a mistake to introduce the bonus on sales system in a store without educating the sales force to GIVE THE CUSTOMER WHAT HE WANTS." . . .

In the end, kinder and more equitable treatment, welfare work, training, and incentives through wages, premiums, and promotion failed to replace the shopgirl with a skilled saleswoman who met department-store managers' complex and contradictory specifications. Four decades of effort to produce a skilled selling force left retail managers nearly as unsatisfied with the performance of the women behind their counters as they had been in 1900. One despairing writer complained that, "In spite of the efforts of training departments, the standard of service remains mediocre. . . . [F]ew clerks can be depended upon really to facilitate an intelligent choice." . . .

Each of the methods for remodeling saleswomen had serious flaws as well as strengths. Attempts to moderate and regularize discipline produced clear rules which governed both managers and workers, but often at the price of thwarting salespeople's initiative. Some managers treated their subordinates in a newly respectful manner, but others persisted in the old retailing pattern of quirky and personalistic supervision. Welfare work could awaken loyalty and help to decrease class-based tensions, but it could also arouse resentment against its paternalism; it could set the mood for efficient selling, but it did little to translate that mood into effective action. Training programs attempted to prescribe selling skill, but that skill flourished on the sales floor where managers' power was limited. They tried to convey an idea of the dignity and professional nature of selling, but too often resorted to cut-rate methods that demeaned the message of skilled selling. Financial incentives might produce higher sales tallies or speed the sale of slow-moving merchandise, but they could also reward overbearing selling tactics that ran roughshod over the customers. Promotion opportunities could raise the quality of saleswomen's performance, but only if the opportunities were numerous enough and only if women were interested in a long-term career.

But the failure of efforts to remake saleswomen went beyond flaws in tactics; the crusade was doomed by more general features of department-store life. First, managers' conduct often belied their rhetoric about selling. While they argued in theory that they must reorient themselves from buying merchandise to selling it, in fact they clung to the buying role because it was more comfortable and more controllable. Selling, and the people who did it, remained solidly on the bottom rungs of the store's prestige ladder. The development of true selling skill would have demanded a transformation in the roles of manager and salesperson alike, a thoroughgoing revision of the store's prestige and reward system. In fact, most managers shied away from the disruptive possibilities of such a change and were satisfied with limited measures to mollify their critics and marginally improve their balance sheets. The price of skilled selling was too high in two senses: wage, training, and welfare-work costs would have been prohibitive, and skilled workers had a dangerously subversive potential.

Second, managers had set themselves a virtually impossible task. They were trying to systematize and rationalize a highly variable type of human interaction, to teach their saleswomen initiative and independence and yet to control the exercise of these characteristics. Saleswomen were to be thinking but also obedient employees; they were to follow store procedure to the last rigorous detail and yet respond creatively to the special opportunities to sell [to] each customer; they were to develop independent judgment but still display unquestioning loyalty to the store; they were to try very hard to sell but not *too* hard. These contradictions are a measure of the difficulties of managing service workers. The endemic variability of retailing was nowhere more troubling: the infinite possibilities of the exchange between salesperson and customer defied standardization and control.

Third, managers were tinkering with two fundamental social categories: class and gender. They tried to modify the class-related personal characteristics of their employees, to narrow the gap between saleswomen on the one hand and managers and customers on the other. But they did so without offering saleswomen either the social or economic power of members of the class they were urged to emulate. They tried to exploit their saleswomen's gender-based personal characteristics, but only dimly understood the difficulties of integrating women's culture with business culture. . . .

✦ FURTHER READING

Loren Baritz, *Servants of Power* (1956)

Susan Porter Benson, *Counter Cultures: Saleswomen, Managers, and Customers in American Department Stores, 1890–1940* (1986)

Harry Braverman, *Labor and Monopoly Capitalism: The Degradation of Work in the Twentieth Century* (1974)

Richard Edwards, *Contested Terrain: The Transformation of the Workplace in the Twentieth Century* (1979)

David Hounshell, *From the American System to Mass Production, 1800–1932* (1984)

David Gartman, *Auto Slavery: The Labor Process in the American Automobile Industry, 1897–1950* (1986)

Sanford Jacoby, *Employing Bureaucracy* (1985)

Nelson Lichtenstein and Stephen Meyer, eds., *On the Line: Essays in the History of Auto Work* (1989)

Stephen Meyer, *The Five Dollar Day: Labor Management at the Ford Motor Company, 1908–1921* (1981)

Daniel Nelson, *Managers and Workers: Origins of the New Factory System in the United States, 1880–1920* (1975)

David Noble, *Forces of Production* (1985)

Sumner Slichter, *Union Policies and Industrial Management* (1941)

CHAPTER
9

Industrial Unionism
During the Great Depression

✣

The 1930s are the pivot upon which twentieth-century labor history turns. Millions of workers joined a newly energized trade-union movement in these years, many of them under the banner of the Congress of Industrial Organizations, the breakaway union federation that burst upon the national scene in 1936 and 1937.

The new unionism had three notable features. First, it organized mass-production industries like auto, steel, and electrical products and vital services like intercity truck transport, longshore freight handling, and municipal buses and subways, all of which stood at the core of the U.S. economy in the first half of this century. By 1945 the unions enrolled almost 15 million workers, five times the number at the depth of the Great Depression. About a third of all nonagricultural workers were now trade-union members, a proportion far above that of any previous era in U.S. history.

Second, many of these unions were organized on an industrial basis. Therefore they enrolled all *workers in a given plant or mill, regardless of their job title, skill level, or AFL claims that they belonged in one of its craft unions. Because of their inclusiveness, the new industrial unions enrolled many workers whom the AFL had spurned: Eastern European immigrants, African-Americans, Mexican-Americans, and white women in unskilled occupations.*

Finally, the unionism of the 1930s had a radical flavor unseen since the era of Eugene V. Debs. Communists and socialists had played key roles in organizing workers in the maritime industries, in auto manufacturing, and in steel and electrical products. Once organized, these new unions often fought with foremen and managers to slow the pace of production, limit management prerogatives, and win a whole series of new rights, among them seniority, which had rarely before been codified in a binding collective-bargaining contract.

Of course, historians do not agree about the full meaning of this experience. How was it that these unions proved so successful at a time when unemployment rates stood at such high levels? Were the unions as radical as many of their contemporary opponents claimed? Were they an effective counterweight to managerial Taylorism? Did ordinary workers see the new unions as merely an instrument to increase their pay and ameliorate the conditions under which they labored, or did they invest their larger aspirations in this new social movement, finding in its struggles some of that transcendant meaning hailed by anticapitalist radicals of old?

In the first document, John Steuben, a communist organizer in Youngstown, Ohio, describes the Communist party's large role in the CIO's Steel Workers Organizing Committee. Out of two hundred SWOC organizers, about sixty were communists. Company recognition of the new unions hardly resolved worker-management conflicts, as the second document demonstrates. In it, Margaret Nowak describes her husband's resourceful leadership in a 1937 slowdown strike in Detroit. Disputes over pay, job content, transfers, and promotions remained endemic in all workplaces, so most union contracts contained an elaborate grievance procedure to resolve them. But union leaders often saw their shop-floor role in quite different ways, as the last two documents illustrate. The first of these offers advice to United Automobile Worker shop stewards on how to win grievances, fight factory supervisors, and strengthen the union, while the second reveals the far more conservative approach of two high officials of the United Steelworkers, who successfully worked to transform their union into one that cooperated with the corporations and tempered the militancy of the rank and file.

Communist John Steuben Organizes in Steel, 1936

Youngstown, Ohio
August 31, 1936

Dear Comrade Stachel:

. . . The drive in the Youngstown steel district like throughout the country has not yet assumed a mass character. However, this does not express the real sentiment of the steel workers, meeting hundreds of them every week, both American and foreign-born, I have yet to find one case of real hostility towards the union. On the contrary, I am met with open arms and the steel workers are keenly interested in the drive and are anxiously hoping to see the drive go over big. I am absolutely convinced that the greatest majority of the steel workers will join the union in the next few months to come.

Why then is there this great discrepancy between the favorable sentiment and the actual growth of the union? The way I see it, these are some of the reasons:

1. The open warning of the companies to fire the men who join the union, still constitute the greatest obstacle. Although we can already observe a definite break down of this fear.
2. Many old foreign-born workers are still bitter against the American steel workers who didn't back them in the 1919 strike and want to see the Americans come in first.
3. The self-satisfaction of the SWOC [Steel Workers Organizing Com-

Max Gordan, "The Communists and the Drive to Organize Steel, 1936" in *Labor History* 23 (Spring 1982), pp. 260–265. Reprinted by permission of *Labor History*.

mittee] on the top with the progress of the drive. This results in a failure to press the field organizers to produce better results. . . . These people on the top (SWOC) also picture the steel drive as a mere series of mass meetings and a mechanical signing up of members without developing any partial struggles and obtain certain initial victories for the workers, without necessarily calling local strikes. . . .

4. The work of the organizers, especially the UMWA [United Mine Workers of America] organizers, is perhaps one of the weakest links in the whole drive. . . .

This is so important a question that I therefore must deal with it in detail. The organizers' staff in Youngstown can be divided into two categories: The UMWA organizers and the Party forces. There is a vast difference between the two. It is amazing how people can be so long in the labor movement and know so little! Not only are they political babies, they are not even good union organizers. To give you an example, a UMWA official from the anthracite (Gwyn) was in Youngstown five weeks and recruited three men. Another from the soft coal (Buhaley) was here six weeks and recruited five men and these were supposed to be well trained organizers. Then take the man who is in charge here (Frank Shiffka) completely incompetent and if not for our forces he would have left the field long ago. . . . On the other hand our forces that are on the staff are the best organizers and produce more results than any of them. I, personally, have established myself as the best recruiter and on the average I recruit close to fifty percent of the total recruits. Our youth organizer and the other comrades are also doing fine.

In face of such a vast difference between our and the UMWA forces, it was necessary to establish a proper relationship. Having in mind that these people don't know what criticism and self-criticism means, we have to avoid any head-on-collision with them. Instead we pursued a policy of winning their confidence. This was fully accomplished with the result that our suggestions and our policies are unquestionably accepted. We have also from the very start, decided that the Party comrades must be the best organizers and by our example bring up the rest of the crew. This is just what is happening now.

A few remarks about the methods of organization. . . . If you receive accurate reports from the field you then know that as yet in no place are the mass meetings a real success and in many places these "mass" meetings only expose the weaknesses of the union and sometimes make it look even worse than it really is. For example, I think it is crazy to now call mass meetings in towns like Alliquippa. On the basis of the experiences in other places and on the basis of Foster's lessons in Youngstown (1919), we have decided not to call any mass meeting until we have at least two thousand men signed up. Then when we have such a number of workers signed up and these are involved in preparation for a mass meeting, we are sure that at least five thousand steel workers will attend the meetings. The workers like this policy very much, as they would be afraid (and with full justification) to attend open meetings. However, we have engaged a radio station in Akron and we broadcast from there twice a week, this will go on till after Labor Day and then we will fight for a further allowance for the radio. The radio and STEEL LABOR are the medium through which we are reaching thousands of workers with the voice of the union. . . .

A few words on the method of recruiting. Of course we are using Comrade Foster's three point theory of organization as our starting point. On the basis of this theory, I have developed a method which has been proven and tested to be the best and the whole crew in Youngstown is now practicing it. I call it the "chain form of recruiting." In brief, it works like this—when I sign up a worker, I ask him to recommend three or five other men from his department. Then I ask him to talk to these workers in the mill and prepare the ground for me. Then two days later I visit these workers, most of them already expect me and when I come to their house and present my credential, they already know who I am and I find no difficulty in signing them up. These men in turn recommend others and the chain is endless. Right now, for example, over a hundred workers are expecting me at their homes. This week, every house that I went to, as soon as I present my credential, the reply was, "Come in, I have been waiting for you." My list is already so big that another organizer will be attached to me so that the workers will not be kept waiting too long. Those organizers that begun to practice this chain form of organizing are also meeting with similar success.

Another method that I am using is not to spread out too much. Instead, I am concentrating on certain departments. For example, I have already signed up the majority of the men in the Condroit Department of the Ygstn Sheet and Tube (over 40 men). From there I began to move into the 40 inch mill. The experience is that once you establish a base in one department it is much easier to spread out into the other departments.

To summarize this point: the tempo in recruiting depends entirely on the organizers, the methods they use, the hours they put in, the ability to convince the worker not to fear signing up and even enthusing them for active participation in the drive. . . .

While it is absolutely correct to discourage local strikes at this stage of the game and even be on guard against any strikes that may be contemplated by the steel companies, yet, the union must already begin to develop certain partial struggles that will result in some immediate victories for the workers. These can be developed through progressive company union representatives, through committees and petitions. The companies are terribly nervous and it is possible to obtain all kinds of concessions that in turn will help to build the union. It is unfortunate that the SWOC don't realize the importance of such actions. Then, there is another aspect to the same problem: when a worker joins the union he expects some kind of help and if this is not forthcoming he will fall for the company propaganda of "Why pay dues?" I think that our forces on the staff should raise this question everywhere and bring it to the attention of the CIO. . . .

Present Policies of Steel Corporations

Our secret method of recruiting and organization created a very difficult situation for the companies. They are really not aware of the degree of progress we have made so far. The decentralized form of organization is an additional obstacle to them. However, we know that they are careful in firing union men. Sixteen of our people were uncovered . . . including many of our comrades. But so far only the YCL [Young Communist League] organizer was fired out of the Sheet & Tube. All the others were called in, warned but not yet fired.

Through a friendly federal man we have also learned that the companies have brought in a lot of ammunition inside the mills. Sheet & Tube has deputized 151 men, Republic 50 men. We have also learned that when the first public meeting is held, they will provoke a fight and open a barrage of tear gas.

Meanwhile, they are publishing every Sunday a full page ad. I will send you a sample of this Sunday ad. They are also circulating a petition among wives of steel workers against the CIO. The spies continue to shadow the organizers and all our wires are tapped. Recently I moved to a new house hoping to keep it secret, several days later two cars with the stool pigeons were in front early in the morning. I figure it is no use to move again, I have arranged for another sleeping place in case of emergencies. I have also learned from the same source that they are especially out to get us and to link us up with the CIO and then make a big splash in the papers. We are now expecting it to break soon and we are prepared for it. . . .

On the Party

. . . The functioning of the Party is very unsatisfactory. . . . At present I devote all my time to the drive. However, as soon as I personally recruit 500 into the union (I have already reached the 200 mark) and the other comrades recruit another 500 steel workers, it will no longer be necessary for me to devote my time on individual recruiting and I will have more time for direct Party work. However, I have already established dozens of splendid contacts for the Party. I look forward that within six months from now the bulk of the Party will be composed of powerful nuclei inside the mills. We have already made a start by recruiting one of the organizers into the Party. . . . I am now working on several other leading people in the drive and I am sure we will soon have them in the Party.

The Party comrades inside the mills are doing splendid work and they are coming forward very nicely. Up to now the active comrades were busy with putting the Party on the ballot, now we're through with this work, we will get busy on stabilizing the units and involve our Party forces in the steel drive. . . .

Comradely yours,

Steuben

Stanley Nowak Organizes a Slowdown Strike, 1937

. . . Ternstedt's was one of the greatest aggregations of women workers in the automotive industry. The vast majority of the twelve thousand employees were women, and all previous organizing attempts had netted only about a dozen members. On some floors of Main Plant No. 18 hardly a man was to be seen, as men worked mainly in the tool and die section.

At the organizational meeting, considerable doubt was expressed as to whether women could be organized, especially since previous attempts had accomplished so little. Finally Stanley spoke up. "I disagree," he said, "that women are difficult to organize. In every shop I have organized, and in every activity in which women have participated with me, I have found them very dependable, vocal, and militant, often more so than men."

"Well, you can have it, Stanley," said the others, who willingly turned over to him the Ternstedt assignment. . . .

Stanley began stopping in at a neighborhood bar, where he learned of grievances in Ternstedt's different departments and featured them in the next day's leaflet. This caught the attention of the workers, and some of them began to stop for a word or two.

The tool and die men and some of the machine repair men began to stop at the sound truck to ask questions. Because of their skills they were less vulnerable than other workers, and soon they began to sign applications and hand out leaflets to fellow employees.

Stanley felt it was time to call meetings. The Slovenian Benefit Society owned the Slovene Hall on Livernois and South streets, about a block away. The sympathetic and cooperative manager permitted the hall's use as a temporary union headquarters and meeting place. Membership meetings grew until forty or fifty people were attending after each shift. . . .

One reason for so many women employees was that the company manufactured small parts easily manipulated by women—door handles, chromium trim, and so on. Many women hired during World War I had been allowed to remain because they would work for less than men. Ternstedt's reputation for low wages was widely known. The bonus system was juggled so that it was almost impossible to earn more than the hourly rate, no matter how much production was turned in. . . .

Another unfair practice was the "shape-up." Employees coming to work gathered around in a semicircle while the foremen selected workers for certain machines or tasks. After all the jobs for that shift were assigned, the remaining workers went home without pay, not even for carfare, since they were paid only for actual working time no matter how many hours they had waited for assignment. . . .

Margaret Collingwood Nowak, *Two Who Were There: A Biography of Stanley Nowak* (Detroit: Wayne State University Press, 1989) pp. 103–104, 109–114. Reprinted with permission.

Since Ternstedt was a division of GM [General Motors], the successful ending of the Flint sit-down on 11 February gave a tremendous boost to the Ternstedt organizing drive. The master contract between GM and the UAW [United Auto Workers] covered all GM plants, thus entitling Ternstedt workers to union recognition. . . .

The workers had begun to publish a paper, the *Ternstedt Flash*. When it announced the coming meeting between [plant manager S. E.] Skinner and the Bargaining committee, a wave of enthusiasm swept the plants, resulting in hundreds of new members. This meeting was regarded as the first step toward victory. However, the workers soon discovered the truth of the old adage, "You can lead a horse to water, but you can't make him drink." Skinner complied with that part of the agreement calling for meeting with the bargaining committee, but granted no concessions. This went on for weeks, creating a serious crisis.

Workers had joined the union for its benefits, yet Skinner refused to agree to any of the demands presented. The new GM contract specifically ruled out strikes. Moreover, there was tremendous antistrike agitation in the press. What could be done to compel Skinner to bargain, short of a strike? . . .

Shop stewards were now functioning in every department at Ternstedt's, numbering almost two hundred, all impatiently demanding action. Unless something was done quickly, further organizing would be stymied, and membership would drop. Stanley anxiously turned the matter over in his mind. Then he recalled reading about a strike in Vienna before World War I, where workers stood at their machines and went through the motions of working, yet produced very little. An old Polish worker in Chicago, who had participated in that strike, had told him about it years before and had given him a book in Polish describing it. He located the book in our library and spent most of the night reading it long after I was asleep. The next morning he seemed relieved.

Smiling, he said over breakfast, "Since the union contract cannot compel Skinner to grant concessions at the bargaining table, neither can it compel workers to produce while at their machines. If Skinner can make a farce of bargaining, I don't see why we can't use this tactic in return." . . .

And so was born the first slowdown in UAW history. The problem now was to organize the new tactic. Of the twelve thousand Ternstedt workers, only a handful had any union experience. They had never heard of a slowdown but were ready for any kind of action.

The new technique was first carefully explained to the bargaining committee, then to the two hundred or more stewards, who then had to explain and demonstrate the idea to trusted workers in each department—all this while maintaining absolute secrecy. Fortunately, there were no company agents in the union leadership in the plants. Finally, the plan was ready to be put into operation. Production was not to be cut all at once in all plants but rather in each department at a different time. On the appointed day and hour, the cue was to be given successively in each department. A meeting of the bargaining committee with Mr. Skinner had been scheduled for the very morning when all this was to take place, and there was some apprehension among the group as they headed for Mr. Skinner's office.

"Good morning, Stanley," greeted Skinner as Stanley came in with his committee that morning in early April 1937.

"Good morning to you, Mr. Skinner," returned Stanley.

The committee members filed into the office and took their places around the big table in the center. Mr. Skinner looked every inch the business executive in his smart suit with his sleek, graying hair and trim build. He sat at his desk a few feet away, greeting each one with a great display of amiability, waving his long cigarette holder and moving papers around as he made conversation. At the bargaining table, small talk and laughter masked an undertone of uneasiness and tension. Skinner's unusual affability and exaggerated courtesy made the committee members wonder, "Does he know?" A surreptitious wink or shrug in reply to questioning glances expressed their hopes and uncertainty. . . .

As each demand was presented, Skinner appeared to weigh it carefully, discussed it with the group, then turned it down for one reason or another. This had been the pattern of the meetings for weeks.

As the farce proceeded, a telephone call interrupted Mr. Skinner. The committee members looked at each other hopefully, and listened eagerly. Skinner was somewhat less genial when he returned to the table, but he continued with negotiations. In a few moments another call came. Skinner looked searchingly around the table as he resumed his seat. His good humor had vanished. Two more calls came. With each one he grew more disturbed. As he hung up the receiver from the last one, his face contorted with anger and he pointed an accusing finger at Stanley.

"You son of a bitch, *you* did this to me!"

"I did what?" Stanley asked innocently.

"*You* know what I'm talking about. How dare you have the gall to come here and go through the motions of bargaining when there's a strike in the plant?"

"A strike?" Nowak repeated. "Aren't the workers on the job? We don't know of any strike."

"Oh yes you do!" insisted Skinner.

"I don't believe it, Mr. Skinner. Take me through the shop and show me where there is a strike."

"Like hell, I will! Get out of here! All of you! You have a hell of a nerve to negotiate with a strike going on." . . .

That night, the day-shift workers joyfully reported what had taken place in their departments. It hadn't taken long for department heads to notice the lag in production and reprimand the workers.

"I'm doing the best I can," workers maintained. "Maybe it's the machine."

Machines checked out okay, but production was still slow. At first, workers were somewhat clumsy at appearing to work while producing little; however, they soon caught on, and then it became a wonderful game, each worker trying to outdo the others in making as many motions as possible and doing the least work. Production slowly dropped. Management had been taken completely by surprise. A new wave of enthusiasm brought hundreds of new union applications, until more than 80 percent of the work force had joined. . . .

The slowdown continued. Production dipped to about 40 percent or 50 percent of the norm. In some departments it dropped to as low as 5 percent or 10 percent on some days. Skinner still refused to budge.

UAW vice president Wyndham Mortimer later told Stanley that William F. Knudsen, GM's president, had approached him and asked if he couldn't pressure Ternstedt workers to end their slowdown.

"They wouldn't even listen to such an idea," Mortimer declared, "unless Skinner begins to bargain in good faith."

Skinner must have been advised to abandon his hard-nosed attitude, for when Stanley phoned him soon after, he said, "Well, Stanley, I guess it's about time we got together again. Bring your bargaining committee and we'll get down to business."

In one three-hour session more was accomplished than in all previous meetings combined. Apparently Skinner realized that he was the one "over the barrel" this time. Union recognition was granted at once, and piecework was abolished, with hourly rates to be negotiated in place of piecework. . . .

For UAW Shop Stewards: "How to Win for the Union," 1941

[The] power of organized labor is brought to bear against management through the shop stewards and plant committeemen, who are the elected representatives of the organized workers. *On these committeemen or stewards depends the success or failure of labor in the automobile industry.*

But the conduct of negotiations with management is only half the job of these committeemen and stewards. Not only must they carry the union's grievances to management: they must insure the continued organization of the men whom they represent.

The best negotiator in the world will not get to first base if he allows the men he represents to fall away from the union. Without organization behind him and working with him, no steward, no committeeman, no officer can win victories from management. Unless he speaks for solidly organized workers, he is as futile and helpless as the individual auto worker back in the days of the open shop.

In other words, the committeemen and stewards have a double responsibility: responsibility for conduct of negotiations and for the men whom he represents united behind the policy of organized labor. He is at once a diplomat negotiating with a foreign power and a general preparing his troops for possible conflict. . . .

From *How to Win for the Union: A Discussion for UAW Stewards and Committeemen*, 1941. Reprinted by permission of UAW Education Department.

In plants where contracts have been signed between the UAW and management a procedure for handling grievances is usually written into the contract itself. In all plants where collective bargaining is carried on, a good steward knows the contract practically by heart.

The contract is a constitution governing union-management relationships. No one can hope to handle grievances successfully without a full knowledge of its provisions. A lawyer must know something of the law before he is allowed to plead cases in court. You must know your plant law before you handle grievances. . . .

The contract is your constitution, and the settlement of grievances under it are the decisions of an industrial supreme court. *A complete record of such decisions is sometimes more important than the contract itself.* . . .

The best contract in the world may be signed between union officers and corporation executives; but, unless that contract is enforced and put into life throughout the shop it is worth a little bit less than the paper it's written on. This is the job of the steward in his dealing with company foremen.

Where union organization is new, the problem of educating foremen to collective bargaining may be one of the toughest jobs the union has to face. Before organization came into the plant, foremen were little tin gods in their own departments. They were accustomed to having orders accepted with no questions asked. They expected workers to enter into servile competition for their favors.

With the coming of the union, the foreman finds the whole world turned upside down. His small-time dictatorship has been overthrown, and he must be adjusted to a democratic system of shop government. Naturally many foremen resent this change and continue a hostile attitude toward the union even after higher company officials may have decided to "work along with the union."

This makes the steward's problem difficult. He must convert the foreman to the democratic processes of collective bargaining and establish a sound working relationship with him as an individual.

Many inexperienced committeemen and stewards feel that the way to do this is to get tough with their foremen. They feel that threats and fistbanging will do the job for them. In 1937 some UAW committeemen used these methods.

Experience has shown that this approach does not work forever. . . .

Although the foreman represents the interests of the company as opposed to the workers, he is also a human being. Approach him like one. Find out what he is interested in. If he is a baseball fan, a little talk about batting averages won't hurt anything. Or if he likes fishing, you can discuss that. Occasional talk of this kind will not make it any harder to get down to business on grievances.

Don't give your foreman reason to believe that you are trying to bluff him. A reputation for honesty and good judgment is essential to your success in collective bargaining.

Hold down on personalities and name-calling. It won't help to settle grievances. And you can be even more forceful, when the occasion demands, if you have something in reserve. Try to avoid personal spite against a foreman because of unfair policies he is ordered to carry out by top management.

If a foreman tries to bully you or talk you down, talk back quick and hard, but keep your temper. A lost temper usually means a lost argument.

Various forms of pressure will bring results from foremen who are trying to be hard. With some men publicity in local union papers or bulletins brings results. With others, reports to top management on trouble-making foremen are the best medicine.

In plants where top management is sincerely anxious to work along with the union, a chronically disruptive foreman will be disciplined by his superiors.

Your relationship with the foreman should be that of equals seeking a solution to a common problem. But don't forget: the stronger the organization behind you, the more powerful your arguments will be. . . .

The steward's greatest difficulty will come on grievances which do not appear to be covered by the terms of the contract. On a demand for action from a worker which is directly contrary to the written contract, the steward has no choice but to say no. But many cases will arise in which justifiable complaints do not seem to be covered one way or another by provisions of the contract.

In such a situation the steward or plant committeeman goes through his contract with a fine-tooth comb to find some provision which will cover this particular situation. If the issue is one of any importance he will get the help of his local union officers in this.

In practically all cases where a worker has a legitimate complaint it will be possible to find some clause of the contract which, with a little pulling and hauling, can be made to cover the situation. Lawyers have been able to use a Constitution written over 150 years ago to cover the complex issues of modern life. A bright steward should be able to do just about as well with his contract. . . .

The union's system of shop stewards and committeemen is a weapon of democracy. That is its fundamental meaning. Where the foreman's power is handed down to him from the corporation owner on top, the steward's power comes from the workers below. The foreman, in the last analysis, is responsible to the directors of the corporation. His job is done successfully when their interests are served. In the same way the steward is responsible to the majority—to the workers; and his job, likewise, is well done when their interests are well served. . . .

A steward or committeeman cannot take action without the backing of the men in his department. This is a truth which cannot be repeated too often.

But this fact is no excuse for inaction. No steward can sit on his hands and allow the company to break down union conditions, simply because the men in his department have not taken the bit in their teeth to demand action of him.

It is the steward's job to go out and win democratic support for the union policies which his experience and knowledge of the labor movement prove to be right.

The steward should remember that forces hostile to labor inside and outside the plant are at all times seeking to win influence over his men. Unless the steward gives positive leadership in behalf of CIO principles, he will find his men pulled away from him.

To make democracy work, therefore, the steward or committeeman must be prepared to put a solid program before his men and, if need be, fight for its support. He must awaken and encourage his men to take part themselves in working out union policy. He should fight at all times against the "card carrier" spirit. He should know, and teach others, that the union is no slot machine into which men drop a dollar a month and receive automatic returns in the form of better wages, hours, and conditions. . . .

The union is opposed to unauthorized strikes. This is not because a milk and water policy has been adopted. It is primarily because the unauthorized strike or stoppage is undemocratic.

Were the unauthorized strikes to be tolerated it would mean simply that any small group within the union would have the power to dictate to the union as a whole. A handful of men in a single plant cannot be given the right of involving tens of thousands of workers, without their consent, in a costly and dangerous struggle. That would mean that a contract covering thousands of workers could be broken down at the whim of a few individuals. To give a minority such power is the very opposite of democracy. It would mean that the UAW-CIO could not exist as a stable organization— could not prepare itself for meeting the tremendous problems that loom in the future of the industry.

That is why every steward, committeeman and officer is duty-bound to fight for the observance of the Constitution and rulings of the International Executive Board for the elimination of all unauthorized stoppages and strikes. . . .

Union Leaders Oppose Shop-Floor Agitators, 1941

. . . On Sunday, March 2, 1941, Stanley Orlosky, lifelong union worker, a pipe fitter in a steel mill, was expelled from his union after a trial on charges of "violation of obligation to the Steel Workers Organizing Committee." To add to his disgrace, Stanley was tried by union officers whom he had solicited to join the union a few years earlier. He came to our office to appeal the decision of the trial board of his local union. Stanley was powerfully built, stood six feet tall, and the few strands of gray in his black hair belied his forty-five years. He exhibited a soiled membership card in the United Mine Workers of America, Local 405, Loyalhanna, Pennsyl-

Excerpt from *The Dynamics of Industrial Democracy* by Clinton Golden and Harold Ruttenberg. Copyright 1942 by Clinton Golden and Harold Ruttenberg. Reprinted by permission of Harper & Row, Publishers, Inc.

vania, dated March 17, 1911. This was secured in his first strike. He lost out in it. Stanley worked the coal fields until 1928, when he was blacklisted and forced to go into the steel mills. The ABC Steel Company fired him in 1933 for being president of the NRA local union, but hired him back in 1934 when the union died. In 1936 he became vice-president of the SWOC [Steel Workers Organizing Committee] local union in his section of the mill and was chairman of the grievance committee until 1940, when the SWOC director removed him from office for violating the contract.

"Being a good union man is agitating—that's what I always knew as a union man—and I got fired for agitating," Stanley complained to us. "The union was organized to have freedom, and not to be fired for talking. The men that tried me in the local, I had a hard time getting to join the union a few years ago. Now they're big union shots. The company has had it in for me since 1933. I'm a thorn in the flesh to it. Now the union sides with the company, and I'm out. That ain't justice. The national office should give me another hearing, and give me back my membership card," he pleaded.

We investigated his case. The talking for which Stanley was fired consisted of charging the incumbent union officers with "selling the men down the river," since they settled grievances on their merits. His idea of a grievance settlement was to get everything or strike. Stanley's leadership was essential to the establishment of the union against bitter resistance, but after it had been fully accepted by management such leadership was a handicap to the development of co-operative union-management relations. His expulsion was sustained by the SWOC national officers.

In this huge mill of more than ten thousand workers, SWOC has five local unions, instead of one, to facilitate the administration of union affairs. Two of the locals are still led by leaders of Stanley's type. Carl Rossi, young high-school graduate, is president of one of the remaining belligerently led locals. He boasts, "I've never lost a grievance case." At joint meetings of the officers from the five locals Carl charges the co-operative ones with "running company unions." He disposes of arguments that costs do not permit granting a particular request with "They're always crying poor mouth." When told his unrelenting pressure for wage adjustments might cut employment, might even put the company out of business, Carl smiles. "Them birds are always crying wolf, and you guys [SWOC district director and co-operative leaders] fall for that scarefish stuff. Not me— that mill will be there when I got whiskers a mile long." Carl and the countless other local union leaders he typifies view the union's relations with management as being predicated upon a continual fight. In those cases, unfortunately still a majority, where management keeps the union at a respectful distance, such a union approach is unavoidable; but where the union has been taken into management's confidence, greater responsibilities face the union and its leaders.

Carl has only one concern in pressing a case of a union member: get for the member what he wants or as close to it as possible. The problem of finding the means to meet the demand is exclusively management's. In winning a case Carl takes all the glory; in losing one Carl gives management all the blame. But Carl never loses a case. A negative reply merely puts the case on the unfinished-business agenda; Carl keeps pressing it until management yields or the member dies. Management . . . encourages this kind of approach by insisting that union membership be voluntary, despite the union's majority enrollment. Repeatedly we have been told by management, "It is your job to sell the union to the employees." Local union leaders know no better way to do this than to "get things" for their followers, and let management worry about how to pay for them.

Eventually this honeymoon comes to an end. Carl's company has taken SWOC into its inner councils, abandoned its policy of keeping the union at a distance, and says to SWOC's top leaders, "We are co-operating fully with SWOC, have granted the union shop as evidence of our sincerity; but some of your local union leaders still serve us with ultimatums to grant demands by a certain time or they will strike. What are you doing to have them approach these problems in a co-operative spirit, as matters for which they must assume joint responsibility?"

At this point union members, their national officers, intermediary field staffs, and local union leaders face the acid test. They have to demonstrate that under a union shop unions can assume and discharge their responsibilities to the best interests of both their members and the business enterprises upon which they depend for a livelihood. This is primarily the job of top union leaders, since they must show to their followers, on the union staff and in the mines, mills, and factories, the way toward industrial peace and fruitful union-management relations. Before this, however, they must show newly recognized unions how to make collective bargaining work under the difficult conditions of partial union membership.

There are two stages in the development of labor leadership: one is the contract stage; the other is the union-shop stage. In signing the initial contract with a firm, top union leaders automatically assume the task of showing the local union involved, and the union field staff directing its affairs, how to bargain contractually. Likewise in signing a union-shop contract, the national union leadership automatically assumes the responsibility for directing the union involved toward co-operative relations with management. We find ourselves in the peculiar position of having to do both jobs simultaneously with different groups of workers, because SWOC's relations with the eight hundred and twenty-six firms under contract are in varying stages of maturity. . . .

✣ *E S S A Y S*

These essays offer two sharp contrasts of what the union movement meant in the 1930s. Historian Melvyn Dubofsky of the State University of New York at Binghamton offers in the first selection a provocative interpretation emphasizing the failures and limits of the new unionism, both as a political institution and as a vehicle for transforming popular consciousness. He points out that most workers did not take part in militant strike actions, Congress of Industrial Organizations' (CIO) union leadership was often quite conservative, and the decade ended with the social and political structures of American life fundamentally unchanged. Most important, Dubofsky asserts a social inertia at the heart of working-class consciousness that failed to engender a cultural or ideological value system capable of standing apart from that of marketplace capitalism.

In contrast, in the second essay, historian Bruce Nelson of Dartmouth College celebrates what he calls the Pentecostal era of worker militancy and class consciousness that transformed the social and economic world of West Coast longshoremen after the Big Strike of 1934. Nelson finds that many workers willingly followed the leadership of political radicals, oppositional values did emerge, and working conditions were so changed that some longshoremen now referred to themselves as the "Lords of the Docks."

Did the meaning of working-class Americanism change during the 1930s? Do these two historians define worker militancy and political radicalism in the same fashion? To what extent is the CIO an heir to the tradition of the Knights of Labor, the Industrial Workers of the World, or the AFL in the Gompers era?

Not So Radical Years: Another Look at the 1930s

MELVYN DUBOFSKY

Our conventional view of the 1930s was aptly caught in the title of Irving Bernstein's history of American labor during that decade, *Turbulent Years*, a title that the author borrowed from Myron Taylor's annual report to the Board of Directors of the United States Steel Corporation in 1938. That liberal historians and corporate executives perceive the 1930s as a "turbulent" decade should today occasion no surprise. For the American business elite especially, their social, economic, and political world had turned upside down during the Great Depression and New Deal. After nearly a full decade of corporate hegemony, class collaboration, and trade union retreat, the United States during the 1930s seemed chronically beset with class conflict, violence, and ubiquitous labor radicalism. In the words of one of the decade's radicals, Len DeCaux, a "new consciousness" awakened workers from lethargy. . . .

The picture one has of the 1930s, then, whether painted by a liberal scholar such as Bernstein, an activist like DeCaux, or a tycoon like Taylor, is of conflict and struggle. The foreground is filled with militant and radical workers, the masses in motion, a rank and file vigorously, sometimes violently, reaching out to grasp control over its own labor and existence.

Given the conventional portrait of the American 1930s, conventional questions arise, the most obvious of which are the following: (1) Why did labor militancy decline? (2) Why did militant, radical rank-and-file struggles produce old-fashioned, autocratically controlled trade unions in many cases? (3) Why did the turbulence create no lasting, mass radical political movement? . . .

Melvyn Dubofsky, "Not So 'Turbulent Years' A New Look at the 1930s," in Charles Stephenson and Robert Asher, *Life and Labor: Dimensions of American Working Class History*, 1986, pp. 205–223. Reprinted by permission of State University of New York Press.

In examining the 1930s, how should we go about creating the history of that era? Two convenient models are at hand. In one we can seek lessons for the present in an instrumental view of the past. That approach suggests the might-have-beens of history. If only Communists had behaved differently; if nonsectarian radicals had pursued the proper policies; if the militant rank and file had been aware of its true interests (as distinguished from the false consciousness inculcated by trade-union bureaucrats and New Deal Democrats); then the history of the 1930s would have been different and *better*. The second approach to our turbulent decade has been suggested by David Brody. "The interesting questions," writes Brody, "are not in the realm of what might have been, but in a closer examination of what did happen." Brody's approach, I believe, promises greater rewards for scholars and may even be more useful for those who desire to use the past to improve the present and shape the future. As Karl Marx noted in *The Eighteenth Brumaire*, man indeed makes his own history, but only "under circumstances directly encountered, given and transmitted from the past. The tradition of all the dead generations weighs like a nightmare on the brain of the living." . . .

Let us now see if we can uncover or glimpse the reality of the American 1930s. Certainly, the turbulence, militancy, and radicalism of the decade existed. From 1920 through 1939, the American economic and social system remained in crisis. Despite two substantial recoveries from the depths of depression, unemployment during the decade never fell below 14 percent of the civilian labor force or 21 percent of the nonagricultural work force. Those workers who once believed in the American myth of success, who dreamed of inching up the occupational ladder, acquiring property of their own, and watching their children do even better occupationally and materially, had their hopes blasted by the Great Depression. . . .

The thwarted aspirations of millions of workers combined with persistent mass unemployment produced a decade of social unrest that encompassed every form of collective and individual action from mass marches to food looting. One historian has pointed out that between February 1930 and July 1932, at least seventeen separate incidents of violent protests occurred. In Chicago in 1931, after three persons were killed during an anti-eviction struggle, sixty thousand citizens marched on City Hall to protest police brutality. Indeed in nearly every city in which the unemployed organized and protested, violent confrontations with the police erupted.

More important and more threatening to the established order than protests by the unemployed and hungry, which punctuated the early depression years, were the more conventional forms of class struggle which erupted with greater incidence after the election of Franklin Roosevelt and the coming of the New Deal. In 1934, after twelve years of relative quiet on the labor front, industrial conflict broke out with a militancy and violence not seen since 1919. In Toledo, Ohio, National Guardsmen tear-gassed and drove from the city's streets Auto-Lite Company strikers who had the support not only of the radical A. J. Muste's American Workers party and Unemployed League, but also of the citywide central labor council, an AFL affiliate. And the following month, July 1934, witnessed still more violent struggles. A strike by maritime workers in the San Francisco Bay area brought battles between police and longshoremen, several dead strikers, and the dispatch of state troops. In protest, the San Francisco central labor council declared a citywide general strike for July 16. Here, too, a labor radical, Harry Bridges, an Australian immigrant and a Marxist, led a strike unsanctioned by the AFL. Only a day after the San Francisco general strike ended, Americans read in their newspapers of July 21 that on the previous day in Minneapolis, Minnesota, fifty men had been shot in the back as police fired on strikers. Within a week of the bloody July 20 battle between police and teamsters in the city's main square, Minnesota Governor Floyd Olson placed the Twin Cities under martial law. Once again, in Minneapolis, as earlier in Toledo and San Francisco, left-wing radicals led the strike, in this instance the Trotskyists, Farrell Dobbs and the brothers Vincent, Miles, Grant, and Ray Dunne. And only a week after the shootings in Minneapolis, on July 28, 1934, deputy sheriffs in the company town of Kohler, Wisconsin, killed one person and injured twenty in what the New York *Times* characterized as a "strike riot."

Few areas of the nation seemed untouched by labor militancy in 1934. In the spring a national textile strike called by the United Textile Workers of America brought out 350,000 workers from Maine to Alabama, and violent repression of the strikers proved the rule in the South's Piedmont mill towns. Throughout the spring auto and steel workers flocked into trade unions, like coal miners the previous year, seeming almost to organize themselves. And when auto manufacturers and steel barons refused to bargain with labor, national strikes threatened both industries. Only direct presidential intervention and the equivocal actions of AFL leaders averted walkouts in autos and steel.

If 1934, in Irving Bernstein's chapter title, amounted to an "Eruption," 1937 experienced an epidemic of strikes. The year began with the famous Flint sit-down strike in which the United Auto Workers conquered General Motors; saw United States Steel surrender to the Steel Workers Organizing Committee (SWOC)-CIO without a struggle less than three weeks after the General Motors strike ended; and culminated in the late spring with perhaps the most violent and bloodiest national strike of the decade: the Little Steel conflict that led to the Memorial Day "massacre" outside Republic Steel's South Chicago plant. In between Flint and Little Steel, more than four hundred thousand workers participated in 477 sit-down strikes. Twenty-five sit-downs erupted in January 1937, forty-seven in February, and 170 in March. "Sitting down has replaced baseball as a national pastime," quipped *Time* magazine.

The labor militancy and strikes of 1934 and 1937 created a solidarity that hitherto eluded American workers. During the 1930s, it seemed, the United States had developed a true proletariat, more united by its similarities than divided by its differences. Mass immigration had ended in 1921, and hence the last immigrant generation had had more than a decade to integrate itself into the social system and for its children to have been

"Americanized" by the public schools and other intermediate social agencies. Male-female role conflicts appeared notable by their absence, and strikers' wives provided their husbands with substantial assistance as members of women's auxiliaries. "I found a common understanding and unselfishness I'd never known in my life," wrote the wife of one Flint sitdowner. "I'm living for the first time with a definite goal. . . . Just being a woman isn't enough any more. I want to be a human being with the right to think for myself." "A new type of woman was born in the strike," noted an observer of the struggle in Flint. "Women who only yesterday were horrified at unionism, who felt inferior to the task of speaking, leading, have, as if overnight, become the spearhead in the battle for unionism."

Even racial tensions among workers seemed to diminish during the 1930s, especially after the emergence of the CIO whose "new unionists" often crusaded for civil rights as vigorously as for trade unionism. The changes wrought by CIO led two students of black labor to conclude in 1939 "that it is easier to incorporate Negroes into a new movement . . . than to find a secure place in an older one." . . .

One must not, however, romanticize working-class solidarity and thus lose sight of the tensions that continued to pit American workers during the 1930s against each other rather than a common enemy. In New Haven, Connecticut, American-born workers still denigrated Italians as "wops," and "it's dog eat dog all right," retorted an Italian-American machinist "but it's also Mick feeds Mick!" A Hollywood film of the late 1930s, *Black Legion*, starring Humphrey Bogart as a frustrated white American-born Protestant machinist, captured the still lingering resentment harbored by the American-born against the foreign-born (and even their children), and depicted the sort of worker more likely to listen to Father Coughlin [conservative radio priest] than to John L. Lewis [United Mine Workers president], Franklin D. Roosevelt, or perhaps [the Communist party's] William Z. Foster. Or, listen to an official of an AFL union with jurisdiction in an industry that employed many Afro-Americans. "I consider the Negroes poor union men. You know as well as I do that they are shiftless, easily intimidated and generally of poor caliber. . . . What should have happened is what is being done in Calhoun County, Illinois, where Negroes are not allowed to stay overnight. As a result there are no Negroes there and no Negro problem."

But it was the CIO, not the AFL, that symbolized the labor upheaval of the 1930s. And in 1937 when CIO-organized autos, steel, rubber, and other former bastions of the open shop, between three and a half and four million workers joined the labor movement, a larger number than the entire AFL claimed as of January 1, 1937. Now, for the first time in its history, organized labor in America wielded power in the strategic core of mass-production industry, and it did so under the aegis of a labor federation (CIO) whose leaders consciously repudiated the AFL tradition of class accommodation and collaboration. The CIO during the late 1930s exemplified solidarity rather than exclusiveness, political action in place of nonpartisanship, biracialism and bisexualism instead of racial and sexual chauvinism, and militancy rather than opportunism. "CIO started as a new kind of labor movement," recalled Len DeCaux in his autobiography. "A challenge to the old AFL and the status quo it complacently guarded. It was new in its youth and fervor, new in the broad sector of the working class it brought into action, new in the way it accepted and integrated its radicals, new in its relative independence of corporate and government control, new in its many social and political attitudes." . . .

Had Lewis decided to lead . . . an independent political movement, the time never seemed riper. The Great Depression and the New Deal had wrought a veritable political revolution among American workers. Masses of hitherto politically apathetic workers, especially among first-generation immigrants and their spouses, went to the polls in greater numbers. And Roosevelt broke the last links that bound millions of workers across the industrial heartland from Pittsburgh to Chicago to the Republican party. Lewis exulted at the results of the 1936 election in which for the first time since the depression of the 1890s, Democrats swept into power in the steel and coal towns of Pennsylvania and Ohio, winning office on tickets financed by CIO money and headed by CIO members. . . .

All this ferment, militancy, radicalism, violence, and perhaps even an altered working-class consciousness were part of American reality during the 1930s. Yet, as we know, American socialism expired during the depression decade, communism advanced only marginally, Roosevelt seduced the farmer-laborites and populists, the CIO came to resemble the AFL, and John L. Lewis once again reverted to behaving like a "labor boss of the most conventional kind." Why? To answer that question we have to examine other aspects of social, economic, and political reality during the 1930s. . . .

Just as one can claim that the 1930s represented a crisis for American capitalism that expressed itself most overtly in the eagerness and militancy with which workers challenged their corporate masters, one might just as easily assert that for most Americans, workers included, events during the decade reinforced their faith in the "justness" of the American system and the prospects for improvement without fundamental restructuring. For many workers capitalism never collapsed; indeed, for those employed steadily, always a substantial proportion of the work force, real wages actually rose as prices fell. For other workers, the tentative economic recovery of 1933–34 and the more substantial growth of 1937 rekindled faith in the American system. The two great strike waves of the decade, 1934 and 1937, erupted not in moments of crisis, but when hope, profits, employment, and wages all revived. Crisis, in other words, induced apathy or lethargy; economic recovery, a sign that the system worked, stimulated action. And when the recovery of 1936–37 was followed by the "Roosevelt depression," a more rapid and deeper decline than the Great Crash of 1929–33, the number of strikes diminished markedly and the more militant CIO affiliates concentrated in the mass-production industries suffered severe membership and financial losses. Perhaps this final crisis of the depression decade left unresolved might have snapped whatever bonds still tied workers to the

American system. That, however, remains a problematic historical might-have-been, as the coming of World War II resolved the contradictions in American capitalism and substituted patriotic unity for class conflict.

An analysis of the statistics of working-class militancy during the 1930s—the incidence of strikes, the number of workers affected, the man-days lost—also leads to divergent interpretations. One can stress the high level of strike activity, the fact that only 840 strikes were recorded in 1932 but 1,700 erupted in 1933, 1,856 in 1934, 2,200 in 1936, and in the peak strike year, 1937, 4,740. One can argue that no area of the nation and, more importantly, no major industry escaped industrial conflict. For the first time in United States history, strikes affected every major mass-production industry and paralyzed the towering heights of the economy: steel, auto, rubber, coal, electrical goods; the list goes on and on. For the nation and its workers, the 1930s were indeed "turbulent years."

But the statistics of industrial conflict reveal another story, an equally interesting one. When the 1934 strike wave erupted, President Roosevelt sought to understand its origins and implications. He asked the Commissioner of Labor Statistics, Isidore Lubin, to analyze and interpret the 1934 outbreak. Lubin prepared a report that he transmitted to the President in late August 1934. Seeking to place the 1934 strikes in historical perspective, Lubin acted logically. He compared what had happened in the first half of 1934 to the last previous year in which the United States had experienced such massive labor militancy, 1919. And he concluded that the 1934 strike wave could not match 1919 in intensity, duration, or number of workers involved. More than twice as many strikes began each month in the first half of 1919, reported Lubin, than in the same period in 1934; moreover, more than two and a half times as many workers were involved in the 1919 strikes. He then proceeded to assure the President that July 1934, the month of the San Francisco and Minneapolis general strikes, witnessed no mass working-class upheaval. Only seven-tenths of one percent, or seven out of every thousand wage earners, participated in strikes. Only four-tenths of one percent of man-days of employment were lost as a result of strikes. "In other words," Lubin reassured the President, "for every thousand man-days worked four were lost because of strikes." . . .

But what of 1937, the decade's premier strike year, when more than twice as many workers struck as in 1934? Well, according to official statistics, only 7.2 percent of employed workers were involved in walkouts (practically the same percentage as in 1934) and their absence from work represented only 0.043 percent of all time worked.

Questions immediately arise from a reading of such strike statistics. What was the other 93 percent of the labor force doing during the great strike waves of 1934 and 1937? More important, how were they affected by the upsurge of industrial conflicts which did not involve or affect them directly?

Such questions are especially important when one bears in mind the continental size of the United States. Geography could, and did, easily dilute the impact of industrial conflict nationally. The United States lacked a London, Paris, Berlin, or Rome, where massive, militant strikes affected the national state directly as well as private employers. Few of the major strikes of the 1930s occurred even in state capitals, most of which were isolated from industrial strife. When teamsters tied up Minneapolis and longshoremen closed down San Francisco in July 1934, truckers continued to deliver goods in Chicago and Los Angeles, and waterfront workers remained on the job in New York, Baltimore, and San Pedro. For trade unionists and radicals it was exceedingly difficult . . . to transform well-structured local and regional organizations into equally effective national bodies. Just as the millions of unemployed during the 1930s did not experience the shock of joblessness simultaneously, so, too, different workers experienced industrial conflict at different times and in different places. As we will see below, what workers most often experienced in common—participation in the American political system—was precisely what most effectively diluted militancy and radicalism.

Despite the continental size and diversity of the American nation, it is possible to glimpse aspects of working-class reality in local settings that disclose uniformities in belief and behavior which do much to explain the dearth of durable radicalism in the United States. We are fortunate that two truly excellent, perceptive sociological field studies were completed during the 1930s that dissect the social structure and culture of two characteristic smaller American industrial cities. We are even more fortunate that the two cities investigated—Muncie, Indiana, and New Haven, Connecticut—proved so unlike in their economic structures, population mixes, and regional and cultural milieus. Muncie was dominated by two industries—Ball Glass and General Motors—characterized by an almost totally Americanborn, white Protestant population, and situated in the heartland of American agriculture, individualism, and evangelical Protestantism. New Haven, by contrast, claimed no dominant employers, encompassed a population differentiated by nationality, race, and religion as well as class, and was set in a region traditionally urban (also urbane) and non-evangelical in culture. Yet after one finishes reading Robert and Helen Lynd on Muncie and E. Wight Bakke on New Haven, one is more impressed by the similarities rather than the differences in working-class attitudes and behavior.

Let us examine Muncie first. The Lynds had initially gone to Muncie in the mid-1920s in order to discover how urbanization and industrialization had affected American culture, how the city and the factory had altered beliefs and behavioral patterns developed in the country and on the farm. They returned a decade later in order to see what impact, if any, the "Great Depression" had had on local culture and behavior. Surprisingly, for them at least, they found labor organization weaker in 1935 than it had been in 1925, yet the Muncie business class seemed more united and more determined than ever to keep its city open shop (nonunion). The Lynds discovered objectively greater class stratification in 1935 than in 1925 and even less prospect for the individual worker to climb up the ladder of success . . . , yet they characterized Muncie's workers as being influenced by "drives . . . largely those of the business class: both are caught up in the tradition of a rising standard of living and lured by the enticements of salesmanship." As one Middletown woman informed the sociologists: "Most of the families that I know are after the same things today that they were after before the depression, and they'll get them the same way—on credit."

Union officials told the Lynds a similar tale of woe. Union members preferred buying gas for their cars to paying dues, and going for a drive to attending a union meeting. Local workers were willing to beg, borrow, or steal to maintain possession of their cars and keep them running. Despite seven years of depression, Muncie's workers, according to the Lynds, still worshipped the automobile as the symbol of the American dream, and, as long as they owned one, considered themselves content.

"Fear, resentment, insecurity and disillusionment has been to Middletown's workers largely an *individual* experience for each worker," concluded the Lynds,

> and not a thing generalized by him into a "class" experience. . . . Such militancy as it generates tends to be sporadic, personal, and flaccid; an expression primarily of personal resentment rather than an act of self-identification with the continuities of a movement or of a rebellion against an economic status regarded as permanently fixed. The militancy of Middletown labor tends, therefore, to be easily manipulated, and to be diverted into all manner of incidental issues.

So much for Muncie—what of New Haven with its more heterogeneous and less culturally individualistic working class that, in some cases, the investigator could interview and probe after the CIO upheaval of 1936–37? Again we see in Bakke's two published examinations of the unemployed worker in New Haven an absence of mass organization, collective militancy, or radicalism, despite an apparent hardening of class lines. New Haven's workers, unlike Muncie's, apparently did not share the drives of the business class and they did in fact develop a collective sense of class. "Hell, brother," a machinist told Bakke, "you don't have to look to know there's a workin' class. We may not say so—But look at what we do. Work. Look at where we live. Nothing there but workers. Look at how we get along. Just like every other damned worker. Hell's bells, of course, there's a workin' class, and it's gettin' more so every day." Yet New Haven, like Muncie, lacked a militant and radical working class. Why?

Bakke tried to provide answers. He cited the usual barriers to collective action and working-class radicalism: ethnic heterogeneity; fear of the alien; fear of repression; and capitalist hegemony that was cultural as well as economic and political. Yet he also discovered that answers to the absence of militancy and radicalism lay embedded deep within the culture of New Haven's workers. In most cases, their lives had disproved the American dream; rather than experiencing steady upward mobility and constantly rising material standards of living, Bakke's interviewees had lived lives of insecurity and poverty. They regularly had had to adjust their goals to actual possibilities, which almost always fell far below their aspirations.

As one worker after another informed Bakke, life involved putting up with it, grinning and bearing it, and using common sense to survive. Explaining how the unemployed managed in a period of general economic crisis, a brass worker noted in a matter of fact fashion, "The poor are used to being poor." . . .

Just so with New Haven's workers. For the majority of them, alternatives to the existing system seemed most notable for their absence. The only alternatives the city's workers cited, German Nazism, Italian Fascism, and Soviet Communism, none of which to be sure they had experienced, held no allurement, promised them "no better, more just social order." Workers repeatedly referred to Soviet Russia to explain both Socialism's and Communism's lack of appeal. . . .

Ah, one might say, Muncie and New Haven were atypical and their working class more so.

Look at Flint and Youngstown, Akron and Gary, Minneapolis and San Francisco. In those cities workers acted collectively and militantly. But a closer look at even such *foci* of labor struggle reveals a much more complex reality than suggested by conventional romanticizations of working-class solidarity and rank-and-file militancy.

Without militants, to be sure, there would have been no Flint sit-down strike, no San Francisco general strike, no walkout by Akron's rubber workers. Without rank-and-file participation, that is, collective struggle, there would have been no union victories. Yet, in reality, solidarity rarely produced collective action; rather, more often than not, action by militant minorities (what some scholars have characterized as "sparkplug Unionism") precipitated a subsequent collective response. And rank and filers frequently resisted the radicalism of the militant cadres who sparked industrial confrontations. In Flint . . . only a small minority of the local workers belonged to the UAW and paid dues on the eve of the strike, and the sit-down technique was chosen consciously to compensate for the union's lack of a mass membership base. . . . Lee Pressman, general counsel to the Steel Workers Organizing Committee, recalls that as late as the spring of 1937, after the UAW's success at Flint and United States Steel's surrender to SWOC, labor organizers had still failed to enrol in SWOC more than a substantial minority of the steelworkers employed by firms other than United States Steel. For most rank and filers, then, militancy consisted of refusing to cross a picket line, no more. As one observer noted of the Flint sit-downers, a group more militant than the majority of auto workers, "Those strikers have no more idea of 'revolution' than pussy cats."

Even the most strike-torn cities and regions had a significantly internally differentiated working class. At the top were the local cadres, the sparkplug unionists, the men and women fully conscious of their roles in a marketplace society that extolled individualism and rewarded collective strength. These individuals, ranging the political spectrum from Social Democrats to Communists, provided the leadership, militancy, and ideology that fostered industrial conflict and the emergence of mass-production unionism. Beneath them lay a substantial proportion of workers who could be transformed, by example, into militant strikers and unionists, and, in turn, themselves act as militant minorities. Below them were many first- and second-generation immigrant workers, as well as recent migrants from the American countryside, who remained embedded in a culture defined by traditional ties to family, kinship, church, and neighborhood club or tavern. Accustomed to following the rituals of the past, heeding the advice of community leaders, and slow to act, such men and women rarely joined unions prior to a successful strike, once moved to act behaved with singular solidarity, yet rarely served as union or political activists and radicals. And below this mass were the teenage workers caught halfway between liberation from their parental families and formation of their own new households, more attracted to the life and rituals of street gangs and candy-store cronies than to the customs and culture of persistent trade unionists and political activists.

A word must now be added concerning those scholars who have argued that during the 1930s a spontaneously militant and increasingly radical rank and file was either handcuffed or betrayed by bureaucratic and autocratic labor leaders. For those who accept the Leninist thesis that trade unions are, by definition, economist and hence nonrevolutionary, there is no problem in comprehending the behavior of American trade unions and their members during the 1930s. But for those who seek to understand why the militant beginnings of the CIO terminated in an ideological and institutional deadend, why, in Brody's words, "the character of American trade unionism . . . made it an exploiter of radicalism rather than vice versa"—questions remain. And it may seem easiest to answer . . . that the blame for the failure of radicalism rests with such labor leaders as John L. Lewis and Sidney Hillman who sold out to the New Deal, collaborated with employers, and restrained rank-and-file militancy through the instrument of the nonstrike union contract. That hypothesis, commonly subsumed under the rubric "corporate liberalism," contains a grain of truth. But the small truth tends to obscure a greater reality. As J. B. S. Hardman [labor intellectual] observed a half century ago, labor leaders are primarily accumulators of power; and, need it be said, no man was more eager to accumulate power than John L. Lewis. A businessman's power flowed from his control of capital; a politician's from influence over voters and possession of the instruments of government; and a labor leader's power derived from his union membership, the more massive and militant the rank and file, the more influential the labor leader. Bereft of a mass membership or saddled with a lethargic rank and file, the labor leader lost influence, and power. All labor leaders, then, necessarily played a devious and sometimes duplicitous game. Sometimes they rushed in to lead a rebellious rank and file; other times, they agitated the rank and file into action; whether they seized leadership of a movement already in motion or themselves breathed life into the rank and file, labor leaders obtained whatever power they exercised with employers and public officials as a consequence of their followers' behavior. Yet, while they encouraged militancy, labor leaders also restrained their troops, in John L. Lewis's phrase, "put a lid on the strikers." They did so for several reasons. First, not all rank-and-file upheavals promised success; and nothing destroyed a trade union as quickly or diluted a labor leader's power as thoroughly as a lost strike. Second, leaders had to judge at what point rank-and-file militancy would produce government repression, an ever-present reality even in Franklin D. Roosevelt's America. Third, and more selfishly, rank-and-file upheavals could careen out of control and threaten a labor leader's tenure in office as well as strengthen his external power. Throughout the 1930s such labor leaders as John L. Lewis alternatively encouraged the release of working-class rebelliousness and "put the lid back on." The labor leader was truly the man in the middle, his influence rendered simultaneously greater and also more perilous as a result of working-class militancy.

A final word must also be said about the union contract, the instrument that allegedly bound workers to their employers by denying them the right to strike. With historical hindsight, such seems to be the end result of the union-management contract under which the union promises to discipline its members on behalf of management. But one must remember that during the 1930s ordinary workers, the romanticized rank and file, risked their jobs, their bodies, and their lives to win the contract. And when they won it, as in Flint in February, 1937, a sit-down striker rejoiced that it "was the most wonderful thing that we could think that could possibly happen to people." . . .

Paradoxically, the one experience during the 1930s that united workers across ethnic, racial, and organizational lines—New Deal politics—served to vitiate radicalism. By the end of the 1930s, Roosevelt's Democratic party had become, in effect, the political expression of America's working class. Old-line Socialists, farmer-labor party types, and even Communists enlisted in a Roosevelt-led "Popular Front." Blacks and whites, Irish and Italian Catholics, Slavic- and Jewish-Americans, uprooted rural Protestants and stable skilled workers joined the Democratic coalition, solidifying the working-class vote as never before in American history. Roosevelt encouraged workers to identify themselves as a common class politically as well as economically. As with David Lloyd George in Britain's pre–World War I Edwardian crisis, Franklin D. Roosevelt in the American crisis of the 1930s found revolutionary class rhetoric indispensable. It panicked the powerful into concessions and attracted working-class voters to the Democratic party. Just as Lloyd George intensified the earlier British crisis in order to ease its solution, Roosevelt acted similarly in New Deal America. By frightening the ruling class into conceding reforms and appealing to workers to vote as a solid block, Roosevelt simultaneously intensified class consciousness and stripped it of its radical potential.

The dilemma of John L. Lewis showed just how well Roosevelt succeeded in his strategy. During the 1930s, no matter how much Lewis preferred to think of himself as an executive rather than a labor leader, however little he associated personally with the working class, he functioned as the leader of a militant working-class movement. Whereas Roosevelt sought to contain working-class militancy through reforms, militant workers pressured Lewis to demand more than the President would or could deliver. The more evident became the New Deal's economic failures, the more heavily labor militants demanded a fundamental reordering of the economy and society, demands that Lewis, as leader of CIO, came to express more forcefully than any other trade unionist. "No matter how much Roosevelt did for the workers," recalls DeCaux, "Lewis demanded more. He showed no gratitude, nor did he bid his followers be grateful—just put the squeeze on all the harder." But Lewis, unlike the British labor leaders of Lloyd George's generation who found in the Labour Party an alternative to the Prime Minister's "New Liberalism," had no substitute for Roosevelt's New Deal. In the United States, the President easily mastered the labor leader.

Lewis's lack of a political alternative to the New Deal flowed from two sources. First was the refusal of most American leftists to countenance a third-party challenge to the Democrats and the intense loyalty most workers felt to Roosevelt. Between the winter of 1937–38 and the summer of 1940, however much Lewis threatened to lead a new third party, his public speeches and private maneuvers failed to create among workers a third-party constituency. It was Lewis's radical speeches that made his eventual endorsement in 1940 of Wendell Wilkie so shocking to many of the labor leader's admirers. Had those Lewis sycophants known that in June 1940, the CIO president plotted to win the Republican nomination for Herbert Hoover, they might have been even more startled. And it was his support first of Hoover and then of Wilkie that exposed the second source for Lewis's lack of a radical alternative to the New Deal. That was the extent to which Lewis, other labor leaders, and perhaps most workers had assimilated the values of a business civilization. This union, Lewis told members of the United Mine Workers at their 1938 convention, "stands for the proposition that the heads of families shall have a sufficient income to educate . . . these sons and daughters of our people, and they go forth when given that opportunity. . . . They become scientists, great clergymen . . . great lawyers, great statesmen. . . . Many of our former members are successful in great business enterprises." And two years later in 1940, he told the same audience: "You know, after all there are two great material tasks in life that affect the individual and affect great bodies of men. The first is to achieve or acquire something of value or something that is desirable, and then the second is to prevent some scoundrel from taking it away from you." Notice the substance of Lewis's remarks to a trade-union crowd, the combination of urging the children of the working class to rise above it, not with it, and the materialistic stress on possessive individualism. Lewis, the most militant and prominent of the depression decade's labor leaders, remained too much the opportunist, too much the personification of vulgar pragmatism and business values to lead a third-party political crusade.

What, then, follows logically from the above description of the 1930s and the implied line of analysis? First, and perhaps obviously, however turbulent

were the American 1930s, the depression decade never produced a revolutionary situation. Second, one observes the essential inertia of the working-class masses. Once in motion, the mass of workers can move with great
acceleration and enormous militancy—but such movement remains hard
to get started. Such social inertia combined with the inability of most
workers and their leaders to conceive of an alternative to the values of
marketplace capitalism, that is, to create a working-class culture autonomous from that of the ruling class, was more important than trade-union
opportunism, corporate cooptation, or New Deal liberalism (though the last
factor was clearly the most potent) in thwarting the emergence of durable
working-class radicalism. Third, and finally, it suggests that a distinction
must be drawn between class struggle as a historical reality and workers
as a class fully aware of their role, power, and ability to replace the existing
system with "a better, firmer, more just social order [than] the one to be
torn down."

Radical Years: Working-Class Consciousness
on the Waterfront in the 1930's

BRUCE NELSON

This essay will examine the activity and consciousness of maritime
workers—longshoremen and seamen—on the Pacific Coast of the United
States during the 1930s. In many ways, the thirties were decisive years in
the history of the American working class. Perhaps nowhere else was the
turbulence, or the distance travelled, greater than in the maritime industry,
where workers who had long been regarded as social scum suddenly developed an exhilarating sense of power and self-respect; unions that had
been moribund for many years were infused with new energy or, in some
cases, pushed aside in favor of more dynamic labor organizations; and a
working-class subculture that had often displayed evidence of militancy and
rebellion provided the foundation of a renaissance of consciousness that
affected many workers beyond the confines of the waterfront. In particular,
the experience of the maritime workers on the West Coast provides a
portrait that contrasts sharply with the recent historiographical emphasis
on the narrow, episodic character of worker militancy and the allegedly
deep "social inertia" beneath the turbulent surface of events in the 1930s.

The West Coast maritime strike of 1934 and the era of insurgency which
followed it for several years constituted a dynamic historical moment. I
have chosen to describe and analyze several aspects of this renaissance—
particularly, the struggle to transform conditions on the job, the relationship
between radical political activity and the language of "Americanism," and
the persistence of a "mood of syndicalism" on the waterfront—rather than
to trace the institutional development of unions, the role of the Communist
Party, and the careers of rank and file leaders who rose to prominence

From Maurice Zeitlin, ed., *Political Power and Social Theory* (Los Angeles: JAI Press, 1984),
pp. 141–152, 154–162, 165–170, 174.

during this era. This choice of focus may tend to obscure the constant motion which characterized the period and may also imply a greater ideological coherence than in fact existed. I do not mean to underestimate the changing (even chaotic) character of events and circumstances on the West Coast waterfront. In fact, given the renewed emphasis on the inertia and persistent conservatism of the working class, my intention is to highlight the reality of ideological ferment, at least among a particular group of workers.

Because Communists played an important role in the maritime industry throughout the 1930s, it has been common to attribute the upheaval on the waterfront to their influence and to discuss the development of maritime unionism from the standpoint of the sharp changes in Communist line and program which occurred from 1929 to 1941. Again, however, my focus will be quite different. This essay will concentrate mainly on the middle years of the 1930s, when the maritime union movement displayed an independent dynamic which, to some degree, eludes the usual periodization of "Third Period," "Popular Front," etc. The key to this independent dynamic is the coming together of a way of life and work with a set of distinct historical factors that included the desperate conditions brought on by the Great Depression, the sense of opportunity and hope generated by New Deal labor legislation, and the worldwide rise of fascism and its apparent manifestations in the United States. The coalescence of these sparks with an already volatile subculture was more important than the influence of a particular left-wing party or trade union leader in shaping this era of insurgency.

In the early 1930s conditions on the West Coast waterfront were barbaric, even by the standards of the Great Depression. Among the longshoremen, the defeat of a number of local strikes in 1919 and 1920 had destroyed the International Longshoremen's Association (ILA) in almost every port and left the men at the mercy of the employers. In San Francisco, the stevedores were forced to endure a despised company union, a notorious speed-up, and the degrading "shape-up," where a few men were "hired off the streets like a bunch of sheep," as longshore leader Harry Bridges put it, while hundreds of others were turned away without work. Depression conditions aggravated the problem of an already swollen work force, and the ILA later recalled that many experienced longshoremen were forced to seek government relief while others "worked like slaves in shifts from 24 to 36 hours without sleep." As the "favored" few worked themselves into a state of exhaustion, crowds of hungry men would hover by the pierheads, on the chance that someone would get hurt on the job or fail to keep pace with the speed-up.

The seamen fared no better than the dockworkers. The humiliating loss of a nationwide strike in 1921 had reduced the venerable International Seamen's Union (ISU) to an empty shell. Wages were slashed and many of the favorable working and living conditions which had been won during an earlier period of insurgency were eliminated. In most ports, seamen were forced to hire through employer-controlled "Fink Halls," where a union partisan, or anyone else who "kicked," was systematically black-balled. When the Great Depression hit the shipping industry, many veteran seamen found themselves in the ranks of the unemployed, while inexperienced "workaways"—who agreed to ship out in exchange for a bunk, substandard food, and a wage payment of one dollar a month—received an alarming proportion of the available jobs. . . .

But, more importantly, the men themselves were not mere flotsam who lacked the capacity to resist the shipowners' ruthless hegemony. The twenties were lean years to be sure, and conditions in the early 1930s were leaner still. But there was among the longshoremen and seamen a tradition of militancy and spontaneous radicalism that was bound to surface again when the historical conditions were ripe. This tradition had its roots in the structure of life and work among the maritime workers and the seamen in particular. Seafaring men had long been victimized by low wages and abysmal conditions of life and work. They knew well the meaning of deprivation and were keenly aware of the enormous distance between the lifestyles of rich and poor. Moreover, they lived on the fringes of society and had little or no recourse to family, religious, ethnic, and other institutions which served the purpose of reconciling working people to the hegemony of the employing class or of creating a stable subculture which reinforced an alternative value system. Although many seamen were literate and well-read, few had had much formal education. Likewise, the transiency inherent in their calling meant that few seamen voted or showed much interest in the activity of the major political parties. The very nature of their trade made it difficult to lead a normal family life, and their low wages made it nearly impossible to support themselves, not to mention wives and children. They were, in the words of *Fortune*, "homeless, rootless, and eternally unmoneyed"—free of the responsibilities of home and family and yet, in many cases, wistful for the comfort and security of a more normal life.

While the seaman lived on the fringes of American society, he routinely saw a good deal more of the rest of the world than his shoreside counterpart. Oftentimes this experience opened his eyes to the breadth of injustice and suffering and rendered him somewhat cynical about conventional repre-sentations of reality. Harry Bridges, who came from a comfortable British middle-class family which had emigrated to Australia, grew restless with a clerk's life and went to sea at the age of fifteen. Long after he had settled down on the San Francisco waterfront and become the principal leader of the West Coast longshoremen, Bridges vividly recalled the profound effect that his stint as a seaman had had upon his outlook:

> . . . I took a trip that gave me a look at India and another at Suez, and what I saw there didn't seem to line up with what my father had told me about the dear old British. Then I got "home" and saw London. It was the filthiest, most unhealthy place I had ever seen. . . . I kept traveling around, and the more I saw the more I knew that there was something wrong with the system.

. . . Of course, not every seaman was radicalized by such encounters. Some shipped mainly in the coastwise trade, along the shores of North America, and many in the foreign trade confined themselves to the "gin mills" and whorehouses that were meant to ensnare the sailor in every port. But a breadth of experience, a worldliness, existed among seafaring men, and it undoubtedly contributed to their relative openness to radical and revolutionary ideas. . . .

The structure of life and work among longshoremen and seamen naturally gave rise to a syndicalist orientation. The close affinity between working and living conditions, the rootlessness and isolation from mainstream American institutions, and the cosmopolitanism of the waterfront created the elements of a mood that, in its most dynamic form, sought to transform the world by fundamentally reshaping the patterns of authority and organization in the realm of work. However, this impulse was at once broader and more elusive than the program of American syndicalism as represented by the Industrial Workers of the World (IWW). The Wobblies focused a lot of energy on the waterfront, and they were able to maintain a foothold among marine workers long after they had become little more than a fading memory in most other industries. The "mood of syndicalism" had at least four readily identifiable dimensions: first, the impulse toward workers' control of production; second, the belief that "direct action" at the point of production was the most effective means for the achievement of working-class objectives; third, the determination to cross traditional craft union barriers in order to build solidarity with other workers; and, finally, a striving for fundamental social transformation embodied in the Wobblies' exhortation to "bring to birth a new world from the ashes of the old." But this "mood of syndicalism" in maritime went far beyond the Wobblies' limited appeal, and survived their eventual demise, because it was rooted not in the doctrine of a particular Left organization but in the subculture of life and work on the waterfront. In the thirties, as in earlier periods of syndicalist upsurge, the world of work became the principle focus and arena of struggle and transformation. As we shall see, it was mainly from this base that the marine workers sought not only to transform conditions on the job, but also to affect the outcome of more overtly political struggles. . . .

Every year, in early March, International Seamen's Union President Andrew Furuseth sent an anniversary message to the ISU's pioneer affiliate, the Sailors' Union of the Pacific, [SUP] to commemorate its founding in 1885. In 1929, when the union's fortunes were at an all-time low, Furuseth's letter to the few diehard members and their guests burned with a zeal that was peculiarly out of character with the times. "*I wish we could all of us be saturated with the spirit of the crusader,*" he said. "Let us make this meeting a Pentecostal one, and go away from it with the determination to achieve, to live up to the highest and best that is in us."

Five years and two months later, maritime workers erupted with the "spirit of the crusader," and for 83 days they waged one of the great battles in the history of the American working class. Even by the standards of

1934, one of the most extraordinary years in the annals of labor, the "Big Strike" fully merited the superlatives which its partisans assigned it. For this drama transformed labor relations in the Pacific Coast maritime industry, ushered in a "Pentecostal" era of unionism and workers' self-activity that confounded and alarmed the AFL old guard as much as it did the employers, and triggered the formation of the Maritime Federation of the Pacific, an organization that many hoped would be a stepping stone toward "One Big Union" of all the marine crafts.

The upheaval began on May 9 as a coastwide longshore strike, but almost immediately seamen began walking off the ships and joining the ILA picket lines. Within ten days virtually all of the maritime unions were on strike, and rank and file Teamsters, in defiance of their officials, were refusing to haul cargo to or from the docks. This remarkable solidarity continued to grow and reached its high point in the San Francisco General Strike in mid-July.

On July 3 the employers declared the port open and the waterfront became "a vast tangle of fighting men" as 700 police tried to move scab cargo through massive picket lines. After regrouping on the July 4th holiday, both sides resumed the battle on July 5, or "Bloody Thursday," as it was soon to become known. The strikers defended themselves and their cause with magnificent courage and discipline. As one observer put it, "In the face of bullets, gas, clubs, horses' hoofs, [and] death . . . [t]hey were fighting desperately for something that seemed to be life for them." But in a physical confrontation of this magnitude, the workers were no match for the superior firepower at the employers' disposal. By the end of the day, two pickets were dead, shot in the back by police; hundreds more were injured, and National Guard troops patrolled the waterfront. It appeared that the strikers had been defeated.

However, "Bloody Thursday" was about to take on a new symbolic meaning. In the funeral procession for the strike's martyrs, tens of thousands of people took to the streets in a silent tribute that must surely rank as one of the most dramatic moments in the history of the American working class. Eyewitnesses spoke of "a river of men flowing up Market Street like cooling lava" and of "a stupendous and reverent procession that astounded the city." One employer spokesman acknowledged this event as "the high tide of . . . united labor action in San Francisco." It was, indeed, the general strike in embryo.

A week later more than 100,000 workers "hit the bricks" in solidarity with the maritime unionists. . . .

The general strike ended inconclusively after four days, with both sides claiming victory. By the end of July, an arbitration procedure had been established, and the maritime workers returned to the job, with none of their demands resolved. To many, it appeared that the strikers were exhausted, and that the inconclusive termination of the general strike had been a setback to the cause of unionism. The *New Republic* complained that "fighting spirit and funds have been used up" and "public opinion has been alienated." The *Nation* expressed the fear that "the maritime unions have now been abandoned to their fate." San Francisco banker William H. Crocker exulted that "Labor is licked." But appearance and reality were sharply at variance. The 83-day maritime and general strike had been but a prelude. The "Pentecostal" era was about to begin. . . .

The Big Strike had involved particular demands that now faced the prospect of arbitration. The National Longshoremen's Board appointed by President Roosevelt would soon make important concessions to the stevedores on the questions of wages, hours, overtime, and control of hiring. But, meanwhile, longshoremen and seamen demonstrated that they had an additional agenda requiring immediate attention. This agenda included the determination to rid the docks and ships of men who had scabbed during the strike, a campaign to make every work unit 100 percent union and to extend unionism into the ranks of unorganized waterfront workers, and the determination to tame the gang bosses and ships' officers who had driven the marine workers with relative impunity during the long non-union era.

Any confusion, fear, and tendencies toward recrimination generated in the aftermath of the general strike seem to have been swept aside as soon as the men returned to work. Longshoreman Henry Schmidt recalled that "somehow or another the men discovered . . . when they went back to work that morning that they had terrific power; they also had some courage, and they changed the working conditions immediately." Bill Rutter, another longshoreman, remembered that "some very good [working] rules . . . were made up, on the pierhead before we went into work that morning." Rutter was a member of a gang scheduled to load sacks of barley, and the men informed their bosses that they would work only fifteen sacks, rather than the customary twenty, per load. After about an hour, a load with twenty sacks came down, and then another. "The guys all went and got their coats and were standing there waiting to pull out," when the bosses relented and agreed to the gang's demand.

Moreover, there was widespread agreement with the opinion of a rank and file stevedore that "we must have a good housecleaning on the waterfront" because "it is filthy with rats, finks, [and] scabs." The "housecleaning" also began immediately. On the American-Hawaiian docks in San Francisco, for example, more than a dozen longshore gangs shut the piers down for a few days until the company agreed to fire several notorious scabs. Employer spokesman Gregory Harrison stated that from July 31, the day the men returned to work, until the day the presidential mediation board rendered its decision on the longshore dispute, "there were repeated strikes and stoppages of work along all of the waterfronts of the Pacific Coast." According to Harrison, "Twenty-nine such strikes and stoppages were actually recorded" during this 74-day period. And, when the longshore arbitration award was handed down on October 12, "far from diminishing, the strikes and stoppages of work increased in frequency and intensity." . . .

The first major confrontation came on September 20, when 600 longshoremen and seamen struck in support of the latter's demand that the

Dollar Line fire seventeen non-union workers who had sailed on the *President Taft* during the maritime strike. When the company balked at this demand, 200 seamen walked off the ship, and 400 longshoremen working the Dollar Line docks immediately joined them. Ship scalers and teamsters soon rallied to the walkout, and union taxi drivers refused to bring passengers to the pier. According to one report, "a crowd of over a thousand men" picketed the docks. After several hours of stalemate, the Dollar Line capitulated and provided the non-union men with a police escort from the ship. The *President Taft* then sailed with a crew that was 100 percent union. . . .

One of the major focal points of rank and file combativeness concerned the pace of work, the weight of sling loads, and relations between gang bosses and men on the docks. In the aftermath of the Big Strike, many of the gang bosses assumed that conditions on the docks would quickly return to "normal" and that they would be free once again to drive the men at the old relentless pace. But the longshoremen quickly introduced them to a new reality. In one instance, a boss demanded that his gang increase the weight of their sling loads, or "you can go home." No longer intimidated by such threats, the gang started to walk off the job; and when the outraged boss took a swing at the gang steward, the union representative "grabbed the big fink around the neck and put him to the floor."

This confrontation and its outcome provide an apt symbol of the enormous change taking place on the West Coast waterfront. The results can be measured in many ways, including statistics on productivity. Spokesmen for the shipowners were soon complaining that the cost of handling cargo in San Francisco had become "probably the highest in the world." Almon Roth, the president of two major waterfront employers' associations, claimed that "a gang of longshoremen used to handle as high as 3,000 sacks of sugar per hour in the unloading operations at Crockett," but that a recent check-up showed "we were getting only 950 sacks per hour per gang. . . . Observation of this operation proved that the men in the hold were resting 60 percent of their time." Roth acknowledged that "there was a day when employees complained of speed-ups." Now, however, "the pendulum has swung the other way. Today employers suffer from deliberate slow-downs."

The transformation lamented by Roth was not the result of spontaneous upsurge alone. The unions established rules designed to spread the work evenly and to prevent "chiselers" from spearheading a return to the old order. Among the longshoremen, there were numerous examples of entire gangs walking off the job early in order to abide by the regulation limiting hours of work to 120 per month. The membership of the ILA voted a $25 fine for anyone who worked more than the 120-hour limit without the union's permission, and there were also penalties for other infractions. While most of these rules were job-related, some were considerably broader in focus. The San Francisco ILA local placed a gang boss on trial for "slandering colored brothers." Among the sailors, there was a regulation fining any union member who set foot in the Seamen's Church Institute, which symbolized shipowner paternalism and a "pie in the sky" attitude toward the seamen's conditions of life and work. The Marine Firemen's Union placed a severe penalty on any of its members caught buying a Hearst newspaper.

Soon after the conclusion of the Big Strike the ILA organized a system of dock and gang stewards to coordinate the activity of the men on the front. According to the employers, this brought about a virtual revolution in the locus of effective power on the docks. Gregory Harrison complained that, because of the steward system,

> authority to direct work upon the docks passed from the hands of the foremen into the hands of dock and gang stewards. The dock and gang stewards are appointed by the Union. They have an organization of their own. They meet regularly; they adopt rules; they establish the manner in which, and the speed at which, work is to be performed on the waterfronts of the Pacific Coast.

Although Harrison may have exaggerated the extent of the longshoremen's control of the work process, he was certainly correct in indicating that a dramatic transformation had taken place. Even the *Waterfront Worker*—a rank and file sheet, with obvious left-wing ties, that had played a vital role in the organization of the ILA local in San Francisco—expressed amazement at "the great change that has come over the workers on the waterfront." . . .

The most eloquent testimony about the depth of this change came from the workers themselves. A longshoreman's wife stated that:

> Before the strike my husband was always complaining about conditions on the waterfront, how hard he was working and how much the bosses were hollering and so forth.
>
> Since returning to work after the strike he is a changed man entirely. He seems different and happier, and even finds time to pay a little attention to his wife. . . .
>
> Thanks to the strike, a change for the better has come for the men on the front and a change has taken place in our home life.

. . . A rank and file longshoreman recalled that "not so very long ago, when we first organized, I was fired and discriminated [against] for being a union man and wearing an I.L.A. button. I have seen my wife and two daughters go hungry." But, he proclaimed, "the old order of things shall never come back to us. . . . We are all brothers now—one for all, and all for one. The spirit of comradeship and Unionism prevails amongst us and we have learned a bitter lesson."

An "Admiral Line Stevie" [a worker on the Admiral Line docks] declared that "We must all fight to the last man to see to it that the old conditions shall never come back to the waterfront again." This determination to put the misery of the past behind them forever was strengthened in the longshoremen and their families by an almost lyrical sense of the glories of the emerging new era. The "Admiral Line Stevie" was convinced that "at this time on the waterfront we have the finest conditions in the world." An "Oldtimer" who had first joined the ILA in 1915 declared that "we are the most militant and organized body of men the world has ever seen." In a letter to the *Waterfront Worker*, a group of "stevies" proclaimed that the longshoremen had truly become the "Lords of the Docks."

This was no small affirmation for men whose status had generally been held in such low esteem that many of them had preferred to call themselves "laborers" rather than longshoremen. . . .

For longshoremen and seamen alike, the foundation of the new order was control of hiring. The dock workers had established the union hiring hall as their number one demand during the strike. Although the arbitration award of October 1934 provided for the establishment of hiring halls operated in each port by labor relations committees of employer and union representatives, the ILA won the sole right to select the job dispatchers. With the union in charge of dispatching, and the men on the docks ready to "hang the hook" on any employer who refused to accept candidates sent from the hall, full control of hiring quickly passed into the hands of the ILA. The shipowners were soon complaining that "the award provisions for [joint] operation of the longshore hiring halls, and the rights of employers thereunder, have been entirely defeated . . . , although the employers have always contributed one-half of the expense of their maintenance." . . .

. . . [I]f this example and many others have demonstrated a significant transformation of work relations and practices, what of the realm of consciousness? Did the maritime workers of the 1930s fit the allegedly normative American mold of "job consciousness" and "militant pragmatism," or were they moving in the direction of a more thoroughly radicalized consciousness?

I realize that any consideration of working-class consciousness is an invitation to polemics. My own understanding of this phenomenon is based on a recognition of the primacy of complexity and diversity over simplicity and unity. Such factors as national boundaries, different time periods, ethnicity, race, and sex have played a major role in creating diversity. Even at the point of production the simple equation "labor versus capital" has not been an adequate description of reality. For, in addition to the above factors, the development of capitalism has led to a continual recomposition of the working class, creating ever new internal divisions and, therefore, a complex and often contradictory consciousness.

In a study of workers in a specific industry and geographic location at a particular historical moment, it is perhaps all the more important to acknowledge that their ideology does not possess normative dimensions that can and should be measured against an enclosed ideal category called "working-class consciousness." On the other hand, it would be equally wrong to take refuge in pure empiricism. For, as English historian E. P. Thompson has reminded us, there is a *logic* if not a *law* in "the responses of similar occupational groups undergoing similar experiences." Without falling prey to notions of historical inevitability, it is possible to affirm that history has demonstrated a persistent if uneven tendency on the part of working people toward the formation of ideas, institutions, and values that have transcended time periods and national boundaries and have reflected a striving toward a collective affirmation of self. At some moments, this tendency has resulted in an inwardly-focused, politically passive subculture. In other circumstances, it has led to an expansive consciousness, based on a lively sense of class relations and class struggle, and seeking to create a more just social order.

For many years our understanding of working-class consciousness was circumscribed by rigid and essentially static models. The two most prominent examples, the Leninist model and that of the Commons/Perlman school of labor economists in the United States, have much in common, in spite of their ideological antagonism. Both view the normal focus of working-class activity as essentially narrow and pragmatic, and both regard the intellectual as playing a crucial role in changing the workers' consciousness. Lenin declared that "the history of all countries shows that the working class, exclusively by its own efforts, is able to develop only trade union consciousness." In the Leninist idiom, the Marxist section of the intelligentsia rescues the workers from the narrow economism and parochial immediacy of the factory world by bringing them the "scientific" truths of socialism. The Commons/Perlman school would agree with Lenin's declaration, but far from denigrating the spontaneous perceptions of the workers, sees their alleged pragmatism as appropriate and beneficial. For Commons and his disciples, the normal outlook of the worker is "job consciousness," seeking only "an enlarged opportunity measured in income, security, and liberty in the shop and industry." When the worker deviates from this normative path, it is because of the intrusion of intellectuals and their abstract, essentially alien formulas. While Lenin characterized the true working-class spokesman as a revolutionary "tribune of the people," Commons and Perlman exalted the "philosophy of organic labor" which had its roots in the craft guilds of the Middle Ages and was developed to its highest level by Samuel Gompers and the American Federation of Labor in the United States.

The last two decades have witnessed a powerful challenge to these static conceptions of working-class consciousness. The most formidable assault has come from Thompson, whose studies of the "making" of the English working class have demonstrated the existence of humane traditions, deeply-held values and powerful currents of thought which shaped the response of working people to changing forms of exploitation. Although intellectuals sometimes played an important role in articulating the ideas and aspirations of the common people, they were not the motive force in the development of working-class consciousness. Rather, Thompson has stressed the richly-textured traditions and the often disciplined and creative self-activity of millions of ordinary folk who too often have been regarded as inert and inarticulate.

The worldwide popular insurgency of the 1960s provided further impetus for a major assault on the reigning orthodoxies. With millions of people taking to the streets on behalf of civil rights and in opposition to U.S. intervention in Vietnam, many young historians in the United States developed a new appreciation for the dynamic role of class struggle and other forms of conflict in American history. The widespread labor militancy of the 1930s once again became a focal point of admiration and study, although there was much speculation and controversy about why the upsurge did not result in a more thoroughgoing social transformation and a more enduring Left movement. In some quarters, the Communist Party and the leadership of the CIO unions came in for a good deal of criticism for allegedly blunting and undermining the spontaneous radicalism of millions of industrial workers.

In recent years the dynamism of the "new labor history" has shown no signs of abating, but on the question of working-class consciousness in the 1930s the pendulum has been swinging back toward a view which reaffirms the essential conservatism and narrow "job consciousness" of American workers, even among those who formed the base of the CIO upsurge. In particular, studies of the auto workers have emphasized that their fabled militancy was not as widespread as we once supposed, and that where there was militancy it often reflected a "myopic" and even "backward" outlook. . . .

In a provocative essay . . . Melvyn Dubofsky offers "another look" at what he calls the "Not So 'Turbulent Years' " of the 1930s. Dubofsky explores the widespread "passivity beneath the turbulent surface of violent events as well as the persistence of many pre-depression era beliefs and behavioral patterns of American workers." For him it is not the Communists and the CIO leaders who are responsible for the circumscribed outcome of the 1930s upsurge, but rather the workers themselves, or "the essential inertia of the working-class masses." . . .

The experience of the maritime workers challenges several major themes of the new labor history, including its emphasis on the distance between the aspirations of workers and the goals of trade unions and union leaders. In the case of the hidebound International Seamen's Union, there certainly was such a distance even when the union followed the initiative of rank and file seafarers and joined them on the picket lines during the 1934 strike. But to suggest a similar pattern in the case of militants like Bridges and the maritime workers from whose ranks they emerged would be ludicrous. For one thing, "Unionism" became almost a sacred cause on the West Coast waterfront. The great majority of longshoremen and seamen flocked into the maritime unions in the period surrounding the Big Strike. For another, the resurgent marine unions became vivid examples of rank and file democracy in action. Their membership meetings were well attended—often to the point of overflowing—and were generally characterized by vigorous debate, with broad participation from the ranks. Moreover, the unions submitted most major policy questions to coastwide membership referendums. In this setting, it was precisely the militant activists who emerged as elected officials and whose leadership was endorsed by the rank and file over and over again, in the face of frequent attempts by the employers and the media to discredit these "radicals" and replace them with more amenable representatives. In a typical broadside, the San Francisco *Examiner* characterized "the line-up in the waterfront labor situation" as

> Harry Bridges vs. responsible union labor
> Harry Bridges vs. the shipping industry
> Harry Bridges vs. San Francisco, the Pacific Coast, the entire American seaboard.
> Put in one phrase—the issue is:
> COMMUNISM VS. AMERICAN LABOR.

Bridges denied being a Communist Party member, but he solicited advice and assistance from Communists and openly endorsed much of the Party's program. Some of the insurgent maritime unionists *were* Communists. Others moved in the direction of self-conscious syndicalism and claimed to be more consistently radical than the Communists. While there remained an inevitable distance between the militant strains in the maritime subculture and the commitment to a specific left-wing program, it is clear that the radical affiliations of Communists and syndicalists did not isolate these activists from their fellow workers in the marine industry. To some degree, the radicalism of the leadership was a reflection of the insurgent spirit and ideological ferment in the ranks. . . .

The record of the West Coast maritime workers indicates a pattern that differs markedly from the portrait which emerges from Dubofsky's essay and the recent studies of the auto workers. In the Big Strike and the "Pentecostal" era that followed on the Pacific Coast, we see not only militant pragmatism but the flowering of radical class consciousness among significant numbers of workers in the marine industry. There were indeed strong syndicalist overtones to their movement, but the character of their activity was often dramatically different from the shop-floor syndicalism . . . among auto workers during the CIO upsurge. The longshoremen and seamen did not limit their sights to the maritime equivalent of a single plant or department. Increasingly, they believed that their struggle rightly included not only walkouts and job actions to transform the world of work, but strikes to defend workers faced with stiff legal penalties, the refusal to load cargo designed to aid Mussolini's war effort in Ethiopia, and opposition to German ships bearing the hated swastika. Moreover, to the growing dismay of the employers, the government, and the press, they insisted on engaging in much of this political activity right at the "point of production."

The dynamic cultural and ideological phenomenon that sociologist Charles R. Walker perceived in Minneapolis, another focal point of the upheaval of 1934, was also evident in port cities up and down the Pacific Coast. Walker observed that "in times of crisis . . . the working class for brief periods develops ideas of its own interest apart from the middle class. . . . It produces leaders, thinks up fresh forms of organization and strategy, and above all scans skeptically its relations to the rest of society." Writing more than a decade later, journalist Richard Boyer argued that this development of an "original culture" had been more than a momentary or transitory phenomenon. Basing his observations mainly on the maritime workers, but also upon broader currents within the labor movement, he saw a "qualitative change" that:

> extended to the values and mores of millions. The ancient American shi-boleths of success—save your money, keep your shoes shined and get to work on time—were being replaced by newer precepts: never pass a picket line, in unity there is strength, and other variations of the statement that individual success can only be attained by collective struggle. The word *union* acquired a new significance and a new dignity. To many it had a majestic ring that summarized a complete and a noble philosophy.

While the consciousness of broad masses of people may be too contradictory a phenomenon to describe as "a complete and a noble philosophy," the marine workers demonstrated a marked tendency to integrate broader political and social themes with the central concerns arising from the world of work. Moreover, they forged a relatively coherent symbolic universe characterized not only by a heightened sense of antagonism toward their employers but by a broad awareness of social and political roles based upon class analysis. Although they reserved a special animosity for the shipowners and their agents on the job, the maritime workers also developed a set of adversary symbols that included such diverse representatives as Adolph Hitler, newspaper magnate William Randolph Hearst, California elected officials Frank "Big Fink" Merriam, the governor, and Angelo "Little Fink" Rossi, the mayor of San Francisco, and University of California football coach "Navy Bill" Ingram and his "Phi Beta Kappa finks" who scabbed during the 1934 strike.

The shipowners were quick to blame this ideological ferment on the Communist Party and its representatives within the maritime unions. To the employers, the ideas and activity of the marine workers represented a deviation from the "safe, sound Americanism" which allegedly had prevailed on the waterfront before the 1934 strike. They longed for the more congenial unionism of the AFL's old guard, even though for more than a decade they had refused to recognize the unions headed by these men. What the shipowners conveniently overlooked, however, was the fact that the consciousness and activity of longshoremen and seamen in the new era had long been an inherent part of the subculture of the marine industry and had been expressed by the workers, episodically if not consistently, during the 50 years that maritime unionism had had a foothold on the Pacific Coast. The tendency to override craft separation and form cooperating federations—at its highest level, the demand for "One Big Union" in the industry—had existed side by side with craft divisions and jealousies and had often swept aside the latter during periods of upsurge. Moreover, the marine workers' internationalism was as much a product of their subculture as it was a reflection of "derived" ideas brought to the men from without. And, given the long history of harsh exploitation, and the fact that there were few institutions that served to mitigate their suffering and draw them closer to the American mainstream, longshoremen and seamen did not need Communists to tell them about the reality of the "class struggle."

On the other hand, it is undeniable that the Communists were a major force in the maritime industry. They provided the workers with a number of disciplined cadres who were not only more able and energetic than the AFL incumbents but were far more in tune with the sentiments and aspirations of the men. Of course, in most cases these disciplined Communist cadres were themselves marine workers of many years standing. Their main role was to help shape an effective trade union program, sum up and popularize the lessons of strikes and other mass actions, and sharpen the focus and intensity of the workers' antagonism toward their principal adversaries. Whereas the Communists did indeed bring "ideas" to the workers in marine, the ones that took hold were not so much new as they were a more sophisticated distillation of popular experience and of tendencies that were inherent in the maritime subculture. As Harry Bridges put it, during the first of four government inquisitions on his relationship to the Communist Party, "I have been a member of a trade union since 1916. There was no Communist Party in 1916, and a lot of my views on trade unionism I had before there was ever a Communist Party. The labor movement in Australia is a pretty old one, and was a pretty militant and progressive one, and I learned a few things there that maybe came in handy later."

The maritime workers' expanding field of vision is evident in the tradition of longshoremen and seamen on the march which developed in the aftermath of the Big Strike. As they marched in Labor Day parades, "Bloody Thursday" memorials, and other events which galvanized the ranks of labor, as they strode forward with heads held high, clad in their work uniforms of jeans, hickory-striped shirts, and white caps, the marine workers became a vivid representation of working-class pride. In these same events, they also demonstrated their increasing integration of job-related concerns with broader, more overtly political issues. . . .

The most powerful symbol of maritime workers on the march was the annual memorial for the martyrs of the Big Strike. Beginning on the first anniversary of "Bloody Thursday," maritime labor stopped work up and down the Pacific Coast, initiating a tradition that the longshoremen have continued ever since. It was, and is, a one-day strike in honor of those who sacrificed their lives in the cause of waterfront unionism. Ironically, in 1935, a coastwide ILA ballot resulted in a vote not to observe a 24-hour "memorial holiday," but in many ports units of the Maritime Federation engaged in such action anyway. In San Francisco, where the ILA local had voted overwhelmingly in favor of a memorial strike, all maritime labor stopped work until 1:00 PM, while stores and bars on the front cooperated by closing their doors for part of the day. The *Voice* claimed that 25,000 people marched up Market Street while "tens of thousands of quiet, awed San Franciscans" watched. Even the conservative *American Seaman* praised the event as a "Monster Parade" whose size "astounded" the city of San Francisco. . . .

Meanwhile, at "the point of production," in addition to the job actions and "quickie" strikes aimed at transforming work relations, there were a growing number of work stoppages around broader, more overtly political issues. Characteristically, San Francisco was the headquarters of this insurgency, but there was similar activity in other ports as well. There were, for example, brief work stoppages to protest the "frameup" of maritime workers charged with murder and conspiracy in a number of celebrated instances during strikes and organizing activities. . . . To support their fellow workers, "approximately 20,000" men—members of the Maritime Federation and rank and file Teamsters—walked off the docks for half an hour during the trial. Three days later a San Francisco jury acquitted the accused ILA members after deliberating for *seven minutes!*

Given the international dimensions of the seamen's experience, and the cosmopolitanism which pervaded the waterfront, the issues of war and fascism proved to be especially volatile during the mid-thirties. . . .

The maritime workers were especially active in their opposition to fascism. The immediate spark was twofold: first, Germany's policy of arresting seamen from many countries, including the United States, for smuggling anti-Nazi literature into the Third Reich; and secondly, Italy's war of aggression against Ethiopia. Already, many seamen had witnessed the destruction of the trade unions and any semblance of democratic rights in Germany and Italy. As early as July 1933, the *Waterfront Worker* reported from Washington State that sailors from a U.S. Navy ship, along with crew members from American and Danish merchant ships, joined together to pull the swastika from a German vessel in Olympia harbor. When the swastika entered San Francisco Bay in March 1935, on the bow of the German cruiser *Karlsruhe*, 7,000 longshoremen, machinists, and ship scalers struck for half an hour, dampening the official welcome which city officials had prepared for the crew of the German naval vessel. When the *Karlsruhe* entered the harbor at Vancouver, British Columbia, the angry response of workers there forced the ship to drop anchor in the stream and forego any plans to visit the city. In Seattle, longshoremen held a protest strike against the arrest of American seaman Lawrence Simpson—who was seized by Nazi police for alleged possession of "Communist" literature in his shipboard locker—while seafaring unions picketed the German ship *Schwaben*. . . .

Although the maritime workers demonstrated a strong sense of internationalism, they often justified their activity in terms of "Americanism." On the surface, this may seem paradoxical, and it certainly does not conform to the dogma which places working-class consciousness in opposition to any form of nationalism or patriotism. But, in fact, the maritime workers were expressing a very different form of Americanism from their employers, who often wrapped themselves in the flag while they endeavored to thwart the most elementary demands of labor. Early in the maritime strike, a major spokesman for capital had defined the conflict as one between "American principles and un-American radicalism." This kind of invective continued to characterize the shipowners' and the news media's descriptions of the marine unions and their leadership for several years. Every insurgent act on the part of the longshoremen and seamen was presented as evidence of the "alien" and "subversive" character of their movement.

The maritime workers were only too well aware that their bitterest enemies voiced their opposition to the new unionism in the language of "Americanism." Even acts of criminal violence and the denial of basic human rights were justified in terms of the defense of "American principles." But in spite of the way their opponents degraded the term, the maritime workers were by no means ready to concede the mantle of Americanism to the shipowners. On the contrary, the workers saw themselves as true patriots, defenders of democracy, and inheritors of the progressive and revolutionary dimensions of America's historical experience. In the eyes of the marine workers, it was the capitalists and their allies who were "unAmerican," because they were trying to deny broad sections of the people their fundamental democratic rights and to rob the workers of an "American standard of living." A resolution passed unanimously by the San Francisco Bay Area District Council of the Maritime Federation stated: " . . . the growth of fascist tendencies and organizations in the State of California . . . [is] in direct opposition to the Democratic principles upon which our government was formed, which guarantee the right of free speech, assembly, the right to organize and fight for better conditions." The *Voice of the Federation* declared that "American citizens are now faced with the choice of fighting for their Liberties or being crushed under the iron heel of a ruthless mob despotism, organized and led by 'unAmerican' employers."

It is vitally important to understand the context in which this heated discussion of Americanism took place. If the employers were unable or unwilling to distinguish between unionism and communism, the maritime workers saw the overtones of fascism in the policies of capital. The *Waterfront Worker* warned that "not prosperity, but insane, bloody fascism is just around the corner." Although the benefit of hindsight may tempt us to dismiss such a prediction as inflammatory and even paranoid, the marine workers had good reason to fear that what they saw and experienced was more than a passing phenomenon. Having, in many cases, witnessed the true meaning of fascism in the port cities of Germany and Italy, they saw parallel developments in the United States, particularly in California, where it seemed that every effort to assert labor's most elementary rights met with a wave of legal and vigilante repression. Nowhere was this truer than in the vast realm of "farm factories" which dominated the Golden State's landscape. On July 20, 1934, the day the San Francisco General Strike ended, police in Sacramento had arrested seventeen leaders of the Cannery and Agricultural Workers' Industrial Union (CAWIU) on the sweeping and conveniently vague charge of "criminal syndicalism." Eventually, eight of them were found guilty and sentenced to prison terms. But this legal persecution was only a small part of what developed into a major offensive in which the state's leading industrial interests mobilized growers large and small, law enforcement authorities, the American Legion, and other zealots in a frenzied effort to destroy unionism in agriculture and weaken it in the cities. . . .

On the waterfront itself, the violence which had peaked during the General Strike continued to take its toll. A year and a half after the eruption of 1934 it still remained commonplace for individuals wearing marine union buttons to be attacked and beaten up at night by roving bands of thugs. In October 1935, Harry Bridges reported "that at least one ILA man is beaten up every night on the Waterfront and . . . a longshoreman was killed by vigilantes last week." Author Louis Adamic recalled that, as he was interviewing Bridges in April of 1936, a man interrupted their conversation to "inform him that a worker had just been found slugged unconscious on a dock." . . .

Meanwhile, in the California state legislature, more than a score of bills calling for restrictions on civil liberties were introduced in one session of the Assembly. Speaking of California, the *Nation* said: ". . . nowhere else has there been such a flagrant denial of the personal liberties guaranteed by the Bill of Rights; nowhere else has authority been so lawless and brazen; nowhere else has the brute force of capitalism been so openly used and displayed." Although criticizing what she regarded as excessive use of the term "fascism" to describe the reactionary offensive in California, journalist Lillian Symes acknowledged: "It was like this, I imagine, in Rome in 1922, in Berlin in 1932."

The maritime workers shared none of Ms. Symes' skepticism about how their tormentors should be characterized. Turning the tables on their accusers, they argued that any talk of "alien" and "subversive" activity should be directed at the employers, the Hearst press, the reactionary ISU officials, and the vigilante groups whose watchword was "intimidation and terror carried out in the dark of night." Ole Olsen, a popular official of the Sailors' Union, characterized William Randolph Hearst as "a madman . . . trying to rule us with his un-American principles" and "Hitler's American prototype." Whereas Hearst was an "aggressor" against democracy, said Olsen, "We are defending our rights as American Workers. . . . Ours is the strength and the vitality of America!" . . .

Clearly there was a tension between this tradition, with its long litany of the victims of capitalist injustice, and the broader symbolism of American history. For the most part, however, the maritime workers did not see a sharp distinction between allegiance to their class and loyalty to their country. In fact, they were anxious to present themselves and their movement in harmony with what they perceived as the mainstream of American history and values. In response to an anti-Communist diatribe from "A LOYAL AMERICAN," who concluded with the familiar taunt—"You always have the privilege of going back to Russia if you do not like it in the United States"— the *Waterfront Worker* stated that "this country of ours" is one "whose wealth we have built with our sweat and blood. . . . *WE are the loyal Americans,* Mister, not you! We are struggling to better the conditions of the workers on the waterfront. *Our struggles are the same as the overwhelming majority of Americans.*" . . .

As they thought about the present struggle and the future goal there was a general, if often unconscious, tendency for maritime workers to resort to a syndicalist frame of reference. Even the Communists on the waterfront sometimes spoke of the object of their struggle in a manner that seemed to envision a "Syndicalist"—more than a "Soviet"—America. This may seem contradictory for members of an organization that declared itself the enemy of syndicalism. But Communists themselves were forced to acknowledge that the soil in which syndicalism flourished was more persistent than the organizations which had been its bearers. As late as November 1935, William Z. Foster complained that traces of syndicalist ideology remained within the Communist Party, in spite of longstanding efforts to eradicate them. Nowhere would this have been more true than on the waterfront, where the close affinity between work and life, and the absence of integrative institutions, made syndicalism—less as doctrine than as mood and tendency—a natural component of the maritime workers' worldview. Moreover, a significant number of the Communists in the maritime industry came from the ranks of the Wobblies, and many of them continued to identify with the ideas and agitational style which had characterized the IWW. Tommy Ray, a seaman who served as a Communist Party cadre on the waterfront for more than fifteen years, recalled with bitterness that "Bon[a]fide seamen"—including Communist seamen—"were considered syndicalists or anarchists by most of the officials of the C.P."

In any case, syndicalist themes cropped up again and again among Communists and non-Communists alike. Harry Lundeberg once said that the maritime workers were willing to "fight capitalism to a finish," but neither he nor any of his colleagues were very specific about the kind of new beginning that would follow capitalism's "finish." Certainly the few efforts of the Communists and their sympathizers to hold up the Soviet Union as the alternative to capitalism met with indifference or defeat. For the most part, the workers, including the Communist workers, fell back on broad formulations that reflected their own experience on the job and in the unions. An "Oldtimer" on the docks declared that "Our mission will not be completed until the unionization of all who toil for a living becomes a reality. . . . Our slogan should be: Long Live Unionism, Forever and Forever." SUP activist Sam Usinger called on his fellow workers to "form a one-big-union where poverty and unemployment shall be unknown." Communist longshoreman Henry Schrimpf characterized the maritime workers as "pioneers into a new era" whose goal was "to lead the workers in the right direction, to feed the little hungry children; make happy homes and elevate the standard of living and generally advance the human cause."

Another longshoreman spoke of the shape of the future as a "Universal Federation," meaning a world bearing the mark of the Maritime Federation of the Pacific. This theme was developed more explicitly in a poem which appeared in the *Waterfront Worker*, whose editors were widely regarded as Communists. An anonymous poet saw a "mighty army" marching

> Toward a great goal, workers paradise
> A government of the workers is their fight
> And now in sight that goal we can see
> For we are joined in solidarity.

What instrument would bring about this "great goal," this "workers paradise"? The author called on his fellow workers to "Form a Pacific Coast Federation," whose example would spread to the Eastern and Gulf ports.

> And when that is complete we're on our way,
>> We'll be over the top a new day,
> And a worker's dream we'll realize
>> The slaves will live in a paradise.

How similar this conception is to the statement of a French syndicalist that "The workers' trade union is . . . the living germ of future society" and the declaration in the IWW preamble that "By organizing industrially we are forming the structure of the new society within the shell of the old."

. . . In the case of the maritime workers, apart from a large and colorful stock of colloquialisms reflecting the particularities of their environment, they expressed themselves in conventional terms derived from the mainstream of American language and culture. As we have seen, they defined their values in terms of Americanism every bit as much as the employers, and their unifying theme was unionism far more than class. In other words, they did not speak the language of Marxism, because for the most part that vocabulary had never taken root in the American soil. However, beneath the surface of common language there was a distinctive meaning that was often profoundly different if not fundamentally opposite from the meaning attributed to the same terms by their employers. To fail to see the deeply-rooted class distinctions in the use of symbolic language and the interpretation of historic events is to obscure and distort a fundamental reality of the experience of American workers.

It is also important to note, however, that the maritime workers did not limit their frame of reference to the commonly accepted historical symbols exemplified by Jefferson and Lincoln. They also drew on a specifically working-class tradition that was, implicitly at least, antagonistic to the mainstream of American historical development. George Woolf, president of the Ship Scalers' local in San Francisco, compared the four members of his union who were arrested on murder charges during an organizing drive to the celebrated California labor martyrs and "class war prisoners" J. B. McNamara and Tom Mooney. "An active Unionist is dangerous to capital," said Woolf, "so he is arrested and framed." Ole Olsen of the SUP called on his fellow workers to learn from the "school of oppression." Every time the employers "send one of our numbers to prison," said Olsen, "every time they have one of us shot in the name of LAW AND ORDER, every time they send their vigilantes to assault one of us they are adding to our education." Advocating a coastwide work stoppage in observance of "Maritime Memorial Day," the anniversary of "Bloody Thursday," Harry Lundeberg [SUP leader] declared that the entire labor movement and all friends of labor should be invited to participate, because the "cause of the maritime workers is the cause of all labor." Said Lundeberg: "The martyrs of the [1934] strike [will] take their place in history with the martyrs of labor, with the victims of Ludlow, Haymarket, Everett, Centralia, Imperial Valley, San Francisco Preparedness Day and Modesto.''

. . . In concluding, it is necessary to acknowledge that the ''Pentecostal'' era was relatively short-lived. It foundered on the rocks of resurgent craft antagonism, clashing personalities, and divergent strategic orientations within the Maritime Federation. As the alliance between the San Francisco longshoremen and the Sailors' Union of the Pacific gradually came apart, so did the threads which had given the Federation its distinctive radical hue. What we are left with, then, is a brief renaissance of consciousness that burned brilliantly for an historical moment. From the standpoint of the conventional wisdom in labor relations, it has been judged as an era of massive ''irresponsibility'' which gradually gave way to a more ''reasonable'' pattern of behavior. But, viewed from the standpoint of the workers themselves, this renaissance represents a long overdue festive upheaval, a search for more humane and just patterns of work relations, a struggle between labor and capital that invaded the realms of culture and politics and provoked a vigorous and healthy debate on the meaning of Americanism and the place of workers in the social hierarchy.

Moreover, in important and enduring ways, the victories of the 1930s transformed the lives of the maritime workers. Conditions on the waterfront changed to the point where, in Henry Schmidt's words, ''the supervisorial personnel had practically nothing to say.'' The longshoremen were no longer merely ''laborers.'' Now they proclaimed themselves ''Lords of the Docks.'' The seamen were no longer transients and pariahs. They struggled for years to create the conditions which made it possible for them to have homes and families. The material gains and their new sense of pride turned these workers into widely respected members of the larger community. In fact, among many of their fellow workers, the longshoremen and seamen took on the stature of heroic proletarian rebels. ''The Staccato Beat of Marching Feet'' became a vivid symbol of their historic advance. The acknowledgment that this forward march was to some degree disrupted and diverted should not detract from our appreciation of the power of the ''Pentecostal'' era and the indigenous foundation upon which this historical moment was constructed.

✣ F U R T H E R   R E A D I N G

Irving Bernstein, *Turbulent Years: A History of the American Worker, 1933–1941* (1970)

John Bodnar, *Workers' World: Kinship, Community, and Protest in an Industrial Society, 1900–1940* (1982)

David Brody, *Workers in Industrial America: Essays on the Twentieth Century Struggle* (1981)

Bert Cochran, *Labor and Communism: The Conflict That Shaped American Unions* (1977)

Melvyn Dubofsky and Warren Van Tine, *John L. Lewis: A Biography* (1977, 1987)

Sidney Fine, *Sitdown: The General Motors Strike of 1936–1937* (1969)

John Freeman, *In Transit: The Transport Workers Union in New York, 1933–1966* (1989)

Peter Friedlander, *The Emergence of a UAW Local, 1936–1939: A Study in Class and Culture* (1975)

Gary Gerstle, *Working Class Americanism: The Politics of Labor in a Textile City, 1914–1960* (1989)

Nelson Lichtenstein, "Auto Worker Militancy and the Structure of Factory Life, 1937–1955," *Journal of American History* 67 (September 1980), 335–353

Alice Lynd and Staughton Lynd, *Rank and File: Personal Histories by Working-Class Organizers* (1973)

Staughton Lynd, "The Possibility of Radicalism in the Early 1930s: The Case of Steel," in James Green, ed., *Workers' Struggles Past and Present: A "Radical America" Reader* (1982)

Bruce Nelson, *Workers on the Waterfront: Seamen, Longshoremen, and Unionism in the 1930s* (1988)

Art Preis, *Labor's Giant Step: Twenty Years of the CIO* (1964)

Ron Schatz, *The Electrical Workers: A History of Labor at General Electric and Westinghouse, 1923–1960* (1983)

CHAPTER
10

Labor and the State

⚕

Although the social history of U.S. workers and their families is an important focus for labor historians, scholars have only recently rediscovered the role of the state as agent of repression and change, and as regulator and administrator of the work environment. There is some irony here because renewed interest in the state returns labor historians to some of the same questions first posed by turn-of-the-century scholar-activists like John R. Commons and Florence Kelly. These reformers were highly conscious of labor law's role in creating an environment that sustained trade unionism and ameliorated the conditions under which all workers—but especially women and children—labored in homes and factories.

When labor historians and other contemporary scholars use the term the state, *they mean the government in all its manifestations: the executive, of course, but also the courts, regulatory agencies, and the police power—in every case, both local and national. During the nineteenth century and much of the twentieth, the judiciary proved the most active arm of the state when it came to regulating the relationship between labor and capital. Reflecting the viewpoint of the Anglo-Saxon elite who governed the country, the courts ruled that most efforts by unions or reformers to alter working conditions threatened the sanctity of contracts or the free play of commerce. Judges frequently enjoined use of the strike and boycott on these grounds. Only the culturally and legally defined dependency of women and children allowed for an aggressive use of the police power to protect working conditions—the protective legislation viewed more problematically by later generations of feminists.*

Spokesmen for organized labor, along with their Progressive allies, protested bitterly, but it was not until the First World War that the state—with its new interest in production, patriotism, and social harmony—began to seek a legal framework that provided for the orderly empowerment of unions and the transformation of social relations at the work site. The breakthrough finally came in the 1930s, when laws were passed that limited court power to halt most strikes, facilitated the organization of trade unions, and laid the basis for an American welfare state.

Through the early 1970s most historians applauded these New Deal reforms, seeing in them first, a fitting culmination of the half-century battle waged by labor reformers, and second, an American version of the welfare state constructed in most other industrial societies. But the history of these legal reforms seems much more complicated and problematic today. The New Deal's pioneer-

ing labor legislation, once dubbed "Labor's Magna Carta," has revealed itself both ineffective and burdensome to the trade-union movement. Likewise, New Deal welfare legislation that mostly affected women—including laws regulating wages, hours, and "sweatshop" work at home—was framed by reformers whose understanding of the complex social relationship among women, their families, and their work is certainly not that of the present.

Why did this failure occur? Were the laws passed in the 1930s flawed at their conception? Is the state merely a creature of ruling-class interests that make temporary and episodic concessions to those below during moments of extreme crisis? Or have the trade unions and their allies failed, in a political sense, to make their weight felt in the administration and revision of the laws passed in more liberal times?

✤ D O C U M E N T S

The first three documents illustrate some of the ways in which the Supreme Court set national labor policy before the New Deal. In the first selection, lawyers for Eugene Debs's American Railway Union argue for the lawfulness of the 1894 railway strike, while the Supreme Court insists that an injunction against such union action, which halted mail delivery nationwide, is entirely necessary and constitutional. Little more than a decade later, the Court sustained positive state action on behalf of women workers, arguing in the second document, *Muller* v. *Oregon*, that Oregon's maximum-hour law was necessary to protect the health and physical well-being of women workers. When it came to regulating wages, however, the Court reversed itself fifteen years later, finding, as the third document, *Adkins* v. *Children's Hospital*, shows, that once women had won the vote, they were no longer dependents who needed state protection. Individual women were therefore "free" to make the same kind of employment contract with an employer as were men.

During the New Deal, the state's relationship to employment regulation underwent a major change. The National Labor Relations Act, the preamble of which appears as the fourth document, asserted that industrial peace could be assured only when employees bargained with their employers on a basis of real economic and organizational equality. The state could foster this condition by promoting the organization of trade unions. The National Labor Relations Board (NLRB) therefore intervened directly at the work site. In the fifth document, the NLRB investigates the case of a textile-mill worker fired for his pro-union views, and orders his reinstatement with back pay. Under the New Deal, maximum-hour and minimum-wage legislation would be extended to men as well as women. Indeed, the very power of the federal government over interstate commerce, which the Supreme Court had relied upon to crush the Pullman boycott, now justified federal regulation of labor standards. In the sixth document, CIO leader John L. Lewis defends government regulation of hours and wages, while John Edgerton, a spokesman for low-wage southern industry, attacks the proposal for the Fair Labor Standards Act.

But the U.S. government smiled on trade unions only briefly. In the conservative political climate after World War II, Congress passed the Taft-Hartley Act, which limited unions' rights to organize, strike, and participate fully in the political life of the nation. Among its most controversial provisions was that allowing states to ban the union shop, a contract device mandating that all employees of a firm must pay dues to the union representing the workers at that company. In the seventh selection, the pro-employer U.S. Chamber of Commerce defends the Taft-Hartley Act and attacks what it calls union "labor monopoly." In the final document, the newly merged AFL-CIO denounces the Taft-Hartley Act and calls for its revision.

In re Debs, 1895

Mr. Lyman Trumbull, for Petitioners.

. . . The bill states that the prisoners are officers and members of an organization known as the American Railway Union; that in May, 1894, a dispute arose between the Pullman Palace Car Company and its employés which resulted in the employés leaving the service of the company; that the prisoners, officers of the American Railway Union combining together, and with others unknown, with the purpose to compel an adjustment of the said difference and dispute between said Pullman Co. and its employés, caused it to be given out through the newspapers of Chicago, generally, that the American Railway Union would at once create a boycott against the cars manufactured by said Pullman Palace Co., and that in order to make said boycott effective, the members of the American Railway Union who were some of them employed as trainmen or switchmen, or otherwise, in the service of the railroads mentioned, which railroads or some of them are accustomed to haul the sleeping cars manufactured by the Pullman Palace Car Co., would be directed to refuse to perform their usual duties for said railroad companies and receivers in case said railroad companies thereafter attempted to haul Pullman sleeping cars.

Such is the gist of the bill. All that is subsequently alleged as to what was done by the prisoners, was for the purpose of compelling an adjustment of the difference between the Pullman Company and its employés. To accomplish this, the American Railway Union called upon its members to quit work for the companies which had persisted in hauling the Pullman cars. Was there anything unlawful in this? If not, then the prisoners and the members of the American Railway Union were engaged in no unlawful combination or conspiracy. The allegation that the prisoners, officers and directors of the American Railway Union did issue and promulgate certain orders and requests to the members of the union in the service of certain railway companies in pursuance of said unlawful purpose or conspiracy, did not make the purpose unlawful, when the facts stated in the bill show that the purpose was not unlawful. All that the prisoners are charged with threatening to do, or having done, was for the purpose, primarily, of bringing about an adjustment of the differences between the Pullman Company and its employés. It is only incidentally in pursuit of this lawful purpose that prisoners are charged with obstructing commerce.

The boycott of the Pullman sleepers was, as the bill shows, not to obstruct commerce, but for an entirely different purpose.

It was not unlawful for the American Railway Union to call off the members of the organization, although it might incidentally affect the operation of the railroads. Refusing to work for a railroad company is no crime, and though such action may incidentally delay the mails or interfere with interstate commerce, it being a lawful act, and not done for that purpose, is no offence. . . .

Mr. Justice Brewer, After Stating the Case, Delivered the Opinion of the Court.

The case presented by the bill is this: The United States, finding that the interstate transportation of persons and property, as well as the carriage of the mails, is forcibly obstructed, and that a combination and conspiracy exists to subject the control of such transportation to the will of the con-spirators, applied to one of their courts, sitting as a court of equity, for an injunction to restrain such obstruction and prevent carrying into effect such conspiracy. Two questions of importance are presented: First. Are the relations of the general government to interstate commerce and the trans-portation of the mails such as authorize a direct interference to prevent a forcible obstruction thereof? Second. If authority exists, as authority in governmental affairs implies both power and duty, has a court of equity jurisdiction to issue an injunction in aid of the performance of such duty. . . .

It must be borne in mind that this bill was not simply to enjoin a mob and mob violence. It was not a bill to command a keeping of the peace; much less was its purport to restrain the defendants from abandoning what-ever employment they were engaged in. The right of any laborer, or any number of laborers, to quit work was not challenged. The scope and purpose of the bill was only to restrain forcible obstructions of the highways along which interstate commerce travels and the mails are carried. And the facts set forth at length are only those facts which tended to show that the defendants were engaged in such obstructions.

A most earnest and eloquent appeal was made to us in eulogy of the heroic spirit of those who threw up their employment, and gave up their means of earning a livelihood, not in defence of their own rights, but in sympathy for and to assist others whom they believed to be wronged. We yield to none in our admiration of any act of heroism or self-sacrifice, but we may be permitted to add that it is a lesson which cannot be learned too soon or too thoroughly that under this government of and by the people the means of redress of all wrongs are through the courts and at the ballot-box, and that no wrong, real or fancied, carries with it legal warrant to invite as a means of redress the coöperation of a mob, with its accompanying acts of violence.

We have given to this case the most careful and anxious attention, for we realize that it touches closely questions of supreme importance to the people of this country. Summing up our conclusions, we hold that the government of the United States is one having jurisdiction over every foot of soil within its territory, and acting directly upon each citizen; that while it is a government of enumerated powers, it has within the limits of those powers all the attributes of sovereignty; that to it is committed power over interstate commerce and the transmission of the mail; that the powers thus conferred upon the national government are not dormant, but have been assumed and put into practical exercise by the legislation of Congress; that in the exercise of those powers it is competent for the nation to remove all obstructions upon highways, natural or artificial, to the passage of interstate commerce or the carrying of the mail; that while it may be competent for the government (through the executive branch and in the use of the entire executive power of the nation) to forcibly remove all such obstructions, it is equally within its competency to appeal to the civil courts for an inquiry and determination as to the existence and character of any alleged obstructions, and if such are found to exist, or threaten to occur, to invoke the powers of those courts to remove or restrain such obstructions; that the jurisdiction of courts to interfere in such matters by injunction is one recognized from ancient times and by indubitable authority; that such jurisdiction is not ousted by the fact that the obstructions are accompanied by or consist of acts in themselves violations of the criminal law; that the proceeding by injunction is of a civil character, and may be enforced by proceedings in contempt; that such proceedings are not in execution of the criminal laws of the land; that the penalty for a violation of injunction is no substitute for and no defence to a prosecution for any criminal offences committed in the course of such violation; that the complaint filed in this case clearly showed an existing obstruction of artificial highways for the passage of interstate commerce and the transmission of the mail—an obstruction not only temporarily existing, but threatening to continue; that under such complaint the Circuit Court had power to issue its process of injunction; that it having been issued and served on these defendants, the Circuit Court had authority to inquire whether its orders had been disobeyed, and when it found that they had been, then to proceed under section 725, Revised Statutes, which grants power "to punish, by fine or imprisonment, . . . disobedience, . . . by any party . . . or other person, to any lawful writ, process, order, rule, decree or command," and enter the order of punishment complained of; and, finally, that, the Circuit Court, having full jurisdiction in the premises, its finding of the fact of disobedience is not open to review on *habeas corpus* in this or any other court. . . .

The petition for a writ of *habeas corpus* is

Denied.

Muller v. Oregon, 1908

Mr. Justice Brewer Delivered the Opinion of the Court.

. . . It is undoubtedly true, as more than once declared by this court, that the general right to contract in relation to one's business is part of the liberty of the individual, protected by the Fourteenth Amendment to the Federal Constitution; yet it is equally well settled that this liberty is not absolute and extending to all contracts, and that a State may, without conflicting with the provisions of the Fourteenth Amendment, restrict in many respects the individual's power of contract. . . .

That woman's physical structure and the performance of maternal functions place her at a disadvantage in the struggle for subsistence is obvious. This is especially true when the burdens of motherhood are upon her. Even when they are not, by abundant testimony of the medical fraternity continuance for a long time on her feet at work, repeating this from day to day, tends to injurious effects upon the body, and as healthy mothers are essential to vigorous offspring, the physical well-being of woman becomes an object of public interest and care in order to preserve the strength and vigor of the race.

Still again, history discloses the fact that woman has always been dependent upon man. He established his control at the outset by superior physical strength, and this control in various forms, with diminishing intensity, has continued to the present. As minors, though not to the same extent, she has been looked upon in the courts as needing especial care that her rights may be preserved. Education was long denied her, and while now the doors of the school room are opened and her opportunities for acquiring knowledge are great, yet even with that and the consequent increase of capacity for business affairs it is still true that in the struggle for subsistence she is not an equal competitor with her brother. Though limitations upon personal and contractual rights may be removed by legislation, there is that in her disposition and habits of life which will operate against a full assertion of those rights. She will still be where some legislation to protect her seems necessary to secure a real equality of right. Doubtless there are individual exceptions, and there are many respects in which she has an advantage over him; but looking at it from the viewpoint of the effort to maintain an independent position in life, she is not upon an equality. Differentiated by these matters from the other sex, she is properly placed in a class by herself, and legislation designed for her protection may be sustained, even when like legislation is not necessary for men and could not be sustained. It is impossible to close one's eyes to the fact that she still looks to her brother and depends upon him. Even though all restrictions on political, personal and contractual rights were taken away, and she stood, so far as statutes are concerned, upon an absolutely equal plane with him, it would still be true that she is so constituted that she will rest upon and look to him for protection; that her physical structure and a proper discharge of her maternal functions—having in view not merely her own health, but the well-being of the race—justify legislation to protect her from the greed as well as the passion of man. The limitations which this statute places upon her contractual powers, upon her right to agree with her employer as to the time she shall labor, are not imposed solely for her benefit, but also largely for the benefit of all. Many words cannot make this plainer. The two sexes differ in structure of body, in the functions to be performed by each, in the amount of physical strength, in the capacity for long-continued labor, particularly when done standing, the influence of vigorous health upon the future well-being of the race, the self-reliance which enables one to assert full rights, and in the capacity to maintain the struggle for subsistence. This difference justifies a difference in legislation and upholds that which is designed to compensate for some of the burdens which rest upon her.

We have not referred in this discussion to the denial of the elective franchise in the State of Oregon, for while it may disclose a lack of political equality in all things with her brother, that is not itself decisive. The reason runs deeper, and rests in the inherent difference between the two sexes, and in the different functions in life which they perform. . . .

Affirmed.

Adkins v. Children's Hospital, 1923

Mr. Justice Sutherland Delivered the Opinion of the Court.

In the *Muller Case* the validity of an Oregon statute, forbidding the employment of any female in certain industries more than ten hours during any one day was upheld. The decision proceeded upon the theory that the difference between the sexes may justify a different rule respecting hours of labor in the case of women than in the case of men. It is pointed out that these consist in differences of physical structure, especially in respect of the maternal functions, and also in the fact that historically woman has always been dependent upon man, who has established his control by superior physical strength. . . . But the ancient inequality of the sexes, otherwise than physical, as suggested in the *Muller Case* . . . has continued "with diminishing intensity." In view of the great—not to say revolutionary—changes which have taken place since that utterance, in the contractual, political and civil status of women, culminating in the Nineteenth Amendment, it is not unreasonable to say that these differences have now come almost, if not quite, to the vanishing point. In this aspect of the matter, while the physical differences must be recognized in appropriate cases, and legislation fixing hours or conditions of work may properly take them into account, we cannot accept the doctrine that women of mature age, *sui juris*, require or may be subjected to restrictions upon their liberty of contract which could not lawfully be imposed in the case of men under similar circumstances. To do so would be to ignore all the implications to be drawn from the present day trend of legislation, as well as that of common thought and usage, by which woman is accorded emancipation from the old doctrine that she must be given special protection or be subjected to special restraint in her contractual and civil relationships. In passing, it may be noted that the instant statute applies in the case of a woman employer contracting with a woman employee as it does when the former is a man. . . .

If now, in the light furnished by the foregoing exceptions to the general rule forbidding legislative interference with freedom of contract, we examine and analyze the statute in question, we shall see that it differs from them in every material respect. It is not a law dealing with any business charged with a public interest or with public work, or to meet and tide over a temporary emergency. It has nothing to do with the character, methods or periods of wage payments. It does not prescribe hours of labor or conditions under which labor is to be done. It is not for the protection of persons under legal disability or for the prevention of fraud. It is simply and exclusively a price-fixing law, confined to adult women (for we are not now considering the provisions relating to minors), who are legally as capable of contracting for themselves as men. It forbids two parties having lawful capacity—under penalties as to the employer—to freely contract with one another in respect of the price for which one shall render service to the other in a purely private employment where both are willing, perhaps anxious, to agree, even though the consequence may be to oblige one to surrender a desirable engagement and the other to dispense with the services of a desirable employee. The price fixed by the board need have no relation to the capacity or earning power of the employee, the number of hours which may happen to constitute the day's work, the character of the place where the work is to be done, or the circumstances or surroundings of the employment; and, while it has no other basis to support its validity than the assumed necessities of the employee, it takes no account of any independent resources she may have. It is based wholly on the opinions of the members of the board and their advisers—perhaps an average of their opinions, if they do not precisely agree—as to what will be necessary to provide a living for a woman, keep her in health and preserve her morals. It applies to any and every occupation in the District, without regard to its nature or the character of the work. . . .

Preamble of the National Labor Relations Act, 1935

. . . The denial by employers of the right of employees to organize and the refusal by employers to accept the procedure of collective bargaining lead to strikes and other forms of industrial strife or unrest, which have the intent or the necessary effect of burdening or obstructing commerce by (a) impairing the efficiency, safety, or operation of the instrumentalities of commerce; (b) occurring in the current of commerce; (c) materially affecting, restraining, or controlling the flow of raw materials or manufactured or processed goods from or into the channels of commerce, or the prices of such materials or goods in commerce; or (d) causing diminution of employment and wages in such volume as substantially to impair or disrupt the market for goods flowing from or into the channels of commerce.

The inequality of bargaining power between employees who do not possess full freedom of association or actual liberty of contract, and employers who are organized in the corporate or other forms of ownership association substantially burdens and affects the flow of commerce, and tends to aggravate recurrent business depressions, by depressing wage rates and the purchasing power of wage earners in industry and by preventing the stabilization of competitive wage rates and working conditions within and between industries.

Experience has proved that protection by law of the right of employees to organize and bargain collectively safeguards commerce from injury, impairment, or interruption, and promotes the flow of commerce by removing certain recognized sources of industrial strife and unrest, by encouraging practices fundamental to the friendly adjustment of industrial disputes arising out of differences as to wages, hours, or other working conditions, and by restoring equality of bargaining power between employers and employees.

It is hereby declared to be the policy of the United States to eliminate the causes of certain substantial obstructions to the free flow of commerce and to mitigate and eliminate these obstructions when they have occurred by encouraging the practice and procedure of collective bargaining and by protecting the exercise by workers of full freedom of association, self-organization, and designation of representatives of their own choosing, for the purpose of negotiating the terms and conditions of their employment or other mutual aid or protection.

A Union Man Gets His Job Back, 1938

. . . Pursuant to notice, a hearing was held in Greenville, South Carolina, on October 4 and 5, 1937, before D. Lacy McBryde, the Trial Examiner duly designated by the Board. The Board and the respondent were represented by counsel and participated in the hearing. Full opportunity to be heard, to examine and cross-examine witnesses, and to produce evidence bearing upon the issues was afforded all parties. . . .

The respondent, a South Carolina corporation, is engaged in the manufacture of cotton cloth. It operates three plants, all in Greenville County, South Carolina. The main plant, known as the Woodside plant, with which this case is concerned, is located at Greenville while the other two are located at Simpsonville and Fountain Inn. . . .

Textile Workers Organizing Committee is a labor organization affiliated with the Committee for Industrial Organization and admits to membership employees of the respondent at its Woodside plant. The predecessor of the unit of the Textile Workers Organizing Committee here involved was known as United Textile Workers of America, Local 1684, and was affiliated with the American Federation of Labor. In 1936 the local was absorbed by the Textile Workers Organizing Committee. . . .

On October 10, 1935, John R. Kirby, an employee of the respondent at the Woodside plant, was discharged. Kirby had been a member of the Union since 1934, then holding the office of warden. During September of that year there was a general strike in the cotton textile industry, affecting also the Woodside plant. At that time Kirby acted as captain of the pickets around the Woodside plant. In November 1934, following the strike, Kirby was elected president of the Union for 1 year, an office he held at the time of his discharge. Avery Hall, an employee at the Woodside plant, in response to the question whether he knew Kirby to be an active Union man replied, ''I sure did.'' And when asked whether this fact was generally known in the plant Hall testified, "Most all the hands knowed it." Another witness, Roy Dryman, an employee at the Woodside plant, when asked whether and how he knew Kirby was a Union man testified, "Because he told me he was and he asked me I guess fifty times to join." Dryman further testified, "I don't guess there was a half dozen people in the mill who didn't know he was an active Union man." From the record it is clear that Kirby was an active Union member and that this fact was generally known throughout the plant.

The Woodside plant was divided into two sections, known as Mill No. 1 and Mill No. 2, though both were in the same building. Prior to Kirby's discharge each section had worked on a day and night shift. In February 1935, pursuant to a predetermined plan, the respondent commenced to make alterations in the plant by which the production would be so changed that the night shift in Mill No. 2, as well as 22 jobs, including those of 15 frame hands, would be eliminated. . . .

On Monday, September 23, 1935, which was the next working day, Kirby started at his regular job when S. N. McConnell, at that time the second hand in Mill No. 1, told Kirby he was wanted by Bray. Grover Hardin, until then employed on the night shift in Mill No. 2, was placed in Kirby's position. Kirby reported to Bray and was told that he was to be transferred to the night shift in Mill No. 2, that being the shift which was to be eliminated as soon as the improvements had been completed. Kirby asked Bray why this was being done, and when no reason was given said, "Mr. Bray, I know why you are transferring me out there. It is because I belong to the Union." From the inception of the improvements in the plant the night shift in Mill No. 2 had been continually reduced until at the time of the transfer only three employees were working there. Kirby was the only man to be transferred from the carding room in Mill No. 1 to the carding room in Mill No. 2, where he took Hardin's place. The Monday following his transfer Kirby was notified by the respondent that his services would be terminated at the end of that week, as the particular set of frames on which he was working were not to be used longer. Accordingly, about 2 weeks after his transfer Kirby was discharged. Shortly thereafter the night shift in Mill No. 2 ceased operating.

Bray testified that in eliminating the night shift in Mill No. 2 he tried to retain the best men. He testified he tried "to pick out the people [he] thought would fit better . . . from an efficiency standpoint, and the people that could get along with people, and cause no confusion in the mill . . . regardless of the time they have been there." Bray testified that neither the pay nor the employment was regulated by seniority, but "everything being equal we try to take care of the people that has been there."

We shall endeavor to apply this test of the respondent to Kirby, on the basis of the evidence presented in the record. Kirby started to work for the respondent during the latter part of April 1933, having had previous experience elsewhere. Though it was up to Bray to make the selection of the men to be kept, the second hand was the employee most familiar with the relative efficiency of the various frame hands in the carding department as he was their immediate superior, worked with them continuously, and kept a written record of their mistakes. From the time of the strike in 1934 to the time Kirby was transferred to Mill No. 2, McConnell was the second hand in charge of the night shift in Mill No. 1. Prior to McConnell's arrival as second hand, the evidence adduced at the hearing was to the effect that Kirby's work was always satisfactory. McConnell testified that Kirby was an average hand, that of the group of approximately 16 frame hands on the night shift in Mill No. 1 there were "two or three that would get better production," but there were "Some didn't get the production he got, couldn't get about as well." Bray admitted he did not seek McConnell's advice before deciding to remove Kirby from the night shift in Mill No. 1 and discharging him shortly thereafter. Bray testified he did not want McConnell's advice because McConnell was Kirby's uncle. . . .

The respondent tried to imply that Kirby did not work regularly by endeavoring to show in his cross-examination that he was not regular in his attendance at the plants at which he had worked since his discharge by the respondent. But if any conclusion is to be drawn from the only record available, the pay-roll record . . . , it would seem that Kirby was rarely absent. For the period of 16 weeks noted in the record he was absent but 2 days. . . .

On the basis of his efficiency, his ability to "get along with people," and his attendance at the plant, it appears that Kirby was one of the better frame hands of the 16 on the night shift in Mill No. 1. This being so, and "everything" not "being equal" as to this group of 16, the question of seniority need not be considered. It must be noted that Kirby was the only man to be transferred from the carding room in Mill No. 1 to the carding room in Mill No. 2. On the basis of the respondent's own test it is clear that if anyone were to be transferred Kirby should not have been that one. . . .

The Union, besides admitting employees of the Woodside plant, also admitted employees from other cotton mills in Greenville. However, there were more members from the Woodside plant than from the others. Though at the time of the strike the membership was quite large, after the strike it had become fairly small. Nevertheless the Union under Kirby held regular meetings and continued active. Following his discharge and departure from Greenville to find other work, however, it became inactive. A few weeks after his departure the Union did not hold further meetings.

The respondent contended that it never knew Kirby was president of the Union and did not even know he belonged to it until his comment to Bray at the time of the transfer. We find, however, in view of the clear testimony that Kirby took an active part in the 1934 strike, and that almost everyone about the plant knew Kirby was active in Union affairs, that the respondent must have been aware of his Union activities. From the record it is clear that Kirby was discharged for his activities in behalf of the Union and the employees of the respondent at the Woodside plant.

We find that by the above acts the respondent has discriminated in regard to the hire and tenure of employment of Kirby, and that it has thereby discouraged membership in the Union. We also find that by the above acts the respondent has interfered with, restrained, and coerced its employees at the Woodside plant in the exercise of the rights guaranteed in Section 7 of the Act. . . .

Upon the basis of the findings of fact and conclusions of law and pursuant to Section 10 (c) of the National Labor Relations Act, the National Labor Relations Board hereby orders that the respondent, Woodside Cotton Mills Co., Greenville, South Carolina, and its officers, agents, successors, and assigns shall:

1. Cease and desist from:

(a) Discouraging membership in Textile Workers Organizing Committee or any other labor organization of its employees at its plant in Greenville, South Carolina, by discrimination in regard to hire or tenure of employment or any terms or conditions of employment;

(b) In any other manner interfering with, restraining, or coercing its employees at its plant in Greenville, South Carolina, in the exercise of their right to self-organization, to form, join or assist labor organizations, to bargain collectively through representatives of their own choosing, and to engage in concerted activities for the purpose of collective bargaining or other mutual aid or protection, as guaranteed in Section 7 of the Act.

2. Take the following affirmative action which the Board finds will effectuate the policies of the Act:

(a) Offer to John R. Kirby immediate and full reinstatement to his former position or to a position corresponding to that formerly held by him at the plant in Greenville, South Carolina, with all rights and privileges previously enjoyed;

(b) Make whole said John R. Kirby for any loss of pay he has suffered by reason of his discharge by repayment to him of a sum of money equal to that which he would have earned as wages during the period from the date of his discharge to the date of such offer of reinstatement, less the amount he has earned during such period;

(c) Post notices in conspicuous places throughout its plant at Greenville, South Carolina, and maintain such notices for a period of at least thirty (30) consecutive days from the date of posting, stating that the respondent will cease and desist as aforesaid;

(d) Notify the Regional Director for the Tenth Region in writing within ten (10) days from the date of this order what steps the respondent has taken to comply therewith.

Testimony for and Against the Fair Labor Standards Act, 1937

John L. Lewis in Defense.

. . . We, of the United Mine Workers of America, and of the Committee for Industrial Organization, wish to pledge our general support to the principle of a minimum wage and maximum workweek. . . .

First. It will increase mass purchasing power, which is an essential condition to permanent economic recovery and stable prosperity.

Second. It will, through reduction in hours of work, make way for the employment of hundreds of thousands of industrial workers who are now without work or on relief.

Third. From a humanitarian standpoint it will bring a greater measure of leisure and economic well-being. It will mean at least a glimmer of sunlight to millions of submerged American workers who now live in economic darkness and despair.

Fourth. From the viewpoint of industrial democracy the pending measure will offer to these unfortunate victims of our existing economic system an opportunity to rise to industrial citizenship or, in other words, a chance through unionization to attain to collective bargaining with their employers and thus achieve industrial emancipation. . . .

I am firmly opposed to wage differentials based on geography. Usually this is no more than a plea for the continuance of low living standards in the Southern States. Such a differential has absolutely no justification. Its proposal is based on an alleged difference in cost of living between the North and the South. I maintain that this is pure allegation. There is not a scrap of evidence to support such a statement. Indeed, so far as data are available, they indicate that the prices of the various items in a family budget are, by and large, just as high in the South as in the North.

Of course, it is a matter of common knowledge that the standard of living of the average southern wage earner, particularly the cotton-mill worker, is somewhat lower than that of the northern wage earner. This is so because wage scales on the whole are lower in the South, and in consequence the southern worker has less money to spend. The difference, in other words, is due not to the fact that prices of individual commodities are lower in the South, but simply to the fact that, because of this lower income, the southern worker gets fewer of the good things of life.

His food may cost him less, but that is because he gets less milk, less fresh vegetables and fruits, and less fresh meats. His housing may cost less, but that is because he gets an inferior type of housing.

Certainly the Government cannot put its approval upon this unfortunate condition. The southern worker is entitled to as good a standard of living as the northern worker. And, if the standard is to be the same, I reiterate, there is absolutely no ground for believing that its cost would be less in the South than in the North. . . .

It is rather a sad commentary on American wage rates to say that no matter how low a minimum may be established, it will benefit great numbers of workers. For instance, suppose that the irreducible minimum wage rate is placed at 40 cents an hour such as provided in the pending bill, and the maximum working week placed at 35 hours. This would mean, under the assumption of steady employment, weekly earnings of $14, monthly earnings of about $60, and annual earnings—on the basis of 50 weeks of employment—of about $700. A wage scale such as this would be of material benefit to hundreds of thousands possibly even millions of American workers. For this reason I regard the adoption of such a minimum standard as provided by this bill as a most desirable step forward. It may be that at the present time, and in view of all the circumstances, even such a short step as this is all that is practicable.

But I think it would be a calamity if such a wage minimum as that referred to should in any way be construed as a living wage. The labor movement with which I am associated is interested in securing for every American unskilled or semiskilled worker a living wage—that is to say, a minimum income upon which he can maintain himself and his family at a level of healthy and decent living. The skilled worker should, of course, receive a higher wage in accordance with his skill and training. But every worker, no matter how humble his job, should be able to secure at least the essentials of what, for lack of a better term, we may term an American standard of living.

Nor should this wage be set by the standards in those industries in which a "family wage" prevails. It is possible, for instance, that a cotton-mill family, in which the husband, the wife, and say three adolescent children, are all employed in the mill, may obtain a very good income by their combined efforts. But this practice is destructive to all that we cherish most in our American institutions. Normally, a husband and father should be able to earn enough to support his family. This does not mean, of course, that I am opposed to the employment of women, or even of wives, when this is the result of their own free choice. But I am violently opposed to a system which by degrading the earnings of adult males, makes it economically necessary for wives and children to become supplementary wage earners, and then says, "See the nice income of this family."

For these reasons we must keep fighting for the principle of a real living wage. Nor is such a conception the nebulous thing that certain of its opponents would have one believe. On the contrary, the principle of the living wage has been quite generally accepted. Moreover, a series of studies by responsible public and other authorities of the amount of income necessary for a living wage has placed the subject on a factual basis. We now know, with sufficient accuracy for practical purposes, the approximate income which an individual or a family must have in order to maintain what may be described as a minimum standard of living for American wage workers. . . .

John E. Edgerton in Opposition.

. . . Mr. Chairman and gentlemen of the committee, although I am president of a textile corporation which employs enough labor to be directly affected by the act under consideration, I appear before you primarily as president of the Southern States Industrial Council for the purpose of presenting the views of the constituency of that organization, which embraces approximately 10,000 industrial units in 15 southern States. . . .

Southern industry will welcome any scheme of control of minimum wages, maximum hours, and the abolition of child labor that would be fair in its application to all industries, to all sections, and to all elements of our working population, and that would not have in it those dangers of con-centrated power and arbitrary authority that do not belong to a democratic government.

What southern industry is mortally afraid of is the result of domination of all industry in the United States by a board with headquarters in Wash-ington—be it a five-man board or any kind of a board. Inevitably, the majority of such a board would represent majority interests in other sections with which the South must compete. Such was the experience under the N. R. A., and more recently under the Wash-Healey Act. The latter spe-cifically provides that the Secretary of Labor shall determine [reading]—

> prevailing minimum wages for persons employed on similar work, or in the particular or similar industries or groups of industries currently op-erating in the locality.

But, under this act the administrative board which has set minimum wages for only one industry—the men's work-clothing industry—set a rate that was practically the same as the union rate in the New York City area, despite the fact that there is a decided concentration of this industry in the South, thus disregarding the specific provisions of the law.

. . . The fact of the tremendously wide variation in the physical or mental abilities of people to earn and of their efficiencies or inefficiencies in performing the tasks for which they are to be compensated does not appear to have been taken into anything like serious consideration.

Since we have been accustomed to thinking of compensation for labor in the light of not only its physical and moral needs but in the light of its demonstrated capacity to produce and thereby justify on a competitive basis the compensation which it gets, it is difficult to think wholly in terms of what workers may want or actually need for their sustenance. We do not think, therefore, that this act in anything like its present form would be at all practical in its operation or helpful to even that segment of society which it is primarily intended to benefit. But, assuming that it would be imme-diately and permanently beneficial to a considerable number of wage earn-ers, we can see no good or logical grounds for withholding such benefits from even larger numbers of wage earners. Why should such favors be held from workers on the farms, in the kitchen, and in other places where fewer people are employed? Whose purchasing power at this time is more important to industry and the Nation than that of the farmers and those engaged in agricultural pursuits? In our view, the purchasing power of the farming population of this country is far more fundamental to the Nation's welfare and progress than is the purchasing power of any other group of consumers. Would not the natural and inevitable effect of this act be to either raise violently the wages of farm labor and thereby throw out of economic balance the entire scheme of agricultural adjustment or to ac-celerate the abandonment of farms by farm labor to the great embarrassment of the Nation's industrial centers? Would there not be in these circum-stances, a multiplication of the already daily calls upon industry to get busy and absorb the unemployed? Would not the philanthropic agencies, both public and private, have more embarrassing problems in trying to take care of the increased number of the inefficient, the untrained and the otherwise incapacitated to earn a fixed minimum wage?

Our second point is that because an act of this sort which leaves out of consideration both the obligation to earn and the wide diversity in earning power, cannot be made fair and beneficial to all the people in all sections and of all races; therefore, it is not justified as an instrument of progress.

But, Mr. Chairman and gentlemen, whatever the other particular objections to this bill may be, or whatever improvements may be suggested or made in any of its details, the most repugnant of all its features is the manner of its administration. It is at that point where most of the dangers lie. There is to be another board, which is to have virtually the power of life or death over practically every industry in the Nation. That means, in the first instance, another stupendous subtraction from the rights and powers of both the States and the individuals thereof, and a transference of all the power and rights thus subtracted to the Central Government in Washington. The forcible taking away of the rights of States and individuals, however constitutional it may be declared to be, is still odious, we believe, to most of the natives of this country. Upon that most vital and most dangerous point, we stake our chief objections to this bill. . . .

Employers Attack the Union Shop, 1958

Our country is dedicated to the protection of individual liberties—freedom for the individual, including protection of his right to choose or reject, so long as the rights of others are not infringed upon.

Laws protecting this right are necessary to insure the freedom of *all* Americans.

Right-to-work laws provide protection, in this instance for the employee, by assuring him the right to work at his job without being *forced* by anyone—the government, an employer, or a union—to join or contribute to a particular labor organization.

Like federal law, state right-to-work laws recognize and protect an employee's right to join with other employees for the purpose of collective bargaining. Unlike federal law, however, the state laws recognize and protect his right to *choose* which, if any, labor organization he wishes to join. . . .

When a person is *compelled* to join an organization, he is *forced* to accept the obligations of membership in that organization required by its constitution, by-laws, and rules of discipline.

If, of course, he voluntarily accepts these obligations, and bears the duties and discipline willingly, that is his right and his privilege.

But when offensive discipline or duties are imposed on one *forced* to join such an organization, he is placed in a position of being compelled to compromise.

A typical example of the compromising position an involuntary member is placed in stems from the vague disciplinary clauses in union constitutions that virtually deny a member the right to disagree with, or criticize union officers. A union member, for instance, has been penalized heavily for writing to his home-town paper, demanding the ousting of labor racketeers.

When union constitutions forbid this type of criticism, a member is forced into a position where his only choice is to disavow earlier promises *or* to give up his right to act according to his own conscience without any restraint except that imposed by public laws.

Also, there are religious groups whose members believe as a basic premise in their worship of God that they should refrain from joining with others in organizations similar to labor unions.

American citizens belonging to these religious groups have been forced from their employment because they could not, in good conscience, join a labor organization.

The meaning of compulsory unionism to an individual thus assumes tremendous proportions, much greater than a simple clause in a collective bargaining agreement. . . .

The ultimate aim expressed by those who favor compulsory unionism is to bring *all* employees, without choice, solidly behind union policies and objectives.

The theory set forth is that when a worker takes employment he becomes a member of an economic society; that the union, armed with the powers and responsibilities of a government, is the government of this society; and that union membership must be compulsory.

The aim is clear. It is to gain, through compulsory unionism, *complete control of all employees,* and *complete control of all jobs.* This means a *monopoly* control over all employment of labor, even though the history of the legal and economic development in this country is to legislate *against* monopolies.

Any contentions that a *labor monopoly* would improve discipline, reduce waste effort, and increase the ability of union officers to serve the interests of the employee, are no different from the contentions which any businessman might make if he were to attempt to justify an *industrial monopoly.* Neither is desirable nor acceptable in the American economy.

If an individual worker can no longer earn a living except by pledging his support to a union, he becomes a subject of a private group. This is, to put it bluntly, government without the consent of the governed. . . .

When unions ask for compulsory unionism they are seeking to achieve solidarity by force rather than merit. This is an old device in the development of our social system that has inevitably led to social evils.

If union officials acquire power by compulsion, rather than by consent of those over whom it is exercised, they are freed from the necessity of winning support on the merits of their policies and programs. In such circumstances, there does not exist for the membership a genuine and full freedom to withdraw their support from these policies and programs, if they should prove harmful to the members.

The result is that the personal power of union officials is increased, since the membership is a captive membership and one from which allegiance does not have to be *won;* the financial and economic strength of the organization is assured and increased, despite the good or bad stewardship of the officials; and revenue is assured for those in command to pursue varied and sometimes questionable activities according to their virtually ungoverned whims.

Good organizations are made good and kept good by vigilance and effective strength on the part of the membership.

Compulsory membership, especially when tied to an individual's livelihood, reverses this process and gives great power to the few instead of resting it in the many. But great power to do good carries with it great power to do evil.

The American labor movement is blessed with many honest and worthy leaders. However, like all other great movements, it is also cursed with dishonest and unworthy men. When good men develop powerful machines for good purposes, it is certain that bad men will operate them for bad purposes if they are given the chance.

A permanent safeguard against the danger of bad operation is voluntary unionism.

The Unions Denounce the Taft-Hartley Act, 1957

The stated purpose of the Taft-Hartley Act is to establish harmonious labor-management relations. Instead, the law has created greater conflict, and has, in some industries, restored near jungle warfare.

Taft-Hartley was passed with punitive intent and has been administered in the same spirit. There is no room in a free America for punitive legislation aimed at a major group of our people.

Industrial unions believe that corrective legislation is needed to restore an even balance in the labor-management relationship in industry. They believe that the American people will see to it that punitive measures are removed from the law and that the law will be rewritten to bring into being the equitable labor-management relations called for by our stated national policy. . . .

Most of Taft-Hartley's 46 major sections, 102 basic subsections, and its many other provisions are designed to protect the employer and entangle workers' rights in a legal blockade of red tape, limitations, and restrictions. . . .

Taft-Hartley attacks the very heart of the American trade union movement by restricting collective bargaining and legitimate organizing activities.

In the area of collective bargaining, the Act turned back the clock to the day of the hated and discredited theory of government by injunction. The so-called "national emergency injunction" has had, in the words of the Federal Mediation and Conciliation Service, "the effect of interfering with collective bargaining" and "tends to delay rather than facilitate settlement."

The right of workers to picket has been curtailed. The right to refuse to cross picket lines has been seriously challenged. The right to strike has been abridged and the right to vote in Labor Board elections has been denied strikers and turned over to strikebreakers. Perhaps even more important, Taft-Hartley has enabled reactionary employers to oppose the organization of their employees with campaigns of subtle and open intimidation.

If this were not enough, Taft-Hartley also makes possible endless and unnecessary delays in the functioning of the National Labor Relations Board. Following the old axiom that justice delayed is justice denied, some employers have made use of these anti-union devices to stall, harass, and ultimately defeat union organization.

Strewn throughout the Act are these provisions and others aimed at restricting unionism. That Taft-Hartley has not destroyed the labor movement is true, but for its existence the labor movement owes no thanks to the law. That our nation's unions have survived under Taft-Hartley is a testimonial to their strength and to the determination of American workers to maintain their union organizations. . . .

The Taft-Hartley Act is so intricate that it can hardly be understood by either the workers or the employers who look to it for protection and help. It has been termed a "gold mine for lawyers" and many lawyers admit inability to understand it. . . .

Taft-Hartley puts its faith in labor injunctions in order to insure labor peace. Nothing could be more false than the belief that the power of the courts is a substitute for free collective bargaining and the voluntary assumption of responsibility by both labor and management. . . .

As temporary restraining orders, injunctions can go into effect with the stroke of a judge's pen and without giving a union the right to be heard. Hearings to determine whether or not an injunction is legal often are held weeks later—after the strike has been weakened and after, for all practical purposes, the issue has become academic.

Even worse, by their sheer weight in numbers, are the mass of easily obtained state anti-labor injunctions. In the Taft-Hartley era of suspicion and mistrust, state injunctions have multiplied and become one of the employer's most potent—and always available—weapons for breaking strikes.

Taft-Hartley makes provision for the so-called national emergency injunction. This kind of injunction is both unfair and one-sided. By prohibiting strike action, it penalizes employees but never the employer. In creating a mandatory 80-day "cooling off period," national emergency injunctions discourage the give-and-take bargaining Taft-Hartley claims to encourage. . . .

There is, of course, no question that employers have the right to express their views on unions and unionism. This right is guaranteed under the First Amendment to the Constitution, but freedom of speech includes neither the right to bully nor the right to coerce.

The Taft-Hartley "free speech" clause states that employers are prohibited only from expressions containing "threat of reprisal or force or promise of benefits." . . .

Taft-Hartley permits an employer to claim a vote for the union may mean a strike, his plant may close if the union wins, and present company benefits may end if the union represents his employees. As such, the sacred principle of "free speech" in the Constitution is being twisted to thwart the rights of America's working men and women. . . .

Taft-Hartley denies to striking workers the very job protection required to assure a strong labor movement in the United States. The law specifically denies to workers replaced by strikebreakers during a legitimate economic strike the right to vote in any representation election conducted by the NLRB.

On the other hand, strikebreakers are given the full right to vote. Employees with years of service may find the union they have built up by hard work and sacrifice over the years voted out by strikebreakers. The vested right a worker acquires in his job over the years as well as his right to refuse to work under conditions he has found to be unfair is completely brushed aside.

An anti-union employer, utilizing the Act, can replace strikers, petition the NLRB for an election, and then sit back while the replacements he has hired vote against the union that previously was legally certified as the collective bargaining representative of his employees.

Taft-Hartley denies unions and their members the right to refuse to handle goods produced under sub-standard conditions or originating in a struck establishment. In effect, this provision forces workers to undercut and undermine their own standards established through collective bargaining. In doing so, the workers hurt themselves, their fellow union members, and fair employers as well.

Unions can be charged with an unfair labor practice for refusing to handle struck or sweatshop-produced work under a provision in Taft-Hartley that defines this action as "forcing or requiring" their employer to break off his business dealings with another employer.

Unions seeking to use the secondary boycott as a legitimate weapon to protect wages and working conditions risk a mandatory injunction. Employers, however, are legally free to contract out work to other employers during labor disputes. Workers, therefore, are left without the right to help each other for legitimate ends—while employers are free to lean upon one another to destroy hard-won labor standards in a given industry.

✤ E S S A Y S

In the first essay, Howell Harris of the University of Durham, United Kingdom, charts the transformation of state labor policy, from judicially led repression in the late nineteenth century through the effort to regularize labor-capital conflict that began in World War I and culminated during the New Deal. Harris acknowledges that the state's intervention in labor relations deprived unions of much of their autonomy and militance. Yet he points out that American capital's historic opposition to the organization of employees has been so fierce and longstanding that a powerful and intrusive state labor-relations apparatus was essential to unions' limited gains in the 1930s and 1940s. State efforts to improve the work lives of unorganized women and children have also been ambiguous. Both the early twentieth-century courts and the New Deal administrative agencies forged labor policies that were, as Eileen Boris of Howard University reminds us in the second essay, profoundly influenced by early twentieth century conceptions of proper family structure and gender roles. The New Deal tried to establish a body of protective labor laws that applied to the entire working class, not just women. But this effort could not be divorced from contemporary ideas about the sexual division of labor, the proper functions of motherhood, and the life experiences of immigrant women.

To what extent have state labor laws and regulations liberated American workers? To what extent have they constricted workers' activities? How might Howell Harris's history of the transformation of industrial relations be structured if it systematically included the effort to reform home-based industrial work and establish labor standards for women and the unorganized?

Politicians, Bureaucrats, and the Shaping of Federal Labor-Relations Policy

HOWELL HARRIS

Between 1932 and 1947 the United States government adopted a fairly coherent set of policies encouraging the organization of workers into unprecedentedly strong unions, independent of employer control. Under this dispensation they secured members, recognition, permanent bargaining relationships, and overall legitimacy. The regulation of industrial relations became primarily a federal rather than a state responsibility; and federal policy was articulated in a series of laws which were given force by powerful and autonomous administrative agencies. The higher federal courts, which had acted as positive creators of industrial-relations policy from the 1890s through the 1920s, played a relatively modest part in this process: for several years after 1937, in particular, they did little more than settle some marginal issues where legislative intent was unclear, or where administrative discretion had been exercised in ways clearly beyond the bounds of the developing political consensus on the proper role and behavior of America's newly powerful unions.

Changes in the substance and processes of industrial-relations policy in this period were certainly dramatic enough to deserve the epithet "revolutionary"—insofar as any policy changes in a sluggish, decentralized and consensual liberal democracy like the United States ever can. And the results were equally dramatic: aided by changes in public attitudes accompanying the Depression of 1929–40, and by the tight labor market during the hectic years of war mobilization 1940–5, American labor unions in-

Howell Harris, "The Snares of Liberalism? Politicians, Bureaucrats, and the Shaping of Federal Labour Relations Policy in the United States, ca. 1915–47," in *Shop Floor Bargaining and the State*, ed. Steven Tolliday and Jonathan Zeitlin (Cambridge, Cambridge University Press, 1985), pp. 148–191.

creased in numbers, in membership (from less than three million to almost 15 million), in labor-force coverage, in bargaining power, and in political influence. Industrial conflict also increased, reaching a high point, by one conventional measure, in the great reconversion strike wave of 1945–6. But that conflict was very different from what America had experienced before the New Deal. It was relatively peaceful, largely because local law-enforcement authorities maintained a surprisingly even-handed approach in policing picketing. Also, employers generally did not use the injunction weapon against strikers, even where they could, and made few attempts to maintain production or employ strikebreakers. The issues of industrial conflict involved the "proper" subject-matter of collective bargaining—wages, hours, working conditions, job control, and the details of the unions' institutional status in the employment relationship. They did not, for the most part, raise fundamental questions about the very existence and essential practices of the labor movement—as, for example, the post–First World War strike wave had. America was on the way to acquiring the mature industrial-relations system, the institutionalized industrial conflict involving orderly, predictable mass strikes. . . .

The State and Labor Before the New Deal

. . . The independent policy-making role of the American judiciary, especially its higher and federal courts, was one of the distinctive features of the American polity. In addition, given the highly politicized and class-biased nature of judicial appointments and decisions, it was impossible that the mystifying belief that judges were law-finders, not law-makers, could persist unchallenged in the United States. Between the 1880s and the 1920s, even the most "conservative" spokesmen for organized labor in America came to an inescapable conclusion, the lesson of bitter experience, that the all-important judiciary played a role of contestant, rather than referee, in cases involving trade-union organization and industrial conflict. Less important agencies of the state, by their actions, won the same general condemnation.

Before the 1930s, most American industrial conflicts were inevitably local affairs, for most union organization and bargaining was decentralized, and major national-market industries, apart from coal mining and the railroads, were citadels of the open shop. And local governmental power was usually to be found arrayed on the side of capital, particularly at such times of crisis.

So when the organized working class looked at the judiciary, both state and federal, and at the local state, not surprisingly it conceived a deep suspicion of, and aversion towards, their intervention. The "voluntarism" of the American Federation of Labor (AFL) was a craving for autonomy, some legitimate sphere of activity within which it would not be disturbed, that the state was unwilling to allow it. Labor's only hope of deliverance lay in putting pressure on the most responsive branches of government. From local authorities, it could try to obtain police neutrality or abstention in times of conflict, and many other everyday advantages. Between the 1870s and 1920s, in areas with relatively mature industrial economies and organized, articulate working classes, state governments began to take a constructive interest in the "labor problem," partly in response to industrial conflict, but also to labor's local political action. They collected statistics and investigated the facts about working conditions, established agencies for mediation and conciliation in industrial disputes, and on occasion attempted, ineffectually, to limit the powers of courts to intervene coercively in industrial disputes, and to outlaw some of the effective tactics of belligerent anti-union employers. More positively, state and local governments enacted laws under their police powers to regulate some conditions of employment for especially vulnerable classes of workers. Most dramatically of all, in the years before the First World War, state legislatures confronted the problem of compensation for America's appalling toll of industrial accidents, breaching the common-law defenses that the judiciary had erected around employers' liability, and substituting a regulated, insurance-based system.

The federal government was slow to be similarly active. It had no clear constitutional responsibility for employment relations other than those of its own civilian workers, and of employees indisputably engaged in interstate and foreign commerce; and in any case most industrial conflicts were small-scale affairs that hardly attracted its attention. In addition, there was no nationally organized political articulation of working-class interests to compel its concern. When it did intervene, it was generally by sending in federal troops which, like the National Guard, "restored order" in industrial disputes in a manner favoring employers. . . .

This situation began to change in the 1890s. The federal government was eventually compelled to take a positive interest in the "labor problem" first by the formation of strong nationwide craft Brotherhoods on the railroads—a federal responsibility under the interstate commerce clause of the Constitution—and later by the emergence of large unions in other basic industries, especially coal mining, of vital importance to an increasingly urban population.

The federal government began to perform a mediatory role: *ad hoc* courts of inquiry into particularly large or bloody strikes were appointed; President Theodore Roosevelt himself intervened in the great anthracite strike of 1902, offering the government's good offices to bring about a compromise settlement. This set a new pattern of executive involvement, and signalled a new conception of the "public interest"—in industrial peace, yes, but not at any price, and not necessarily on the employer's terms or in strict defense of the status quo. The federal government's new role was increasingly institutionalized: a permanent, if ineffective, system of mediation and conciliation in railroad labor disputes was developed by trial and error, and in 1913 the new Department of Labor was charged with providing impartial third parties to help settle strikes in other industries.

Public policy evolved alongside the institutions through which it was expressed and implemented. Official actions and pronouncements came to reflect a newly sophisticated understanding of the workings of the industrial relations system within a capitalist democracy, and promote social change to bring realities into line with the new model. Unions were to be given a useful and legitimate role within industry for collective bargaining over wages, hours, and conditions of employment, with the idea that this would lead to a more stable, peaceful and just relationship between management and workers; and the AFL was to be granted a recognized status as *the* political representative of America's wage earners, which it somewhat ambitiously claimed on the basis of having organized about 10% of them.

Such recognition was first extended by a private organization of enlightened capitalists, the National Civic Federation (NCF), but the federal government soon followed suit. The necessity of collective organization, the desirability of collective bargaining, the national interest in securing some kind of "industrial democracy," became commonplaces of respectable and official rhetoric. And if Presidents or Congress wanted to talk to some "responsible" representatives of the organized working class—numerically small but politically significant for the Democratic Party after 1910—they had little choice but to turn to Samuel Gompers and his AFL. In consequence, Gompers became a public figure, and the AFL acquired a certain legitimacy. Congress responded, however ineffectually, to some of its requests, notably for protection against anti-trust suits and other common forms of legal harassment, via the 1913 Clayton Act, and under the Wilson administration it acquired a seat in the cabinet.

The First World War: Making America Safe
for "Industrial Democracy"?

The nascent functional representation of the AFL and its ability to exact political and economic concessions were given a mighty push forward by the war emergency of 1916–19. That period was both a false dawn and a forcing-house for the ideas and institutions which shaped the development of the American industrial relations system in the 1930s and 1940s. The AFL, particularly its national leadership, played an important role in defending the Wilson administration's foreign policy to the working class, both at home and abroad; in tune with its new-found super-patriotism, it assisted the federal government—and some states—in their repressive activities directed against the anti-war section of the socialists and the Industrial Workers of the World (IWW). But this cooperation was not offered without calculation. The AFL aimed to free itself and its members from the taint of un-Americanism, and from unsympathetic state attentions; it expected immediate, concrete, economic and organizational gains; and it looked forward to a permanent alteration in the relations between unions and employers, the labor movement and the state, in the postwar world. It expected the public rhetoric about "industrial democracy" in Progressive Era America to be turned into reality.

The AFL succeeded in attaining most of its short-term objectives, but not the last and most important. Membership nearly doubled between 1916 and 1920 from 2.073 to 4.079 millions. Apart from a few important occasions in 1919–22, state repression did not affect it or its affiliates directly. Particular sections of the labor force—railroad workers and seamen—received dramatic improvements in their conditions of employment by federal laws enacted in response to astute and persistent lobbying and, in the former case, the real threat of an all-out national strike. The "labor movement" as a whole—meaning the "legitimate" unions of the AFL and the Railroad Brotherhoods—was granted representation on the advisory committees overseeing the mobilization and preparedness effort, and on the all-important committee which determined wartime labor-relations policy, as well as on the National War Labor Board (NWLB) of 1918–19 and subsidiary authorities in specific industries which implemented it. This political recognition was symbolic of the permanent status to which the AFL laid claim. Even more significant was its immediate outcome.

The cardinal features of wartime federal policy were that there should be no strikes or lock-outs, no interference with union-organized shops, and no attempts by unions or workers to win new formal recognition agreements, extend collective bargaining, or increase membership by "coercive measures." Most significantly, "[t]he right of workers to organize in trade unions and to bargain collectively through chosen representatives [was] recognized and affirmed."

Obviously there were some unresolved inconsistencies here. . . . It represented a part of the state's response to a crisis of manpower, inflation and industrial conflict which dictated a new departure in public policy, amounting to an explicit recognition of the unions' claim that their status as autonomous bargaining institutions should be protected against that ingrained and pervasive employer hostility which the state had hitherto generally assisted. So great were those obstacles, so comparatively weak the existing labor organizations which it was now public policy to foster and manipulate, so extreme the emergency, that the United States took the course of basing its industrial-relations system on a framework of positive rights and administrative intervention, rather than simply extending legal immunities for trade-union organization and behavior. In so doing, it decisively rejected . . . the AFL's normally preferred model of voluntarism, and began to carve out its very own distinctive path. When another national emergency presented itself less than a generation later, the war experience offered a persuasive model of how to meet it, and many helpful precedents.

In 16 months' activity the NWLB developed a number of procedures to give effect to its policies and resolve disputes coming before it. First, some common employer practices were prohibited—blacklisting, the imposition of individual non-union ("yellow-dog") contracts, espionage, interrogation, and surveillance aimed at hampering legitimate self-organization. Secondly, effective remedies were devised for workers discriminated against because of legitimate union membership or activity—which might include a strike provoked by an employer's breach of contract; reinstatement with back pay (less any interim earnings) was the remedy for individuals. To enforce public policy, administratively supervised orders prohibited discriminatory discharges, demotions, or suspensions, and required that discharges be for "just and sufficient" causes capable of standing up to impartial investigation. Arbitrary employment practices were further restricted by the imposition of the seniority principle in layoffs.

The Board could not compel companies to begin collective bargaining with unions "as such." But it could and did require them to maintain relationships already established, and to meet and negotiate with committees representing their employees. Firms could not compel membership of a company union, nor satisfy the requirement that they negotiate by "bargaining" with one while refusing to deal with a representative workers' committee. In numerous cases the Board ordered the establishment of works committees in non-union plants, supervising secret-ballot elections for the purpose, and determining election districts and representation ratios. In these cases, to be sure, unions were not recognized "as such"; and the machinery of representation and bargaining was not what the AFL and its affiliates preferred. But under an acceptable compromise formula, unions were assisted to establish themselves in practice as an important, even controlling, element in some of the works committees whose birth the NWLB oversaw. This was admittedly a temporary measure; but NWLB officers, AFL leaders, and businessmen foresaw that such novel arrangements among unskilled and semiskilled workers, and in mass-production industries, for the most part previously unorganized, might well provide the basis for open collective bargaining with an "outside union" once the no-strike rule was removed and employers were unprotected against labor militancy. The NWLB's *de facto* recognition of unions even went so far as to protect local officers' right to have time off to engage in union business outside the plant, without pay but without loss of job either.

Managerial autonomy and its unilateral authority to determine employment policy were well and truly violated by NWLB orders. In the short run, given the necessity of industrial peace, the bargaining power and militancy of workers enjoying an unprecedentedly strong labor market, and the lack of cost constraints, employers were generally willing to go along with NWLB orders. Some even accepted that some form of "collective dealing," possibly formalized via a "trade agreement," had a real contribution to make to the improvement and stabilizing of in-plant labor relations.

But few employers indeed were prepared to accept the AFL's claim that independent, outside unions represented, not just the best, but the only legitimate channel for collective bargaining. And fewer still were prepared to go along with the AFL's underlying vision of bilateral trade agreements covering wages, hours and other employment conditions at the level of the firm, or better, employers' association, as the basis for a co-determined collective control of the economy.

The 1920s: Managerial Counteroffensives, Conservative Polity, Private Initiatives

The troubled postwar years 1919–22 saw first inflation, continuing over-full employment, and a sustained rise in union membership accompanied by massive, formal industrial conflict; then a frightened, repressive reaction by the propertied classes and the state, on the grounds that aliens and radicals were subverting American institutions, its private capitalist economy first of all; and finally, a short, dramatic recession, with massive unemployment in the short term, from which recovery was very patchy and slow in hitherto strongly unionized sectors. The recession brought wage cuts, and helped stimulate employer attacks on the gains in union membership, recognition and job controls, won in the hectic years 1916–20. This was no fitting context for the realization of the collectivist dreams of the AFL and its liberal or social democratic allies.

Instead, it nourished an impressive and successful reactionary movement. As America moved into peacetime, the extraordinary powers of the federal government, which had underpinned the NWLB's success, lapsed. . . . Industry would not accept organized labor's claim to the exclusive right of representation of workers' interests: instead, large firms moved to convert works councils into company unions, or to install the latter themselves to forestall outside unionization; while trade associations orchestrated a nationwide drive against union organization in the name of the "open shop," the "American Plan," and the "right to work." In the great coal and railroad strikes, the Wilson and Harding administrations initiated anti-union actions; the state and federal judiciary developed extreme doctrines to further restrict picketing, prevent union organization, and penalize strikes, boycotts, or sympathetic actions. The United States reverted to its anti-union normalcy. Unions were confined to sick industries, like coal, railroads, and textiles; to some competitive local-market industries, including construction and the needle trades; to their craft bastions, for example, printing; and to employees of some public utilities and branches of government service.

Labor's dreams of 1917–19 were easily, and utterly, dashed. It made no difference whether the unionized minority worked for nationalization of basic industries, establishment of a labor party, or achievement of employer recognition by the promise of cooperation. In the 1920s, all roads led to failure, except for the railroad operating crafts, entrenched in a major industry under federal supervision, and with a uniquely well-developed national political machine for mobilizing congressional support. The railroad unions gained a measure of legal protection by the 1926 Railroad Labor Act, but at a price. Collective bargaining as a means to settle disputes and ensure industrial peace was endorsed, and employer interference with employees' freedom of association condemned. But the unions were enmeshed in a complex and unsatisfactory *federal* procedure governing contract negotiation, which provided for temporary prohibitions against strikes, and were saddled with a grievance-handling system in which company unions might still find a place.

This thoroughly interventionist law did not offer a model capable of general application. Even if it had been otherwise attractive or acceptable, the constitutional obstacles to an active federal policy covering the bulk of extractive, manufacturing and processing, and local-market industries seemed insuperable. Instead, the AFL and its allies still hoped to import into the United States the principles of British labor law, to establish and protect an arena for collective action and voluntarist, adversarial labor relations free from judicial meddling. The role the AFL and its friends wished the state to play was one that would be passive and even-handed. They neither wished nor expected the federal government actively to promote unionization in peacetime by extending aspects of railroad labor policy to all industry, or by permanent intervention along the lines the NWLB had mapped out.

In one important respect, however, the 1920s was a decade of preparation for the New Deal "revolution." This period saw the consolidation of the infant discipline of industrial relations in the universities and the emergence of influential streams of ideas such as those associated with John R. Commons' circle at the University of Wisconsin. Groups such as these were destined to play a key role in New Deal policy-making and to provide the Roosevelt administration with legislative draughtsmen, advocates and administrators. In the 1920s they perfected their ideas about what sort of industrial relations system they wanted. Collective bargaining would be an essential component of a system of industrial peace, social justice, economic progress and political stability. They found their blueprint for this system in microcosm in the responsible industrial unionism of the needle trades. . . .

Arbitration . . . was a decentralized, voluntarist mechanism for the settlement of disputes, promoting peace and order in industry, but not at the expense of "justice," or of the right to strike in the last resort. It offered labor-relations academics jobs and a satisfying policy-making role in association with some of America's most progressive industrial unions. Early arbitrators used the "governmental" analogy of collective bargaining as the American way to "industrial democracy" so common in the aftermath of the First World War. Unionization introduced "constitutional government" into industry via the trade-agreement mechanism. And they were to be that constitution's judges.

Arbitrators . . . exercised an equitable jurisdiction, developed standards of "due process" in employment relations, built up a common law, case by case, and codified it into new agreements and understandings. They helped lay a firm foundation of ideology and practice on which they and those they trained or influenced would help build a larger, more progressive, but "responsible" American labor movement. Before this could happen, however, a revolution in public policy, informed by historical experience, but developed in response to immediate pressures, would be needed.

1932–1935: Voluntarism Transcended

Organized labor and its liberal allies had responded to the judiciary's perfection, and employers' increasing use, of the injunction weapon in the 1920s with a counterattack involving persistent lobbying and propaganda. In 1932, all that effort finally bore fruit. The progressive elimination of right-wing Republicans at the polls—and the consequent reduction of

Congressional sensitivity to business pressures—which began in 1930, and continued for the next three elections, gave them their opportunity. The Supreme Court had already declared that, on the railroads, the state had the power to make company unions and other forms of employer interference with workers' rights to free self-organization unlawful. But that was no green light for a generally interventionist federal labor relations policy, given the same court's restrictive interpretation of the Constitution's "commerce clause." . . .

Norris–La Guardia [which curbed employer ability to win an antistrike injunction from the courts] was the almost perfect expression of the AFL's attitude towards the role of the "law" (i.e., the courts) in labor-relations: that there should scarcely be one. Eventually, the courts themselves seemed to agree, extending the Act's protection of union organization and practices—including concerted refusals to work or patronize, inducements to strike or boycott, and picketing, regardless of objectives—from injunctive restraint, to include immunity against civil actions for damages and, in large measure, criminal prosecution. But the belated triumph of voluntarism in American labor law took years to achieve: in 1932, Norris–La Guardia's importance was chiefly symbolic. It only applied to federal courts, and was not, in any event, upheld as constitutional by the Supreme Court until 1938.

By that time, the United States had rejected such thoroughgoing voluntarism as the basis for its labor-relations policy, and put continuous administrative intervention and deliberate institution-building in its place. For a few years, the courts were busy scrapping one traditional set of restraints on unions, while the NLRB was busy inventing another, with those same courts' active encouragement and passive consent. . . .

The radical transformation in public policy, and partial opening of the floodgates to a surge of unionization, which occurred with the enactment of Section 7(a) of the National Industrial Recovery Act (NIRA) in summer 1933, was so largely the unintended result of an incredibly confused legislative process that it is still difficult, 50 years on, to explain quite how or why it happened. . . .

In the NIRA's corporatist scheme, Section 7 explicitly recognized organized labor as a part of the "social compact" it envisaged; it provided for the possibility of labor representation on the industry authorities designated to draw up codes of "fair competition," including labor standards. And in addition, of course, it seemed to endorse the spread of free trade unionism and collective bargaining as instruments and objectives of public policy. But the business community was determined to exploit its advantages—including the wavering resolve of the Roosevelt administration, the lack of any real enforcement mechanism, and the weakness of the labor movement—to make sure 7(a) did not have the effects that some of its draughtsmen intended. The administration seemed to expect that in return for this grant of rights the labor movement would peacefully participate in the work of economic reconstruction, without acknowledging that encouraging union organization in an environment of employer hostility and chronic economic stagnation must inevitably result in increased industrial conflict—at least in the short term, though in the longer run one might reasonably anticipate a restoration of industrial peace within the newly democratized employment relationship. And the labor movement and its liberal allies had great hopes that 7(a) really meant what they thought it said, giving labor that voice in economic planning at the level of the work-place, industry and nation that they had claimed for a generation, with the objective of redressing the skewed balance of social power and income distribution which they thought explained America's economic collapse and political malaise.

The NIRA was not, however, self-enforcing. Given the preponderant economic power of organized business, and the administration's major com-mitment towards using the NIRA for economic stabilization and recovery, not power redistribution, the way the Act worked bitterly disappointed the AFL and its liberal allies, notably Senator Robert Wagner, a New York Democrat. In particular, under the "Blue Eagle" business managed to increase the numbers of employees covered by company unionism faster than resurgent independent unions added to their membership.

Though workers were mostly unable to form viable unions and establish bargaining relationships in 1933–4, there was nothing to stop them trying. The resulting strikes troubled an administration set on building national unity and a synthetic social harmony across the lines of party, class and interest, with uninterrupted economic recovery its primary objective. It had to find some way of defusing industrial conflict, policing and enforcing NIRA's labor provisions, and thereby allaying criticism from its own . . . supporters.

Accordingly, a National Labor Board (NLB) with no clear policies, uncertain authority, and no independent enforcement powers, was estab-lished in August 1933, with Senator Wagner at its head. It was tripartite in membership, at both the national and local level; its major purpose was the speedy restoration of "industrial peace" through mediation and con-ciliation. But the most intractable strike issues were organization and rec-ognition. Employers were belligerent and imaginative in their defense of the "open shop," denounced the Board and resisted its proposed settle-ments; the administration and the courts failed to support it. Still, the NLB did have some achievements. It began the business of recruiting and training a federal labor relations bureaucracy, and it completed the education of Senator Wagner in the realities of American industrial relations and em-ployer behavior.

The NLB devised a formula for ending strikes which drew on the experience of the NWLB, Railroad Labor Board, and private dispute-settlement. Strikers were to return to work without discrimination, bargain-ing on wages and hours was to begin, representatives were to be selected by secret ballot under NLB auspices, and any unresolved matters or dis-putes over interpretation of resulting agreements were to be settled by NLB arbitration. All the "Reading Formula" needed to become effective was employer acceptance, or administration and judicial support. It had neither in adequate measure. By summer 1934, the NLB was a busted flush.

Through 1935 Wagner, his few congressional allies, the AFL, and his corps of NLB-experienced advisers, accordingly tried to win some independent legislative mandate for the NLB to develop and enforce what they thought national policy was, or should be. But the Roosevelt administration resisted. It was only willing to go so far as to create a somewhat stronger, quasi-judicial NLRB, in 1934. Congress accepted this reform of the NLB's structural weaknesses—the new Board was administratively autonomous, staffed exclusively with impartial "experts"—which had not addressed the basic problems of jurisdiction and power. Congress and the administration acted in this way to stave off an impending national steel strike, and to satisfy the Democratic Party's pro-labor supporters before the 1934 elections. . . .

The most consistent pressure for a clear declaration of federal policy came from the NLR and first NLRB themselves. Ignoring their agencies' marginal status and wavering official support, the Boards' pro-labor and liberal pluralist staff members acted as if they were empowered to be vigorously innovative policy-makers and enforcers. They fleshed out vague words of the 7(a) and gave them practical meaning: with more conviction than helpful precedent, they tried to restrict employers' ability to form or dominate company unions, and to protect workers' right to organize from other employer interference. They determined that the choice of the *majority* of employees voting in a Board-supervised election should be the exclusive bargaining representative of *all;* and they began to define, procedurally and substantively, what such bargaining would amount to—including the presumption that it would result in a written, fixed-term contract covering the major issues of union recognition, wages, hours and working conditions.

This surely was a case of bureaucratic audacity, scarcely comprehensible if one neglects the prior experience and beliefs of the New Deal's "experts," which told them what kind of labor-relations system America had to have, and that they must intervene creatively to build it. They were able to get away with this audacity, though not to see their policy preferences enacted until 1935, or enforced until after 1937, only because of the extraordinary openness and confusion of the policy-making and administrative process in the mid-1930s. Roosevelt himself had no great interest in the organization of labor, but was, for the most part, benignly indifferent to the Wagner camp's initiatives, as he was to workers' self-help activities. The business community had committed everything to a strategy of obstruction and reaction. From 1934 to 1937, this did not pay off because it relied for success on the declining Republican party, whose right wing was nearing extinction, and did not impress the new, uncommitted or pro-labor Democrats. The organized labor movement supported its bureaucratic and congressional friends' legislative proposals, but played little part in determining what they were, and scarcely understood their detailed implications.

Wagner, almost singlehandedly, and against the odds, sustained the campaign for federal labor law reform in 1934 and 1935. When it finally received the administration's belated and half-hearted endorsement, it was largely because the Supreme Court's vetoes had created a policy vacuum, and because Wagner had made it clear that he was going to force the issue to a vote, and that he had sufficient support in Congress to get it through, with or without the administration's help. . . . The fact and manner of the Wagner Act's passage in 1935 may have been quite accidental, but the *content* of the Act was quite otherwise, because it had the benefit of two years' detailed experience of the problems of employer opposition to independent unionism, and because it was unusually cleverly drafted to give a carefully established bureaucracy a broad discretionary power to implement a clearly declared public policy. The Act was as proof against judicial meddling and attack as its draughtsmen could make it, and the new NLRB it created set about its business in September 1935 with care and confidence.

The Wagner Act: Meaning and Impact, 1935–1941

As far as the Wagner Act's draughtsmen were concerned, the NLRB could now eliminate employer obstruction, by intervening, with the support of a changed public opinion, and hopefully of the courts, to strike down and prevent the recurrence of specified "unfair labor practices." This would remove one particularly frequent source of bitter industrial conflict, the recognition dispute. The NLRB's powers to determine appropriate bargaining units, to hold elections, or in other ways discover the wishes of the majority of workers in such a unit, as to which organization, if any, should represent them all, would help shape the emerging structure of labor organization in collaboration with the initiatives of workers and their unions. Such designated representatives would have a clear status when they came to the bargaining table, and the legitimacy which derived from serving a clear public interest: the "equalization" of bargaining power in industry and the redistribution of income in such a way as to satisfy institutional economists' prescription for regenerating and then stabilizing the economy. The net result of workers' initiatives, employers' concessions, and state sponsorship would be a "democratic" form of "industrial government" resting on representation, due process, compromise, and the development of industrial codes governing, in the first instance, wages, hours and working conditions. All of this would be conducive to industrial peace, as grievances about employer autocracy would be removed, and permanent institutions established to resolve the remainder, which were much more amenable to settlement by negotiation, compromise and third-party mediation or conciliation.

The Wagner Act was not without ambiguity of language and inconsistency of purpose, but its main lines were clear. . . . It should be read in the light of the ideology and intentions of the "experts" who drew it up and administered it, and of what they had already done on the NLB/NLRB. . . .

Building on their limited experience with collective bargaining in labor-intensive, decentralized, disorderly industries, whose undercapitalized firms lacked managerial resources, they expected similar "beneficial results" as collective bargaining "matured" in the core firms of basic manufacturing industry. There would be "progress" towards an increase in the scale of the bargaining unit—from the plant to the firm, to the entire industry— and in the scope of bargaining, going beyond immediate job regulation to include some kind of union–management cooperation in productivity improvement and economic planning. This was, they thought, a logical evolution, conducive to the appearance of responsible labor leadership and stable industrial relations, as well as to real efficiency gains.

This collectivist vision appealed to some managerial progressives, Catholic corporatists, and numerous labor activists who had moved within the orbit of the Socialist Party and/or League for Industrial Democracy. But it had no constituency to compare with that of the plant- or firm-based, narrowly job-conscious unionism that the 1930s and 1940s actually encouraged. There was little practical interest in the labor movement in working towards any such vision, no comparable political consensus to support such a revolution in America's economic structure as existed for the Wagner Act's more modest and immediate objectives, and unremitting employer hostility to any such entrenchment of labor in the strategic decision-making heart of the enterprise, where it had no right to exist and could make no useful contribution. . . .

So one of the visions of labor law reformers was destined to be frustrated. But, in the event, the transformation which actually occurred in American labor relations in 1935–47 was sufficient to convince them that they had wrought well, and achieved everything of importance.

What actually happened was that, in a way exceeding the most optimistic forecasts of the NLRB's lawyers, the Supreme Court in 1937, acting under severe political pressure, removed the constitutional uncertainty which had made the law something of a dead letter in the two years since its passage—the two years which saw the formation of the Committee for Industrial Organization (CIO) and the breakthroughs in union organization and recognition in the steel, automotive, rubber, electrical and other core sectors of the economy. Those breakthroughs owed little to the NLRB's direct assistance—until 1937, it could do nothing against an employer determined to obstruct or delay in his compliance with the law. Afterwards, it could do more, but only slowly, uncertainly, and retroactively. More important was the uniquely favorable political context created by the ability and willingness of workers to help themselves, the structural capacity of unions to assist them, and the support or complaisance of public opinion and agencies of the local state, responsible to the electoral strength of workers remaking the Democratic Party into a close approximation to a labor party in numerous industrial districts. To this conjuncture of forces must be added the effects of the "boomlet" of 1936–7 on workers' ability to strike, and employers' willingness to concede direct wages-and-hours benefits, in addition to limited union recognition and bargaining rights, as the price of resumed production and the *promise* of industrial peace.

The NLRB became much more important after the Supreme Court unshackled it in 1937 and, in surely the most extraordinary *volte-face* in its long history, went on to give the Board fairly consistent support. Indeed, in many instances the Court abstained altogether and allowed the NLRB's policy-making to proceed unhindered. Simultaneously, the Court extended the meaning of the Norris–La Guardia Act far beyond what its sponsors had dared hope, and went so far as to determine that picketing was "free speech," and thus protected against local prohibitions and regulations by the full force of the Bill of Rights.

What happened in the field of public policy, then, was a somewhat contradictory set of developments. As conservatives began to regain power at the state level in and after 1938, federal law became the chief defense of workers' and unions' rights. The higher federal judiciary cleared away many of the most important legal restraints on industrial conflict, whatever its purposes and methods, that they and their predecessors had painstakingly fashioned over generations. And the NLRB, implementing the Wagner Act with unsurpassed vigor, began to modify the behavior of employers in relation to unions at the same time as it began to show unions that federal aid did not come without strings. Even as the courts were freeing the labor movement from the burden of hostile local and judicial regulation which had been voluntarism's target, the Board was developing a much more thoroughgoing regulation of the structure and functions of collective bargaining, and of the organizational and conflictual behavior of workers and their unions. The AFL's leadership had not bargained on this when they pressed hard for the Wagner Act's passage, and was understandably miffed. Organized labor supported the Democratic cause in the 1936 election and lobbied Congress intensively for adequate funds to enable the NLRB to handle the massive caseload that almost swamped it in 1937–9. But the Board did not respond by behaving as the labor movement's grateful client. Instead, it acted more like a patron, confident that it alone had the strategic vision and the public responsibility to shape the labor movement to fit in with the requirements of its conception of the national interest.

Modification of employer behavior *vis-à-vis* unionization struggles, recognition disputes, and the establishment of routine collective bargaining was much the greater part of the NLRB's achievement. . . . Especially after the return to economic recession and stagnation in the summer of 1937, and the recovery of conservative strength in local and state politics which followed, the NLRB offered the safest route to bargaining status for fledgling unions, particularly in the mass production industries. The NLRB was a vigorous and dedicated agency, certainly a partisan of the labor movement, and perhaps preferred its newer and weaker organizations in the CIO which actively besought its aid and fitted its model of the kind of labor unions large-scale industry "needed." The La Follette Committee of the Senate gave sterling service in revealing the most discreditable and violent aspects of the employers' anti-union tactics, creating a public opinion hostile to them and a disinclination on the part of many firms to use such crude and overt modes of anti-unionism. The NLRB backed that work up, ordering reinstatement of individuals dismissed for union membership or activity, with appropriate restitution for lesser discrimination, dis-establishing company unions and voiding "sweetheart" contracts negotiated between AFL unions and employers which ignored workers' wishes. Employers were required to "cease and desist" from a wide range of anti-union behavior, and to post notices around their plants admitting their guilt and promising not to misbehave in future. They were required to negotiate with unions in "good faith," which the Board proceeded to define, on a range of mandatory issues, which it determined in developing case law. And they were obliged to formalize their agreements in written, fixed-term contracts, to confine their recognition and negotiations *exclusively* to a certified majority representative, and in effect to obey a code of positively acceptable labor practices which the Board developed and the judiciary, with relatively few exceptions, endorsed.

So much for the good news. Before proceeding to the less good, or positively bad, it is worth emphasizing that even during the peak years 1937–9 when the NLRB was providing "the outstanding instance during the present century of an aggressive programme sustained over powerful opposition of regulated parties" (and) "the most high powered and effective law enforcement in our history," and when it was dealing with a massive caseload both in unfair labor practice and representation cases, its work was not entirely successful, even by its own standards. Delays created by a burgeoning load which grew faster than staff could be recruited and trained, exacerbated by the need to take decisions ignored or appealed by employers to successive stages of the judicial system for review and enforcement, reduced the effectiveness of NLRB intervention. Employers *could* perfectly well ignore and obstruct NLRB orders if they chose. The cost was high in legal fees and possibly in back pay, and could result in workers who were dissatisfied with the rewards of following orderly procedures deciding to strike to try and win recognition or effective bargaining rights. But those were costs many firms were willing to incur, because the course seemed *right* and because the rewards of weakening and demoralizing a union unable to win anything for its new, imperfectly attached members, or to strike with equanimity in a stagnant economy, looked worthwhile. Growth in union membership still depended on organizing initiatives, grass-roots militancy, good tactics and strategy, and persistence, as much as on the NLRB. And, as the years 1940–5 were to prove, it was far more responsive to the course of economic recovery and re-employment than it was to a favorable turn in federal policy after 1937. Perhaps the most that can be said for the NLRB's work in its heroic period, 1937–9, is that the NLRB prevented too severe a fall-off, and facilitated slight recovery in union membership after the shock of the 1937–8 recession when worker militancy, and union activists' *élan*, visibly diminished, along with public tolerance of the most effective organizational tools—especially the sit-down strike—deployed to such effect in 1936–7.

The Government Tightens Its Grip

And now for the really bad news. The Wagner Act, by making policy-making in labor relations a matter of continuous administrative regulation, progressively denied unions the autonomy they had long cherished. From 1937 onwards, they discovered that the decisive turn away from voluntarism meant that their *own* institutional prerogatives were open to NLRB and judicial challenge as well as those of the employers who were the Act's prime—and, in their eyes, exclusive—targets. The AFL, in particular, . . . was horrified to discover that, by order of a Board it had played a large part in creating and nurturing, some of its customary organizing tactics (e.g., signing up with employers rather than, or before, enrolling workers into membership) were outlawed, and the resulting contracts, sometimes containing valuable closed-shop provisions, declared null and void. In the name of protecting the individual employee's right to choose, the Board denied AFL unions full freedom to exploit employer preference for them over those of the novel and less respectable CIO as a shortcut to the unions' institutional objectives—expanded membership, however recruited, and bargaining rights, however unfavorable the terms of those bargains might be to the workers' concerned.

The NLRB went beyond this. It used its exclusive power to determine what was an appropriate unit for collective bargaining *and fulfilling the purposes of the Act*—increasingly defined as industrial peace and stabilized, efficient labor relations—in order to establish the structure of collective bargaining, whether on a single or multi-plant basis, employing industrial or craft units. It did this in a way which ignored established AFL unions' pretensions to define their own jurisdictions, and to suit their bargaining structure to their own best estimates of what suited each situation. The NLRB's unit determinations could favor one union over another in a competition for members and exclusive bargaining rights. They even came to define the conditions under which craftsmen (or those the AFL was ready to call such) would be granted, at the Board's entire discretion, the privilege of an election to determine whether they wanted to be separately represented or not. Increasingly, NLRB policies dictated an appropriate structure for union organization and collective bargaining responsive to "experts' " readings of what public policy required rather than workers' or unions' attempts to follow their ingrained traditions and the dictates of their own interests. Simultaneously, NLRB decisions, judicial rulings, and limitations on strike activity imposed by the economic stagnation of 1937–9 and the unions' wartime no-strike pledge of 1941–5, blocked off the possibility that unions might ignore NLRB rulings and escape their impact by using the age-old techniques of the recognition strike, boycott, or secondary action. Even before Taft-Hartley was enacted in 1947, unions were finding themselves increasingly entrapped within a formal and legalistic structure of rules, which declared orderly resort to NLRB machinery and acceptance of Board decisions, however unpalatable, to be the only way to win the valuable status of legitimate, legally protected, collective bargaining representative.

NLRB policy, increasingly influenced by the Supreme Court after 1939, became positively unhelpful in certain areas. Definition of subjects where collective bargaining was mandatory showed employers where they need not even go through the forms of negotiation on union demands on non-mandatory issues, since any attempt to enforce them would not enjoy the law's protection. "Economic" strikers' right to strike was in practice restricted by permitting employers permanently to replace them, and giving them no right to be rehired. Even before Taft-Hartley specified unfair labor practices that workers and unions might commit, thereby running into legal penalties, the Board and the courts had already written some of them into case law—even though the Wagner Act had been silent on this and had, indeed, stated that none of its provisions were to be so interpreted as to infringe upon the right to strike. That did not stop the Board identifying certain kinds of strike whose methods or objects disqualified the strikers from the Act's protections. The unluckiest workers of all were those, like foremen and supervisors, whom the Board and the courts decided were not "workers" at all, when it came to enjoying Wagner Act protection; their self-organizational efforts were fully exposed to employer hostility. . . .

The course of administrative and, to some extent, judicial decision-making is explained partly by the fact that the Wagner Act gave the Board wide discretion to implement a policy some of whose premises were contradictory. The Board, prodded by the courts, had to resolve them. Thus, for example, employees' exercise of their right to self-organization, unfettered by employer actions *but under NLRB supervision,* was supposed to lead more or less automatically towards the establishment of satisfactory collective bargaining relationships, industrial peace, etc. As time went on, the NLRB increasingly ruled that employee self-organization was only the *means;* orderly collective bargaining (enshrined in ongoing contractual relations) was the Act's major objective. What if employees exercising their free choice should want to break away from an existing bargaining unit unsatisfactory to them, or seek a new union to represent them while an existing union had a valid contract? In such a situation, the Board came to rule that order and stability came first: breakaway unionism threatened bargaining structures it had deemed satisfactory to effect the purposes of the Act, and the institution of the fixed-term contract. Accordingly, the Board would only allow craft or professional groups the privilege of separation from an existing unit if they met stringent conditions and the Board judged that the situation merited it; and would deny any dissidents the opportunity to challenge an existing duly-certified representative for a year after a Board certification, or up to two years if a valid contract ran that long. The Congress made it even harder for changes of representative to take place; and the NLRB and the courts devised sanctions to protect NLRB certifications and established contractual relationships from disturbance by "direct action."

But why did the Board, the courts, and Congress decide these difficult and ambiguous questions as they did? The answer is that the Wagner Act irreversibly politicized industrial relations. Disputes between managers and workers, employers and unions, unions and unions, unions and the NLRB, were not finally resolved by the NLRB's ambitious bureaucrats, even when the federal judiciary upheld its decisions rather than, as on occasion, overturning them or pushing them in new and "safe" directions. The theory of administrative regulation was that the Board was impartial, expert, autonomous. But in practice it was not perceived as such by contending parties; and in truth it was far from autonomous. From 1935–9 the NLRB ignored rising opposition to its policies from employers, the press, conservative politicians and finally the disillusioned AFL, much the stronger of the rival labor organizations. It did not enjoy the Roosevelt administration's favor—indeed, it was treated as a political liability. The NLRB achieved four years of autonomy, acted as if it were invulnerable, did not trim its policies to accommodate presidential unease, AFL grievances, or business and conservative hostility. It neglected the vital task of winning itself a constituency—it did nothing to attempt to counter its bad press, built no political bridges. This was dangerous folly: it made the NLRB an unnecessarily easy target for its enemies, at the same time as alienating friends or neutrals. . . .

The simple fact is that, once labor relations had become politicized, the NLRB found itself with only one constituency to which to appeal for protection, the organized labor movement. By its own policies it had succeeded in alienating the AFL, the most significant part of the movement. And when it came to the crunch, the NLRB was dependent on the actions of a Congress where rural districts were flagrantly over-represented and where there were far more legislators responsive to the dominant economic interests of their constituencies as reflected by the anti-union local elites who provided party finance and organization, than there were from the metropolitan and industrial districts where the Democratic Party had turned into an approximation of the British Labour Party. In such a situation, there was only one way the heavily politicized federal labor policy could develop, and that was in the direction of promoting order, stability, efficiency, and industrial "peace"—and even then that proved insufficient to fend off the business/conservative attack which eventuated in Taft-Hartley.

The Pressures of War, 1941–1945

There is a further important reason for the conservative, institution-building turn clearly taken by federal labor relations policy after 1940. That is, quite simply, the demands of wartime economic mobilization for freedom from "unpatriotic disruption" (as strikes were generally perceived) and from destabilizing wage inflation. Those great pressures led to the creation of two more temporary, but vastly important, federal labor relations bureaucracies which took over the primary responsibility for shaping and controlling the American labor movement.

The National Defense Mediation Board (NDMB) of March–November 1941, and its stronger successor, the National War Labor Board (NWLB) of January 1942–August 1945 (which actually kept operating until 1946, but with only a shadow of its former authority after V-J Day), were much more powerful than the NLRB had ever been. They did not have to worry about judicial review, though a heavy caseload led to long delays for the NWLB in 1943 in particular. They had full authority, as a result of executive orders under the war powers of the presidency, to settle any labor dispute by conciliation, mediation, or compulsory arbitration. They were supposed to act in conformity with relevant federal statutes (particularly the Wagner Act), and generally did so; and their autonomy in setting wage policy was increasingly restricted as the war progressed. Nevertheless, the NDMB and, even more, NWLB enjoyed a wide-ranging freedom that the NLRB never possessed, and they had a full panoply of enforcement devices at their disposal—from persuasion and horse-trading, through moral black-mail, up to and including denial of union security and revocation of favorable contract terms (for labor), and federal seizure and operation of plants (for management).

They were tripartite in structure, so that 'voluntarism' was in theory preserved by moving bargaining from the level of the plant or firm to that of the industry commission, or the regional or national board, in each of which organized business and labor were represented. But, in practice, voluntarism came to mean simply the right to participate, to be informed, to share responsibility for Board decisions *and for their acceptance* by the interested parties' 'constituents'. The Boards worked, in that they produced 'practical', conservative, compromise solutions, more or less acceptable to both sides and to the federal government. Industrial production was rarely inconvenienced by strikes; the lid was kept on increases in workers' basic rates of pay; the 'national interest' was served.

NDMB/NWLB experience pointed the way towards continued federal intervention to determine the outcome of important collective bargains in peacetime—via 'fact-finding' boards in 1945–7, Taft-Hartley's emergency disputes provisions, or successive counter-inflation policies. In the short term, they perfected the decentralized, 'private' institutions for controlled industrial conflict developed under state sponsorship since 1933. They were far stronger than the NLRB: it could not determine the terms of a collective agreement, but simply state that on certain subjects bargaining in good faith was obligatory on management (and, increasingly, on labor too); it could push both sides to negotiate and observe written, fixed-term contracts, but could not order them to establish machinery to guarantee observance.

The NDMB and NWLB operated under no such limitations. As representatives of labor and management were opposed on all the most important issues coming before them, it was the *public members* of the Boards who came to occupy the balance of power. They had a continuous, expert presence; they had significant prior experience, and a 'received wisdom' to guide them in their institution-building task. While the NLRB continued with the important business of operating its machinery for unions to win recognition, even against employer hostility, without the dangers of a strike, and policing the conduct of both sides in routine collective bargaining, the NWLB had a much more interesting job. Accordingly, many NLRB staffers migrated to the rival agency with the free-wheeling style, higher salaries, and draft exemptions. It selected the most useful and acceptable precedents of 'mature collective bargaining' in prewar industry, and imposed its model of labor relations on unions and employers over their strong protests. It *generalized* certain characteristics of America's relatively few stable labor relations systems, applying them to the industrial unions and core firms in the durable goods industries; these lay at the vital heart of the war economy and had no indigenous bargaining history to speak of at all. . . .

Conclusions

By the end of the war, as a result of the combined efforts of the NLRB and NWLB, the American labor movement was unprecedentedly strong, at least as measured by statistics of membership, contractual relationships, closed shop, union shop, maintenance of membership, or dues checkoff agreements, and other conventional indices. But it was also unprecedentedly dependent on the federal government, trapped in a situation where it was defenseless against intervention from new "friends" (the NLRB) as well as familiar old antagonists—unsympathetic courts, actively hostile state and federal legislatures, recovering their power and reactionary self-confidence.

During the 1930s, the labor movement had actively sought federal assistance for the straightforward purpose of weakening or even neutralizing the power of its opponents. In those terms, the Norris–La Guardia and Wagner Acts had been unqualified successes. What the labor movement had not generally seen (but could have) was that, once the unions became agents of public policy—whether its objectives were the defense of employee rights, the "equalization" of their bargaining power, the redistribution of income, the elimination of violent and potentially destabilizing industrial conflict, or any other of the Wagner Act's liberal purposes—they were undeniably "affected with a public interest." They owed a substantial measure of their power, if not their existence, to the state. Accordingly, they could expect continuous interference from it, and had no credible intellectual defenses, nor sufficient independent political strength, to set against that unwanted development. . . .

Labor's dilemma was real, and was probably inevitable. In politics, it had nowhere to go but the Democratic Party, however unreliable a friend that proved to be. In labor relations matters, against persistent employer opposition, in a situation where the direct action alternative to NLRB and NWLB procedures was uncertain at best, dangerous at worst, it had to use the channels the federal government provided, however constricting. And, by and large, it *chose* to. For the simple fact is that "responsible unionism" *paid off*. During the war, unions observing the no-strike pledge, not pressing their members' economic demands with the full weight of their bargaining power, obtained institutional security of income and membership, a recognized status in the plant or firm, liberal fringe benefits, some extensions of joint consultation and even bargaining, and arbitration-terminated grievance systems which denied employer demands for unilateral authority *at the same time* as they confined unions and their members within the language of contract and the time-consuming, legalistic procedures. It is not self-evident that "irresponsible" unionism would have secured more than this, given the willingness and ability of Congress and the administration to strike at non-complying unions in a variety of harmful ways. . . .

Federal labor relations policy from 1932 to 1947 simultaneously strengthened the unions as institutions and circumscribed their role. The unions were fortunate indeed that a liberal, but not a very interested or sympathetic, administration was brought to do this in probably the only set of circumstances when American public policy *could* have taken such a dramatic deviation from its past courses. Only the collapse and chronic stagnation of the economy, the desperate search for answers and palliatives, the massive turnover of state and federal politicians, the partial "revolution" in the balance and social bases of the two main parties' support, and the accompanying erosion of the political influence of the business community could have created an opportunity for something like the Wagner Act. Only the advent of full employment in a time of war, when the state had to intervene directly and continuously in industrial relations to preserve a working social harmony, guarantee uninterrupted production, and maintain economic equilibrium could have provided such a favorable environment for the new unions of the 1930s to become entrenched, and continue to grow. They did so under the auspices of a relatively liberal regime that preferred to rely on manipulation in its management of the clash of domestic class interests, and which was itself probably saved by the war from the full effects of the conservative reaction already setting in 1937–8.

In this conjuncture, America's labor movement enjoyed 15 years when, at different times, the political climate, the tightness of the labor market, the spontaneous militancy (*or* organizability) of its potential membership, all favored it. And America's budding labor relations experts had unprecedented opportunities for employment, on-the-job training, and real creative influence on that "responsible" labor movement and pluralistic, rational industrial relations system they were dedicated to building. From 1932 to 1947 both the labor movement and its nurturing, confining, nanny-like bureaucracy enjoyed an extended period of extraordinary freedom to develop a new industrial relations system which may well have come to serve a system-sustaining function, but which was created only over the strenuous, but unsuccessful opposition of a business community displaying an unusual degree of unity in its hostility, of a press which served as its mouth-piece, and of a conservative political establishment only temporarily weakened by economic collapse and political disorder.

Given the American labor movement's pre–New Deal weakness—its ideological subordination, political dependence, marginal legal status, organizational impotence—it is scarcely possible to conceive of the creation and entrenchment of what was, for all its glaring deficiencies, the nearest thing to a dynamic, inclusive, mass movement that the American industrial working class has ever managed to put together, without the transformation in public policy after 1932. . . .

New Deal Reformers Use the Government to Protect Women Workers

EILEEN BORIS

. . . The history of homework regulation in the 1930s illustrates the complex relation between the quest for labor standards . . . and protective legislation for women. On one hand, homework laws and regulations appeared as part of a broad arsenal of devices to protect and improve labor standards; homework abolition benefitted all workers to the extent that homework undermined wages, hours, health and safety standards. On the other hand, homework laws addressed the work environment of women and children, the "commercialization of the home" and degradation of motherhood so condemned by the Women's Bureau and women's reform organizations. Such laws were gender specific; thus Commissioner of Labor Elmer F. Andrews called New York's 1935 Esquirol-Neustein Act regulating homework, "a historic step in the liberation of women and children from parasitic exploitation." Thought of as gendered (referring to women) and ungendered (referring to workers) at the same time and by the same people, regulation of industrial homework reflected the economic realities and political possibilities of the New Deal. This double identity, genderless but female, makes the regulation of homework a particularly rich case study in the interweaving of class, gender, and race/ethnicity in labor legislation. Analysis of its legislative history also suggests that labor standards need not be based on biological difference.

Protective Legislation and Female Difference

Homework regulation, because it barred an exploitative but customary practice from the home, belongs to the history of protective legislation for women. Although *Commonwealth* v. *Hamilton Mfg. Co.* provided a ten-hour day to women in textile manufacturing without mentioning their gender, courts began to uphold state labor protections for women on the basis of their dependent status. Because they were viewed apart from men, women like children, were considered wards of the state; limiting their working hours became a legitimate public health measure. In contrast, the courts had struck down most labor standards legislation that applied to men. When New York passed legislation seeking to regulate the hours of bakers, the Supreme Court rejected the regulations as an infringement of

Eileen Boris, "The Quest for Labor Standards in the Era of Eleanor Roosevelt: The Case of Industrial Homework," *Wisconsin Women's Law Journal*, 2 (1986), pp. 53–74.

the right to contract: the right to work for whatever wages the laborers chose. The justices underlined qualities reserved for male workers alone:

> There is no contention that bakers as a class are not equal in intelligence and capacity to men in other trades or manual occupations, or that they are not able to assert their rights and care for themselves without the protecting arm of the State interfering with their independence of judgment and of action. They are in no sense wards of the state.

The Court did grant exceptions to the general interpretation of the Fourteenth Amendment for certain categories of workers, however. Earlier, in *Holden* v. *Hardy*, the Court upheld a state maximum hour law for miners as a proper public health measure. It based its decision on the reasonable difference between miners and other kinds of workers.

Women reformers learned from this ruling and began to characterize women as belonging to one of the protected categories due to their potential ability to reproduce.

Thus, in *Muller* v. *Oregon* the reformers defended Oregon's ten hour law for women by arguing that industrial conditions particularly weakened female health and destroyed the reproductive system. The Supreme Court agreed and in this landmark decision upheld protective legislation for women. . . .

A similar marshalling of "scientific" facts by reformers convinced the Supreme Court in *Bunting* v. *Oregon* to uphold a maximum hours law not restricted only to women. However, state courts generally ignored this decision. They continued to cite *Muller* with its defense of female "difference."

Minimum wage laws for women subsequently were rendered noncompulsory as a result of *Adkins* v. *Children's Hospital*, a decision which extended the right to contract doctrine. In essence, the Court reversed its previous expansion of the state's police powers to protect potential and future motherhood. By according women who had just received the vote their equality before the law, the Court considered women workers to be on the same level as men, at least in terms of labor standards legislation. Because labor standards legislation generally did not cover male workers, adhering to *Adkins* had the effect of invalidating all labor standards. But reviving *Muller*, with its emphasis on different treatment, would leave protective legislation for women intact. *Bunting*, with its acceptance of labor legislation for both sexes, seemed forgotten as the right to contract dominated 1920s legal thought.

The Arguments of Women Reformers

As First Lady, Eleanor Roosevelt popularized the thought of a generation of women reformers who fought for both protective legislation for women and labor standards legislation for all workers. She understood the significance of minimum wage, maximum hour, and other legislation to guarantee a decent standard of living. In the 1920s she had served her political apprenticeship as a member of the National Consumers' League (NCL) (founded in 1899 to improve labor conditions of women through consumer white lists and boycotts) and the Women's Trade Union League (WTUL) (established in 1903 to unionize women workers). She articulated the views of women from these and other reform organizations, as well as those of Democratic party stalwarts, whose presence in her husband's administration did so much to shape its social legislation. As Roosevelt stated at a benefit concert for the WTUL in 1932, "the very fact that in order to live, people will work any number of hours, people will take any wages that they can get, and that this is a necessity during this crisis, means that we must guard against having these standards remain permanently as prosperity returns to us."

When speaking about "labor standards," Eleanor Roosevelt often referred to "labor" or the "worker" without any explicit gender distinction, relying on the plural, perhaps, to avoid the universal masculine pronoun. She called for the protection of the health of current and future generations without any link to the fragility of female reproduction, a concept central to earlier defenses of protective legislation. She understood that Depression conditions had eroded whatever gains workers had won through union organization or during economic good times, that unemployment threatened to undermine employer compliance with existing voluntary labor standards. "Limiting the number of working hours by law," she claimed, "spreads the employment, thereby giving more people work." Moreover, sweatshop wages and hours were bad for business; they created "unfair competition," by penalizing those employers who desired to be "fair," and they contributed to the underconsumption which many New Dealers saw as a major cause of the depression.

Presenting what would become the goals of the 1933 NRA [National Recovery Administration], she felt "it is self-preservation to treat the industrial worker with consideration and fairness at the present time and to uphold the fair employer in his efforts to treat his employees well by preventing unfair competition." Her emphasis on industrial workers, rather than women workers, certainly fit into the New Deal's proposed industrial recovery codes under the NRA. Such codes eventually mandated minimum wages, maximum hours, and other standards for all workers, regardless of sex, even though the codes ultimately maintained differentials based on sex, region, and race.

Nonetheless, Roosevelt also consciously considered women to be a special class of worker. "Many women," she wrote, "are not unionized and even unions have temporarily lowered their standards in order to keep their people at work." Thus women needed state protection. . . .

Advancement of protective legislation became the strategy of Roosevelt and other reformers because of the exploitative working conditions faced by women, the difficulty in organizing them, and the likelihood that the courts would uphold the laws. As explained by Mary Robinson, director of the Women's Bureau's Division of Public Information, "women are at a disadvantage in the wage-earning world because of traditions, prejudices, and other circumstances connected with their sex" leading to "a much greater tendency to exploit women because of their having a weaker status than men in the industrial world and thus lack of equality of bargaining power between themselves and their employers." However, their vulnerable condition as workers alone did not justify minimum wage and maximum hour legislation. Robinson also drew upon the reasoning of *Muller*: "the State's stake in the health of women extends beyond the individual to the race." Expressing the dualistic thinking of reformers, Women's Bureau Chief Mary Anderson further stated, women "are homemakers and mothers and also the victims of excessive exploitation by unscrupulous employers."

Though the courts previously emphasized female biological weakness (an argument that the reformers would employ to their advantage), Roosevelt stressed the social necessity for protective legislation rather than its biological base. She agreed with [National Consumers League leader] Florence Kelley that "sex is a biological fact. The political rights of citizens are not properly dependent upon sex, but social and domestic relations and industrial activities are." Roosevelt believed that "women *are* different from men." Her emphasis lay in the way that difference shaped the social roles that placed female industrial workers at an economic disadvantage. During a 1937 interview on Roosevelt's radio series, Rose Schneiderman [of the Women's Trade Union League] explained their shared position:

> In all seriousness, we aren't interested in maximum hours and minimum pay for professional women. Let's face facts—as they are. Of course, I want the best possible working conditions for all people, men and women. It's obvious to me that when working conditions for women are bettered, those of men automatically rise too. But because women do have home responsibilities, they need them most.
>
> I have never known a man to go home at the end of a day and do the housework—except intermittently, dropping it again as soon as possible. . . .

Neither Schneiderman nor Roosevelt questioned women's responsibility for home and children, but neither would they deny women the right to work as well as care for the home. In fact, during a period of relentless assault on that right, Roosevelt stood as a staunch defender of the married women's right to work. . . . [Her] pleas for protective legislation reflected an acute assessment of women's double day: "Surely the woman who works so that her children may have the necessities as well as some of the advantages of life, needs an eight hour day!"

Though Eleanor Roosevelt accepted gender difference and women's primary role as wife, mother, and homemaker, she based her support for protective legislation on the social conditions which turned that biological difference into a disadvantage. As had other women reformers, she focused on transforming those conditions, using the state as the agent of change. The massive economic crisis, however, had transformed labor standards for all workers. The changed economic and political landscape of the thirties provided the terrain on which protective legislation became labor standards legislation for all workers.

From Protective Legislation to the Fair Labor Standards Act

The economic conditions of the Great Depression justified gender inclusive and state-mandated labor standards. As Secretary of Labor Frances Perkins, a leading member of the women's reform network, stated in 1933, "after . . . the abnormal amount of unemployment, men's wages are at such a low ebb that temporary federal control of industry guaranteeing minimum wage rates to both sexes is being urged in many quarters." The economic crisis provided a reason for extending minimum wage and maximum hours laws to men as part of the police power of the state. The applicability of the laws to men became a reality as a result of the politics of the New Deal: Roosevelt's massive 1936 victory, the Supreme Court's more favorable approach to New Deal social legislation and the growing power of the union movement.

The NRA of 1933 was the first attempt at legislating minimum wages and maximum hours for all workers. Initial legislative efforts had focused on a federal law to provide a short work week with minimum wages for both men and women for a two year emergency period. The NRA promised a more permanent solution. It incorporated standards of fair competition into industry-wide codes developed by tripartite boards representing business, labor, and government. Section 7 (a) of the NRA encouraged collective bargaining and required all codes to include wage and hour provisions. Under the NRA codes, women and men gained higher wages, shortened hours of work, and increased employment.

However, the codes also reinforced existing sex-discrimination, as reported by the Women's Bureau in its evaluation of the impact of the NRA on women. The act covered "industries in or affecting interstate or foreign commerce" but did not extend to domestic service, agricultural and public service work, and non-factory laundry and garment work. Thus it excluded nearly one-half of employed women, a majority of whom were women of color and older women. Major industries employing women also lacked codes during 1933–34, the first year of the act. Moreover, as the Women's Bureau found, many women "were affected in some codes by the lowered minimum wages fixed on various differential bases, such as geographic location, sex, or size of city; by lower minimum for handicapped workers and for learners sometimes not carefully defined, by lack of provisions for eliminating homework . . . and by the allowance of many exceptions from the hour maxima."

Even though the Women's Bureau argued that men's wages also suffered in industries dominated by lowly paid women, it failed to point out that few men did "women's work." Thus lower rates in such industries collectively affected women more than men. The NRA raised the basic minimum wage, but because it treated men's and women's work differently and set codes on the basis of industries rather than creating one national standard, it replicated the existing segmentation of the labor market by sex, race, and age. In effect, these state-sponsored labor standards actually contributed to inequality.

During the NRA period, long time supporters of protective legislation for women began to endorse wage and hour laws that covered both sexes. They believed that the NRA experience would aid passage of these laws, inasmuch as they were necessary "to maintain and extend desirable standards achieved under the NRA." The 1934 conference on labor legislation, called by the Department of Labor (and including numerous state departments of labor and state federations of labor), urged that " 'the time seems ripe for the enactment of State laws applicable to all workers,' both men and women." But the same conference also recommended state laws for women only.

The women of the Labor Department—particularly Mary Anderson and Katherine Lenroot (chief of the Children's Bureau)—did not completely trust the courts to uphold gender-neutral laws. They feared leaving women and children unprotected. Moreover, since legislation for women in the past had paved the way for the NRA, in their mind, future legislation for women would also indirectly benefit male workers. Again, as it had from its beginnings in the 1920s, the Women's Bureau was attempting to use sex-based legislation as a form of class legislation. Yet, its numerous studies, particularly the 1928 *The Effects of Labor Legislation on the Employment of Women*, refused to take into account occupational segmentation by sex and thus showed the impossibility of improving the wages of men and women on the basis of legislation for women only. Because men did not work in the same occupations as many women, men did not face the particular obstacles that confronted women. Accordingly, the Bureau inflated the potential benefits for men resulting from protective legislation for women.

Even in the early years of the New Deal, Frances Perkins continued to urge state minimum wage and shorter hours laws for women "to take care of the future when temporary Federal control will cease." After the Supreme Court declared the NRA unconstitutional in May 1935, the search for labor standards progressed on both a state and national level. When the Depression began only nine states had variously enforced minimum wage legislation for women; another six states did so during the early years of the crisis. By 1938, twenty-two states, the District of Columbia and Puerto Rico had minimum wage laws. While most states had some kind of hours regulation, only fourteen states, the District of Columbia, and Puerto Rico mandated the eight hour day, and a 48 hour week for specific industries.

These gains hardly broke the back of exploitative labor conditions. State legislation did not control interstate commerce and thus could not bring about uniform labor standards. Moreover, Franklin Roosevelt's first term saw as much failure as success. . . . It must be remembered that reformers faced stiff opposition in state legislatures from local business interests and the Catholic church (which opposed the Child Labor Amendment).

Nevertheless, on the federal level, the Labor Department, guided by assistant director Clara Beyer of the newly-formed Bureau of Labor Standards, continued to push for federal hours and wages legislation. In 1936, Congress passed the Walsh-Healey Public Contracts Act which mandated a basic eight hour day and forty hour week, overtime pay, and no child labor in contracts entered into by the federal government in excess of $10,000. Yet here too the minimum wage was set according to the "prevailing" rate in that industry or similar ones "currently operating in the locality," a loophole leading to a lower female wage. The Fair Labor Standards Act finally became law in 1938 after more than two decades of fighting for such legislation on the part of Perkins and the women's network of reformers. The Act set minimum wages, maximum hours, and ended child labor in all industries engaged in interstate commerce.

While social reformers were pressing for state protection of workers, the labor movement was organizing an unprecedented number into the Congress of Industrial Organizations (CIO). Aided first by the NRA guarantee of the right of collective bargaining and then by the passage of the Wagner Act (1935), workers in auto, steel, rubber, and other heavy industries founded and solidified industrial unions that encompassed both the skilled and the unskilled. Though union organization developed among predominantly male workforces, drives in electronics and meatpacking protected large numbers of women. As the impact of collective bargaining reverberated throughout the marketplace, the CIO promised to increase the number of organized women while upgrading the standards of unorganized women.

The Amalgamated Clothing Workers of America and the International Ladies Garment Workers Union also gained in strength. They represented industries particularly vulnerable to sweatshops and industrial homework. The Amalgamated's leader Sidney Hillman joined the reformers in advocating labor legislation, including restrictions on homework. At the same time, organizers of female-concentrated industries took heart from the overall level of militancy and initiated organizing drives in clerical work, textiles, tobacco, sales, and even laundry and domestic service. The revival of the union movement suggested that both sexes would be able to gain labor standards through collective bargaining, although the movement's major successes came in sectors dominated by male workers. In the meantime, to protect its gains and aid its future prospects, organized labor added its voice to the political arena in support of labor standards legislation for all workers.

By mid-decade, shop floor advances helped sustain political pressure for labor standards while decisions by the Supreme Court cleared the way for future legislative action, particularly the Fair Labor Standards Act. Franklin D. Roosevelt's attempt to pack the Supreme Court with justices who would favor his policies contributed to the Court becoming more receptive to social legislation. This transformation was nowhere more apparent than in its aboutface on the minimum wage for women.

In *Morehead* v. *New York ex rel Tipaldo*, the Court relied on its previous decision in *Adkins* and overturned New York's state minimum wage law. However, in rejecting sex based legislation, this decision actually opened the way toward class legislation. The justices declared,

> While men are left free to fix their wages by agreement with employers, it would be fanciful to suppose that the regulation of women's wages would be useful to prevent or lessen the evils [of exploitative working conditions] listed in the first section of the act. Men in need of work are as likely as women to accept the low wages offered by unscrupulous employers.

Although the court in *Tipaldo* adhered to "right to contract," it also agreed with those legislators who saw in the depression a reason to consider the situation of men. . . .

Less than two years later in *West Coast Hotel Co.* v. *Parrish*, the Court upheld an almost identical Washington minimum wage law and overturned *Adkins* in the process. Returning to the reasoning of *Holden*, Chief Justice Hughes reiterated the rationale behind that earlier decision, "that both parties are of full age and competent to contract does not necessarily deprive the state of the power to interfere, where the parties do not stand upon an equality, or where the public demands that one party to the contract shall be protected against himself." The minimum wage, then, became a legitimate device to maintain the public interest in the health of women . . . Moreover, since low wages led to high relief rolls, Hughes contended, "The community is not bound to provide what is in effect a subsidy for unconscionable employers. The community may direct its lawmaking power to correct the abuse which springs from their selfish disregard of the public interest."

Though the court here did not direct the legislature to regulate "all cases which it might possibly reach," though it affirmed protecting only women because of their "relative need," it based its holding not on the abstract "right to contract," but rather on the legislature's discretionary use of the police power. Thus, Frances Perkins wrote Governor Stark of Missouri that even though she supported "protection of underpaid men as well as women through the establishment of minimum wage rates by law [.] . . . the Supreme Court's decision in the Washington case applied only to the power of the State to regulate the wages of women." Laws directed solely at women were still necessary. Yet, with *Adkins* out of the way, the Court could return to its reasoning in *Bunting*, which upheld hours legislation for both sexes, and sustain the Fair Labor Standards Act in *U.S.* v. *Darby*.

Homework Regulation and Labor Standards

The regulation and eventual abolition of industrial homework was crucial to the success of the FLSA [Fair Labor Standards Act] and the entire quest for labor standards. Reformers had long argued that homework regulation would protect the health of women and children. . . . In the thirties, however, homework legislation became linked with the larger political economy. As the National Child Labor Committee argued before one NRA hearing, allowing homework to exist "would make the maintenance of maximum hour and minimum wage schedules and the prohibition of child labor practically impossible." In 1934, the first Conference on Labor Standards, which had endorsed minimum wages—when possible—for men as well as women, called for the elimination of homework through state regulatory legislation, interstate compacts, the NRA codes, and other federal legislation, or whichever proved "most effective." In 1935, Frances Perkins further explained to the Southern Regional Conference on State Labor Legislation, that "[T]he trick of manufacturers of sending work to be done in homes at low wages is breaking down our standards in some industries. We must think seriously of prohibiting this. We must also think about safety and sanitation which are a part of every sound labor program." In meeting after meeting throughout the thirties, the Labor Department included industrial homework among its topics of discussion; the restriction of homework became another device to improve the working conditions of both sexes.

Even though they classified homework regulation under the gender neutral category of labor standards, reformers understood homework to be a form of women's work. The studies of the Women's Bureau confirmed that the overwhelming majority of homeworkers were married women in their childbearing years, another cluster of women over fifty, primarily either ethnic immigrant or Spanish-speaking. Their households seemed to have more children and/or younger, pre-school children as well as an underemployed or unemployed primary (male) breadwinner. Many of these women defined childcare as their main responsibility and were reluctant to work in a factory. . . .

Thus reformers called for a ban on industrial homework precisely because homeworkers were mothers and worked in the home. As assistant director Beyer questioned, "Is it socially desirable for a mother with a four month [sic] old baby and three other children under 6 to work 33 hours a week for $1.75; or for a mother with 4 children under 5 to work an average of 4 hours a day and receive 63 cents for her week's work?" For Beyer and the others, homework disrupted the true purpose of home and motherhood by transforming the nurturing mother into the employer of her own children.

After the Supreme Court found the NRA unconstitutional, the Labor Department attempted to coordinate state actions; the many conferences of labor law administrators that resulted passed numerous resolutions condemning homework. The administrators called for a ban on industrial homework in order to maintain factory wages. They also tried to abolish homework indirectly by applying minimum wage decrees to homeworkers in industries under such orders. By forcing manufacturers to pay the same wages to factory and home workers, the administrators wanted to make homework less profitable and thus less attractive to employers. Though

neither Walsh-Healey nor FLSA specifically addressed homework regulation, Congress—as well as Perkins, Beyer and the Women's and Children's
Bureaus—certainly saw an administrative ban as a crucial step toward the
implementation of these acts.

In the more conservative atmosphere of 1939 and 1940, Congress rejected a call to amend the FLSA to ban homework, even as it passed a
bill to regulate rather than abolish homework in Puerto Rico. Though reformers persisted in viewing their fight against homework as eliminating an
exploitative labor system, they legally curtailed homework only by considering its abolition as a means toward enforcing the wages, hours, and
child labor provisions of FLSA. The Secretary of Labor in the early 1940s
used the FLSA to prohibit homework from seven industries—knitted out-
erwear, jewelry, handkerchiefs, embroidery, gloves, women's apparel and
button and buckle. In *Gemsco* v. *Walling*, the Supreme Court upheld this
exercise of authority by the Secretary of Labor. According to the Court,
homework was not "an independent industry but an operation conducted
largely by [the] same employers who maintain factories" and thus it represented a "competitive practice with factory work" detrimental to the
goals of FLSA.

By Fall of 1938, then, after passage of the FLSA, the Division of Labor
Standards, the State Commissioners, the AFL, and the CIO agreed that
"the States should follow the example of the Federal Government and
proceed with wage and hour legislation applicable to both" sexes. The
women of the Labor Department had been drafting bills to safeguard the
protection of women even if the courts invalidated coverage of men. Wom-
en's Bureau chief Mary Anderson actually attempted to subvert the inclu-
sion of men in the state laws. Because the FLSA was new, Anderson
wanted to wait until its provisions and constitutionality were tested and
expenses evaluated. She did not want the states to risk losing the protections
granted to women in existing legislation by amending their statutes to cover
men. Behind Anderson's fears lurked strongly held assumptions about wom-
en's difference forged in the 1890s and the first decade of the twentieth
century.

The Significance of Homework Legislation Today

In the 1930s, Eleanor Roosevelt and her generation of women reformers
agreed that men and women should benefit from labor standards legislation.
They could not abandon the fight for minimum wage and other labor standards for women, even though political conditions had freed them from
gender-based strategies as a means toward gaining class-based legislation.
To Mary Anderson and others in the Women's and Children's Bureaus,
the concept of women's place as childbearer and rearer had justified protective legislation and shaped the debate over industrial homework restrictions. These assumptions made it difficult to chart a new course after the
passage of the FLSA; in fact, social reform women in the forties, fifties

and even the sixties still refused to endorse the ERA because they understood it to undermine protective legislation for women. Yet the FLSA promised a new, genderless basis for the quest for labor standards, despite its replication of existing labor market segmentation by sex and race.

The prohibition of homework, a type of women's work, would regulate labor standards for both sexes, but only if men and women had equal access to the labor market. Such equality did not exist in 1940 and does not exist today; women still have the responsibility for caring for children and other dependents. This cultural assignment leads to less opportunity for education, lower job expectations, and, most importantly, employer discrimination. The labor market remains segregated by sex and race, making it more likely that certain groups of women, especially women of color, will earn only a minimum or sub-minimum wage. For these women, history has borne out the fear of the AFL in the 1930s, that the minimum wage actually would become the maximum.

The amount of industrial homework subsided during the quarter century boom following WWII, perhaps as much because the practice no longer made economic sense than because the government could enforce FLSA with any great precision. Though restriction of industrial homework succeeded as protective legislation for women workers, embroidery, handkerchief, and related work apparently became mechanized and/or was undertaken by the even cheaper labor markets in the Third World. Other types of garment homework seemed to enter unionized factories. Loss of homework, however, did not necessarily mean economic devastation; the expansion of clerical and service work provided jobs for daughters of white immigrant families previously engaged in homework and unionization of their men's work made a family wage more of a reality in the immediate post war years.

In the unstable economy of the 1970s and 80s, homework has apparently resurged as a production strategy in old industries, like garments, as well as new ones, like microcomputers and clerical work. It has become part of the economic decentralization and underground economy central to the current restructuring of capitalism in the industrialized nations and also part of the problem of the informal sector in the Third World periphery. Today, the homeworker remains a married woman with small children, but she is more likely to be a recent immigrant from Latin America or Asia than one of those native-born and rural knitters whose challenge of the homework laws captured public attention in recent years.

In the 1980s, homework has reemerged as a political issue. Contemporary proponents of homework continue to argue, as in the past, that women should have the right to work at home and care for their children at the same time. Labor liberals warn of the return of the sweatshop and its erosion of labor standards for all workers. But feminist rhetoric has entered both sides of the debate about homework. Proponents equate women's "rights" with "the right to work," while liberal reformers, unionists, and feminists argue for women's rights on the job—and to a job. These opponents of homework are less concerned with defending the integrity of the home than with providing childcare and other services so that women can work outside of the home.

In this controversy, women must confront the meaning of female "difference" as boldly as did Eleanor Roosevelt and her generation of women reformers. A half century of history has taught women to be leary of the stress on female biological difference: all too often "difference" has justified patriarchal thinking, legal inequality, and economic subordination. . . .

In the words of Eleanor Roosevelt, "This is a time which should teach us all one lesson—namely, that the prosperity of the few is very precarious indeed if the many are in really poor circumstances."

✦ *F U R T H E R   R E A D I N G*

James B. Atleson, *Values and Assumptions in American Labor Law* (1983)

Jerold Auerbach, *Labor and Liberty: The LaFollette Committee and the New Deal* (1966)

Judith Baer, *The Chains of Protection: The Judicial Response to Women's Labor Legislation* (1978)

Eileen Boris, "Regulating Industrial Homework: The Triumph of 'Sacred Motherhood'," *Journal of American History* 71 (March 1985), 745–763

Valerie Jean Conner, *The National War Labor Board* (1983)

Melvyn Dubofsky, "Abortive Reform: The Wilson Administration and Organized Labor," in James Cronin and Carmen Sirianni, eds., *Work, Community, and Power* (1983)

Nancy S. Erickson, "*Muller* v. *Oregon* Reconsidered: The Origins of a Sex-Based Doctrine of Liberty of Contract," *Labor History* 30 (Spring 1989), 228–250

Daniel Ernst, "The Yellow-Dog Contract and Liberal Reform," *Labor History* 30 (Spring 1989), 251–274

Leon Fink, "Labor, Liberty and the Law: Trade Unionism and the Problem of the American Constitutional Order," *Journal of American History* 74 (December 1987), 904–925

William E. Forbath, "The Ambiguities of Free Labor: Labor and the Law in the Gilded Age," *Wisconsin Law Review* (1985), 767–817

——, "The Shaping of the American Labor Movement," *Harvard Law Review* 102 (April 1989), 1109–1256

Steve Fraser, "Dress Rehearsal for the New Deal: Shop-Floor Insurgents, Political Elites, and Industrial Democracy in the Amalgamated Clothing Workers Union," in Michael Frisch and Daniel Walkowitz, eds., *Working Class America* (1983)

James A. Gross, *The Reshaping of the National Labor Relations Board: National Labor Policy in Transition, 1937–1947* (1981)

——, *The Making of the NLRB: A Study in Economics, Politics, and Law* (1974)

Howell Harris, *The Right to Manage: Industrial Relations Policies of American Business in the 1940s* (1982)

Vivian Hart, "Minimum-Wage Policy and Constitutional Inequality: The Paradox of the Fair Labor Standards Act of 1938," *Journal of Policy History* 1 (1989), 319–343

Herbert Hill, *Black Labor and the American Legal System* (1985)

James A. Hodges, *New Deal Labor Policy and the Southern Cotton Textile Industry* (1986)

Raymond Hogler, "Labor History and Critical Labor Law: An Inter-Disciplinary Approach to Workers' Control," *Labor History* 30 (Spring 1989), 185–192

Wythe Holt, "The New American Labor Law History," *Labor History* 30 (Spring 1989), 275–293

Karl E. Klare, "Judicial Deradicalization of the Wagner Act and the Origins of Modern Legal Consciousness, 1937–1941," *Minnesota Law Review* 62 (1978), 265–339

———, "Labor Law as Ideology: Toward a New Historiography of Collective Bargaining Law," *Industrial Relations Law Journal* 4 (1981), 450–482

Nelson Lichtenstein, *Labor's War at Home: The CIO in World War II* (1982)

Staughton Lynd, "Ideology and Labor Law," *Stanford Law Review* 36 (1984), 1273–1298

———, "Thesis and Antithesis: Section 7 of the NLRA, the First Amendment, and Workers' Rights," in Jules Lobel, ed., *A Less Than Perfect Union* (1988)

Theda Skocpol, "Political Response to Capitalist Crisis: Neo-Marxist Theories of the State and the Case of the New Deal," *Politics and Society* 10 (1980), 155–201

Katherine Van Wezel Stone, "The Post-War Paradigm in American Labor Law," *Yale Law Journal* 90 (1981), 1509–1580

Steven Tolliday and Jonathan Zeitlin, eds., *Shop Floor Bargaining and the State: Historical and Comparative Perspectives* (1985)

Christopher Tomlins, *The State and the Unions: Labor Relations, Law, and the Organized Labor Movement in America, 1880–1960* (1985)

Stanley Vittoz, *New Deal Labor Policy and the American Industrial Economy* (1987)

Margaret Weir, Ann Orloff, and Theda Skocpol, *The Politics of Social Policy in the United States* (1988)

CHAPTER 11

Race, Gender, and Industrial Unionism: World War II and Its Aftermath

✧

World War II lasted only half a decade, and most of the killing and destruction took place far away from the United States, yet this most massive of all twentieth-century military conflicts had an enormous impact on American society. Above all, the war ended the Great Depression. With the military accounting for about 47 percent of all production and services at the peak of the fighting, the gross national product doubled in the wartime years. And unlike so much of the military spending of the 1970s and 1980s, this war was a metal-bending, engine-building, gasoline-powered conflict that required an enormous amount of relatively unskilled labor. Unemployment, still 14 percent in 1940, vanished in just a couple of years. Wages went up, infant mortality declined, and life expectancy increased. Indeed, jobs were created for 17 million new entrants into the work force, enabling millions of people once consigned to the bottom of the labor market—white women, black laborers, teenagers, and older workers—to take high-paying, defense-related jobs for the first time; or if they were already employed in industry, to improve their positions and their pay.

But how much of a social revolution did this full-employment economy generate? The war clearly had a huge impact on the status of black workers. The unprecedented demand for new sources of industrial labor, combined with Allied denunciations of Nazi racism, weakened longstanding racist structures within the workplace. Three million blacks surged out of the rural South and into factories, shipyards, steel mills, and military-training camps where union contracts and government policy gave them a measure of industrial citizenship. Blacks were increasingly well organized and self-confident, and their advances generated enormous tensions. By the summer of 1943, race riots and "hate strikes" con-

vulsed many war-industry centers. But the modern civil-rights era clearly had
dawned.

Historians of American women have been fascinated as well by the new demographic patterns generated by the war. The imagery of Rosie the Riveter has
been a compelling one, but just what were the thoughts and opinions of the
millions of housewives, sales clerks, and female farm laborers who took over traditionally male jobs? Were they motivated by wartime propaganda or by a
proto-feminist consciousness? Or did they merely respond to the lure of higher
pay and new jobs? And scholars are puzzled because this great migration of female labor seems unaccompanied by the kind of change in social consciousness
that made the movement of black workers into industry so politically and socially
explosive. After the war many women simply left, or were forced out of, high-
profile, heavy-industry jobs. Despite popular myths about the 1950s, there was
no wholesale return to the kitchen: within less than a decade, a higher proportion of women were at work—about 35 percent—than at the height of World
War II.

And while the trade-union movement itself boomed during the war, it
found itself ambiguously transformed. The powerful War Labor Board (WLB)
guaranteed unions protection against hostile managers, raised the wages of
many lower-paid workers, and called upon employers to offer equal pay for
equal work. But the government also put a ceiling on wages and demanded a
no-strike pledge from union leaders. This difficult arrangement tended to transform union officials into mere contract administrators who enforced the will of
the bureaucrats in Washington. As might be expected, many workers objected to
the wage limits, long WLB delays in resolving their disputes, and the effort wartime managers now made to restore discipline in their shops and mills. By 1944
a wildcat-strike movement had emerged, largely centered in cities such as Detroit, Akron, and Chicago, where unionists sought to defend the power of the
shop-floor organizations they had built in the 1930s.

✣ D O C U M E N T S

In the first two documents, the War Labor Board mandates equal pay for equal
work, regardless of an employee's race or gender. But note the use of a sweeping ideological argument by this government agency to attack the idea of racial
discrimination, and compare this with the far narrower grounds upon which the
WLB endorses women's rights at work. World War II era civil-rights activism is
apparent in the third document, an excerpt from an article in the NAACP's (National Association for the Advancement of Colored People) The Crisis, which
confidently, and correctly, predicted that the Detroit branch of this organization
would soon enroll 20,000 members. The Communist Party influenced, or actually
enrolled, a substantial number of African-American union activists in the 1940s.
As document four indicates, association with the party made these individuals
and the civil rights issues they championed vulnerable to attack in the early Cold
War era when anti-Communist organizations, like the House Committee on Un-
American Activities, sought to probe party membership and influence. The interplay of ideology and organization was crucial to the rise of a civil-rights consciousness among black workers, but the entrance of white women into the work
force generated no similar rise in feminist ideas. In the final document Marie

Baker, the recently divorced mother of a small child, describes her successful work life in a southern California aircraft factory, which ended abruptly and with little protest on Baker's part at the war's end.

The War Labor Board Assails Workplace Racism, 1943

. . . In this small but significant case the National War Labor Board abolishes the classifications "colored laborer" and "white laborer" and reclassifies both simply as "laborers" with the same rates of pay for all in that classification without discrimination on account of color. The Negro workers in this classification are hereby granted wage increases which place them on a basis of economic parity with the white workers in the same classification. This wage increase is made without regard to the "Little Steel" formula, but with regard simply for the democratic formula of equal pay for work equal in quantity and quality in the same classification. This equalization of economic opportunity is not a violation of the sound American provision of differentials in pay for differences in skills. It is rather a bit of realization of the no less sound American principle of equal pay for equal work as one of those equal rights in the promise of American democracy regardless of color, race, sex, religion, or national origin.

The unanimous decision is in line with the President's Executive Order 8802; with the general policy of the Board; with the union's request; . . . with the unanimous recommendation of the review committee composed of representatives of labor, industry, and the public; with prophetic Americanism; and with the cause of the United Nations. To the credit of the Company this decision, along with other decisions in the case, is accepted by management in good faith and spirit.

Economic and political discrimination on account of race or creed is in line with the Nazi program. America, in the days of its infant weakness, the haven of heretics and the oppressed of all races, must not in the days of its power become the stronghold of bigots. The world has given America the vigor and variety of its differences. America should protect and enrich its differences for the sake of America and the world. Understanding religious and racial differences make for a better understanding of other differences and for an appreciation of the sacredness of human personality, as a basic to human freedom. The American answer to differences in color and creed is not a concentration camp but cooperation. The answer to human error is not terror but light and liberty under the moral law. By this light and liberty, the Negro has made a contribution in work and faith, song and story, laughter and struggle which are an enduring part of the spiritual heritage of America.

There is no more loyal group of our fellow citizens than the American Negroes, north and south. In defense of America from attack from without, they spring to arms in the spirit of Dorie Miller of Texas, the Negro mess boy, who, when the machine gunner on the Arizona was killed, jumped to his unappointed place and fired the last rounds as the ship was sinking in Pearl Harbor.

It is the acknowledged fact that in spite of all the handicaps of slavery and discrimination, the Negro in America has compressed more progress in the shortest time than any race in human history. Slavery gave the Negro his Christianity. Christianity gave the Negro his freedom. This freedom must give the Negro equal rights to home and health, education and citizenship, and an equal opportunity to work and fight for our common country.

Whether as vigorous fighting men or for production of food and munitions, America needs the Negro; the Negro needs the equal opportunity to work and fight. The Negro is necessary for winning the war, and, at the same time, is a test of our sincerity in the cause for which we are fighting. More hundreds of millions of colored people are involved in the outcome of this war than the combined populations of the Axis Powers. Under Hitler and his Master Race, their movement is backward to slavery and despair. In America, the colored people have the freedom to struggle for freedom. With the victory of the democracies, the human destiny is toward freedom, hope, equality of opportunity and the gradual fulfillment for all peoples of the noblest aspirations of the brothers of men and the sons of God, without regard to color or creed, region or race, in the world neighborhood of human brotherhood. . . .

The War Labor Board Orders Equal Pay for Equal Work, 1944

Adjustments which equalize the wage or salary rates paid to females with the rates paid to males for comparable quality and quantity of work on the same or similar operations . . . may be made without the approval of the National War Labor Board. . . .

The application of the Order is quite plain and simple in cases where women are employed to replace men on jobs which are not changed.

Where the plant management, in order to meet the necessity of replacing men by women, has rearranged or lightened the job, perhaps with the employment of helpers to do heavy lifting or the like, a study of job content and job evaluation should afford the basis for setting "proportionate rates for proportionate work." Such questions require a reasonable determination, by collective bargaining or arbitration, of the question whether, or how far, the newly arranged job is of equal quantity and quality with the old job. The new wage set on such a basis does not require the approval of the National War Labor Board. . . .

We have found from experience that there has been some tendency to abuse this rule of equal pay for equal work.

This refers particularly to job classifications to which only women have been assigned in the past. The rates for such jobs, especially when developed by collective bargaining, are presumed to be correct in relation to other jobs in the plant.

Whether a job is performed by men or women, there may be a dispute over correctness of its wage rate in relation to rates for other jobs in the same plant. These are the so-called intra-plant inequality cases. Their discrimination should not be related to the "equal pay for equal work" question; they should be determined on the basis of maintaining or developing a proper balance of wage rates for various jobs based upon job evaluation.

We have even seen instances in which the workers have demanded, or the employers have proposed, that the wages being paid to women in one plant should be increased on the ground that in some other plant similar work is being done by men at a higher wage. Such proposals tend to overlook the fact that wages paid to men in the same occupation generally vary from plant to plant. In such cases, the question whether the work is done by men or women is irrelevant. The claim for increased wages immediately reduces itself to a single question of different wage rates for the same work in different plants. Interplant inequalities in wage rates are quite common in American industry, and often well established. They afford a basis for a wage increase only in very exceptional cases. If the interplant inequality is in fact one that should be corrected at all, its correction is independent of any question of men and women workers.

The Crisis Predicts a Surge in NAACP Membership, 1943

The question has been raised, "Can Detroit get 20,000 NAACP members in 1943?"

Yes—is the answer echoed by the president of the branch, Dr. James J. McClendon, the executive board, the membership committee, the labor committee and interested citizens of Detroit. . . .

Detroit takes pride in building powerful organizations. The largest industrial union in the world—Ford Local 600, UAW-CIO, of which a Negro, Shelton Tappes, is recording secretary—is located in the "motor city." The United Automobile, Aircraft and Agricultural Implement Workers of America, CIO, one of the largest international unions in the world, got its start in Detroit, once an open shop town.

Today, Detroit is a worker's town—dynamic in every respect. The CIO and the AFL embrace a majority of the Negro workers and these organizations are reflected in the NAACP membership. AFL teachers, sanitary workers, street car and bus motormen, conductors and conductorettes laborers, carpenters, postal employees; CIO rubber workers, retail and restaurant employees, maintenance workers, autoworkers, state, county and municipal workers, make up a major portion of the present membership of more than twelve thousand NAACP members. . . .

The labor committee is the largest and most active committee of the branch. Meeting regularly each Sunday afternoon, it hears grievances of workers from plants and industries throughout the city, takes them up through regular union channels, always reserving the NAACP as the court of last appeal. It was the labor committee which saw the need for a demonstration against mounting discrimination, and, together with the Inter-Racial Committee of the UAW-CIO, sponsored the largest gathering held recently on the question of employing more Negro women in Detroit's war industries.

War Brings Problems

Since 1941, more than 300,000 workers have come into the metropolitan area to man the industries, some of them newly created, which are pro-ducing the materiel for victory. More than 50,000 Negro workers are a part of this new group. Bursting at its seams, the city's problems of housing, recreation, delinquency and employment have risen in alarming proportions. Perhaps this accounts for the willingness of Detroit citizens to tackle *any* problem of discrimination with a vitality that amazes the nation—especially Washington!

Aroused by the slow upgrading of trained Negro men, the reluctance of war industries to utilize available Negro woman power, the NAACP labor committee and the Inter-Racial Committee of the UAW-CIO co-sponsored a demonstration in Cadillac Square, Sunday, April 11. More than 10,000 people paraded from the Detroit Institute of Arts to the Square where stands the monument of Sojourner Truth.

The parade was colorful. Huge banners cried: "Down with discrimi-nation," "Jim-Crow must go!", "Bullets and Bombs are Colorblind." Air raid wardens, Women's Volunteer Corps, OCD people, marched in uniform to show that the Negro is taking part in civilian defense activities. The Boy Scouts and the "Majorettes," a group of young girls twirling batons behind the American Legion Drum and Bugle Corps, added youthful color to the parade.

5,000 people marched for more than five miles on a warm Sunday afternoon to give vent to their feelings against jim-crow practices in Detroit. As the procession passed the USO, 24 Negro soldiers on weekend leave from a nearby airfield proudly walked from the building and calmly fell into the line of march. Their action clearly showed that they felt: "This is our fight too!" . . .

Embodying the desire to have democracy practiced at home as well as abroad, the huge assembly ratified the *Cadillac Charter*, which called for: abolition of discrimination in government, housing, the armed forces; ab-olition of the poll tax; security from mob violence, lynching, police brutality and physical violence; equal treatment in hiring, upgrading and training. The preamble stated that "as people of all races" we "declare ourselves wholeheartedly behind the effort of the government to prosecute the war to an ultimate victory." The charter further pointed out that "full and equal participation of all citizens is fair, just and necessary for victory and an enduring peace. . . . [D]iscriminatory practices cannot be maintained if America is to hold out to the world hope of freedom."

The House Committee on Un-American Activities
Harrasses a Black Union Official, 1952

Mr. Tavenner. What is your name, please?

Mr. Hood. My name is William R. Hood.

Mr. Tavenner. When and where were you born, Mr. Hood?

Mr. Hood. I was born in 1910, but I categorically refuse to tell you where I was born. My father and mother are still in Georgia. I will write the name to the committee. My uncle was killed by a mob, I don't want them persecuted. I talked with my mother already and the hysteria created here in this Georgia city—with my father in business and my sister a school teacher in Georgia, I don't want them persecuted or to have reprisals as the result of my behavior in the city of Detroit.

Mr. Tavenner. How long have you lived in Detroit?

Mr. Hood. I came to Detroit in 1942.

Mr. Tavenner. How have you been employed?

Mr. Hood. I traveled for a life insurance company in the State of Georgia.

Mr. Tavenner. I meant here in the State of Michigan.

Mr. Hood. I worked at Chevrolet Gear & Axle, I think it was a short period in 1942 and I left because of discriminatory practices. They wouldn't promote or upgrade me. I was hired by the Ford Motor Car Co., January 26, 1943.

Mr. Tavenner. And you have been working there since?

Mr. Hood. I have been working for the Ford Motor Car Co. with the exception of the time I have been the representative and recording secretary of the largest union in the world, the UAW-CIO, Ford local 600.

Mr. Tavenner. During what period of time did you occupy that position?

Mr. Hood. I have occupied that position for four years and will be running for my fifth term in office this coming June.

Mr. Tavenner. I am sorry, I did not get the beginning of your service.

Mr. Hood. I was elected recording secretary of local 600 four years ago. I hope I will be elected for the fifth time this June in spite of this committee.

Mr. Tavenner. The Daily Worker of September 1, 1951, carries an article on page 1 to the effect that you spoke in New York City on behalf of Louis Weinstock who had been indicted under the Smith Act. Is it correct that you did speak in behalf of Louis Weinstock at that time?

Mr. Hood. I refuse to answer about my appearance in New York in behalf of Mr. Weinstock under the privileges of the fifth amendment; however, I might tell you that I am very sympathetic toward minority people and other people that are kicked around in this Nation.

Mr. Tavenner. Were you sympathetic to Mr. Weinstock, who was

U.S. House, Committee on Un-American Activities. *Communism in the Detroit Area—Part I.* 82nd Cong. 2d sess. (Washington, D.C.: Government Printing Office, 1952), pp. 2878–2898.

charged, under the Smith Act, with advocating the use of force and violence in the overthrow of the Government of this country?

Mr. Hood. I do not advocate the overthrow of the Government by force and violence. The methods and approaches used by the Government in trying to arrive at certain conclusions—I refuse to answer in respect to Mr. Weinstock on the basis of the privileges granted me under the fifth amendment.

Mr. Tavenner. Did Mr. Weinstock live in Detroit at any time?

Mr. Hood. I refuse to answer that question on the basis of the immunities which I have under the fifth amendment.

Mr. Tavenner. Did you know on September 12, 1951, that Louis Weinstock had been a functionary of the Communist Party for a number of years?

Mr. Hood. I refuse to answer any questions similar to that in respect to any individual's participation in anything, under the fifth amendment.

Mr. Tavenner. You spoke of having sympathy, as I understand it, for Weinstock?

Mr. Hood. I didn't say I had sympathy for Weinstock. I said I have sympathy for persecuted people in America and all over the world.

Mr. Tavenner. Did you consider that Weinstock was being persecuted?

Mr. Hood. I refuse to answer any question with respect to Weinstock under the immunities of the fifth amendment.

Mr. Tavenner. According to the Daily Worker of November 19, 1951, page 2, you were reported as being among the speakers at the Twentieth Anniversary National Conference of the American Committee for the Protection of the Foreign Born. Did you make such an address on that occasion?

Mr. Hood. I refuse to testify to this committee about any speeches I made other than those speeches that I made to my activity in local 600 as a functionary of the National Negro Labor Council for which I thought I was here, according to the press releases, anyway, yesterday.

Mr. Tavenner. Are you willing to tell the committee whether or not you were approached, and if so by whom, to assist in the meeting that I referred to, the American Committee for the Protection of the Foreign Born?

Mr. Hood. I think it logically follows that the question asked me now would be refused on the basis of my privileges and on the basis of your first question—on the basis of the privileges granted me under the Constitution of the United States and the fifth amendment.

Mr. Tavenner. Do you refuse to answer?

Mr. Hood. I refuse to answer and I so indicated in my remark. Perhaps you didn't hear me.

Mr. Tavenner. You are reported having been a sponsor of the Mid-Century Conference for Peace held in Detroit in May 1950, is that correct?

Mr. Hood. I refuse to answer that question under the fifth amendment.

Mr. Tavenner. Let me explain, before you give your final answer. I am interested in knowing the circumstances under which your support of that matter was obtained if it was obtained. Does that change your answer?

Mr. Hood. I don't think it would, based upon my knowledge of this committee. I don't think it would change it, counsel.

Mr. Tavenner. As the recording secretary of the CIO, Local 600, UAW—I seem to have it backwards—were you required to sign a non-Communist affidavit?

Mr. Hood. I was, counsel.

Mr. Tavenner. Did you sign it?

Mr. Hood. I did, sir, for four consecutive years. I have been elected and I hope to sign it again. I hope I will be elected.

Mr. Tavenner. In view of that, may I ask whether at the time you signed the affidavit you were a member of the Communist Party?

Mr. Hood. I was not a member of the Communist Party.

Mr. Tavenner. Have you been a member at any time since the time you first signed that?

Mr. Hood. I have not been a member of the Communist Party from the time I first signed it.

Mr. Tavenner. The committee has information indicating that in 1947 you were issued a 1947 card, No. 68126 of the Communist Party.

Mr. Hood. It is a damned lie.

Mr. Tavenner. Have you ever been a member of the Communist Party?

Mr. Hood. I have already answered that question. As a Negro-American, based upon this committee's action, I refuse to testify about my past action in respect to the question that you asked me, under the fifth amendment. That is the answer.

Mr. Tavenner. I do not understand your answer. Have you ever been a member of the Communist Party?

Mr. Hood. I told you I refused as a Negro-American particularly for reasons of my own. I refuse to answer that question under the fifth amendment. I refuse to answer.

Mr. Tavenner. When you say you refuse to answer for reasons of your own, to what are you referring? Are you referring to the fifth amendment or some other reason?

Mr. Hood. Counsel, will you please phrase your question again? Will you repeat the question?

Mr. Tavenner. Will you read the question?

(The question was read by the official court reporter.)

Mr. Hood. I am referring to the fifth amendment. I am not a lawyer but I said the fifth amendment. These are my own reasons.

Mr. Tavenner. Then if I understand your testimony correctly, you denied that you have been a member of the Communist Party at any time within the past four years, which is the period of time you have been the recording secretary of the UAW but you refuse to answer whether or not you have ever been a member of the Communist Party, is that your testimony?

Mr. Hood. I refuse to answer.

Mr. Tavenner. Mr. Hood, according to the Daily Worker of October 23, 1951, page 3, you are said to have been a sponsor of a dinner at 13 Astor Place, New York City, to be given on October 26, 1951, for the defense of Dr. W. E. B. DuBois and sponsored by the trade-union committee to defend Dr. W. E. B. DuBois. If it is true that you were one of the sponsors of that dinner, I would like to know how your sponsorship was obtained.

Mr. Hood. I refuse to answer under the privileges of the fifth amendment.

Mr. Tavenner. The committee is also informed through notices in the Daily Worker of December 5, 1951, on page 2 and in the same paper of September 10, 1951, page 3, that you were scheduled as a speaker at a rally to be held in St. Nicholas Arena in New York City on September 10, 1951, for the repeal of the Smith Act. Do you recall whether or not you spoke on such occasion?

Mr. Hood. I refuse to answer under the fifth amendment.

Mr. Tavenner. Mr. Hood, the Washington, D.C., Evening Star of October 30, 1951, on page 7, carried a paid advertisement which was an open letter to J. Howard McGrath, Attorney General of the United States, protesting the jailing of four trustees of the bail fund of the Civil Rights Congress. Your name appears as one of the signers to that open letter. Will you tell the committee who solicited your signature and what interest was involved in soliciting your signature, if it was so obtained?

Mr. Hood. I refuse to answer under the privileges of the fifth amendment. . . .

Mr. Tavenner. I have no further questions, Mr. Chairman.

Mr. Jackson. I have no questions.

Mr. Potter. No questions.

Mr. Wood. The witness is excused from further attendance and a recess will be taken until 2 o'clock.

(The witness was excused.) . . .

Women's Work in a California Warplane Factory, 1941–1945

. . . I needed a job because I was going to be very independent. I wasn't going to ask for any alimony or anything. I was just going to take care of myself. There was no jobs in Mojave in the desert; you had to come down here.

Women, everyone, was going to work at that time. We were really patriotic in those days. 'Course, we were in a real war. We were being attacked; you know, Pearl Harbor and all. I think the people came together better than they did during Vietnam. 'Course, Vietnam was such a mess; I mean, it was a real tragedy. But during World War II, everybody got real patriotic and got in there and worked. Grandmothers, mothers, daughters, everybody. I was real patriotic and I wanted to help. I was going to work right out in the factory. I wasn't going in for an office job. No, no, I didn't want that.

So I came down and had an interview and went to work at North American. I had a friend and I had a room at her house in L.A. My daughter stayed in Mojave with my sister until I could have her down here.

I started after just a day or two. I was very nervous. I had the impression that women were tough that worked in factories, and I was scared to death, hoping nobody would hit me. That was silly. But it didn't seem like nice people worked in factories. I don't know where I got that idea. So I was nervous about going. Because I had been so sheltered. I was a Caspar Milquetoast, I really was.

Anyway, I just went straight into the plant. You get your badge and someone takes you up to your department, introduces you to the supervision, sets you down to this little table where you're going to sit for all these hours. It was such a huge place and we were upstairs, not near any planes, of course, because it was just this little section where you did all the buffing of the tubes. But it was exciting. In spite of being nervous, it was exciting. Here I was, being a war worker.

The first day I worked at a machine that had like sandpaper on it. When the tubes are cut, they're rough and not smoothed off at the ends. So this is a wheel that goes around and you'd hold the tube up to it to try to smoothe it off. Morons could have done it, sitting there just buffing the tubing.

I was so excited about a job that I didn't really care. But when I got a chance to go into another department, I was delighted. I was hoping that I would be transferred because it was boring, but you didn't think much about that because you were so busy being so patriotic and doing something for your country.

They put me in the empennage department, which is the tail section of the plane, the B-25 bomber. We put the de-icer boot on the vertical and the horizontal stabilizers of the bomber. The men had been doing that and they weren't quite as neat as the women. So we were doing a better job. They just showed us what to do and we did it; it was quite a few little operations. They'd bring in the stabilizers, the horizontal ones, and we had to get a template to put on there—that was like a pattern—and fasten it on. Then we took a drill and drilled holes. When that was taken off, we got a notcher and we'd notch the holes. And then we'd get the boot— made of rubber—and we'd powder it, and then we'd place it on this horizontal stabilizer and use pins to hold it in. Then we'd take out each pin and put a screw in to hold it. Then we'd turn it over and do the other side. And it had to be real smooth. The purpose of the de-icer boot, the planes were going to the countries where ice would form, and from the cockpit they could press a button or something and it would make it expand and the ice would break and fall off because it was rubber.

This girl that came with me from the tube-bending department, she and I got real good at it. Seems like we had it mastered real fast. I think we were the first two in there, and then they kept bringing more girls in and we showed them. The men were thrilled to pieces to get away from that job because they didn't like it. They'd rather be putting the plane together than just standing there putting the boots on.

They were bringing in more girls to do this—because the bombers were really going out fast—and they needed a leadgirl. So they made me a leadgirl. I did have some special training because I had some paperwork to do. At that time Mr. Kindelberger was the president of North American, and his secretary, Bobby Waddell, gave a class on office procedures. It was given through the University of Southern California, and we went right on company time during the day into one of the offices. I think it was once a week for six weeks.

I went in April and this was about August. By that time, there was eighteen girls working in there and eight of them were Negro girls. There were men, too, because the rudders and all that went on right there in the department. After we finished the boots on the stabilizers, then the men put them on the tail sections of the plane. But I just supervised the women.

There was a leadman, a foreman, and an assistant foreman over me, but I had to see if the girls were working and get supplies to do the work and see if they got along. There was a girl from the South. I guess she had never been around Negroes and she didn't want to work near them. I told her I had four brothers out in the Pacific and they were all fighting at the same time, and why couldn't she stand in there and work next to someone no matter who they were? Kind of made me a little angry. Then another girl, she didn't like the perfume one of the girls was wearing. She'd put up a big fuss about that! So minor! But otherwise, they got along pretty good. They finally got over their little funny ways.

I had no problems with the black women. I got along fine with them. The only problem was when two of them got into a fight. The men in the department, the supervision, they're the ones that broke it up. It was a silly fight to begin with. I was terribly upset when I had to go in and be a witness. The union lawyer started throwing questions at me. I was so nervous! They put words in your mouth. By the time I got out of there, I went straight to the little girls' room and had a good cry. It just really shook me up, terribly. But because I was the leadgirl, I had to tell. I didn't like that part at all! . . .

Well, North American had to find me a house because I was a war worker—which they did. A brand new two-bedroom apartment here in Rodondo Beach for $46.50 a month. And my girlfriend, Gwen Thomas, lived in the single apartment downstairs, and we lived in the big one upstairs. She had two children and her husband was in the navy and, of course, gone all the time. My mother was to take care of the two children. . . .

My mother did the cooking and the housekeeping and looked after Barbara. So it was wonderful having her with me. She stayed with me until after I got married the second time. Coming home, mother always had dinner ready for us, and we'd just sit around and listen—we didn't have television, just radio. Sometimes we'd go to the show, or on Saturdays, we'd go into L.A. once in a while, look around. That's about it. And then we had company a lot because my brothers would sometimes come. And there was other friends who were in the service and would drop in once in a while unexpectedly. . . .

Later on, when they quit putting the de-icer boot on the bomber because it was going to a hot country and they didn't need it, then they gave me a choice. I could work on the line, which was putting things together, or I could be the general foreman's clerk. Naturally, I took that. I could stay clean, I could stay dressed. I could do the paperwork which I had been doing anyway, keeping track of each worker. I was right there in the same area. It was just elevated two steps, to like a little box thing. The general foreman sat up there and the foreman, and I had a little desk there looking down into the department.

When a new-start came in, I'd go to the front office and pick them up and bring them back and introduce them to the supervision and show them where to get the tools. And when someone terminated, I'd take them out. And then I got supplies for the department, even for the men. I'd keep a record on each employee and when they were entitled to a raise, I'd type it up for the general foreman. Things like that. I liked it. And I had a shop pass. I could roam around a little if I didn't have anything to do. By that time, I had a sister, two brothers, and a sister-in-law working in the plant.

I thought I would continue as long as I could. I hoped that I would. We didn't think they'd be making that many planes after the war and wouldn't need that many workers, but I'd been there so long and I was pretty sure that they still needed a clerk out in the plant. So I figured that I'd probably still have a job. If I hadn't married, I think I'd still be there. In fact, I did stay for a while until my husband came back. He was an officer in the Merchant Marine. We were married [in] April '45, and he left and he was gone until August. . . .

He was all ready to teach when the war started, but didn't have a chance to. When he came back, he applied at different schools and he was accepted at San Bernardino. I had to terminate—I hated to do it, but I had to. So we left my mother and my daughter in my house here and we went to San Bernardino and he worked there for a semester.

So at the end of the war, I wasn't thinking about working again. I was just thinking of being a wife and maybe a mother, future mother. I wanted another child, but I was happy to be a housewife. . . .

⚓ *E S S A Y S*

In the first essay, Robert Korstad of Duke University and Nelson Lichtenstein of the University of Virginia argue that in the 1940s the organization of thousands of black workers laid the basis for a union-led civil-rights movement whose dimensions approached that of the better known insurgency that so transformed race relations in the 1960s. They found that the formation of a black-led union at the Reynolds Tobacco Company in Winston-Salem, North Carolina, empowered the black community and transformed the politics of that southern city.

But this victory proved short-lived, for the company and its conservative allies used the bitterly anticommunist mood of the early postwar years to attack and destroy this union and the black freedom movement it had so energetically sustained.

White women defense workers also lost a good deal of what they had won during World War II, as Ruth Milkman of the University of California at Los Angeles makes clear in the second essay. While a wholesale purge of black male workers from heavy industry was unthinkable at the war's end, white women had neither an ideology nor an organization to defend their continued presence there. As managers sought to displace women from industrial employment, the United Auto Workers (UAW) offered little or no resistance.

Why was the unionization of black workers of such greater political explosiveness than that of white women? What role did ideology play in management's attitude toward these different groups of workers?

How Organized Black Workers Brought Civil Rights to the South

ROBERT KORSTAD and NELSON LICHTENSTEIN

Most historians would agree that the modern civil rights movement did not begin with the Supreme Court's decision in *Brown* v. *Board of Education*. Yet all too often the movement's history has been written as if events before the mid-1950s constituted a kind of prehistory, important only insofar as they laid the legal and political foundation for the spectacular advances that came later. Those were the "forgotten years of the Negro Revolution," wrote one historian; they were the "seed time of racial and legal metamorphosis," according to another. But such a periodization profoundly underestimates the tempo and misjudges the social dynamic of the freedom struggle.

The civil rights era began, dramatically and decisively, in the early 1940s when the social structure of black America took on an increasingly urban, proletarian character. A predominantly southern rural and small town population was soon transformed into one of the most urban of all major ethnic groups. More than two million blacks migrated to northern and western industrial areas during the 1940s, while another million moved from farm to city within the South. Northern black voters doubled their numbers between 1940 and 1948, and in the eleven states of the Old South black registration more than quadrupled, reaching over one million by 1952. Likewise, membership in the National Association for the Advancement of Colored People (NAACP) soared, growing from 50,000 in 355 branches in 1940 to almost 450,000 in 1,073 branches six years later.

The half million black workers who joined unions affiliated with the Congress of Industrial Organizations (CIO) were in the vanguard of efforts to transform race relations. The NAACP and the Urban League had become

Robert Korstad and Nelson Lichtenstein, "Opportunities Found and Lost: Labor, Radicals, and the Early Civil Rights Movement," *Journal of American History*, 75 (Dec. 1988), pp. 786–793, 799–806, 811.

more friendly toward labor in the depression era, but their legal and social work orientation had not prepared them to act effectively in the workplaces and working-class neighborhoods where black Americans fought their most decisive struggles of the late 1930s and 1940s. By the early forties it was commonplace for sympathetic observers to assert the centrality of mass unionization in the civil rights struggle. A Rosenwald Fund study concluded, not without misgivings, that "the characteristic movements among Negroes are now for the first time becoming proletarian"; while a *Crisis* reporter found the CIO a "lamp of democracy" throughout the old Confederate states. "The South has not known such a force since the historic Union Leagues in the great days of the Reconstruction era."

This movement gained much of its dynamic character from the relationship that arose between unionized blacks and the federal government and proved somewhat similar to the creative tension that linked the church-based civil rights movement and the state almost two decades later. In the 1950s the *Brown* decision legitimated much of the subsequent social struggle, but it remained essentially a dead letter until given political force by a growing protest movement. In like manner, the rise of industrial unions and the evolution of late New Deal labor legislation offered working-class blacks an economic and political standard by which they could legitimate their demands and stimulate a popular struggle. The "one man, one vote" policy implemented in thousands of National Labor Relations Board (NLRB) elections, the industrial "citizenship" that union contracts offered once-marginal elements of the working class, and the patriotic egalitarianism of the government's wartime propaganda—all generated a rights consciousness that gave working-class black militancy a moral justification in some ways as powerful as that evoked by the Baptist spirituality of Martin Luther King, Jr., a generation later. During the war the Fair Employment Practices Committee (FEPC) held little direct authority, but like the Civil Rights Commission of the late 1950s, it served to expose racist conditions and spur on black activism wherever it undertook its well-publicized investigations. And just as a disruptive and independent civil rights movement in the 1960s could pressure the federal government to enforce its own laws and move against local elites, so too did the mobilization of the black working class in the 1940s make civil rights an issue that could not be ignored by union officers, white executives, or government officials.

This essay explores . . . the workplace-oriented civil rights militancy that arose in the 1940s, in particular the unionization of predominantly black tobacco workers in Winston-Salem, North Carolina. The remarkable collective activism of these workers made Winston-Salem a center of black working-class activism in the upper South, but similar movements took root among newly organized workers in the cotton compress mills of Memphis, the tobacco factories of Richmond and Charleston, the auto plants of Detroit, the steel mills of Pittsburgh and Birmingham, the stockyards and farm equipment factories of Chicago and Louisville, and the shipyards of Baltimore and Oakland. . . .

Winston-Salem had been a center of tobacco processing since the 1880s, and the R. J. Reynolds Tobacco Company dominated the life of the city's eighty thousand citizens. By the 1940s whites held most of the higher paying machine-tending jobs, but blacks formed the majority of the work force, concentrated in the preparation departments where they cleaned, stemmed, and conditioned the tobacco. The jobs were physically demanding, the air was hot and dusty, and in departments with machinery, the noise was deafening. Most black workers made only a few cents above minimum wage, and benefits were few. Black women workers experienced frequent verbal and occasional sexual abuse. Reynolds maintained a determined opposition to trade unionism, and two unsuccessful American Federation of Labor (AFL) efforts to organize segregated locals had soured most black workers on trade unionism.

But in 1943 a CIO organizing effort succeeded. Led by the United Cannery, Agricultural, Packing and Allied Workers of America (UCA-PAWA), a new union drive championed black dignity and self-organization, employing several young black organizers who had gotten their start in the interracial Southern Tenant Farmers Union. Their discreet two-year organizing campaign made a dramatic breakthrough when black women in one of the stemmeries stopped work on June 17. A severe labor shortage, chronic wage grievances, and a recent speedup gave the women both the resources and the incentive to transform a departmental sit-down into a festive, plant-wide strike. The UCAPAWA quickly signed up about eight thousand black workers, organized a committee to negotiate with the company, and asked the NLRB to hold an election.

The effort to win union recognition at Reynolds sparked a spirited debate about who constituted the legitimate leadership of the black community in Winston-Salem. Midway through the campaign, six local black business and professional men—a college professor, an undertaker, a dentist, a store owner, and two ministers—dubbed "colored leaders" by the *Winston-Salem Journal*, wrote a long letter to the editor urging workers to reject the "followers of John L. Lewis and William Green" and to remain loyal to Reynolds. In the absence of any formal leadership, elected or otherwise, representatives of Winston-Salem's small black middle class had served as spokesmen, brokering with the white elite for small concessions in a tightly segregated society. The fight for collective bargaining, they argued, had to remain secondary to the more important goal of racial betterment, which could only be achieved by "good will, friendly understanding, and mutual respect and co-operation between the races." Partly because of their own vulnerability to economic pressure, such traditional black leaders judged unions, like other institutions, by their ability to deliver jobs and maintain a precarious racial equilibrium.

The union campaign at Reynolds transformed the expectations tobacco workers held of the old community leadership. Reynolds workers responded to calls for moderation from "college-trained people" with indignation. "Our leaders," complained Mabel Jessup, "always look clean and refreshed at the end of the hottest day, because they work in very pleasant environments. . . . All I ask of our leaders is that they obtain a job in one of the factories as a laborer and work two weeks. Then write what they think." W. L. Griffin felt betrayed. "I have attended church regularly for the past thirty years," he wrote, "and unity and co-operation have been taught and preached from the pulpits of the various Negro churches. Now that the laboring class of people are about to unite and co-operate on a wholesale scale for the purpose of collective bargaining, these same leaders seem to disagree with that which they have taught their people." Others rejected the influence of people who "have always told us what the white people want, but somehow or other are particularly silent on what we want." "We feel we are the leaders instead of you," asserted a group of union members.

Reynolds, the only major tobacco manufacturer in the country not under a union contract, followed tried and true methods to break the union. Management used lower-level supervisors to intimidate unionists and sup-ported a "no union" movement among white workers, whose organizers were given freedom to roam the company's workshops and warehouses. That group, the R. J. Reynolds Employees Association, sought a place on the NLRB ballot in order to delay the increasingly certain CIO victory. Meanwhile, the white business community organized an Emergency Citi-zens Committee to help defeat the CIO. In a well-publicized resolution, the committee blamed the recent strikes on "self-seeking representatives of the CIO" and warned that continued subversion of existing race relations would "likely lead to riots and bloodshed."

In earlier times, this combination of anti-union forces would probably have derailed the organizing effort. But during World War II, black workers had allies who helped shift the balance of power. The NLRB closely su-pervised each stage of the election process and denied the company's request to divide the work force into two bargaining units, which would have weakened the position of black workers. When local judges sought to delay the election, government attorneys removed the case to federal court. In December 1943 an NLRB election gave the CIO a resounding victory. But continued federal assistance, from the United States Concil-iation Service and the National War Labor Board, was still needed to secure Reynolds workers a union contract in 1944.

That first agreement resembled hundreds of other wartime labor-man-agement contracts, but in the context of Winston-Salem's traditional system of race relations it had radical implications, because it generated a new set of shop floor rights embodied in the seniority, grievance, and wage ad-justment procedures. The contract did not attack factory segregation—for the most part white workers continued to control the better-paying jobs— but it did call forth a new corps of black leaders to defend the rights Reynolds workers had recently won. The one hundred or so elected shop stewards were the "most important people in the plant," remembered union activist Velma Hopkins. They were the "natural leaders," people who had "taken up money for flowers if someone died or would talk to the foreman [even] before the union." Now the union structure reinforced the capa-bilities of such workers: "We had training classes for the shop stewards:

What to do, how to do it. We went over the contract thoroughly." The shop stewards transformed the traditional paternalism of Reynolds management into an explicit system of benefits and responsibilities. They made the collective bargaining agreement a bill of rights.

The growing self-confidence of black women, who constituted roughly half of the total work force, proved particularly subversive of existing social relations. To the white men who ran the Reynolds plants, nothing could have been more disturbing than the demand that they negotiate on a basis of equality with people whom they regarded as deeply inferior—by virtue of their sex as well as their class and race. When union leaders like Theodosia Simpson, Velma Hopkins, and Moranda Smith sat down at the bargaining table with company executives, social stereotypes naturally came under assault, but the challenge proved equally dramatic on the shop floor. For example, Ruby Jones, the daughter of a railway fireman, became one of the most outspoken shop stewards. Perplexed by her newfound aggressiveness, a foreman demanded, "Ruby, what do you want?" "I want your respect," she replied, "that's all I ask."

By the summer of 1944, Local 22 of the reorganized and renamed Food, Tobacco, Agricultural and Allied Workers (FTA) had become the center of an alternative social world that linked black workers together regardless of job, neighborhood, or church affiliation. The union hall, only a few blocks from the Reynolds Building, housed a constant round of meetings, plays, and musical entertainments, as well as classes in labor history, black history, and current events. Local 22 sponsored softball teams, checker tournaments, sewing circles, and swimming clubs. Its vigorous educational program and well-stocked library introduced many black workers (and a few whites) to a larger radical culture few had glimpsed before. "You know, at that little library they [the city of Winston-Salem] had for us, you couldn't find any books on Negro history," remembered Viola Brown. "They didn't have books by Aptheker, Dubois, or Frederick Douglass. But we had them at *our* library."

The Communist party was the key political grouping in FTA and in Local 22. FTA president Donald Henderson had long been associated with the party, and many organizers who passed through Winston-Salem shared his political sympathies. By 1947 party organizers had recruited about 150 Winston-Salem blacks, almost all tobacco workers. Most of these workers saw the party as both a militant civil rights organization, which in the 1930s had defended such black victims of white southern racism as the Scottsboro boys and Angelo Hearndon, and as a cosmopolitan group, introducing members to the larger world of politics and ideas. The white North Carolina Communist leader Junius Scales recalled that the "top leaders [of Local 22] . . . just soaked up all the educational efforts that were directed at them. The Party's program had an explanation of events locally, nationally, and worldwide which substantiated everything they had felt instinctively. . . . It really meant business on racism." The party was an integrated institution in which the social conventions of the segregated South were self-consciously violated, but it also accommodated itself to the culture of the black community. In Winston-Salem, therefore, the party met regularly in a black church and started the meetings with a hymn and a prayer.

The Communist party's relative success in Winston-Salem was replicated in other black industrial districts. In the South a clear majority of the party's new recruits were black, and in northern states like Illinois and Michigan the proportion ranged from 25 to 40 percent. The party's relative success among American blacks was not based on its programmatic consistency: during the late 1940s the NAACP and other critics pointed out that the wartime party had denounced civil rights struggles when they challenged the Roosevelt administration or its conduct of the war effort, but that the party grew more militant once Soviet-American relations cooled. However, the party never abandoned its assault on Jim Crow and unlike the NAACP, which directed much of its energy toward the courts and Congress, the Communists or their front groups more often organized around social or political issues subject to locally initiated protests, petitions, and pickets. Moreover, the party adopted what today would be called an affirmative action policy that recognized the special disabilities under which black workers functioned, in the party as well as in the larger community. Although there were elements of tokenism and manipulation in the implementation of that policy, the party's unique effort to develop black leaders gave the Communists a special standing among politically active blacks.

Tobacco industry trade unionism revitalized black political activism in Winston-Salem. Until the coming of the CIO, NAACP attacks on racial discrimination seemed radical, and few blacks risked associating with the organization. A 1942 membership drive did increase branch size from 11 to 100, but most new members came from the traditional black middle class: mainly teachers and municipal bus drivers. The Winston-Salem NAACP became a mass organization only after Local 22 conducted its own campaign for the city branch. As tobacco workers poured in, the local NAACP reached a membership of 1,991 by 1946, making it the largest unit in North Carolina.

Unionists also attacked the policies that had disenfranchised Winston-Salem blacks for more than two generations. As part of the CIO Political Action Committee's voter registration and mobilization drive, Local 22 inaugurated citizenship classes, political rallies, and citywide mass meetings. Union activists challenged the power of registrars to judge the qualifications of black applicants and insisted that black veterans vote without further tests. The activists encouraged the city's blacks to participate in electoral politics. "Politics IS food, clothes, and housing," declared the committee that registered some seven hundred new black voters in the months before the 1944 elections. After a visit to Winston-Salem in 1944, a *Pittsburgh Courier* correspondent wrote, "I was aware of a growing solidarity and intelligent mass action that will mean the dawn of a New Day in the South. One cannot visit Winston-Salem and mingle with the thousands of workers without sensing a revolution in thought and action.

If there is a 'New' Negro, he is to be found in the ranks of the labor movement.''

Organization and political power gave the black community greater leverage at city hall and at the county courthouse. NAACP and union officials regularly took part in municipal government debate on social services for the black community, minority representation on the police and fire departments, and low-cost public housing. In 1944 and 1946 newly enfranchised blacks helped reelect Congressman John Folger, a New Deal supporter, against strong conservative opposition. In 1947, after black registration had increased some tenfold in the previous three years, a minister, Kenneth Williams, won a seat on the Board of Aldermen, becoming the first black city official in the twentieth-century South to be elected against a white opponent. . . .

By the mid-1940s, civil rights issues had reached a level of national political salience that they would not regain for another fifteen years. Once the domain of Afro-American protest groups, leftist clergymen, and Communist-led unions and front organizations, civil rights advocacy was becoming a defining characteristic of urban liberalism. Thus ten states established fair employment practice commissions between 1945 and 1950, and four major cities—Chicago, Milwaukee, Minneapolis, and Philadelphia—enacted tough laws against job bias. Backed by the CIO, the Americans for Democratic Action spearheaded a successful effort to strengthen the Democratic party's civil rights plank at the 1948 convention.

In the South the labor movement seemed on the verge of a major breakthrough. *Fortune* magazine predicted that the CIO's ''Operation Dixie'' would soon organize key southern industries like textiles. Black workers proved exceptionally responsive to such union campaigns, especially in industries like lumber, furniture, and tobacco, where they were sometimes a majority of the work force. Between 1944 and 1946 the CIO's political action apparatus helped elect liberal congressmen and senators in a few southern states, while organizations that promoted interracial cooperation, such as the Southern Conference for Human Welfare and Highlander Folk School, experienced their most rapid growth and greatest effectiveness in 1946 and 1947.

The opportune moment soon passed. Thereafter, a decade-long decline in working-class black activism destroyed the organizational coherence and ideological élan of the labor-based civil rights movement. That defeat has been largely obscured by the brilliant legal victories won by civil rights lawyers in the 1940s and 1950s, and by the reemergence of a new mass movement in the next decade. But in Winston-Salem, Detroit, and other industrial regions, the time had passed when unionized black labor was in the vanguard of the freedom struggle. Three elements contributed to the decline. First, the employer offensive of the late 1940s put all labor on the defensive. Conservatives used the Communist issue to attack New Deal and Fair Deal reforms, a strategy that isolated Communist-oriented black leaders and helped destroy what was left of the Popular Front. The employers' campaign proved particularly effective against many recently organized CIO locals with disproportionate numbers of black members. Meanwhile, mechanization and decentralization of the most labor intensive and heavily black production facilities sapped the self-confidence of the black working class and contributed to high rates of urban unemployment in the years after the Korean War.

Second, the most characteristic institutions of American liberalism, including the unions, race advancement organizations, and liberal advocacy organizations, adopted a legal-administrative, if not a bureaucratic, approach to winning citizenship rights for blacks. The major legislative goal of the union-backed Leadership Conference on Civil Rights in the 1950s was revision of Senate Rule 22, to limit the use of the filibuster that had long blocked passage of a national FEPC and other civil rights legislation. The UAW and other big unions cooperated with the NAACP in the effort, but the work was slow and frustrating and the struggle far removed from the shop floor or the drugstore lunch counter.

Finally, the routinization of the postwar industrial relations system precluded efforts by black workers to mobilize a constituency independent of the leadership. Focusing on incremental collective bargaining gains and committed to social change only if it was well controlled, the big unions became less responsive to the particular interests of their black members. By 1960 blacks had formed oppositional movements in several old CIO unions, but they now encountered resistance to their demands not only from much of the white rank and file but also from union leaders who presided over institutions that had accommodated themselves to much of the industrial status quo. . . .

Like most labor intensive southern employers, R. J. Reynolds never reached an accommodation with union labor, although it signed contracts with Local 22 in 1945 and 1946. Minimum wage laws and collective bargaining agreements had greatly increased costs of production, especially in the stemmeries, and the black women employed there were the heart and soul of the union. Soon after the war, the company began a mechanization campaign that eliminated several predominantly black departments. When the factories closed for Christmas in 1945 new stemming machines installed in one plant displaced over seven hundred black women. The union proposed a "share the work plan," but the company was determined to cut its work force and change its racial composition by recruiting white workers from surrounding counties. The black proportion of the manufacturing labor force in Winston-Salem dropped from 44 to 36 percent between 1940 and 1960.

The technological offensive undermined union strength, but by itself Reynolds could not destroy Local 22. When contract negotiations began in 1947, the company rejected union demands for a wage increase patterned after those won in steel, auto, and rubber earlier in the spring. Somewhat reluctantly, Local 22 called a strike on May 1. Black workers and virtually all of the Negro community solidly backed the union, which held out for thirty-eight days until a compromise settlement was reached. But, in a pattern replicated throughout industrial America in those years, Communist influence within the union became the key issue around which management and its allies mounted their attack. The *Winston-Salem Journal* soon denounced Local 22 as "captured . . . lock, stock and barrel" by the Communist party, warning readers that the strike would lead to "open rioting." This exposé brought Local 22 officers under the scrutiny of the House Committee on Un-American Activities (HUAC), which held a highly publicized hearing on the Winston-Salem situation in the summer of 1947.

Communist party members contributed to the volatility of the situation. In the late 1940s, Local 22 found itself politically vulnerable when foreign policy resolutions passed by the shop stewards' council followed Communist party pronouncements. The party's insistence on the promotion of blacks into public leadership positions sometimes put workers with little formal education into union leadership jobs they could not handle. Moreover, the party's obsession with "white chauvinism" backfired. After the 1947 strike, Local 22 made a concerted effort to recruit white workers. Some young veterans joined the local, although the union allowed most to pay their dues secretly. The party objected, remembered North Carolina leader Junius Scales, " 'If they got any guts,' they would say, 'let them stand up and fight,' not realizing, as many black workers and union leaders realized, that for a white worker to just *belong* to a predominantly black union at that time was an act of great courage."

With its work force increasingly polarized along racial and political lines, Reynolds renewed its offensive in the spring of 1948. Black workers remained remarkably loyal to the union leadership, but the anticommunist campaign had turned most white employees against the union and eroded support among blacks not directly involved in the conflict. The company refused to negotiate with Local 22 on the grounds that the union had not complied with the new Taft-Hartley Act. The law required union officers to sign an affidavit swearing they were not members of the Communist party before a union could be certified as a bargaining agent by the NLRB. Initially, all the CIO internationals had refused to sign the affidavits, but by 1948 only Communist-oriented unions such as FTA still held out. When Reynolds proved intransigent, there was little the union could do. FTA had no standing with the NLRB, and it was too weak to win another strike.

At the same time, Local 22 began to feel repercussions from the conflict within the CIO over the status of unions, like the FTA, that had rejected the Marshall Plan and endorsed Henry Wallace's Progressive party presidential campaign in 1948. A rival CIO union, the United Transport Service Employees (UTSE), sent organizers into Winston-Salem to persuade black workers to abandon Local 22. In a March 1950 NLRB election, which the FTA requested after complying with the Taft-Hartley Act, UTSE joined Local 22 on the ballot. The FTA local retained solid support among its black constituency, who faithfully paid dues to their stewards even after the contract had expired and in the face of condemnation of their union—from the company, the CIO, and HUAC. Even the black community leader Alderman Williams asked workers to vote against the union and "send the Communists away for good." Yet Local 22 captured a plurality of all the votes cast, and in a runoff two weeks later it won outright. But when the NLRB accepted the ballots of lower-level white supervisors, the scales again tipped against the local.

Local 22 disappeared from Winston-Salem's political and economic life, and a far more accommodative black community leadership filled the void left by the union's defeat. Beginning in the mid-1940s, a coalition of middle-class blacks and white business moderates had sought to counter the growing union influence within the black community. They requested a study of local race relations by the National Urban League's Community Relations Project (CRP). Largely financed by Hanes Hosiery president James G. Hanes, the CRP study appeared in late 1947 and called for improved health, education and recreational facilities, but it made no mention of workplace issues. The Urban League foresaw a cautious, "step by step approach" and proposed that an advisory committee drawn from the black middle class discuss community issues with their white counterparts and help city officials and white philanthropists channel welfare services to the black community. The *Winston-Salem Journal* called the CRP's recommendations a "blueprint for better community relations" but one that would not alter "the framework of race relations."

The Urban League's program helped make Winston-Salem a model of racial moderation. Blacks continued to register and vote in relatively high numbers and to elect a single black alderman. The city high school was integrated without incident in 1957, while Winston-Salem desegregated its libraries, golf course, coliseum, and the police and fire departments. But the dynamic and democratic quality of the black struggle in Winston-Salem would never be recaptured. NAACP membership declined to less than five hundred in the early 1950s, and decision making once again moved behind closed doors. When a grievance arose from the black community, a group of ministers met quietly with Hanes; a few phone calls by the white industrialist led to desegregation of the privately owned bus company in 1958.

A similar story unfolded in the plants of the R. J. Reynolds Tobacco Company. After the destruction of Local 22, the company blacklisted several leading union activists, yet Reynolds continued to abide by many of the wage standards, benefit provisions, and seniority policies negotiated during the union era. The company reorganized its personnel department; rationalized procedures for hiring, firing, and evaluating employees; and upgraded its supervisory force by weeding out old-timers and replacing them with college-educated foremen. To forestall union activity, Reynolds kept its wages slightly ahead of the rates paid by its unionized competitors.

In February 1960, when sit-ins began at segregated Winston-Salem lunch counters, the voices of black protest were again heard in the city's streets. But the generation of blacks who had sustained Local 22 played little role in the new mobilization. College and high school students predominated on the picket lines and in the new protest organizations that confronted white paternalism and challenged the black community's ministerial leadership. NAACP membership rose once again; more radical blacks organized a chapter of the Congress of Racial Equality (CORE). Public segregation soon collapsed.

The subsequent trajectory of the freedom struggle in Winston-Salem was typical of that in many black communities. Heightened racial tensions set the stage for a 1967 riot and a burst of radicalism, followed by the demobilization of the protest movement and years of trench warfare in the city council. The political career of Larry Little, the son of Reynolds workers who had been members of Local 22, highlighted the contrasts between the two generations of black activists. Little moved from leadership of the North Carolina Black Panther party in 1969 to city alderman in 1977, but despite the radicalism of his rhetoric, crucial issues of economic security and workplace democracy were not restored to the political agenda in Winston-Salem. Because black activists of his generation confronted the city's white elite without the organized backing of a lively, mass institution like Local 22, their challenge proved more episodic and less effective than that of the previous generation. . . .

E. P. Thompson once asserted that most social movements have a life cycle of about six years. And unless they make a decisive political impact in that time, that "window of opportunity," they will have little effect on the larger political structures they hope to transform. For the black freedom struggle the mid-1940s offered such a time of opportunity, when a high-wage, high-employment economy, rapid unionization, and a pervasive federal presence gave the black working class remarkable self-confidence, which established the framework for the growth of an autonomous labor-oriented civil rights movement. The narrowing of public discourse in the early Cold War era contributed largely to the defeat and diffusion of that movement. The rise of anticommunism shattered the Popular Front coalition on civil rights, while the retreat and containment of the union movement deprived black activists of the political and social space necessary to carry on an independent struggle.

The disintegration of the black movement in the late 1940s ensured that when the civil rights struggle of the 1960s emerged it would have a different social character and an alternative political agenda, which eventually proved inadequate to the immense social problems that lay before it. Like the movement of the 1940s, the protests of the 1960s mobilized a black community that was overwhelmingly working-class. However, the key institutions of the new movement were not the trade unions, but the black church and independent protest organizations. Its community orientation and stirring championship of democratic values gave the modern civil rights movement a transcendent moral power that enabled a handful of organizers from groups like the Student Nonviolent Coordinating Committee, SCLC, and CORE to mobilize tens of thousands of Americans in a series of dramatic and crucial struggles. Yet even as this Second Reconstruction abolished legal segregation and discrimination, many movement activists, including Martin Luther King, Jr., recognized the limits of their accomplishment. After 1965 they sought to raise issues of economic equality and working-class empowerment to the moral high ground earlier occupied by the assault against de jure segregation. In retrospect, we can see how greatly they were handicapped by their inability to seize the opportunities a very different sort of civil rights movement found and lost twenty years before.

How Women Were Purged from the War Plants

RUTH MILKMAN

One of the most important questions facing historians of American women involves the defeminization of basic industry at the end of the Second World War. The economic mobilization for war dramatized the possibility of employing women in "men's jobs" on an unprecedented scale and seemed to throw into question the sexual division of paid labor as a whole. Yet, in the course of postwar reconversion, women were systematically purged from their wartime jobs, and the prewar sexual division of labor in manufacturing was effectively reconstructed. The automobile industry is a prominent case in point. At the peak of wartime employment, women workers comprised over one-fourth of the labor force in auto; by September 1945, a month after V-J Day, the female share of employment in the industry had dropped below 10 percent, where it would remain for many years to come.

The question, of course, is why women were not retained in the postwar years, despite the success with which they were integrated into the production workforce of industries like auto during the war. This is ultimately a specific—and extreme—version of a more general problem, namely, why the sexual division of labor, as it has developed historically within and between industries, has been so resistant to change. Although this is by no means a new problem, in the period since the war it has become increasingly urgent. Despite the rapid growth of female labor force participation over the postwar decades and despite the fact that the resurgence of feminism has undermined the legitimacy of sex discrimination in the labor market, occupational segregation by sex and the wage inequality that accompanies it have remained largely intact. . . .

Recent research has greatly deepened historians' understanding of the complex relationship between women and industrial unions in the 1940s. However, it does not adequately explain the exclusion of women from the postwar auto industry. And, because it focuses primarily on the role of the union, this body of scholarship is ultimately quite misleading. Although it is true that the UAW colluded with management and that effective union resistance to the policy of purging women from the postwar workforce might have altered the situation, to understand why the postwar sexual division of labor in auto took the form it did, one must look to *management*

Ruth Milkman, "Rosie the Riveter Revisited: Management's Postwar Purge of Women Automobile Workers" in Nelson Lichtenstein and Stephen Meyer, *On the Line: Essays in the History of Auto Work* (Univ. of Illinois Press, 1989), pp. 129–130, 132–141, 143–147.

first and foremost. Indeed, the central question remains: Why was management so intent on excluding women from postwar employment in the first place? During the war, women auto workers won enormous praise for their performance from all sides. Why should employers have been so reluctant to retain them in the postwar? Given the historical "cheapness" of female labor, management's postwar policy seems especially paradoxical. . . .

The historic structure of the industry and the character of its labor process proved the most important reason female substitution was not an attractive option for automotive management in the immediate postwar period. The Fordist revolution, which organized mass production around the moving assembly line, laid the basis for automobile manufacturing to develop as a high-wage, capital-intensive industry; thus, employers had little incentive to substitute female labor for its more expensive male equivalent. Despite the fact that the obstacles to substitution were minimal in the early days—auto was a rapidly expanding and completely new industry with no tradition of union organization and no history of sex-stereotyped jobs—management showed negligible interest in employing women workers.

Because they have historically been performed by men, production jobs in the auto industry are frequently described as "heavy," completely reversing the actual line of causality. In fact, however, the need for workers capable of great physical exertion was eliminated early in the history of the industry, given mechanization and streamlined organization of production. . . . [In] a 1924 essay on the auto industry Charles Reitell observed that

> quickly—overnight as it were—the machine, gigantic, complex and intricate, has removed the need of muscle and brawn. As Frederick W. Taylor put it, "The gorilla types are no more needed." Instead we have a greater demand for nervous and mental activities such as watchfulness, quick judgements, dexterity, guidance, ability and lastly a nervous endurance to carry through dull, monotonous, fatiguing rhythmic operations.

These were precisely the characteristics of manufacturing jobs commonly thought to be most appropriate for women workers in the early part of the century, according to the prevailing stereotypes. So one might have expected management, ever eager to maximize profits, to have had an enormous incentive to utilize the ample supplies of "cheap labor" available in the female population in this period. However, this did not occur. Women remained a tiny minority of the auto manufacturing labor force throughout the pre–World War II period. They were employed mostly in parts plants and in the "cut-and-sew" (upholstery) departments of body plants. Although occasionally women were substituted for men, and at lower pay, management's apparent disinterest in any serious effort at large-scale feminization is far more striking. . . .

Most women employed in auto manufacturing were engaged in the production of auto parts. Unlike the rest of the auto industry, parts manufacturing had many characteristics of the secondary sector of the economy. Machine pacing was used far less extensively, and piece rates—the standard form of wage payment in the heavily female "sweated" manufacturing industries of the day—remained the predominant form of wage payment as late as 1950. The auto parts industry was also relatively competitive, with some notorious sweatshop operations like Briggs, where women's labor was used quite extensively and wage rates were reported to be as low as 4 cents per hour in the 1930s. But this was atypical. In the major auto firms, the predominant policy was to pay high wages in exchange for subordination to the machine-paced organization of production. In fact, . . . even the five-dollar day was an economy. The combination of dramatically lowered turnover rates and the extra production extracted by means of the speed-up meant Ford workers produced more per dollar of wages after the implementation of the five-dollar day than before. Ford himself justifiably called it "one of the finest cost-cutting moves we ever made."

That classic comment captures the essence of management strategy at Ford, a model for the auto industry generally. There was no incentive to seek supplies of cheap female labor in this situation. On the contrary, Ford, and the other auto firms as well, were in a position to offer their predominantly male workforce pay rates approximating a "family wage," an ideal with great resonance in the early twentieth-century working-class community. In his 1924 autobiography, Ford explicitly embraced the concept:

> If only the man himself were concerned, the cost of his maintenance and the profit [sic] he ought to have would be a simple matter. But he is not just an individual. He is a citizen, contributing to the welfare of the nation. He is a householder. He is perhaps a father with children who must be reared to usefulness on what he is able to earn. . . . The man does the work in the shop, but his wife does the work in the home. The shop must pay them both. . . . Otherwise, we have the hideous prospect of little children and their mothers being forced out to work.

. . . Once the auto industry's basic pattern of employment by sex had been established, with men in the vast majority of jobs and women concentrated in small parts production and in cut-and-sew operations, the sexual division of labor proved extraordinarily stable. . . . In day-to-day managerial practice, the established system of sex labeling guided decisions as to whether to hire a male or female in each job opening. Thus, auto employers—and auto workers as well—came to view certain jobs as quintessentially male and others, a far more limited group, as suitable for women. Neither the 1921 recession, the Great Depression, nor the rise of industrial unionism significantly altered the sexual division of labor in auto; it remained unchanged throughout the prewar era.

Even during World War II, employers were initially quite resistant to the idea of hiring women for war jobs in auto plants. They did so only when military conscription had exhausted the supply of male labor in an era of rapidly increasing war production. The federal government intervened in 1942, setting male employment ceilings and giving the War Manpower

Commission the power to enforce them. The results were quite dramatic: the proportion of women employed in the auto industry swelled from only 5 percent just before Pearl Harbor to 25 percent two years later.

Once it became clear that there was no alternative, managerial attitudes about the employment of women in production jobs also seemed to shift dramatically. As early as June 1942, George Romney, then head of the Automotive Council for War Production, reported to a meeting of automotive managers and government planners on wartime labor supply problems that "the consciousness of the capability of women is growing all through the [auto] industry." . . . During the war, numerous testimonials from management conceded that women's production record exceeded that of men on the same or similar jobs. For example, women hired to do "men's jobs" at the four largest plants of the Ford Motor Company "job for job . . . outproduced the men in most cases," according to a 1943 report.

Despite this general enthusiasm for the performance of women war workers, wage differentials between the sexes did not disappear during the war years—a consideration one might expect, given the glowing praise for the performance of women war workers, to have generated some management interest in retaining women permanently in the kinds of jobs they held during the war emergency. The UAW, to be sure, contested wage discrimination, rather successfully, in a series of "equal pay for equal work" cases before the War Labor Board. Although sex differentials in pay in the auto industry were narrowed considerably following these struggles, they were not fully eliminated. In August 1944, women's average straight-time hourly wage in Michigan's auto plants was 90 percent of the male average. . . .

[In] the aftermath of the war, just as in the early development of the industry, automotive employers ignored the opportunity to feminize the workforce. Indeed, in the massive layoffs immediately following the end of the war, women were thrown out of work at a rate nearly double that for men in the manufacturing sector as a whole. The disparity was even greater in auto and other "heavy" industries that had employed very few women in the prewar period. In the month following V-J Day, there was a precipitous drop in women's share of the automotive workforce, from 18 percent in August 1945 to 10 percent in September. The dramatic wartime employment gains of women in the industry were thus rolled back even more rapidly than they had been made. As postwar hiring resumed, it became clear that auto would once again rely on an overwhelmingly male labor force. Wage levels remained high, even increasing during the postwar years. As in the prewar era, management's efforts to boost productivity focused on tightening control over labor, not on reducing pay levels. Management continued to nourish the basic conviction, historically rooted in the logic of Fordism—as operative in the postwar situation as in the prewar—that women were simply not suitable for employment in automotive production jobs. Employers saw the successful performance of women war workers as, at best, a fortunate outcome of an experiment in which they had participated with great trepidation and only because there had been no alternative. Women had performed better than anyone had expected during the war, true enough, but now the emergency was over, and men's jobs were men's jobs once again. . . .

Studies of the impact of the postwar transition on women auto workers have focused primarily on the issue of women's seniority rights and the role of the UAW. . . .

The starting point is the observation that women's departure from the automotive labor force, contrary to popular belief at the time, was not voluntary. In fact, the overwhelming majority of women working in the industry during the war intended not only to continue working after the war but to stay in the same type of work. Eighty-five percent of the women war workers responding to a 1944 UAW survey wanted to remain in the labor force after the war, and almost all of them preferred to continue doing factory work. . . . The same employment preferences persisted in the immediate aftermath of the war. In July 1946, the Detroit office of the U.S. Employment Service had nearly twice as many applications on file for semiskilled and unskilled manufacturing jobs from women as from returning male veterans, but the applicants for clerical and service work included a higher proportion of veterans than of women. . . .

This situation presented the UAW with a serious dilemma. After the war ended, the full employment economy, the crucial precondition for female incorporation into "men's jobs" in industry in the first place, could no longer be sustained. As a result, women war workers now directly competed for jobs with their male counterparts—a problem intensified by the influx of large numbers of returning veterans into the industrial labor force. Moreover, fear of a return to the high unemployment levels of the depression years after the war was widespread, especially among workers in durable goods industries like auto, always particularly sensitive to cyclical economic changes. This situation naturally produced considerable hostility toward women.

In the late 1930s, the fledgling UAW had fought long and hard for the establishment of seniority systems to distribute employment equitably in just such situations as this. During the war, it was already obvious that postwar demobilization would bring the first real test of the seniority principle. At the same time, the UAW's commitment to eliminate all forms of discrimination provided an opening for women union activists to work toward the equalization of seniority rights. They pursued this goal energetically and relatively successfully. By the end of the war, the UAW's official policy stance was that women should enjoy the same seniority rights as men. Locals were urged to eliminate separate women's seniority lists and other sex-discriminatory contract provisions, and many did so.

However, in the absence of full employment, the principle of seniority, even if properly enforced, had mixed implications for women war workers. Because their employment gains were so recent, concentrated in the three-year period of war production, the "last hired, first fired" principle embedded in the seniority system meant women would be laid off in disproportionate numbers. Indeed, this is the basis for the argument *against* strict seniority systems advanced in recent years by advocates of affirmative action for women and other industrial minorities; however, this view did not enjoy much credibility in the 1940s. Female union activists concerned about women's postwar employment pressed not for preferential treatment for women, but simply for the enforcement of the limited seniority rights women war workers already had.

But preferential treatment was widely advocated for one group of workers: returning veterans. Popular appreciation of the hardships of military service thoroughly legitimized the idea that veterans should not be further penalized for their absence from the labor market during the war, and UAW contracts granted seniority equal to the time spent in military service to veterans previously employed by an auto company as well as to those newly hired after their military discharge. At the same time, the union, wary of the potential division between veterans and other workers, strongly opposed so-called super-seniority rights for veterans, which would have given them preferential status over virtually all other workers. To this extent, the UAW's official policy unambiguously protected women's seniority rights, limited as they were.

Official union policies were one thing, but their enforcement was another matter altogether . . . There was tremendous ambivalence about women's rights to postwar jobs in industry on the part of both UAW leaders and the rank-and-file, despite the union's formal opposition to sex discrimination. Internal battles over women's seniority rights raged within the UAW, and all too often the union's practice was inconsistent with its official policy. Separate women's seniority lists remained in effect at the war's end in some locals, although in many others women activists had succeeded in eliminating them during the war. There were other blatantly discriminatory arrangements as well. The national General Motors contract, for example, provided that women employed on "men's jobs" during the war would accumulate temporary seniority, applicable "for the duration only."

In many plants, women did have equal seniority rights according to the contract, and the main problem was lack of enforcement. . . .

> In our plant, and I guess it is the same in most plants, we have women laid off with seniority . . . and every day they hire in new men off the street. They hire men there, they say, to do the heavy work. The women do light work. During the war they didn't care what kind of work we did, and still we have to work on hard jobs now, and some of the men with lesser seniority get the small jobs.

Explicit job classification by sex was still prevalent at this time; thus, management had only to reclassify jobs in the course of postwar reconversion—from female to male, or from light to heavy—in order to justify not recalling women. Protective legislation, temporarily eased during the war, now became another mechanism by which jobs that women had performed quite adequately during the war, and wanted to keep, were reclassified as "men's jobs." . . .

It is indisputable that the seniority system was stacked against women, even where nominally nondiscriminatory, and that women war workers' seniority rights, limited as they were, were honored more in the breach than in the observance. However, the seniority system and the UAW's failure to protect women's limited job rights still do not *explain* the virtual absence of women in the postwar auto labor force because this line of argument ignores management's crucial role in shaping the postwar sexual division of labor. Far more important than the seniority system, properly enforced or not, in determining the composition of the future labor force in auto was *hiring policy*. Here, managerial control was virtually complete. So many new workers were hired in the industry after the war that the seniority lists were of marginal significance. Contrary to general expectations, the postwar years saw enormous expansion in the auto industry, after a relatively brief interlude of reconversion unemployment. The postwar boom was based on a vast consumer demand for automobiles, as a result of both the unavailability of cars during the war and the general prosperity of the period. By 1947, the number of production workers in the nation's auto factories already exceeded that at the peak of war employment. . . .

Perhaps the most convincing way to demonstrate that women's low seniority standing was not the cause of their poor postwar representation among auto workers is to compare the impact of reconversion on women with that on black workers in the industry. Like women, black workers as a group had relatively low seniority standing at the conclusion of the war. They, too, had first entered the auto industry in large numbers during the war mobilization period. The proportion of blacks in Detroit's automotive plants rose from 5.5 percent in May 1942 to 15 percent by the spring of 1945. Black workers gained access to semiskilled auto jobs on a significant scale for the first time during the war years, in a process paralleling the expansion in the number of jobs open to women.

The experiences of these two groups, so similar during the war, diverged sharply with reconversion to consumer automobile production. While women were ousted from their new positions in the industry at the end of the war, and in most cases not recalled, blacks were more fortunate. "Once the painful transition to peacetime was over," [historians] August Meier and Elliott Rudwick conclude, "blacks found that they retained the foothold in semiskilled machine production and assembly-line work which they had won during the war." Data on black employment in individual auto firms confirm this. The proportion of blacks in Chrysler's production workforce actually rose just after the war, from 15 percent in 1945 to 17 percent in 1946, in stark contrast to the "exodus" of women from the industry. By 1960, blacks were 26 percent of the labor force in Chrysler's Detroit plants and 23 percent of GM's production workforce in that city. Ford, the one auto manufacturer that had employed blacks in significant numbers before the war, also increased its black employment in the postwar years; by 1960 blacks comprised over 40 percent of the production workforce at the huge River Rouge plant.

This divergence between the experience of women and blacks can only be understood in the context of management's hiring policies. The female proportion of the workforce might have been marginally greater in the postwar years if the UAW had more effectively defended women's seniority rights. But given the high turnover rates for all auto workers and the vast postwar expansion of the industry, even if the UAW had secured the reinstatement of every woman war worker, there would still have been a sharp decline in female representation in the industry's labor force, unless additional women were added as well. Only an insistence on sex-blind hiring policy—which the UAW had no means to enforce—could have substantially altered the situation.

But why was postwar hiring policy different for blacks vis-à-vis women? In the prewar period, management's lack of interest in hiring blacks—like women, a source of "cheap labor"—for auto production jobs had the same basis as its disinterest in feminization. Both were by-products of the industry's general program of labor discipline, to which high wages were central. And, again paralleling the case of women, racial stereotypes rationalized and legitimized racially exclusive hiring. Yet, by the late 1940s, at least in the North, race discrimination had already lost much of its former legitimacy. A large and vital civil rights movement enjoyed substantial UAW support, and management might have expected vigorous protests if it pursued racially discriminatory employment policies.

When blacks were first hired in large numbers in Detroit's auto factories during the period of economic mobilization, there had been considerable opposition among white workers, most dramatically expressed in the numerous "hate strikes" which erupted in the plants and in the "race riot" of the summer of 1943. But by the end of the war, there was no longer any legitimate basis for excluding blacks from postwar jobs in the Detroit auto industry. During the war, Detroit had become a major center of the civil rights movement. The Motor City had the largest branch of the National Association for the Advancement of Colored People (NAACP) of any city in the nation, with a membership of 20,000 by 1943. And the UAW had developed into a strong ally of the NAACP and other civil rights groups. Although discrimination persisted in the auto industry regarding promotion of blacks to the elite skilled trades, no one contested their claim to semi-skilled jobs.

The sharp regional variations in patterns of racial hiring within the auto industry suggest the critical importance of the legitimacy or illegitimacy of racial exclusion in shaping employment policies. The proportion of blacks in Detroit's auto plants rose quite dramatically in the 1940s and 1950s, reaching well over 25 percent of the production workforce by 1960, but in the United States as a whole the percentage of nonwhite workers in the auto industry grew much more modestly, from 4 percent in 1940 to only 9 percent in 1960. The national figures reflect the continuing practice of excluding blacks from employment in southern plants. As a manager at a GM plant in Atlanta told the *Wall Street Journal* in 1957, "When we moved into the South, we agreed to abide by local custom and not hire Negroes for production work. This is no time for social reforming and we're not about to try it.''

The situation of women auto workers was quite different from that of northern blacks. The incorporation of women into the industry provoked no riots or "hate strikes," precisely because female employment was explicitly understood as a temporary expedient "for the duration" of the war. There was no parallel expectation regarding black men, whose interests were aggressively defended by a growing interracial constituency of liberals, unionists, and civil rights supporters throughout the North. Although women war workers wanted to remain in the auto industry, their preferences seemed to have little social or political legitimacy. No significant feminist movement existed, nor did a popular consciousness of women's job rights emerge at this critical juncture when the sexual division of labor which would characterize the entire postwar period was crystallizing. Unlike race discrimination, which might have proven politically and socially costly, management could rely upon minimal resistance, either from women themselves or from the UAW, to purging women from the auto workforce in the war's aftermath.

Although there were some protests against postwar sex discrimination, these were both rare and generally unsuccessful. At best, they secured postwar employment for small groups of women war workers with contractual seniority rights. Demanding that management also refrain from discriminating against women in hiring new workers, once the seniority lists were exhausted in the course of postwar expansion, was never "on the agenda." But this is precisely what would have been required for women to maintain their wartime gains in the industry.

Instead, the typical pattern was collusion between male workers and management in excluding women from postwar employment. This was due to not only the general cultural setting but also the particular structural features of the auto industry. The response of male workers to the postwar transition was quite different in some other industries. In electrical manufacturing, for example, the same fear of unemployment which led to union collusion with management's violation of women auto workers' seniority rights produced strikingly opposite results. In the electrical case, it was impossible to think of excluding women from employment; the industry had been one-third female even before the war. Instead, male workers responded to the wartime upheaval in the sexual division of labor (and the anticipated postwar upheaval as well) by fighting *against* sex discrimination and challenging the whole system of job segregation by sex in a struggle for equal pay for jobs of comparable worth. As in auto, the goal was to decrease the likelihood of permanent (i.e., postwar) female substitution. Because auto management had never seriously attempted to replace men with women, except, of course, during the war emergency, the UAW had little incentive to protest hiring policy; in electrical manufacturing, management's extensive use of female labor generated a radical challenge to sex discrimination in the form of a comparable worth demand. In this way, management policy not only shaped the sexual composition of the labor force in each industry but also profoundly influenced the character of labor struggles over women's position. . . .

Except for the brief interlude during World War II, women have always remained a small minority among auto production workers. Even in the 1970s, when the proportion of women in the industry's blue-collar workforce increased slightly, the changes were quite modest, particularly given the dramatic rise in female labor force participation in the economy as a whole. The effect of the women's movement of the late 1960s and 1970s on auto employment in some respects paralleled the impact of the civil rights movement in the 1940s; however, since there was no comparable expansion of employment in the 1970s, the scale of change was far smaller. Gains made through affirmative action have been significantly eroded since 1978, when women's employment peaked, as a result of the increased plant closings and layoffs. In general, the continuity of the sexual division of labor in the auto industry is far more striking than the changes which have occurred. The reconstruction of the prewar situation in the aftermath of World War II is but the most extreme instance of that general continuity, rooted in the structural characteristics of the industry and its labor process.

✣ F U R T H E R   R E A D I N G

Karen Anderson, "Last Hired, First Fired: Black Women Workers During World War II," *Journal of American History* 69 (June 1982), 82–97
——— , *Wartime Women: Sex Roles, Family Relations and the Status of Women in World War II* (1981)
Jack Bloom, *Class, Race and the Civil Rights Movement* (1987)
Alan Clive, "Women Workers in World War II: Michigan as a Test Case," *Labor History* 20 (1979), 44–72
Herbert Garfinkel, *When Negroes March: The March on Washington Movement in the Organizational Politics of FEPC* (1959)
William Gould, *Black Workers in White Unions* (1977)
Barbara Griffith, *The Crisis of American Labor: Operation Dixie and the Defeat of the CIO* (1988)
William Harris, *The Harder We Run: Black Workers Since the Civil War* (1982)
Herbert Hill, *Black Labor and the American Legal System: Race, Work and the Law* (1985)
Maureen Honey, *Creating Rosie the Riveter: Class, Gender and Propaganda During World War II* (1984)
Julius Jacobson, ed., *The Negro in the American Labor Movement* (1969)
Amy Kesselman, *Fleeting Opportunities: Women Shipyard Workers in Portland and Vancouver During World War II and Reconversion* (1990)
Nelson Lichtenstein, *Labor's War at Home: The CIO in World War II* (1982)
——— , "The Making of the Postwar Working Class: Cultural Pluralism and Social Structure in World War II," *The Historian* 51 (November 1988), 42–63
August Meier and Elliott Rudwick, *Black Detroit and the Rise of the UAW* (1979)
Ruth Milkman, *Gender at Work: The Dynamics of Job Segregation by Sex During World War II* (1987)
Robert Norrell, "Caste in Steel: Jim Crow Careers in Birmingham, Alabama," *Journal of American History* 73 (December 1986), 669–701

Trade Unions in
the Postwar Order

⚓

Historians once wrote as if labor history ended in about the year 1950. The giant strikes and factional struggles of the 1930s and 1940s were over, and many companies, once bitterly antilabor, bargained routinely with the big trade unions, whose members enjoyed the highest standard of living in the world. At this point the social scientists and economists took the lead. These scholars recognized that change could still take place but they nevertheless thought of the relationship among workers, unions, employers, and the state as a relatively fixed and harmonious system. Indeed, by the mid 1950s, most observers thought that the union movement had grown up, almost as an adolescent moves inevitably into adulthood. Thus, Richard Lester, an influential industrial-relations expert of the early postwar years, entitled one of his books As Unions Mature.

But social systems do not simply evolve; they are the product of economic change and political struggle. And in recent years this postwar "settlement," or "labor-capital accord," has come under sharp attack. The end of liberal, political hegemony and the decline in the fortunes of the union movement have prompted many historians to take a closer and more critical look at the peculiarly American interclass accommodation that jelled in the late 1940s: a decentralized system characterized by extremely detailed, firm-centered collective-bargaining contracts; management power at the point of production; and a labor movement whose procapitalist, antiradical politics placed it far to the right of any other in the industrial world. Compared to other advanced industrial countries, the United States offers its workers a low "social wage": that is, no system of national health insurance, relatively low public pensions and unemployment payments, and few restraints on the mobility of capital.

How was this system created? First, the inauguration of the Cold War brought enormous pressures to bear on the labor movement, especially the CIO, whose leadership concluded that the very survival of their organizations depended upon the exclusion of those unions in which the communists still played an influential role. This purge proved a disaster, not because communist-influenced unionists themselves represented a workable alternative leadership for the labor movement, but because the bureaucratic ejection of these radicals so decisively narrowed the limits of internal political debate within the unions.

Second, the rightward shift in national politics after World War II blocked the labor-liberal effort to construct an American version of the European welfare state. Unions like the auto workers and the steel workers had to turn to the bargaining table to secure those welfare benefits—health insurance, pensions, inflation protection, and so forth—that in other countries were the nearly exclusive responsibility of the government. The system worked well for a couple of decades, but it gradually became clear that the collective-bargaining relationship could not support this burden. Not all firms were equally profitable, and not all workers were enrolled in unions that could win such generous contracts. By the 1970s the wage scales and benefit schedules of American workers were characterized by far greater inequality than a quarter-century before.

Finally, American managers successfully halted the erosion of their ability to control production at the shop-floor and office level. It was here, far from the bargaining tables, that shop stewards and supervisors waged a bitter and protracted conflict. During World War II, the War Labor Board (WLB) had encouraged unions and managers to collaborate in a system of routine grievance-handling that proscribed the tradition of militant self-help often characteristic of shop bargaining in the 1930s. The postwar Taft-Hartley Act advanced this process, as did the system of centralized bargaining and grievance arbitration that evolved in these same years.

What were the key events that made this process irreversible? What impact did this postwar system have on the activity and consciousness of ordinary workers?

✢ D O C U M E N T S

The CIO's 1949 indictment of the United Electrical, Radio and Machine Workers of America (UERMWA) is reprinted in the first selection. This 600,000-member union, the third largest in the industrial-union federation, was expelled on the grounds that its leadership followed the communist line. The charge was rendered in brutal language, and such anticommunist sentiment worked its way deeply into the consciousness of American workers, as the second document reveals. Here delegates to a United Auto Workers (UAW) convention decisively reject a 1980 effort by their leaders to delete from the union constitution a forty-year-old section barring the election of communists to union office. The shop floor was also an arena of struggle. In the third document, Harry Shulman, the influential arbitrator who adjudicated disputes between the UAW and Ford Motor Company, admonishes union militants for failing to respect the authority of Ford supervision. Although Chrysler had one of the best traditions of shop-floor activism in the auto industry, even here strict adherence to the contract could become a trap, as chief shop steward B. J. Widick indicates in the fourth document. In the final selection, the conventional labor-relations wisdom of the era is summed up by a 1951 *Fortune* magazine essay applauding the conservatism of the union movement and asserting the embourgeoisement of American workers.

The CIO Attacks a Communist-Led Union, 1949

We can no longer tolerate within the family of CIO the Communist Party masquerading as a labor union. The time has come when the CIO must strip the mask from these false leaders whose only purpose is to deceive and betray the workers. So long as the agents of the Communist Party in the labor movement enjoy the benefits of affiliation with the CIO, they will continue to carry on this betrayal under the protection of the good name of the CIO.

The false cry of these mis-leaders of labor for unity and autonomy does not deceive us.

In the name of unity they seek domination.

In the name of autonomy they seek to justify their blind and slavish willingness to act as puppets for the Soviet dictatorship and its foreign policy with all its twists and turns from the Nazi-Soviet Pact to the abuse of the veto in the UN, the Cominform attack upon the Marshall Plan, . . . , the Atlantic Treaty and arms aid to free nations.

Now that they are at the end of the trail, these Communist agents cry out against "raiding and secession." What they call raiding and secession is simply a movement of workers throwing off their yoke of domination. These workers seek refuge from a gang of men who are without principle other than a debased loyalty to a foreign power.

Their masters have long decreed the creation of a new labor federation into which they hope to ensnare the labor unions they think they control. This has already taken place in many countries of the world. It will not happen in America.

When they saw that their attempt to use UERMWA to subvert the CIO was failing, they resorted to the typical Communist tactic of systematic character assassination against the National CIO, our President, Philip Murray, and all affiliated unions and officers who opposed the Cominform policy.

Their program of vilification reveals the degradation of men who have surrendered the right and lost the ability to think for themselves. It brands them as unfit to associate with decent men and women in free democratic trade unions.

The CIO is a voluntary association of free trade unions dedicated by its constitution to the protection and extension of our democratic institutions, civil liberties, and human rights. Free unions are voluntary associations of free men, held together by common loyalties and the elements of decency and honesty. We will fight with conviction and vigor against all enemies within or without the CIO who would trample or seek to destroy these sacred principles.

The certificate of affiliation of the CIO is a symbol of trust, democracy, brotherhood and loyalty in the never-ending struggle of working men and women for a better life. There is no place in the CIO for any organization whose leaders pervert its certificate of affiliation into an instrument that would betray the American workers into totalitarian bondage.

By the actions of its leadership, by their disloyalty to the CIO, and their dedication to the purposes and program of the Communist Party, contrary to the overwhelming sentiment of the rank and file membership who are loyal Americans and loyal CIO members, the leadership of the United Electrical, Radio and Machine Workers of America have rendered their union unworthy of and unqualified for this certificate of affiliation.

The UERMWA has been selected by the Communist Party as its labor base from which it can operate to betray the economic, political, and social welfare of the CIO, its affiliates and the general membership. The program of the UERMWA leadership that has gradually unfolded is but an echo of the Cominform. At the signal of the Cominform, the Communist Party threw off its mask and assumed its true role as a fifth column. Its agents in the labor unions followed the Communist Party line. The UERMWA leadership abandoned any pretense of loyalty to the CIO and its program. The record is clear that wherever the needs of the Communist Party in the Soviet Union dictated, the leadership of the UERMWA was always willing to sacrifice the needs of the workers. . . .

Anticommunist Sentiment in the UAW, 1980

Section 8. . . . [of UAW Constitution]　No member of any Local Union shall be eligible to hold any elective or appointive position in this International Union or any Local Union in this International Union if he is a member of or subservient to any political organization, such as Communist, Fascist or Nazi Organization which owes its allegiance to any government other than the United States or Canada, directly or indirectly.

Vice President Greathouse

On this one . . . we have been told there isn't much sense of having a philosophical argument on this. The Sixth Circuit Court of Appeals has ruled that this is illegal. The Labor Department said to us it should be taken out, and the Public Review Board has recommended that it be taken out, that you cannot really police this kind of an operation. As we know, these political parties have been made legal in both the United States and Canada, and it's based upon those recommendations that we're proposing the change.

It is the philosophy of the UAW that we are recommending that the Constitution be cleaned up and that it be taken out.

The floor is open for further discussion. . . .

Delegate Guy Messina, Local Union No. 595,
Region 9

I certainly am not a polished speaker such as Michael Harrington, who is an admitted democratic socialist, but I can tell you one thing in plain English. I am an anticommunist. I do speak against the deletion. You say that they recommend it. Well, I say you make them do it to us, because I say it should stay in the way it is now until they force us to do it. . . .

Delegate William Kommenich, Local Union No. 719, Region 4

I stand highly opposed to this. I spent my time in Korea fighting the Communist Party. We spend all our efforts in this country fighting the Communist Party, and now you're telling me the government says they can run our union. . . .

Delegate Richard Harrison, Local Union No. 426, Region 2

I'd like to remind all the delegates here at one time the law said that we could not organize anybody like this, we could not sit in a convention like this. And I stand wholly opposed to removing this until the law makes us do it.

(Applause.) . . .

Delegate Michael Messina, Local Union No. 893, Region 4

Mr. Chairman, I rise in support of the deletion of this section. The junior senator from Wisconsin, Joe McCarthy, is dead, is dead, is dead, and I say good riddance to the S.O.B.

I encourage the members of this convention to take a look at the history of this union and of the American labor movement. If it had not been for progressive left-wing leaders in our movement we would not have the movement that we have today; we would not have the right to be here at this convention.

I urge this convention to delete Section 8 of Article 10, and let us move out of the 1950s and into the 21st Century. . . .

Delegate Lillian Hawkins, Local Union No. 1141, Region 1C

I am against this. We have people here starving to death and we're feeding the communists, the fascists and everything else that disagree with us. And I say we do not delete this from our Constitution.

(Applause.) . . .

Delegate Myrna Reynolds, Local Union No. 268, Region 1C

I am opposed. I lost a brother in Korea. That's all I have to say. . . .

Delegate Richard Graham, Local Union No. 892, Region 1E

I know everyone is saying the same thing that I want to say. But I've got to say it anyway.

We run these clowns off when they come to our plant handing out this bullshit. We don't even allow them in there doing it. I'll be damned if I want to give up the right to stand here and give you guys hell, if you want to be a communist and cut my throat for me. Bullshit.

We're opposed, and we're staying opposed. . . .

Delegate Charles Strackbein, Local Union No. 140, Region 1

I stand opposed to this amendment. You don't know the damage that can be done to a local union when these people infiltrate your ranks. We have had chief stewards elected at our local that's torn the guts out of it. They've taken good people, talked them into their ways and got them fired, people with high seniority.

It's easy to lead some of our members, and it does a lot of damage to them people. I really stand opposed to this motion. Let the government make us take it out. . . .

Delegate Robert Pulliam, Local Union No. 468, Region 1D

I believe we have an emotional issue here. The people are not thinking. You can go back to the United States Constitution which gives every person in the United States the right to form any political party, oppose any type of government, or state your own ideas.

Now, the other thing about it, basically by law, and it being a violation of the Constitution as interpreted by the courts, this can be deleted. But I would hope that these people, the International and the delegates in this convention would have enough intelligence to know the background of anyone running and that we would not elect a damn communist, a damn fascist or any of these people.

This is a highly emotional thing because all of us are against communism and fascism and even against the multinational corporations. But that doesn't mean we can't instill our own thoughts on other people. They have a right to make their own decisions. And I think the convention delegates, if they would think about it for a moment, would realize we would be too intelligent to elect these type of people in office. Thank you. . . .

Delegate Elizabeth Bishop, Local Union No. 1695, Region 9

I stand against this motion. Brother, I'm sure when they elected Castro they didn't know he was a communist until after he was elected.

We came out of the CIO and the AFL because of communism. We don't need these kind of people in our union. If the law says they can be card carrying communists, fine, but not in our union. . . .

Delegate Lewis Moye, Local Union No. 110, Region 5

I rise in support of the deletion, and I'll tell you why. I think anybody should have the right to run for office, regardless of their political beliefs. I think in most organizations nowadays they require that this be a part of their constitution. I think that what is happening here now is that people are venting their anger against the communists, when it's been stated here yesterday and all day today our real enemy is the corporate powers of America.

I think this whole thing about anticommunism has been used down through the years to make working people forget who their real enemy is. We know it, and it's been stated here all day today that the real enemies of America are the corporations of America, and anticommunism has been used throughout the years to divert our real struggles in this country, and it's being expressed here now.

It is being expressed here now.

I support the deletion. It never should have been in the Constitution. It probably was put in there by McCarthy.

Thank you. . . .

Delegate Herbert Wyatt, Local Union No. 23, Region 3

I rise opposed to the motion. Part of the reason is, you can just see what the Communists are doing in Cambodia right now. You can see what they did in Vietnam, Korea, and what they are trying to do to the entire world.

I can look down the road 10 years from now and see the delegates here in one hell of a fight because the communists and the Nazis, they can come into the local unions and they can con the people into getting elected. They will be here at this convention disrupting it until they take over the whole union.

Now, I realize the court to a certain extent has said that it might be illegal. But the court has also given us the right to make reasonable rules as far as our union officials go and how we operate. I say vote it down. . . .

Delegate Robert Whalen, Local Union No. 1073, Region 3

I rise against this for the reason that a lot of people I think sometimes forget history. I have always heard all my life that anything that suits the communists is the truth to them, regardless of how they go about it.

I have read these things that it is unconstitutional for us to feel this way, but what about the things that we have taken over the past years to our government for the American worker that we ask and are denied time and time again?

I say let's show our government that we can also deny certain things that we feel are unconstitutional for us. . . .

Delegate Daniel Vergari, Local Union No. 245, Region 1A

I move for the previous question.

Vice President Greathouse

All right, the motion has been made to close debate. Let's see if there are 125 people who are ready to put the motion to close debate. All in favor to close debate raise your hand. Yes, there are. Down.

All right, all in favor of closing debate raise your right hand. Down. Those in opposition.

There are a very small number opposed to the motion. Debate is closed.

On the motion. The motion is to adopt the committee report to delete this section from the Constitution. All those in favor of the motion signify by raising your right hand. Down.

All those in opposition.

The motion is defeated and the committee will be aware of your action. . . .

An Arbitrator Upholds the Authority of Ford Supervision, 1944

As a result of the blockade of Gates 9 and 10 of the Rouge Plant, incident to the memorable disturbance in the Aircraft Building on March 15, 1944, many employees in other buildings were unable to report to work. The Spring & Upset building was undermanned by some forty per cent that day. It was desirable to keep the Supercharger job going in that building, not only because of the great need for that product in the war effort, but also to avoid the shutting down of jobs involving numerous men in other buildings which were dependent on the Supercharger job. Accordingly, Spring & Upset Supervision sought to assign men temporarily to work out of their classifications on the Supercharger and other jobs. The Company found that X, a district committeeman in this unit, had instructed employees not to work out of their classifications and that, as a result of his instructions, certain employees, though otherwise willing to accept the assignments, refused to do so, with the consequence that the needed production was not maintained—at least not until top officers of Local 600 came into the building and straightened the matter out. X was thereupon suspended pending further investigation and on March 24th he was discharged. The grievance in this case protests his discharge.

Some men apparently think that when a violation of contract seems clear, the employee may refuse to obey and thus resort to self-help rather than the grievance procedure. That is an erroneous point of view. In the first place, what appears to one party to be a clear violation may not seem so at all to the other party. Neither party can be the final judge as to whether the Contract has been violated. The determination of that issue rests in collective negotiation through the grievance procedure. But in the second place, and more important, the grievance procedure is prescribed in the Contract precisely because the parties anticipated that there would be claims of violations which would require adjustment. That procedure is prescribed for all grievances, not merely for doubtful ones. Nothing in the Contract even suggests the idea that only doubtful violations need be processed through the grievance procedure and that clear violations can be resisted through individual self-help. The only difference between a "clear" violation and a "doubtful" one is that the former makes a clear grievance and the latter a doubtful one. But both must be handled in the regular prescribed manner.

Some men apparently think also that the problems here involved are evils incident to private profit enterprise. That, too, is a totally mistaken view, as a moment's reflection will show. The problems of adjustment with which we are concerned under the Contract are problems which arise and require adjustment in the management of an enterprise under any form of economic or social organization. Any enterprise—whether it be a privately owned plant, a governmentally operated unit, a consumer's cooperative, a social club, or a trade union—any enterprise in a capitalist or a socialist economy, requires persons with authority and responsibility to keep the enterprise running. In any such enterprise there is need for equality of treatment, regularity of procedure, and adjustment of conflicting claims of individuals. In any industrial plant, whatever may be the form of the political or economic organization in which it exists, problems are bound to arise as to the method of making promotions, the assignment of tasks to individuals, the choice of shifts, the maintenance of discipline, the rates of production and remuneration, and the various other matters which are handled through the grievance procedure.

These are not incidents peculiar to private enterprise. They are incidents of human organization in any form of society. On a lesser scale, similar problems exist in every family: who shall do the dishes, who shall mow the lawn, where to go on a Sunday, what movie to see, what is a reasonable spending allowance for husband or daughter, how much to pay for a new hat, and so on. The operation of the Union itself presents problems requiring adjustment quite similar to those involved in the operation of the Company—problems not only in the relations of the Union to its own employees but also in the relations between the members of the Union. Anyone familiar with seniority problems knows that the conflict of desires within the Union are quite comparable to those between the Union and the Company. And any active member of Local 600 knows that the frictions and conflicts within a large Union may be as numerous and difficult as those between the Union and the Company. Such "disputes" are not necessarily evils. They are the normal characteristics of human society which both arise from, and create the occasion for, the exercise of human intelligence. And the grievance procedure is the orderly, effective and democratic way of adjusting such disputes within the framework of the collective labor agreement. It is the substitute of civilized collective bargaining for jungle warfare.

But an industrial plant is not a debating society. Its object is production. When a controversy arises, production cannot wait for exhaustion of the grievance procedure. While that procedure is being pursued, production must go on. And someone must have the authority to direct the manner in which it is to go on until the controversy is settled. That authority is vested in Supervision. It must be vested there because the responsibility for production is also vested there; and responsibility must be accompanied by authority. It is fairly vested there because the grievance procedure is capable of adequately recompensing employees for abuse of authority by Supervision.

It should be definitely understood, then, that a committeeman has no authority to direct or advise an employee to disobey Supervision's instructions; that his authority is expressed in the duty to take the matter up with Supervision and seek an adjustment through negotiations and the grievance procedure; that an employee must obey Supervision's instructions pending the negotiations or the processing of his grievance, except only in the rare case where obedience would involve an unusual health hazard or similar sacrifice; and that disobedience by the employee, or counsel of disobedience by a committeeman, is proper cause for disciplinary penalty.

A Shop Steward on the Frustrations of the Contract System, 1954

I have been elected Chief Steward for six consecutive years. Being a Chief Steward has a lot of advantages. Some days you do not have any grievances. It's not too exhausting if you know your way around. Under the Chrysler Contract the stewards have more freedom than under the Ford or GM contracts because the former is vague. It says in effect: "A chief steward is to work when not engaged in grievance procedure." This is given a very elastic interpretation. In the 1948 negotiations, Chrysler tried to put in the GM system with specific time limits. They were not able to do that, mainly due to our local union, so that we still have this flexible, vague wording, which means in effect that a man takes the time for union business that he can get away with, and in practice it means that most of the stewards never work. . . .

We had a very famous case on trim work. Back in Dodge in 1946 they changed from tacking trim on with hammer and tacks to using an instrument like a putty knife and sticking the trim in, and they changed the rate since it was no longer a "trim job," which is where a man uses a hammer and tacks. They cut the men's wages ten cents an hour. That went to Umpire, who ruled that the new operation was an assembly operation—just ordinary, unskilled labor. . . .

It is difficult to get at these issues via the "strikeable issues" (clause in the UAW-Chrysler contract) because the strike is a very, very limited weapon, too costly in most cases, and has in the past, in view of all the great strikes we have had since the war, exhausted the people in the shops. It's a bluff. You can't get the rank and file to strike on those kind of issues for a very good reason: things are too tight. The Company knows that, they know the feeling of the people as well as we do. All of this changes depending on the economic situation, how steady the work is, etc. In the first postwar years, when the Company could sell anything it could build, they were too busy making money to bother with disputes on minor grievances, or trying to take things away from us, or anything like that—we had our own way. Now, the opposite is true, and the Company knows it. It will take something like the guaranteed annual wage issue to mobilize the workers for any kind of serious struggle.

Although it is a rule of the Contract, supported by the International Union, that grievances are to be written, we never write them. I have had only one written grievance in six years. I do not believe in them. If I can't win it on the floor—this is our way of looking at it—you can't win it. The Company seldom deliberately violates the Contract. Actually, our fights are almost always around this business of the "fat" we have built up. If you are going to keep that fat, you are going to keep it only by not going into the bargaining procedure, because you can't win there.

I do not have any objection to the Umpire system in principle. I think that the Umpire should have limited authority on certain limited issues. But I think our contracts are becoming such legalistic documents as to be unworkable in terms of real, genuine labor relations; and we are getting this whole new body of law, which is just fantastic. With that and the Taft-Hartley Law we are getting a complexity which is out of this world. The average Chief Steward is incapable of bargaining seriously under our Contract, on many issues. . . . In the old days, he was the Union, he was the Contract. Everything he did was decisive in the plant. Now he is a Philadelphia lawyer. It's embarrassing. Time and again Management does things that I know it has a right to do under the Umpire system, but the men don't know it. If I explain to them that the Company has that right under four or five rulings made previously, they get sore at me. They will say, "You don't represent us; you represent the Company."

As a result—in our setup, and I'm sure its true elsewhere—the Stewards tend to become demagogues. They tend to fake on all this stuff. They write grievances when they know they shouldn't. All he does by that technique is avoid his responsibility by passing it on to the Shop Committeeman. . . . Instead of an education in the actual meaning of the Contract and the establishing of a decent relationship in the shop, you get the art of buck-passing to the nth degree, and that's really why we have all this trouble in the plants. The Stewards, instead of being real leaders, tend to become more and more political fakers, and that's how they win elections.

[*Like so many other long-time union radicals, chief shop steward B. J. Widick eventually left the shops. After 1960 he taught, wrote, and lectured on union and industrial relations subjects.*]

Fortune Magazine Applauds the U.S. Labor Movement, 1951

The transformation of American capitalism has been due in large part . . . to the rising power of labor, which has forced a revision of capitalist thinking and capitalist practices. Yet the fact that this change has been no more than a *transformation,* the fact that capitalism in America has not been overthrown or seriously damaged by the power of the workers, is of equal importance to a real understanding of America. And this fact, which can scarcely be duplicated anywhere in the world, can be accounted for only by reference to the U.S. labor movement itself.

What utterly baffles the European intellectual concerning the American labor movement is its stubborn refusal to behave in accordance with the so-called "laws of history." American labor has exhibited none of the ideological uniformity that characterizes continental or British labor. A vast philosophical distance separates arch-Republican Bill Hutcheson of the carpenters from ex-Socialist Dave Dubinsky of the ladies' garment workers; yet they work together as vice presidents of the American Federation of Labor. And while the younger Congress of Industrial Organizations shows greater cohesion, the differences between Emil Rieve of the textile workers and Walter Reuther of the automobile workers might be enough to disrupt most European trade-union organizations. This diversity runs all the way to the individual local. Within the same union, within the same industry, within the same city, union practices, union policies, and even union oratory vary all over the lot.

American labor is not "working-class conscious"; it is not "proletarian" and does not believe in class war. Some parts of it are as uncompromisingly wedded to rugged individualism as the National Association of Manufacturers. Others want to "reform capitalism." If there were a standard or typical labor view on this subject, it would probably come close to that of George W. Brooks of the strong and tough pulp, sulfite, and paper-mill workers (A.F. of L.), who says "labor's objective of 'making today better than yesterday' is predicated on its acceptance of capitalism."

Yet the American union is a militant union—more militant, perhaps, than its European counterparts. Not only can the average union point to steadier gains for its members in the form of wages and benefits than any counterpart of it elsewhere; it has also been demanding for itself more and more managerial power within the business enterprise. And it is capable of fighting for both its economic and its power demands with a ferocity and bitterness (to say nothing of a vocabulary) that could hardly be matched by any class-war union.

For however much similarity there may be between the objective conditions that gave rise to unionism throughout the industrialized world, the American union is unique in the meaning it has for its member, in the purpose and function it serves for him: *it is his tool for gaining and keeping as an individual the status and security of a full citizen in capitalist society.* That the union has made the worker to an amazing degree a middle-class member of a middle-class society—in the plant, in the local community, in the economy—is the real measure of its success. . . . Never have left-wing ideologies had so little influence on the American labor movement as they have today. The Communists still control a small but strategic sector of American labor and have scattered but dangerous beachheads elsewhere, notably in the Ford local of the automobile workers. But in glaring contrast to twenty or even to ten years ago, the Communists stay in control only by claiming to be "bona fide unionists"; the mask is dropped only in the closed conventicles of the faithful. David Dubinsky pointed out in 1950 that the old radical, socialist, and idealist movements which formerly were the source of union leaders have been drying up. There are no Wobblies today, no Jewish Bund, no Italian anarchists, no Debs, no Mother Jones. If there is any ideological influence in American labor today it is Catholic union theory—spread by a growing number of labor priests and Catholic labor schools. It is of considerable importance in several C.I.O. unions as well as in the building trades of the A.F. of L.

In historical perspective it appears that the flare-up of left-wing ideologies in the middle thirties was a freak, no more typical of the basic trends of American unionism since the 1890s than the economic stagnation of the period was typical of the basic trends of the American economy. In origins (Knights of Labor, etc.) the American labor movement was more socialist than the British, and in 1902 the A.F. of L. convention barely defeated a resolution endorsing socialism (4,897 to 4,171). This date corresponds to the date when British labor took the opposite turning—1899, when Keir Hardie committed the [Trade Union Congress] T.U.C. to the borning Labor party. Since then British labor has been increasingly dominated by the socialist intellectual. By contrast, the creed of the American labor movement, as summed up in that famous sentence of the Clayton Act of 1914, "The labor of a human being is not a commodity or article of commerce," traces back not to the *Communist Manifesto* but to that blackest of "black Republicans," Mark Hanna, whom Gompers joined in the leadership of the National Civic Federation. There is a price for these achievements of democratic unionism. The less class war, the more group greed: a quiet division of loot or assumption of privilege at the expense of less organized members of society. Here is the peculiar danger posed by American labor to a free and mobile society: the danger of social thrombosis, of union feudalism.

Last November, Pan American Airways pilots threatened to strike. Their objective was not higher wages, shorter hours, or different working conditions. It was to deny jobs and benefits to a group of fellow pilots. Pan American had just acquired American Overseas Airlines. But the Pan American pilots refused to let the American Overseas pilots come in except at the very bottom. Union leaders and government agencies both urged full acceptance of the seniority gained by the American Overseas men during their years of service—in vain. The demand of the Pan American pilots was not motivated so much by fear of damage as by desire to gain a better position for themselves—at the expense of fellow pilots who had been unlucky enough to work for the less successful company.

The pressure for *exclusive* kinds of job security usually comes from the men and is often resisted by union leaders. It is in part an instinctive assertion of the property right—a property right in a certain job. The blame, if blame there be, lies not at the door of unionism but in the technical conflict between machine modes of production and American democratic ideals. It seems harder nowadays (though it may not be) to reach the top through individual effort in an industrialized economy. The workers respond to this supposed sacrifice of vertical mobility by claiming more security— and when this claim is asserted in a particular job, the result may be a real loss of horizontal mobility.

Union policy is not responsible for this danger, but the structure of U.S. unionism has paralleled and sharpened it. The value of the union card is highest in a small unit: there is one local per company, if not per plant or even per department. Seniority rights tend to be bounded by the local's membership. So are the "fringe benefits"—pension rights, severance pay, vacations, sick pay, profit shares, life insurance, etc.—benefits worth as much as 30 cents in some companies for every dollar paid in straight wages. The growing demand for these benefits is in itself a sign of the middle-class character of the American worker and of his union. They are among our major tools of integrating the worker into industrial capitalism as a full and responsible citizen. And they are necessarily grounded in his membership in one particular enterprise or in one particular industry. But these privileges and benefits are usually not transferable. They thus create the danger of tying the worker to his job. After a few years of service a man has amassed too big a stake to be willing to leave, even for a better job. They may also tend to convert the job into a property and the work group into a closed guild. In the typographical union a "priority system" protects a preferred job for a linotype operator even if the worker is forced out for years by illness—or, as in the last war, even leaves the industry for a defense job. Companies with generous pension or profit-sharing plans are under increasing pressure to restrict the hiring of new workers to sons or relatives of their present employees. The fear of just such "un-American" developments was partly responsible for the no-closed-shop provision of the Taft-Hartley Act.

But to halt or reverse this trend will require more than restrictive legislation. It will require considerable imagination in devising new techniques and procedures—above all, techniques to make job benefits transferable. It may also require enabling legislation, the kind that encourages and rewards voluntary action. In attempting to solve this problem we will have to be careful not to weaken the desire of the American worker and of his union for a stake in the enterprise.

✣ E S S A Y S

In the opening essay, David Oshinsky of Rutgers University offers an early critique of the CIO's decision to expel several communist-led unions from the industrial-union federation. He argues that this decision was influenced heavily by the government and aided by the Roman Catholic church, whose reach extended to many CIO officials as well as to the hundreds of thousands of union members who were Catholic. Yet in a point that would be supported by historians writing somewhat later, Oshinsky asserts that anticommunism itself never proved as popular as many top union officials might have thought: hence their recourse to the expulsion, rather than to the electoral defeat, of the communist-allied unionists they so attacked.

In the second essay Nelson Lichtenstein of the University of Virginia outlines the expansive postwar vision of the industrial unions and the political developments that gradually forced them to abandon it. Taking the New Deal and World War II experiences as a guide, unionists like the UAW's Walter Reuther had hoped to exert direct political influence on the government to regulate favorably wages, prices, and the postwar deployment of capital. This gambit failed, and in its wake came a struggle with the big corporations in the field of collective bargaining alone, a terrain far narrower and less advantageous than that of the policy-making political arena.

What is the relationship between the fight against the communists and the evolution of postwar collective bargaining? Why were business leaders so hostile to even noncommunist union leaders? Was the Taft-Hartley Act really a "slave labor law," as many unionists charged?

Labor's Cold War: The CIO and the Communists

DAVID OSHINSKY

In 1950, the Congress of Industrial Organizations expelled its Communist-dominated affiliates to the overwhelming approval of America's liberal community. Since that time, scores of historians and journalists have continued to applaud the purges. They were necessary, we are told, to rid the labor movement of devious ideologues who placed the interests of a foreign power above the interests of the union members they represented; to re-affirm the CIO's commitment to trade union democracy; to aid the free world in its "death struggle" against totalitarianism; and to enhance the CIO's credibility as a responsible political force dedicated to the ideals of democracy. In the words of Max Kampelman, whose book, *The Communist Party vs. The CIO*, [was] the most influential work in the field, "not only was the integrity and survival of the trade union heritage at stake, but more important was the national interest of the United States. For the CIO to have remained aloof from the battle between Communism and democracy would have stopped it from playing any significant role on the American scene."

In recent years, . . . historians have begun to question the necessity of these expulsions. While freely admitting that the Communists followed a pro-Soviet line, they insist that this bias did not affect their performance any more than CIO President Philip Murray's pro–New Deal bias affected his performance. Indeed, they argue that the Communists were often excellent "bread and butter" unionists whose affiliates were actually more democratic than their right-wing counterparts. The Communists were punished, they conclude, not because of their subordination of trade union goals to the interests of a foreign power, but because "they were Communists and saw the world in a different way"—a way that could no longer be tolerated in Cold War America. As soon as the CIO national office realized which way the wind was blowing, it not only capitulated to this anti-Communist hysteria, but actively encouraged it within the labor movement.

This new interpretation raises some very significant questions. First, to what extent did the Communists' adherence to the Stalinist line hinder their effectiveness as trade union leaders? Was it, in fact, any more damaging to independent trade union action than the right wing's strict allegiance to the Democratic party? Second, what were the motivating forces behind

Text by David Oshinsky from Robert Griffith and Alan Theoharis, eds., *The Specter: Original Essays on the Cold War and the Origins of McCarthyism*, 1974, pp. 118–132, 135–144, 146–151. Reprinted by permission of the author.

the expulsions? Were CIO leaders simply responding passively to Cold War pressures, or were these pressures willingly exploited in an attempt to rid the federation of a vocal, and often troublesome, minority. Third, what forces were exerting these pressures? How influential, for example, was the business community, or the Truman administration, or the Catholic church, in bringing about these expulsions? . . .

Shortly before the CIO was formed, the Communist Party [CP] abandoned its attempts at dual unionism in favor of "boring from within" existing labor organizations. This new policy, part of a larger CP strategy to unite with other "progressive forces" in a Popular Front against fascism, encouraged party organizers to work within established AFL unions, and wherever possible, to capture them from below. Yet, despite the intensity of their efforts, the Communists were never able to mobilize much support within the Federation. Virtually every affiliate passed a resolution barring them from membership, while the AFL Executive Board amended the national constitution so that "no organization . . . controlled by Communists or advocating the violent overthrow of our institutions shall be allowed representation in any Central Labor Body or State Federation of Labor." By 1937, the Communists could claim control of only a few unskilled affiliates, including Harry Bridges' Pacific Maritime Federation and "Red Mike" Quill's Transport Workers Union.

The formation of the CIO in 1936, however, provided the Communists with an unprecedented opportunity to establish themselves in the new industrial unions. From the very outset, CIO President John L. Lewis made it known that he would accept aid from any group willing to go out and recruit workers. Although Lewis had a long history of red-baiting within his own union, the United Mine Workers, he sympathized with the Communists' belief that the growing class militancy of unorganized and unskilled workers should be encouraged, not crushed. Unlike Sidney Hillman of the Clothing Workers, David Dubinsky of the Ladies Garment Workers, or Philip Murray of the Steel Workers, Lewis felt that a large degree of rank-and-file insurgency—including the type displayed in the bloody strikes at Toledo, Minneapolis, and San Francisco and in the sit-downs at Flint and Cleveland—was vital to a movement employing mass organizational techniques. And Lewis realized that few groups in America could identify with this working class militancy better than the Communists. During the Depression's early years, the CP organized regional councils for the unemployed which sought to radicalize the jobless through massive demonstrations for more relief. These councils were also instrumental in preventing the eviction of rentless tenants and in organizing gas and electric squads to turn on these utilities after they had been shut off by local companies. On the labor front, the most dramatic strikes of this period were led by Stalinists and Trotskyists. As Len DeCaux so well put it: "The Communists brought misery out of hiding in the workers' neighborhoods. They paraded it with angry demands through the main streets to the Public Square, and on to City Hall. They raised particular hell."

While this initial commitment to working class militancy, coupled with a superb sense of organizational discipline, made the Communists top-flight labor recruiters, their effectiveness within the CIO still varied greatly from union to union. In the established affiliates—like Lewis' United Mine Workers or Dubinsky's Ladies Garment Workers' Union—which were well organized and controlled by strong leaders, the Communists made no headway at all. Indeed, it is one of the great ironies of labor history that at the very time Lewis was recruiting Communists as CIO organizers, his own union had a law on the books barring them from membership. Similarly, the CIO's new unions in steel, textiles, and meatpacking, which began as national organizing committees governed from the top by Murray, Hillman and Van Bittner, proved difficult to penetrate. By 1938, in fact, Hillman and Murray had quietly removed all known Communists from their organizations. The Communists did succeed, however, among the affiliates—such as the Fur and Leather Workers and the Mine, Mill and Smelter Workers—that had a legacy of radicalism, and among several industrial unions, particularly the United Automobile Workers and the United Electrical Workers, whose devotion to the principle of local autonomy precluded any CIO attempt to organize them from above.

Because of their ability to organize at the local level, the Communists were able to build a powerful faction within the CIO. In less than three years, they obtained "complete or partial control" of about 40% of the CIO unions. On the national level, where their influence was sharply curtailed by the opposition of Hillman and Dubinsky, the Communists still placed Len DeCaux as editor of the *CIO News*, Lee Pressman as CIO General Counsel, and a significant number of party supporters in middle and lower level administrative positions. However, since most of their support was at the grass roots, the Communists exerted greater authority within the CIO's local and regional councils. By 1939, pro-Communist forces had taken over the Industrial Union Councils of New York, Illinois, California, Wisconsin and Minnesota.

In the CIO's early years, the tenuous relationship between the left-wing and right-wing factions was based on their common desire to organize mass production workers and to unite in a Popular Front against Hitlerism. Temporarily, at least, basic political and ideological differences were cast aside. From a political standpoint, this meant that both sides unanimously endorsed the New Deal's alleged commitment to industrial unionism, its social welfare programs, and its obvious sympathies for the Soviet Union and the "western democracies" in their relations with the Axis powers. The main difference was that the right-wingers truly believed in the social-reformist philosophy of the New Deal and were determined to channel the CIO's political power through the Democratic party in an effort to make their voices heard, while the Communists believed the concept of a government-labor coalition was anathema to the interests of the working class. Only the Stalinist line of class collaboration, coupled with Roosevelt's enormous popularity among industrial workers, kept most Communist trade unionists in the New Deal camp.

Because the Communists in the CIO adhered so rigidly to the Stalinist line, they were often forced into dangerous political situations. A good example occurred in 1939 when the Soviet Union signed a non-aggression pact with Nazi Germany. As one labor historian noted: "The self-effacing affability of the Communists came to an end with the . . . pact. The Communists stopped deferring to the Roosevelt administration and the liberal CIO leadership and began once again to articulate rank-and-file demands." More specifically, the Communists now viewed Roosevelt's foreign policy, as well as his mobilization program, as a thinly-veiled attempt by the "Wall Street interests" to involve the nation in an unwanted, utterly senseless foreign conflict aimed at protecting the imperialist interests of England and France. And they responded with a series of wildcat strikes in the defense industries—most notably at Allis-Chalmers and North American Aviation. . . .

All attempts to deal with the "Communist problem" were postponed by the German attack on Russia, and America's subsequent entry into the war. As soon as Russia was invaded, the pro-Communist unions discarded their opposition to the defense effort by promising an all-out effort to increase production and to decrease the possibility of labor-management disputes. Yet even after the political differences dividing the two factions were temporarily put aside, disputes arose over the extent to which organized labor should moderate its demands to conform with the war effort. In this case, it was the Communists who became the most ardent defenders of wartime cooperation. While both sides generally endorsed the "no strike" pledge, for example, several prominent Communist union leaders ignored national CIO policy by supporting the Smith-Connolly Act, which advocated the prohibition of strikes in defense industries and jail terms for strikers, as well as Roosevelt's own proposal for a labor conscription act covering all workers between 18 and 65. Indeed, Harry Bridges told a meeting of longshoremen in San Francisco that strikes were "treason"; that the government should "refuse to give consideration to the demands of any section of labor on strike"; and that "the strike weapon is overboard, not only for the duration of the war, but after the war too."

This strict adherence to the concept of wartime cooperation took other forms as well. The Communists actively supported contracts calling for speed-ups, incentive pay, and the reintroduction of piecework; they were also particularly adamant in their determination to break "wildcat" strikes at the local level. Since these policies were often in direct conflict with the wishes of the workers, the left-wing leadership was forced to discard the concept of local union autonomy in favor of strict consolidation at the national level. By war's end, the Communist-controlled unions could hardly claim to be more democratic than any of the other CIO affiliates; to the contrary, their wartime "sellout" of the rank-and-file was soon to serve as a pretext for expelling them from the CIO.

Shortly after the war ended, America began the troublesome process of "reconversion." Most labor leaders saw the need for a reconversion with modified government supervision; this meant the rigid enforcement of price controls and the scrapping of wage controls. Industry, on the other hand, desired the retention of wage controls and the elimination of price controls. It soon became clear that this dichotomy was reaching alarming proportions. . . .

The country was soon plagued by a wave of strikes. In the year's time since Japan's capitulation, 4.9 million workers were involved in 4630 work stoppages totaling 119.8 million man days of labor. The following year was even worse; within a six month period the major industries of America— steel, coal, auto and transportation—were shut down. As one strike would end only to be followed by two more, there was a noticeable increase in anti-labor sentiment. A Gallup poll conducted in December of 1946 on the question "Should Congress in this coming legislative session pass new laws to control labor unions?" indicated sixty-six percent affirmative, twenty-two percent negative, and twelve percent undecided. . . .

To make matters worse, the onset of the Cold War offered America's conservative, anti-union forces an opportunity to link these labor disturbances to the "international Communist conspiracy." In part, the conservatives were reacting to a new change in the Communist party's post-war line. After five years of open support for President Roosevelt and the war effort, the American Communists were suddenly condemned by Moscow (through the famous Duclos letter) for their conciliatory attitude towards progressive capitalism and their abandonment of the class struggle. In the future, they were told, Communists must work to strengthen the American left and to reconstitute the party's working-class base. Not surprisingly, the conservatives publicized the letter as yet another example of Joseph Stalin's ability to manipulate large sections of the American labor movement. The Hearst-owned *San Antonio Light*, for example, declared that the post-war strikes were part of a "clear and distinct revolutionary pattern . . . timed to serve Russia's political interests," while Charles Wilson, president of General Motors, claimed that the two great problems facing America were "Russia abroad" and "labor at home." . . .

The Cold War also renewed factional animosities within the labor movement. . . .

In the years 1945–1950, the infusion of Cold War issues into union politics was so complete that the major factional battles centered almost exclusively around the Marshall Plan, the Henry Wallace campaign, and the Taft-Hartley non-Communist affidavits. For the CIO's right-wing leaders, of course, the Cold War was a tremendous asset. Walter Reuther rose to the UAW's presidency during this period by red-baiting his opponents into submission, while James Carey, ousted president of the United Electrical Workers, recaptured many of his former constituents by organizing a rival union under the banner of rabid anti-Communism. For the CIO's left-wing leaders, however, the Cold War meant either a rapid adjustment to the realities of domestic anti-Communism, or the possibility of virtual extinction. A few left-wingers, like Joe Curran of the National Maritime Union and Mike Quill of the Transport Workers Union, broke off ties with the Communist party in time to save their careers. But a good many of their former colleagues were simply swept away by the force of these Cold War attacks. By 1950, eleven left-wing unions had been expelled from the CIO; and the remaining affiliates were controlled by vehement anti-Communist leaders.

As CIO delegates moved into Atlantic City for the 1946 national convention, the "Communist issue" clearly dominated their thoughts. In the wake of the 1946 congressional elections, where Republicans won control of Congress with a campaign stressing New Deal subversion and Soviet aggression, the CIO was in a most precarious position. As the major power base for domestic Communists, it was becoming a prime target for red-baiters, legislative committees and the right wing press. The choice facing CIO leaders seemed ominous indeed. On the one hand, they could turn on the Communists, thereby encouraging a factional dispute which might destroy the federation; on the other, they could ignore them, waiting helplessly as the albatross of treason was hung around their necks.

At the convention, the leadership could not reach immediate agreement upon a suitable course of action. The more vehement anti-Communists headed by Walter Reuther and James Carey, wanted a showdown on the issue; the pro-Communists, headed by Ben Gold of the Fur and Leather Workers, and James Matles and Julius Emspak of the United Electrical Workers, were trying desperately to avoid one. And somewhere in the middle was CIO President Philip Murray, who wanted some sort of national policy or statement that would publicly confront the issue without alienating either side. . . .

In an attempt to reach some sort of compromise on the issue, Murray appointed a special committee, composed of three left-wing executive board members and three right-wing members, to respond to "the allegations contained in the newsprints [which Murray, himself, termed "wild and wholly irrational"] . . . that this organization of yours and mine, this great trade union movement, is Communistically inclined." For its part, the committee finally decided on a resolution stating that the CIO "resents and rejects efforts of the Communist Party or any other political party and their adherents in the affairs of the CIO." However, no mention was made of the fact that Communists were presently working within the CIO, and Murray was careful to note that the resolution ". . . should not be misconstrued to be a repressive measure, calculated to do things of a repressive nature."

Considering the hostile political climate surrounding the convention, a resolution which condemned Communist interference but took no action against Communists themselves was surprisingly mild. In fact, it was intended to be mild, and for several good reasons. First, the vast majority of CIO leaders feared that a purge of Communists at this time would tear the organization apart. Indeed, it was only after the overwhelming defeat of Henry Wallace in 1948 that most of them realized the CIO could easily survive such a purge. Second, more than a few CIO leaders were concerned about the constitutional issues involved. They knew that if Communists were legally elected by the rank-and-file of a given affiliate, the CIO could only remove them by expelling the union itself; by this process, the CIO stood to lose upwards of a million members. Third, at this time, the rival factions seemed to be in general agreement on the one issue that usually divided them—foreign policy.

In 1946, the CIO was still unanimous in its opposition to President Truman's handling of foreign affairs. The Communists, of course, were highly critical of the new "get tough" policy towards Russia, and advocated a return to a more "progressive thinking" of Franklin Roosevelt. Interestingly enough, most non-Communist CIO leaders supported this position. As good Democrats, they felt that Truman was moving away from his predecessor's policy of cooperation with Russia in favor of Churchill's proposed Anglo-American alliance against Communism. Therefore, the foreign policy resolution passed at the pro-Communist Fur and Leather Workers' convention of 1946, advocating "friendship with the Soviet Union . . . and strenuous opposition to those who seek to destroy the progressive policies of our great President Franklin Roosevelt and to plunge our country and the Soviet Union into a terrible war," was no different from the ones passed by Hillman's Amalgamated Clothing Workers or Murray's United Steel Workers. . . .

By 1947, however, as relations between the United States and the Soviet Union continued to decline, America's liberal community began to feel the effects of the Cold War. Already two opposing groups had been formed: the Progressive Citizens of America (PCA), and the Americans for Democratic Action (ADA). The PCA, an outgrowth of an earlier Conference of Progressives attended by Philip Murray and several members of the CIO's Political Action Committee (all of whom soon resigned), was organized primarily to oppose Truman's handling of domestic and foreign policies—especially his failure to perpetuate ". . . the progressive global thinking of Franklin Roosevelt." The ADA, supported by Walter Reuther and David Dubinsky, was also critical of Truman's failings, but excluded Communists from membership. Indeed, as one sympathetic journalist has noted, "it was in large part set up as a counterpoise to PCA—to provide a rallying ground for anti-Communist liberals who rejected all associations with Communists."

Although the CIO Executive Board refused to endorse either organization at its general meeting in February, 1947, and issued a statement "deploring the division in the liberal movement," this attempt to remain apart from the conflict proved of short duration. The reason for this change was quite simple: in the following months, Truman began to win back many disenchanted CIO leaders by his veto of the Taft-Hartley bill and his espousal of the Marshall Plan. While the ADA applauded Truman's efforts, the PCA, with strong Communist backing, bitterly attacked the Marshall Plan, and set out to organize a third party movement around the candidacy of Henry Wallace. By the summer of 1947, the CIO's Communist faction was marching in step to the drums of Gideon's Army.

The repercussions caused by this opposition to the Marshall Plan and support for the Wallace movement were particularly damaging to the left-wingers. Philip Murray, who had been on record many times against the formation of a third party, was so disturbed by these incidents that he told the CIO Executive Board members in July, 1947: "It is high time the CIO leaders stopped apologizing for Communism. If Communism is an issue in your unions, throw it to hell out, and throw its advocates out along with it. When a man accepts office . . . to render service to workers, and then delivers that service to other outside interests, that man is nothing but a damned traitor." . . .

Perhaps the most important battles took place within the United Electrical Workers and the United Automobile Workers. Here, the anti-Communist forces, led by James Carey and Walter Reuther, were aided for the first time by powerful outside interests, including the Association of Catholic Trade Unionists, the Truman administration, and the business community, in their attempt to purge the pro-Communist factions.

From its very inception, the United Electrical Workers (UE) was ruled by a coalition of pro-Communist forces, led by Secretary-Treasurer Julius Emspak and Director of Organization James Matles, and non-Communist forces, led by President James Carey. . . .

[T]rouble began after the Hitler-Stalin pact, when the *UE News*, under Emspak's direction, abandoned its Popular Front editorial policy and condemned Roosevelt for violating his former declarations of neutrality. Although Carey was clearly irritated by the shift, he intervened only after receiving a letter from a local union asking whether it could legally pass a resolution barring "Communists, Nazis or Fascists" from positions of authority. Carey used his weekly column in the *UE News* ("Let's Talk It Over") to inform the local union that such a resolution was clearly constitutional. Although his column was not subject to editorial censorship, Emspak wrote a short rejoinder to the column stating that Carey had been asked to postpone discussion of this issue until after a meeting of the union's executive board, but had refused to do so.

The final break came when Germany attacked the Soviet Union in 1941, and the *UE News* again reversed its editorial policy. In his column of July 12, 1941, Carey focused attention on the shift by calling Matles and Emspak "political acrobats in pink tights posing as labor leaders who are a disgrace to the union and insult the intelligence of the membership." In response to this attack, Matles and Emspak mobilized their forces for a convention floor fight on the issue of whether local unions could prevent known Communists from holding office, and sounded out local feeling about the desirability of opposing Carey for the presidency. At the UE's 1941 convention, the pro-Communist forces easily won both battles; they not only passed a resolution stating that "any good-standing member of the Union is entitled to all rights and privileges without discrimination, unless such

member be proven guilty of acts against the nation or against the Union
. . ." but also elected their own candidate, Albert Fitzgerald, to the union
presidency. Interestingly enough, Fitzgerald told the assembled delegates:
"I am not a Communist. I am not dominated by Communists. And as a
citizen of the United States I despise the philosophy of the Communist
party." But it was obvious to all observers that Matles and Emspak, in
selecting a respectable Catholic, a good rank-and-file unionist, and a man
willing to spout anti-Communist epithets while actually submitting to the
party line, had fulfilled their major objective: they had buried the Carey
forces. . . .

Early in 1947, Carey began a campaign to regain control of the UE by
forming a rival faction, the UE Members for Democratic Action (UEMDA).
In a letter to the *UE News*, he drew the battle lines: "The issue between
me and the present UE leadership," he wrote, "goes solely to the proposition that our great International Union has become known as a transmission belt for the American Communist Party." . . .

Carey began his assault upon the left-wing leadership at the UE's 1947
national convention. Here, the UEMDA proposed that the delegates re-
affirm the CIO's 1946 pledge ". . . rejecting the efforts of the Communist
Party or other political parties to interfere in the CIO." Instead, the delegates, by margins of 8–1, passed a series of resolutions which condemned
red-baiting, called for the solidarity of all workers ". . . regardless of craft,
age, sex, race, creed, or political belief," and ordered the UEMDA to
disband. Carey was bitterly disappointed by his poor showing, and claimed
that the convention had ". . . castigated the CIO, not only its leadership,
but its membership as well." . . .

Despite this setback, the Carey faction achieved some notable successes
at the local level. There were several reasons for this, but one of the most
significant was the role played by the Association of Catholic Trade Unionists. Formed in 1937 by a group of Catholic clergymen, the ACTU was
committed to the organization of industrial workers in accordance with the
encyclicals promulgated by Pope Pius XI and Pope Pius XII. In pragmatic
terms, this meant vigorous support for all CIO officials who subscribed to
the doctrines of labor-management cooperation and anti-Communism, and
vigorous opposition to those who did not. As Father John Clancey, a
prominent ACTU spokesman, told the United Rubber Workers convention
in 1940: "We don't want to be faced with a choice . . . between Fascism
and Communism because there is a middle ground. We don't have to turn
right or left, but go straight ahead in establishing industrial democracy.
There is no reason why workers and management cannot democratically
plan the industrial futures of the various industries."

When Carey began his drive to oust the Communists from the UE, he
was offered immediate assistance by the ACTU. In some areas, this assistance proved to be of little value, but in others, where the ACTU was
well-established, the Carey forces were aided immeasurably. In Pittsburgh,
for example, the home base for Father Charles Rice, ACTU's acting president (and a close friend to both Murray and Carey), the local chapter,

while not numerically strong, published a weekly paper, *The Pittsburgh Catholic*, and had the full support of the regional archdiocese.

In 1948, the Pittsburgh chapter organized an opposition group, the "Rank-and-File," within Local 601—a huge UE affiliate of almost 17,000 members, the majority of whom were Catholic. Father Rice personally led the assault. First, he had several of the Catholic churches in Pittsburgh print leaflets urging parishioners to throw out the local UE leaders; second, he combined with other dissidents—including a powerful Socialist faction—to run an opposition slate of candidates in the upcoming local election; third, on the eve of the election, he convinced his close friend Represent- ative Francis Walter of the House Committee on Un-American Activities to subpoena the local's leaders to testify about their Communist back- grounds. The UE's national office was so enraged by this power play that it distributed a pamphlet, "The Members Run This Union," which read: "The ACTU is an organization devoted to capturing control of unions to establish its own kind of domination . . . by fomenting division along re- ligious lines. . . . Undemocratic and authoritarian in the last degree, the ACTU operates to impose its program and policies upon labor unions by capturing key personnel, and favors the extension of undemocratic methods in trade unions to perpetuate the power of ACTU puppets, and, through them, the domination of the ACTU over the union." It was Father Rice, however, who carried the day. Local 601 voted the pro-Communist forces out of office, providing Carey with one of his most important "grass-roots" victories.

The Carey faction was also aided by the new anti-Communist crack- down in Washington. The Atomic Energy Commission, for example, used its "implied powers" to order all companies working on classified projects not to recognize unions that were labeled as security risks; the UE thereby lost its bargaining rights at the Knolls Atomic Power Laboratory in Sche- nectady, New York. Far more serious, however, was section 9(h) of the Taft-Hartley Act, passed in 1947, which provided that no labor union could avail itself of NLRB facilities unless its officers filed non-Communist af- fidavits. When the UE leadership balked at signing these affidavits, some employers refused to negotiate with the union. This recalcitrance proved very beneficial to Carey and the UEMDA. In several instances they won control of local affiliates who feared that a continuation of this boycott policy would destroy their ability to bargain for better wages and working conditions. One survey, conducted by *Fortune*, estimated the 70,000 UE members either went over to the Carey side, or left the UE entirely to join the United Automobile Workers or the AFL's International Brotherhood of Electrical Workers. . . .

Despite these favorable circumstances, the Carey forces were still un- able to oust the Communists at the national level. Each year the UEMDA would go to the UE convention with high hopes for victory, and each year its assaults would be beaten back. (The issue was finally resolved, of course, with the formation of the rival International Union of Electrical Workers in 1949.) The reason for this failure was simple: unlike the more successful anti-Communists—including Walter Reuther and Joe Curran of the National Maritime Union—Carey never made any attempt to prove that the Communists were working against the economic interests of the rank-and-file. At no time, for example, did the UEMDA seriously raise the issue of the UE's wartime advocacy of piecework and incentive pay, or its blatant attempts to break strikes at the local level. As one observer aptly concluded: "The great battles at the UE Conventions of 1946, 1947, 1948, and 1949 were . . . concentrated on political issues: 'red-baiting,' foreign policy, the Progressive Party, etc. . . . On these issues, the opposition documented the pro-Communism of the UE leadership, but the opposition remained somewhat distant from the immediate and day-to-day concerns of the workers. . . . In other words, the UE membership was not uninterested in the issue of anti-Communism. But it refused to make anti-Communism, in and of itself, a primary and decisive criterion for determining loyalty."

The Communists had also been very influential in the formation of the United Automobile Workers Union [, but] the signing of the Hitler-Stalin pact [reduced their influence.] During this period, the Communists bitterly condemned President Roosevelt's defense mobilization program and began a series of unauthorized walkouts at Allis-Chalmers and North American Aviation. In both of these instances, the UAW's national office worked openly to break the strikes. And, at the union's 1941 national convention, violent debates ensued over how to best punish the local Communist leaders involved. . . .

What kept the Communists from total extinction was the simple fact that the anti-Reuther forces, led by R. J. Thomas and George Addes, needed all the votes they could muster to keep Reuther from gaining the union's presidency. Reuther was very popular because of his ability to articulate rank-and-file demands as well as his ability to fight for them. But for years he had been denied the UAW's top post by a coalition of forces, led by Communists, non-Communist radicals and unaligned union officials who were put off by his driving ambition. Unfortunately for Thomas and Addes, their own desire to protect the various elements within this coalition made them the perfect targets for Reuther's red-baiting attacks. And it was on the strength of these attacks that Reuther finally achieved his elusive goal.

With the onset of the Cold War, Reuther began a campaign to rout the opposition by concentrating on "Stalinist influences" within the union. Undaunted by the fact that the Communists were clearly a minor faction within the majority coalition, he claimed that Addes and his supporters had fellow-traveled with the Reds during the war (over the issues of the no-strike pledge, incentive pay and piecework) and would continue to do so in the future. By allowing this left-wing activity to go unchecked, Reuther contended, Addes and Thomas were playing into the hands of right-wing reactionaries who were out to destroy the union.

In his attempt to unseat the Addes-Thomas Administration, Reuther, like James Carey of the UE, had the valuable support of the Association of Catholic Trade Unionists. During the years 1945–1947, the official UAW publication, *The United Automobile Worker*, was controlled by Addes, so Reuther used the ACTU's Detroit organ, *The Wage Earner*, to publicize his own version of the controversy. And not surprisingly, *The Wage Earner* claimed that both Addes and Thomas were fellow travelers.

> Communists and Communist followers began to appear in key staff positions (after their administration took office). The UAW's education department became infiltrated. Soon Thomas himself began to talk the language of the Party line. The same man who, four years ago, angrily rejected Communist support at the Buffalo convention, now claims he couldn't help it if the Commies like him. . . . Thus gradually R. J. Thomas was knitted into the so-called "left-wing" of which Addes has been the leader.

It should also be mentioned, however, that even Reuther was occasionally embarrassed by the ACTU's fanatical anti-communism. When, for example, Michigan Governor Kim Sigler told the House Committee on Un-American Activities in 1947 that Thomas, Addes, and UAW Vice-President Richard Leonard were "Communist captives," *The Wage Earner* complimented him for " . . . performing a service to the people of Michigan in exposing a lot of Communist monkey business." Reuther, on the other hand, claimed that the governor's testimony was a conservative attack "upon the entire UAW and the American labor movement." Unlike Carey, who thrived on government support in his attempt to unseat the Matles-Emspak faction, Reuther believed that government intervention in union affairs was both unnecessary and unwise. . . .

In 1947, the Reuther forces won [a] major victory over the issue of Taft-Hartley. The Addes faction, which by now was clearly on the defensive, backed a resolution opposing compliance with the law. Noting that officials of the United Electrical Workers and the United Steel Workers were both refusing to sign the non-Communist affidavits, they warned that the UAW's compliance would put a "stamp of approval" upon the entire act—an act that most CIO leaders referred to as a "slave labor" measure. In rebuttal, the Reuther forces based their arguments on more pragmatic grounds: if UAW officials refused to sign the affidavits, the union would lose the right to petition the NLRB for its services in cases where union raiding was at issue, or where local elections were in dispute. UAW leaders, therefore, should comply with the law under protest and fight the battle in the courts. The delegates voted overwhelmingly to sign the affidavits—a clear signal that Reuther now held the power to purge his opponents.

Having now complied with section 9(h) of the Taft-Hartley Act, the UAW began at once to reap its benefits. Under the Remington-Rand decision of 1947, the NLRB had ruled that any contract signed by an employer with a union advocating noncompliance could be upset if another qualified union sought an election to determine bargaining rights in a particular plant. Using this decision to its own advantage, the UAW started raiding the membership of the Communist-dominated Farm Equipment Workers Union at the Caterpillar Tractor Plant in Peoria, Illinois. In this particular case, the company had refused to bargain with the union until its officials signed non-Communist affidavits, and the union had responded with a strike to force the company's hand. Almost immediately, the UAW and the AFL's International Association of Machinists rushed hundreds of organizers to the Caterpillar plant to prepare for the new representation election. Since the [Farm Equipment Workers Union] FE could not get its name on the ballot, the UAW picked up 14,000 new members. In the end, the FE was forced to comply with section 9(h) in order to avoid total extinction.

In analyzing Reuther's final victory (which came about, technically, at the UAW's 1947 national convention), most historians have concluded that the Communists did themselves in by consistently working against the economic interests of the rank-and-file. All Reuther did was to hammer away at this obvious point. While it is quite true that, unlike Carey, Reuther generally avoided peripheral political issues like the Marshall Plan and concentrated on vital economic matters, the fact remains that his major opponents in the UAW were neither Communists nor fellow travelers. And their economic policies, while sometimes sympathetic to the Communist line, were hardly governed by it. . . . [B]oth sides in the battle used the Communists: the Addes faction used them to help keep Reuther from gaining the union's presidency, and the Reuther faction used them in an attempt to show the membership that Addes and Thomas were obviously following the Communist line. . . . Reuther's victory was due to the fact that the Cold War made the Communists dangerous allies, but perfect scapegoats. . . .

On the national level, while the pro-Communist faction was badly shaken by the strong support given to the Administration's foreign and domestic policies in 1947, its final defeat came the next year with Truman's stunning re-election. From the very outset, the CIO made it clear that it expected every affiliate to work within the Democratic party, and that support for Henry Wallace would be interpreted as a deliberate attempt "to create confusion and division within the labor movement." Some pro-Communists, like Mike Quill, took the warning to heart. "If being for Wallace will split the CIO, the price is too great," he claimed. "I'm a trade unionist first." A few days after his statement, "Red Mike" broke openly with the third party and began criticizing "the crackpots of the Communist Party." Other left-wingers, however, including Matles, Emspak, Gold and Bridges, were not so easily intimidated. They argued that according to the CIO constitution, the national office had no right to interfere in the political activities of the various affiliates. And Bridges declared that he would vote for Truman only if the CIO conducted a referendum to determine whether a majority of the rank-and-file actually supported him over Wallace.

The CIO responded with a campaign to deprive Wallace of mass labor support by portraying him as a fellow traveler and by harassing his followers. In March, 1948, Murray ousted Harry Bridges from his post as CIO Regional Director for Northern California; two months later, he openly advocated the ouster of any regional council that either condemned the

Marshall Plan or supported the third party effort. CIO-PAC, which spent slightly over $1,000,000 in "voluntary contributions" to put Truman and other Democratic candidates over the top, cooperated with the ADA in distributing Quill's denunciations of the Communist party, and printed thousands of copies of a "Speaker's Book of Facts," in which the question "Is Henry Wallace being supported by Communists? was to be answered with the statement: "Yes. The Communist Party National Chairman William Z. Foster, who is under indictment for conspiracy, announced on August 3, 1948, that the Party will endorse and will support Wallace." And national CIO leaders took every opportunity to denounce Wallace as an unwitting dupe of the Communists. In an address to National Press Club Luncheon in Washington, Walter Reuther stated: "I think Henry is a lost soul. . . . People who are not sympathetic with democracy in America are influencing him. Communists perform the most complete valet service in the world. They write your speeches, they do your thinking for you, they provide you with applause, and they inflate your ego as often as necessary. . . . I'm afraid that's the trouble with Henry."

Truman's resounding pluralities in labor areas, coupled with the disappointing Wallace turnout, provided the final impetus for the Communist expulsions. To begin with, the results indicated (at least to the CIO's national leadership) that the vast majority of CIO members identified strongly with the Democratic party, supported Truman's foreign and domestic policies, and rejected the pro-Soviet attitude of the Gold-Bridges-Matles-Emspak faction. This meant, of course, that the left-wingers were guilty of acting against the political interests of their constituents. Moreover, unlike their stand against Roosevelt, the Communists could not claim to be following the wishes of the CIO's president; indeed, their support for the third party was in direct defiance of Murray and national CIO policy. The Communists were trapped; they had gone out on a limb, only to have Harry Truman saw it off.

The actual purges of the left-wing affiliates took place at the 1949 and 1950 national conventions. Here, they were charged with advocating policies which were " . . . consistently directed to the achievements of the purposes . . . of the Communist Party rather than the objectives set forth in the constitution of the CIO." The charges themselves included opposition to the defense program prior to World War II, wartime collaboration with employers, failure to support the Marshall Plan, and opposition to the re-election of Truman in 1948.

The final question, of course, is why the CIO took such drastic action against these unions. Certainly their adherence to the Communist party line was no more blatant than Murray's adherence to the Democratic party line. Their right to express contrary opinions, moreover, was protected by the CIO's doctrine of local autonomy. Yet, the CIO found the process of "expulsion" to be suitable for two reasons. First, quite clearly the emotional anti-Communist climate brought on by the Cold War (and nursed along by

Murray, Reuther and Carey) *had* reached a point by 1950 where drastic action was absolutely necessary. As one labor historian recently noted: "Aside from the fact that many CIO leaders were themselves ideologically opposed to Communism, most of them were able to perceive that organizations accused of being either pro-Communist or Communist-dominated would face serious and increasing difficulties in post-war America. . . . Given the attitudes which prevailed in this country it would have been extremely difficult for an organization such as the CIO to refuse to take action against known Communists within its ranks." Furthermore, most CIO leaders, having rejected a third party in favor of a labor-liberal alliance channeled through the Democratic party, were forced to move to the right by the vehement anti-Communism of President Truman and his non-labor supporters. The *CIO News* actually put it best by stating that, like the ADA, its new Cold War position would still be ". . . left of center, but not to the extreme left. . . . And that's a good place for a labor organization to be."

Second, given the CIO's new ideological shift, the national office was forced to take action because the anti-Communist factions within the various left-wing affiliates were unable to dislodge the Communists from power. In only three of the sixteen pro-Communist unions were the right-wingers successful in gaining control—an indication, perhaps, that despite their pro-Soviet, anti-Truman position, the Communists were still respected for their ability to run effective trade unions. Indeed, several researchers who analyzed these factional battles have concluded that the anti-Communists made little headway because they concentrated on peripheral issues, and failed to demonstrate that the left-wingers had willingly acted against the interests of the rank-and-file. Not surprisingly, then, despite Murray's statement that the expulsions were necessary ". . . to fight Stalin, to fight Moscow, to fight imperialism, to fight aggression here at home," as well as to remove "the dirty, filthy traitors of American trade unionism from the CIO," few serious attempts were made to save the nearly 1,000,000 expelled workers—the vast majority of whom were non-Communist—from these "dirty, filthy traitors." When the smoke had cleared, CIO leaders simply commended themselves on the thoroughness of the operation, and for the irreparable damage done to the cause of domestic Communism. "To put it bluntly . . .," the *CIO News* boasted, "we have in a year broken the back of the Communist Party in the United States."

With the Communists now gone, the CIO easily replaced the remnants of its Depression ideology with the more respectable rhetoric of Cold War liberalism. Its publications, free at last from the fear of stinging left-wing rebuttals, wrote comfortably about the problems raised by Communist expansion in Europe and Asia, and by leftist influence in the American labor movement. As Paul Jacobs, a willing participant in the purges, later wrote, "an inevitable consequence of the expulsions was to bring all serious political debate inside the CIO to a standstill. . . . Unions could now be counted on to give automatic approval to any action undertaken by the government in its struggle against world Communism."

The Unions' Retreat in the Postwar Era

NELSON LICHTENSTEIN

The dramatic growth of the organized working class put the American system of industrial relations at a crossroads in 1945. In the years since 1933 the number of unionized workers had increased more than fivefold to over fourteen million. About 30 percent of all American workers were organized, a density greater than at any time before and a level that for the first time equaled that of northern Europe. Unions seemed on the verge of recruiting millions of new workers in the service trades, in white collar occupations, across great stretches of the South and Southwest, and even among the lower ranks of management. "Your success has been one of the most surprising products of American politics in several generations," Interior Secretary Harold Ickes told a cheering CIO convention just after Roosevelt's 1944 reelection. "You are on your way and you must let no one stop you or even slow up your march." Three years later, the sober-minded Harvard economist Sumner Slichter still counted U.S. trade unions "the most powerful economic organizations which the country has ever seen."

It was not size alone that contributed to this assessment. The élan so noticeable in many sections of the labor movement rested upon a degree of union consciousness, in some cases amounting to working-class loyalty, that would today seem quite extraordinary. The mid-1940s were no period of social quiescence, for the war itself had had a complex and dichotomous impact on working Americans. On the one hand it had provided them with a taste of postwar affluence and had attuned them to the daily influence of large, bureaucratic institutions like the military and the government mobilization agencies. But the labor shortages of that era and the social patriotic ideology advanced by government and union alike engendered a self-confident mood that quickly translated itself into a remarkable burst of rank-and-file activity. Led by shop stewards and local union officers, hundreds of thousands of workers had taken part in a wildcat strike movement that had focused on a militant defense of union power in the workplace itself. And the now forgotten series of postwar general strikes called by central labor councils in Oakland, California; Lancaster, Pennsylvania; Stamford, Connecticut; and Akron, Ohio are indicative of the extent to which working-class activity still retained an occasionally explosive character even in the later half of the 1940s.

The economic power wielded by American trade unions was by its very nature political power, for the New Deal had thoroughly politicized all relations between the union movement, the business community, and the state. The New Deal differed from previous eras of state activism not only because of the relatively more favorable political and legislative environ-

Steven Fraser, Gary Geistle, eds., *The Rise and Fall of the New Deal Order, 1930–1980.* Copyright © 1989 Princeton University Press. Excerpt, pp. 123–124, 137–145, reprinted with permission of Princeton University Press.

ment it created for organized labor but, perhaps even more important, because the New Deal provided a set of semipermanent political structures in which key issues of vital concern to the trade union movement might be accommodated. Although the industry codes negotiated under the National Recovery Administration were declared unconstitutional in 1935, the Fair Labor Standards Act established new wage and hour standards three years later. The National Labor Relations Board established the legal basis of union power and provided the arena in which jurisdictional disputes between the unions might be resolved, while the National War Labor Board had provided a tripartite institution that both set national wage policy and contributed to the rapid wartime growth of the new trade unions. The successive appearances of these agencies seemed to signal the fact that in the future as in the past, the fortunes of organized labor would be determined as much by a process of politicized bargaining in Washington as by the give and take of contract collective bargaining.

As a result of the wartime mobilization the United States seemed to advance toward the kind of labor-backed corporatism that would later characterize social policy in northern Europe and Scandinavia. Corporatism of this sort called for government agencies, composed of capital, labor, and "public" representatives, to substitute rational, democratic planning for the chaos and inequities of the market. The premier examples of such corporatist institutions in 1940s America were the War Labor Board and its wartime companion, the Office of Price Administration—administrative regimes that began to reorder wage and price relations within and between industries. Although union officials often denounced both agencies for their accommodation of politically resourceful business and producer groups, the maintenance of institutions such as these were nevertheless seen by most liberal and labor spokesmen as the kernel of a postwar "incomes" policy. That policy would continue the rationalization of the labor market begun during the war, set profit and price guidelines, and redistribute income into worker and consumer hands. These agencies were usually staffed by individuals somewhat sympathetic to their consumer and trade union constituencies and headed by New Dealers like Chester Bowles and William H. Davis who recognized the legitimacy of labor's corporate interests.

The War Labor Board, for example, socialized much of the trade union movement's prewar agenda, thus making seniority and grievance systems, vacation pay and night-shift supplements, sick leave and paid mealtimes, standard "entitlements" mandated for an increasingly large section of the working class. Likewise, the Little Steel wage formula, although bitterly resisted by the more highly paid and well-organized sections of the working class, had enough loopholes and special dispensations to enable low-paid workers in labor-short industries to bring their wages closer to the national average. Thus black wages rose twice as rapidly as white, and weekly earnings in cotton textiles and in retail trade increased about 50 percent faster than in high-wage industries like steel and auto. By the onset of postwar reconversion, [War Labor Board] WLB wage policy was explicitly egalitarian. "It is not desirable to increase hourly earnings in each industry in accordance with the rise of productivity in that industry," declared a July 1945 memorandum. "The proper goal of policy is to increase hourly earning generally in proportion to the average increase of productivity in the economy *as a whole.*"

Since contemporary trade unions have often been equated with "special interest politics," it is important to recognize that the American trade union movement of the immediate postwar era, and especially its industrial union wing, adopted a social agenda that was broad, ambitious, and not without prospects for success. The unions thought the welfare of the working class would be advanced not only, or even primarily, by periodic wage bargaining but through a political realignment of the major parties that would give them a powerful voice in the management of industry, planning the overall political economy and expansion of the welfare state. The union agenda was never an entirely consistent one, but its thrust meshed well with the corporatist strain that characterized late New Deal social policy.

This perspective was most graphically manifest in the demand for tripartite industry governance, embodied in the Industry Council Plan put forward by CIO president Philip Murray early in the war. The industry council idea represented an admixture of Catholic social reformism and New Deal era faith in business-labor-government cooperation. Under the general guidance of a friendly government, the Industry Council Plan contemplated the fusion of economic and political bargaining at the very highest levels of industry governance. Here was the essence of the CIO's corporatist vision: organized labor would have a voice in the production goals, investment decisions, and employment patterns of the nation's core industries. "The Industry Council Plan," wrote Philip Murray, "is a program for democratic economic planning and for participation by the people in the key decisions of the big corporations." Such important elements of the union movement's wartime agenda as the Guaranteed Annual Wage, industry-wide bargaining, and rationalization of the wage structure could be won only through this initiative.

If the CIO plan had something of an abstract air about it, the proposals put forward by the young autoworker leader, Walter Reuther, had a good deal more political bite. Reuther rose to national prominence in 1940 and 1941 with a widely publicized "500 planes a day" plan to resolve the military aviation bottleneck through a state-sponsored rationalization of the entire auto/aircraft industry. Reuther proposed a tripartite Aircraft Production Board that would have the power to reorganize production facilities without regard for corporate boundaries, markets, or personnel. It would conscript labor and work space where and when needed and secure for the United Auto Workers (UAW) at least a veto over a wide range of managerial functions. Winning wide support among those New Dealers who still retained a commitment to social planning, the Reuther plan was ultimately delayed and then defeated by an automobile industry both hostile to social experimentation and increasingly well represented within the government's wartime production agencies.

The Reuther plan nevertheless cast a long shadow, for it contained hallmarks of the strategic approach so characteristic of labor-liberalism in the 1940s: an assault on management's traditional power made in the name of economic efficiency and the public interest, and an effort to shift power relations within the structure of industry and politics, usually by means of a tripartite governmental entity empowered to plan for whole sections of the economy. Thus did auto executive George Romney declare, "Walter Reuther is the most dangerous man in Detroit because no one is more skillful in bringing about the revolution without seeming to disturb the existing forms of society."

Indeed, the union movement defined the left wing of what was possible in the political affairs of the day. Its vision and its power attracted a species of political animal hardly existent today, the "labor-liberal" who saw organized labor as absolutely central to the successful pursuit of his political agenda. After 1943 the CIO's new Political Action Committee put organizational backbone into the northern Democratic party, and the next year its "People's Program for 1944" codified many of the central themes that would define liberalism in the immediate postwar years: big-power cooperation, full employment, cultural pluralism, and economic planning. "Labor's role in our national progress is unique and paramount," affirmed Supreme Court justice William O. Douglas as late as 1948. "It is labor, organized and independent labor, that can supply much of the leadership, energy and motive power which we need today."

The CIO hoped to take the tripartite, corporatist model of wage-price bargaining that had emerged during the war and use it to bridge the uncertain political currents of the reconversion era. The industrial union federation wanted a National Production Board that would preside over the reconversion of defense plants to civilian production, maintain a semblance of price control, and establish a set of wage guidelines designed to defend working-class incomes. As CIO president Philip Murray told a 1944 labor meeting, "Only chaos and destruction of our industrial life will result if employers look to the war's end as an opportunity for a union-breaking, wage cutting, open-shop drive, and if labor unions have to resort to widespread strikes to defend their very existence and the living standards of their members." To forestall such a prospect, the CIO in March 1945 sponsored a "Labor-Management Charter" with William Green of the AFL and Eric Johnston, the corporate liberal president of the U.S. Chamber of Commerce. Consisting of a list of often irreconcilable platitudes hailing the virtues of unfettered free enterprise and the rights of labor, the charter nevertheless symbolized the CIO's hope for cooperation with the liberal wing of American capitalism in stabilizing postwar industrial relations along roughly the lines established during the war. "It's Industrial Peace for the Postwar Period," headlined the *CIO News*. In return for management support for the unamended Wagner Act and a high-wage, high-employment postwar strategy, the unions pledged to defend "a system of private competitive capitalism" including "the inherent right and responsibility of management to direct the operations of an enterprise."

The businessmen with whom the CIO hoped to work were collective bargaining progressives and moderate Keynesians who favored a counter-cyclic fiscal policy and a degree of structural reform as the minimum program necessary to stabilize postwar capitalism. Often influenced by the Committee for Economic Development and the Twentieth Century Fund, they also supported the 1946 Full Employment Act in something like its original, liberal form. Among these progressive industrialists with whom the CIO sought an alliance, in addition to the Chamber of Commerce's Eric Johnston, who called for a "people's capitalism" in the postwar era, was Paul Hoffman of the Studebaker Corporation, who took pride in his company's harmonious relationship with organized labor. But the most famous of these progressives was undoubtedly Henry J. Kaiser, the maverick West Coast industrialist who had built his empire on New Deal construction projects and wartime contracts. Hardly an opponent of government planning or public works spending, Kaiser's good relations with the unions and the pioneering health-care facilities at his shipyards and mills added to his reputation as a social liberal. In 1945 he won strong UAW cooperation for a well-publicized effort to convert the giant Willow Run bomber plant to civilian car production.

Implementation of a new wage-price policy was one of the key elements in such an accord with the liberal wing of the business community, so state action was essential. The CIO wanted a 20- or 30-percent increase in real wages to make up for the elimination of overtime pay at the end of the war, and many New Dealers like Commerce Secretary Henry Wallace and William Davis, now head of the Office of Economic Stabilization, considered such a wage boost essential to maintaining living standards and avoid the long-feared postwar downturn.

Such forecasts were music to CIO ears, but the political and social base for such a liberal postwar prospect had already been eroded. Since 1938 labor-liberalism had been on the defensive, stymied by the defection of Southern agriculture from the New Deal coalition, by the political rejuvenation of a conservative manufacturing interest during World War II, and by the reemergence of long-standing ethnic and social tensions within the urban Democratic party. Certainly emblematic of this stalemate was Harry Truman's selection as vice-president in 1944, replacing Henry Wallace, the labor-liberal favorite. FDR's successor was not a New Dealer, but a border-state Democrat, a party centrist whose political skill would lie in successfully presiding over an increasingly factionalized party coalition. . . .

The CIO had also profoundly misjudged the tenor of the postwar business community. The progressive industrialists with whom the industrial union federation hoped to achieve an accord were in fact a relatively uninfluential minority. Key business spokesmen were those practical conservatives who presided over the core manufacturing firms in the unionized steel, electrical, auto, rubber, and transport industries. Led by men such as John A. Stephens of U.S. Steel, Ira Mosher of the National Association of Manufacturers, and Charles E. Wilson of General Motors, these industrialists had emerged from the war with enormous sophistication and self-confidence. Unlike their counterparts in continental Europe, or even in the British Isles, who had been tarred with the brush of collaboration or appeasement, American business leaders found the wartime experience one of both commercial success and political advance. They felt in little need of the kind of state-sponsored labor-management collaboration that helped legitimize a mixed capitalist economy in Germany, France, and Italy in the immediate postwar era.

These industrialists recognized the potential usefulness of the new industrial unions as stabilizers of the labor force and moderators of industrial conflict, but they also sought the restoration of managerial prerogatives that wartime conditions had eroded in the areas of product pricing, market allocation, and shop-floor work environment. They were intensely suspicious of the kind of New Deal social engineering favored by labor, and only with some reluctance did they accommodate themselves to the modest degree of economic stimulation that would later go by the name "commercial Keynesianism." Looking forward to a postwar boom, they wanted to be free of government or union interference in determining the wage-price relationship in each industry. Thus the long-awaited Labor-Management conference that President Truman convened in November 1945 was doomed to failure. No accord proved possible on either the prerogatives of management or the scope of legitimate union demands, and on the critical issue of a general wage policy, the CIO got nowhere. Philip Murray offered industry a de facto policy of labor peace in return for a pattern wage increase, which Truman had endorsed in a speech of October 30, but the opposition was so great that the issue never secured a place on the formal conference agenda.

The CIO faced resistance not only from industry but from within the labor movement itself. The AFL unions had never been as committed as the CIO to the tripartite bargaining arrangements of the war era, and these unions demanded a return to free and unrestricted collective bargaining. In part this stemmed from the AFL's tradition of Gompersarian voluntarism, but it also reflected the contrasting organizational base of the two labor federations. The CIO industrial unions were overwhelmingly concentrated in the manufacturing sector of the economy where they faced oligopolistically organized employers who were themselves capable of imposing a new wage pattern. But only 35 percent of AFL membership lay in this heavy industrial sector, while construction, transportation, and service trades proved the federation's most important centers of strength. These decentralized, and now booming, sectors of the economy were less subject to the pattern-setting guidelines established by core firms like General Motors and U.S. Steel. With almost seven million members in 1945, the AFL was not only 30 percent larger than the CIO but actually growing more rapidly, in part because its flexible model of mixed craft and industrial unionism seemed to fit more closely the actual contours of the postwar economy than did the CIO brand of mass organization. This meant that, although CIO unions like the Steelworkers and the UAW remained innovative and powerful institutions, their political and organizational weight was often less impressive than it seemed.

Although he was an industrial unionist, John L. Lewis spoke most forthrightly for the AFL viewpoint. Repeated clashes between the United Mine Workers (UMW) and the Roosevelt administration during the war had soured the mine leader on the kind of state-sponsored industrial planning arrangements he had once advocated as the CIO's first president. Lewis was now determined to exercise his union's power unfettered by a new set of federal regulations. "What Murray and the CIO are asking for," declared Lewis at the Labor-Management conference, "is a corporate state, wherein the activities of the people are regulated and constrained by a dictatorial government. We are opposed to the corporate state."

This stalemate led directly to the General Motors strike, actually begun while the conference remained in session, and then to the general strike wave that spread throughout basic industry in the winter of 1946. Like Walter Reuther's other wartime "plans," the GM strike program made a strong appeal to the "national" interest, this time not so much in terms of rationalized production and democratic control, but as part of the emerging Keynesian consensus that a substantial boost in mass purchasing power would be necessary to avoid a postwar depression. The UAW's demand that industry pacesetter GM raise wages by some 30 percent without increasing the price of its product seemed adventuresome in a collective bargaining negotiation; even more so was its demand that GM "open the books" to demonstrate its ability to pay. The company quickly denounced these UAW demands as European-style socialism, but they were in fact little more than standard OPA price-setting procedures now translated into the language of collective bargaining.

While this program was formally directed against the giant automaker, it was in practice a union demand against the state as well, for its ultimate success rested upon the ability of an increasingly embattled OPA to resist industry pressure and enforce price guidelines well into the postwar era. This program won Reuther a wave of support, both within the UAW, where it prepared the way for his election as union president, and among influential liberals who identified with the union effort. A union-sponsored "National Citizens Committee on the GM-UAW Dispute" lauded the UAW's determination to lift "collective bargaining to a new high level by insisting that the advancement of Labor's interest shall not be made at the expense of the public." And a strike support committee, headquartered at NAACP offices in New York, quickly enrolled such luminaries as Eleanor Roosevelt, Wayne Morse, Reinhold Niebuhr, Walter White, and Leon Henderson.

Reuther and the rest of the CIO won an 18.5-cent wage increase during the postwar round of strikes and negotiations that ended in the late winter of 1946. But the effort to turn this struggle into a downward redistribution of real income was decisively repulsed, first by the adamant opposition of industrial management, second by Truman administration vacillation, and finally by division and timidity within trade union ranks, especially after

Philip Murray made it clear that the Steelworkers' union would not turn its mid-winter strike into a political conflict with the Truman administration over the maintenance of price controls.

The 1946 strike settlement ended left-liberal hopes that organized labor could play a direct role in reshaping class relations for the society as a whole. Thereafter Reutherite social unionism gradually tied its fate more closely to that of industry and moved away from a strategy that sought to use union power to demand structural changes in the political economy. Instead the UAW worked toward negotiation of an increasingly privatized welfare program that eventually succeeded in providing economic security for employed autoworkers. But just as postwar liberalism gradually reduced its commitment to national planning and eschewed issues of social and economic control, so too did the UAW abandon the quest for labor participation in running the automobile industry. And just as liberalism increasingly came to define itself as largely concerned with the maintenance of economic growth and an expansion of the welfare state, so too would the UAW and the rest of the labor movement define its mission in these terms.

Although the immediate postwar strike wave had proven the largest since 1919, the pattern wage increases won by the UAW and other major unions soon evaporated under the galloping inflation let loose when government price controls were cut back during the summer. In the fall, therefore, all the major unions had to return to the bargaining table to demand another round of wage increases. Unions that sought to improve on postwar wage patterns, such as the Railway Brotherhoods and the UMW, now found that "free" collective bargaining of the sort advocated by John L. Lewis brought them into bitter confrontations with the government. The frequent strikes and annual pay boosts of this era, which industry used to raise prices, were at least partially responsible for creating the conservative, antilabor political climate that gave Republicans their large victory in the 1946 elections and then culminated in the passage of the Taft-Hartley Act in 1947.

Passage of the Taft-Hartley Act over President Truman's veto proved a milestone, not only for the actual legal restrictions the new law imposed on the trade unions, but as a symbol of the shifting relationship between the unions and the state during the late 1940s. The law sought to curb the practice of interunion solidarity, eliminate the radical cadre who still held influence within trade union ranks, and contain the labor movement to roughly its existing geographic and demographic terrain. The anti-Communist affidavits, the prohibition against secondary boycotts, the enactment of section 14b allowing states to prohibit the union shop, the ban on foreman unionism—all these sections of the law had been on the agenda of the National Association of Manufacturers and other conservative groups since 1938. Of course, Taft-Hartley was not the fascist-like "slave labor law" denounced by the AFL and CIO alike. In later years, unions like the Teamsters prospered even in right-to-work states, while the bargaining relationship between employers and most big industrial unions was relatively unaffected by the new law. But if Taft-Hartley did not destroy the union movement, it did impose upon it a legal/administrative straitjacket that encouraged contractual parochialism and penalized any serious attempt to project a classwide political-economic strategy.

This explains the union movement's enormous hostility to Taft-Hartley. As CIO counsel Lee Pressman put it in 1947, "When you think of it merely as a combination of individual provisions, you are losing entirely the full impact of the program, the sinister conspiracy that has been hatched." Union leaders correctly recognized that the act represented the definitive end of the brief era in which the state served as an arena in which the trade unions could bargain for the kind of tripartite accommodation with industry that had been so characteristic of the New Deal years. At the very highest levels a trust had been broken, which is why Philip Murray declared the law "conceived in sin." Taft-Hartley had altered the whole texture of the sociopolitical environment, and the failure of the congressional Democrats to repeal the law in 1949 proved the final blow for many unionists. As Arthur Goldberg, who replaced Lee Pressman as CIO lawyer, sadly put it in late 1949, the law had "in its most fundamental aspect created great changes in our industrial *mores* with incalculable effects."

The cold war's chilling effect on domestic politics . . . sealed the fate of labor-liberal efforts to find an effective vehicle that could stem the rightward drift in national politics. Until the spring of 1948 labor-liberals almost uniformly repudiated Truman as their presidential candidate and proposed replacing him with men as different as Dwight D. Eisenhower and William O. Douglas. More significant, the structure of the Democratic party also came under scrutiny. The CIO, the new Americans for Democratic Action, and the AFL favored its "realignment," either by liberalization of the South or, if that failed, the expulsion of the Dixiecrats. Moreover, there was still enough interest in the formation of a third party to create at least a serious debate within some of the major unions—notably the UAW—and within sections of the liberal community.

Ironically, it was the actual formation of a third party—the Progressive party, which ran Henry Wallace for president—that put a decisive end to such political experimentation and brought the industrial union wing of the labor movement even closer to the Democratic party. . . . His candidacy brought into sharp relief two issues that would prove crucial to the political reformulation of postwar labor-liberalism. The first was the Marshall Plan, and more generally the effort to integrate into an American-dominated world order the shattered economies of the industrialized West and commodity-producing South. Although initially greeted with some skepticism even by anti-Communist union leaders like Walter Reuther, the Marshall Plan won strong endorsement from most liberals as their hopes for the construction of a purely domestic full-employment welfare state declined, and as the Truman administration advanced the European Recovery Program as a key to international trade and North Atlantic prosperity.

The second issue raised by the Wallace candidacy was the legitimacy of the Communists in American political life, and more broadly the possibility that Popular Front politics might have a continuing relevance in postwar America. Wallace refused to accept the postwar settlement that was emerging abroad and at home. He wanted détente with the Soviet Union (accepting its control of Eastern Europe) and saw the Marshall Plan as little more than an effort to drive Western Europe into the straitjacket constructed by a newly hegemonic American capitalism. At home he denounced Taft-Hartley, defended those unions that defied its sanctions, and tried to ally himself with the most advanced forms of civil rights militancy.

By 1948 the Wallace candidacy was therefore anathema, for it represented a break with what was becoming fundamental in postwar America: alignment with the government in the battalions of the new cold war and exclusion of the Communists from the political arena. This was made explicit in a January 1948 CIO executive council resolution rejecting the Progressive party and endorsing the Marshall Plan. A powerful Wallace movement threatened to taint the CIO with the badge of disloyalty. "The real issue," asserted the ever cautious Philip Murray, "is the jeopardy in which you place your Unions." Truman's well-crafted opening to the labor-liberals—his Taft-Hartley veto message in June 1947, his accommodation of the urban coalition's pressure for federal civil rights action in the summer of 1948, and his pseudopopulist "Give 'm Hell, Harry" presidential campaign in the fall—solidified labor-liberal ties with the Democratic party. Although the trade unions might still differ privately on bargaining goals or even their approach to Taft-Hartley, any divergence from the CIO election strategy was tantamount to organizational treason, which was in fact one of the charges leveled against several unions expelled from the CIO in 1949.

Organized labor's failure to build its own political party may well have been overdetermined, even in an era when its organizational strength reached a twentieth-century apogee. The peculiarities of the American electoral system, the concentration of union strength in a relative handful of states, the ideological pressures generated by the cold war, and the continuing ethnic and racial divisions within the working class are but the most obvious factors that sealed labor's alliance with the Democratic party. But the costs of this political marriage still require calculation. Even in the urban North the Democratic party rarely offered the representatives of organized labor more than a subordinate role in the development of its political program. The CIO bargained with the Democratic party "much as it would with an employer," admitted Political Action Committee (PAC) head Jack Kroll in the early 1950s.

Two important consequences flowed from this dilemma. At the level of national policy formation, organized labor had no effective vehicle through which it could exert systematic pressure upon either the Democratic party or the state apparatus. The trade unions maintained an extensive lobbying operation in Washington and in most state capitals, but on any given issue of interest to their membership, they were forced to rebuild the labor-liberal coalition all over again. Thus labor took justifiable credit for the reelection of Truman in 1948, but it proved incapable of translating this vote into a coherent congressional majority after Congress convened three months later. In turn, this radical disjunction between the relative solidity of the working-class vote and the weakness of its political representation contributed to the demobilization and depoliticization of a large part of the American working class in these years. Denied access to a political leadership that could articulate their specific class-oriented interests, workers found their consciousness shaped either by the parochial interests of their union, or, more likely, by the vaguely populist rhetoric of mainstream Democrats.

After 1947 the defensive political posture adopted by even the most liberal of the CIO unions enhanced the apparent appeal of a narrowly focused brand of private-sector collective bargaining. For example, the conservative victory in the 1946 congressional elections had a dramatic impact on Walter Reuther's own thinking. In a radio debate of May 1946, well before the elections, Reuther told his audience that rhetoric about a "government controlled economy" was a big-business scare tactic. The real question, he said, is "how much government control and for whose benefit." But in the wake of the massive Republican victory of November 1946 Reuther made a rhetorical about-face, now urging "free labor" and "free management" to join in solving their problems, or a "superstate will arise to do it for us." Or as Reuther put it in another context, "I'd rather bargain with General Motors than with the government. . . . General Motors has no army."

General Motors and other big companies also sought a long-range accommodation with their own unions. General Motors wanted to contain unionism within what it considered its "proper sphere"; otherwise, declared Charles Wilson, the "border area of collective bargaining will be a constant battleground between unions and management." To executives like Wilson this fear was exacerbated by the realization that inflationary pressures generated by cold war military spending would be a permanent feature of the postwar scene. The UAW effort to link company pricing policy to a negotiated wage package in 1946 had been staved off by GM, but the company realized that disruptive strikes and contentious annual wage negotiations, especially if couched as part of a broader offensive against corporate power, merely served to embitter shop-floor labor relations and hamper the company's long-range planning.

Therefore in the spring of 1948—just after the Czech coup and during the months when Congress debated an administration request for a $3.3 billion military procurement package—GM offered the UAW a contract that seemed to promise social peace even in an era of continuous inflation. Two features were central to the new social order: first, an automatic cost-of-living adjustment keyed to the general price index; second, a 2-percent "annual improvement factor" wage increase designed to reflect, if only partially, the still larger annual rise in GM productivity. To GM, such permanently escalating labor costs would prove tolerable because this industrial giant faced little effective competition, either foreign or domestic, so it could easily "administer" any price increases made necessary by the new labor contract.

The agreement was a dramatic, even a radical, departure from past union practice. Reuther himself had rejected wage escalation until early 1948, and a Twentieth Century Fund survey of union leaders taken later the same year revealed that more than 90 percent opposed COLA clauses in their contracts. With the general wage declines of 1921, 1930–32, and 1938 still a living memory, most union leaders instinctively rejected the premise upon which the GM-UAW contract was based: the emergence of a new era of inflationary prosperity and relative social peace. Labor leaders thought such schemes foreclosed the possibility of a large increase in the real standard of living, and they continued to fear that such a wage formula would become a downhill escalator when the inevitable postwar depression finally arrived. The UAW, for example, described the 1948 GM pact as only a "holding action" that protected GM workers until the labor-liberal coalition could replace it with more comprehensive sociopolitical guidelines.

But when the 1949 recession turned out to be less than the depression many had expected, the gateway was open to the further elaboration of such an accommodation between the big unions and the major corporations. Again, the UAW pioneered the way, with a new agreement, a five-year "Treaty of Detroit" that provided an improved COLA, a wage increase, and a $125-a-year pension. *Fortune* magazine hailed the 1950 UAW-GM contract as "the first that unmistakably accepts the existing distribution of income between wages and profits as 'normal' if not as 'fair.' . . . It is the first major union contract that explicitly accepts objective economic facts—cost of living and productivity—as determining wages, thus throwing over-board all theories of wages as determined by political power and of profits as 'surplus value.' " By the early 1960s the COLA principle had been incorporated in more than 50 percent of all major union contracts, and in the inflationary 1960s and 1970s it spread even wider: to Social Security, to some welfare programs, and to wage determination in some units of the government and nonunion sector.

Just as the negotiation of COLA agreements came in the wake of the union movement's forced retreat from the effort to reshape the Truman administration's early economic policy, so too did the new interest in pension and health and welfare plans represent a parallel privatization of the labor movement's commitment to an expanded welfare state. Initially, American trade unionists overwhelmingly favored a public, federal system for financing social benefits like pensions, health care, and unemployment insurance. Both the CIO and AFL worked for the passage of the Wagner-Murray-Dingell bill, a 1945 proposal that would have liberalized and fed-eralized the American social welfare system in a fashion not dissimilar to that envisioned by the British government's pathbreaking Beveridge Report of 1942, which laid the basis for the welfare state constructed by the postwar Labour government.

But the same forces that gutted the Full Employment Act of 1946 also destroyed labor-backed efforts to raise the social wage in these same postwar years. "Nothing more clearly distinguishes the post-war political climate of the USA from that of Great Britain than the almost unqualified refusal of its legislature to respond to proposals for social reform," wrote the British political scientist Vivian Vale. The United States devoted about 4.4 percent of GNP to Social Security in 1949, a proportion less than half that of even the austere economies of war-torn Western Europe.

Organized labor still found company-funded pension and health schemes distasteful—their coverage was incomplete, their financing was mistrusted, and they smacked of old-fashioned paternalism—but the political impasse faced by postwar unionists seemed to offer no alternatives. . . .

Indeed, mainstream union leaders never abandoned their formal commitment to an expanded welfare state, but at the same time they retreated, if more subtly, to a more parochial outlook. Immediately after the disastrous midterm elections of 1946, CIO leaders announced that they were not going to wait "for perhaps another ten years until the Social Security laws are amended adequately." Instead they would press for pensions and health benefits in their next collective bargaining round. Some unionists of a more explicitly social democratic outlook, like Walter Reuther and William Pollock of the Textile Workers, theorized that if employers were saddled with large pension and health insurance costs, they would join "shoulder to shoulder" with labor-liberal forces to demand higher federal payments to relieve them of this burden. But such assumptions proved naive. The big unions themselves no longer saw an increase in federal welfare expenditures as an urgent task. And after the steel and auto unions established the heavy-industry pension and health benefit pattern in 1949, employers were more than ready to fold these additional costs into their product prices. Moreover, managers recognized that company-specific benefits built employee loyalty, and at some level they understood that a social wage of minimal proportions was advantageous to their class interest, even if their own firm had to bear additional costs as a consequence.

Despite these limitations, it looked as if the "key" wage and benefit bargains negotiated by the big unions would generate the kind of classwide settlement in the United States that was characteristic of industry-labor relationships in northern Europe. Beginning in 1946 there were four distinct collective bargaining "rounds" in which the wage pattern hammered out in the steel or auto industry became the standard applied in rubber, meatpacking, electrical products, and other core industries. Similarly, pensions, health benefits, and supplemental unemployment payments were also copied by many large employers, both union and nonunion, private and public.

But this sort of pattern bargaining had a remarkably anemic life. It never spread much beyond the oligopolistically structured core industries, and even there it required a strong union that could take labor costs out of competition to make the pattern stick. Where unions were weak, as in electrical products and textiles, or where competition was fierce, as in automotive parts and food processing, wage and benefit guidelines established in Detroit or Pittsburgh were reproduced only imperfectly. For example, in the Detroit-area auto parts industry only about a quarter of all companies, employing 40 percent of the work force, followed the big-three pattern. Similarly, cost-of-living adjustments were rarely extended to workers in those segments of the labor market outside the core industrial/governmental sector. As a result, wage disparities increased dramatically within the postwar working class. The relatively egalitarian wage patterns of the mid-1940s began to erode even in the high employment years of the Korean War, but they underwent a truly radical deterioration in the inflationary era after 1965 when workers outside of the primary labor market found themselves defenseless against renewed inflation and labor-cost competition. . . .

The weakness of the postwar welfare state and the extreme fragmentation inherent in the American system of industrial relations did much to redivide the American working class into a unionized segment that until recently enjoyed an almost Western European level of social welfare protection, and a still larger stratum, predominantly young, minority, and female, that was left out in the cold. Because so much of the postwar social struggle has taken place at the level of the firm rather than within a broader political arena, this American system has reinforced the postwar economy's tendency to construct segmented and unequal labor markets. This multi-tiered system of industrial relations has served to erode solidarity within the working class and has made it difficult to counter claims that welfare spending and social equity are harmful to economic growth. The classic resentment felt by many blue-collar workers toward those on state-supported welfare has one of its roots in the system of double taxation the organized working class has borne in the postwar era. Union workers pay to support two welfare systems: their own, funded by a "tax" on their total pay periodically renegotiated in their contract, and that of the government, paid for by a tax system that grew increasingly regressive as the postwar years advanced. In turn, organized labor has come to be perceived (and all too often perceives itself) as a special-interest group, in which its advocacy of welfare state measures that would raise the social wage for all workers has taken on an increasingly mechanical quality.

Among other consequences, these divisions within the working class and between labor and its erstwhile allies have progressively weakened political support for the structures of the welfare state erected in the New Deal era. American unions remain supporters of Social Security, national health insurance, and minority-targeted welfare programs, but their ability to mobilize either their own members or a broader constituency on these issues declined during most of the postwar era. A militant civil rights movement, not the unions, put these issues back on the national agenda for a time in the 1960s. Moreover, labor's postwar abdication from any sustained struggle over the structure of the political economy has had its own debilitating consequences. As older industries decline, it has both sapped the loyalty of the labor movement's original blue-collar constituency and at the same time deprived the unions of any effective voice in the contemporary debate over the reorganization of work technology or the reindustrialization of the economy.

⚓ *F U R T H E R   R E A D I N G*

John Barnard, *Walter Reuther and the Rise of the Auto Workers* (1983)
Daniel Bell, *The End of Ideology* (1960)
David Brody, *Workers in Industrial America: Essays on the Twentieth Century Struggle* (1980)
David Caute, *The Great Fear: The Anti-Communist Purge Under Truman and Eisenhower* (1978)
Mike Davis, *Prisoners of the American Dream* (1987)
James Foster, *The Union Politic: The CIO Political Action Committee* (1975)
J. David Greenstone, *Labor and American Politics* (1970)
Martin Halpern, *UAW Politics in the Cold War Era* (1988)
Howell Harris, *The Right to Manage: Industrial Relations Policies of American Business in the 1940s* (1982)
Richard Lester, *As Unions Mature* (1957)
Harvey Levenstein, *Communism, Anticommunism, and the CIO* (1981)
Nelson Lichtenstein, "UAW Bargaining Strategy and Shop Floor Conflict, 1946–1970" *Industrial Relations* 24 (Fall 1985), 360–381
George Lipsitz, *Class and Culture in Cold War America: "A Rainbow at Midnight"* (1982)
Mary Sperling McAuliffe, *Crisis on the Left: Cold War Politics and American Liberals, 1947–1954* (1978)
Ronald Radosh, *American Labor and United States Foreign Policy* (1969)
Katherine Stone, "The Post-War Paradigm in American Labor Law," *Yale Law Journal* 90 (June 1981), 1509–1580
Steven Tolliday and Jonathan Zeitlin, "Shop Floor Bargaining, Contract Unionism, and Job Control: An Anglo-American Comparison," in Nelson Lichtenstein and Stephen Meyer, eds., *On the Line: Essays in the History of Auto Work* (1989)
Robert Zieger, *John L. Lewis* (1989)
———, *American Workers, American Unions, 1920–1985* (1986)

CHAPTER
13

The Postwar Working Class

⚜

For nearly a third of a century, from the end of World War II until the early 1970s, American capitalism enjoyed high economic growth. Even with five short recessions, the production of goods and services more than doubled, while unemployment and inflation remained at levels well below those of other twentieth-century decades. The standard of living of the average family just about doubled in the three decades after 1941, high-school graduation became the norm for most working-class youth, and college enrollments tripled. People lived half a decade longer than in the 1930s (blacks fared even better), and women, on average, had 25 percent more children than in the years of the Great Depression and World War II.

Impressed with the stability of U.S. capitalism and the rise in education levels and white-collar jobs, many social commentators concluded that the American class structure was undergoing a radical transformation. There were still workers, employers, and middle-class professionals, of course, but the differences between one group and another seemed of increasingly less importance since all seemed to share common values and, within limits, common life-styles. The cross-class appeal of right-wing demagogues like Joseph McCarthy and George Wallace suggested that class no longer served as an operative political category, while the integration of the working class into a culture of middle-class prosperity was advanced by the revival of the nuclear family as the key unit of consumption.

However, none of this amounted to a social revolution. After 1945 the American class structure, as measured by relative income distribution, remained static. And within the working class, the difference between a good job and a poor one grew larger. Work at the core of the economy—in the big firms, the middle reaches of the government bureaucracies, and the military—was relatively well-paid, lifetime employment. This sector expanded modestly in the quarter-century after the war: the corporations were earning money, the government hired more teachers and policemen, and the unions made many once transient and unstable job situations more secure. But there were still millions of jobs—perhaps as many as 40 percent of all positions—that shared none of these characteristics. Farm laborers, insurance-company clericals, cab drivers, cannery workers, and dime-store clerks were poorly paid, were insecure, and had few prospects for promotion. Many economists have come to see these jobs as part of a distinct and fast-growing "secondary" labor market, rigidly segregated from the more secure work of the core economy yet essential to the functioning of the ever-changing business system itself.

Of course, such casual and insecure employment has always been a part of the American working-class experience. However, in the postwar era, the typical worker in this sector was not the ditch digger or farm hand, but the female office or sales clerk. Despite the celebration of the male wage earner at the head of a nuclear family, as in television shows like "Father Knows Best," women more than doubled their presence in the work force, steadily and without much notice in the 1950s and 1960s, but far more dramatically in the years after 1969, when a rising feminist movement highlighted the trend. Although the entrance of college-educated women into male-dominated professions like law, medicine, and academe has captured much attention, women's wages actually dropped relative to those of men in most occupations. And women continued to work in sex-segregated jobs. In fact, 95 percent were employed in just five traditional job categories: light manufacturing, retail trade, clerical, health, and education. Not unexpectedly, the high-status work within these sectors was usually male; the low-status work, female. Thus the job of bank clerk, once an exclusively male preserve (when money handling carried high status), abruptly shifted to an almost exclusively female occupation in the mid-1950s, when bank managers routinized and downgraded the job.

What determines the class standing of a family: its total income, life-style, or occupation of the breadwinner(s)? In the relative conservatism of the American postwar working class, what factor registers most decisively: the Cold War, the crusade against the left, or the economic growth of the era?

⚓ D O C U M E N T S

Among the most influential students of the postwar working class was the sociologist Daniel Bell. In the first document, he argues that the long-term shift from agriculture to manufacturing to service- and information-based enterprises culminated in America's "post-industrial society," whose class structure was different from that of the traditional hierarchy. But a glimpse inside some white-collar service-industry jobs reveals a more prosaic world of work. In the second document, accountant Fred Roman describes the steep and treacherous career ladder at his large accounting firm, while in the third selection, an office worker, interviewed by sociologist Louise Howe, describes the managerial attitudes that make so much clerical work a dead-end job. Aside from outright discrimination, women have lower wages and less opportunity for promotion because the burdens of child care and family illness rest most heavily on them. In the late 1980s, the average salary of a working women who gave birth dropped about $3,000 the year a child was born and about $5,000 annually for the next two years. Thus child care is in great demand, as reporter Tamar Lewin makes clear in the fourth document. So too is legislation ensuring that firms will grant workers leave when family emergencies arise, as Tina Hurst, a mother of two, graphically reveals to a congressional committee in the final document.

Sociologist Daniel Bell's "Post-Industrial" Vision, 1973

In *The Communist Manifesto*, which was completed in February 1848, Marx and Engels envisaged a society in which there would be only two classes, capitalist and worker—the few who owned the means of production and the many who lived by selling their labor power—as the last two great antagonistic classes of social history, locked in final conflict. In many ways this was a remarkable prediction, if only because at that time the vast majority of persons in Europe and the United States were neither capitalist nor worker but farmer and peasant, and the tenor of life in these countries was overwhelmingly agrarian and artisan. . . .

Marx's vision of the inexorable rise of industrial society was thus a bold one. But the most important social change in Western society of the last hundred years has been not simply the diffusion of industrial work but the concomitant disappearance of the farmer—and in a Ricardian world of diminishing returns in land, the idea that agricultural productivity would be two or three times that of industry (which it has been in the United States for the last thirty years) was completely undreamed of.

The transformation of agrarian life (whose habits had marked civilization for four thousand years) has been the signal fact of the time. In beholding the application of steam power to a textile mill, one could venture predictions about the spread of mechanization and the extension of factory work. But who would, with equal confidence, have made similar predictions following the invention by Cyrus McCormick of the reaper in 1832 and its exhibition at the Crystal Palace in London in 1851? Yet in the United States today, only 4 percent of the labor force is engaged in agriculture; the work of little more than three million persons (as against more than twice that number two decades ago) feeds 207 million persons, and if all crop restraints were released, they could probably feed fifty million more.

In place of the farmer came the industrial worker, and for the last hundred years or so the vicissitudes of the industrial worker—his claims to dignity and status, his demand for a rising share of industrial returns, his desire for a voice in the conditions which affected his work and conditions of employment—have marked the social struggles of the century. But beyond that, in the utopian visions of Marx and the socialist movement, the working class, made conscious of its fate by the conditions of struggle, was seen as the agency not only of industrial but of human emancipation; the last great brakes on production and abundance would be removed when the working class took over control of the means of production and ushered in the socialist millennium.

Yet if one takes the industrial worker as the instrument of the future, or, more specifically, the factory worker as the symbol of the proletariat, then this vision is warped. For the paradoxical fact is that as one goes along the trajectory of industrialization—the increasing replacement of men by machines—one comes logically to the erosion of the industrial worker himself. In fact by the end of the century the proportion of factory workers in the labor force may be as small as the proportion of farmers today; indeed, the entire area of blue-collar work may have diminished so greatly that the term will lose its sociological meaning as new categories, more appropriate to the divisions of the new labor force, are established. Instead of the industrial worker, we see the dominance of the professional and technical class in the labor force—so much so that by 1980 it will be the second largest occupational group in the society, and by the end of the century the largest. This is the new dual revolution taking place in the structure of occupations and, to the extent that occupation determines other modes of behavior (but this, too, is diminishing), it is a revolution in the class structure of society as well. This change in the character of production and of occupations is one aspect of the emergence of the "post-industrial" society. . . .

A post-industrial society is based on services. Hence, it is a game between persons. What counts is not raw muscle power, or energy, but information. The central person is the professional, for he is equipped, by his education and training, to provide the kinds of skill which are increasingly demanded in the post-industrial society. If an industrial society is defined by the quantity of goods as marking a standard of living, the post-industrial society is defined by the quality of life as measured by the services and amenities—health, education, recreation, and the arts—which are now deemed desirable and possible for everyone.

The word "services" disguises different things, and in the transformation of industrial to post-industrial society there are several different stages. First, in the very development of industry there is a necessary expansion of transportation and of public utilities as auxiliary services in the movement of goods and the increasing use of energy, and an increase in the non-manufacturing but still blue-collar force. Second, in the mass consumption of goods and the growth of populations there is an increase in distribution (wholesale and retail), and finance, real estate, and insurance, the traditional centers of white-collar employment. Third, as national incomes rise, one finds . . . that the proportion of money devoted to food at home begins to drop, and the marginal increments are used first for durables (clothing, housing, automobiles) and then for luxury items, recreation, and the like. Thus, a third sector, that of personal services, begins to grow: restaurants, hotels, auto services, travel, entertainment, sports, as people's horizons expand and new wants and tastes develop. But here a new consciousness begins to intervene. The claims to the good life which the society has promised become centered on the two areas that are fundamental to that life—health and education. The elimination of disease and the increasing numbers of people who can live out a full life, plus the efforts to expand the span of life, make health services a crucial feature of modern society; and the growth of technical requirements and professional skills makes education, and access to higher education, the condition of entry into the post-industrial society itself. So we have the growth of a new intelligentsia, particularly of teachers. Finally, the claims for more services and the inadequacy of the market in meeting people's needs for a decent environment as well as better health and education lead to the growth of government, particularly at the state and local level, where such needs have to be met.

The post-industrial society, thus, is also a "communal" society in which the social unit is the community rather than the individual, and one has to achieve a "social decision" as against, simply, the sum total of individual decisions which, when aggregated, end up as nightmares, on the model of the individual automobile and collective traffic congestion. But cooperation between men is more difficult than the management of things. Participation becomes a condition of community, but when many different groups want too many different things and are not prepared for bargaining or trade-off, then increased conflict or deadlocks result. Either there is a politics of consensus or a politics of stymie.

As a game between persons, social life becomes more difficult because political claims and social rights multiply, the rapidity of social change and shifting cultural fashion bewilders the old, and the orientation to the future erodes the traditional guides and moralities of the past. Information becomes a central resource, and within organizations a source of power. Professionalism thus becomes a criterion of position, but it clashes, too, with the populism which is generated by the claims for more rights and greater participation in the society. If the struggle between capitalist and worker, in the locus of the factory, was the hallmark of industrial society, the clash between the professional and the populace, in the organization and in the community, is the hallmark of conflict in the post-industrial society.

This, then, is the sociological canvas of the scheme of social development leading to the post-industrial society. . . .

Fred Roman on the Life of an Accountant, 1972

I usually say I'm an accountant. Most people think it's somebody who sits there with a green eyeshade and his sleeves rolled up with a garter, poring over books, adding things—with glasses. (Laughs.) I suppose a certified public accountant has status. It doesn't mean much to me. Do I like the job or don't I? That's important.

He is twenty-five and works for one of the largest public accounting firms in the world. It employs twelve hundred people. He has been with the company three years. During his first year, after graduating from college; he worked for a food chain, doing inventory.

The company I work for doesn't make a product. We provide a service. Our service is auditing. We are usually hired by stockholders or the board of directors. We will certify whether a company's financial statement is correct. They'll say, "This is what we did last year. We made X amount of dollars." We will come in to examine the books and say, "Yes, they did."

We're looking for things that didn't go out the door the wrong way. Our clients could say, "We have a million dollars in accounts receivable." We make sure that they do, in fact, have a million dollars and not a thousand. We ask the people who owe the money, "Do you, in fact, owe our client two thousand dollars as of this date?" We do it on a spot check basis. . . .

We work with figures, but we have to keep in mind what's behind those figures. What bugs me about people in my work is that they get too wrapped up in numbers. To them a financial statement is the end. To me, it's a tool used by management or stockholders.

We have a computer. We call it Audex. It has taken the detail drudgery out of accounting. I use things that come out of the computer in my everyday work. An accountant will prepare things for keypunching. A girl will keypunch and it will go into the monster. That's what we call it. (Laughs.) You still have to audit what comes out of the computer. I work with pencils. We all do. I think that's 'cause we make so many mistakes. (Laughs.) . . .

I'm not involved in keeping clients or getting them. That's the responsibility of the manager or the partner. I'm almost at the bottom of the heap. I'm the top class of assistant. There are five levels. I'm a staff assistant. Above me is senior. Senior's in charge of the job, out in the field with the client. The next level is manager. He has overall responsibility for the client. He's in charge of billing. The next step is partner. That's tops. He has an interest in the company. Our owners are called partners. They have final responsibility. The partner decides whether [a debt] is going to go or stay on the books.

There are gray areas. Say I saw . . . five hundred thousand dollars as a bad debt. The client may say, "Oh, the guy's good for it. He's going to pay." You say, "He hasn't paid you anything for the past six months. He declared bankruptcy yesterday. How can you say he's gonna pay?" Your client says, "He's reorganizing and he gonna get the money." You've got two ways of looking at this. The guy's able to pay or he's not. Somebody's gotta make a decision. Are we gonna allow you to show this receivable or are we gonna make you write it off? We usually compromise. We try to work out something in-between. The company knows more about it than we do, right? But we do have to issue an independent report. Anyway, I'm not a partner who makes those decisions. (Laughs.)

I think I'll leave before I get there. Many people in our firm don't plan on sticking around. The pressure. The constant rush to get things done. Since I've been here, two people have had nervous breakdowns. I have three bosses on any job, but I don't know who's my boss next week. I might be working for somebody else.

Our firm has a philosophy of progress, up or out. I started three years ago. If that second year I didn't move from SA–3, staff assistant, to SA–4, I'd be out. Last June I was SA–4. If I hadn't moved to SA–5, I'd be out. Next year if I don't move to senior, I'll be out. When I make senior I'll be Senior–1. The following year, Senior–2. Then Senior–3. Then manager—or out. By the time I'm thirty-four or so, I'm a partner or I'm out. . . .

It's a very young field. You have a lot of them at the bottom to do the footwork. Then it pyramids and you don't need so many up there. Most of the people they get are just out of college. I can't label them—the range is broad—but I'd guess most of them are conservative. Politics is hardly discussed.

Fifteen years ago, public accountants wore white shirts. You had to wear a hat, so you could convey a conservative image. When I was in college the big joke was: If you're going to work for a public accounting firm, make sure you buy a good supply of white shirts and a hat. They've gotten away from that since. We have guys with long hair. But they do catch more static than somebody in another business. And now we have women. There are several female assistants and seniors. There's one woman manager. We have no female partners.

If you don't advance, they'll help you find another job. They're very nice about it. They'll fire you, but they just don't throw you out in the street. (Laughs.) They'll try to find you a job with one of our clients. There's a theory behind it. Say I leave to go to XYZ Manufacturing Company. In fifteen years, I'm comptroller and I need an audit. Who am I gonna go to? Although their philosophy is up or out, they treat their employees very well. . . .

When people ask what I do, I tell them I'm an accountant. It sounds better than auditor, doesn't it? (Laughs.) But it's not a very exciting business. What can you say about figures? (Laughs.) You tell people you're an accountant—(his voice deliberately assumes a dull monotone) "Oh, that's nice." They don't know quite what to say. (Laughs.) What can you say? I could say, "Wow! I saw this company yesterday and their balance sheet, wow!" (Laughs.) Maybe I look at it wrong. (Slowly emphasizing each word) *There just isn't much to talk about.*

Women Office Workers Face
Dead-End Clerical Work, 1977

. . . Claire, the supervisor, was demonstrating the new word-processing machines. "There's no way I could go back to a regular electric typewriter after using this. Just watch." She inserted a small plastic card, pushed a button and in less than a minute the machine typed a full page perfectly.

"It's really something, isn't it?" Claire marveled.

In parallel rows young women, about half of them black, sat silently typing away. Or watching the typewriters type away.

"How many do you have working here now?" Bonnie asked, knowing the answer.

"As of this month we're down to ten."

"And just a few years ago there were how many?" Bonnie continued.

"Twenty-three."

"And I bet you're getting out as much work as before."

"Oh, yes. Probably more."

Although she was exactly the same age as Bonnie, Claire looked years older. Perhaps it had something to do with her position, with her slightly prim manner, the totally serious attitude with which she approached her work, the dedication even. She considered herself not simply a supervisor, but also a teacher, she told me a few days later when we met outside the office for a talk. Ever since the company had sent her to a lecture series on How-to-Supervise she had become "a nut about training," about "developing my girls," but for reasons beyond her control things rarely seemed to work out as she planned.

. . . I asked what it would be like to be starting out in her department.

"Okay, it's your first day. You're probably scared to death so I'd try first of all to make you feel at ease. I'd take you around the department. Introduce you to everyone. I'd assign you a lunch partner so later you wouldn't have to go out all alone.

"Then I'd sit you down and explain our training program. This is something, frankly, I'm rather proud of. It's something I worked out myself, using as a basis our company's own *Tips for Typists* pamphlet which has an index of insurance terms. First to get some general ideas about your skills, what kind of practice you're going to need, I'd start you on a sample letter on a simple electric typewriter. I wouldn't be too concerned about your mistakes at this point, more about the setup of the letter. Frankly our executives are extremely fussy about how things look and to be honest I think they have a perfect right.

"Then for about your first week, I'd give you a choice of simple jobs. There's a bin of handwritten stuff we all have to type up, reports, letters, charts, memos, everything you can think of, and usually we take these things in rotation. You finish something, you take the next, that's the fairest way. But since you're new, you'd be able to pick out what you want.

"As a beginner here you'd be starting out at grade-level two. For some reason, maybe they think it would be insulting, we have no grade-level one. With our latest salary schedule that means you'd be getting $108 a week to start.

"Probably I'd keep you on this simple typing for about a month. Then if everything was going smoothly I'd put you on the word-processing machines. Now you'd be learning all about our different form letters, about inserting different standardized paragraphs with others, and I'd be encouraging you all the time, following your progress. You'd stay on this for a while, coupled with ordinary work on the regular typewriter.

"Then, usually in the beginning of the second month, I'd start giving you training on the dictaphone. This is very important. We get tapes from all over the field, some are transmitted on the telephone as well as by hand and through the mail. It takes a while to learn how to do it, the voice can be fuzzy, or they're mixing things up, but I'd be right there helping you out as much as I could.

"In about a month after that, say about the beginning of your third month, if you're progressing okay you'd be advanced to level three, which means a five- or eight-dollar raise, so that now you could be up to $113 or $116. You really should be if everything is going right. Certainly by six months you should be at level three. If there's a problem, I'll try to work it out with you.

"By the way, when you get to the dictaphone stage, I wouldn't have you doing that all the time. So that your day will be varied as much as possible I'd rotate the different kinds of work—word processing, simple typing, dictaphone. That is my policy anyway. At the moment, however, we've been having a lot of sickness in the department, colds, flus, I don't know what's the matter with everybody, we've been very shortstaffed and that makes it difficult to spread the work around the way I like. But if it's at all possible I do.

"Now you'd be building up to level four—that's a senior transcription clerk. And that means you'd have more responsibility and could handle the most difficult jobs. To get to level four should take you between a year, say, and a year and a half."

"And then?" I asked.

"Well, frankly, the trouble is after level four there's nowhere else for you to go. Nowhere except for assistant supervisor and supervisor—and the people who get these jobs generally stay forever. I was a senior transcriber myself for over three years before the assistant supervisor got pregnant and left and that was unusually lucky for me. And then a few months ago the supervisor quit, another incredible break. As I say it rarely happens. Supervisors hardly ever leave around here."

I asked Claire about the company's affirmative action program.

"What's that? Oh, yes, I think I heard something. They've made a few women assistant managers and two have become managers. And I think they've started hiring some women college graduates for other kinds of jobs. But that hasn't anything to do with our department. The girls in our department don't get to go anywhere else usually."

I asked about the company's tuition refund program.

"Well, I think someone in our department used it a few years ago to learn steno, but that's the only one I can remember. And since we have so little call for secretaries here—you have to be on a really high level to get one—it didn't do her any good. At least not here. She left. And now with those two departments moving there'll probably be less call for secretaries."

I asked about the turnover in her department.

. . . She pursed her lips. "Okay, last year we had fifteen girls come and go in just twelve months. In a department of only ten or so you can see how bad that is." . . .

"How would you change your department if you could?"

"Let's see. Well, first I'd give them a full hour for lunch so they'd have time to go out if they wanted to. And I'd raise their salaries so they could afford to—particularly those who have been here for a while. What they're getting . . . it's really not enough with today's prices, is it? And then, last, I'd create another level, a new level five between senior transcriber and assistant supervisor. Maybe then they wouldn't be leaving us all the time."

Claire obviously assumed that the company really wanted all the women in her department to stay for years and years. Yet, as I told her, I had long been under the impression that giant insurance companies (as well as other large corporations) traditionally expected, no, traditionally *depended* on what they blithely called A&P (attrition and pregnancy) to keep their clerical salary levels down. Except for a select proportion—the cream— who were to be groomed, like Claire, for somewhat higher roles, they counted on the exit of many noncollege employees after several years and the entrance of new high school graduates to take their places at beginners' wages. Which is partly why they usually preferred young women to older women (who were less likely to quit) for such "entry" (dead-end) positions in the first place. . . .

Claire frowned. "Probably they do expect some to leave but not as many as we've had, I don't think. And as far as getting the girls cheaper, I hear that's why they're moving those departments. The small town where they're going has lower salaries, generally."

"Will your department be affected by the move?"

"I can't say. It's all pretty uncertain. Just a lot of rumors so far. No one knows what's going to happen."

"What about your own future?"

"Don't know. I don't see moving by myself, all alone. There's nothing else going on in that town. I'll tell you the truth. I like my work. I think the company's great, but sometimes I can't help wishing I was married, taking care of my own kids at home."

And if and when you do that, I thought, will the company be able to find someone cheaper to replace you, too? Another happy statistic for the A&P file? No, at your level they do believe in paying for experience— don't they? "By the way," I asked, "how much are you paid for all the responsibility you now assume?" (I'd read that the president, whom Claire and Bonnie were privileged to call by his first name, made well over $200,000 a year.)

"I just got a raise," Claire said. "Before taxes, $177 a week."

The Day-Care Nightmare, 1988

To the well-documented strains associated with day care, add another: as more women leave home for work and careers, fewer are available to take care of other people's children.

While the number of day care centers is growing, the greatest proportion of child care does not take place in these formal settings. Instead, families send their children to a friend across town or the lady down the street who watches several children besides her own.

According to the Census Bureau's 1984–85 data . . . , 37 percent of the nation's 8.2 million preschool children whose mothers work are in such arrangements, known collectively as family day care. Another 23 percent spend most of their time in day care centers or preschool programs, about twice the percentage that were in such programs in 1977. . . .

Family day care, staffed almost entirely by women, has been hard hit by the backwash from the social trend that created them in the first place: the growing number of working mothers.

"It's a nightmare," said Dr. Michael Rothenberg, the Seattle pediatrician who is co-author of the latest edition of "Dr. Spock's Baby and Child Care."

"We all know that by 1990, 80 percent of the mothers with children under 1 will be working and looking for child care, and where the hell are they going to find it?"

Since there is little reliable up-to-date data on the child care industry, in part because 60 to 90 percent of all family day care is unlicensed, it is impossible to say how many child care providers there are, or how many are leaving the field. But both national data on working women, and anecdotal evidence from those concerned with child care, suggest a brewing crisis.

"Three years ago, we used to get one or two calls a month from parents in this area who were looking for child care, and now we probably get 25 a week," said Kay Hollestelle, a spokeswoman for the National Association for Family Day Care, in Washington. "Some of them are desperate, saying they've been looking for weeks and they're due back at work July 1 and what can they do. We're not set up to give them names, so about all I can do is send them to a referral agency, or suggest that they think about becoming child-care providers themselves." . . .

Last year, two-thirds of all school-age children had working mothers, and for the first time, even most mothers of babies under a year old were employed. Indeed, since United States employers, unlike those in most other industrialized countries, are not required to provide maternity leave, many infants now go into group care when they are only a few weeks old.

"Those neighbors and aunts and grandmothers who have been going out and getting jobs are the very same women who would have been taking

"Daycare Becomes a Growing Burden," by Tamar Lewin, June 5, 1988. Copyright © 1988 by The New York Times Company. Reprinted by permission.

care of kids in the days when women stayed home," said Ellen Galinsky, director of Work and Family Life Studies at Bank Street College of Education in New York. "Now that those people aren't around, there's an enormous demand for more formal child care programs."

But the search for good-quality day care is difficult for families that can not afford the fees—as much as $215 a week for a child in some large cities—of formal day-care centers, or the even higher cost of an individual babysitter. Generally full-time care is 40 to 50 hours a week.

Family day care usually costs less, generally from $30 to a little over $100 a week, with unlicensed day care at the low end of the scale. Family day care also has the added appeal to some parents of a home setting rather than an institutional one. . . .

But child-care experts worry that because so much family day care is unregulated—often quite legally—many of the homes are overcrowded and unsafe. Licensing requirements vary widely from state to state, but over the last few years there has been a general trend toward stricter requirements, although enforcement is often lax.

The experts point to a steady stream of incidents like the one . . . in which 18-month old Jessica McClure of Midland, Tex., fell into a well shaft at the unlicensed day care program where her aunt watched nine children.

About a third of all working parents still manage to look after their children without paying for child care at all, either by leaving the child with a relative, or splitting care with a nearby friend or relative or a spouse who works a different shift.

But as families become more spread out, and more women work, such arrangements are increasingly difficult to work out.

"Ten years ago, when my oldest son was born, my mother lived with us and looked after him and I didn't worry," said Mary Robinson, a researcher who lives in Palo Alto, Calif. "And when my second child was born, my mother wasn't living with us anymore, but my mother-in-law was available to take care of her. But when Britney was born, there wasn't anybody in the family who could do it."

Mrs. Robinson found a family day care home for her two youngest children, but after four weeks, she decided they were not getting enough attention, and she moved them to a different home.

"Now that lady, who is a nurse, is going back to work," said Mrs. Robinson.

Turnover among family day care providers is a staggering 60 percent a year, as against about 40 percent among those who work at day-care centers.

The lack of stability can be a terrible strain on both the children whose routines and attachments are suddenly disrupted, and on their parents.

"One of the things that's critical to child development, especially in the first year of life, is constancy of care," said Dr. Rothenberg.

But it can be hard to find. Theresa Canada of Hillsborough, N.C., went back to work when her daughter, Elizabeth, was 4 weeks old—and by the time Elizabeth was 6 months old she had been cared for in eight different homes. "Each time, on a Friday, they'd tell me I had to find someone else for Monday," said Mrs. Canada, adding that the women gave different reasons for their decisions. "It made me miss a lot of work, and I was tearing my hair out." . . .

While child care has gained wide social acceptance in recent years, the salaries and job benefits are not improving fast enough to attract people to the field. Most full-time child-care workers earn less than $10,000 a year, which is less than either parking lot attendants or animal caretakers are paid.

"It's always been seen as something between a market service and an informal exchange," said Sheila Kamerman, a social-policy professor at Columbia University's School of Social Work. "As labor market opportunities for women increase, the number who stay in family day care is going to decrease, and we're going to have the same kind of crisis we're seeing with foster care and homemakers and all the other things women used to do without much compensation. I think we're going to have to see more professionalization of family day care."

A Worker Pleads the Case for Family and Medical Leave, 1987

My name is Tina Hurst. I live in Newark, Delaware, with my husband and two children, Heather, age 8, and Ian, age 3. . . . The Family and Medical Leave Act is important legislation for all parents of minor and adult children with disabilities. One never thinks about the need for the minimum requirements provided in this legislation until something happens to your family.

We are an example of the average American family. We needed two incomes to support ourselves and our two children. In May 1985, I started working at a large pharmaceutical company, as a handpacker. The company's leave policy allowed for three days off, unpaid, every six months.

Nearly a year later, my three year old son Ian had his first seizure. We rushed him to the hospital where he was diagnosed with pneumonia and high fever which set off the initial seizure. He was hospitalized for four days. My husband and I alternated taking time off from work to be with him. I was working the third shift, so I was able to be at the hospital during the day, but I still missed two nights of work. The doctors advised us to stay with him at all times in the hospital. In late August Ian had a very serious asthma attack and was admitted to the hospital in serious condition. Once again I missed two nights of work to be with him. When I returned to work the next day, my supervisor warned me that I had taken more than the three days of the unpaid sick leave allowed and that I should watch my absenteeism.

In September Ian had a severe allergic reaction to the drug he was taking for his epilepsy. He continued to have seizures. In mid-October Ian was again hospitalized for high fever and pneumonia. I missed two nights of work. Then my supervisor and personnel manager said that if I missed one more night of work in the next six months they would fire me or I would be asked to resign. I explained Ian's condition and asked if I could have a leave of absence, rather than being fired. They said no, but assured me that they would rehire me with seniority if my son's health improved.

I did not feel any other option but to resign—which I did. In late November Ian's seizures came under control. I called the personnel manager, who told me that they were not hiring and to check back in March. I was shocked. I expected them to keep the promise they had made to me when I resigned. I lost my job because I was forced to choose between caring for my seriously ill child or working to help support my family.

I missed only *six nights* of work in seven months, and the company was well aware that each of my absences was due to my son's hospitalizations. This is an emotionally stressful period for me and my family. Losing my job has made this difficult experience even harder. We still need my income to support our children and to help take care of our medical expenses.

✢ E S S A Y S

In the first essay, journalist Andrew Levison challenges the idea, widely held in the 1950s and 1960s, that most American workers had joined a broad, homogeneous middle class. He does this in two ways: first, by demonstrating that blue-collar, manual labor has hardly disappeared, and second, by deconstructing Census Bureau categories to show that much manual, routine labor is in fact hidden within the white-collar sectors of the economy, namely, service, sales, and clerical work. Thus whatever the color of the collar, a working-class majority still exists in the postwar United States. In the late 1960s, male wages and family income began to stagnate, prompting a vast increase in the proportion of women who entered the labor force in the 1970s and 1980s. In the second essay, economist Heidi Hartmann, director of the Institute for Women's Policy Research, argues that, regardless of their motivation, women's entry into the labor force serves to boost the power and independence of women in the home and in a marriage. Writing in the 1980s, a decade later than Levison, she suggests that the decline of heavy industry and the shift to a service economy will indeed blur the lines between work that was once considered white-collar or blue-collar, male or female, to create the possibility of greater homogeneity within the working class and a new era of collective struggle.

The Working-Class Majority

ANDREW LEVISON

It was one of the cold, chilly, gray days of fall, for which the Midwest is famous, when I sat in a university classroom and took notes in a bored and abstracted fashion from one of the faceless army of professors who drag one from freshman to senior year in the colleges of the "Big Ten."

Andrew Levison, *The Working Class Majority*. Copyright © 1976 by Andrew Levison. Abridgements by permission of the Putnam Publishing Group, pp. 17–51.

I was sitting toward the back with a friend who was equally distracted and bored. He was a Vietnam vet who was born in a working-class suburb of Milwaukee. The topic of the lecture was "The Working Class," and had there been a spark of interest in the professor's presentation, my blue-collar friend, at any rate, would have been roused from his doldrums.

But instead of anything dramatically new, the professor was simply reciting the common wisdom of postwar American society. "The working class," he asserted, "is, for several reasons, no longer a central force in American society.

"First, they have become a minority. White-collar workers now out-number blue-collar.

"Second, rising income levels have eliminated the rigid distinctions between blue-collar and white-collar—some blue-collar workers, like plumbers and mechanics, make more than white-collar workers like clerks and teachers.

"Third, the suburbs have created social and cultural integration, a common life-style that makes the distinctive working-class neighborhood or culture a thing of the past."

The professor went on to declare the political implications of this change, which, in his view, was the end of any distinctive "working-class" political attitudes.

This lecture was delivered in the fall of 1967—and within six months George Wallace would end the idea that the man who works in a factory was politically the same as his university professor cohort in suburban America.

The other points, about the percentages, life, and conditions of American workers, would not die so easily. In one form or another they have continued up to today and many still believe them.

. . . But, each of these conclusions is wrong and politically dangerous . . . They are, in fact, simply myths that must be put aside. . . .

The first conclusion, that a majority of Americans are white collar, seems hard to deny. If a student in that classroom, for example, had not been convinced by his professor's assertion, he would have found little to support his skepticism. His economics textbook had a full-page chart which made the white-collar occupations appear to be spreading throughout America like some advancing army charging across a map of Europe. . . .

But, while it is understandable that a note-taker in that class would give up in despair, it is a shame. If he had pressed on one more step, he would have found that the terms white collar and blue collar were used in a specific and technical way that was not the way we use them in ordinary conversation. . . .

In terms of occupation, the division is basically between manual, essentially physical or menial, labor and managerial or intellectual work. Blue-collar workers mean people who work with their hands, not with their minds. The images are the factory worker or the garbage collector, the construction worker or the man who carries your bags in the airport. People instantly recognize that there is something fundamental that separates all the people who "punch a clock" or just "bust my ass all day" from the doctors, lawyers, and executives whose jobs are an important, creative part of their lives and mean something to them. Working-class jobs are almost inevitably relatively low paying and low in prestige. Day to day, they offer little independence or control, certainly in comparison with a doctor or lawyer.

On the other hand, "white-collar jobs" bring to mind the image of the man behind the desk: William L. White's *The Organization Man*, angling for the vice-president's job. Or else the doctor or lawyer, the "professional" man comes to mind.

These jobs are relatively high in status and pay, and offer more in-dependence, control, and satisfaction than work which requires only rote, mechanical labor.

Some jobs fall in a gray area between these two poles. These are, in general, the lowest level clerical positions. But this basic brain vs. brawn dichotomy is how we really think about class in America. In 1970, when construction workers beat up students in downtown New York, the horrified reactions of many intellectuals clearly expressed the real way class is viewed. Liberals said, "Those thugs are beating up our kids. *They* don't understand. *They* must all be fascists. *We* have to do something!"

All of the clichés which said construction workers were really middle-class and shared the life-style of the intellectuals were forgotten. It was *us* and *them* and *they* meant working class. Thus, if we want to think in practical political terms about American workers, this simple commonsense division is what we must use as a guide.

In a way, it shouldn't even have been necessary to justify this point of view. Since most people use blue-collar and white-collar as synonyms for brawn and brain, for manual labor vs. professional and managerial work, one would reasonably expect that when statistics are quoted, they are based fairly concretely on this dichotomy.

But the problem is that they are not. . . . The precise definition of the category "blue-collar" limits it to production and distributive workers, who are only a fragment of all the Americans who are still employed in essentially rote, manual labor.

First of all, the "service" workers were excluded from the blue-collar classification. But within this group are such occupations as janitors, wait-ers, porters, ushers, elevator operators, doormen, and even shoeshine boys. These jobs just listed are a "who's who" of the most menial and low-paying occupations in America. Yet, when writers quoted the percentage of "blue-collar" workers at 37.5 percent they were automatically including everyone else, including the service workers, in the middle class. Other workers in the service category are equally manual: guards, watchmen, cooks, housekeepers, hospital and other attendants, barbers, police, and firemen. Only a tiny handful of people who hold jobs such as FBI agents and detectives could even be suggested as middle-class.

In addition, the male clerical and sales category, considered as part of the white-collar group, proves to have many working-class jobs concealed within it. The postman is a clerical worker. So is the young man in the supermarket who punches the prices on the cans. Baggagemen, messenger boys, bill collectors, newsboys, auctioneers, peddlers, office machine operators, bus and train dispatchers, telegraph operators, and so on, are all contained in the white-collar category and hence called middle class.

All of this becomes clear just by looking at the specific occupations for men. But on turning the page to the breakdown for women, suddenly we realize we have been thoroughly bamboozled.

When people read those quotes about the end of manual labor and the new white-collar majority they automatically thought of doctors and lawyers and "corporation" men as the "new class." But what they were reading were statistics not only about men, but about all women too, even those who only worked a few hours a week.

These women comprise 70 percent of clerical and sales workers, a key part of the "middle-class majority." They work as telephone operators, cashiers, salesgirls, typists, and in other low-paying, low-status jobs. The euphoric image of a society of professionals and executives is irrevocably lost. Eighty percent of the labor force are either manual or clerical workers, with the majority in manual jobs.

Some sociologists have tried to salvage the "middle-class majority" by suggesting that these women clerical and sales workers are a "new" social group, a lower-middle-class "salariat." This is an appealing solution since one would hesitate about calling these women "working-class."

Many writers have been seduced by this concept since it seems to apply to the many "career girls" whom one meets and who seem more middle-class than working-class. The image of the women clerical and sales workers that these writers have is the New York single girl, perhaps a Vassar graduate, who is working as a secretary, but dreams of "getting into publishing." She lives with two other girls in an expensive East Side apartment, reads *Ms.*, takes courses at the New School on some strange subject like existential pottery, smokes pot on occasion, and goes skiing on the weekends. Such a person, however, is not at all typical of the clerical and sales category. Most women clerical and sales workers are married and about half are *married to working-class men.*

Suddenly the career girl secretary is joined by a somewhat less romantic figure, a welder's wife who works part time as a cashier in the A&P. Instead of *Ms.*, imagine *Reader's Digest*, instead of ski slopes, it's Wednesday night bowling. Lastly, not pot but one of her husband's beers. If a sociologist met her on the street, she would be one of "them," not one of "us."

The best way to clarify this confusion is to look at the occupational structure for men alone. Most women are married and therefore live in the class and culture of their husbands. They follow their husbands lead in politics and all their social life is with their husbands' class. Thus the occupations for men give a much clearer indication of the relative size of the working class and middle class in America.

The following chart shows the proportions quite clearly:

Major Occupation Groups for Males, 1969

Professional and Technical	14.6% 29.2		
Managers, Officials and Proprietors	14.6	/ ....42.4 Middle Class	
Clerical	7.4 ....13.2		
Sales	5.8		
Craftsmen and Foremen	21.4		
Operatives	21.4 ....57.5 Working Class		
Laborers	7.6		
Service	7.1		

When we remember that there are many working-class jobs like mailmen hidden in the clerical and sales category, the true manual figure is probably 60–62 percent. Thus, three-fifths, 60 percent of America is working-class. The euphoric concept of a middle-class majority, the end of manual labor, and the new age in human history were all based on including the wives of steelworkers who went to work as cashiers and salesgirls as middle-class.

This chart, however, includes black and white Americans. Since blacks are disproportionately employed as manual workers, one might suspect most *white* people could be white-collar.

This, however, is not the case: 55.3 percent of white men are in the four manual categories, and with the misclassified clerical workers one can estimate about 58 percent, perhaps more, are what we would call working-class. Thus, the difference is about 2 percent—57.5 to 55.3. . . .

America is not a white-collar or middle-class society. Sixty percent of American men still work in essentially rote, manual jobs.

For all practical purposes this is the key point. Next Monday 60 percent of American men will begin a new week at nine to five jobs which they do basically with their hands. To anyone who is involved in organizing communities, winning elections, or passing legislation this is the reality they must face.

But, it does leave open the possibility that blue-collar work may be rapidly disappearing and perhaps in a few years we will have our beloved middle-class majority after all. Social analysts most certainly jumped the gun in announcing the end of manual labor, but perhaps they were right in saying that fundamental changes occurred in the postwar period and that the long range trend is toward the end of manual labor. . . .

If we look at the actual number of people in different occupations, there is one absolutely stunning fact. The number of working-class Americans has not decreased at all—in fact, since 1950 it has increased by roughly four million! There are four million more workers in America today than in 1950. The declining trend the analysts notice is totally relative— as the population grew, the working class increased, but the minority of Americans who are middle-class increased at a faster rate.

Here are the figures for men in terms of our commonsense definitions and rounded off:

	1950	1969	CHANGE, 1950–69
Middle Class	13,000,000	19,000,000	+6,000,000
Working Class	22,000,000	26,000,000	+4,000,000

This white-collar increase is significant, but let us put it in perspective. The relative percentage of workers goes down, from 62.4 percent to 57.5 percent, a 5 percent drop in twenty years (not counting the misclassified clerical and sales workers).

But first of all, that still leaves us with 26 million working-class American men and 19 million middle-class. That is a raw social and political fact that cannot be denied.

Second, the middle class needed an increase of three million people just to stay even with the working class and hold the working-class majority at 62 percent. So there are only a bit less than three million middle-class people who indicate something new in the occupational structure since 1950.

Again, the raw number is striking. The whole "great change," the postwar "revolution," the end of manual labor comes down to less than three million men in a male labor force of 45 million. It may be significant, but it hardly constitutes a fundamental change in the very nature of society. At this rate there will be a working-class majority until the next century. At least another generation of Americans will be predominantly working-class. Seven presidents and thousands of congressmen will be elected by a working-class majority. . . .

A closer look at changes in the particular occupational categories since 1950 shows some further points of interest:

Employed Men by Occupation (in Thousands), 1950 and 1969

MIDDLE CLASS	1950	1969
Professional and Technical	2,700	6,800
Managers, Officials, and Proprietors	5,400	6,700
Clerical	3,000	3,400
Sales	2,400	2,700

WORKING CLASS	1950	1969
Craftsmen and Foremen	7,500	9,900
Operatives	8,800	9,900
Laborers	3,400	3,500
Service	2,700	3,300

In the white-collar category the striking fact is that the three million "new" workers are clearly in the professional and technical category, whose growth can be largely traced to two concrete events of the postwar period. One is the sudden growth of the educational system in response to the postwar baby boom and Sputnik. A second is the massive allocation of resources to scientific research and development, much of it directly related to military projects.

Obviously, a large part of the "great change" was the result of some very concrete political decisions on how to spend the taxpayers' money and not an earth-shattering revolution in the nature of American capitalism. This is not as exciting as "postindustrial states" or "new eras in human history" but it is very likely closer to the truth.

The lower half of the chart also blows the whistle on some other cherished illusions. For one thing, skilled workers have clearly been growing rapidly, and the least-skilled blue-collar category hardly at all. But in 1969, the majority of American workers, 61 percent in fact, were unskilled or semiskilled. We will see that skilled workers have been the victims of many myths, but at this point, we can at least dismiss the belief that they are typical blue-collar workers. A significant minority yes, but a majority no. . . .

If manual workers live exactly like white-collar workers, however, then the fact that they work in factories instead of offices is probably not of great political significance.

This is, of course, what most commentators have told us. The message that blue-collar workers are now "middle class" or "middle Americans" has been repeated so many times that no one ever thinks of questioning it. Although no longer called affluent, they are never called poor. . . .

[T]he Bureau of Labor Statistics calculates "standard budgets" which tell us what we need to know. Each budget is geared for a family of four.

Although they use the neutral terms, upper, middle, and lower to describe three standards of living, these budgets automatically define the three distinct socioeconomic cultures in the United States, the culture of poverty, working-class culture and the life-style of middle-class affluence. Most affluent people, for example, buy a certain kind of clothing, rent or buy a distinct kind of house or apartment, buy a certain kind and amount of food, and so forth.

Every year the B.L.S. sends its employees out into the stores, car lots, and real estate agencies to find out how much these characteristic kinds of purchases cost.

The result is three budgets which reflect the average cost of obtaining the basic goods and services on each of the three levels. Thus, in 1970, for example, the lower standard of living budget was $6,960. This meant that a poor family needed $6,960 to obtain the typical shelter, clothing, etc., of most "lower-income" people in America.

The intermediate budget is immediately recognizable as the world of the blue-collar worker, the world of Sears, Roebuck furniture, four-dollar bourbon and two-year-old cars, traded in every six years. It is not a standard of affluence or anything remotely resembling the American dream. It constitutes the cost of living that some unions call a "shabby, but respectable, life."

In 1970, this intermediate budget required $10,670 and the affluent budget required $15,950. . . .

Working Class Family Income, 1970

INCOME IN THOUSANDS	PERCENT	PERCENT OF ALL WORKING-CLASS FAMILIES BELOW THIS LEVEL
1–7	29.5	29.5—30% Poor
7–8	8.1	37.6
8–9	8.6	46.2
9–10	8.2	54.5—60% "Below Intermediate"
10–12	14.8	69.4
12–15	15.2	84.4—85% "Below Affluence"
15+	15.5	100.0

. . . The majority of American working people do not even earn enough for the "middle American," "intermediate" budget. . . .

Thirty percent—almost a third of employed American workers, are living in what is really poverty. They made less than $7,000 in a year when the "lower" budget called for $6,960. This means a total family income of $135 per week *before taxes*. Another 30 percent were above the poverty budget, but below that "shabby" intermediate level. Thus, 60 percent of the working class is either poor or hovering between poverty and the very modest level contained in the intermediate budget. A United Auto Workers study shows just how "modest" that budget is.

It assumes, for example, that the family will own:
      . . . A toaster that will last for 33 years;
      . . . A refrigerator and a range that will each last 17 years;
      . . . A vacuum cleaner that will last 14 years;
      . . . A television set that will last ten years.
The budget assumes that a family will buy a two-year-old car, and keep it for four years. In that time they will pay for a tune-up once a year, a brake realignment every three years, and a front-end alignment every four years . . .
The budget assumes that the husband will buy one year-round suit every four years . . . and one topcoat every 8½ years.
It assumes that the husband will take his wife to the movies once every three months, and that one of them will go alone once a year. The two children are each allowed one movie every four weeks. A total of $2.54 per person per year is allowed for admission to all other events, from football and baseball games to theater or concerts.
Finally, the budget allows nothing whatever for savings.

. . . The affluent worker, who until recently was supposed to be typical, constitutes 12 to 15 percent of the working class, white and black. . . . The average worker earned $9,500 in 1970, much closer to poverty than to affluence. It is an ironic fact that, while many commentators spoke of the affluent worker with two cars in the garage and a color TV, even today, the majority of blue-collar workers have neither.

These statistics do include black workers. But a simple calculation shows that excluding them would only increase the "well-being" of white workers by about 2.5 percent—this is more than counterbalanced by the simple fact that these figures are the before-tax income. They are also the income of the entire family, working wives and children included. These statistics do not include the long-term unemployed, the ill, or old people on pensions. These figures describe the working poor, not poverty in general. . . .

In fact, more than anything else, it is working wives who have made possible even the modest standard of living workers enjoy. The earnings of the husband, even if employed full time, shows very clearly what a worker's paycheck looks like:

Median Working-Class Income by Occupation, 1970	
Craftsmen and Foremen	$9,253
Operatives	7,644
Laborers	6,462
Service	6,964

In May 1970, the typical manufacturing production worker with three dependents had earnings of $132.93 weekly and spendable earnings (i.e., after taxes, etc.) of $115.27. . . . It is worth keeping this in mind when one imagines a working class family which has an income of $10,000 a year— he earned only seven or eight thousand and his wife the rest. Or the skilled worker's family who has $12,000. He often gets $9,000—she, the balance.

Suddenly, all the analyses which say workers don't really have any legitimate economic complaints look rather doubtful.

As we will see, a single illness, a period of unemployment or the loss of the wife's income when she becomes pregnant can wipe out a lifetime of savings and send many working-class families into a permanent cycle of debt and economic crises. The conclusion is inescapable: millions are still living far below the level needed for a full, decent life.

But, if the objective situation of most workers comes as a surprise, when we compare it to the middle class, the conclusion is so stunning and so disruptive of anything that we have heard that some people may find it difficult to accept despite the facts.

To make the comparison clear, let us first look at something we know, the economic inequality between black and white.

The average family income of blacks is 60 percent of whites, a difference of about $4,000. What this means is that in order for black people to be on the same economic level as whites, once a year we would have to give every black family a check for an average of $4,000. This 60 percent or $4,000 is a shorthand way of understanding the degree of inequality between black and white in America. . . .

When we turn to working class vs. middle class, however, the clichés about the similar life-styles and a narrowing income gap lead us to expect something far different. . . .

However, the average white-collar income is about $12,500, while blue-collar, as we saw, is $9,500. This is a difference of about $3,000 or, to put it another way, blue-collar income is about 77 percent of white-collar.

But, as we noted, the white-collar total includes many clerical and sales workers who are really manual workers. If we look at the two predominant categories, professional and technical, and managers and proprietors (75 percent of all white-collar men), we find their average income is about $14,500. Manual workers earn only 65 percent of the upper-middle-class average, and the difference between them is $5,000. We would have to give every worker in America $5,000 to create real equity in income between the professional and managerial middle class and the working class. In percentage terms, the inequality between manual workers and most white-collar workers is almost as great as the gap between black and white, and in the absolute number of dollars that separate them, the distance between manual and professional and managerial workers is, in fact, greater.

This doesn't mean that workers are as poor or as exploited as blacks. They are not. What it does mean is that the inequality, the distance a factory worker sees between himself and the middle class is almost as great as the distance the average black person sees between himself and white America. There is a profound economic inequality between black and white America, but there is also a profound inequality between social classes, as well. If a black skin means economic inequality, so does a blue collar. Economic inequity and injustice in America come in both colors. . . .

If one doesn't personally know and talk with blue-collar workers it is possible to think that this inequality has little practical impact on the average worker. Yet the fact is, blue-collar workers really are deeply aware of it. All through the fifties and sixties, while intellectuals were talking about the disappearance of class, workers saw the chasm between themselves and the theorists who wrote about them. The auto assembly line worker, who owns a five-year-old Chevy he bought second hand, spends eight or nine or even ten hours a day building Cadillacs or Torinos he will never buy, and he knows it is the middle class that is buying them. As middle-class people go flying to Acapulco or San Juan for Christmas, they leave under the watchful eyes of mechanics, maintenance men and cabdrivers, who get two weeks vacation a year, and usually spend it at home, or perhaps take a drive with the family to Disney World or a national park for a few days. Social inequality is not abstract for these people. It is a visible daily reality. . . .

The one myth which remains is the "suburban worker." According to the authorities, it was here that the American dream of social and economic equality became a practical reality. The blue-collar worker no longer came home to his dreary tenement, still dressed in his work clothes, where he was packed together with his fellows. Now he changed clothes in the factory and drove to his suburban home, looking just like his middle-class neighbor who arrived alongside him. The common suburban life-style and daily personal contact, they said, was rapidly eliminating all of the distinctive "working-class" qualities of blue-collar America. America was a country of suburbs and the great social problem was crabgrass.

In the last few years this euphoric image has been tarnished by white resistance to residential integration, and suburbs are now counterposed to the image of the decaying inner cities. But, the vision of the suburbs as a single, undifferentiated mass of middle Americans still remains. Suburban whites and ghetto blacks define the way most people think of American society. . . .

[W]orking-class suburbs [do not] offer a life-style the same as the affluent ones. . . . First, the median value of a worker's home in 1964 was $13,237, while that of the upper middle class's was $20,375. In addition, fewer workers owned houses than did the upper middle class (61 percent vs. 83 percent). . . .

In general, working-class suburbs get the freeways, airports, or public housing which lower community values.

One could assemble a staff and spend a year confirming this reality with detailed studies of every city in America. But in fact we know that the middle class does not go to the bars and bowling alleys of working-class America, and that workers do not go to the same "art" films or expensive restaurants. If we think about it we realize that the suburbs we pass on the way to work are different from our own.

The truth is that working-class people are shadowy figures to most middle-class people. Contact is limited to a quick glance at a knot of construction workers sitting on the sidewalk eating lunch. Or else it is a few words exchanged with a postman, doorman, or telephone installer. Beyond this, few have gone.

. . . If one lives in a middle-class suburb and works in an office, one never sees blue-collar workers and, naturally, one never talks to them. From this distorted frame of reference, it is easy to believe that workers are disappearing, or living like the middle class. . . .

The discontents of blue-collar workers have been dismissed as unimportant, their economic demands called greedy, and their particular interests almost systematically ignored. Condescending and elitist theories of working-class psychology have been developed to explain their behavior, inevitably assuming workers have no legitimate complaints. . . .

The condition of blacks in America is, ironically, easier to deal with than that of white workers. . . . [M]any people have in their memories certain statistics like the fact that there are almost 25 million, perhaps more, black people in America, that the unemployment rate is usually double that of whites, and so forth.

However, the undeniable injustices of unemployment and welfare have often led to a visual image of the black community as entirely composed of unemployed ghetto youths and welfare mothers. This, along with the social crises of bad housing and medical facilities, narcotics, and crime results in a liberal vision of the black community as some unique "underclass" or "culture of poverty."

The problem with this "underclass" view is that, while it highlights some of the most critical problems, it obscures certain key facts. Most black people are not welfare recipients or "street dudes." They are blue-collar workers who work in some of the dirtiest, lowest paying, and often most dangerous jobs in America. This means that, in economic terms, the problems of black people, although significantly worse than the problems of white workers, are part of the general pattern of social and economic inequality in America, and not some accidental, special case in an otherwise egalitarian society. Most black people, for example, are poor because of *low wages,* not inadequate welfare payments or unemployment. Although concern with the poverty of unemployed youths and welfare mothers is valid and important, it should not lead us to ignore the poverty of black janitors and dishwashers, maids and laundry workers. In an economic sense, the most important source of black poverty is the exploitation of black workers through low-paying jobs. Even among black youths, whose unemployment is at crisis level in some communities, nationally, the majority are still employed. . . .

One young, southern black, who joined a job training program which paid a certain salary to people as they learned, provided an ironic case in point. He described how, in addition to being given training in some rather dubious skill, the white instructor spent a good deal of time talking about the cultural factors and how he truly understood the desperation and despair that the trainees felt about finding work.

The irony was that this young black and several of his friends had been employed before they joined the program. They started the program because it literally paid more than the jobs they had held. Their previous work, with a temporary employment agency, gave them a take-home pay of about nine and a half dollars a day—$8.75 after busfare to the agency and back. To be sure of work they had to get up at 4:30 and be at the agency by 5:15–5:30 A.M., although their pay did not start until they actually began work at 8 or 9.

So, here were men who had been spending over twelve hours a day to earn $8.75 a day now in a training program whose central thesis was that psychological, social, and cultural factors were their real problem, not the $8.75.

In general, the scandalous conditions and real discontents of black workers have been the most ignored aspect of the conditions of blacks in America. Yet it is a central factor in the current crisis.

The census figures in this area are especially untrustworthy. There is ample evidence that blacks are often undercounted. So, although we will use census statistics, it is with the caution that they are not as trustworthy as they are for whites.

Of the 22–23 million blacks the census counts in America, about 6 million are adult men outside institutions such as school, jail, and the army. Of these:

Employed	4,770,000
Unemployed	410,000
Out of the labor force	889,000

The unemployed figure includes 266,000 who were actively seeking work, and 144,000 which the AFL-CIO estimates were unemployed but not actively seeking work, which excludes them from the census calculations. Even this number is an underestimation because it includes as "employed" anyone who worked even one day in the two weeks before the survey as "employed." It also understates, due to the undercounting of blacks by the census. The unemployment noted above is about equal to 9 percent of the black labor force, and a complete figure would probably be 12–15 percent, if it included the people who only worked a few hours. This is confirmed by a study of black and white unemployed in central cities, which suggests that about 13 percent are unemployed or subemployed. For black youth, the situation is far worse, and in some cities the unemployment figure is 25–40 percent or more.

1969 Percent Distribution, Black and Other Male Employees by Occupation Group and Median Income

OCCUPATIONAL GROUP	PERCENT		'70 MEDIAN INCOME, YEAR-ROUND, FULL-TIME WORKERS
Professional and Technical	7.4		$8,675
Managers, Officials, and Proprietors	4.5	22%	8,752
Clerks	8.1	Middle Class	7,668
Salesworkers	1.9		Not Available
Craftsmen and Foremen	15.1		7,353
Operatives	29.9	78%	6,273
Service	14.3	Working Class	5,670
Laborers	18.9		5,410

When we compare these incomes, which are only for those lucky enough to find year-round employment, with the national averages the magnitude of black working-class poverty becomes clear, as does their concentration in the less skilled end of the working class occupational spectrum. The service and laborer categories, in particular, are huge compared with the occupational distribution of all Americans.

However, it is worth noting that operatives are the largest single category, constituting nearly 30 percent of the total. While this often hides the continuing pattern of occupational segregation of blacks into the worst "black" jobs, the sixties did see a dramatic increase in the number of black factory workers in industries like auto and steel. There has been a corresponding increase in black union membership. Today there are more blacks in unions (3,000,000) than in any other organization, aside from the black church. . . .

The basic point is clear. The majority of black Americans are working people, and for these close to five million black men, their discontents and poverty result from being the most oppressed sector of the working class. An increase in the minimum wage and serious enforcement of the minimum wage laws would do more to end black poverty than anything an army of social workers will ever accomplish. The problem is not values or culture. For the majority it is the typical working-class issue—the size of the paycheck. . . .

As we have seen, a great deal of the confusion about the class structure of America resulted from the role of women. When we turn to an examination of women as a special group, the reason becomes clear.

Essentially, there are two parallel but different occupational hierarchies in America, one for men and one for women. When one looks at the two combined, one sees strange cases of white-collar workers earning less than blue-collars. But when they are separated, both the male and female hierarchies show very clearly the continuing superiority of white-collar over blue-collar and service jobs. The unskilled or low-skilled jobs in service and sales, like maids, salesgirls, and waitresses, are the lowest paid. Semi-skilled women factory workers do a bit better and the huge clerical category, which is split between skilled and semiskilled workers (for example, the secretaries, stenographers, and receptionists), are better still. At the top of the hierarchy are the small group of managers and proprietors and the far larger group of professional workers like grade school and high school teachers, medical technologists, nurses and so on.

Thus, the brain vs. brawn distinction that we used for men is equally valid for the female hierarchy, even though the specific jobs they do are different. If we divided these jobs up into unskilled, semiskilled, skilled, and the college-trained professional and technical workers, we would find that the female labor force is, in its majority, unskilled or semiskilled workers with rote, repetitive jobs. In fact, the major difference between women and men is the almost total absence of a true professional and managerial sector. Many of the "professional" jobs women hold, like medical lab assistants, are really more comparable in training and skill levels to the highest male skilled workers' jobs.

However, the most important fact is the profound difference between the salaries of men and women. In every category, women receive thousands of dollars less than men for jobs which are at approximately the same skill level.

The low wages paid to these women workers have two important consequences. First, for the 58 percent of married women who are married to blue-collar workers as we saw, it can make the difference between almost literal poverty and a less than adequate, but tolerable, life. Although some commentators with an unshakeable optimism have seen the startling growth of women workers as a result of "widening horizons," a desire to find self-expression, careful studies show that economic necessity is the more probable cause.

Second, the low wages paid to these women are the margin of profit for many industries, such as clothing or electronics which are hard pressed by cheap foreign imports. Women factory workers often get a starting salary of $2.15 or $2.25 in these industries, which would be below the poverty level for a man. The same is true for occupations like salesgirls, who often receive less than $90–100 a week.

These figures indicate that, although the women's liberation movement has, up till now, received far more publicity for its personal and social grievances than for its economic discontents, there are very serious issues involved. Although very different from blacks, both blacks and women have been shunted off into separate occupations and industries with the lowest wages, and so the more visible injustices of racial and sexual inequality conceal the general issue of class inequality. But the economic position of women, like blacks, is clearly part of the general question of work and inequality in America. And, if only because so many blue-collar workers' wives are working today, the condition of women workers is inseparable from the standard of living of the American working class as a whole. . . .

Working Women Change Their Lives

HEIDI HARTMANN

A great deal can be said about the effect on women of changes in the economic structure. The current structural transformation of the economy, sometimes viewed as a set of long-term trends in motion since World War II and sometimes viewed as a short-term economic crisis of recent origin, can be held responsible for the feminization of poverty, the high divorce rate, the increased labor force participation of women, and a host of other changes affecting how we live our intimate lives.

While many decry these changes, particularly for their supposed negative impact on women, children, and families, I argue that on the whole the economic changes of the past several decades have been positive for women. Women in advanced industrialized countries today have more access to economic resources independently of men than ever before in human history. They have more control over the conditions of their lives, and probably have a higher standard of living relative to men than at any time previously. Of course, I do not deny that the recent economic downturns (in 1980 and 1982), coupled with cutbacks in social welfare programs, have affected women negatively. I argue only that they have not erased the progress of the past thirty to forty years. Confining my analysis to the United States, I will attempt to show how this general progress has occurred and demonstrate the potential for further, positive changes in women's

Heidi Hartmann, "Changes in Women's Economic and Family Roles in Post-World War II United States," in *Women, Households, and the Economy*, Lourdes Beneria and Catharine R. Stimpson eds. (Rutgers University Press, 1987), pp. 33–36, 41–49, 54–59 with some abridgements. Reprinted by permission of Rutgers University Press.

status, as gender relations continue to evolve and to affect economic change as well. . . .

In order to describe the economic context for gender relations since World War II, let me digress for a moment to summarize some of the economic changes that have occurred during this period. . . . [T]he current economic situation has its roots in long-term economic and political changes within the United States as well as changes in the position of the United States relative to other countries in the postwar period. . . . Most obvious among the long-term changes have been the decline in U.S. military hegemony since WW II; the deterioration of U.S. leadership in the international economy; increasing competition for world markets in manufactured goods from Western Europe, Japan, and other countries; increasing demands from third world providers of raw materials; and the movement of U.S. capital to more profitable production sites abroad. The competitive difficulties of U.S. manufacturing have contributed to the continuing decline in the proportion of manufacturing in the GNP [gross national product] and to the increase in output that originates in services. Many have argued that this shift to services is necessarily accompanied by a decline in average wages and a tendency toward a bifurcated income distribution . . .

These structural changes are reflected in a remarkable lack of economic progress for many people, at least on some indicators. Real incomes have not risen for U.S. families since 1970, although they rose substantially in the decade of the 1960s. Unemployment in 1982–84 was at its highest levels since the Great Depression.

This uneven economic performance, increases in military spending, and the tax cuts of Reagan's "supply-side" national fiscal and monetary policies have combined to produce an enormous deficit in the federal budget accounts. Though they are certainly exacerbated by the [Reagan] administration's policies, the factors generating pressure for cuts in social welfare spending have a longer history. Federal social welfare outlays as a proportion of GNP actually peaked in 1976 at 12.1 percent, the year Carter was elected . . . Even with cuts in discretionary programs and slower growth in entitlements such as social security, the deficit looms large and is expected to remain so if tax policy or military spending policy is not reversed or moderated. Both continuing to live with a large deficit and taking drastic action to reduce it threaten prospects for sustained economic recovery. The long-term roots of the current fiscal crisis, then, lie in the generalized restructuring of the U.S. economy that has occurred over the past several decades. The future capacities of the U.S. economy are unclear, but the public expectation of substantial social welfare spending that has been generated by public programs developed over this same period is likely to create continued demand for social services, despite current pressures to reduce the deficit.

The real change in social welfare spending comes not from the recent Reagan cutbacks but from the previous, more gradual evolution that increased federal social welfare spending from 4 percent of GNP in 1950 to 11.5 percent in 1979 . . . This long-term growth in social welfare spending has had significant effects on women's abilities to live independently of men outside of traditional families. The current cutbacks . . . have to be seen not only as an attempt to discipline labor generally by reducing the social wage (an attempt made necessary by long-term economic difficulties), but also as an attempt to reassert patriarchal control and to turn back gains made by women in this same period. Reductions in social programs have the effect of forcing many back into traditional family forms for economic support, health care, child care, and so on. . . .

Equally as striking as the postwar changes in U.S. economic structure and economic position vis-à-vis other countries are the postwar demographic changes that have occurred in fertility, family and household formation, and women's labor force participation in the United States. Briefly stated, since 1950 women are delaying marriage and childbearing, having fewer children over their lifetimes, and spending more time over their lifetimes living alone or as heads of their own households—living neither with parents nor husbands. And, of course, women's participation in the labor force is at an all-time high. . . .

[T]he tendency for women to form and head households on their own has increased tremendously over the past thirty years in all age groups across all nonmarried statuses . . . And while heading families or households means poverty for some women, in general the tendency to form households is associated with the increases in economic well-being that make it possible, particularly the large increases in the labor force participation of women of all ages. Even the fact that young women with early first births establish their own households rather than live with their parents can be seen as an indicator of increased resources. And although a larger proportion of poor families are headed by women alone than heretofore (48 percent in 1979 versus 23 percent in 1959), actually a decreasing proportion of such households are poor. In 1959, 42.6 percent of families headed by women alone were poor; twenty years later the percentage of such families who were poor had fallen to 30.4 . . .

[T]he experiences of marriage and childbearing have become more universal for women over the course of the twentieth century (and for childbearing, particularly since 1940), but as fertility has fallen and divorce has increased, living in families and raising children has become limited to a shorter period of the average woman's life. A substantial and increasing proportion of women raise children in households that do not include a husband or male partner. At any point in time, fewer people are living in marriages. Overall between 1950 and 1980, husband-wife couples decreased from 78 percent of all households to 61 percent . . . Single-person households have increased dramatically, and increasing numbers of couples are living in nonmarriage relationships. Thus, a general diversification of family and household types has occurred. . . .

Over this same period, as women's fertility has declined and household types have diversified, women's educational attainment and labor force participation have increased dramatically. Changes in educational attainment for women in the post–World War II period have been less dramatic than changes in labor force participation, but nonetheless substantial. . . . For the population over age twenty-five, a statistic that reflects past as well as current trends, 20 percent of the men versus 13 percent of the women have completed college (these proportions have approximately tripled since 1950 for both sexes). . . .

Labor force participation rates, it is now well known, have increased dramatically since 1950 for every age group of women except those over age sixty-five. . . . And increases have been greatest among women of childbearing age and among women who have children under six (their rate of labor force participation has nearly quadrupled). . . . [T]here is no longer a dip in labor force participation during the childbearing years. Average expected years of work at birth have increased from twelve years to twenty-nine years between 1940 and 1979–80 . . . Women, collectively, are earning more money than ever before (even though their average earnings relative to men have not increased), simply because more women are in the labor force for more of their lives than formerly. Women are thus contributing more financially to the support of themselves and their families; many are entirely self-supporting. Through increased labor force participation, women probably have access to more economic resources, independently from men, than ever before in human history. . . .

One response to all these changes is to certify a family crisis and to bemoan the increased exploitation of women who must support households and children on their own or who bear the brunt of the speed-up that occurs when both adults must work outside the home. But another interpretation . . . is to see these changes as largely positive for women because they contribute to women's increased autonomy from men and their increased economic independence, whether or not they live with men. These changes probably raise women's own standards of living, since having their own sources of income probably allows them literally to spend more money on themselves. . . . [E]ven though women earn less than men, their own earnings can bring them a standard of living comparable to that provided by men in the 1950s. Even with respect to total hours worked by women (housework plus wagework), women are probably better off now than they were just ten years ago. When women enter the labor market, total time spent working increases because wage work is added to housework: even though time spent on housework decreases substantially (from about fifty-five hours to thirty-five hours per week), the combined total represents a work week of about sixty-five to seventy hours. In the past few years, however, several studies show that housework time for working women has fallen, not because husbands are picking up more, but because women are simply doing less. . . .

It is somewhat risky, of course, to infer a great deal about changes in gender relations from aggregate data such as these. My argument amounts to saying that patriarchy is weakening, and that women have benefited from these observed changes in living arrangements. But not all women have benefited equally. The fact that single black women who head households with children on their own are especially likely to be in poverty raises the

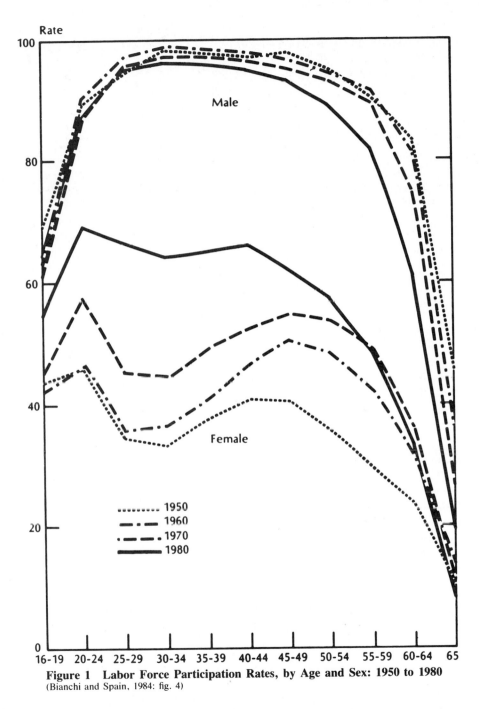

Figure 1   Labor Force Participation Rates, by Age and Sex: 1950 to 1980
(Bianchi and Spain, 1984: fig. 4)

Table 1 Labor Force Participation Rate of Women

YEAR	*BIRTH COHORT	AGE GROUP 20–24	25–29	30–34	35–39	40–44	45–49	50–54	55–59	60–64	65–69	70+
1955	1931–35	46.0	35.3	34.7	39.2	44.1	45.9	41.5	35.6	29.0	17.8	6.4
1960	1936–40	46.2	35.7	36.3	40.8	46.8	50.7	48.8	42.2	31.4	17.6	6.8
1965	1941–45	50.0	38.9	38.2	43.6	48.5	51.7	50.1	47.1	34.0	17.4	6.1
1970	1946–50	57.8	45.2	44.7	49.2	52.9	55.0	53.8	49.0	36.1	17.3	5.7
1975	1951–55	64.1	57.0	51.7	54.9	56.8	55.9	53.3	47.9	33.3	14.5	4.8
1980	1956–60	69.2	66.8	64.1	64.9	66.1	62.1	57.8	48.6	33.3	14.7	4.6
1985	1961–65	71.8	71.4	70.3	71.7	71.9	67.8	60.8	50.3	33.4	15.1	4.3

Note: Labor Force Participation Rates of Women, 20 years and over, by age, annual averages selected years, 1955–1979. * Women born between indicated years.
Sources: For 1955–1975: U.S. Department of Labor, Bureau of Labor Statistics. *Perspectives on working women: A Data Book.* Bulletin 2080. (Washington, D.C.: Government Printing Office October 1980.) For 1980 and 1985: Employment and Earnings, January 1981 (Annual Data table 3). Employment and Earnings, January 1986 (Annual Data table 3).

issue of interpretation starkly. Does this greater autonomy from men represent choice or necessity? Is family break-up caused by poverty? Does it result from abandonment by men? . . .

The changes observed in the aggregate demographic data support the contention that changes in the degree, extent, and form of male domination have occurred. Three types of changes are considered: the trend toward nonmarriage and toward women maintaining households alone; the changes within marriage; and changes in responsibility for children.

First, as we have seen, the diversification of family forms has led to women having greater autonomy from men in their living situations; this is reflected in larger numbers of women living alone or heading families. The choice to maintain an independent household as a single woman has become common and socially acceptable. Only a minority of divorced women headed their own households in 1950, but most do so now. The possibility of "doubling-up" or living with other family members still exists, but it is no longer necessary. With the elderly, we have come to recognize and accept their desire to be independent, to live separately from adult children. . . . Even among low-income women, maintaining a household on one's own generally became more possible over this period. . . .

If it is relatively easy to conclude that maintaining one's own household once one becomes a single parent or is divorced is a preferred choice, it is more difficult to say that divorce itself, or parenthood without a male partner, is a result of choice, especially choice by women. . . . First, divorce has increased over time as incomes have risen. People seem to want more divorce when they can afford it. . . . [F]or black women, undergoing a transition to a single-parent-female household is not associated with a transition to poverty status in a majority of cases; rather, poor black women heading their own households tended to be poor in their prior households as well. This finding suggests that it is not abandonment by males that makes these women poor. Rather, given their poverty, many apparently choose to live apart from men and head their own households. . . . Many older, single, professional women are choosing to have children without men (as noted, extramarital fertility is increasing for women of all ages). And women with the highest incomes and the best educations have the highest rates of divorce. . . . [T]hese developments are on the whole indicators of the preferences of many women for an unmarried state. We also know that women living without men do less housework, with and without children; the presence of men in the household seems to create about eight hours of additional housework for women per week . . . Is it not likely that faced with men's intransigence with respect to taking on more housework (housework by men, on average, has barely increased, despite women's increasing wage-work), and given that women have always been the primary child rearers anyway, that the increased propensity of all women to form their own households is in many ways a matter of choice?

A second set of observations about changes in the shape of male domination concerns changes within marriage. Women are achieving greater equality with men; through wage earning, they are changing family consumption patterns toward purchases that benefit them and toward greater personal consumption . . . ; they are doing less housework; and their greater willingness to leave marriages may be bringing about some improvements within marriages. . . . [I]ncome per hour of labor (including both wage work and housework) has increased considerably for married women over the decade of the 1970s because their wage work has increased; their return per hour has increased relative to their husbands' as well. Further, an increasing proportion of women earn more than their husbands—12 percent in 1981 . . . versus 10 percent in 1976 . . .

A third kind of evidence concerns children and here the picture is more mixed. . . . Decreased fertility and increased control of fertility through contraception and abortion is especially liberating to women. Intensive childcare represents a much more predictable and much shorter period of a woman's life. Beyond that, however, women have come to bear more of the responsibility for children alone, as single parenting has increased. On the one hand, this indicates their increased ability to do so. The right to have children without being dependent on men is no doubt important to many women. On the other hand, it indicates men's lessened responsibility for children, both in their daily care and financially. Few men pay child support faithfully after divorce or separation. This failure has clearly had a negative economic impact on women and children. . . .

We do not know enough about all the ramifications for men's, women's, and children's lives, but taken together they do suggest that in general men exercise less authority over women and children in families than heretofore.

I would argue, then, that to the extent that there is a family crisis, it is by and large a healthy one, particularly for women. Even if it were not healthy, however, these changes are here to stay and are likely to continue in the same direction. Women are not going to go back home. The rapid changes we have been experiencing in family organization and in women's employment do cause hardship. Wageworking women with young children work long hours between work and family care. Many newly divorced women, especially older women who did not expect to support themselves, are left without labor market skills or experience. Some single women with children live in poverty, and/or bear the total burden of financial support and physical and emotional care of their children. And as we have noted, many men seem to have abrogated their responsibilities for children. Nevertheless, although some of the changes have negative implications, especially for particular groups of women, furthering these changes and reducing their negative implications will work to women's advantage. . . .

It may be instructive to consider one of the changes discussed above, women's increased labor force participation, in order better to understand the sources of change. The increase in women's labor force participation can be seen as a result of contradictions inherent in an earlier accommodation of gender and economic relations. Specifically, the previous, pre–World War II arrangement of patriarchal capitalism (or capitalist patriarchy) contained the seeds of the current changes, and the current situation will lead to further changes. . . . [I]n the twentieth century a partnership between capitalism and patriarchy emerged in which the interests of both were served by allowing women a secondary place in the wage labor market, which kept them dependent on men and thus assured men of their continued services. Women's place in the labor market has been characterized by the sex segregation of jobs and by low wages. Women's place in the labor market should be seen primarily as the result of patriarchal gender relations (operating in this case in a capitalist production environment).

Prior to World War II, the majority of married women did not work in the labor market; female-dominated jobs were populated by single women, young and old, who had to support themselves. The labor of married women, though it often contributed to cash income via various forms of homework, was largely family-centered in childcare and housework. Married women generally relied on their husbands' incomes. When they worked, they were viewed as secondary earners; their positions as wives in some sense justified their lower wages. Thus, by ensuring a pool of low-wage workers (wives and by extension, all women), patriarchy created an attractive pool of additional workers who could be drawn into capitalist relations on favorable terms for the capitalists. As women are drawn into the labor market, the work they formerly did at home also became increasingly available on the market. The service sector grows because the availability of cheap female labor provides the supply and because the use of women in the labor market rather than at home also provides the demand for replacement services (fast-food replacing home cooking, for example).

In this way, the enormous growth of the service sector, an important aspect of the structural transformation discussed here, can be seen as a direct result not only of capitalist development but also of patriarchal relations. Without the availability of large numbers of low-wage women workers, it is not clear that capitalist expansion would have taken this direction so strongly. The growth of much of the business service sector is required by a shift toward large-scale, multinational business with its consequent need for more communication, management, record keeping, and so forth. Women's labor allows this shift to occur. And the shift toward the commercialization of personal services is required by women's increased labor force participation. Changes in economic structure, then, can be seen as the result of changes in gender relations as well as in class behavior.

Hence, capital may be gaining in the centuries-old struggle between capital and men over the deployment of women's labor power (and men may be losing). More of women's labor power is being deployed outside the home, where it is not under the direct control of fathers and husbands. Moreover, . . . women, too, are gaining in this struggle.

The increased labor force participation of women also sets the stage for further transformation. As women work more and work more continuously over their lifetimes, they have come to challenge their low-wage, secondary positions. The women's movement has contributed to this general process of consciousness-raising concerning the value of women's work. Two examples of this challenge are the development of the comparable worth strategy and the beginnings of large-scale clerical worker organizing.

The comparable worth strategy challenges the relative pay levels of men's and women's jobs—nurses and plumbers, librarians and engineers, secretaries and sales representatives. Comparable worth is a direct assault on the economic, social, and cultural system that has undervalued women's work relative to men's. Such claims are usually initiated when groups of women workers begin to investigate the relative wage levels of men's and women's jobs at their workplace, the qualifications required for the jobs, and the methods of setting pay. Arguments are then couched in terms of entire groups of women workers being underpaid . . . The most significant part of this type of campaign may be its ideological and consciousness-raising elements. Such studies convince some women who might not have thought about it or articulated it that their jobs are underpaid, that they do deserve more for the work they do. Moreover, by bringing the bases for wage differentials into the realm of public discussion, comparable worth campaigns politicize the wage determination process. In both these ways, such campaigns set the stage for the unionization of women.

But the more revolutionary aspect of the comparable worth strategy arises because it creates the possibility that women will be able to support themselves financially on equal terms with men. Such an eventuality would revolutionize gender relations and create the possibility of true autonomy for women. Moreover, by raising issues about how women's work is valued, obvious parallels are drawn to the undervalued work women do in the home. Whether in a capitalist wage labor market or a socialist one, issues of the value of the work performed traditionally by men and by women must be raised. Such questions directly challenge patriarchal norms and patriarchal power bases.

While capitalists would undoubtedly have continued to profit from women's secondary position in the labor market, women's own challenge to their secondary status creates a new opportunity for working-class unity between men and women. Men are being presented with a second chance to incorporate women into the labor market as equals. This progressive response to the changes we have observed can improve women's and children's lives more than a return to greater economic dependence on men. Men, and society in general, should have greater responsibility for children, and women should have higher incomes. While men have something to lose from this approach, in the long run they also stand to gain. . . .

To conclude, let me outline briefly the progressive social policies that would enhance women's ability to be self-sufficient, clarify what I am not arguing in this essay, and comment on the importance of understanding social change as the outcome of both gender and class struggle.

Employment-related policies that would be important to women's advancement toward autonomy include increased collective bargaining and unionization, continued emphasis on equal employment opportunities and affirmative action, and, of course, comparable worth. For these policies to be effective, consistent full employment must be achieved. This in turn will no doubt require greater public control over what have generally been up to now private investment decisions. Improving working conditions on the job will also require a greater degree of employee involvement in work decisions. Hence, advancing women's specific interests as workers will also lead to the enhancement of workers' rights and economic prospects in general. Moreover, that women have greater responsibility than men for children needs to be recognized, and social programs to ameliorate the effects of this difference must be developed. Policies to provide subsidized child care, parental leave, and so forth, will at least initially benefit women more than men, but they obviously benefit male parents as well.

A central demand that should be raised and supported by feminist and progressive groups now is for universally available free child care. Because childbearing has become more universal and is limited to a shorter period of adult life, achieving consensus about supporting families for this limited period should become increasingly possible. Social security provides a useful analogy; it supports people for a limited (though growing) period of their lives, and everyone pays for it through payroll taxes. Universal, employment-related parental insurance financed via a payroll tax could provide parental leaves as well as funds for child care. Child care itself could be available free (or at modest cost in addition to the normal payroll tax) to the actual current users.

In general, I believe most benefits should be tied to employment or participation in training programs. As working for wages increasingly becomes the norm for all women, the fact that poor, young, minority women are "stockpiled" on welfare programs increasingly disadvantages them. They, like all women, need to learn labor market skills and progress toward self-sufficiency. Of course, not everyone is able to work, and social programs that provide a decent standard of living for those unable to work are needed as well.

In my view, enhancing economic autonomy for women so that they need not be dependent on individual men should be the central goal of the women's movement; greater social responsibility for children is a critical component of that goal. One would also hope that individual men would adjust to the new realities and take on their share of child care and housework.

I am *not* arguing that women, who would be able to be truly economically autonomous with these new arrangements, would not choose to live with or even marry men. They might. They might also choose to live in groups or with other women or alone. But whatever their choices they would be less coerced by economic considerations than they are presently. Marriage would no longer be the central path to economic survival that it now is. I am also not arguing that the transition to this new arrangement has been painless. Some women have been negatively affected. But I am arguing that social policies such as those described above can do much to ameliorate the negative effects. In the long run we will gain more than we lose.

. . . It seems inevitable that fewer and fewer men will have "macho" jobs in the economy—those associated with hard physical labor and rugged working conditions. With technological change and sectoral shifts, more and more men will, like women, work in the service sector. The recent emphasis on sex role research, the new androgynous personality, and so forth, might be seen as an effort to retrain men for "women's" jobs, or at least to make these jobs increasingly ideologically acceptable to men. Although men will increasingly enter the service sector, I would not expect sex segregation in the labor market to be eliminated entirely over the next few decades; that will require many, many years. But the lines between blue-collar and white-collar jobs and professional and support jobs will most likely blur. These developments hold the promise of progressive change if we can develop new strategies that build upon them. Just as the increased mobility of capital . . . calls forth new solutions, so might these sectoral and structural shifts. The new solutions will undoubtedly require a new consciousness on the part of men as well as of women. . . .

✣ *F U R T H E R   R E A D I N G*

Stanley Aronowitz, *False Promises: The Shaping of American Working Class Consciousness* (1973)

Lourdes Beneria and Catharine R. Stimpson, eds., *Women, Households, and the Economy* (1987)

Barbara Bergmann, *The Economic Emergence of Women* (1988)

Paul Blumberg, *Inequality in an Age of Decline* (1980)

Clair Brown and Joseph A. Pechman, eds., *Gender in the Workplace* (1987)

Ely Chinoy, *Automobile Workers and the American Dream* (1955)

Sara M. Evans and Barbara J. Nelson, *Wage Justice: Comparable Worth and the Paradox of Technocratic Reform* (1989)

David Halle, *America's Working Man* (1984)

Irving Howe, ed., *The World of the Blue Collar Worker* (1972)

Louise Kapp Howe, *Pink Collar Workers* (1977)

Mirra Komarovsky, *Blue-Collar Marriage* (1967)

William Kornblum, *Blue Collar Community* (1974)

Steven McLaughlin et. al., *The Changing Lives of American Women* (1988)

Helen Remick, ed., *Comparable Worth and Wage Discrimination* (1984)

Lillian Rubin, *Worlds of Pain: Life in the Working-Class Family* (1976)

Richard Sennett and Jonathan Cobb, *The Hidden Injuries of Class* (1972)

Patricia Cayo Sexton and Brendan Sexton, *Blue Collars and Hard Hats* (1971)

Bertram Silverman and Murray Yanowitch, eds., *The Worker in "Post-Industrial" Capitalism* (1974)

Ronnie Steinberg-Ratner, ed., *Equal Employment Policy for Women* (1980)

Studs Terkel, *Working* (1972)

Donald Treiman and Heidi Hartmann, eds., *Women, Work, and Wages* (1981)

CHAPTER
14

Workers and Their Unions
in Troubled Times

⚶

*In the 1970s and 1980s, U.S. capitalism stumbled badly. The Vietnam War had
sapped American strength, touched off a round of inflation at home, and given
oil-producing countries the opportunity to jack up the prices of their vital commodity abroad. Profits and productivity stagnated, corporate debt soared, and
the stable industrial order established just after World War II began to crack.
The U.S. government abandoned Keynesian efforts to sustain working-class incomes and fought the chronic inflation of the 1970s and early 1980s by boosting
interest rates, thereby plunging the economy into two deep recessions and pushing unemployment to levels not seen since the 1930s. Big employers, led by New
York City and Chrysler (and their bankers), responded to this crisis by trying to
roll back wages and other labor costs.*

*As a result, working-class living standards have remained just about the
same for a generation, work time has grown well above 40 hours a week, and
the trade-union movement has suffered an absolute decline in its numerical
strength and economic power. By 1990 a thirty-year-old blue-collar man earned
about one-quarter less than his father did at the same age. Women's wages increased relative to those of men in the 1980s, but this rise represented the
shrinkage in the number of high-paying blue-collar jobs in manufacturing and
construction rather than growth in women's earning power. Only the massive
influx of women and teenagers into the work force and the increase in the
length of the work week kept family incomes at about the same level as that of
the early 1970s.*

*The decline of the unions proved both cause and symptom of these difficult
economic times. After 1970 almost all private-industry unions lost members: the
unionized sector of the work force shrank from about 28 percent in the late
1960s to 17 percent in the late 1980s. This decline in union density flowed not
only from the growth of unorganized employment in service and sales jobs, but
from the de-unionization of industries like coal, steel, meatpacking and lumber,
which had once been among the fortresses of organized labor. The unions fared
much better in the public-employment realm, especially in the 1960s and early
1970s, when about half of all state- and local-government workers became*

union members. But organized labor's success among these workers merely highlighted the retreat of the unions from the private sector. In the business world,
only one worker out of eight held a union card, a statistic making the United
States a unique industrial society: the only large nation still calling itself democratic without a substantial union movement.

Why this decline in union power? Historians and social scientists have not
reached a consensus, in part because all their answers are so ideologically
charged. The most widespread view, but also the most ahistorical, holds that
trade unions are no longer necessary to ensure social justice on the job. The
1930s are over; managers are more enlightened; and most work, even that in
factories, requires cooperation rather than conflict between labor and capital.
While this argument is itself part of the larger ideological assault against the
contemporary union movement, it gains some credibility because so many trade
unions are in fact stolid, highly bureaucratic institutions that have failed to respond to the needs of their members and potential recruits.

Another explanation for union decline is grounded in what some see as a
rapid shift in the cultural and sociological contours of the working class. Jobs
are moving from the relatively well-organized Northeast and Midwest to the
union-resistant South and West. Factory work is in relative decline, whereas
employment in the traditionally non-union, white-collar sector is expanding rapidly. Such employment shifts and cutbacks have indeed eroded membership in
the old industrial unions, but workers in such expanding sectors as health care,
education, and government service have been far from hostile to unionism. Indeed, by the early 1990s, white-collar workers (about 60 percent of whom are
women) composed more than half of all organized workers in the United States.

The most compelling explanation, both for the union-movement decline and
for the stagnation in working-class living standards, has been a political one:
rising costs and steep foreign competition, have forced U.S. employers to inaugu-
rate a long-term offensive against the welfare state and the wage standards and
working conditions that evolved when U.S. capitalism had a more expansive
character. Beginning in the early 1970s, a bipartisan conservative coalition,
largely dominant in both Congress and the White House, has shifted government
policy, economic and legal, far to the right. High levels of unemployment have
been used to fight inflation, the right to strike has been curbed, taxation has
become more regressive, and the social wage has eroded.

How have these policies affected different sectors of the working class: for
example, racial minorities, white women, and skilled workers? Has unionism's
appeal declined? Why have conservatives won the votes of almost half of all
workers in recent years? Why do so many of the poor fail to vote?

✢ D O C U M E N T S

By the mid-1970s, the relative decline in the competitiveness and profitability of
U.S. capitalism pushed many companies determined to limit their labor costs. In
the first document, *Business Week* argues that the health of U.S. corporations
can be restored only by sacrifice from the American people—"doing with less
so that big business can have more." In practice this meant that employers
would take a tough line against unions. In document two, *Wall Street Journal*
reporter Douglas Martin profiles the activities of one of the new breed of anti-
union lawyers; while in the next reading, *Business Week* reports how large con-

struction firms used the recession of the early 1980s to cut wages and de-union-ize large sections of their industry. In earlier years, unions might have appealed to the National Labor Relations Board (NLRB) to help them resist hostile employers, but as the AFL-CIO charges in the fourth document, the federal labor law no longer served the interests of organized labor. The recession and the double-digit interest rates of the late 1970s and early 1980s also made the modernization of much basic American industry unprofitable. Among the victims of this economic environment were the workers at two South Chicago steel mills, Wisconsin Steel and U.S. Steel's South Works. The fifth document records the experiences of three of the 15,000 workers permanently laid off between 1980 and 1983.

Immigrant workers, many of them illegal, often were blamed for taking jobs away from U.S. citizens, as journalist Dan La Botz reports in the sixth selection. And in a similar vein *New York Times* reporter Peter Kilborn found in document seven that the high levels of unemployment made it easy for companies to recruit strikebreakers during several of the most bitter labor-management conflicts of the 1980s. But employers were not always successful, as the next two documents reveal. With enough organization and effort, and with a return to some of the militant tactics of earlier years, trade unions recorded some impressive victories at the end of the 1980s. At Harvard University, clerical workers won their first collective-bargaining contract after an organizing struggle of many years. In southwestern Virginia, the United Mine Workers, one of America's oldest unions, defended workers' health-care benefits and pension rights in an epic strike that saw more than 3,000 miners arrested over an eleven month period.

The Options Ahead
for the Debt Economy, 1974

JOHN CARSEN-PARKER

The U.S., like the world around it, is in sad shape today. Having borrowed too much in the expectation of perpetual plenty, Americans are desperate for answers to questions for which there are no pat answers.

If there is a remedy for today's inflation except recession, it has not been found, all of President Ford's brave hopes this week notwithstanding. It is not certain that the $1-trillion transfer of wealth from oil-consuming to oil-producing nations can be carried out peacefully, and if the oil bill is hurting the U.S. less than most nations, it hardly matters because all nations are so closely tied together today. Even if this country's oil bill is comparatively modest, the U.S. already carries a burden of debt so heavy that it is doubtful that all of it can be repaid and almost certain that not enough more can be borrowed to keep the economy growing as it has since World War II.

Finally, and most distressing of all, it is not at all certain how graciously Americans, or any other people for that matter, will accept what is plainly today's (and history's) economic reality: that there is no such thing as perpetual plenty and no party that does not eventually end.

No More to Borrow

The U.S. has tried to do too much with too little, and that cannot go on forever. Even if the U.S. is not overborrowed now—a most debatable point—it cannot continue to pile up debt as it has in the postwar era because the sort of government policies that would permit that to happen would simply feed inflation. "We have passed the point of no return," mourns Albert M. Wojnilower, an economist at First Boston Corp. in New York.

It is inevitable that the U.S. economy will grow more slowly than it has. Government economic policy will be more restrictive—and, at the same time, more imposing because it is also inevitable that government will attempt to take on still more of the job of channeling what capital there is to where it seems needed the most.

Some people will obviously have to do with less, or with substitutes, so that the economy as a whole can get the most mileage out of available capital. There will be fewer homes and more apartment houses built because apartment houses represent a more efficient use of capital. It will be harder to launch risky new ventures because the needs of existing businesses will be so great.

Indeed, cities and states, the home mortgage market, small business, and the consumer, will all get less than they want because the basic health of the U.S. is based on the basic health of its corporations and banks: the biggest borrowers and the biggest lenders. Compromises, in terms of who gets and who does without, that would have been unthinkable only a few years ago will be made in coming years because the economic future not only of the U.S. but also of the whole world is on the line today.

First Things First

Put simplistically, as long as corporations stay healthy, they can pay taxes and provide people with jobs. As long as people have jobs, they, too, can pay taxes, and they can buy goods. But when corporations fall sick, people lose jobs and stop buying. Nobody pays taxes, governments and local authorities are not financed, and everyone—corporations, consumers, federal and local administrations alike—goes broke or gets embedded more deeply in the debt spiral.

If corporations are healthy, these things do not have to happen. Corporations are the key to whatever can be done to unwind the Debt Economy with the least possible pain, partly because it is in the corporate area that debt has increased most spectacularly and partly because it is in the corporate area that the increase is doing the most damage. Chairman Reginald H. Jones of General Electric Co. put it very bluntly in testimony before the Senate Subcommittee on Economic Growth, headed by Lloyd M. Bentsen (D-Tex.). "We have," said Jones, "a picture of business going deeper into debt, faced with declining return on investment, unable to attract sufficient equity funding, unable to keep up with inflation in its depreciation charges, and subsisting on a thinner and thinner diet of retained earnings.''

Yet it will be a hard pill for many Americans to swallow—the idea of doing with less so that big business can have more. It will be particularly hard to swallow because it is quite obvious that if big business and big banks are the most visible victims of what ails the Debt Economy, they are also in large measure the cause of it. President Ford's anti-inflation package may make perfect economic sense, but he will find it very difficult to sell Congress on his proposal to levy the same 5% tax surcharge on the worker making $7,500 a year and the corporation making a thousand times that much—especially when the package also contains some tax breaks for corporations.

Facing It Squarely

Nothing that this nation, or any other nation, has done in modern economic history compares in difficulty with the selling job that must now be done to make people accept the new reality. And there are grave doubts whether the job can be done at all. Historian Arnold Toynbee, filled with years and compassion, laments that democracy will be unable to cope with approaching economic problems—and that totalitarianism will take its place.

Governments find it handy to blame the oil-producing nations for all that has gone wrong, but it is in the nature of elected officials to find others to blame for their own mistakes. The world's great economies were running out of control long before the first shot in the Yom Kippur War was fired, and all that the oil situation has done is to hasten an inevitable day of reckoning. Moreover, it is a day of reckoning made inevitable by forces set in motion three decades ago, in those heady days after the end of World War II.

The first promise that every postwar government made to people sickened by both depression and war was that a new era had dawned in which there would be neither—only limitless growth and prosperity for all. The industrial nations would regain their glory, the developing nations would achieve it. And for a quarter-century, governments actually did seem to be making good on that promise. Between 1945 and 1970 the world enjoyed the longest boom on record—fueled in large part by borrowed money. Business borrowed at a prodigious rate to make the stuff, consumers borrowed at a prodigious rate to buy it, governments borrowed at a prodigious rate to support armies and build roads and schools. The $2.5-trillion debt load of the U.S. is just a part of a total world debt load that could top $10-trillion.

Too Many Dollars

And then, suddenly, it all began coming unstuck for reasons that are not totally clear even today—except that no boom goes on forever.

Among other causes, the U.S. flooded the world with an unprecedented quantity of unwanted, inflationary dollars. The death throes of the international monetary system sent billions of dollars crossing frontiers faster than anyone could count them—far faster than any government could counter them. Most basic, though, was that the world's hunger for goods—for cars instead of bicycles, for beef instead of chicken—simply outstripped its financial resources. That bred inflation, which bred more debt, which bred more inflation, and so on in an ever-worsening spiral. And then came the oil situation to make an awful situation unbearable.

But promises, once made, are not easily forgotten. The world's financial resources may be strained to the breaking point, but the demand for money has hardly slackened at all. It requires money beyond the ability of the average person to imagine just to keep the world's great economies where they are—some $200-billion in net new external capital to support the U.S. economy alone in 1974.

Finding the Capital

Looking beyond this year, the U.S. demand for capital through 1985 will total—according to a study just completed by the New York Stock Exchange—no less than $4.69-trillion, counting internal as well as outside funds. The total expenditure of other countries will be even more if the Debt Economy does not drag them down. According to GE's Jones, in 1973 Japan put 37% of its gross national product into gross private domestic investment. The figures for France and Germany were 28% and 27%—and for the U.S. only 15.7%.

But whether the U.S. or any other country will in fact be able to make this kind of investment depends very largely on its ability to finance by some means other than going deeper into debt. For stock markets all over the world have been making it horribly clear that corporations are sick—and they are sick largely as a result of their overdependence on debt.

The recent destruction of stock prices reflects, more than any other single factor, the extraordinary recent build-up of debt. In the U.S., this build-up has been gaining momentum, and its acceleration has coincided with the debacle in equity values. As economist Henry Kaufman of Salomon Bros. points out, the increase in U.S. debt averaged a relatively reasonable 6.2% annually in the 1950s and 6.9% in the 1960s, but it zoomed past 9% in the first three years of this decade: The stock market, as measured by the average price of equities, has been sinking like a veritable stone since 1970.

If corporate debt continues to increase so rapidly, corporate interest payments will regularly exceed the combined total of dividends and retained earnings. And when this happens, corporations are not only intensely vulnerable to cyclical downturns but are also being run for the benefit of creditors rather than stockholders.

At least one solution must be to make capital more easily obtainable in the form of equity—and in the U.S., at least, it is not too late for this to be done. What is essential, in the opinion of John C. Whitehead, a senior partner of Goldman, Sachs & Co., is to increase both the incentive to save and the incentive to place savings in "opportunity" investments.

Looking at the U.S. picture alone, nonfinancial corporations invested nearly $540-billion between 1969 and 1973. About $290-billion came from depreciation, $60-billion from retained earnings, and a net $40-billion from stock sales. On the debt side, a net $75-billion was raised by bond issues, and $75-billion more was raised through bank loans and through commercial paper.

The NYSE estimate for plant, equipment, and inventory additions through 1985 is $2.65-trillion. If this were to be raised in the proportions of the last five years, corporate equity would rise by $500-billion, but debt would soar $750-billion. Since the resulting interest burden would certainly bring about—well before 1985—the bankruptcy of most U.S. corporations, it is something less than desirable. One alternative would be to reduce the level of expenditure. But if this were taken far enough to bring debt down to safe levels, it would result in such painful unemployment—and hence such dislocation of world trade—as to be equally undesirable.

Another alternative would be to correct the imbalance between equity and debt, and although this would certainly not provide a panacea for the world's problems, it would do a great deal to get the economy back on a sounder footing—and permit the U.S. to help keep other economies afloat. Among the steps that might be taken:

Avoid Credit Allocation.   Through the Federal National Mortgage Assn. and other agencies, there has been allocation of credit—and it has been something less then successful. It has failed to provide enough funds for the mortgage market, but it has made funds unavailable to other markets. If debt in the economy is to be reduced to reasonable levels, the first step is to put these agencies back into the budget and finance them through taxes rather than through borrowings—thus at least avoiding additions to the debt burden.

Encourage Investment from Abroad.   The NYSE strongly endorses increasing the supply of funds by eliminating the withholding taxes on dividends and interest from U.S. securities held by foreigners. The exchange's committee on International Capital Markets has estimated that an additional $4-billion to $6-billion of capital could flow into U.S. securities if these taxes were eliminated—and the committee was working with information accumulated before the rise in oil prices vastly increased the dollars in foreign hands.

Change Depreciation Basis.   Chrysler Corp. Chairman Lynn Townsend believes business should be allowed to base depreciation on replacement cost rather than on historical cost. "The net book value of plant, property, and equipment in the steel industry is about $14-billion," he says, "but the replacement cost at today's prices would approach $78-billion." If depreciation were put on a more realistic basis, retained earnings would of course be reduced. But since business' tax burden would be reduced considerably more, cash flow would be improved—and the need for external financing substantially cut.

Make Dividends Tax Deductible.   Robert Eisner of Northwestern University favors the idea that dividends, like interest payments, should be tax deductible for the corporation paying them. To avoid revenue loss to the Treasury, it might be more practical to gradually reduce the amount of debt interest that is deductible—at the same time progressively increasing the deductible percentage of dividend payments.

A corollary of this plan, intended to encourage savings, would be to increase the deductibility of dividends to individuals while reducing that of individuals' interest payments. Since deducting interest is of less benefit to low-income than to high-income borrowers, its gradual elimination would insure that the benefits of the discouragement of debt and the encouragement of savings were not confined to any single group.

Reduce Capital Gains.   An alleviation of the capital gains tax is essential, in Senator Bentsen's view, if the individual investor is to return to the equity market, and President Ford's new proposals favor the principle. Bentsen has introduced legislation that would increase the amount of an individual's income that could be offset with capital losses and would progressively reduce the taxability of capital gains according to how long an asset is held.

The Effects

It is obviously impossible to quantify precisely the improvements in the Debt Economy that might be brought about by these suggestions. There are too many imponderables involved. To take just one: It is far more likely that large quantities of oil dollars would be reinvested long term in the U.S. economy if the economy were seen by potential investors to be sounder. And if large quantities were reinvested long term, the whole capital supply picture would change for the infinitely better.

In any case, it seems fair to speculate that the amount to be raised in the public markets through the sale of equity might be increased so that the additional amount of debt required would be no more than the additional amount of equity.

There would thus be a relatively minor deterioration in debt-equity ratios. And the removal of governmental demand from the debt market, coupled with the infusion into the capital pool of an indeterminable but substantial sum from overseas as a result of eliminating withholding, would make interest rates substantially lower—so that interest coverage would be greatly improved.

It is hardly necessary to add that initiatives such as these could not instantly repair the damage done by 30 years of ever-increasing reliance on debt. But they would go a long way toward undoing the harm—and toward insuring that capital formation provides a much more solid base for the future than it has for the past.

A Consultant's Techniques for Smashing Unions, 1979

Stephen J. Cabot makes nearly as much as the President of the United States by helping companies fight labor unions. "I've been called the biggest, no-good, union-busting, S.O.B. that ever lived," he says.

On a recent afternoon, the 37-year-old Philadelphia attorney maneuvered his silver Mercedes past a group of pickets in front of Kardon Chevrolet here. Inside the $30,000 air-conditioned car, he derided the strikers as "nincompoops" and "bastards." Mr. Cabot was guiding owner Michael Kardon's campaign against Teamster Local 676, which had represented the 24 Kardon salesmen since 1973.

On Mr. Cabot's advice, Mr. Kardon rejected the union's money demands and swiftly hired replacements when the resulting strike began seven months ago. Then, workers petitioned the National Labor Relations Board for an election to oust the union, a step that is illegal for management to encourage but was fairly predictable under the circumstances. Because the voting unit now was dominated by replacements and nonstriking union members, Mr. Cabot judged that the union couldn't win.

The vote took place in September; the results haven't been made known, because the union challenged the election before the NLRB. But those figures now are a meaningless formality. Ten days ago, strikers tendered their resignations and stopped picketing. "They saw the handwriting on the wall," Mr. Cabot says.

Owner Kardon, who says he talks with Mr. Cabot more than with his wife, is grateful. "It's like David and Goliath," he says; unions "literally hold an ax" over businessmen's heads; "I need somebody to help me."

The strikers, who earned an average of $36,000 a year in pay and benefits, took a decidedly different view. "It's a dirty deal," shop steward Ronald Dengel declared. He said Mr. Cabot "shows an employer how he can take a man who's had a job for 10 or 15 years, get rid of him and blackball him so he can't get a job again—all perfectly legally."

A Growing Field

Mr. Cabot denies blackballing but generally accepts the characterization. He specializes in keeping unions out, dislodging unions that are already in and extracting the best possible deal from unions that can't be removed. He is increasingly fighting in areas of growing importance to the labor movement: white-collar employees, public sector workers and smaller companies. "It's a nasty business," he says, asserting that his life is occasionally threatened. . . .

Labor observers say that Mr. Cabot's hardball style exemplifies a trend. Greater management aggressiveness has played an important role in slashing labor's success in representation elections to 46% last year from 51.1% in 1973 and over 60% in the mid-1960s. "There are some (lawyers) that are just unbeatable," acknowledges Charles McDonald, the AFL-CIO's assistant director of organizing.

The number of specialists—including lawyers, consultants and social scientists—who are on the companies' side in these fights has ballooned, though statistics are sketchy. Last year, the Labor Department chronicled the involvement of such specialists in 159 labor disputes, a 127% increase from 1975. . . .

Labor leaders rail mightily against the proliferation and growing sophistication of all this expertise directed against them. Present-day workers "face the law of the jungle and the professional strikebreakers just as surely as their grandfathers did," George Meany, who until today was president of the AFL-CIO, has proclaimed. "Today's labor-relations consultants carry briefcases instead of brass knuckles."

Two in Firm Indicted

. . . But Mr. Cabot believes that management's experts aren't hard-bitten enough. "Most management labor lawyers fight with kid gloves," he scoffs. His partner Martin J. Sobol is blunter: "The union can play hardball, but we're supposed to play spongeball. When we start throwing rocks, they don't like it." . . .

. . . The smartest thing management can do, Mr. Cabot says, is to keep unions out in the first place. "I have seen very few instances where the smart company, planning in advance, has been unionized," he says. That planning, he says, should start with improved employe communication, in part to determine workers' real desires. He says that this knowledge is valuable ammunition even if the employer doesn't intend to satisfy those desires.

Mr. Cabot says employes will be happier if rules and privileges are written down rather than arbitrarily applied. "Workers are crying to know where they stand," he says. He also urges firms to pay wages as high as competitors are paying and to comply with every workplace law. He says unions leap on any employer misfeasance as a persuasive argument for organizing, and he warns that "most companies have some work rules that violate federal law."

In one current assignment, Mr. Cabot represents a chain of women's exercise salons. The chain faces federal charges of cheating its instructors— who earn just above the minimum wage—by not paying for their leotards. The first step of his suggested strategy is to bring the firm into compliance with a strict interpretation of all labor laws.

Mr. Cabot and his competitors also urge that supervisors be trained to serve as anti-union leaders. "The front-line supervisor is the best possible communicator in a campaign," says Herbert Melnick, chairman of Modern

Management Methods Inc. "He can talk to somebody without fear of breaking the law." Also, supervisors are sensitive to management pressure in that they can easily be fired.

Some experts advocate selective hiring to avoid unions. Businessmen at a North Carolina seminar, according to a union infiltrator's report, were advised by Chicago consultant Woodruff Imberman to hire as many women as possible because "It's obviously legal to scare the bejesus out of your female employes with threats of strikes, violence and picket lines." Mr. Imberman says he did advise the businessmen to hire women, but he denies the colorful language. He says he also advised them to hire only as many blacks as legally necessary, because blacks are more prone to unionize.

Along similar lines, Mr. Cabot gives advice on what localities are best for avoiding certain unions, going so far as to pinpoint specific sections of a given city. And he suggests that a nonunionized company lose a grievance fight or two to show that the grievance system works.

. . . Mr. Cabot says he really gets tough when an organization attempt begins. "You catch 'em with their pants down," he says.

For example, he devises ways for companies to circumvent laws barring criticism of unions during a campaign. One favorite tactic: a true-false test, with the highest achiever getting an inexpensive prize. Among other things, the exam will ask, say, whether the president of the particular union makes $150,000 and has a personal chauffeur, (The correct answer will be "true.") More crucial, Mr. Cabot will fashion countless delays of the vote. "With every month that goes by," he says, "the union's strength is lessened."

Through it all, Mr. Cabot insists that he isn't anti-union and that he tries to discourage a "Let's bust the union" attitude. But critics find that hard to swallow. "You don't respect somebody who's perpetuating slavery in the workers," says Henry Nicholas, a leader of the predominantly black hospital workers' union in Philadelphia.

Others suggest that Mr. Cabot sometimes skirts the law. In particular, they cite a bitter 1975 dispute between the Teamsters and the trucking firm of W. C. McQuaide Inc. of Johnstown, Pa. In a brief filed with the administrative law judge who was hearing the case, an NLRB field attorney alleged that Mr. Cabot himself lied on the stand, instructed a witness to lie and performed other unprofessional acts. Mr. Cabot calls these allegations "patently untrue," argues that they reflect the emotions of a heated battle and points out that the allegations weren't ever pursued.

(He further suggests that the two principal NLRB lawyers who worked on the case couldn't have been too distressed over his ethics; they subsequently came to work for his firm of Pechner, Dorfman, Wolffe, Rounick & Cabot.) . . .

Mr. Cabot has also fought public-employe unions, labor's fastest-growing segment. Two years ago, he offered to work without fee helping Edward A. Hanna, then the maverick mayor of Utica, N.Y., fight that city's unionized public-works employes. Mr. Hanna, who at one point fired the workers, jokes, "I needed Steve Cabot to fight city hall." Among other things, Mr. Cabot says, his tough stance at least ended "hour coffee breaks."

Although he represents corporate heavyweights like Dravo Corp. and Clorox Co., Mr. Cabot is also capitalizing on what he views as an aggressive push to unionize small businesses. His reasoning: With much of big industry already organized, labor has nowhere else to turn. "Hey, small business-men, wake up—you're sitting ducks," he says.

Small-businessman Norbert Beisterling, owner of Plunkett Motor Freight in Zehenople, Pa., recounts a 1973 battle in which he was the only driver still on the job after his seven teamster employes walked out. Strikers, armed with picket signs, followed him around in automobiles. "It was like an instant strike every place I went," he says. But a mixture of Mr. Cabot's legal efforts and "street-fighting" style defeated the union and "got me born again," Mr. Beisterling says. His conclusion: "You have to be a bastard."

Mr. Cabot, who is married and has two daughters, seems to have hit upon a winning formula. His time can be purchased for $150 an hour (making for an annual income between $150,000 and $200,000), he cruises to many appointments in a private plane, and he's building a modernistic $300,000 house. He also sandwiches "union-avoidance" seminars into his 15-hour-a-day schedule for as much as $1,000 each.

Construction Unions Try to Shore Up a Crumbling Foundation, 1985

For years contractors pleaded with the building trades to trim back the unwieldy tangle of costly union provisions on construction projects. Some unions yielded to the demands—but only on a local basis. But the slump in construction is forcing national union leaders to take drastic steps. Some-time this spring, leaders of the 15 building trades unions in the AFL-CIO will sign off on a "national project agreement" that will significantly ease work rules on all major construction. This turnabout is a belated admission that the 40% gap between union and nonunion pay scales is much too wide. Says one union leader: "It is a matter of do or die."

The unions are in bad shape. They now claim only about 30% of the nation's 4 million construction workers, down from about 65% a decade ago. Nearly 400,000 skilled workers have abandoned unions since the late 1970s because their locals could not find them jobs. With unemployment in construction still hovering near 14%, there is a ready labor pool for nonunion contractors who can provide good wages and benefits and still undercut union labor costs. And as the gap between union and nonunion pay narrows, ex-members have less incentive to return to the fold. Says Richard B. Munn, executive vice-president of Associated General Con-tractors of California: "Workers, especially young people, will go wherever the work is."

Although the building trades have never been very strong in residential construction, until the mid-1970s they held a vise-like grip on the $200-

billion-a-year commercial and industrial construction business. In many regions, the unions were able to negotiate rigid work rules and high wages, ranging up to $40 an hour in wages and benefits for plumbers, for example. But no longer.

In Cincinnati, the Iron Workers have agreed to a 20% cut in wages on medium-size commercial projects, where the competition among builders is stiffest. In the traditionally antiunion South, the Painters union is letting contractors hire a larger proportion of apprentices, who earn half the $14-an-hour rate for journeymen. In South Texas, where the union share of work has dropped to 15%, from 85% a decade ago, building trades are taking the unprecedented step of letting union members work on the same job with nonunion workers. In center-city Philadelphia, a labor bulwark, some 2,000 carpenters will forgo a 9% wage hike scheduled for May 1.

These and similar concessions held construction wage hikes in 1983 to 2.2% and in 1984 led to the smallest average wage increase in four decades: 0.4%. This trend will be a big plus for the economy. During the past two decades, the $300-billion construction industry was a major contributor to inflation. Financing and land costs have recently been the biggest factors in construction inflation. But holding down labor costs, which account for up to 36% of building costs, should help moderate prices during the remainder of the 1980s. This is true partly because there are no behemoth projects such as steel mills, nuclear power plants, and refineries on the drawing board—and the lead time for these is as long as 10 years. Declares an official of a large contractor: "We don't see any possibility of another construction boom."

"Crazy Practices"

In an effort to regain some of their former clout, building trades leaders are trying to make union construction competitive and the impending national project agreement is one approach. Although its authors decline to discuss the arrangement for fear of stirring worker opposition, the pact may be "the best thing ever to come from the building trades," declares Jackie W. St. Clair, executive secretary of the Texas Building & Construction Trades Council. Among its provisions will be uniform work hours for all unions on the same project. In the past, each union insisted on a separate schedule of hours and holidays that made impossible an efficient scheduling of work. "These practices are crazy," concedes Edward J. Carlough, president of the Sheet Metal Workers Union. "They drive a contractor who wants to use unions right out the door."

A few individual unions are mounting similar efforts. Among them, the Bricklayers union has set up its own labor-management committee, which is monitoring nearly 400 agreements a year. The committee can order a local to accept a modest contract without striking. This is one way that an international union can influence contract settlements that are typically negotiated at the local level. The Bricklayers union also has started a planning group that will focus on organizing new members—and one of its proposals may be to expand into residential construction. In addition, the union's new International Masonry Institute is trying to create jobs by promoting research into new types of masonry construction.

Other union experiments have not been successful, however. A "market recovery program" begun in 1982 by the AFL-CIO's Building & Construction Trades Dept. and the National Construction Employers Council (NCEC) is one of several attempts to reform work practices on a city-by-city basis. The two sides are trying to set up joint labor-management committees to supervise local bargaining. But there has not been enough monitoring to tell how well these committees are functioning. Critics say they are not doing well.

Cost-conscious union leaders also are meeting fierce resistance from some rank-and-file workers who want to keep hard won gains. In Tacoma, Wash., Atlantic Richfield Co. recently wrung a 20% wage cut, plus permission to use lower-paid apprentices and helpers as one-third of the work force, from seven of the eight unions involved in the construction of industrial building modules for the North Slope of Alaska. But when the plumbers balked at the deal, ARCO made good on its threat to move the work to nearby Seattle, where all of its unions had accepted givebacks. But, explains an official of Tacoma's seaport, "If you were a union with 65% unemployment, you would not want to sign a contract that requires a third of the work force to be apprentices and sub-apprentices."

Biggest Enemy

With the unions on the defensive, every move they make is being countered with almost missionary zeal by antiunion employers. The Associated Builders & Contractors (ABC) has set up a network of law firms in 100 cities to dispense advice on how to go "double-breasted," or set up nonunion subsidiaries. The ABC also sponsors seminars on union-busting and operates a training program that it says is graduating 50,000 craftspeople a year. This competes with apprenticeship programs that the building trades traditionally have used to control the entry of workers into the industry.

But the biggest enemy of the unions is weak construction activity. As long as this continues, says William E. Besl, chairman of the NCEC, "things never will be the same as they once were for the building trades."

The AFL-CIO Condemns the Federal Labor Law, 1985

In 1935, Congress enacted the Wagner Act which declared that "Employees shall have the right to self-organization, to form, join or assist labor organizations, to bargain collectively through representatives of their own choosing, and to engage in other concerted activities for the purpose of collective bargaining or other mutual aid or protection." By the 1950s and 1960s, this principle had gained at least some measure of acceptance, and to a large extent employers did not choose to interfere with their employees' exercise of the right of self-organization; to some extent, employers resisted unionization by improving their employees' wages and working conditions. And if workers chose a union, employers by and large complied with their legal duty to bargain with that union in an honest effort to reach a contract.

In recent years, this trend has been reversed. The norm is that unions now face employers who are bent on avoiding unionization at all costs and who are left largely free to do so by a law that has proven to be impotent and a Labor Board that is inert.

It is difficult to quantify this change in employer attitudes and actions, but we all know it is there. A study of organizing campaigns in the private sector shows that 95 percent of employers actively resist unionization, and 75 percent of all employers hire so-called "labor-management consultants" to guide their efforts to avoid unionization at an estimated cost of over $100,000,000 annually. Many employers—how many thousands each year cannot be determined—discharge union activists. In 1957, the NLRB secured reinstatement for 922 workers who had been fired for union activity. By 1980, that figure had reached 10,000. . . .

Even when workers opt for unionization, unions often face massive resistance in securing a contract; the rate of employer refusal to bargain has been rising twice as fast as even the rate of unlawful discharges. Consequently, after a bargaining unit organizes, the employees are not able to obtain a collective bargaining agreement approximately 35 percent of the time—a substantial increase since the 1960s. And the law's remedy—when it comes—is most often too late to matter.

Nor are anti-union actions confined to not-yet-organized or just organized employers. Employers with longstanding collective bargaining relationships are closing unionized plants and diverting work to their established non-union plants or to new plants established in non-union areas in the United States and elsewhere. The owners of unionized companies are creating new, paper corporations to do the same work as the organized corporations and are transferring all or most of the work done to these new entities. And unionized employers are engaging in intransigent, bad-faith bargaining in order to provoke a strike so that the employer can replace his employees and oust their bargaining representative.

Two principal factors have combined to make it possible for employers to engage in such hostile actions against employees who wish to bargain collectively. First, . . . the United States has become a society with persistently high levels of unemployment. Unless current policies are changed, this will continue; under even relatively optimistic projections, there will be a structural shortage of at least 4,000,000 jobs throughout the 1980s.

Second, the federal government has done its part to encourage hostile employer actions by providing less and less protection to workers who exercise their right to organize and by setting an example for the most virulently anti-union employers. The Reagan Administration's handling of the air traffic controllers provided a signal to, and the model for, anti-union employers. Thereafter, the Administration turned over the labor law to an NLRB Chairman who has publicly declared that "collective bargaining frequently means . . . the destruction of individual freedom and the destruction of the marketplace," and that "the price we have paid is the loss of entire industries and the crippling of others." Not surprisingly, the Board he chairs has, at every turn, cut back on the extent of protection the law provides to workers who desire to unionize.

Because of these developments, the costs associated with organizing are increasing while the resources available are declining. The experience in this country is that a catalyst is usually needed for a group of individuals to shake the habits of a lifetime and to assert themselves by taking advantage of the opportunities provided by collective action; that is especially true when those individuals are subject to economic reprisal. Union members have always accepted it as their responsibility to start the process of organization. But in recent years, as the size of the workforce has expanded rapidly, the number of union members has declined and the needs of the already organized have increased, it has become increasingly difficult for union members to meet that responsibility.

Steelworkers Face a Bleak Future After Layoffs, 1984

Carl Stezko, White Male, Mid-50s

I worked at Wisconsin Steel for almost thirty years. I get a partial pension of $300 a month, that's all. No other benefits. Nothing. I had a hernia. The doctor said I could die if I didn't have an operation. I didn't have any hospitalization, no money to pay for it. I tried to get a green card [Medicaid] to pay for it, but they said sell your house and car if you want it. I couldn't do that. Finally, my doctor says if you can get into the hospital, I'll do the operation. So I lied to the hospital, just went in there and told them I had insurance. I never could have imagined doing such a thing.

I've been everyplace looking for a job—White Castle, Burger King, McDonald's, Sears, K Mart. I've been to hospitals and cemeteries. I went to Jays Potato Chips. They gave me a test and said, "You're overqualified." I said, "I'll tell you what, you said you're paying $5 an hour, well I'll work for $3." They still wouldn't take me. I'm a skilled electrician, plumber, a pipe fitter. But they ain't gonna hire a guy like me. I still go out every day and look.

My wife isn't healthy. She can't work. We have a two-flat [two-family house], but the mortgage isn't paid off. I get $160 a month in rent on the other apartment. I'm paying $200 on the mortgage and $160 in gas bills. So you can't make ends meet. I only eat one meal a day. Food stamps turned me down. I don't know where to turn. I'm ashamed to ask for anything. I always swore I'd never go on pension—I'd work till the day I died.

I did go to the alderman for a year and a half trying to get a job. I was

David Bensman and Roberta Lynch, *Rusted Dreams: Hard Times in a Steel Community*, (New York: McGraw-Hill, 1987), pp. 93–94. Reprinted by permission of McGraw-Hill Publishing Company.

begging, pleading. I saw him at least twenty times. They kept telling me, "You're at the top of the list." You know you get desperate: one day I approached him in the parking lot to ask about the job. The next time I saw him, he really went after me, just about spit on me cause I did that. You're never supposed to come up to him about something like that outside of his office. I just had to sit there and take it. I'm a big guy. Fifteen years ago, maybe I would have knocked him down. But when you got nothing, you've got to take that kind of stuff. Maybe the good Lord will come down and help me. I pray every day. That's all I have faith in anymore.

Mary Morgan, Black Female, Early 50s

I started in at South Works in 1973. I had two kids still at home and was just separated from my husband. He died a few months later.

I really liked that job. By me being a widow, I could support myself. I didn't have to go out and ask somebody for money. I didn't have to go on Aid. I could support my own self. That's very important to me.

I've been off work since January of '82. I haven't been able to find anything else. And all my benefits is ran out, even my little savings. My children help a little. I have six—all grown now. They're all unemployed. Three of them worked at one company that was sort of like the mill. It's all but closed down now. They had been going on unemployment and trying to find a job, but that has ran out now. I have my youngest son, my oldest daughter, and one little grandchild living with me. Altogether I have ten grandchildren. That's what makes it rough.

I've been looking for other jobs. I've been to Sweetheart, Tootsie Roll, Sure-Plus, Libby's, Soft Sheen. I've been to places to find something in the line of what maybe I could do. 'Cause, you see, some of these jobs you can't apply for them if you don't have the ability or education. Most of them just say they're not hiring. It gets discouraging.

I definitely blame Reagan. Because you know like they say, you're supposed to clean up your own backyard before you go and clean up somebody else's. And all this money he's got going for all these other things, like nuclear, he could be using that to put people back to work. I hope and pray—if I live—if they do get another president, that he'll do better than this one has been doing. Because he just don't care about women—he don't understand that we've got to live just like the men do. We've got to make a living.

I have very little hope—very, very little. I'm praying that I can find me a job somewhere. But if they don't open up something where peoples can get a job, it don't look very good at all. I guess they just want us all to dig a hole and get in it.

Victor Gonzalez, Hispanic Male, Early 50s

I spent most of my life at Wisconsin Steel. I thought I was set. In four more years, I'd have had my thirty years and got my pension.

I'm a carpenter. I've tried everything to get a job. But you don't have the opportunity to prove to anyone what you can do. When you tell people you're a former steelworker, they won't hire you. I went down to the Job Service [Illinois Bureau of Employment Security] and they were going to send me out for an interview. But when I told the guy I'd worked for Wisconsin, he said, "Forget it, they won't want you."

Then I went to Florida to look for work because my wife's mother lives there. I got a job in the fields trimming trees for $2 an hour. Then I got into construction; I was hauling cement bricks for $4 an hour. The boss really liked me, but the job ended and there wasn't any more work. So we came back up here.

We had just moved from South Chicago to Dolton [a nearby suburb] the year before the mill closed. The mortgage payments were $310 a month and we couldn't handle them on top of all our other bills. Our unemployment ran out. We lost the house—and our car too. We went to live with our daughter in South Chicago. But that's hard. You feel like you're intruding. You wish you had a place of your own.

Our children are hurting too. Out of six, only one has a regular job. One daughter worked at South Works, another at Wisconsin; our son was at Wisconsin; one son-in-law was there, another at South Works. So it's the whole family.

So many people that I know, they just gave up. But I'm not giving up. Right now, I'm trying to get into construction. It's hard, though. I feel like I've been robbed—robbed of twenty-five, twenty-six years of my life really.

Latino Workers: A Scapegoat for Mass Unemployment? 1982

James Gonzalez ran in panic from the agents of La Migra who raided the Boulder Valley Poultry Farm in Boulder, Colorado. He ran from the farm into the main road and was run down by a gravel truck and killed. Gonzalez's real name turned out to be Jose Morales, an undocumented worker.

My friend Juana, who works in a laundry, called me up at the community organization on the north side of Chicago where I work. "Daniel," she said. "I'm afraid to go to work. My husband is out of town, and the children will be home all alone. What shall I do?"

Jose Morales was killed, thousands of workers were deported, and hundreds of thousands like Juana lived in fear in the early weeks of May as the U.S. Immigration and Naturalization Service (INS) carried out "Operation Jobs"—a reign of terror in the immigrant communities and workplaces.

Throughout the country, workers stayed away from work; some businesses were forced to close. Church attendance in Spanish-speaking congregations dropped off; students' attendance at English G.E.D. classes

Dan La Botz in *Labor Notes*, May 26, 1982. Reprinted by permission of the Labor Education and Research Project.

declined. A panic seized the immigrant communities, particularly the Central Americans for whom deportation can mean death at the hands of the dictators in El Salvador, Guatemala or Honduras.

Some 400 INS agents in many major cities arrested 5,440 undocumented workers and deported 4,071. Over 90% of those arrested were Hispanic; most of them were from Mexico but they included immigrants from El Salvador, the Dominican Republic, Brazil, and Guatemala. In Chicago, a number of Poles were arrested.

Many ethnic, religious, civil rights, and labor organizations—including the International Ladies Garment Workers Union in Chicago—protested these raids.

Ted L. Georgetti, assistant director of the INS in Chicago, said, "There is widespread unemployment . . . and there are indications that a number of illegals are holding jobs that should go to citizens. If this is politically motivated, I don't think it is wrong."

The government clearly doesn't expect to solve the problem of over 10 million unemployed workers by arresting some 5,000 undocumented workers. Nor does its raid make a dent in the estimated 7.5 million undocumented workers in the country or those entering at a rate of 500,000 a year. Why then the raids?

The Reagan administration is attempting to blame the undocumented workers for unemployment and to make white and black workers see the "foreigners" as responsible for taking away their jobs. It is an attempt, as crude as it is cruel, to divide the U.S. working class.

But Reagan chose the wrong targets. Blacks won't rally around the flag-draped agents of the INS while Haitians remain in INS detention camps, and La Migra also made the mistake of picking up Poles, when the Solidarnosc movement has made the Poles heroes to many U.S. workers. The arrest of Poles, given the concentration of citizens of Polish descent in the big cities and in unionized industry, will hurt Reagan's attempt to rally white U.S. workers to his side. . . .

The INS arrests were not only carried out by the same President who arrested PATCO [Professional Air Traffic Controllers Organization] strikers, they are part of the same attack—an attack on labor. Remember, the PATCO strikers were made "illegal." Reagan struck first at a somewhat better-paid group of professional workers, feeling they would be isolated from the bulk of the organized labor movement. Now he strikes at the lowest-paid immigrant, minority workers, feeling they too are isolated from the mass of unionized workers. The strong sectors of organized labor have a responsibility to support the weaker, to defend the undocumented worker.

PATCO proved the government was prepared to bust unions. The INS raids prove the government is willing to use a national police force against workers. We had better stick together today or tomorrow we may find that we are all "illegals." . . .

Management's Weapon: Scab Labor, 1990

To keep operating in a strike, more and more companies have been deploying a weapon they long shunned—hiring permanent replacements for workers who are on the picket lines.

When 6,300 drivers for the Greyhound Corporation abandoned their buses . . . , management had 700 new recruits on hand to drive its fleet and 900 more in training. Thousands of new pilots, mechanics and flight attendants who have been assured careers with Eastern are keeping the airline aloft. And long after the end of the strikes in which they were hired, thousands of new workers remain on the job at the International Paper Company, the Boise Cascade Corporation, the Phelps Dodge Corporation and at Continental Airlines. . . .

Labor experts maintain that management's wide use of permanent replacements has upset the symmetry that has been a tradition of labor disputes. On the one hand, management has said it has a right to lock workers out at the risk of losing profits; on the other, labor has said it can withhold its services at the risk of losing income.

"The balance has shifted," said Mark A. de Bernardo, director of the Labor Law Action Center at the United States Chamber of Commerce [in Washington]. "Labor's trump card in a dispute, the strike, is no longer trump."

Robert M. Baptiste, a Washington attorney for labor unions, said that in a strike "there was always a sense that people would eventually say, 'Enough, let's sit down and get serious.' " But he added, "Now, companies just want to get rid of unions."

One reason that companies now think that goal is possible is the lesson they drew from the illegal strike of 11,500 Federal air traffic controllers in August 1981, seven months into Ronald Reagan's first term as President. After the striking controllers defied a back-to-work order, Mr. Reagan dismissed them, filled their ranks with permanent replacements [, and] the union collapsed.

"A Signal to Other Employers"

The government's success in keeping the air traffic system working impressed many unionized companies.

"Reagan made it respectable to bust unions," Mr. Baptiste said.

Gary Burtless, a labor economist at the Brookings Institution, said Mr. Reagan emboldened management to risk the strain to its business of taking on less experienced workers. "The fact that the President was able to keep the air traffic system going indicated that there was a lot more scope for replacing workers than people imagined," Mr. Burtless said. "If you can replace air traffic controllers you can certainly replace bus drivers."

The permanent replacements, often recruited from the ranks of the

---

unemployed or from low-paid employees of other businesses, are a variation on the temporary substitutes vilified by trade unionists as "scabs" or "strikebreakers" but nevertheless regarded as a part of management's legitimate arsenal. Temporary replacements leave at the end of a strike, but permanent replacements are assured the strikers' jobs. After a strike, the law allows strikers first claim on their old jobs, but only if replacements vacate them.

Risk of Permanent Replacements

Many companies still shun permanent replacements, in part because they run some risk in using them. Even if they decide they can get by without the expertise of skilled workers, companies must weigh the potential costs of incurring the wrath of workers who are not involved in the strike and of losing customers because of consumer doubts about the quality of the service provided by replacement workers.

This change in management's attitude has occurred along with a change in workers' loyalties, both to their unions and to their companies, which makes it harder for unions to sustain strikes and easier for management to persuade workers to move into the strikers' jobs.

Workers no longer think unions can deliver the gains in wages and benefits that made blue-collar members the world's best paid workers. For several years, union workers in private industry have been winning smaller wage increases than nonunion workers, and trade union membership as a part of the national work force has declined from 30 percent in the 1970s to 16.4 percent in 1989.

And for all that attention that recent strikes at companies like Greyhound, Eastern, the Pittston Coal Group Inc., Boeing and the Nynex Corporation have received, unions are increasingly wary of using their ultimate weapon, the strike, and risking both their members' jobs and the embarrassment of failing to win concessions from management. In the 1970s the Bureau of Labor Statistics recorded an average of 289 strikes a year involving 1,000 or more workers. In the last five years [1984–1989] the average was 52.

The Seeds of Acrimony

Furthermore, some companies have found it easier than they expected to find replacement workers.

That is what happened in an especially vitriolic strike in 1987 and 1988 involving three International Paper mills in Jay, Me. The company proposed eliminating premium pay for work on Sundays and holidays, and the paperworkers union walked out. The company started bringing in permanent replacements just 13 days later, planting the seeds of acrimony that local officials say will persist for years.

"It's something you do only as a last resort," said James W. Gilliland, the company's director of employee relations. "It's not fun for anybody."

In Jay, he said, the company has reduced its work force from 1,250 to 1,062, and 80 percent of the employees are permanent replacements. They started at $9 to $10 an hour, about $4 less than the strikers, Mr. Gilliland said, and premium pay was abolished.

Once the company decided to proceed, Mr. Gilliland said it found a surprisingly large pool of candidates for the strikers' jobs despite the nation's relatively low unemployment rate.

"As more and more young people have entered the labor market, they have found fewer and fewer high-paying industrial jobs," he said. "So when an industrial company enters the market to hire permanent replacements, it has no trouble whatever."

Clerical Workers Win at Harvard University, 1989

Harvard University holds a special place in the American imagination. Steeped in tradition, its ivy-covered walls conjure up images of Puritan divines and Brahmin transcendentalists: a timeless world, where the debate is over the life of the mind, not making a living. In this world a labor union has no place.

This past October, however, Harvard signed a collective bargaining agreement with its white-collar employees—secretaries, lab technicians and others, a work force composed mainly of women. On May 17, 1988, those workers had voted to be represented by the Harvard Union of Clerical and Technical Workers, an affiliate of the American Federation of State, County and Municipal Employees (AFSCME). The agreement provides for wage increases and greater job security, and also for maternity and paternity leave, child care and a decentralized system of joint labor-management problem solving.

The success of the Harvard union stands as a landmark in the drive of university clerical workers to organize. Blue-collar workers at Harvard and other schools have been organized for decades, but clerical and technical employees only recently. In 1983 clerical workers in the University of California system voted to be represented by AFSCME, at Columbia they joined the United Automobile Workers and at Yale the Hotel Employees and Restaurant Employees. In 1984 clerical workers at state universities in Iowa joined AFSCME. And in 1988 clerical workers at Adelphi, Cincinnati and Bridgeport universities voted for union representation. Almost 40 percent of the clerical work force is organized at public universities and a quarter of it at private universities.

Last spring John Sheridan Associates, a management consulting firm, sent a letter to university presidents warning that the Harvard " 'model' of labor-management relations" will be "*exported* by the union to other colleges." Workers will be urged, " 'If it's good enough for Harvard . . . it's good enough for you.' " To "meet this threat," Sheridan offered its

Craig Becker, "Lessons of the Harvard Drive," *The Nation* magazine. Copyright 1990 by the Nation Company, Inc. Reprinted with abridgements by permission of the publisher.

union-busting skills, honed while serving clients from Ramada Inn to Carnegie-Mellon University.

Such solicitations highlight the difficulties university workers face in organizing. Virtually every private university has opposed unionization. At Harvard, the administration provided supervisors a 104-page manual detailing antiunion arguments. It distributed glossy pamphlets and a series of letters to the entire staff, disputing the union's "false claim." Supervisors invited small groups of workers to tea, serving cookies and lecturing on the evils of unions. Harvard president Derek Bok sent a letter to each employee. "I am not at all persuaded," he wrote, "that union representation and collective bargaining will improve the working environment at Harvard." The university appointed Anne Taylor, an attorney formerly with the National Labor Relations Board, to run its campaign.

Not surprisingly, organizing at Harvard was slow going (the union drive began in 1974, in the medical school), and the margin of victory was slim— only 44 votes, of more than 3,000 cast, with 41 challenges. Nor did the university acquiesce in the result. It filed objections with the NLRB, alleging election-day misconduct. Not until an NLRB judge ruled against Harvard did the university begin bargaining. "Nothing came easy," as the lead organizer, Kris Rondeau, put it, "from signing a union card, to wearing a button at work, to voting yes." At other universities the pattern of events was similar: initial losses, narrow victories, university opposition. Nonetheless, since 1971, 70 percent of campus clerical organizing drives have ended in union certification.

What lessons can be learned from the union's victory at Harvard? Can organizing on campus offer an example for labor elsewhere? Not easily, it would appear, because of the seemingly unique features of the university workplace. But a closer study shows that campus workers have overcome barriers to organizing that are similar to those existing outside the academy.

State universities and established private institutions cannot flee across borders like runaway shops in other industries. Offsetting this physical stability, however, is the high rate of employee turnover, which impedes organizing. At Harvard, calculations of annual turnover range from 40 percent to 26 percent. Even the lower figure (which Harvard claims is "about average for universities") means that half those involved in a union drive will be gone after two years.

Equally distinctive is the openness of the academy. Union organizers often cannot get through factory gates or office doors. The Supreme Court has upheld the right of most employers to post their property against trespass. In universities, however, many employees work in places open not only to students and the public but also to organizers and fellow employees interested in talking union. Such access during the workday is especially important when, as in universities, employees are mainly women, who bear a disproportionate share of domestic responsibility and have little time for meetings after work.

But openness on campus has its flip side. University workers tend to be more dispersed and isolated than workers in other settings; often they work more closely with their boss than with one another. The jobs are less collective and more varied than in factories or offices. At Harvard, employees work in more than 400 buildings, spread out across Cambridge, Boston and farther away at the Harvard Forest. They are divided into 150 classifications, from secretary to piano technician, sous chef to animal facilities assistant. The administration exploited this diversity in arguing against the union. According to Bok, a union would homogenize working conditions by seeking "uniform treatment" of wages and employment terms, whereas the university offered "flexibility and personal choice."

Universities are also singular in granting job security to some of their unorganized employees—tenured faculty—and allowing them a limited governance role. The Supreme Court has stressed the unusual features of the professor's position. Under federal labor law, managers (as the Court defines most professors) are not protected when engaging in union activities. But the Court has also noted that "collegiality and tenure insulate the professor" from sanctions that can be applied to an "industrial manager" who defies company policy. University customs inhibit administrators from fully mobilizing managerial staff against unions.

Privileged with job security, professors may prove willing to challenge the administration's authority over labor matters. . . .

. . . At Yale, the strike of white-collar workers in 1984 prompted the largest faculty meeting since the turbulent debates of the early 1970s, but the faculty decided to endorse the administration's refusal to enter into binding arbitration. As if to underscore the faculty's marginality, the administration not only rejected arbitration by an outside third party but also a union proposal to submit the dispute to a panel of professors.

Typically, professors serve merely as a buffer, inhibiting administrators from adopting management's dirtiest tricks. At Harvard, the union successfully blocked the administration's effort to postpone the election until the end of the school year. In part, the administration simply wanted a longer time to counter the union drive. But union supporters also believed that in the summer, without faculty and students on campus, administrators would be less constrained and the staff more vulnerable.

Finally, universities are distinctive in being nonprofit. Even more so than other institutions that do not measure their accomplishments in cash, universities pay deference to ideals different from those of the market. Ideally, the university is a place of dialogue, where ideas have special currency and speech is unfettered. But workers argue that in seeking to check unions, administrators betray the university's ideals. Sometimes this betrayal is obvious. During the strike at Yale, the Connecticut Civil Liberties Union protested on behalf of staff and students who had been disciplined for "engaging in strike-related speech." At other times, it is more subtle. At Harvard, the union questioned whether the administration's campaign was simply communication, as the university said, or rather a sophisticated form of coercion. The union's statement of principles declared: "No employer should use its power, financial influence, prestige and access to all channels of communication to influence its employees not to join a union." . . .

In bringing unions on campus, university employees take seriously the image of the university as more than a workplace. At Harvard, the union focused on wages and child care, but its appeal transcended bread-and-butter unionism, raising issues of participation and dignity. From card signing to bargaining over pension formulas, rank-and-file employees controlled the process. Although most were relatively young and did not expect to stay long at Harvard, they stressed the needs of older workers. Taylor, speaking for an institution that claims to further human values, dismissed all this "feel-good stuff." Using the cold idiom of market analysis, she told the workers "to array the pros and cons, to do a cost-benefit analysis and decide if it's best for you. It's not a moral choice."

On campus, workers are carving out a place for their unions befitting the ideal of the academy. But their conception has not been persuasive to administrators in the nation's foremost universities, who have refused to recognize unions voluntarily or remain neutral before elections. The principle of managerial prerogative operates as powerfully within the university as within any profit-making corporation. Harvard's campaign to defeat the union differed from those of companies like J. P. Stevens and Adolph Coors, but less because Harvard is a nonprofit, scholarly institution than because the university has a different work force. From the choice of a female attorney to run its antiunion drive to its carefully crafted communications, university strategy was tailored to its employees' sensibilities. Harvard did not use bare knuckles; rather, to borrow an apt phrase from the Supreme Court, it extended "the fist inside the velvet glove."

What, then, does the Harvard contract portend for workers who do not toil within ivy-covered walls? The victory took too long, was too hard fought and came to too close a vote to offer a model readily "exportable." But neither was Harvard an isolated case; during the past decade, employees in colleges across the country have organized. Nor are conditions on campus so exceptional that organizing there cannot apply to other workplaces.

Indeed, the new university unions exemplify the changing nature of the labor movement. Since 1970, more than half of all new union members have been women. At Harvard, more than 75 percent are women. And the concerns animating campus unions are the same as elsewhere. At Yale, workers organized around pay equity and comparable worth, issues that have been the subject of union-backed litigation from the state of Washington to Long Island. At Harvard, day care was a rallying point. These issues transcend the specifics of campus economics, as the arguments mustered against union demands show. Yale's provost termed the undervaluing of women's work "a national problem, which Yale can't be expected to solve." Taylor admitted child care was inadequate, but explained, "it's a social problem." At both universities, administrators maintained that deep-rooted problems could not be cured by collective bargaining. But, as at other workplaces, employees came to different conclusions.

Still, the events at Harvard have a special significance. The university—and Harvard stands as an exemplar of university ways—defines its stance in society as one of critical distance. As Emerson, himself a Harvard graduate, wrote in his essay "The Transcendentalist," intellectuals "withdraw themselves from the common labors and competitions of the market and the caucus, and betake themselves to a certain solitary and critical way of living." It is from this detachment, paradoxically, that universities draw their influence. But in employing others to perform their "common labors," universities enter the market. Here, they cannot avoid Emerson's exhortation to "learn to act, and carry salvation to the combatants and demagogues in the dusty arena below."

Harvard's actions spoke volumes to other universities and nonacademic corporations about acceptable management tactics in union elections and the place of unions in white-collar industry. Over time, however, it may be that those who perform Harvard's common labor will prove to be the ones who teach its most enduring lessons.

The *UMW Journal* on How the Mine Workers Won at Pittston, 1990

. . . From the beginning, it looked like Pittston was out to break the union. A giant conglomerate based in Greenwich, Conn., Pittston withdrew from the Bituminous Coal Operators' Association in 1986 and announced it would seek independent negotiations with the union when its contract expired in February 1988.

The company opened new nonunion coal subsidiaries and began a massive shift of assets and jobs away from its union mining operations, leaving thousands of UMWA [United Mine Workers Association] members on layoff.

Negotiations began in November 1987 with the company seeking to slash health care and pension rights and gut work rules. In February 1988, with no new agreement reached, the company cut off health benefits to 1,500 pensioners, widows and disabled miners.

But the company underestimated its UMWA workforce.

"My father, my grandfather and I have over 100 years of coal mining with Clinchfield Coal Co. [now owned by Pittston]," said Carson Wise Jr., a [UMWA] member.

"And the company took away my father's hospitalization. My mother-in-law's a widow and they took her hospitalization, too. So I decided I'd fight 'em 'til hell freezes over to see 'em do right by these people."

Developing a "no-holds-barred" strategy, the union used a host of new tactics to force the company to act more responsibly, continue to negotiate and ultimately settle the strike. Union members and supporters:

From *UMW Journal*, March 1990. Reprinted with permission.

- Led boycotts of two banks—Crestar and Manufacturers Hanover—to protest loans made to Pittston for the company's strikebreaking fund.
- Put constant pressure on members of Pittston's board of directors, asking them to resign or call for a fair agreement.
- Conducted the first sit-down strike in the United States since the 1930s at Pittston's Moss No. 3 preparation plant, peacefully shutting down the company's largest coal-processing operation for four days.
- Enlisted the support of the 2-million-member Miners International Federation and of the International Confederation of Free Trade Unions, which represents over 100 million workers worldwide.

. . . But the cornerstone of the strike's success was good old-fashioned solidarity.

Supporters from across the country and around the world worked to help win the strike. And over 50,000 people, including UMWA members from the United States and Canada and trade unionists from all over North America and abroad, traveled to southwest Virginia to bring moral and material support to the strikers.

Pittston miners were quick to cite this solidarity, along with good leadership, as the foundation of their successful strike.

"We got this contract because we have great leadership in this union and because of the support we got from our communities, the surrounding counties, the churches, local merchants and other unions. Everybody came in and gave us great support, and without that we wouldn't have got this far," said [UMWA] member Mike Kennedy.

"Public support is really how you take on a big corporation," said Kennedy, a miner at Pittston's McClure No. 1 mine.

"A group of people back in southwest Virginia probably couldn't have beat Pittston alone. But when we got other people involved I think we put enough pressure on the company to where we were capable of winning this fight."

At the height of the dispute, the union received 15 to 20 speaking invitations a week from groups in the United States and Canada who wanted to hear more about the strike. Rank-and-file miners travelled as representatives of the union to tell their story. . . .

The speaking tours generated thousands of dollars to help support the strikers and applied more public pressure to Pittston.

. . . Another key to gaining public attention and support was the union's use of large-scale non-violent strike activities.

"It was the only way we could get nationwide attention; otherwise, we'd still be striking," said [UMWA] member Roy C. Sauls, a 20-year mine worker.

During the strike, over 3,000 Pittston miners, family members, supporters and other UMWA members were arrested for peaceful protest actions. . . .

Tom Yates, a [UMWA] member from Lebanon, Va., and a 19-year veteran coal miner, knows all about tightening his belt and about picket duty. He spent more than 200 evening shifts at the picket shack outside the entrance to Pittston's Moss No. 3 prep plant.

During the strike, he saw his wife start working outside the home for the first time and his daughter, a college student, take a part-time job to help pay the bills. On Feb. 26, after two days of retraining and a union safety inspection of the plant, he—like most Pittston miners—returned to work under a new contract.

But mine workers like Tom Yates did more than win a new contract. Their solidarity became a rallying point for the entire labor movement.

Pittston miners both received encouragement from and supported members of dozens of other unions. Camouflage, adopted as a symbol of solidarity at Pittston, began showing up on workers hundreds of miles from the strike region.

"This was the classic David beats Goliath story," said Mary Blue, a member of the Communications Workers of America . . . from Denver, Colo.

"The victory at Pittston sends a clear message to corporate America: if you want to push us, we're willing to take a stand for what we believe."

"There's a new labor movement out here and the Pittston strike definitely played a role in that," said Dan Ross, a former miner now working with United Auto Workers . . .

"The '80s was the era of givebacks. The '90s is our turn."

"Pittston thought they was gonna bust the UMWA," added Tom Yates.

"What they did instead was turn all the unions in this country around."

Joel Phillips, Castlewood, Va.

. . . What amazed me was how the women and children got involved. In most strikes only the men are involved and the women are at home taking care of the family. The women and children played a very significant role. They participated by sitting in the roads, getting carried to jail and bringing food to the picket line. The kids even spent time at school telling friends the strike dealt with more than money.

To add to our success, other labor organizations, along with religious and community people, came in to help us, not only financially but physically. Never before have I seen different religious groups joining together for one cause. Once we were able to get everybody to see that Pittston was out to destroy us, everybody realized our fight was their fight.

Their support was the spark we needed to win. People working together can mean a better way of life for all working people in the future.

John Cox, Dillner, Pa.

I went to work in Richmond, Va., on something we called the Richmond Project. Our goal was to maintain a presence in the state capital to keep the issues behind the Pittston strike alive. We leafletted and spoke to different unions and church groups about the problems Pittston miners were faced with.

We even set up a small tent city on the Capitol grounds for more than a week. We had the place secured and it was all well organized and peaceful.

A lot of the people we talked to had never voted and really hadn't cared to vote. But, after we talked about how important political action was, many registered to vote and even helped us with the phone banks in the Douglas Wilder campaign for governor.

I believe government needs to hear the cries of labor and it needs to apply the labor laws as they were written, not just to benefit some company that wants to take away workers' rights.

We need to do something as far as labor law changes go. Other countries seem to be obtaining freedom and we seem to be losing ours. We need everybody to keep the ball rolling.

Stanley Zuber, Summit Hills, Pa.

Without question, the Pittston strike was the single most important issue for the UMWA in the past decade. The strike changed a lot of the younger people. It opened their eyes to what the big picture really is. It also instilled confidence and renewed pride in the rank and file.

The timing of the tentative agreement couldn't have been better for us up here in northeastern Pennsylvania. We were just getting into negotiations with Lehigh Coal & Navigation and the Pittston agreement gave us some additional bargaining power—it showed the companies the UMWA's commitment to its members.

Even if it seems like the deck is stacked against us with all these Republicans in office, it's the little people that make the difference. It's the individuals that make up the union.

But we can't sit back and revel in our victory. We have to continue to use all the things that made this strike a win, like the working relationship with other unions. Every union member should know what their brothers and sisters in other unions—their neighbors—are up against, and we gotta support them. It's a two way street.

David Fisher, Avonmore, Pa.

When we met with the New Jersey Industrial Labor Council last summer about the Pittston strike, we were surprised to find that nobody there knew much about our situation. But, once we told them our story, they set us up with our own office in Newark.

From there we started talking to the union memberships throughout New Jersey about how our people were being treated in Virginia. After that, we started getting phone calls from all kinds of people and organizations wanting to know more. Some of them wanted to take convoys down to Virginia to see the situation first hand and we helped set that up, too.

Through these kinds of efforts, our outreach committee was able to get out the word even when the media refused to tell our story. I think this type of outreach was a very big factor in getting public support on our side.

The Pittston strike gave the labor movement a shot in the arm that it needed. We learned we must help one another to fight for everyone's survival. Solidarity is the key word and we must continue with nonviolence, education and the support of the community and religious groups in order to win.

✣ E S S A Y S

In the first essay, labor journalist Kim Moody argues that the Chrysler bailout of 1979–1980 broke the system of pattern bargaining in the core industrial sector, touching off a wave of concessions and givebacks that weakened the unions and lowered wages. Initially, many unionists thought that such concessions were mere temporary retreats designed to save jobs and help out hard-pressed employers. However, Moody shows that, while relatively few jobs were saved, dozens of employers demanded—and won—wage concessions of their own, regardless of the financial health of their enterprises.

In the second essay, Deborah E. Bell of the American Federation of State, County, and Municipal Workers explores the historical development of public-worker unionism and explains the process by which pay equity and other women's issues assumed special prominence within public-sector unions in the 1970s and 1980s. Women working in the public sector were not organized into unions as women, Bell argues, but rather as part of a broader effort to unionize specific occupational groups that happened to be heavily dominated by women. Nevertheless, the rise in the proportion of unionists who are female, as well as the general resurgence of feminist ideas in U.S. society, has made these public-sector unions staunch advocates of women's rights on the job and in the labor movement as a whole.

Concession Bargaining and the Decline of Industrial Unionism in the 1980s

KIM MOODY

Modern business unionism in the United States has never developed a method of dealing with large-scale business failure. In the postwar period, companies came and went, but most of the industries in which unions were based continued to provide jobs. If Packard went under, it was probably because GM, Ford, or Chrysler beat it in the US market. But as long as the US market grew and the players were US firms producing for a domestic market, the failure of one firm probably meant more work at another— minus the tolerated annual loss of jobs due to new technology and higher productivity. Business unionists therefore didn't worry much about corporate failures.

In the automobile industry, however, the rules changed. For one thing, the number of passenger car producers dwindled to four, meaning that any

Kim Moody, *An Injury to All: The Decline of Industrial Unionism* (London: Verso, 1988), pp. 152–153, 165–169, 171–177, 179–190. Reprinted with permission of the publisher.

failure would have a significant impact. The growing penetration of the US market by imports, particularly following the oil price increases of 1973 and the recession of 1974–75, meant that the production lost from a failure could be picked up by an overseas firm. US producers stuck with big cars, so the Japanese and others took a larger piece of the market by introducing smaller, more fuel-efficient products. By 1981 they had captured 29% of the market. This might not have mattered if the US market had continued to expand rapidly, but it didn't. The US and Canadian market shrank from 61% of total world demand for cars in 1960 to 37% in 1980. . . .

[N]ew investment by US industrial firms was increasingly financed by borrowing from banks rather than by using internally generated funds. In auto, the Big Three all adopted the same growth strategy: first, in the 1950s, expansion in the large, more profitable big-car market; second, expansion abroad. GM was the leader in both strategies, with Ford a close second. Chrysler, however, was in bad shape. . . . By mid-1979 Chrysler had a total debt of $1.5 billion and a payment schedule it could not meet. In 1979 Chrysler unveiled its high-priced New Yorker and St. Regis models, which had cost $57 million in retooling, just as OPEC announced another oil price increase. In mid-1979 the company had 80,000 cars in unsold inventory valued at $700 million.

Negotiations for a bailout had begun even before the disaster of 1979. John Riccardo had been in close touch with the forty or so banks that had held Chrysler's debt since 1976. Negotiations with the Carter administration and the UAW [United Auto Workers] had been under way during 1978 even before Lee Iacocca became president of the company in November 1979. Indeed, by early 1979 Chrysler had worked out a $750 million line of credit with domestic banks and another $400 million with Japanese banks. On 9 August 1979, Secretary of the Treasury G. William Miller announced that the US government would provide $750 million in loan guarantees. But the banks wanted more than federal guarantees. . . . They wanted concessions from the union as part of a plan to reorganize Chrysler.

. . . The wage and benefit concessions made to the Chrysler Corporation in October 1979 were pushed through by the UAW leadership as a sign of good faith to Chrysler's bankers and an incentive to Congress to pass the Chrysler Loan Guarantee Act. Certainly no one thought a six-month wage freeze, the surrender of six paid holidays, and the deferment of pension increases would solve Chrysler's financial problems. But the bankers were still hesitant about extending Chrysler's line of credit, President Carter was not yet committed to the plan, and congressmen outside the Rust Belt states were wondering how all this would look in the 1980 elections. The concession agreement was more a political act than an economic one.

The consequences of this political act, however, were profoundly economic. One of the largest, most powerful industrial unions in the US had demonstrated that wage and benefit bargaining was not a one-way street. Congress got the message right away. In January 1980 it made passage of the bill contingent on further concessions. The UAW accepted the loss of seventeen paid holidays and the continued delay of all pay raises for Chrysler's hourly workers. A year later, Lee Iacocca asked the union for an additional concessions package worth $673 million. The Federal Loan Guarantee Board backed Iacocca. These concessions . . . put Chrysler workers about $3 an hour behind workers at Ford and GM, introducing a new economic element in Big Three bargaining. The pattern, established four decades earlier, was broken.

From the start, the UAW leadership pushed hard to sell the cuts to the members. At each stage, the UAW sent out letters to all Chrysler workers. . . . By 1981 the union had the concessions formula down pat: ". . . without the sacrifices, there will be no loan for Chrysler and those jobs will go under along with the company."

UAW Vice President Mark Stepp, who was in charge of selling the 1981 agreement to the Chrysler Council, tried to convince the delegates that the agreement was another one of the UAW's "precedent-setting" breakthroughs. He claimed that Chrysler had signed a letter of agreement granting "the right for workers to have something to say about their destiny." What Chrysler agreed to were joint union/management committees that could discuss problems voiced by employees. Far from being some new instrument of power, they were another step toward the surrender of autonomous union power. . . .

Neither this fact nor the economic logic of breaking the pattern were lost on the other automakers. A Ford spokesman told the *Detroit Free Press*, "You can bet we're watching Chrysler's efforts with a good deal of interest. We haven't done it [ask for concessions] yet, but we'll see what happens on this go-around with Chrysler." GM Chairman Roger Smith was even more to the point: "You cannot have a two-tier industry." In other words, Chrysler now had a competitive advantage. In February, *Business Week* carried an article entitled "Pleas for Wage Relief Flood into the UAW." In the first nine months of 1981 the UAW's Research Department assessed seventy-five requests for concessions. The union's early plea that the Chrysler case was exceptional went out the window.

The pressure mounted on the UAW all through 1981, and in December the International Executive Board reversed its previous refusal to reopen the Ford and GM contracts. In February 1982 the UAW agreed to sweeping concessions at Ford. All paid personal holidays (a shorter worktime program initiated in 1976 to help create jobs) were ended. The 3% annual improvement factor, first negotiated in 1948, was dropped, and three COLA [cost of living adjustments] and all pension increases were deferred. The deal was estimated to be worth $1 billion to Ford. In April GM got the same agreement, saving $3 billion over twenty-nine months. . . .

The Chrysler concessions were not the first such give-backs. Companies in rubber, aerospace, meatpacking and other industries had demanded and sometimes received concessions. But the Chrysler bailout was a highly visible public event. And the UAW contracts with the Big Three were arguably the backbone of the entire pattern structure of industrial collective bargaining. If the UAW, a strong union with a reputation for militancy, could put bargaining based on company performance and competitiveness ahead of the traditional pattern, why not others?

The spread of concessionary bargaining was rapid. Following the GM settlement, the seven corporations covered by the Basic Steel Agreement asked the USW [United Steel Workers] to open the contract and make concessions. This proposal was rejected by Steelworkers local union presidents in 1982. But by the end of the year, major concessions had been negotiated in airlines, meatpacking, agricultural implements, trucking, grocery, rubber, among smaller steel firms, and in public employment. The years 1979 through 1982 might be termed the first round of concessionary bargaining. These were recession years and a number of the industries in which give-backs were made were experiencing financial or competitive problems. Labor, therefore played down the importance of concessions, calling it a temporary phenomenon. . . .

But employers didn't see it that way. A 1982 survey of four hundred corporate executives (from both profitable and ailing firms) by *Business Week* revealed that 19% of them said that, "although we don't need concessions, we are taking advantage of the bargaining climate to ask for them." Profitable firms that received concessions during the first round included GM, Kroger, Iowa Beef, Gulf Oil, Texaco, Caterpillar Tractor, and United Parcel Service. Furthermore, some of the industries involved were not declining industries like auto or steel, but growing ones like trucking, meatpacking, and even airlines. In these industries, the specific problem was the growth of a nonunion, substandard sector within an industry that had become competitive in the domestic market. The airline unions, with their history of craft, company-by-company bargaining, were unprepared for the competitive atmosphere that deregulation brought. In the case of trucking (which was also deregulated) and meatpacking, the Teamsters and United Food and Commercial Workers, respectively, adopted policies of granting concessions—piecemeal in trucking, across the board in meatpacking—which inevitably accelerated the employer drive for concessions.

The second round of concessions bargaining, beginning in the economic recovery year of 1983 and going through 1985, opened with major concessions in the Basic Steel Agreement. . . . In February 1983 the USW granted the seven major steel firms a $1.25-an-hour wage cut, the loss of six COLA payments, reductions in vacation time, and the reduction of Sunday pay to time and a quarter. The pact was said to be worth $3 billion to the steelmakers. It specified that the wage cut would eventually be restored, but future rounds of concessions negated that part of the agreement. Phelps Dodge also took on members of the USW at its copper-mining facilities in the Southwest. This led to a long, bitter and ultimately unsuccessful strike, with the company imposing deep cuts on a nonunion workforce. The Teamsters signed the second National Master Freight Agreement to contain across-the-board concessions, including a two-tier wage scale, loss of the COLA, and concessions on production standards. The second round also saw profitable firms such as Greyhound, the three major aerospace corporations, the major oil refiners, Hormel, and growing service industries like the hotel industry demand concessions with all the insistence of Chrysler or General Motors.

By the end of the second round of concessions, the nation was in its third year of economic recovery. Concessionary bargaining had crossed industry lines, and unions in some industries had made their second set of give-backs. The notion that concessions were a temporary phenomenon visited only on ailing industries and firms was no longer tenable. . . .

The impact of concessions goes beyond wage rates, however. It has hit other benefits with increasing force. The Bureau of Labor Statistics [BLS] publishes data on total compensation (wages and benefits) only for new contracts covering 5,000 or more workers, but this series reveals the same downward trend. The average first-year adjustment for total wages and benefits fell from 10.2% in the private nonfarm economy in 1981 to 1.1% in 1986, indicating that declines in the larger bargaining units were even greater than in the others. Cost-of-living clauses have been another major casualty of concessionary bargaining. In 1979 about 60% of all workers under major contracts (covering 1,000 workers or more) were covered by COLAs. According to the BLS's figures, only 50% of those covered by major contracts had COLAs by 1983; by 1986 the figure had fallen to 31%.

In the face of worker impatience with second and third rounds of demands for concessions, the employers looked for new formulas that would induce employed workers to ratify concessionary contracts. One such device was the lump-sum or bonus payment—a one-shot amount of money that would not be folded into the wage rate, but would be large enough to produce ratification or cooperation for the moment. The effect of lump-sum payments on worker income was substantial. According to the *Wall Street Journal*, "While many corporate executives are promoting the bonus programs as a tool to share the wealth and increase productivity, the plans clearly mean less money for most workers." Because of the compounding effect of regular annual increases in the wage rate, lump-sum payments over the life of a contract can mean a lot less money. For example, a worker making $8.00 an hour just before a new contract would gain about $2,000 over the three-year life of the contract if his/her wage rate were increased 2% a year. A 2% annual bonus, on the other hand, would produce only $1,000 in three years.

Further, a lump-sum payment would mean that in the following bargaining round the wage "platform" would be the same as it had been three years earlier. In both these ways, bonuses perpetuated wage deceleration and avoided cost increases in premium pay (overtime, weekends, holidays, and so on) or benefits based on wage rates. . . .

Another device that captured capital's imagination for a period was the two-tier wage system. It allowed the employer to hire new workers at wage rates below those of current employees. Short-term "starting rates" were not new, but the two-tier plans of the 1980s either created a permanent lower stratum of employees, at least until all the higher paid workers retired, or a prolonged wage gap between the two groups of workers. Since a two-tier system required no sacrifice from those currently employed, it was often easier to sell than a straight wage cut or freeze. Of course, it also undermined the potential solidarity of the workforce because two groups of workers were performing the same work for different pay. These schemes became popular in 1983, and 800,000 workers were covered by contracts with two-tier structures by 1984. . . . The largest single contract to adopt two-tier pay was the Teamsters' 1985 National Master Freight Agreement. The union that negotiated the largest number of two-tier agreements was the United Food and Commercial Workers, which signed 87 of the 261 two-tier agreements negotiated in 1983–85, most of them in the retail grocery industry. . . .

The first round of concessions had focused on wages and benefits, but concessions on working conditions, work rules, production standards and other aspects of the workplace regime became increasingly common in the second and third rounds. . . .

The significance of contract language regulating working conditions through such means as job classifications, work rules, and production standards is often seen by the public or even by unaffected groups of workers as something anachronistic or irrational. In fact, such regulations are necessary for the functioning of most systems of production. Workers engaged in the collective production of goods or services must know what they are doing, where their responsibilities begin and end, and agree on a manageable rate of work so that the different operations are properly coordinated. The more complex the operation, the greater the need for universal rules. Otherwise, the result is simply chaos. Frederick Taylor and the "scientific management" school recognized this principle as much as any trade union. The difference, of course, was that management wants the right to set these rules as it sees fit, while labor needs to shape the rules to protect itself.

There is no greater efficiency inherent in management's version of work regulation than labor's. . . . [M]anagement's attempts to define work rules are shaped by its need to control labor, not by any technically objective standard of efficiency. Indeed, the literature of industrial relations underlying such programs as Quality of Work Life recognizes the inevitability of management inefficiency. This is because the workers who collectively perform the complex operations of modern industry have a better understanding of what is really involved in their work than do managers who have no hands-on experience. Management attempts to increase efficiency often simply produce low-quality products or services. In the end, all forms of workplace regulation reflect a large element of subjective self-interest.

From the standpoint of labor, work rules, job classifications and other methods by which the union attempts to regulate the organization, pace, and quality of work are essential and rational forms of protection. Management cannot arbitrarily load one individual or group with more tasks, combine jobs to reduce the workforce, or deprive a worker of the work he or she was hired to do. Union regulations are also important to safety. Management's disregard for safety in large-scale operations is well-known.

Workers can be endangered if they are pushed to perform work they are not familiar with. The existence of clearly defined jobs also provides some choice for workers with different abilities and temperaments. It is a fact that workers often bid for jobs with no difference in pay and will even take a pay cut if the work suits them better. Finally, the existence of established rules gives the workplace union some power. Work-to-rule is, of course, an important means of asserting union power—one reason management would like to dump such rules.

In general, modern industrial unionism preferred to leave the workplace regime to the control of management and its modification to the local union. Job classifications are often spelled out in national contracts for the purpose of establishing wage rates, but detailed work rules are seldom a part of national agreements. Employer demands for modifications in work rules during national negotiations usually take the form of getting the international union's permission to bargain with locals for such changes. Work-rule concessions at the plant and local union level accelerated in the second half of the 1980s, further undermining pattern bargaining and the trade union principle of common work standards. . . .

Standard wages, benefits and conditions are the economic foundation of unionism. They underwrite the solidarity of the membership by establishing an egalitarian means of determining wages and benefits in place of employer favoritism or external economic criteria. But standardization is also the objective basis for both the defense of living standards and for future improvements. In 1909 John R. Commons noted that in order for any group of workers to raise their wages above a given market level they would have to "take wages out of competition." This meant standardizing wages throughout a particular labor market regardless of the competitive pressures on the employers.

Except for rare cases of true monopoly (for example, AT&T until very recently), all employers producing and selling the same (or substitutable) goods or services are in competition in a capitalist society. Labor, no matter how well organized, cannot eliminate the competition among employers, but it can eliminate the competition among workers. In Commons's time, most labor markets and unionized employers were local or regional. The major exceptions were coal, firearms and rail transport. The new basic industries such as steel were still nonunion. Most unions were craft unions. They attempted to "take wages out of competition" by establishing a standard union rate and forcing employers to hire only from the union. This involved either organizing all the workers in the same craft in a given market or driving nonunion workers out of the market in one way or another. In general, only the building trades unions were successful in this effort, and their success was often based on ethnic exclusivity and racial discrimination. This craft approach to suppressing competition among workers was basic to the old business unionism of the American Federation of Labor.

Industrial unionism approached the question of eliminating competition among workers in an entirely different way. Rather than working to limit the labor market or exclude potentially competitive workers, the industrial unions attempted to organize all the workers in the industry. The industrial union approach was inclusive rather than exclusive, national or even international rather than local or regional. The unions then fought to standardize wages, benefits and conditions for all the workers. Industrial unionism was egalitarian in that all workers performing similar work received the same package of wages and benefit standardized through the mechanism of pattern bargaining. . . .

[A]s long as the economy grew these patterns functioned as a means of protecting and improving the living standards of millions of workers. They provided a measure of protection not only for those directly covered by the major industrial patterns, but for workers performing similar or related work in the thousands of new plants built during the three decades following 1950—at least those fortunate enough to be organized into unions. Workers outside of manufacturing—for example, in transportation and communications—also benefited from the first major patterns as they established their own in the 1950s and 1960s. Eventually, after the mid-1960s, even public employees were able to bargain on the basis of "comparability," that is, the standards set in private industry for similar work. There is even evidence that union pay levels and benefits have a spillover effect on nonunion employers in the same industry.

For this system of pattern bargaining to work, the major patterns must remain intact. But . . . the structure of the patterns started to deteriorate in 1948, when the major industrial unions ceased to present the same demands at the same time. Pattern bargaining then became specific to each industry. Beginning in the 1960s, nonunion sectors developed in most industries, slowly at first, then rapidly, putting increased competitive pressure on the patterns. In the 1970s import competition in some industries added to this pressure. The main effect here, however, was not to put US workers into direct wage competition with overseas workers (a situation the employers could not have imposed due to the magnitude of the wage gap) but to intensify domestic competition. The simultaneous crisis of profitability gave the employers the incentive they needed to break the "social compact" on which US labor relations were based. The rise of a competitive, nonunion sector in one industry after another gave them the first lever. Ultimately, however, it was the cooperative posture of business unionism in accepting concessions that turned a crack in the patterns into a flood of concessions.

In October 1979 the UAW's acquiescence to concessions put Chrysler workers' wages into competition. Beneath all the language about saving jobs, the UAW leadership demonstrated its willingness to make wages, benefits and then working conditions subject to competitive bargaining. The pattern in auto was broken, and the standard that upheld worker solidarity eliminated. Naturally, the other US automakers moved to end Chrysler's advantage by reducing the pay and fringe benefits of their own workers. A degree of wage parity was reestablished in 1985, but by that time the automakers had imposed bidding between plants (in which work rules were bartered for alleged job security) and the dynamic of competition was out of control.

In other industries, concessions were made on a "pattern" basis—that is, all the firms covered by the pattern agreement were given wage relief. This was the case in meatpacking in 1982 and 1984, steel in 1983, and trucking in 1982 and again in 1985. The unions believed that this strategy would prevent the breakup of the patterns because it preserved a standard. In fact, it simply opened the door to competitive bargaining. The wage freeze granted major meatpackers by the United Food and Commercial Workers [UFCW] was aimed at reducing pressure on the local unions to grant concessions by giving the companies under the pattern a break in relation to the lower wages of newer nonpattern firms, union and nonunion alike. The Teamsters granted concessions to make union firms more competitive with nonunion operators. The USWA gave the seven basic steel corporations wage cuts to help them meet overseas competition. But once a union agreed to concessions in an industry with a lower pay, nonpattern sector (union or not), wages and other forms of compensation were put into competition, and the resulting centrifugal forces were hard to reverse. Smelling blood, the employers refused to limit their demands for concessions to the orderly process the unions hoped for.

If many labor leaders did not seem to grasp the economics of the situation, capital and its advisers understood it perfectly. Charles Lieberman, an economist for Shearson/American Express, explained it to *Wall Street Journal* readers: "Unlike the major industrial economies of Europe, the US labor market is becoming progressively more competitive. This development reflects the gradual erosion of the power of labor unions as well as the impact of deregulation." . . .

The centrifugal force of concessionary bargaining was nowhere more graphically demonstrated than in meatpacking. The meatpacking industry went through a series of structural changes in the 1960s and 1970s. Many old plants were closed as the companies opened new ones outside the industry's traditional centers in Chicago and Kansas City. Conglomerates bought several of the major packers, in many cases divesting them later. Meatpacking faced no serious competition from imports, nor was the industry as a whole in crisis, unlike auto or steel. But as new firms entered the industry, a substandard, competitive sector developed. Toward the end of the 1970s pressure from numerous companies, both profitable and unprofitable, began to convince UFCW local unions that they had no choice but to make concessions. One UFCW staffer said at the time: "After Chrysler went down, we started getting hit by very aggressive moves from the companies for mid-term concessions. They were hitting the local unions and trying to turn them against the International."

In 1981 the UFCW leadership came up with the utterly remarkable idea that the best way to stem the tide of concessions being made by locals in the pork-producing sector of meatpacking was to grant a wage freeze to all the companies under the pattern agreement. In a letter to all affected meatpacking locals dated 18 December 1981, UFCW President William Wynn announced the four objectives of the union's new strategy: 1) to "preserve and expand master agreements," 2) "to bring lower wage operators more in line with master agreement companies," 3) to resist "midterm contract concessions," and 4) to "minimize the wave of plant closings." Predictably, Wynn's strategy achieved none of these aims.

The voluntary offer of a wage freeze put the pattern wages into active competition by granting relief to the pattern employers. Here, as elsewhere, this simply unleashed the desire of employers for a further improvement in their competitive position. The master agreement in the pork sector fragmented. Lewie Anderson, head of the UFCW's Packinghouse Committee, told the *Wall Street Journal* that in the first eighteen months of the new agreement the number of workers receiving the pattern rate of $10.69 an hour had dropped from 50,000 to 30,000. Far from creating an orderly closing of the wage gap as other firms raised wages, the industry experienced a rapid downward spiral in wages. According to US Labor Department figures, the average hourly wage in meatpacking plants went from $9.19 in January 1982, when the UFCW's voluntary 44-month wage freeze went into effect, to $7.93 in January 1985. In addition, a number of the substandard firms got further concessions during that period, fouling the union's plans to raise off-pattern wages. . . .

. . . The situation in the industry remained chaotic, and the companies pushed for further concessions in 1984. The UFCW did not have to reopen the contract, which didn't expire until September 1985, but it did, granting a $1.69-an-hour wage reduction to those employers still under the pattern. The basic labor rate in plants still under the pattern, mostly Hormel and Oscar Mayer plants, was $9 an hour. The new agreement called for an increase to $10 an hour in September 1985. The UFCW claimed that by 1985 concessions would be over, but it was wrong. In Tennessee, where Oscar Mayer workers had avoided the $1.69 wage cut, the company demanded a $.69 cut in October 1985 to bring that plant's rate down to the level of the others. In Detroit, UFCW Local 26 suffered three defeats in late 1985 and early 1986. Kowalski Sausage broke the UFCW at its plant and cut wages. Hygrade workers took a cut from $10.69 to $9.50 with an additional $.80-an-hour reduction in benefits in February 1986 after a six-week strike. Thorne Apple Valley, which already paid below the pattern rate, imposed a wage freeze in February 1986 after a three-week strike. . . .

Beginning in 1986, the UFCW did manage to win wage increases at some plants. At Swift and Armour Dial (but not the ConAgra-owned plants) wages were raised to $10 an hour in September 1986. Most Hormel and Oscar Mayer plants went to $10.25 in September 1986 and were slated to reach $10.70 in September 1988. By 1988, the best of the new contracts would recover a rate first negotiated in 1979 and implemented in 1981. Real wages would be far below the level reached at the beginning of the decade. And there was no longer an industry pattern. These contracts, which represent a tiny minority of the workers once covered by the pattern, no longer cover the same period—that is, Swift, Armour Dial, and Morrell are behind by a year and below the wage levels at Hormel and Oscar Mayer, which means that the former companies have a competitive advantage. Even within the two remaining single-company "chain" agreements, not all of the plants at Hormel or Oscar Mayer receive the same rate. For example, workers performing slaughtering at Oscar Mayer's Perry, Iowa, plant receive less than workers doing processing. These contracts were negotiated at the height of an economic recovery; given the domination of competitive rates in the industry, it is quite likely that another round of concessionary demands will emerge in the next recession. . . .

The competitive logic that shatters industry-wide patterns also tends to penetrate any company with duplicate operations or the ability to outsource production. Companies demanded that local unions make concessions, usually on working conditions or work rules, with the threat that if they didn't give in the work would go elsewhere. This tactic emerged in the auto industry after the Chrysler bailout. . . .

In the fall of 1981, Ford told workers at its Sheffield, Alabama, aluminum casting plant that it would close the plant if they did not agree to a 50% cut in wages and benefits. The casting could be done elsewhere. At the same time, Ford asked Local 182 at its Livonia, Michigan, plant for a number of work-rule changes, making explicit the threat to move work away from the plant. Bill Grenham, financial secretary of the local, said: "Management told us there were other manufacturers that want this job. They're looking to get it done for the lowest possible price." At the same time, Ford won concessions from three Detroit-area UAW locals, awarding them work on new projects. In the case of two of the locals, Ford let it be known that it was considering sending the projects to Toyo Kogyo, a Japanese firm that is 25% Ford-owned. The notion of bidding for future work then supplemented the threat of plant closings. . . .

Bidding wars between plants thus became a regular feature of labor relations in the auto industry. As one UAW local official put it: "The threat to close plants also helps these large corporations pressure different plants into a bid war against each other for their jobs. The corporations want to cut labor costs and the workers are giving without receiving any return value." . . .

By 1987 competitive bargaining on a local union basis was widespread. The *Wall Street Journal* noted that "12 of GM's 22 assembly plants now have 'competitive' agreements, in most cases because the local unions agreed to reopen local contracts before their September 1987 expiration." Most of the local contract changes involved reducing job classifications and changing other work rules. By 1987, Chrysler had negotiated "modern operating agreements" at five of its remaining thirty-one plants.

The trend toward competitive local bargaining on the basis of working conditions suggested that even wage bargaining might be put on a plant-by-plant basis. In these cases, the competition is not limited to plants within the same firm, but to those performing similar work in the industry, even where outsourcing is not likely. This has already occurred in meatpacking, where workers performing slaughtering in the higher wage companies are paid less than workers doing other jobs because of the existence of sub-standard plants in the industry. At Firestone Tire, four of the company's eight plants pay wages below the national contract, meaning, as the *Wall Street Journal* pointed out, that "the company really doesn't have a national wage rate." Taking the collapse of pattern bargaining in steel one step further, the 1986 contract at Armco established different wage rates at most of the company's four plants. The Ashland, Kentucky plant accepted a wage freeze, two plants in Kansas City took wage and benefit cuts of $2.25 an hour, and the Baltimore plant took a $3.25-an-hour reduction. In all likelihood, the Armco agreement will set a precedent for future bargaining in a number of industries that employ dual or multisourcing of their components or products. . . .

The entire rationale for making concessions has been that they will, in one way or another, save jobs. This rationale has advanced from an argument for a temporary or exceptional modification of bargaining practices and contracts to a basic component of business unionist ideology for many union officials—committed as they are to shifting the union to a nonadversarial relationship with industry. However, few have put it as bluntly as UAW Vice President Don Ephlin, who announced that the role of the union in this era is to "reverse the rapid decline of America's manufacturing industries and help restore US competitiveness where it counts, in the battle for markets and jobs." In this view, concessions, like protectionism or labor-management cooperation, are just one means to that end.

Top union leaders do not mean by such statements that they plan to save all existing jobs. Since they share the company's concern about being competitive, they accept that rationalizations, new technology and other labor-saving steps will be needed. Nevertheless, when selling a contract to the members who are worried sick about losing their jobs, this more businesslike view of saving *some* jobs by allowing the company to cut labor costs is seldom mentioned. The concessions, they argue, will save jobs. But do they?

By the mid-1980s the record indicated that the answer is no, concessions do not save jobs or plants. A study of twenty-two tire plants that made concessions between 1977 and 1981 showed that all but five of them closed anyway. In 1983, the same year that it received concessions from the USW, US Steel announced plans to close one-third of its remaining steel capacity as well as various finishing and fabricating mills. Chrysler, of course, closed several plants as part of the bailout operation and continued closing plants after returning to profitability. . . .

One reason that concessions don't save jobs is that labor costs are seldom the cause of a corporation's or industry's financial problems. . . . [D]uring the 1970s labor costs as a proportion of total costs shrank in the economy as a whole and in manufacturing. On an industry-by-industry basis, the manufacturing industries . . . saw labor costs decline or remain stable as a proportion of sales in 1976–80. Wages and benefits rose, but the cost of other industrial inputs rose faster.

Business itself did not see concessions as a means of salvation. One steel industry executive told *Business Week*, "I don't think you can get enough money out of wage cuts in the long run to save the industry." Ernest Savoie, Ford's director of labor relations, was even more specific: "The factors outside collective bargaining far outstrip the gains we can make in wages and benefits. We could cut labor costs in half and still be uncompetitive."

Indeed, labor costs are about 25% to 35% of total costs in most manufacturing industries where concessions have become common. Concessions to this or that firm make little real difference to a large multinational corporation. If concessions are to make a difference they must be generalized so that the entire cost structure of the economy is transformed. This was a goal that the Business Roundtable sought through legislation in the 1970s. In the 1980s, concessions and union cooperation in making other changes that reduce costs in the long run became central to capital's strategy for enhancing the overall competitiveness of the US economy. Ford's Savoie explained that what employers wanted was "a bending of the labor cost trend line." He went on to say that he saw the concessionary contracts of recent years as a "transference from *we* vs. *they* to *us;* from adversarial to converging; from rigidity to flexibility; and from partisan to common interest." . . .

The team concept, or the "transference from *we* vs. *they* to *us,*" became popular with management in the late 1970s and early 1980s for precisely the same reasons that they began to demand concessions: to involve the union in improving the competitive position of the company, the industry, and the nation in the interests of capital and at the expense of labor. Concessions relieve capital of burdens that it believes undermine its ability to increase profits. But what capital really seeks is an entire change in the rules. When it is able to rid itself of unions completely, it does so. When the union is entrenched, it looks for another way. The "team concept" provides a permanent, institutional change in day-to-day company operations and labor relations. Concessions seek to tie worker compensation to company performance and to eliminate work rules that stand between the workers and management's will. The team approach bypasses such rules altogether. Its focus is not on wages or benefits per se, but on productivity, the exploitation of the workers' understanding of the production process, and above all the consciousness of the worker.

These sorts of programs go by various names: team concept, employee involvement, labor/management participation team, quality circles, and perhaps most commonly, quality of work life (QWL). Whatever the name, they share the purpose of getting workers to identify with company goals. Depending on the particular scheme, the union is either integrated into this process or marginalized altogether. . . . Obviously, it is more difficult to eliminate union functions where an entrenched union exists. So most QWL programs set up parallel or alternative structures that involve rank-and-file members, shopfloor union officials, and supervisors as part of the same team or group.

However, QWL programs are ultimately directed at the consciousness of the workers. They seek not simply to get union leaders to cooperate or to integrate the union, but to change how the workers perceive their own position in production and, hence, how they see unionism as well. . . .

QWL programs do this by appealing to genuinely felt needs. Like concessions, they seem to offer a way to protect jobs by helping the employer. But unlike concessions they offer a positive-sounding approach. They are designed to appeal to the worker's need to be treated as an intelligent human being who understands what he or she is doing either individually or as part of a group. QWL programs promise to listen to the workers, to take their suggestions about production methods seriously, to give them "a say." The workers are encouraged to "participate" in solving the company's problems. . . .

The point of departure of QWL programs and the team concept is the language of industrial democracy and worker participation, but the goal is something quite different: acceptance by the workers of management's competitive imperative as a day-to-day guiding principle of behavior. Obviously, workers with that sort of consciousness would not see much point in "arbitrary" union standards beyond the pension and social insurance provided for in the union contract. It is hardly surprising, then, that some of the most aggressive companies, like GM and USX, not to mention nonunion companies like IBM, are among the greatest proponents of QWL programs. . . .

In spite of the disastrous effect of concessions on union bargaining power, the clear intent of QWL programs as a "union substitute," and the complete failure of the "power-sharing" approach to alter real power relations one iota, much of the US labor leadership continues to hold out labor-management cooperation or nonadversarial labor relations as some sort of alternative to the collapse of the old system of collective bargaining based on pattern bargaining supported by governmental regulation. In fact, the popularity of nonadversarial labor relations reflects the conversion of a large number of union leaders to the competitive logic of the business enterprise, a fact that has given rise to the term *enterprise unionism*. Enterprise unionism differs from company unionism in that the union involved is still controlled and administered independently of the employer. Its identity with the goals of the employer is less an ideological preference for business norms than an adaptation to the effects of intensified competition in a global economy. But in the end, it signals the decline of industrial unionism.

Women and the Rise of Public-Sector Unionism Since the 1960s

DEBORAH E. BELL

A new emphasis on women and women's issues has emerged in the American trade union movement in recent years. Unions representing state and local government workers are at the forefront of this trend. They have

---

Deborah E. Bell, "Unionized Women in State and Local Government," in Ruth Milkman, ed. *Women, Work and Protest* (University of Illinois, 1985), 180–197.

organized large numbers of women, and, equally important, they have reformulated traditional trade union issues in ways that have particular relevance for women. Most private-sector labor organizations lag far behind. . . . [Over] 40 percent of the 7.7 million women workers in the public sector are represented by a union or association—more than twice the level of organization among women workers in the economy as a whole.

Women work in all areas of government. The majority are in jobs providing educational services, a sizeable minority (about 30 percent) work in health services, and the balance are in social services or public-administration jobs. Because of the public character of certain traditionally female professions—teaching, library and social work—women employed in government are significantly more likely to be working in jobs classified as professional than are women working in the private sector. Twenty percent of women workers in the public sector are classified as professionals, while another 24 percent are paraprofessionals or technical workers. In contrast, in the economy as a whole, only 17 percent of all women workers (public and private) are in the combined "professional and technical" category. On the other hand, clerical workers are also overrepresented in the public sector, making up 42 percent of its female workforce, as compared to 35 percent in the economy as a whole.

In spite of the high level of unionization and the greater proportion of professionals, the median salary for full-time women workers in government is comparable to the average for all full-time women workers. Non-white women are more often employed in the public sector than in the economy as a whole, making up 24 percent of all women employed in government, as compared to 14 percent of all employed women. One in five public-sector women workers is employed part-time, slightly below the level in the female workforce as a whole. While public-sector employment is in some ways atypical, none of the differences just reviewed account for the extraordinarily high level of unionization, relative to the private sector.

The majority of public-sector labor organizations represent workers in a single occupational category—police officers or nurses, for example—or workers in a cluster of occupations delivering one service—education or health care are instances. Some unions are structured along "industrial" lines, most notably the American Federation of State, County and Municipal Employees (AFSCME) and the Service Employees' International Union (SEIU), whose members work in a wide range of occupations, performing a variety of services. Some public employees, usually those employed by state governments, have opted not to join international unions but to bargain through independent associations. . . . There are also professional associations which engage in collective bargaining, but are not unions.

The largest all-public unions are AFSCME, with slightly over one million members, 40 percent of whom are women, and the American Federation of Teachers (AFT), with about 550,000 members, two-thirds of whom are women. The National Education Association (NEA) is a professional association with over 1.6 million members, most of whom work in public education. (No sex breakdown is available for NEA members, but the proportions are probably similar to the AFT's.) Among the mixed public/private labor organizations, SEIU probably represents the largest number of public workers. About 250,000 of its members, or one-third of the total, are public workers; of this group, an estimated 45 percent are women. The Communication Workers of America (CWA) represents an estimated 50,000 public workers, about half of whom are women, and the American Nurses' Association represents about 35,000 public-sector nurses, almost all of them women. The Teamsters and the Laborers also represent sizeable numbers of public workers, but most are men.

Women public-sector workers are as likely as their male coworkers to be unionized—more than two in every five—and, for working women, that rate is higher than in any other industry except communications. The high degree of unionization among women in public employment cannot be attributed to organizing efforts directed specifically at women workers. Such efforts were almost non-existent until the 1970s. Rather, their extensive organization is an historical byproduct (indeed, a necessary one) of the general project of organizing public workers, which began in the postwar period. . . .

The Rise of Public-Worker Unionism

The unionization of the public sector is one of the most significant developments in the US labor movement in the postwar era. The overall decline in union membership over the past thirty years would have been far greater if it were not for the dramatic increases in organization among public workers. By 1978, 6.1 million government workers were represented by labor organizations, compared to 3.9 million in 1968.

Public-sector unionization occurred in three stages. The first, in the years before 1965, was a period of initial efforts to pass collective bargaining laws covering public workers. This period also saw the instigation of organization drives, largely among blue-collar workers and in cities and states where there was a tradition of private-sector trade unionism. The second stage, between 1965 and 1975, saw the rapid expansion of both employment and unionization in the public sector, with service workers, many of them black, at the center of the organizing. Only in the third stage, from 1975 to the present, a period of reduced growth in unionization and in government budgets, have women workers, especially clericals, emerged as the primary focus of organizing efforts.

Civil service rules constitute the traditional personnel structure in government. Laws establishing civil service systems and regulations, covering primarily white-collar workers, have been passed by states and localities since the late nineteenth century. The designation of collective bargaining rights for public workers also rests with the individual states, for public employees are not covered by the National Labor Relations Act. While some groups of public-sector workers had organized themselves earlier, they rarely gained formal recognition or collective bargaining rights before the 1950s. Important symbolic steps in the development of public-sector unionism were taken with Mayor Robert Wagner's agreement to recognize unions representing New York City workers in 1958, and the executive order issued four years later by President Kennedy, which extended limited bargaining rights to federal employees. Most states passed public-employee collective bargaining laws after 1962, but they vary considerably with respect to categories of employees that can bargain, terms of employment that are bargainable, and dispute-resolution mechanisms. A critical point of difference between the private and public sectors is that most public employees do not have the legal right to strike. Public-sector arbitration procedures are therefore more highly developed.

Before 1965, male blue-collar workers employed in local-government-run parks, sewers and highways were often part-time or seasonal workers and hence not covered by civil service agreements. These workers actively sought unionization in order to achieve full-time status and full-time benefits. They were willing to strike and were loud and forceful in their demands. Their militance often led to the passage of collective bargaining laws, thereby reducing the need for other groups to strike for recognition. Several unions—the Laborers, the Teamsters, SEIU and AFSCME—recognized the implications of this blue-collar militancy. These unions readily signed up workers who came to them, and also initiated their own organizing drives.

Another group which favored unionization, although much less important numerically at the time, was professional white-collar workers in public administration. Covered by state and local civil service systems, many of these workers, particularly at the state level, had historically organized themselves into employees' associations. They tended to be heavily involved in state and local politics, lobbying for improvements in wages and civil service rules and supporting friendly candidates. While employees in some associations steadfastly opposed unionization, others sought collective bargaining over wages and non-politicized grievance mechanisms in order to win greater protection from the vagaries of politics. Unlike the blue-collar workers, they seldom engaged in job actions, but they did use their political leverage to win first informal and later formal bargaining procedures, which ultimately were codified in state law. This general pattern would repeat itself in state after state in the 1960s and 1970s.

During the initial stage of public-sector unionization, politically committed organizers and activists played a critical role. Their politics were usually informed by the experience of CIO organizing drives or left-wing political movements. From the former came a vision of trade unions as a means of gaining institutional legitimacy for the largely immigrant industrial working class, as well as economic gains. From the latter (the Communist Party, the Socialist Party, the "Wallace for President" campaign), came experience in organizing techniques, a notion of what good government services ought to be and, perhaps most important, political bases of support in several major cities. In New York City, San Francisco, Cincinnati, Philadelphia and elsewhere, the presence of left-wing and progressive political organizations and strong private-sector unions was as important as any other factor in early organizing successes among government workers.

Once the groundwork was laid, public-worker unionization accelerated rapidly. In the period of national economic growth and expanded government budgets under President Johnson in the mid-1960s, the service functions of government, particularly local government, grew enormously. Massive amounts of federal aid were passed down to states and localities to implement the socio-political agenda of the "Great Society," a trend which continued until the economic contraction of the mid-1970s. The effort to buy urban peace through more public services and more public jobs also extended to providing improved wages and benefits for organized government workers. The successes of the previous decade—getting laws passed, effective organizing drives, winning more comprehensive contracts—multiplied. Employees' associations began to reconstitute themselves as collective bargaining organizations, or to affiliate with established unions.

Many of the new jobs created in this period were clerical and service jobs in such entities as school districts, hospital corporations and "Model Cities" programs. There was no legal mandate that such jobs should have civil service protections—job security or pension coverage, for instance. These jobs served a dual purpose: to expand government services and to create openings for the unskilled and the unemployed, frequently women and non-whites. The work was often part-time, for with less than full-time hours and few benefits, more jobs could be created and more people employed. The unions viewed this kind of public-employment policy as a threat, and opposed it, both in the political arena and by organizing the new workers.

Black workers were critical to public-sector organizing in this period. In many cities in the 1960s, blacks were the explicit targets of public-employment programs. Once employed, blacks wanted the rights and protections which they perceived unionization could provide. The multi-occupational unions, most importantly AFSCME and SEIU, responded by actively organizing service-workers, including large numbers of blacks. Their goal was to achieve full-time rights and privileges and higher salary rates. Organizing black government-workers also led to breakthroughs in traditionally non-unionized areas of the country, most notably the South. Here, black sanitation- and highway-workers receiving low wages and no job security or rights asked public unions to organize and represent them. "Dignity" was a common theme in these drives, and links to the civil rights movement were more than rhetorical—civil rights activists were often pro-union activists as well. The civil rights movement defined social enfranchisement as an end; public-sector jobs and public-sector unions became part of the means. It was hardly coincidental that when Martin Luther King, Jr., was killed in 1968, he was visiting Memphis to support striking AFSCME sanitation-workers.

Public-sector job growth and unionization between 1950 and 1975 brought women nearly half the state and local government jobs. Large numbers of women were organized in this period, but very few rose to leadership positions in the burgeoning public-sector unions. During 1965–75, activists were more likely to be male than female—even in organizing drives among professional groups such as teachers and social workers, where female presence was strong. For example, in New York City, the greatest support for the organizing efforts of the United Federation of Teachers (UFT) came from high school teachers, of whom a relatively high proportion were men.

Women clerical workers were organized somewhat selectively prior to 1975. The factors favoring organizing drives seem to have been either large numbers, as in New York City, to make it worth the effort, or small numbers concentrated in one or two locations, such as a hospital, to make it relatively easy. Receptivity to unionization on the workers' part was also a consideration, but when there were large numbers involved or the clericals were the only unorganized group in a jurisdiction, the multi-occupational unions would often try to organize them regardless of their initial receptivity. The strategic reasoning was, first, concern that politicians and administrators might play off unionized and non-unionized workers against one another, and, second, the conviction that a fully unionized public workforce meant power—both at the bargaining table and in the legislature. In localities where clericals were few in number, dispersed locationally, and expressed no interest in being organized, they were more often than not ignored by unions in the pre-1975 period.

But since the mid-1970s, this has begun to change. In May 1977, 34 percent of government clerical workers were represented by a labor organization, compared with 46 percent of government professionals, 44 percent of government blue-collar workers, and 41 percent of government service-workers. Since then, however, the biggest increases in public-sector unionization have been among clerical workers. Between 1977 and 1980, the number of unionized government workers in blue-collar and service occupations increased only about 1.5 percent, while in the white-collar occupations the increase was 20 percent; and among clerical workers in particular, the increase was 22 percent.

What accounts for this upsurge in unionization among clerical workers? First, the simple fact that women have entered the workforce in large numbers in the past few years and plan to remain working suggests an imperative to maximize job security and economic benefits. Also, an ongoing impact of the women's movement has been to legitimate the economic and political activism of women on their own behalf, part of which is a more positive attitude toward unions. The absence of any comparable increase in unionization among private-sector clericals, however, identifies the primary catalyst—the change in the multi-occupational public-sector unions themselves. Part of the change is structural. Over the past twenty years, their occupational distribution has been steadily shifting from predominantly blue-collar to predominantly white-collar. Because there are far more women in white-collar jobs, an increase in the proportion of female members has accompanied the occupational shift and has affected union policy-making in favor of organizing women and women's issues.

Women's Issues and Women's Leadership in Public Unions

Policy shifts in unions have resulted from increased participation by women members in union activities. Women are becoming more active as shop stewards and running for office. In a survey of its local union officers, AFSCME found that 33 percent of local presidents in 1982 were female, compared to 25 percent several years before, and that women hold 45 percent of all local union offices. In recent years, a woman was elected an international vice-president of SEIU for the first time, and two women were elected to the International Executive Board of AFSCME. Black women have also moved into local leadership positions; this is significant because unions are one of the few places in American institutional life where this is possible in the 1980s. An increased emphasis on skills development among women unionists has helped to increase women's leadership. . . . At the local level, women's committees often serve the role of stimulating discussion and training among women. There are also more women union staff-workers than ever before. Although they tend to be concentrated in social service, research and editorial staff jobs, women increasingly hold legal, education, safety and health, organizing and collective bargaining positions.

As the number of women members grows and as more women gain concrete organizational, leadership and staff experience, issues of concern to women are more likely to be raised and addressed. Women's issues in the public sector can be categorized in traditional trade union terms—job security, the changing structure of the workplace, and wages and benefits. Because women are concentrated in service and white-collar office jobs, however, the specific issues emphasized are somewhat different.

Changing economic conditions threaten to determine women's job security in government. Long-term reductions in the rate of growth of government budgets will result in reduced public services and a smaller public-employment base. The push to reduce public services has ideological as well as economic goals: (1) to eliminate institutionalized mechanisms for income redistribution; and (2) to leave service gaps that the private profit-making service sector can fill, in order to stimulate growth in that part of the economy. Under the Reagan administration, there [was] also an explicit effort to undermine public-sector unionism and gain greater control over the public workforce, as seen in the federal government's conscious destruction of the air traffic controllers' union in 1981.

. . . Much of the budget-cutting that occurred at the local level in the late 1970s was due to reduced local revenue growth, and the services suffering the most were those financed primarily from local revenues—police, fire, sanitation, highways and sewers—with male-dominated workforces. Health and welfare services, with a much higher proportion of female workers and a larger share of federal funding, were less hard hit. However, the federal domestic-spending cuts called for since 1980 . . . have a devastating effect on employment for women in the local government growth areas of the past fifteen years—education, health and social services.

A related problem is the increasing support for privatization of the delivery of services traditionally provided by government. Private management companies employing low-paid, non-unionized workers with few benefits are already being hired to run public hospitals and to provide food-preparation and cleaning services for many state and local government agencies. There are even proposals for a nation-wide federal voucher system for primary through high school education, with the vouchers redeemable at public or private schools. Though the rationale for privatization is better-quality services at reduced costs, there is not much concrete evidence that a profit-making company can improve quality *and* reduce costs unless workers are paid the minimum wage with no benefits. Especially vulnerable are entry-level workers, often women, in service jobs where wages and benefits are significantly higher in the public than in the private sector (usually due to unionization), because privatization could lead to immediate savings in labor costs alone.

Even more significant for women are the changes likely to result from automation in office and service jobs. The introduction of technologically advanced equipment—word processing, computerized record-keeping, more automated testing, new types of food-preparation and cleaning equipment—is inevitable, but it has not occurred as frequently or as rapidly in the public sector as in the private, usually because state and local governments cannot afford to buy the equipment as quickly.

The workforce adjustments and changes in the work process that will result from automation are already evident. The popular catch-phrase accompanying these changes is "increased productivity"—more output per person-hour, which essentially means performing services with fewer workers. New technology is likely to have especially dramatic effects on the structure of the many white-collar and professional functions entailed in maintaining and processing data involved in financial records, welfare cases, medical records and property tax assessments. . . . Many of the jobs affected by this "de-skilling" are female-dominated. This change will also lead to fewer advancement opportunities, because most office jobs will be at the low end of the clerical/administrative career ladder.

Because of "de-skilling," automation in the public sector may lead to net gains rather than losses in clerical jobs, but there will be other negative effects, such as the potential for greater control and monitoring of both the content and the pace of clerical jobs. Questions have been raised over possible safety and health hazards associated with the computerized equipment itself (particularly the video display terminals), but perhaps more hazardous are the physical effects—eye strain, back and neck aches, etc.— of the repetitive, monotonous tasks which the equipment imposes on the work process. Further, the pace of work can be monitored, and even preset, electronically, making it possible to measure (or to claim to measure) the output and productivity of many public-service functions which were not previously quantifiable. This, in turn, might provide a rationale for productivity-based job cuts without adequate consideration of the effects on the quality of service.

In regard to wage and benefit issues, women's expanded role in public unions has come in an era of sharply reduced budgetary latitude in government and while many private-sector unions are engaged in "concession bargaining." Nevertheless, public unions have been moderately successful in raising and addressing some economic issues of concern to women. For example, in addition to negotiating across-the-board wage increases, unions have increasingly exerted pressure for enforcement of affirmative action and equal employment opportunity policies to help women get jobs in nontraditional, often higher-paying, occupations. Public unions are also demanding restructuring of civil service classifications to create career ladders with more promotional opportunities. Demands for training and skills upgrading are also common, and many unions use their own educational resources to provide them.

Dollars alone will not solve the problems facing women who move in and out of the labor force, particularly those with children; alternative work schedules are also needed. Flextime, which permits variation in arrival and departure times as long as the required number of hours per week are worked, often sharply reduces absenteeism among women with children. "Compressed time" (i.e., three twelve-hour days per week) and job sharing are other approaches of increasing interest to women.

Child-care is a particularly critical issue for working women. Nevertheless, it is one on which the unions have made little progress. As long as women drop out of the labor force to care for children, they will lose ground over the course of their working life. Studies demonstrate that "breaks in service" have a seriously depressing effect on wage growth and career advancement for women, particularly in clerical and service jobs, where the effect becomes institutionalized in the "dead-endedness" of those jobs.

Child-care is costly and usually benefits only a relatively small proportion of a union's members at any one time. Demands for child-care are fairly common, but, in actual negotiations, bargaining committees are rarely willing to give up part of a wage increase to fund such programs, and most public employers are not willing to bear the cost themselves. . . . Full-time enrollment in a child-care center costs upward of $65 per week, more than many working women can afford. Serious attitudinal barriers remain, as well. Women are still viewed as primarily responsible for the care of children by all social institutions, including unions, and there is a deep-rooted ambivalence about making it easier for mothers to work.

The public sector offers unusual opportunities—potentially available physical facilities, concentrations of large numbers of employees and, in some areas, the experience of running day-care programs for the population at large. What is still lacking, however, is a commitment on the part of public-sector unions to experiment with those opportunities, to find ways to provide child-care and to insist on employers' obligation to help provide it. . . .

The most important women's issue to emerge from the public-sector unions has been pay equity. The concept of pay equity, or comparable worth, posits that the principle of "equal pay for equal work" is inadequate to address the issue of economic discrimination in the workplace because women and men do different jobs in a sex-segregated economy. Rather than arguing for equal pay for all workers performing the same job, pay equity advocates argue for equal pay for work of comparable value. In this view, occupational segregation, combined with wage discrimination, has depressed wage rates for traditionally female-dominated occupations. Moreover, the sex gap in wages is not adequately explained by differences in job requirement (skills, level of responsibility, hazards, and mental and physical effort required) and is therefore discriminatory.

Advances around the pay equity issue have been made in the public sector not only because a lot of working women are concentrated there in female-dominated occupations, but also because wages and job descriptions are public information. Civil service systems offer an easily available basis for job-evaluation studies to demonstrate lack of equity. Generally speaking, this kind of information is not readily accessible in the private sector. Further, public-sector collective bargaining laws and practice and civil service laws and practice contain explicit references to the principle of just and equitable wages. They thus provide a basis for challenging or threatening to challenge existing wage levels and job classifications. Also, politicians are concerned about the voting power of women, and some are receptive to legislative proposals on pay equity for public employees because they provide an opportunity to have a direct effect on the salaries of women in that sector.

A variety of tactics are being employed to achieve pay equity. Legislation and collective bargaining are the primary ones, with litigation and Equal Employment Opportunity Commission complaints as back-up pressure tactics. In many instances, collective bargaining and legislative gains have led to job-evaluation studies which have identified discriminatory wage inequities, but have not yet led to actual wage adjustments. In the context of reduced government growth, implementing pay equity will be costly. AFSCME estimates that winning its pay equity lawsuit on behalf of 10,000 workers against the State of Washington will cost $500 million in back pay and raise the state budget by 2 percent annually for ongoing increases. There are cases, however, where wage adjustments have been made or are scheduled, often because of women unionists, working in coalition with women's organizations and women politicians. For example:

- In March 1982, legislation was passed in Minnesota to determine which state-employee job classes are underpaid relative to others and to make wage adjustments, beginning in July 1983. . . .
- Municipal workers in San Jose, California (members of AFSCME), won a commitment to pay equity wage adjustments in addition to general wage increases through a six-day strike in June 1981. . . .

- In collective bargaining, the state of Connecticut committed 1 percent of the total state payroll (about $1 million) for pay equity adjustments to state clerical and health care titles. . . .
- Clerical workers in Santa Clara County, California (members of SEIU), bargained in 1974 for an evaluation of their job classifications. This resulted in wage adjustments such as: extra pay for skills like fast typing and bilingual ability; a new bridge classification between clerical and paraprofessional jobs to provide career opportunities; and establishment of a classification review board to decide on upgradings. After years of bargaining and expedited arbitrations, the clericals received inequity wage adjustments ranging from 1.5 to 15 percent in July 1981, in addition to a general wage increase.

These examples illustrate the importance of generating support for pay equity in the political arena, as well as in collective bargaining, using traditional and non-traditional techniques.

For the public-sector unions that have been active around the pay equity issue, there have been institutional rewards. A strong stand on an issue like pay equity lends credibility to unions as aggressive representatives of women's concerns. This has appeal to potential as well as current members, so that gains on pay equity can be an important part of an organizing strategy. In addition, pay equity represents an innovative wage strategy in public-sector collective bargaining for current members, offering a rationale for shaking loose money for higher wages from a tight-fisted state or local legislature coping with budget-cuts. . . . Once established in law or in a contract, the principle of comparable worth as an acceptable imperative for adjusting wage levels—even though it may only be applied to a small number of workers at low initial cost to the employer—provides the basis for a union to negotiate extensions of the principle to greater numbers of workers with each succeeding contract.

In the short run, women in female-dominated professional and managerial occupations in the public sector will benefit disproportionately from pay equity. Their numbers are relatively small, which keeps costs down, and while government professional and managerial salary rates in general are far below comparable private-sector salaries, pay equity is a more palatable excuse for increasing wages than private-sector comparability. . . .

The mass of women, in clerical and service jobs, probably will not benefit right away from pay equity; the cost of closing the male/female wage gap is just too great. An indirect approach to pay equity, job reclassification, may offer more immediate relief. The cost of raising wages through reclassification can be rationalized by expanding the range of duties of a particular job, theoretically increasing the productivity associated with that job as well as management's flexibility in assignments. Reclassification can also lead to creating more advancement opportunities at increased wages.

Although some unions have emphasized reclassification as a pay equity strategy, it has some serious pitfalls. For one thing, workers may not want more responsibility, only more equitable wages for the work they are currently doing. The widespread discussion of career ladders may divert attention from the needs at the bottom rungs. The reality is that there will always be many fewer jobs at the top than at the bottom of these ladders. Further, public management has been known to have quite different motives in acceding to reclassification demands. For instance, reclassification may be used to reduce the number of supervisory jobs permitted union recognition rights, or less specific job descriptions may be enlisted by management to give greater flexibility in task assignment. . . .

Conclusion

. . . As government negotiators become more aggressive in trying to hold down increases in wage costs and become more willing to tolerate strikes, public-sector unions will have to develop greater creativity in their bargaining demands, including pressing for some that will only be applied to select groups of workers. The complexity of the pay equity issue provides a range of strategic options for unions to pursue, depending on specific circumstances.

Success in winning wage adjustments for public-sector, female-dominated job categories, based on the pay equity concept, may have a spillover effect into the private sector. For organizing women workers, however, particularly clerical workers, the public-sector experience is less applicable as a model. The differences are just too great. Pre-existing employees' associations throughout much of the public sector have made it much easier to unionize women public workers than those in comparable private-sector jobs. Furthermore, there is generally less resistance by most public officials to unionization than there is in a private company. In addition, in government, some part of the workforce is usually unionized already, which both lowers management resistance and increases worker receptivity, even when most of the unionized workers are in male-dominated blue-collar or uniformed jobs.

Successful organizing of women workers in government will carry on, and significant union resources will be expended to win these new members. The competition among the multi-occupational unions to win recognition rights has been fierce, and will continue to be. In recent years, for example, clerical workers at state universities and colleges have frequently been the targets of organizing drives by competing unions. . . .

Today, unionized public-sector women are at the forefront of the fight for improved employment conditions for women. This did not result from a long-range strategy on the part of public-sector unions. Rather, it is the unexpected consequence of the vast influx of women into the growing number of government jobs, and the effects of the complex relationship between the trade union, civil rights and women's movements. An enormous momentum has been generated, and in spite of budget-cuts, the public sector has become a central arena for addressing women's issues. . . .

⚘ F U R T H E R   R E A D I N G

Diane Balser, *Sisterhood and Solidarity: Feminism and Labor in Modern Times* (1987)

David Bensman and Roberta Lynch, *Rusted Dreams: Hard Times in a Steel Community* (1987)

Barry Bluestone and Bennett Harrison, *The Deindustrialization of America* (1982)
————, *The Great U-Turn: Corporate Restructuring and the Polarizing of America* (1988)

Samuel Bowles, David Gordon, and Thomas Weisskopf, *Beyond the Waste Land* (1982)

Mike Davis, *Prisoners of the American Dream* (1986)

Leon Fink and Brian Greenberg, *Upheaval in the Quiet Zone: A History of Hospital Workers' Union 1199* (1989)

Richard Freeman and James L. Medoff, *What Do Unions Do?* (1984)

Michael Goldfield, *The Decline of Organized Labor in the United States* (1987)

Thomas Kochan, Robert McKersie, and Harry Katz, *The Transformation of American Industrial Relations* (1986)

Ruth Milkman, "Women Workers, Feminism and the Labor Movement Since the 1960s," in Ruth Milkman, ed., *Women, Work and Protest* (1985)

Kim Moody, *An Injury to All: The Decline of American Unionism* (1988)

Mike Parker and Jane Slaughter, *Choosing Sides: Unions and the Team Concept* (1988)

Karen Brodkin Sacks, *Caring by the Hour: Women, Work and Organization at Duke Medical Center* (1988)

CHAPTER
15

The Future of Work

⚶

Americans have come to reexamine the content and organization of their work, perhaps more so today than at any time since Henry Ford first deployed the moving assembly line. The sharp decline in productivity growth during the 1970s and 1980s, combined with the competitive challenge mounted by German and Japanese capital, has forced American employers to take a critical look at the way work has been organized in U.S. factories and offices. Whatever one thought of Japanese management or German labor, the highly successful firms in these nations clearly had evolved work structures quite different from those that had once made the United States the world leader. Was it therefore possible to organize work more democratically and more efficiently? Had Taylorism outlived its usefulness? Could worker participation be built into the job?

The dramatic appearance of computers, robots, and new forms of telecommunication equipment in the 1980s indicated that the tools were now at hand to begin a fundamental restructuring of work—not only in the routine assembly and paper shuffling at the bottom of the organization, but also in the more autonomous work of technicians, professionals, and middle managers at higher levels of pay and responsibility. Even the location of the work site seemed up for grabs, for the same system of computers that reorganized the work flow within a firm also facilitated the detailed and daily coordination of production across town or across an ocean.

Scholars of work and labor nevertheless have adopted quite different perspectives on this new industrial revolution. A majority, largely management-oriented, have concluded that the competitive and fast-changing economic environment requires a more cooperative, flexible, and reskilled work force, ready and willing to participate with management in a joint effort to make their organization more effective and efficient. In this view the rapidly changing character of world markets and the dramatic increase in work-site technology have reversed what many saw as the twentieth century's historic tendency to subdivide the labor process and deskill individual workers. The new economic and technological conditions also have eliminated the usefulness of the traditional adversarial relationship fostered by unions and managers at the point of production, and have replaced it with a participative model that reduces the need for carefully defined work rules, grievance systems, and wage standards.

This viewpoint has its adherents even within the union movement, but other observers, in labor and academe, argue that unilateral employer initiatives *designed to reorganize production and computerize the work site will ultimately reduce American workers' power, actual or potential. Computerization, they say, advances managerial efforts to appropriate labor's on-the-job knowledge and gives managers the upper hand in strikes and other forms of conflict. The easy flow of information from one office and factory to another may well globalize production, but in such a way that high-tech design rooms and low-wage sweatshops complement each other within the same production system. Simultaneously, quality circles and team-production schemes serve merely to undermine the elementary forms of the "we versus them" solidarity long felt by many workers, replacing it with a firm-centered ideology that further divides employees into competing production units loyal to their company, region, or nation.*

✝ D O C U M E N T S

In the first document, *New York Times* business writer Doron Levin reports that the new generation of "smart machines" deployed by U.S. manufacturers requires self-reliant workers whose knowledge of the production process must be expert and extensive. But labor activists Mike Parker and Jane Slaughter find that the supposedly democratic and multiskilled character of work in the new generation of Japanese-style auto factories has a dark and exploitative underside. Focusing on a GM-Toyota joint venture in California, Parker and Slaughter perceive in the production process more old-fashioned Taylorism than high-tech teamwork. Indeed, the computerized workplace can also eliminate even the simplest skills, as journalist Barbara Garson demonstrates in the next document, an account of an interview she conducted with a young McDonald's employee. A computerized cash register, which enables management to keep track of almost every hamburger and French fry sold, has stripped the company's minimum-wage sales workers of the need for elementary mathematical skills, and the opportunity to make decisions for themselves. Morton Bahr of the Communications Workers of America (CWA) finds extensive computerization a threat to worker interests because of the ease with which employers can transfer work to distant, low-wage locations, a few examples of which he recounts in the fourth document.

This condemnation of decentralized production was not the official U.S. government viewpoint, however. In the fifth document, former Secretary of Labor Ann McLaughlin attacks unions for resisting decentralized production and applauds the new telecommunications technologies that enable many women to perform their clerical work at home. In contrast, the sixth reading, a report on the work of the New York State Labor Department's Apparel Industry Task Force, suggests that the relationship between low- and high-tech work is a complex one. Thus the same economic conditions and technical innovations that offer white-collar women the possibility of electronically based work in the home also generate inner-city garment-industry sweatshops that exploit Hispanic and Asian families. Finally, the regulation of the new technology is a central theme in the seventh document, the International Association of Machinists' (IAM), "Technology Bill of Rights." This 1984 manifesto calls on management to share with workers and the larger community the decision to deploy a new technology, and it seeks to ensure that a portion of any benefits will be won by workers in the form of higher wages, shorter hours, and greater on-the-job autonomy.

Smart Machines Make Smart Workers, 1988

. . . A decade ago, robots and computerized manufacturing equipment were rapidly appearing on the assembly line as industry sought to automate the nation's factories.

As workers worried that they would be replaced by intelligent machines, engineers and executives spoke of the "lights out" factory of the future, one automated enough to operate in the dark, unattended.

But this enthusiastic reliance on highly automated production lines has been disappointing. Factory managers are finding that a key to superior performance is smarter workers who can handle the smarter machines.

Now, workers are being given more powers—for example, the authority to deal with a problem involving one of the machines instead of turning to a superior, or to make production-line decisions. And they are being given more information about day-to-day operations so as to become more deeply involved in the factory's work.

Manufacturing experts have coined a term for this new strategy: the "informated" factory.

The People Factor

"Automation doesn't work when the organizational structure doesn't accept it," said Ramchandran Jaikumar, a professor at the Harvard Business School. "Management of intellectual assets is the key, and that hasn't been done in enough factories."

The personality of an informated factory is striking to a visitor. Workers spend a significant part of their day collecting and sorting data about subjects like quality control, inventory and shipments that are available on television monitors near their machines.

At the new Mazda car plant in Flat Rock, Mich., for example, charts and graphs about the plant's operations fill bulletin boards at nearly every work place. At the Weyerhaeuser Company's plant in Longview, Wash., every one of the more than 1,000 workers has access to a TV screen and the same production data as the plant manager. In an earlier era, workers would not have been privy to such information.

Workers in these factories attend numerous meetings, on company time, to help decide everything from vacation scheduling to the number of units to be produced in the coming week.

Managers and foremen, on the other hand, seem to have relinquished some of their roles as bosses. Instead, they are spending more time dispensing advice and solving problems. Harold Epps, manager of the Digital Equipment Corporation keyboard plant in Boston, was forced to transfer some old-line supervisors who could not adjust to this new approach. To sharpen his own coaching skills, Mr. Epps said, he now puts himself through two weeks a year of classroom or on-the-job training and teaches at night at a local college.

At Weyerhaeuser's Longview plant, knowledge of production data generated by smart machines has enabled workers on the computer-operated sodium hydroxide manufacturing line to save the company millions of dollars in energy costs in the past three years. Machine operators learned who was using too much water in the process, and corrective steps were taken.

The General Electric Company's Salisbury, N.C., factory, which makes electrical distribution equipment, is a showcase of worker-driven automation. G.E.'s top manufacturing executive, Frederick Garry, said G.E. wants to replicate what it has accomplished in Salisbury in its worldwide network of more than 300 manufacturing plants.

By scientific and engineering standards, G.E.'s manufacturing process is advanced, but not at the leading edge. To be sure, the machines are more capable than those of a decade ago. And by reprogramming the mainframe computer that controls them, G.E. Salisbury can swiftly build a seemingly endless variety of electrical boards.

A Do-It-Yourself Attitude

The biggest change is the way people work. G.E. wanted to avoid cumbersome delays caused by the bureaucratic chain-of-command relationships between worker and plant manager. In the past, workers were not allowed to correct automation glitches, or they did not know how. Instead plant maintenance workers were called to do the job.

Four years ago, as a way to cut through bottlenecks on the plant floor, G.E. decided to give its factory staff far more information and far more power to make decisions.

As a result, when Bob Hedenskog, automation equipment operator, has a problem, he may now telephone a manufacturing engineer in G.E.'s Plainville, Conn., office. Previously, he would have had to call his foreman, who would have dealt with the problem.

Mr. Hedenskog, who used to be a machine "setup man," recently ordered $40,000 worth of parts on his own initiative, to replace parts he expects will wear out in the coming year. And, using his knowledge of what it takes to run his machine, he has served on a committee that hired a new worker to operate the machine on another work shift. According to G.E. management, the new system has been met with overwhelming, though not unanimous, worker approval. Opal Parnell, who has been operating a stamping machine at G.E. for 11 years, put it this way: "You get more work out this way. The majority of people take it as a big opportunity. You're an adult, and you've got to do it."

Ms. Parnell was referring to the fact that she, Mr. Hedenskog and the other 75 or so workers on the plant floor are largely unsupervised and make their own production and scheduling decisions as part of a committee on which they serve.

Some Eschew New Responsibility

Employee turnover at Salisbury was about 15 percent in the first year under the new system. Several workers who left said they did not want additional responsibility, a company spokesman said. But turnover has dropped to 6 percent in the past year, partly because worker-selection committees tend to recommend people for employment who they think will fit in.

"Team spirit and reliability are important," said Roger Gasaway, a G.E. plant manager, "because workers often decide among themselves when to work overtime or on weekends."

Because of enormous manufacturing efficiencies at Salisbury, G.E. since 1985 has been able to close five plants producing the same product, while gaining market share on its rivals. And the number of worker hours per distribution board produced has been reduced by two-thirds.

More important, customer delivery time has been cut by a factor of 10 and quality has improved.

A Long Way to Go

By all accounts, the level of success achieved in Salisbury has yet to be matched by most automated United States plants. A G.E. executive estimated that the company was no more than 30 percent of the way to its goal of operating all its manufacturing the way it is done in Salisbury.

Deere, Polaroid, Harley-Davidson, I.B.M., Motorola, Digital Equipment, General Motors, Xerox, Weyerhaeuser and several other Fortune 500 companies operate at least one automated factory in which workers have a lot of authority, according to several manufacturing experts. The experts think that United States manufacturers must pursue the model of a self-directed and highly automated work force in order to compete worldwide.

Mr. Jaikumar of Harvard studied the use of flexible machines in the United States and Japan and found that Japanese plants can make about 10 times as many products as American plants using similar machines. The Japanese plants, he discovered, also have many more workers with advanced degrees working directly with the machines.

Fewer but Smarter Workers

Government economists predict that employment trends through the next decade will mirror manufacturing's need to have more sophisticated machines that require more sophisticated workers.

The Bureau of Labor Statistics predicts that between 1986 and 2000 the number of jobs in manufacturing in the United States will decrease to about 18.2 million, from about 19 million.

And within manufacturing, the nature of work will change, the economists predict. There will be 165,000 more jobs for engineers, 80,000 more jobs for managers, 23,000 more jobs for computer and other scientists and

70,000 more jobs for engineering and other technicians. At the same time, there will be 203,000 fewer jobs for assemblers, 147,000 fewer jobs for laborers and movers and 319,000 fewer jobs for machine setters, the economists predict.

If these predictions are correct, the typical factory worker of the future will clearly bear only a passing resemblance to his or her blue-collar forebear. The operators of tomorrow's programmable machines must be better educated and possess more abilities to interact with co-workers.

The "Gold Collar" Worker

Robert Kelly, a professor at Carnegie-Mellon University, has dubbed these highly educated and highly socialized employees "gold collar" workers.

Building a work force that can make decisions on its own has been a daunting problem. Mr. Gasaway acknowledges that some G.E. managers, including himself, have trouble giving up power.

Historically, some workers and labor unions have been suspicious of management-led "team building" and "quality circles," fearing they were simply a plot to increase worker output.

"If employees are to learn to operate in new ways and to broaden their contribution to the life of the business, then career ladders and reward systems reflecting that change must be designed," said Shoshana Zuboff, a Harvard professor who coined the term "informate" in her recently published book, *In the Age of the Smart Machine*.

By completing community college courses related to their work, G.E. workers in Salisbury may increase their pay by as much as 40 percent. Moreover, the credits earned qualify them for job openings in the plant.

Lee Sage of Arthur Young & Company said that at the General Motors Corporation outmoded ways of measuring and rewarding performance in factories have presented major obstacles to manufacturing improvements. Arthur Young is a consultant to G.M.'s Buick-Oldsmobile-Cadillac vehicle-building group.

G.M., with more than 150 factories in North America, is widely considered the world's biggest user of programmable manufacturing machines.

A Change in Focus

Historically, G.M. plant workers have been motivated by promotions and bonus systems that reward them for meeting production quotas. Improving manufacturing processes has been given less of a priority.

To change that, plants in the Buick-Oldsmobile-Cadillac group each have a "Quality Council" for managers and hourly workers to share information and decide questions jointly.

In the past, union officials often opposed efforts to expand the responsibilities of workers, preferring instead to force managements to hire additional workers. But officials of the United Auto Workers union have supported initiatives to improve G.M. manufacturing at Buick-Oldsmobile-Cadillac, Mr. Sage said.

"The people I've met from the union are saying, 'Just give me a chance to succeed,' " he said.

The New Taylorism in a Japanese-Managed Auto Factory, 1988

The General Motors–Toyota assembly plant in Fremont, Calif., has probably been the site of more pilgrimages by eager managers than any other factory in the United States. These managers, from throughout the auto industry and from many other industries, are now trying to apply the lessons of this joint venture—called Nummi, for New United Motors Manufacturing Inc.—in their own factories. At conference after conference, academics, engineers, managers and union leaders extol Nummi's successes. These have become legendary:

- Consistently high quality ratings. According to a 1986 Massachusetts Institute of Technology study, Nummi rated 135 to 140 out of a possible score of 145.
- A massive increase in labor productivity—at least 50 percent higher than other General Motors Corporation plants and almost as high as at a Japanese Toyota plant.

But like other great feats, Nummi's achievements are accompanied by myths. The most important of these is that Nummi is productive because of worker involvement or even worker control. According to the stories, the team concept used at Nummi encourages workers to use their brains. For the first time, workers have a say in management by planning how to carry out and share their own work. The old authoritarian foreman is replaced by a "group leader," aided by worker "team leaders."

In fact, Nummi has achieved its gains through far greater regimentation of the work force than exists in traditional American auto plants. Tight specifications and monitoring of how jobs are to be done, a bare-bones work force with no replacements for absentees and a systematic and continuing speedup are the methods used.

We use the term "management by stress" to describe this system, which often goes by the names "team concept" or "synchronous manufacturing." It depends not only on tight control of the work force but also on extensive outside contracting and on organizing all production on a "just-in-time" basis.

Management by stress goes against traditional management notions, at least in the United States. In a traditional system—sometimes called "just in case"—management wants extra parts and extra workers on hand to cover for any glitches that may arise.

Mike Parker and Tom Slaughter, "Behind the Scenes at Nummi Motors," *The New York Times*, December 4, 1988.

Under management by stress, the aim is to methodically locate and remove protections against glitches. Glitches are in fact welcomed because they identify the system's weak points. Breakdowns indicate where a method must be changed, perhaps a way found to perform a particular bottleneck operation more quickly. Just as important, points that never break down are assumed to waste resources. They are targeted as well— human or material resources are removed until the station can keep up, but just barely.

The "andon" board illustrates how management by stress functions. At Nummi and at other Japanese-owned car plants in the United States, a lighted board above the assembly line—called the andon board—shows the status of each work station. When a worker falls behind or needs help, he or she pulls a cord; bells chime and the board lights up. If the cord is not pulled again within a set period of time (say a minute), the line stops.

In a traditional operation, the plant manager would want to see no lights flashing. Not so under management by stress. An unlighted andon board signals inefficiency. Workers are not working as hard as they might. If the system is stressed—by speeding up the line, for example—some workers will fall behind, the lights will flash and management can focus on redesigning those jobs to make them more efficient. The ideal is for the system to run with all stations oscillating between lights on and lights off. . . .

Most glowing accounts of Nummi and other team concept plants contrast their methods to the "scientific management" principles championed by Frederick W. Taylor, the father of time-and-motion study. Former Labor Secretary Ray Marshall, speaking at a recent conference on labor-management cooperation, asserted that Nummi had "done away with Taylorism."

In fact, management by stress is an intensification of Taylorism. Engineers and group and team leaders break the required assembly tasks down into the tiniest of separate "acts" and come up with a detailed written specification of how each worker is to do each job. This chart is posted near the line so the group leader can check to see that the worker does not vary his or her methods. Workers are not allowed to work faster for a short time to create some breathing space—although the jobs are so "loaded" that this is usually not possible anyway. If they discover a method, on their own, that makes the job easier, they must ask the supervisor's permission to use it. The catch, of course, is that another task will be found to fill the time.

Thus no matter how well the workers learn their jobs, there is always room for kaizen, or continuous improvement. At Nummi recently, slow sales caused the company to slow the line speed to reduce inventories of unsold cars. Instead of letting those on the line enjoy the slightly more relaxed pace, some workers were removed from the line and the jobs rebalanced so that the pace was as killing as before. Some of the extra workers were put into kaizen groups to observe their colleagues and make suggestions as to how they could work more efficiently.

This is how management by stress differs from Taylorism. Taylor believed that management's engineers and time-study men could capture workers' knowledge of the production process all at once, after which workers would revert to being nothing but hired hands. Management-by-stress managers understand that workers continue to know more about the actual performance of their jobs than higher management does, and so make the process of appropriating that knowledge a never-ending one. . . .

Under traditional contracts, the amount of work on a job is subject to negotiation between union and management. The union has the right to file grievances over work and health and safety standards and to strike over them during the life of the contract. Management is not allowed to add extra work onto a job once the work standard has been agreed to.

In management-by-stress plants, these safeguards are replaced with a system that supposedly trusts the worker. "Why have all these bureaucratic procedures?" the argument goes. "If the worker is making an honest attempt to keep up but can't, all she has to do is pull the cord."

Of course, pulling the cord that stops the line is only a temporary help at best. It doesn't mean that a worker will be taken off the job, only that the hapless worker will receive immediate attention from the team and group leaders in the vicinity.

The stop cord works well when production has just begun and the bugs are still being worked out. Once production is up to speed, however, any problems are assumed to be the worker's fault. Workers at G.M.'s Van Nuys, Calif., assembly plant complain that management spent most of their early team meetings explaining how rare a stop-the-line situation should be.

Another myth about team-concept/management-by-stress plants is that they want workers who are highly skilled and can exercise judgment in running the highly complex factories of today. In fact, workers often find themselves feeling more like interchangeable parts than before.

Management wants flexibility to respond to the ups and downs of the market quickly. This requires that workers be able to perform many different jobs, and that contractual barriers to the group leader's right to assign workers be abolished. Thus management-by-stress plants break production jobs down into simple actions that require little special training and that can be mastered quickly. Rather than learning a marketable skill, workers become "multiskilled" by learning a series of job-specific tasks that depend mainly on manual dexterity, physical stamina and the willingness to follow instructions precisely. . . .

Related is management's other tool for flexibility—the right to assign workers to any job. Whereas in traditional plants certain workers, usually those with more seniority, could become inspectors, repairers, janitors and material handlers, in management-by-stress plants the assembly line worker is expected to handle these chores in addition to the assigned assembly tasks. One of the workers' biggest complaints about plants where such classifications have been abolished is that "there aren't any good jobs left."

The related complaint is favoritism. Flexibility means that management gets to assign its "pets" to those few "good jobs" that remain instead of using seniority or negotiated work rules. Management also gets to decide which workers get to leave the fast-paced line and serve in the kaizen groups. . . .

The Nummi system is supposed to provide workers with job security in exchange for management flexibility. But the system maintains a strong sense of insecurity as a primary motivation. Nummi workers and others in team-concept plants accept it mainly because they believe that without it they would have no jobs at all. Management constantly reinforces this fear by suggesting—or in many cases threatening—that if the plant is not run the way management wants, it will be closed.

Most of the auto plants in the United States that have gone as far as Nummi in implementing management-by-stress techniques are Japanese-owned or managed. It is important not to be distracted, however, by these methods' country of origin. Managers eager to reap their productivity benefits are introducing these methods the world over and, under different names, in every industry in America. They do not require the particularities of Japanese culture to work. . . .

Computerized Order Taking at McDonald's, 1988

I waited on line at my neighborhood McDonald's. It was lunch hour and there were four or five customers at each of the five open cash registers. "May I take your order?" a very thin girl said in a flat tone to the man at the head of my line.

"McNuggets, large fries and a Coke," said the man. The cashier punched in the order. "That will be—."

"Big Mac, large fries and a shake," said the next woman on line. The cashier rang it up.

"Two cheeseburgers, large fries and a coffee," said the third customer. The cashier rang it up.

"How much is a large fries?" asked the woman directly in front of me.

The thin cashier twisted her neck around trying to look up at the menu board.

"Sorry," apologized the customer, "I don't have my glasses."

"Large fries is seventy-nine," a round-faced cashier with glasses interjected from the next register.

"Seventy-nine cents," the thin cashier repeated.

"Well how much is a *small* fries?" . . .

By then it was my turn.

"Just a large fries," I said.

The thin cashier pressed "lge fries." In place of numbers, the keys on a McDonald's cash register say "lge fries," "reg fries," "med coke," "big mac," and so on. Some registers have pictures on the key caps. The next time the price of fries goes up (or down) the change will be entered in the store's central computer. But the thin cashier will continue to press the same button. I wondered how long she'd worked there and how many hundreds of "lge fries" she'd served without learning the price.

Damita, the cashier with the glasses, came up from the crew room (a room in the basement with lockers, a table and a video player for studying the training disks) at 4:45. She looked older and more serious without her striped uniform.

"Sorry, but they got busy and, you know, here you get off when they let you."

The expandable schedule was her first complaint. "You give them your availability when you sign on. Mine I said 9 to 4. But they scheduled me for 7 o'clock two or three days a week. And I needed the money. So I got to get up 5 in the morning to get here from Queens by 7. And I don't get off till whoever's supposed to get here gets here to take my place. . . . It's hard to study with all the pressures."

Damita had come to the city from a small town outside of Detroit. She lives with her sister in Queens and takes extension courses in psychology at New York University. Depending on the schedule posted each Friday, her McDonald's paycheck for a five-day week has varied from $80 to $114. . . .

The flexible scheduling at McDonald's only seems to work one way. One day Damita had arrived a half hour late because the E train was running on the R track.

"The assistant manager told me not to clock in at all, just to go home. So I said O.K. and I left."

"What did you do the rest of the day?" I asked.

"I went home and studied, and I went to sleep."

"But how did it make you feel?"

"It's like a humiliating feeling 'cause I wasn't given any chance to justify myself. But when I spoke to the Puerto Rican manager he said it was nothing personal against me. Just it was raining that day, and they were really slow and someone who got here on time, it wouldn't be right to send them home."

"Weren't you annoyed to spend four hours traveling and then lose a day's pay?" I suggested.

"I was mad at first that they didn't let me explain. But afterwards I understood and I tried to explain to my sister: 'Time waits for no man.' "

"Since you signed on for 9 to 4," I asked Damita, "and you're going to school, why can't you say, 'Look, I have to study at night, I need regular hours'?"

"Don't work that way. They make up your schedule every week and if you can't work it, you're responsible to replace yourself. If you can't they can always get someone else."

"But Damita," I tried to argue with her low estimate of her own worth, "anyone can see right away that your line moves fast yet you're helpful to people. I mean, you're a valuable employee. And this manager seems to like you.''

"Valuable! $3.35 an hour. And I can be replaced by any [pointing across the room] kid off the street." I hadn't noticed. At a small table under the staircase a manager in a light beige shirt was taking an application from a lanky black teenager.

"But you know the register. You know the routine."

"How long you think it takes to learn the six steps? Step 1. Greet the customer, 'Good morning, can I help you?' Step 2. Take his order. Step 3. Repeat the order. They can have someone off the street working my register in five minutes."

"By the way," I asked, "on those cash registers without numbers, how do you change something after you ring it up? I mean if somebody orders a cheeseburger and then they change it to a hamburger, how do you subtract the slice of cheese?"

"I guess that's why you have step 3, repeat the order. One cheeseburger, two Cokes, three. . . .''

"Yeah but if you punched a mistake or they don't want it after you get it together?"

"Like if I have a crazy customer, which I do be gettin' 'specially in this city, and they order hamburger, fries and shake, and it's $2.95 and then they just walk away?"

"I once did that here," I said. "About a week ago when I first started my research. All I ordered was some French fries. And I was so busy watching how the computer works that only after she rang it up I discovered that I'd walked out of my house without my wallet. I didn't have a penny. I was so embarrassed."

"Are you that one the other day? Arnetta, this girl next to me, she said, 'Look at that crazy lady going out. She's lookin' and lookin' at everything and then she didn't have no money for a bag of fries.' I saw you leaving, but I guess I didn't recognize you. [I agreed it was probably me.] O.K., so say this crazy lady comes in and orders French fries and leaves. In Michigan I could just zero it out. I'd wait till I start the next order and press zero and large fries. But here you're supposed to call out 'cancel sale' and the manager comes over and does it with his key.

"But I hate to call the manager every time, 'specially if I got a whole line waiting. So I still zero out myself. They can tell I do it by the computer tape, and they tell me not to. Some of them let me, though, because they know I came from another store. But they don't show the girls here how to zero out. Everybody thinks you need the manager's key to do it."

"Maybe they let you because they can tell you're honest," I said. She smiled, pleased, but let it pass. "That's what I mean that you're valuable to them. You know how to use the register. You're good with customers." . . .

McDonald's computerized cash registers allow managers to determine immediately not only the dollar volume for the store but the amount of each item that was sold at each register for any given period. Two experienced managers, interviewed separately, both insisted that the new electronic cash registers were in fact slower than the old mechanical registers. Clerks who knew the combinations—hamburger, fries, Coke: $2.45—could ring up the total immediately, take the cash and give change in one operation. On the new registers you have to enter each item and may be slowed down by computer response time. The value of the new registers, or at least their main selling point (McDonald's franchisers can choose from several approved registers), is the increasingly sophisticated tracking systems, which monitor all the activity and report with many different statistical breakdowns.

"Look, there," said Damita as the teenage job applicant left and the manager went behind the counter with the application, "If I was to say I can't come in at 7, they'd cut my hours down to one shift a week, and if I never came back they wouldn't call to find out where I was.

"I worked at a hospital once as an X-ray assistant. There if I didn't come in there were things that had to be done that wouldn't be done. I would call there and say, 'Remember to run the EKGs.' Here, if I called and said, 'I just can't come by 7 no more,' they'd have one of these high school kids off the street half an hour later. And they'd do my job just as good." . . .

A Unionist Blasts Overseas Office Work, 1987

For the past 15 years, we have been occupied with the very real problem of jobs leaving this country. In most cases, these are jobs like the making of a wrench, or making apparel, steel, autos. We have tried to deal with this problem through legislation as well as in collective bargaining. However, with the advent of new technology, such as satellite communication and computers, it is easier than ever for employers to move new technology and capital across borders.

One example of this is American Airlines, which historically used keypunch operators earning between $8 and $10 an hour to process the previous day's used tickets and handle the billing and record-keeping. This is now done in Barbados for $2 an hour!

Each day an American Airlines aircraft flies to Barbados and deposits the tickets which are keypunched at one-fourth or one-fifth the U.S. wage level, and then transmitted back to the United States via satellite in finished form.

Trammel Crow Company, the nation's largest real estate company, has established a series of data bases in the People's Republic of China. They train university students in the English language, not in reading and writing, but in the recognition of letters so they can keypunch them into the data base. Then, upon graduation, they are hired at a wage of a dollar a day!

When questioned, Trammel Crow said that it did not go to China for the dollar a day wage, but that the Chinese workers are more efficient because they cannot read and understand the English language, so they don't become engrossed in what they are punching.

Pier 1 Imports became the first American company to store its inventory records in China. Several hospitals followed, and now American hospitals are storing medical records in China.

The scope of this is endless.

Anyone who has a business where record-keeping is a vital part can store data anywhere in the globe through satellite transmission and a relatively simple computer with a printer. And it can retrieve it at will.

What is on the drawing board is even more frightening. There will be more intelligence stored from now until 2010, less than 25 years from now, than in the entire history of mankind.

That is mind-boggling and raises many questions: Who is going to control that intelligence? How do you retrieve it? How will it be used?

To point out the seriousness of the situation, two years ago, just prior to his retirement, the then chairman of the board of AT&T, speaking at the Aspen Institute, talked about the technology that they now have at the Bell Laboratory. They already have a computer, no larger than a cigar box, into which you can speak in any language to seek information that is stored anywhere in this world, or even in space, and the computer will seek it out, retrieve it, and give it back to you in the appropriate language.

What makes all of this technology frightening as well as exciting is that it was supposed to create a new type of service job that was going to somehow supplement, if not totally offset, the blue collar jobs that have been lost.

But the lesson it teaches us is that notwithstanding our particular occupations or job titles, that job, if not now, in the very near future, is going to be totally done in another country where wages are cheaper.

Therefore, it is important that we face these problems today and take charge of our own destiny, because no one else is going to do it.

Secretary of Labor Ann McLaughlin Makes the Case for Home Work, 1988

One axiom of public life is that great battles are often fought over small issues: case in point, industrial home work.

In November, the Department of Labor lifted a 45-year-old ban on industrial home work in five industries—jewelry, buttons and buckles, embroideries, handkerchiefs and gloves and mittens.

The prohibitions had had some ridiculous consequences. It was illegal, for example, to make women's underwear at home, but boxer shorts you could have sewn to your heart's content.

Nevertheless, given the history of this issue, we expected that the end of the ban would generate controversy and perhaps legal obstructions (courtesy of organized labor), and we were right. Attacks from a number of sources began immediately . . . In truth, the issue of industrial home work has relatively little to do with whether a mother with young children can supplement her family's income by making knitted hats or belt buckles at home. It has everything to do with whether millions in the work force, using new technology such as personal computers and fax machines, will be able to do so. It is the latter that organized labor opposes—it wants to prevent business technology from leaving the traditional work place. As early as 1983, the Service Employees International Union, which represents 780,000 clerical and health workers, forbade its members to work at home.

Organized labor is worried about the millions of new "open collar" workers who will be able to do jobs at home that once required an office setting—that may be about 10 percent of our work force by the year 2000.

Giving workers the freedom to work at home maximizes individual economic freedom, promotes work-force flexibility, provides an opportunity for individual initiative and creates jobs. But because homeworkers are decentralized, they are hard to organize. And organized labor, which finds itself representing an ever-declining portion of American workers, doesn't want to lose the ability to attract one of its few potential growth markets, office and clerical workers.

Suppose, as organized labor claims, industrial home work does have the potential for worker exploitation. The fact is, the Department of Labor is serious about enforcing laws that prevent abuse.

The unions' approach to preventing labor abuse is to prevent labor. They are willing to see workers go idle, including older workers and those in economically depressed areas.

By contrast, our approach is to build an enforcement mechanism, and then allow people to work. If providing job opportunities for America's workers isn't the mission of the Department of Labor, I don't know what is.

So there it is. A small issue with some big symbols attached. As the rhetoric heats up in January, remember what the real debate is about— freedom of choice.

Return of the Sweatshops, 1988

. . . A building that looks like it never saw better days is home to a cramped belt factory on Eighth Avenue.

Here, in the heart of Manhattan's Garment District, are about 20 workers—packed into a windowless room with only one door, partially blocked by stacks of boxes.

Welcome to the sweatshop of the 1980s.

Cats dart across the factory, ignoring the incessant whir of high-speed sewing machines and the clatter of presses stamping holes in the belts. The machines and their operators compete for space.

There is not much room for error. An errant bump or nudge could mean a lost finger or arm.

Against the wall is a broken clock with dusty time cards. But that doesn't matter. Chances are, the employees are being paid "off the books" anyway, at salaries below the minimum wage.

Joe Halik wants to change all that.

"We're looking for victims of opportunity," he said.

Halik is one of the supervisors of the state Labor Department's Apparel Industry Task Force, whose job it is to crack down on the undesirables in the garment industry.

The state Labor Department estimates there are an estimated 4,000 such shops in the metropolitan area, employing about 50,000 workers. The European immigrants who toiled in these shops at the turn of the century have been replaced by poor women and illegal aliens, most of them Hispanic and Chinese.

"They're bypassing California and coming straight here," Halik said.

The 20 investigators on the task force are looking for violations of laws governing the minimum wage, industrial homework and child labor. They also check whether a business is paying for unemployment and disability insurance, as well as making contributions to the workers' compensation fund.

The task force has been able to keep better tabs and more vigorously enforce those laws since January, when makers of women's and children's wear had to register with the state to prove those payments are being made.

During two days spent with task force investigators in Manhattan, Rockland, and Westchester, it became clear that registration has been slow to catch on in an industry leery of outsiders. Perhaps with good reason.

"What they're doing is perpetuating the system to keep everyone low," said another task force supervisor, Charles DeSiervo, who estimated that 70 percent of the apparel makers are not registered.

Eight task force members start their work on a recent day on Eighth Avenue, watching other people go to work.

A slight Hispanic woman walks toward a building on 38th Street carrying a large shopping bag. She soon has company. Two investigators have trailed her to the top floor of a building housing dozens of clothing firms.

They hit paydirt when they arrive at a business and discover that the bag contains hundreds of pieces of lace that will go on gowns and dresses. By all appearances, it is a violation of rules governing doing industrial work at home.

The practice is banned because it usually means the employee is not getting overtime for work done after a full day in the factory. Payment is usually by the piece and is invariably done "under the table."

DeSiervo believes that curbing home work is one of the keys to cleaning up the industry.

"Home work was rampant; it was all through the streets," DeSiervo said. "They're starting to notice us. What it takes is strict enforcement."

While investigator San Bargas quizzes, in Spanish, the woman with the shopping bag, the surprised owner of the shop insists it is the first time this has ever happened. Halik looks mildly amused.

"It's always the first time," he said, noting that it's one of many excuses investigators hear when they make their unscheduled visits.

Other excuses: "I didn't know; I just started this morning."

"It just broke yesterday," is a frequent response when asked why the time clock is broken.

The task force also keeps close tabs on abusers of child labor laws, a vestige of the clothing industry's seamier past.

Halik said children as young as 9 are pressed into service by their parents to cut threads, move clothes, and pack and fold, often near dangerous equipment.

"It's sad. It's sad to see," he said.

A visit to a different Chinatown shop turns up a shy young woman who tries to make a quick exit. Investigator Gene Lee, who speaks Chinese, catches up to the girl and coaxes her into returning.

At first, the girl claims she is 26. Lee gently tells her to try again. She eventually admits to being 16, although she and the office manager make a last-ditch effort to have her listed on the record as 18.

Getting working papers will not be easy. The girl only came to the United States last year, meaning she does not have a Social Security number, without which the Labor Department is loathe to issue working papers.

"Without a Social Security number, you can't pass go," noted veteran investigator Paul Kalka.

What she and other workers don't have to worry about is a raid by immigration authorities after a visit by the labor investigators, who have enough to do without worrying about green cards.

"Whether you're illegal or legal, our job is to make sure you're being paid the minimum wage," DeSiervo said.

The investigators, though, will refer certain factories to the Fire Department if they believe a danger exists. The belt factory fit that bill.

Sweatshops are by no means limited to New York City. Which is why the task force members come to Rockland the following week. It is the first trip in these parts for the 3-year-old task force, and its members don't know what to expect.

They arrive at the sprawling Garnerville Industrial Complex to check out leads provided by the department's White Plains office. A maze of ancient stairs and passageways leads them to Garnerville Knitwear, which manufactures goods for J. C. Penney and Bloomingdales, among others. All of the paperwork appears in order except for the registration.

One of the mill's managers admits there is a problem, but nothing the investigators can help her with.

"We can't get enough people to work here," she said.

To be sure, the labor pool is a crucial difference between the suburbs and New York City, where workers seeking a job need only come out of the subway in the Garment District to find a host of cardboard help-wanted signs in their native languages tied to lampposts.

A tour of the Garnerville complex turns up no other apparel makers. Names that sound promising are actually bedspread and quilt makers or upholsterers. A check of the other aging buildings along Railroad Avenue turns up nothing. Such searches for factories are not uncommon for the investigators.

"Sometimes it's like detective work when they don't advertise. You have to find them," Bargas said.

Rockland is a washout for the task force, which heads next to Westchester and has greater success uncovering violations in Port Chester, Yonkers and Mount Vernon.

The reasons these rules are so frequently broken are many and varied. But they are all inextricably linked to the bottom line. "This is a cutthroat business. Everybody works on a slim profit margin," DeSiervo said.

Most of the places visited by the task force are small contractors for designers and larger manufacturers who farm out their work. Competition is such that the industry is in a continual squeeze.

"It used to be a contractor would say, 'I can sell you that blouse for $1.85 a piece,' " DeSiervo said. Now the manufacturer is saying, 'I will buy that piece for $1.40.' "

When the contractor complains he can't make money on that margin, the designer threatens to take his business elsewhere. To prevent that from happening, some contractors cut costs by avoiding payroll taxes and unemployment and disability insurance payments. Those steps alone can knock 20 percent off the contractor's expenses, DeSiervo said.

It is estimated that about one-third of the contractors are "hard-core" violators who, in order to avoid prosecution, sometimes pack up and set up shop elsewhere, moving back and forth across state lines.

That prompted New York and New Jersey, in July, to join forces to stop the unscrupulous operators, who face fines of $50 to $2,500, and even criminal penalties in some cases.

Regulating the apparel industry is nothing new. Neither is the industry's antipathy to regulation. But in the task force, some manufacturers have an ally in a business where friends are in short supply, Halik said.

"Many of them are happy to see us, and hope we force out the illegals," he said.

"By legitimizing them, we've raised the industry."

A Technology Bill of Rights, 1981

*International Association of Machinists
and Aerospace Workers*

Preamble

Powerful new technologies are being poured into the workplace at a record rate. Based on the expanding capabilities and decreasing cost of computers and microelectronics, new forms of automation will leave few workplaces or occupations untouched. Robots on the assembly line, word processors in the office, numerical control in the machine shop, computer-aided design in the engineering department, and electronic scanners in supermarkets are only a few examples of the widespread changes that are taking place.

While such technologies offer real promise for a better society, they are being developed in a shortsighted and dangerous direction. Instead of benefits, working people are seeing jobs threatened, working conditions undermined, and the economic viability of communities challenged. In the face of these unprecedented dangers, labor must act forcefully and quickly to safeguard the rights of workers and develop technology in a way that benefits the entire society. Key to this is proclaiming and implementing a Technology Bill of Rights. This should be a program that is both a new vision of what technology can accomplish and a specific series of demands that are meant to guide the design, introduction, and use of new technology. This approach is based on the following assumptions:

1. A community has to produce in order to live. As a result, it is the obligation of an economy to organize people to work.
2. The well-being of people and their communities must be given the highest priority in determining the way in which production is carried out.
3. Basing technological and production decisions on narrow economic grounds of profitability has made working people and communities the victims rather than the beneficiaries of change.
4. Given the widespread scope and rapid rate of introduction of new technologies, society requires a democratically determined institutional, rather than individual, response to changes taking place. Otherwise, the social cost of technological change will be borne by those least able to pay it: unemployed workers and shattered communities.
5. Those that work have a right to participate in the decisions that govern their work and shape their lives.
6. The new automation technologies and the sciences that underlie them are the product of a worldwide, centuries-long accumulation of knowledge. Accordingly, working people and their communities have a right to share in the decisions about, and the gains from, new technology.

The choice should not be new technology or no technology but the development of technology with social responsibility. Therefore, the precondition for technological change must be the compliance with a program that defines and insures the well-being of working people and the community. The following is the foundation of such a program, a Technology Bill of Rights:

1. *New technology must be used in a way that creates or maintains jobs.* A part of the productivity gains from new technology can translate into fewer working hours at the same pay or into fewer jobs. This is not a technical but a social decision. Given the pervasiveness of new forms of automation, the former approach is vital. The exact mechanisms for accomplishing this—a shorter work week, earlier retirement, longer vacations, or a combination—ought to be a prerogative of the workers

involved. In addition, comprehensive training must be provided well before any change takes place to insure that workers have the maximum options to decide their future. Moreover, new industries that produce socially useful products must be created to insure the economic viability of regions that are particularly affected by technological change.

2. *New technology must be used to improve the conditions of work.* Rather than using automation to destroy skills, pace work, and monitor workers, it can be used to enhance skill and expand the responsibility workers have on the job. In addition, the hazardous and undesirable jobs should be a first priority, but at the discretion of the workers involved and not at the expense of employment. Production processes can be designed to fully utilize the skill, talent, creativity, initiative, and experience of people—instead of production designs aimed at controlling workers as if they were robots.

3. *New technology must be used to develop the industrial base and improve the environment.* At the same time corporate America has raised the flag of industrial revitalization, jobs are being exported from communities, regions, and even countries at a record rate. The narrow economic criteria of transnational companies are causing an erosion of the nation's manufacturing base and the collapse of many communities that are dependent on it. While other countries in the world have a pressing need and legitimate right to develop new industry, it is nonetheless vital that corporations not be allowed to play workers, unions, and countries against each other, seeking the lowest bidder for wages and working conditions. Instead, close cooperation among unions throughout the world and stringent controls over plant closings and capital movement are in order. In addition, the development of technology should not be at the expense of the destruction of the environment.

⚜ *E S S A Y S*

In the first essay, Harley Shaiken, a professor in the department of communications, University of California at San Diego, argues that employers have used the computerized workplace as a new and potent weapon against unions. Shaiken shows that even such highly skilled professionals as air-traffic controllers are now vulnerable to union busting, as the federal government's 1981 destruction of their union so graphically demonstrated. In the second essay, however, Stanford University Business School professor Paul Adler rejects such a pessimistic reading of contemporary developments. Instead, he argues that technological change in the workplace is hardly the job-displacing, skill-eroding phenomenon attacked by so many of its critics on the left. Certainly, individual jobs and individual skills have been destroyed, but taken as a whole, the new machines and new processes require a more skilled and educated work force than ever before. For Adler, political and social forces, not technology per se, lie behind the loss of union strength and the growth of unemployment.

The authors of the final essay, social scientists M. Patricia Fernández-Kelly of Johns Hopkins University and Anna M. García of the Center for U.S.–Mexican Studies at the University of California at San Diego, similarly stress the role of the overall political economy in shaping the nature of work. In comparing the home-work labor of Cuban women in Miami with that of Mexican women in Los Angeles, the authors emphasize how household relations help shape an underground economy of sweatshops and illegal workplaces, existing side by side with the more visible high-technology society.

What is the relationship between the character of an economic enterprise and the usefulness of a new technology to workers and to managers? How can politics shape technological change at the work site? Can the viewpoints of Paul Adler and Harley Shaiken be reconciled?

Computers Against the Unions

HARLEY SHAIKEN

The ultimate weapon workers can bring to bear against their employer is withdrawing their labor. In most industries, when a union strikes, production stops. The economic resources of the firm are then pitted against the staying power of the people on the picket line until the dispute is resolved. The union's leverage, however, is seriously eroded if the firm is able to continue operating while its employees are on the street. In a number of highly automated industries such as petroleum refining, chemical plants, and the telephone company, this practice has become normal operating procedure, obviously weakening the unions involved. In most industries, however, there are roadblocks to continuing operations, such as the need for hard-to-find skilled workers. The widespread introduction of computer-based machines and systems, however, removes some of these key limits. Computerization in many industries means that operations can be maintained with a less-skilled work force. It also becomes possible to transfer work outside of a strike location since telecommunications do not respect picket lines. Does this mean, then, that computer technology will be used to downgrade or perhaps eliminate labor's most effective weapon? In many cases, the possibility certainly exists. But, computers also provide labor with some potent new opportunities, such as the ability to paralyze highly integrated operations. Which scenario is enacted depends on the nature of the industry, the way the technology is designed and deployed, and the strategies workers and managers pursue in a given situation.

Consider a recent example of the use of computers in a strike. On August 3, 1981, members of the Professional Air Traffic Controllers Organization (PATCO) walked off the job, the culmination of a decade of bitter and often turbulent labor relations in the nation's air traffic control system. The Reagan Administration, determined to thwart a walkout of public employees, gave the strikers forty-eight hours to return to work or face permanent dismissal. The resources and muscle of the federal government were arrayed against a tiny union that threatened to cripple air transport throughout the United States. The stakes, however, went far beyond the air traffic system. . . . For PATCO, the battle ended almost before it was joined in a rout that included the firing of 12,000 air traffic controllers and the decertification of their union.

PATCO was weakened by a lack of public support, lukewarm aid or even hostility from other unions, its own inexperience, and a tough adversary. But what ultimately doomed the union was the government's skillful use of computer technology to keep air traffic moving, gutting the strikers' leverage. Soon after the walkout occurred, 75 percent of commercial flights were operating in spite of the fact that some 75 percent of the air traffic controllers were on the picket line. The centerpiece of the Federal Aviation Administration's [FAA] strategy was "flow control," a computerized procedure to regulate departures and to space aircraft uniformly along air traffic routes, thus maximizing the use of airspace, facilities, and controllers.

The FAA's planning for a controllers' strike began in January 1980. For eighteen months thereafter, the agency worked to refine a plan for operating the nation's airways with minimum demands on controllers, including experiments with existing flow-control procedures. The earlier attempts sought to replace the controllers only during a strike; this evolved into permanently replacing the controllers once they went on strike. Some of the studies were shrouded in the greatest secrecy; computer tapes containing preliminary operating data were stored in locked safes at the leading FAA route-control centers across the country. Even after a tentative agreement was reached with PATCO on June 22, 1981, the FAA continued to improve its contingency plans. . . .

Computers reduce but do not eliminate the need for air traffic controllers, an occupation that remains labor intensive and skill based. According to a Rand Corporation report:

> Much, if not most, of a controller's time is spent on tasks that require distinctly human skills: negotiating flight-plan changes with pilots, vectoring aircraft around rapidly changing severe weather, deciding upon general operational configurations with other controllers, and the like. These tasks also require experience, maturity, and flexibility—the blips on those screens are, after all, real people who change their minds and make mistakes.

As a result, supervisors were requalified as controllers during the planning period so that they could become the core of a group to replace any strikers. But one early study indicated that a work force largely limited to supervisors could maintain only about one third of normal operation, so clearly success depended on the number of controllers who remained on the job. As it happened, the 3,000 supervisors were supplemented by 5,700 nonstriking controllers and 1,000 military personnel when PATCO walked out, bringing the total to over half of the prestrike work force.

This turned out to be enough. With the new flow-control strategies in use and with nearly 10,000 controllers on the job, air traffic was disrupted within politically tolerable limits and the striking controllers were left essentially powerless. In pursuing this strategy, however, the government may have taken a major gamble on safety. In a complex system such as air traffic control where human life is at stake, built-in redundancy assures that if one aspect of the operation fails, the system itself will not. An important element of that redundancy is the skill and experience of the human operators. The administration's gamble has obviously paid off since a major air disaster has not occurred. But, by eliminating so many of the system's most experienced and talented controllers, the redundancy of the system may have been compromised. . . .

An intriguing question is how much of the FAA's hard line at the bargaining table was based on confidence in its secret strike preparations. Or conversely, would PATCO have reacted differently had it known the full scale of the government's efforts to keep the system running? There is little question that the FAA maintained a hard line throughout the negotiations whether or not this was as a result of its contingency plan. . . .

With the strike over, the administration has turned its attention to rebuilding the air traffic system, criticized by many as being overburdened and outmoded even in the pre-walkout days. On January 28, 1982, [FAA chief] J. Lynn Helms announced a twenty-year program, costing between $15 and $20 billion, to replace the system's aging computers and significantly automate air traffic control. An important question is to what extent the design of this program has been influenced by the government's strike experience and its turbulent record of labor relations. Whoever controls technological decision-making has the power to shape technology to conform with their desired goals.

Technically, there are a number of very different options available: These range from seeking total automation to giving controllers and pilots new tools that enhance human judgment. The FAA's proposal leans heavily in the former direction. . . .

The FAA denies that its automation program is an outgrowth of the strike, maintaining that it was begun in March 1981. This denial, however, does not indicate the extent to which the previous decade of labor strife was a factor in the minds of FAA planners. Helms does admit that the walkout heightened an awareness of the need to rebuild the system. One FAA research and development executive told *Aviation Week and Space Technology* magazine that maintaining operations during the strike was in fact a test of the automation program. The dispute certainly seems to have encouraged those forces desirous of eliminating controllers' jobs or at least minimizing their influence. In an editorial during the strike, *Aviation Week and Space Technology* commented:

> Yet one more positive result from the strike will be the acceleration of automation of traffic control. Automation cannot affect the denouement of the strike, but the strike will unlock the decision and funding door to use avionic technology. . . . Few federal bureaucrats have the chance to fire 70% of their departments and replace the victims with junior, lower-salaried recruits—or with computers and black boxes.

. . . The pressures to minimize the role of the controllers conflict with the development of the optimal technical alternatives. The Rand Corporation raises some probing questions about the role of the controller in any new system:

> The critical question in designing the ATC [Air Traffic Control] system of the future is not really what *can* be done but what *should* be done. Exactly how much and what kind of automation should assist or replace the human controller? Should we strive for a system in which the machine has the primary responsibility of control and human expertise is used in a secondary, backup fashion? Or should men, in spite of their intrinsic limitations, retain primary control responsibility and utilize machine aids to extend their abilities?

Rand then blasts the direction of FAA research and development for heading in the first direction:

> The AERA [Automated En-route Air Traffic Control] scenario presents serious problems for each of the three major goals of ATC—safety, efficiency, and increased productivity By depending on an autonomous, complex, fail-safe system to compensate for keeping the human controller out of the route decision-making loop, the AERA scenario jeopardizes the goal of safety. Ironically, the better AERA works, the more complacent its human managers may become, the less often they may question its actions, and the more likely their system is to fail without their knowledge. We have argued that not only is AERA's complex, costly, fail-safe system questionable from a technical perspective, it is also unnecessary in other, more moderate ATC system designs.

Rand proposed an alternative called Shared Control in which the primary decision-making responsibilities remain with the controller but in which the operator has an increasing "suite of automated tools." The role of the controller would be expanded so that "he is routinely involved in the minute-to-minute operation of the system." The system itself would consist of a "series of independently operable, serially deployable aiding modules." Whatever its technical merits, Shared Control would add to the responsibilities of an occupational category in which over two thirds of the existing members had just been dismissed.

The story of the confrontation between PATCO and the FAA underscores the potential importance of computers in labor-management relations in general and strike situations in particular. On the one hand, computer technology and telecommunications make possible central direction of far-reaching activities, concentrating enormous power into relatively few hands. The few dozen controllers in Gander, Newfoundland, for example, demonstrated their ability to halt virtually all trans-Atlantic flights for a number of tense hours near the beginning of the strike. Had a few more PATCO members joined the strike, the air traffic system of the entire country would have been tied in knots. On the other hand, complex computer systems often lend themselves to operation by a reduced and less skilled work force in an emergency situation. The leverage of the air controllers evaporated because less-experienced workers could successfully take over the job.

A much different outcome resulted from a civil service dispute in Britain in the spring of 1981. In this case, a small number of workers used computers to bring an enormous bureaucracy to its knees. The civil service unions challenged the government in a pay dispute, not by pulling out hundreds of thousands of workers in a direct confrontation, but by withdrawing 3,500 workers who use computers to process Britain's national sales tax at tax collection centers. Great financial pain was inflicted with minimal resources in a few months by this devastating campaign of guerrilla warfare. In the first week of the strike, for example, 1,200 strikers reduced the government's revenues from a normal $550 million to $105 million, even though supervisors continued on the job. Within a few months, labor stoppages had delayed between 25 and 45 percent of the government's sales-tax collections, forcing emergency borrowing: 370,000 payment checks piled up, creating a logistical nightmare.

A highly centralized computer system and a highly unionized work force with strong ties to related unions proved to be a formidable adversary for the government. . . . Management, however, has the power to redesign the technology, and in the aftermath of the strike, there have been widespread calls for decentralization of Britain's computer system. One spokesperson for a U.K. trade association, advising its members to use many small computers in place of a highly centralized system, coined the quip "an Apple a day keeps the union away."

In more and more industries, the design of computer technology provides management with some unique options. In operations as diverse as newspapers, insurance, aerospace, and automobiles, the ability of computers to continue production with a fill-in work force—often composed of people with fewer skills—can devastate a union effort. An early example of this was a bitter labor dispute at the *Washington Post* in the mid 1970s. Determined to free itself from restrictive work rules and to achieve lower manning requirements in the pressroom, *Post* management took a hard line at the bargaining table. At the same time, extensive preparations were made to keep the newly installed printing equipment running during a strike that was sure to ensue. These preparations included importing executives from papers with strike experience and sending fifty-five white-collar employees to a special school to learn how to operate the new presses, the automatic features of which were an issue in the dispute.

On October 1, 1975, the strike began. As 205 pressmen walked off the jobs, nine presses were smashed and one set afire. Whoever sabotaged the equipment undoubtedly suspected that this would be no ordinary walkout and that the very existence of the union was at stake. After suspending publication for a day, the *Post* used helicopters to ship printing plates to six nonunion plants in Virginia and Maryland, which would temporarily print the paper while its own presses were being repaired. After the machinery was fixed, a total of 35 managers and nonstriking workers performed the jobs of 205 press operators on the automated equipment. With the union's leverage sapped, the strike rapidly turned into a debacle for the pressmen. Not only was the strike lost, but only fifty-three pressmen were eventually hired back and all resigned from the union before resuming work.

In the printing industry, what happened at the *Post* is hardly an isolated event. A. H. Raskin, the former labor writer at the *New York Times*, who has closely followed labor relations in the newspaper industry, maintains:

> New technology in almost every department has rendered obsolete the union's jealously guarded lines of craft monopoly; now a handful of executives and confidential secretaries with a modicum of special training can do everything necessary to produce a paper.

. . . In the newspaper industry, however, managerial leverage is based on more than being able to print the newspaper during a strike. The paper has to be delivered as well. At the *Washington Post*, this proved to be no problem since the drivers were nonunion, but this is certainly an area of potential union leverage. The value of this broader support was illustrated in a 1978 strike of New York City's three principal dailies, the *Post*, the *Times*, and the *News*. In this convoluted and often bitter conflict, automation was a contributing factor to employer overconfidence as management went into negotiations. The industry's hardline position, particularly concerning control of the pressroom, resulted in a three-month strike, which the pressmen were able to survive. The support of other unions—especially the deliverymen's—proved to be more than a match for the publishers' ability to continue running the presses using automation. . . .

Had PATCO been able to generate this kind of active support from other unions in the air transport industry, principally the pilots, the balance of power might have been changed considerably. The short-lived job actions that did take place overseas proved effective but difficult to sustain in the face of strong government pressures.

The advantages that computers give management in an office workers' strike were made clear during a 1980–81 dispute between Blue Shield of California and 1,100 members of the Office and Professional Employees Union (OPEU) Local 3 in San Francisco. As the 133-day strike began, the company adopted a carefully prepared contingency plan. This plan included assigning all available supervisors to computer banks in the claims-processing area, hiring and quickly training 350 new workers, and routing some claims processing to nonunion offices as far away as Los Angeles. The various offices were linked together through computers and telephone lines irrespective of picket lines. In addition, training the new workforce was made far easier because computers had been used to simplify tasks. As a result, Blue Shield asserted that it was able to maintain near-normal operations with far fewer workers. After the strike, the company refused to return 448 jobs to the main office.

Even manufacturing is affected. The power of skilled workers on the job is rooted in their skills, which in the past have been both difficult to replace and portable. As one machinist at Rolls-Royce Aircraft division put it, "If you have a dispute with the foreman, you take your knowledge home with you." This leverage is undermined, however, with numerical control. Much of the skill is embodied in the parts program, which is no longer under the machinist's direct control. During a walkout, experienced supervisors can instruct nonstriking employees, often with little machining background, on how to keep the machines running. Although the process can be inefficient and often produces considerable scrap, it can serve to pressure unions toward a settlement.

To utilize this capability fully, some companies have transferred experienced machine operators into supervisory and semi-supervisory positions before a strike. This is a particularly prevalent practice in the aerospace industry. At McDonnell Douglas in St. Louis, for example, nonunion managerial staffs are called Free Enterprise Personnel (FEP). During a strike in the late 1970s, Cas Williams, the president of the IAM [International Association of Machinists] local union, maintained that the company was able to operate at about 60 percent of capacity. Similar events have taken place at General Electric's giant jet engine plant in Evandale, Ohio. According to Homer Deaton, the president of the UAW local union in the plant:

> Almost every foreman in the NC [numerical control] area started out as a machinist and many of them are ex-union stewards. The company loads up supervision with machine operators because when we go on strike, they use foremen to set up the NC machines and then they bring in secretaries to run them.

Once the machining knowledge is embodied in the numerical control program, it becomes possible to transfer production from a struck plant to shops that are still working, regardless of whether they are across the street or half way around the world. This ability was demonstrated by General Motors when it brought out a new luxury model in 1975, the Cadillac Seville. It was designed in record time using the computer-aided design techniques available in the early 1970s. The computer also generated NC tapes to manufacture the car's body dies. When the Seville program was being planned, GM engineers decided to machine many of these dies at independent shops in the Detroit area rather than in internal GM facilities. Although the corporation may have preferred to go to nonunion shops, the independent tool and die plants with NC capacity for a job of this size are the largest shops and generally organized by the UAW.

A crisis occurred for General Motors when the UAW struck these plants in 1973. If the introduction of the Seville was not to be delayed, the die work would have to be done somewhere else. Tapes containing all the information necessary to machine much of the dies were sent to a General Motors plant in Flint that was not on strike. The enormous flexibility of NC allowed the Seville die work to be sandwiched between the already scheduled work and all projects were completed on time. GM admits to paying a $1 million premium for doing the work in this way but it was obviously worth the price.

Without NC, it would have been impossible to transfer this project because of the large numbers of skilled workers necessary to complete it on time. Historically, the production of tools and dies has been a key bottleneck that the UAW has been able to use effectively in its struggles with the company. As it was, the leverage of the entire union was undermined in this case.

According to the Wharton School monograph *Operating During Strikes*, once a firm is successful in running a plant during a labor dispute, the practice is addictive.

> The fact that plant operation is a popular option for management with experience suggests that, once tried, plant operation tends to become an integral part of collective bargaining. This has been the case in the oil and telephone industries, is becoming the case in the chemical and newspaper industries, and may become the case in such new entrants to the field as the paper and hotel industries. Once used, plant operation may spread by virtue of example or force of competitive pressure, as in the oil and chemical industries. Once thus entrenched, plant operation seems unlikely to be dislodged until a new set of technological or institutional barriers to successful operation are created by either law or the ingenuity of the labor movement. No such barriers seem likely to emerge in the immediate future, but what lies beyond that limited horizon remains to be seen.

The stakes for unions are obviously quite high. As the Wharton monograph puts it:

> The fundamental effect, if not purpose, of plant operation is to alter the balance of economic power in collective bargaining in management's favor by limiting the loss of revenue and profit resulting from a strike. In the short run, this enhanced bargaining power should enable management to secure a more favorable settlement of strike issues than would have been the case in the event of nonoperation. In the long run, this enhanced bargaining power should result in a series of more modest settlements, possibly to the point of seriously weakening the perceived effectiveness of a union or unions generally in representing employees.

Where then does this leave unions? In simpler times, John L. Lewis— the fiery president of the United Mineworkers Union—told a president who sought to break a miners' strike that "you can't mine coal with bayonets." That still may be true, but computer technology allows more and more processes to be operated by supervisors and other fill-in workers during a labor dispute. Does this mean that John L. Lewis's strategy is outmoded and that the strike is finished as labor's ultimate weapon? No, but it means that unions will require broader strategies and more technical sophistication to use the strike as an effective weapon in the future.

While the labor movement's lack of ingenuity has been all too apparent in many instances, in some other cases innovative strategies have been the key to victory. One vital tool of workers, seeing their power eroded by computer technology, is to broaden the struggle to include those unions who retain considerable leverage. In the newspaper industry, for example, the New York pressmen were successful because the drivers refused to deliver the papers that obviously could have been printed. . . . In other cases, unions have revived older tactics with a new twist. In a recent dispute at the telephone company in British Columbia, for example, the Telephone Workers Union (TWU) knew that the company would be capable of continuing service if they went on strike. Instead, they occupied telephone company headquarters and offices throughout the province. The union, however, went beyond resurrecting the sit-in. Operations were continued "under new management"—the workers themselves—for five days. In a variant of this tactic, workers at the telephone company in Australia also continued working during a dispute in the late 1970s. But while they were providing service to the customer, they were refusing to process any bills for long-distance calls.

If new strategies are not developed by labor, its power could become increasingly eroded—first at the bargaining table, and ultimately in the society itself. The strike of the Communications Workers of America (CWA) against AT&T and the Bell System in the fall of 1983 is one more example of union leverage being sharply curtailed. While the strike disrupted certain services, such as telephone installations, the telephone company nonetheless was able to continue its core operations uninterrupted for over three weeks. Ironically, the strike occurred against a backdrop of near record profits for the telephone company and at a time when its relations with its union were among the most cordial of major U.S. industries. The company was obviously using power to protect its interests not simply in 1983 but for years to come in a deregulated market. If unions are weakened at the bargaining table in this way, then the erosion of the power of the labor movement in the society is not far behind. To the extent that power shifts in management's direction in negotiations, new industries, particularly high-tech industries, could become even more difficult to organize. None of this grim scenario for labor is inevitable. But in an age of high technology, "business as usual" is no longer a tenable strategy for unions.

Technology: Good for the Workers

PAUL ADLER

There seems to be an emerging consensus on the American left that technological change under capitalist conditions is bad news for working people. The line of thought opened up by Harry Braverman in *Labor and Monopoly Capital* . . . leads to a common core of conclusions: that technological change in capitalist societies is a major cause of economic dislocation and unemployment; that it usually leads to a reduction in skill requirements; that only organized worker resistance can limit this damage; and that only fundamental social change can turn the potential offered by technological progress to good purpose.

I believe that these propositions are substantially wrong. Technological

Paul Adler, "Technology and US," *Socialist Review* 85 (January–February 1986), pp. 67–87.

change, even under capitalist direction, is . . . much more an asset than a liability for the forces of progressive change. . . .

This essay outlines some starting points for such an analysis. I will explain why technology has very little to do with unemployment, and why on average it has a positive effect on skill requirements and working conditions. . . .

Technology and Unemployment

Technological change is often blamed for causing unemployment. . . .

At first sight it seems obvious that technological change, by increasing productivity, often reduces employment possibilities. If, in a given industry, the productivity change is faster than the growth in demand for its product, the more or less normal practice of capitalism is to "let people go." And often they won't leave without a struggle.

After all, even when a displaced worker immediately finds another job, the change is often costly to the worker. The new job may be one that pays less; the urgency of finding new employment often forces people to take less remunerative jobs. . . .

Then there is the fact that even short spells of unemployment are costly if you're trying to pay off a house or maintain a family, not to mention the psychological cost of not knowing if and when you're going to find a new job. But it would be silly to blame technology for these very real problems when the culprit is the notorious limitations of current "employment adjustment," unemployment insurance, and retraining provisions and the absence of serious planning for industrial change.

Finally, through such displacements, established bastions of union strength can be undermined. But while this certainly poses serious problems, the issue here is really one of the political context and of how difficult it is to organize workers in their new jobs. Technology doesn't have much to do with that, at least not directly.

The "automation and unemployment" question, therefore, is not so much one of job displacement per se, as whether automation has the effect of limiting the development of new employment opportunities. The short answer to that question is no. . . .

Think of radios: technological advance created a whole new radio-producing industry, and then further advances in automation made radios progressively cheaper to build. In this case, technology created a new set of jobs, and more technological change brought more jobs as more people could afford the product.

After a while, of course, virtually everyone had acquired a radio, the demand for radios peaked, and no matter how cheap they got, radio sales weren't going to grow much. Beyond that point, further productivity improvements start generating displacement. Until, that is, the technical (and marketing) innovation of "Walkman"-style radios boosted demand again.

In this industry, like many others, technological change in different periods created, increased, and reduced employment. Above and beyond the magnitude of the technological change itself, its effect on employment depended critically on how people's willingness to buy a radio responds to price reductions (what economists call its "price elasticity") and to changes in the product itself. What is true for radios is true for any industry. . . .

If it's so difficult to trace employment changes back to technology, could we perhaps reverse the procedure and determine the employment effects of specific technologies? That too turns out to be a disappointing exercise. If, on the one hand, we take a very specific technology, like word processing, its effect on employment is still dependent on changes in the demand for that activity's products, and, as we have seen, sometimes automation ends up increasing that demand. (In the case of word processing, for example, more drafts get written.) On the other hand, if we take a wide span of technologies, lumping together, for example, the various forms of computerization, we find that the net effect of jobs created and jobs lost is not traceable to technology, but is primarily a function of changing social and macroeconomic conditions. For every activity in which computerization can automate and eliminate jobs, there are other activities in which it creates jobs.

There is simply no general rule as to how fast the job-creation progresses relative to job-elimination. The *absence* of such a rule is itself one of capitalism's enduring features and cardinal sins: the uncoordinated nature of such changes means that we end up with sometimes labor shortages and sometimes unemployment and wasted resources. But again, the culprit is not technological change, but the unplanned nature of capitalist development.

It is worth noting that even if demand is constant, the effect of technological change on employment in a specific activity may seem large in magnitude, but usually turns out to be quite small in impact since it's spread out in time. The example of robotics is instructive. . . . [T]he maximum overall job displacement rate due to the introduction of robots in United States manufacturing as a whole will be about ten percent over the 1982–1990 period. If we go down to a finer level of analysis, the worst case is that of auto production painter jobs, of which between twenty-seven and thirty-seven percent might be eliminated by 1990. That, however, turns out to be three or four percent per year, and normal voluntary turnover rates should suffice to handle the reductions. Modest retraining commitments . . . should cover any local imbalances. This is why it can be so effective for unions to focus efforts on negotiating the rate of change, as distinct from fighting the change itself. . . .

How does this general perspective on technological change suggest we tackle the burning issues of today? Over the long run, robotics and other forms of automation may indeed mean that auto jobs, given a saturation of people's need for autos, go the way farm jobs have gone over the last century. But if this change occurs through attrition, on what basis would we oppose it? We might *selectively* oppose displacement in those cases where the jobs under attack are high-wage jobs like, for example, those in the auto industry. (It is important to note that there is no evidence that automation generates more displacement from high-wage jobs than from low-wage jobs. If anything, the long-run effects we will discuss in the next section suggest the opposite.) But there is no good reason at all why we should not fight tooth and nail to maintain those higher-paying jobs—it's not as if even the best-paid auto workers are living in grandiose luxury. And the conservative and liberal argument that higher wages reduce competitiveness only works when economists do their "all else being equal" trick; in the real world, higher wages can serve as a powerful spur for management to automate, to improve business efficiency, and to design better products.

We should nevertheless be lucid in making this "high wages as spur" claim. In a market economy, it can only be effective in defending United States workers if *all three* of the following conditions hold: (1) union clout has not generated a wage-level too far above what feasible technological change and productivity improvements can defend against foreign competition, (2) management is committed to making their profits in this line of business, and (3) the investment thus spurred is located in the United States.

On the first condition, it is sometimes simply unrealistic to expect to maintain employment and wage levels. Given new computerized technologies and given people's demand for newspapers, for example, something had to give in the newspaper industry. . . . In industries under pressures of this kind, the "militant" position against any worker concessions in employment or wage levels can at best serve as a rhetorical stance designed to elicit management concessions that cushion the blow, by generating redlining, hefty severance pay, government retraining and reemployment initiatives, and so forth.

On the second condition, we have to contend with the philosophy expressed in U.S. Steel's famous dictum "We're not in the business of making steel; we're in the business of making money." This attitude . . . expresses a loss of real entrepreneurial commitment that cannot bode well for long-run competitiveness in any industry. In the longer run this loss of commitment is . . . one of the most important forces legitimating socialist ideas of public control: requests for bail-outs can offer important opportunities to argue our case.

On the third condition, plant location, we should of course welcome public debate on whether we need to maintain an auto or a steel industry for the sake of the "industrial coherence" of the United States' economy. But this is a complex issue, involving the interests of both American and foreign workers in a context of seemingly irreversible trends toward economic interdependence. And we should be aware of the pitfalls of the "militant" position that argues for the defense of the status quo when our real concern is with minimizing the pains of change. For having pursued an approach of this kind, Australian unions found themselves in an absurd alliance with local auto companies defending import tariffs that were so high that it would have been cheaper to pay all auto workers in Australia their full wages for the rest of their lives to stay at home (or get another job), rather than subsidizing the profits of the grossly inefficient auto companies.

In the final analysis then, technology is but one amongst very many factors governing the immediate future of employment in specific activities—and not a particularly important factor either. The really imminent threat to auto workers' jobs comes from foreign competitors' more efficient organization and more competitive product designs, not from robots. Technology assumes somewhat greater importance in determining employment in specific industries if we shift our focus from the next few years to the next few decades—by which time it may make a lot of sense to shift workers (gently, hopefully!) to new activities.

In other words, job displacement that happens over a short time-span (years) is hardly ever due to technological change, and displacement that happens over longer periods (decades), while often having much more to do with technology, is something the left can often support. . . .

If this analysis is correct, it is somewhat abusive to talk of "technological displacement," because employment changes in a given industry depend on the joint effect of changes in technology and in demand for that industry's output. But if it's only half meaningful to talk of "technological displacement" with respect to specific activities, it's virtually senseless to talk of "technological unemployment" in the aggregate, because whether or not workers displaced from one industry find new jobs elsewhere has very little indeed to do with technology. Changes in "demand," in what people will spend to satisfy an old or a new need, are in the short run determined less by changes in their needs than by changes in how much money they have to spend on those needs. And that depends on the general state of the economy, not on technological change. . . .

. . . The driving force behind short-run changes in income, positive and negative, is not technological change, but the incoherent, unplanned course of capital accumulation as expressed in the complex interdependent relationships between output, profit, wages, investment, savings, interest rates, etc.—the poorly understood world that economists call "macroeconomics." It is these macroeconomic cyclical fluctuations so characteristic of capitalism that drive unemployment.

One last question remains: Is there any reason to fear that great increases in productivity deriving from the *combined* effect of the whole panoply of "advanced technologies" will render permanently unemployable a significant proportion of the labor force? This scenario is simply groundless, because no one has ever discovered limits to the creation of new human needs or to capitalist greed. Only a macroeconomic downswing or extraordinary political conditions has ever been known to frustrate the desires of business to capitalize on the consumer's wants. The very real possibility of financial collapse means that mass unemployment like we saw in the 1930s is still possible, but it is not technology that will stop willing hands from finding employment in some profitable (if sometimes socially useless) activity.

It is only in a different sort of society, where production is for use rather than for profit, that the productivity increases generated by automation could be consciously used to reduce work time more than incrementally. . . .

Democratic policies designed to attack the root causes of unemployment should focus, therefore, not on the easy scapegoat, technology, but on the chronic instability of market economies. We should be proposing new forms of planning and new ways of socializing the costs of change. Local initiatives to monitor technological change at a firm, industry, regional, or occupational level can help to ease transitions. And these efforts are worthy of support as expressions of the need for economic democracy. But it is irresponsible to present these local efforts or even national technology policies, no matter how vigorous and far-reaching, as capable of significantly influencing the unemployment problem. If blaming technology is an expedient substitute for direct reference to the still unpopular themes of socialization and planning, then it is at best a politically self-defeating expedient.

Technology and Skills

Though I believe technological change to have little relevance to the aggregate number of jobs, I do think that it is a central factor, probably *the* central factor, in determining the long-run evolution of the *quality* of jobs. . . . [T]his evolution is, on average, overwhelmingly positive in character.

. . . Capitalists, in their inevitable competition to accumulate profits, are forced over the long run to seek higher productivity. Apart from inventing new products, productivity growth is their most reliable way of staying competitive. Making operations more productive can be achieved in a number of ways. Radicals like to focus on one way of increasing productivity: intensified work effort. As capitalism develops, however, intensification as a productivity factor becomes increasingly overshadowed by mechanization and automation—getting sufficiently cheap machines to do what workers once did. In this automation process, capitalists often implement technical changes that, quite unintentionally, cause major improvements in working conditions and gradual increases in skill requirements. This process, furthermore, was largely responsible for the concentration of workers in larger plants and offices, which, by breaking the isolation of the small workshop—however convivial—made unionization possible. . . .

For the period that has been studied most adequately, the post–World War II years, the verdict is unambiguous: *not one* of the systematic, nationwide studies shows a deskilling trend in either individual or average job requirements; most show a clear upgrading both for the labor force as a whole *and* for most occupations taken individually.

What about the longer term? Here the data are much harder to assess. . . . The major declines have been in the laborer and farm categories, the major increases in the professional and technical, clerical, operative, and service categories. It is hard to believe that the shift between these categories doesn't represent a net upgrading. For the overall figures to express a net deskilling, one would need to believe that the *worst* examples of deskilling are in fact representative of the evolution of the *great bulk* of jobs (so that the drift towards higher-skilled occupational *categories* was outweighed by the deskilling of most individual *jobs* within each category). Evidence of the post-1945 period as well as common-sense ballpark estimates make this hypothesis seem quite implausible. . . .

[Critic] Braverman's vision is . . . based on a romanticization of the nineteenth-century factory. Braverman (like most of his radical followers) ignores the huge numbers of women, children, and men who spent their days carrying wood, coal, and so forth, on their backs from one craftsman to the next. He also ignores the stultifying world of the domestic helpers. And as for farm work, one can only go so far in glorifying the drudgery of most pre-mechanized agricultural labor.

Whatever doubts one may have about the exact comparability of the various categories then versus now—and these doubts are legitimate—the overall shift in the structure of the economy has almost certainly favored higher-skilled jobs.

This fact is critical. It permeates our everyday consciousness in the form of a widespread feeling that we wouldn't swap today for yesterday. That sentiment is not a manifestation of "false consciousness"; it is based on what is most probably an accurate intuition of fact. Whatever social criticism we want to make on the theme of skills must integrate this fact. . . .

One might object, as has just been suggested, that this improvement in the overall picture has come only very slowly, and that perhaps it results from the creation of new jobs that are more skilled than the old jobs that have been lost, while most *individual* jobs and *individual* workers would have been progressively deskilled and degraded. . . .

Indeed, the work of Braverman and a host of other critics establishes a theoretical argument for such job-level deskilling. They argue that managers want to deskill jobs both to lower labor costs and to give management the control over the shop floor that skilled workers used to have. Indeed, they argue, doesn't mechanization usually amount to "taking the skill out of the job and putting it into the machine"?

The simplest form of the deskilling argument doesn't appeal to technology but is worth appraisal by way of introduction. It rests on the indubitable fact of progressive "fragmentation" and "specialization" of jobs. But do these amount to deskilling? Take fragmentation first. While it is clear that capitalism's obsession with labor cost and shop-floor control pushes towards maximum fragmentation of jobs, there is no evidence that this has gotten worse over the last, say, century. It is true that capitalism *began* with a spurt of job fragmentation. But once the factory system was established, and as technology moved from lower to higher levels of automation, fragmentation has probably been, if anything, alleviated. As for "specialization," which has certainly grown over time, it is not at all obvious that specialization amounts to deskilling: is the specialist doctor less skilled than the generalist?

Developing a more powerful form of the deskilling argument using the example of the numerically controlled (NC) machine-tool, [historian] David Noble has argued that there is usually a hidden capitalist agenda in the way machines are designed. He shows how a design that would have patterned the machine-tool's computer program on the skilled machinist's performance of the task was ignored, in favor of a system that put the program design function into the hands of specialized programmers. He emphasizes managers' objectives in this choice: lowering labor costs and increasing shop-floor discipline by taking control out of the machinists' hands. But he virtually ignores its more important motivation: the simple fact that before NC, certain machining operations thought by the Air Force—the people who financed the development of NC—to be critical were materially impossible for a machinist to perform. More importantly, David Noble mentions but then ignores the fact that on average, and not-withstanding capitalists' intentions, the new machinists' jobs are *not* less skilled. On the contrary, these NC-operator jobs require new skills—skills that bosses would often like to ignore.

This last point is critical. The more automated machines are more powerful and more expensive; they operate with higher-value throughput and often fabricate parts of greater unit value. The responsibility required of the worker is correspondingly increased, even if the job itself seems to require merely pushing the STOP button when the red light goes on. But, as any unionist can testify, such increased responsibility is normally com-pensated in higher job classification and higher pay. Furthermore, it is as unproductive for radical critics as it is unprofitable for capitalist managers to underestimate the scope of the knowledge required of the operator to know when to hit that STOP button. This calls for training in the principles governing the internal workings of the automatic system: NC operators are increasingly being called upon to understand the control program logic in order to collaborate in writing programs and to correct errors on the shop floor. Like the increased responsibility, this training, too, demands remu-neration. And finally, we should not ignore the new programming jobs. Smart employers often retrain the conventional machine-tool operators to do this programming, capitalizing on their intimate knowledge of the pro-duction process (and avoiding labor conflicts over job loss at the same time). And even when the new programmers are not ex-machinists, such jobs represent opportunities for other workers, drawing the average level of all workers' skills upwards.

The NC case is fairly representative. My own research on basic com-puterization found very similar changes in the types of skills and in the general upward drift in the amount of skill even for low-level clerical em-ployees. Even though there are exceptions that warrant our concern and solidarity, new technologies more often than not require new and higher skills. Machines do "embody" skills—but not, typically, those of the op-erator: they embody primarily the technological skills of scientists and engineers. In this process, the requirements of the operator do *change*, but there is no theoretical reason to expect them to be *reduced*. On the contrary, the responsibility and training requirements mostly increase. . . .

. . . As technology develops—and this would hold under any social regime—machine systems grow to encompass broader and broader spans of previously discrete operations. Workers lost their individual autonomy—but not necessarily to the benefit of capitalists. As a general rule, workers lose their individual control to a broader "collective worker," encompassing manual workers, technicians, and engineers. Whether the capitalist's control over this collective worker is greater or less than he had over the individual worker is a subject worth exploring—but one that so far has resisted any simple generalization.

A second "feint" . . . is represented by those who argue that the distribution of skills tends towards a polarization between "bad" jobs of the (supposedly) low-skilled operators and "good jobs" of highly skilled engineers and programmers. Proponents of this thesis usually still want to maintain the idea that through this polarization, average skill levels have declined, but at least they can acknowledge growth of technical occupations.

The skill data do not, however, support the polarization idea whatever average trend its proponents associate with it. Evidence of skill polarization in specific industries or regions is simply not representative of overall trends. There *has,* on the other hand, been some polarization in wages due to the burgeoning of low-paid jobs in recent years. But this is the effect, not of skill changes, but of a decade of economic turbulence and of the influx of youth and educated women into the labor force. Moreover, amongst full-time workers, wage polarization has been restricted to younger men, while the wage structures of older men and of women in general have actually widened around the middle. Finally, it's important to see that both the turbulence and the rapid change in the labor-force demographics are inherently transitory phenomena, not deeply rooted tendencies. . . .

This, however, does not imply that there is no point in pursuing analysis and debate on the broad long-run trends in skill. On the contrary.

Take, for example, the shift from manual to cognitive skills. We should not be indifferent to the fact that machine-surveillance jobs require a type of learning that is more theoretical than the craft-style, experience-based learning characteristic of less automated jobs. Such a shift may have negative effects on job satisfaction, . . . but it also has positive effects. The long-run shift from manual towards intellectual work, while creating its own problems, has the net effect of generally improving working conditions and of creating a broader horizon for the worker's world. The workers' knowledge-base shifts towards training programs that bring them into contact with a world of science and technology that is a far cry from the narrower world of the factory workers of earlier epochs. Something of value is certainly lost in this process, but something else is gained, and in net it is hard to deny that working-class culture is thereby enhanced.

This cultural shift, reinforced by other social trends such as increasing educational levels, poses problems for traditional unionism and working-class politics. With these enlarged perspectives, workers are less inclined to follow old loyalties, and they demand more explanations from and consultations by both management and union. But this challenge is surely one that progressive forces must welcome.

Of course, machine-tending is not the only sort of job created in the process of automation. On the one hand, there is the growing number of technician/engineer positions that automation calls for. On the other hand, there are menial jobs that automation often leaves at its interstices, such as when data from one computer's printout has to be typed into another computer terminal. Our assessment both of how to handle these exceptions and of how to further improve the lot of the majority depend, once again, on our understanding of the nature of automation and the long-run skill trends.

Take first the growth of the technical occupations. If . . . new technologies introduced by capitalists are basically tools of oppression, then the technicians and engineers who are the makers and guardians of these tools are unlikely to be allies of the workers they help to oppress. Formally speaking, the technicians and engineers are "workers" insofar as they are wage-earners who don't own productive property, but in the Braverman perspective they are usually expected to side with their masters. In this view, it would be illusory to expect significant numbers of them to contribute to working-class organizations on an ongoing basis.

If, on the other hand, technological change is . . . basically thrust upon capitalists, and if it has mainly positive effects for workers, then things look very different. Even if bosses sometimes try, and occasionally manage, to rally engineers and technicians to a myopic and, in general, unprofitable use of technology to deskill jobs, the general picture is one in which these new and expanding categories of workers can be counted as probable allies.

Making engineers and technicians allies of the workers who are using their tools is by no means an easy task. There are bound to be some tensions between the NC operator and the programmer, and managers may have a vested interest in fostering such conflicts. . . . But we should not ignore the internal contradictions of such policies, namely, that managers need employees to cooperate if production and profits are to continue to flow. Such tensions between "conception" and "execution" personnel are therefore not . . . fundamental conflicts. Unions *can* hope to overcome them and to organize the technical categories—but only if they make the effort, embrace technical workers' concerns, and find a common ground.

It is critical that this effort be made: the technical work force is the fastest-growing segment of the labor force. It is already larger than the craft category, and may soon overtake the clerical category as well. And when the technical work force moves into action, as they have on many occasions in many countries, they are a potent force. . . .

This long-term prognosis shouldn't, of course, comfort us in exaggerating the speed of the movement towards a more technical labor force—it's painfully slow—nor in exaggerating the weight of this "new working class" in the overall picture—it will be small for many decades to come. After all, at the same time as technological change is creating these technical jobs, it is (re)creating lower-level, relatively simple, and basically boring jobs.

But in the case of these other jobs too, our general understanding of automation and of the overall long-run trends can make a big difference to the way we analyze concrete problems.

How should we interpret the fact that many jobs transformed by new technology—even more skilled jobs like the NC operators'—are characterized by high levels of boredom? When active human intervention in the fabrication of a product is replaced by the machine, productivity will be improved—more goods and services will be available for the same or reduced work effort—but workers have been replaced by machines as the central agents of production. Deprived of the sort of satisfaction that craftsmen feel when the artifact leaves their hands at the end of the cycle, workers often feel less satisfied in automated settings: "Who wants to be just a button-pusher?"

Clearly, some job boredom is due to the peculiarities of capitalist work organization—excessive job fragmentation, for example. These sources of boredom could, with concerted effort, be overcome. But it is critical to understand that another part of job boredom may be the price that humanity, in any form of society, pays to reduce the amount of time people have to spend in producing the nuts and bolts, the cars and highways, the burgers and fries of everyday life. Indeed, as automation progresses, it's hard to see how any form of society could (or would want to) avoid more and more jobs coming to resemble those of the workers in the control rooms of modern chemical refineries and steel mills: highly trained, highly responsible, but basically boring. This part of the boredom problem calls for a different remedy. I believe that it should be grasped by progressive forces in society as an opportunity to popularize a really radical demand—free time.

This is the reason we should be arguing for a shorter work week, and not as a remedy for unemployment. As the European unions have discovered, it's simply wrong to think that a thirty-five-hour work week will make much of a dent in the unemployment rate (the reduction in hours provokes significant and compensating productivity gains). And it's rather curious politics to focus on sharing the symptom rather than on curing the disease. But the free-time idea has real appeal, and can represent a profoundly progressive impulse. . . . A healthy debate could perhaps be fostered if we began by acknowledging that different segments of society will experience the issue differently and indeed that people often feel ambivalent on the issue. A comprehensive program relative to free-time could therefore rest on three policy "legs"; better work, less work, and better free-time. Any one leg or pair of legs will fail to capture the profound impulses expressed in the other(s). But the combination could be powerful.

It's worth noting a second way in which technology can play a powerful supporting role in the emergence of a free-time demand: . . . more complex technologies create such pressing needs for continual learning that the work/free-time split is itself undermined.

Hispanic Women and the Persistence
of the Informal Economy

M. PATRICIA FERNÁNDEZ-KELLY

and ANNA M. GARCÍA

In the latter part of the twentieth century, underground economies are expanding in industrial regions like the United States and western Europe. The proliferation of sweat shops, unlicensed industrial operations, and homework seems incongruous in information-based societies in which multinational corporations rely upon advanced technology. Nevertheless, a growing body of quantitative and qualitative evidence points to economic informalization as a distinctive and ongoing process in advanced industrial nations. Low-tech industries like apparel and high-tech industries like electronics share this feature.

A considerable degree of internal variation characterizes informal economies. An understanding of this differentiation should entail the study of labor market conditions and of the household structures to which informal workers and employers belong. It is within the household that the constraints of class and gender mesh, resulting in various modes of adaptation to the surrounding economic system and in differing patterns of employment. A comparison between Miami and Los Angeles provides an invaluable opportunity to illustrate this point. Homework involving Hispanic women, particularly immigrants and refugees, is widespread in the two locations, especially in the garment industry. On the surface, the two cases seem to be similar outcomes resulting from identical economic processes. However, as we will see, in Miami the existence of an ethnic enclave formed by Cuban entrepreneurs, most of them political exiles, enabled women from the same families and community to transform homework into a strategy for maximizing earnings and for reconciling cultural and economic demands. Theirs is a position of qualified vulnerability when judged against the totality of economic and political interactions. By contrast, in Los Angeles the high degree of proletarianization of Mexican women (partly resulting from their working-class background, undocumented immigrant status, and particular household characteristics) has accentuated their vulnerability in the labor market. For many of these women, industrial homework and even the purchase of small assembly shops are measures of last resort; they are strategies to stay a step above poverty. . . .

Two hypotheses guide this comparative analysis. (1) Proletarianization—that is, dependence on the larger mechanisms of the wage labor market—reduces the possibility of upholding patriarchal norms of reciprocity between men and women. This, in turn, translates into high levels of economic and political vulnerability. (2) Conversely, the existence of an ethnic entrepreneurial class predicated upon patriarchal notions of rec-

From M. Patricia Fernández-Kelly and Anna M. García, *Homework: Historical and Contemporary Perspectives on Paid Labor at Home*, 1989, pp. 165–179. Reprinted by permission of University of Illinois Press.

iprocity can improve the bargaining ability of women in the labor market and raise the political strength of the group as a whole. The first proposition applies to Mexican women employed in garment and electronics manufacture in southern California. The second refers to Cuban garment workers in southern Florida.

Hispanic Women in Wage Labor

. . . Cubans and Mexicans share similar marital profiles and household compositions. Intact marriages as well as a relatively low percentage of households headed by women are distinguishing features in both groups. Seventeen percent of Cuban and 16 percent of Mexican households are headed by females, compared to about 8 percent of white domestic units in the same situation. Sixty-seven percent of Mexican and 64 percent of Cuban women were married and living with their spouses in 1976. Sixty-five percent of Mexican men and 70 percent of Cuban males lived in stable marital unions. Finally, about 74 percent of Mexican women had children living with them. The equivalent figure for Cubans was 62 percent.

Both Cuban and Mexican women have had a prominent representation as remunerated workers in the United States. Their labor force participation rates dispel the widespread notion that work outside the home is a rare experience among Hispanic women. For instance, 50 percent of native-born and 45 percent of foreign-born Mexican women were employed outside the home in 1976. The equivalent figure for foreign-born Cubans was 65 percent (despite the fact that their labor participation rate prior to their arrival in the United States was about 30 percent). Thus, current levels of employment among Mexican and Cuban women in the U.S. approximate or surpass the labor force participation of non-Hispanic white women, of whom 57 percent work outside the home. Moreover, while other ethnic groups in the United States have diminished their participation in blue-collar employment, Hispanic women have increased their relative share in it, particularly in the production of nondurable goods.

The importance of minority women's employment in assembly is readily apparent in southern California, where 67 percent of working women classified as "operators, fabricators, and laborers" belong to ethnic minority groups. Fifty-one percent of those are Hispanic. These findings contradict the assumption that Hispanic women's participation in the labor force is confined to the service sector. Census figures for Los Angeles County further confirm the significance of Hispanic women's employment in manufacturing: 73.7 percent of all female "operators, fabricators, and laborers" (136,937 persons) are members of ethnic minorities. Almost 60 percent of that subgroup (105,621 individuals) are Hispanic. Even more revealing is the composition of workers classified as "textile, apparel, and furnishings machine operators." Approximately 46,219 women are employed in that occupation in Los Angeles. Almost 91 percent of those are minorities; 71.76 percent, Hispanic. Equivalent data for New York and Miami (the two other areas with the fastest growing Hispanic populations) indicate that we are looking at a substantial percentage of the manufacturing labor force. However, census material may underestimate the actual involvement of Hispanic women in wage labor: many are part of the underground economy; they are found in small unregulated assembly shops or doing piece work and industrial homework.

The preceding summary is useful for comparative purposes. However, some features vary when observations are limited to certain industries, their correspondent labor market incorporation patterns, and household characteristics prevalent among their workers. For example, in both southern California and southern Florida most direct production workers in the garment industry are Hispanic. In Los Angeles and Miami apparel firms approximately 75 percent of the operatives are Mexican; 85 percent, Cuban. In contrast to the characteristics of the population at large, among Los Angeles garment workers approximately 29 percent are female-headed households, a figure much larger than that for Mexicans living in the United States in general (16 percent). By contrast, there is little variation when comparing the number of female-headed households in the Florida needle trade industry with the population as a whole. About 17 percent of Cuban households are headed by females; the equivalent figure for the Florida garment industry is 19 percent.

The large number of female-headed households in the Los Angeles garment industry calls for an explanation. Because Cubans and Mexicans share many cultural characteristics, that explanation cannot rely exclusively on differences regarding values and attitudes about family life or sex roles. Instead, it must take into consideration the differential modes of incorporation of the two ethnic groups into their receiving economic milieu. . . .

Structures of the Garment Industry in California and Florida

. . . To understand the current position of Mexican and Cuban home-workers, we must first compare garment manufacture in Los Angeles and Miami.

The two sites differ in the timing of the industry, its evolution, maturity, and restructuring. In Los Angeles, garment production is not only older, developing first in the late nineteenth century with the gold rush and waves of Chinese immigrants. It is also rooted in specific events such as the Great Depression, changing conditions of assembly and unionization in New York, emphasis on new definitions of casual wear, and, finally, continued reorganization during the seventies and eighties as a response to the impact of foreign imports. Restructuring in the Los Angeles garment industry has led to a decreasing number of large firms and a proliferation of small, subcontracted shops, many of which fall partly or totally outside government supervision. . . . Between 30 and 50 percent of the $3.5 billion in 1983 Los Angeles garment industry sales may have originated in home production or unregulated shops, the majority of which are small.

Apparel production in Miami has had a shorter history and a less diversified experience. In the early sixties Miami's industry was highly seasonal, employed fewer than 7,000 workers, and depended on New York entrepreneurs feeding U.S. and European luxury markets in belts, gloves, and purses. As retired manufacturers from New York living in Miami saw the advantages of opening new businesses and hiring large numbers of freshly arrived Cubans, Miami expanded by 1973 to employ more than 24,000 people, the vast majority of whom were Cuban women. This same process led to the predominance of Cuban males among contractors. From its inception, then, apparel manufacturing in Miami illustrated gender and ethnic stratification: 70 percent of the manufacturers were Jewish; 90 percent of the contractors, Cuban men; and 95 percent of the work force, Cuban females. As in Los Angeles in the early eighties, many of the 716 firms in Miami employed fewer than thirty workers, and a substantial proportion of the industry (at least one third) originated in unregulated shops and homes.

However, unlike Los Angeles, since the late seventies Florida has suffered labor shortages caused by the relatively advanced age (over forty) of the work force and the absence of a new labor supply. The decreasing availability of Cuban women's labor has contributed, as we shall see, to the expansion of homework in Miami.

The two locations also differ in the availability of a favored labor supply. The growth of the Los Angeles clothing industry resulted from capitalists' ability to rely on steady waves of Mexican immigrants, many of whom were undocumented. Over the last century this continuous migration has ensured a permanent supply of workers. From the twenties, Mexican women dominated the work force; the majority were below the age of thirty, two-thirds were born in the United States, and nine-tenths were unmarried. By 1944, when the number of garment manufacturers had grown to 900, 75 percent of their 28,000 employees were Mexican women and girls. By contrast, garment production in Miami expanded because of an unprecedented influx of exiles ejected by a unique political event. Cubans working in the Florida apparel industry arrived in the United States as refugees, protected and relatively privileged. Their exile was filled with uncertainty and the possibility of dislocation but not, as in the case of undocumented Mexican aliens, with the probability of harassment, detention, and deportation.

Implicit in the previous point is a differentiation in social class between the two groups of newcomers. For more than a century, the majority of Mexican immigrants have had a markedly proletarian background. Until the seventies, the majority had rural roots; in more recent times the number of urban immigrants has grown. In sharp contrast, Cuban waves of migration have included a larger proportion of professionals, mid-level service providers, and various types of entrepreneurs ranging from those with previous experience in large companies to those able to start small family enterprises. Research has shown that entrepreneurial experience among Cubans and reliance on their own ethnic network accounts, to a large extent, for their success in business formation and appropriation in Miami. . . .

In addition to disparate class compositions, the two groups differ in the degree of their homogeneity by place of birth. Besides the sizable undocumented contingent, the Los Angeles garment industry also employs U.S.-born citizens of Mexican heritage. Although no systematic studies have been done on the subject, first-hand reports and anecdotal evidence indicate a fragmentation between "Chicanas" and "Mexicans," with the latter occupying the lower rungs in the labor hierarchy. Differences in citizenship status, length of residence in the United States, and skill often result in open or latent conflict among the two groups. Recently arrived Mexican immigrants point to discrimination and prejudice from workers with whom they share a common ethnic background. Cubans, on the other hand, were a highly cohesive population until recently, when the arrival of the Port of Mariel refugees resulted in a potentially damaging fragmentation of the community.

Perhaps the most important difference between Mexicans in Los Angeles and Cubans in Florida is related to their distinctive patterns of labor market insertion. Historically, Mexicans have arrived in the U.S. labor market in a highly individuated and dispersed manner. As a result, they have been extremely dependent on labor supply and demand—forces beyond their control. Their working-class background and the stigma attached to their frequent undocumented status has accentuated even further their vulnerability vis-à-vis employers. By contrast, Cubans have been able to consolidate an economic enclave containing immigrant businesses which hire workers of a common culture and national background.

This economic enclave operates as a buffer zone, separating and often shielding members of the same ethnic group from the market forces at work in the larger society. The existence of an economic enclave does not preclude exploitation on the basis of class; indeed, it is predicated upon the existence of a highly diversified immigrant class structure. However, the quantitative and qualitative evidence suggests that commonalities of culture, national background, and language between immigrant employers and workers can become a mechanism for collective improvement of income levels and standards of living. As a result, differences in labor market insertion patterns among Mexicans and Cubans have led to varying social profiles and a dissimilar potential for socioeconomic attainment.

Household Organization and the Politics of Home and Work

Neither proletarian atomization among Mexicans nor participation in an economic enclave among Cubans can be explained without consideration of the role played by households and families in the allocation of workers to different segments of the labor market. Both Mexican and Cuban women have sought homework as one way to reconcile the responsibilities of family and domestic care with the need to earn a wage. Employers, in turn, have found in homework a vehicle to lower the wage bill, evade government regulations, and maintain competitiveness in the market. While these two aspects have remained constant, the circumstances surrounding homework in southern California and southern Florida highlight the varying impact that class has on household composition and that class-defined households have on various types of labor force participation. Differences in class background and household composition have led to the contrasting experiences of Mexican and Cuban homeworkers.

Both Cubans and Mexicans prize the idealized family—long-term, stable unions in which men act as main providers and women as principal caretakers of children. However, the possibility of forming such family units over extended periods of time vary in consonance with several factors including class background. Stable nuclear families and clearly defined sex roles are often found among the middle and upper classes; the poor must often live in highly flexible households in which resources and services flow constantly but adherence to the norms of the patriarchal family are unattainable. . . . [T]he large number of female-headed households in the Los Angeles garment industry can be partly explained as an outcome of proletarianization and the absence of an ethnic enclave in which the injuries of class are mitigated. . . .

The employment history of Amelia Ruiz, a U.S.-born woman of Mexican ancestry, more fully illustrates the ways that economic uncertainty, cultural expectations, and household stability lead women to homework. She was born into a family of six children in El Cerrito, Los Angeles County. Her mother, a descendant of Native American Indians, married at a young age the son of Mexican immigrants. Among Amelia's memories are the fragmentary stories of her paternal grandparents working in fields and, occasionally, in canneries. On the other hand, her father was not a stoop laborer but a trained upholsterer. Her mother was always a homemaker. Amelia grew up with a distinct sense of the contradictions that plague the relationships between men and women. . . .

After getting her high school diploma, Amelia took up odd jobs in all the predictable places: as a counter clerk in a dress shop, as a cashier in a fast food establishment, and as a waitress in two restaurants. When she was twenty, she met Miguel. He was a consummate survivor, having worked in the construction field, as a truck driver, and even as an ESL (English as a Second Language) instructor. At the age of twenty-one and despite her misgivings, Amelia was married: "For a while I kept my job, but when I became pregnant, Miguel didn't want me to work anymore. Two more children followed and then, little by little, Miguel became abusive. He wanted to have total authority over me and the children. He said a man should know how to take care of a family and get respect, but it was hard to take him seriously when he kept changing jobs and when the money he brought home was barely enough to keep ends together." After the birth of her second child, Amelia started work at Shirley's, a women's wear factory in the area. Miguel was opposed to the idea. For Amelia, work outside the home was an evident need prompted by financial stress. At first, it was also a means to escape growing disillusion: "I saw myself turning into my mother, and I started thinking that to be free of men was best for women. Maybe if Miguel had had a better job, maybe if he had kept the one he had, things would have been different. . . . We started drifting apart."

She had worked at Shirley's for almost a year when one late afternoon, after collecting the three children from her parents' house, she returned to an empty home. She knew, as soon as she stepped inside, that something was amiss. In muted shock she confirmed the obvious: Miguel had left, taking with him all personal possessions; even the wedding picture in the living room had been removed. No explanations had been left behind. Amelia was then twenty-eight years of age, alone, and the mother of three small children.

Under the circumstances, employment became even more desirable, but the difficulty of reconciling home responsibilities with wage work persisted. Amelia was well regarded at Shirley's and her condition struck a cord of sympathy among other factory women. In a casual conversation, her supervisor described how other women were leasing industrial sewing machines from the local Singer distributor and doing piece work at home. By combining factory work and home assembly, she could earn more money without further neglecting her children. Mr. Driscoll, Shirley's owner and general manager, made regular use of homeworkers, most of whom were former employees. That had allowed him to retain a stable core of about twenty employees and to depend on approximately ten homeworkers during peak seasons.

Between 1979, the year of her desertion, and 1985 when we met her, Amelia had struggled hard, working most of the time and making some progress. Her combined earnings before taxes fluctuated between $950 and $1,150. In 1985 almost half of her income went to rent for the two-bedroom apartment which she shared with the children. She was in debt and used to working at least twelve hours a day. On the other hand, she had bought a double-needle sewing machine and was thinking of leasing another one to enable a neighbor to help with additional sewing. She had high hopes: "Maybe some day I'll have my own business; I'll be a liberated woman. . . . I won't have to take orders from a man. Maybe Miguel did me a favor when he left after all."

Although there are individual variations, Amelia's life history is shared by many garment workers in southern California. Two aspects are worth noting in this experience. First, marriage and a stable family life are seen as desirable objectives which are, nonetheless, fraught with ambivalent feelings and responsibilities. Second, tensions surrounding home life express a contradiction between the intent to fulfill sexual roles defined according to a shared culture and the absence of the economic base necessary for their implementation. Male unemployment and women's need to become breadwinners militate against the maintenance of patriarchal standards. Male desertion adds to the vulnerability of women. Mexican garment workers, especially those who are heads of households, face great disadvantages in the labor market. They are targeted as a preferred labor force for jobs which offer the lowest wages paid to industrial workers in the United States;

they also have among the lowest unionization rates in the country. Ironically, household atomization, partly caused by proletarianization and the ensuing breakdown of patriarchal norms, has not been followed by the elimination of similar patriarchal standards in the labor market. . . .

Tales like the [one] related above can be found among Cuban and Central American women in Miami. However, a larger proportion have had a different trajectory than Mexicans in Los Angeles. Among the first waves of refugees were many who worked hard to bring the standards of living of their families to the same levels or higher than those they had been familiar with in their countries of origin. The consolidation of an ethnic enclave allowed many Cuban men to become successful entrepreneurs. While their wives toiled in garment factories, they entered the world of business. Eventually, they purchased homes, put their children through school, and achieved comfortable styles of life. At that point, many Cuban men pressed their wives to stop working outside the home. They had only allowed them to work in the first place out of economic necessity. . . . [D]ecisions made at the level of the household can remove workers highly desired by employers from the marketplace, thus endangering certain types of production. In those cases, loyalty to familial values can act against the interests of capitalist firms. Interviews with Cuban women involved in homework confirm this general interpretation. By capitalizing on their skill and experience, many of these women became subcontractors, employing their own neighbors and transforming so-called "Florida rooms" (the covered porches in their houses) into sewing shops.

In one of those improvised sewing shops we interviewed Elvira Gómez. She was thirty-four when she arrived in Miami with her four children, ages three to twelve, in 1961. . . .

Before her marriage Elvira had worked briefly as a secretary. As a middle-class wife and mother she was used to hiring at least one maid. Coming to the United States changed all that: "Something had to be done to keep the family together. So I looked around and finally found a job in a shirt factory in Hialeah. Manolo [her husband] joined a childhood friend and got a loan to start an export-import firm. All the time they were building the business, I was sewing. There were times when we wouldn't have been able to pay the bills without the money I brought in."

In her case, working outside the home was justified as a way to maintain the integrity of her family and as a means to support her husband's early incursions into the business world:

> For six long years I worked in the factory, but when things got better financially, Manolo asked me to quit the job. He felt bad that I couldn't be at home all the time with the children. But it had to be done. There's no reason for women not to earn a living when necessary. But I tell my daughters that the strength of a family rests on the intelligence and work of women. It is foolish to give up your place as a mother and a wife only to take orders from men who aren't even part of the family. What's so liberated about that? It is better to see your husband succeed and to know you have supported one another.

Several points are worth noting in the experience of Cuban garment workers. Exile, for example, did not transform sexual roles; rather, it extended them in surprising ways. The high labor-force participation rates of Cuban women in the U.S. have been mentioned earlier. However, prior to their migration, only a small number of Cuban women had worked outside the home for any length of time. It was the need to maintain the integrity of their families and to achieve class-related ambitions that precipitated their entrance into the labor force of a foreign country.

As with Mexicans in southern California, Cuban women in Miami earned low wages in unskilled and semiskilled jobs. They too worked in environments devoid of union benefits. However, their membership in an economic enclave allowed them to see industrial homework as an expression of relative prosperity and as a means to achieve a supplementary income while minding domestic responsibilities.

Conclusions

The comparison between different experiences among Hispanic women in two distinct geographical locations shows that involvement in informal production can have entirely dissimilar meanings, depending on the type of incorporation into the broader economic context and on the interplay between sexual politics and household composition. . . .

⚜ *F U R T H E R R E A D I N G*

William Abernathy, Kim Clark, and Alan Kantrow, *Industrial Renaissance: Producing a Competitive Future for America* (1982)
Eileen Boris and Cynthia R. Daniels, *Homework: Historical and Contemporary Perspectives on Paid Labor at Home* (1989)
Harry Braverman, *Labor and Monopoly Capital* (1974)
Kathleen Christensen, ed., *The New Era of Home-Based Work* (1988)
——, *Women and Home-Based Work: The Unspoken Contract* (1988)
Barbara Garson, *The Electronic Sweatshop* (1988)
Joan Greenbaum, *In the Name of Efficiency: Management Theory and Shopfloor Practice in Data Processing Work* (1979)
Joseph Grunwald and Kenneth Flamm, *The Global Factory* (1985)
Heidi Hartmann, Robert Kraut, and Louise Tilly, eds., *Computer Chips and Paper Clips: Technology and Women's Employment*, 2 vols. (1986, 1987)
Robert Howard, *Brave New Workplace* (1985)
Harry Katz, *Shifting Gears: The American Automobile Industry in Transition* (1986)
National Research Council, *Office Workstations in the Home* (1985)
David Noble, *Forces of Production* (1984)
Office of Technology Assessment, *Automation of America's Offices* (1985)
Mike Parker and Jane Slaughter, *Choosing Sides: Unions and the Team Concept* (1988)
Michael J. Piore and Charles F. Sabel, *The Second Industrial Divide* (1984)
Robert Reich, *The Next American Frontier: A Provocative Program for Economic Renewal* (1983)
Harley Shaiken, *Work Transformed: Automation and Labor in the Computer Age* (1985)
Stephen Wood, ed., *The Degradation of Work* (1982)
Shoshana Zuboff, *In the Age of the Smart Machine: The Future of Work and Power* (1988)

APPENDIX

American Labor:

A Statistical Portrait

⚕

Farm Laborers' Average Monthly Earnings with Board, 1818–1948

YEAR	UNITED STATES	WEST NORTH CENTRAL	SOUTH ATLANTIC	PACIFIC
1948	$91.00	$107.00	$57.00	$158.00
1940	28.05	28.12	17.46	42.84
1929	40.40	42.10	25.23	59.90
1919	41.52	50.81	30.23	65.30
1909	21.30	26.47	14.64	34.28
1899	14.56	18.04	9.32	25.10
1890	13.93	15.84	9.46	22.64
1880	11.70	14.88	8.81	24.77
1870	16.57	17.10	9.95	29.19
1860	13.66	13.76	11.08	34.16
1850	10.85	12.00	8.20	68.00
1830	8.85	10.15	7.16	
1826	8.83	10.15	7.18	
1818	9.45	10.15	8.10	

U.S. Bureau of the Census, *Historical Statistics of the United States, Colonial Times to 1970* (Washington, D.C.: Government Printing Office, 1975), p. 163.

Figure 1   Total U.S. Work Stoppages, 1881–1970

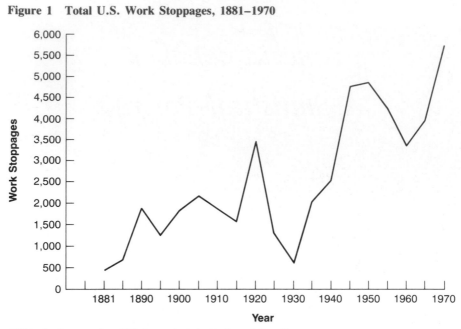

1959 is the first year for which figures include Alaska and Hawaii.
U.S. Bureau of the Census, *Historical Statistics of the United States, Colonial Times to 1970* (Washington,
D.C.: Government Printing Office, 1975), p. 179.

Figure 2   Work Stoppages Involving 1,000 Workers or More, 1947–1989

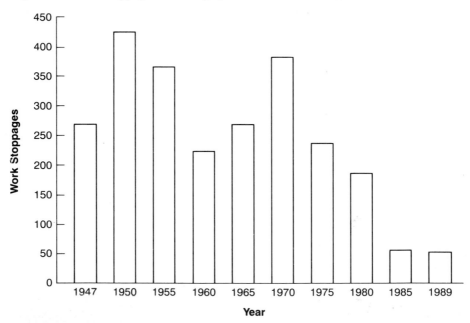

Bureau of Labor Statistics.

Figure 3   Trade-Union Membership as a Proportion of All Workers

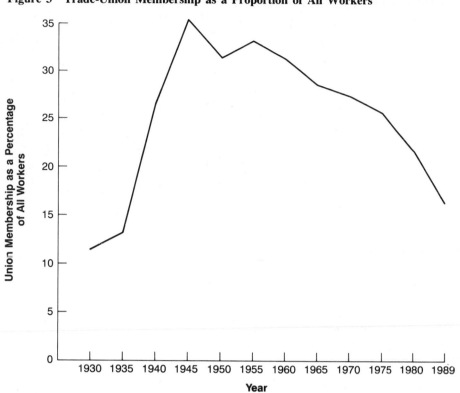

U.S. Bureau of the Census, *Historical Statistics of the United States, Colonial Times to 1970* (Washington, D.C.: Government Printing Office, 1975), p. 178; Bureau of Labor Statistics Press Release, 1990.

Figure 4   Women in the Labor Force by Marital Status, 1890–1988

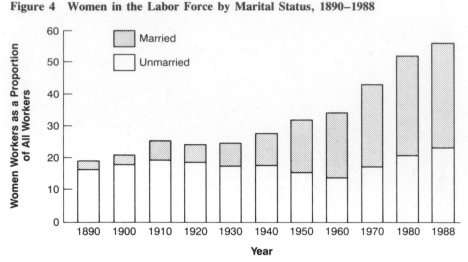

U.S. Bureau of the Census, *Historical Statistics of the United States, Colonial Times to 1970* (Washington, D.C.: Government Printing Office, 1975), p. 133; U.S. Bureau of the Census, *Statistical Abstract of the United States, 1989* (Washington, D.C. 1990, 109th ed.), p. 285.

Figure 5   Unemployment as a Percentage of the Civilian Labor Force, 1890–1989

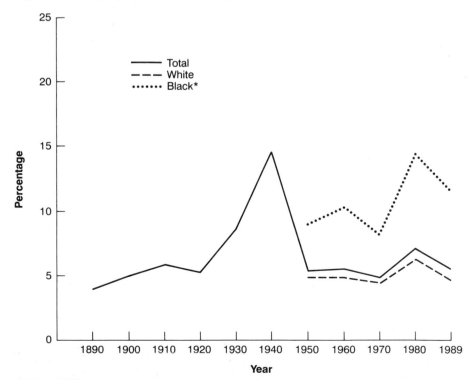

*Black unemployment statistics include other minorities before 1971.
U.S. Bureau of the Census, *Historical Statistics of the United States, Colonial Times to 1970* (Washington, D.C.: Government Printing Office, 1975), p. 135; Bureau of Labor Statistics Press Release, 1990.